LEAVING
ISLAM

Edited by
IBN WARRAQ

LEAVING ISLAM

Apostates Speak Out

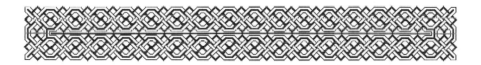

Prometheus Books

59 John Glenn Drive
Amherst, New York 14228-2197

Published 2003 by Prometheus Books

Inquiries should be addressed to
Prometheus Books
59 John Glenn Drive
Amherst, New York 14228–2197
VOICE: 716–691–0133, ext. 207
FAX: 716–564–2711
WWW.PROMETHEUSBOOKS.COM

07 06 05 04 03   5 4 3 2 1

Library of Congress Cataloging-in-Publication Data

Leaving Islam : apostates speak out / edited by Ibn Warraq.
    p. cm.
    Includes bibliographical references and index.
    ISBN 1–59102–068–9 (alk. paper)
    1. Apostasy—Islam. 2. Liberty of conscience (Islam). 3. Religious tolerance—Islam. 4. Christian converts from Islam. 5. Islam—Controversial literature. I. Ibn Warraq.

BP168.L43 2003
297—dc21

2003041377

Printed in Canada on acid-free paper

To my children

"I refuse to belong to a religion that will not not have me as a member."
　　　　　　　　—Ibn Warraq
　　　　　　　　(with apologies to Groucho Marx)

"You hate our Cassandra cries and resent us as allies, but when all is said, we ex-Communists are the only people on your side who know what it's all about."
　　　　　　　　—Arthur Koestler

"The predicament of Western civilization is that it has ceased to be aware of the values which it is in peril of losing."
　　　　　　　　—Arthur Koestler

CONTENTS

PART 2: TESTIMONIES SUBMITTED
TO THE ISIS WEB SITE

PART 3: TESTIMONIES
OF BORN MUSLIMS: *MURTADD FIṬRI*

PART 4: TESTIMONIES OF WESTERN CONVERTS: *MURTADD MILLI*

APPENDICES

PREFACE

A ll the testimonies here are witnesses to the authors' courage, for a free discussion of Islam remains rare and dangerous, certainly in the Islamic
world and even in our politically correct times in the West. A surprising number of
the apostates decided to write under their real names, a triumphant gesture of defiance and freedom. Many, on the other hand, have chosen to write pseudony-
mously, and since this is a fact that seems to irritate many in the secular West, I
shall briefly indicate the reasons why. Apostasy is still punishable by long prison
sentences and even death in many Islamic countries such as Iran and Pakistan, and
as many of our authors have relatives in those countries, whom they regularly
visit, it is common sense and simple prudence not to use their real names. Others
still do not wish to unnecessarily upset husbands, wives, parents, and close relatives who, for the most part, remain ignorant of their act of apostasy.

The opinions expressed, and their manner of expression, in the testimonies
are the individual responsibility of each author. As editor, I do not always or necessarily share the sentiments of the contributors, some of whom would now
describe themselves as deists, agnostics, or even Christians. We are all, however,
united in totally rejecting Islam, and prefer living in a democracy, where a firm
separation of religion and state is in place, to living under an Islamic theocracy.

After the name of each author in part 3 I have added in brackets the author's country of origin, to give an idea of the geographical range of the apostates and their cultural background. In one case, although the author was born in the United States, I have indicated the country of origin of his parents, again to indicate the cultural background of the kind of Islam in which he grew up.

Where does one go for spiritual and intellectual sustenance once one has abandoned Islam? One could join and participate in the activities of the following organizations founded expressly for former Muslims, for a totally uninhibited but necessary critique of the religion they have left behind but which they see as a danger for democratic societies:

♦ Institute for the Secularisation of Islamic Society (ISIS)
♦ Faith Freedom International
♦ Advocates of Article 18
♦ Apostates of Islam

I have devoted some more pages to the above organizations in appendix B.

I have tried not to be too pedantic about the diacritical marks necessary for a scientific system of transliterating Arabic proper names and words. In part 1 I have tried to be as rigorous as possible, while in the appendices I have carefully transliterated the names of Muslim authors and the Arabic titles of their works. However, I have not transliterated each and every Arabic name or Arabic word in the extensive quotes given in the appendices. In the forty-five or so testimonies, I have only occasionally—though not, I hope, obsessively—intruded to add the correct transliterated form of an Arabic name or religious term.

At the beginning of appendix A, part 3, I have explained that for the *verse numbering* (and only for the verse numbering) of the Koranic quotes, I have used M. Pickthall's translation, *The Meaning of the Glorious Koran* (London, 1930). Pickthall was a Muslim, and his translation is highly respected by all Muslims and is easily available. However, for the actual translation of the verses I have employed various works indicated in appendix A, part 3.

PART 1

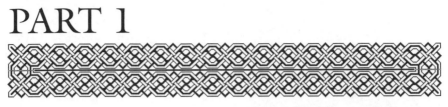

THEORY
AND PRACTICE
OF APOSTASY
IN ISLAM

1

APOSTASY

Introduction: Apostasy in Judaism, Greek and Roman Religions, and Christianity

A postasy in some form or other seems to have occupied Judaism, Christianity, and even Greek and Roman religions, despite the fact that the notion of exclusivity was alien to the two Classical religions. The attitudes and acts toward those these religions regarded as apostate developed over several centuries. In Judaism, the apostate who abandons his ancestral religion for Christianity, for example, is considered a traitor, and by 100 C.E. the rabbis had in place a prayer that read, "For apostates let there be no hope. The dominion of arrogance do thou speedily root out in our days. And let Christians and the sectarians perish in a moment. Let them be blotted out of the book of life." By the third century C.E., the rabbis had legal power to expel apostates from Judaism. In the Classical world, we had the edict of Diocletian against the Manichaeans (297 C.E.), which read, "It is the most serious crime to reject what once and for all has been arranged and established by the ancestors." In Christianity from the third century onward, apostasy meant paganism, and was punished ever more severely. Indeed, for the early church "apostasy was an inexpiable offense. After baptism there was no forgiveness of this sin." [1] By 445 C.E., "two edicts directed that persons having betrayed the holy faith shall be segregated from the community of all men, shall not have testamentary capacity, shall not inherit, shall forfeit their position and status, and shall be branded with perpetual infamy." [2] Interestingly enough, the Christians carried on the persecution of the Manichaeans started by Diocletian in 297 C.E.

While Christianity and Islam each claimed to be the sole custodian of God's final revelation to mankind, and neither admitted salvation outside its own system of beliefs,[3] Hinduism and Buddhism have never entertained any notion of exclusivity; hence the total absence of any idea of apostasy. Articles on apostasy in encyclopedias pass the latter two religions by.[4]

APOSTASY IN ISLAM: KORAN, ḤADĪTH, DOCUMENTS, AND CASE STUDIES[5]

Definitions

The Arabic word for apostate is *murtadd*, "the one who turns back from Islam," and apostasy is denoted by *irtidād* and *ridda*. *Ridda* seems to have been used for apostasy from Islam into unbelief (in Arabic *kufr*), and *irtidād* from Islam to some other religion.[6] A person born of Muslim parents who later rejects Islam is called a *Murtadd Fiṭri*; *fiṭri* meaning "natural," it can also mean "instinctive, native, inborn, innate." One who converts to Islam and subsequently leaves it is a *Murtadd Milli*; from *milla*, meaning "religious community." The *Murtadd Fiṭri* can be seen as someone unnatural, subverting the natural course of things, whose apostasy is a wilful and obstinate act of treason against God and the one and only true creed, and a betrayal and desertion of the community. The *Murtadd Milli* is a traitor to the Muslim community and equally disruptive.

Any verbal denial of any principle of Muslim belief is considered apostasy. If one declares, for example, that the universe has always existed or that God has material substance, then one is an apostate. If one denies the unity of God or confesses to a belief in reincarnation, one is guilty of apostasy. Certain acts are also deemed acts of apostasy: for example, treating a copy of the Koran disrespectfully, by burning it or even soiling it. Some doctors of Islamic law claim that a Muslim becomes an apostate if he or she enters a church, worships an idol, or learns and practices magic. A Muslim becomes an apostate if he defames the Prophet's character, morals, or virtues, and denies Muhammad's prophethood and that he was the seal of the prophets.

The Koran

It is clear quite clear that under Islamic law an apostate must be put to death. There is no dispute on this ruling among classical or modern Muslim scholars,[7] and we shall return to the textual evidence for it. However, there is some controversy as to whether the Koran prescribes any punishment for apostasy in this world. Some modern scholars have argued that the apostate is threatened with punishment only in the next world, as, for example, at XVI.106:

> Whoso disbelieveth in Allah after his belief—save him who is forced thereto and whose heart is still content with the Faith—but whoso findeth ease in disbelief: On them is wrath from Allah. Theirs will be an awful doom.

Similarly in III. 90–91:

> Lo! those who disbelieve after their (profession of) belief, and afterward grow violent in disbelief: their repentance will not be accepted. And such are those who are astray. Lo! those who disbelieve, and die in disbelief, the (whole) earth full of gold would not be accepted from such an one if it were offered as a ransom (for his soul). Theirs will be a painful doom and they will have no helpers.

However sura II.217 is interpreted by no less an authority than al-Shāfiʿī (d. 820 C.E.), the founder of one of the four orthodox schools of law of Sunnī Islam, to mean that the death penalty should be prescribed for apostates. Sura II.217 reads: ". . . But whoever of you recants and dies an unbeliever, his works shall come to nothing in this world and the next, and they are the companions of the fire for ever." Al-Thaʿālibī and al-Khazan concur. Al-Rāzī, in his commentary on II.217, says the apostate should be killed.[8]

Similarly, IV.89:

> They would have you disbelieve as they themselves have disbelieved, so that you may be all like alike. Do not befriend them until they have fled their homes for the cause of God. If they desert you seize them and put them to death wherever you find them. Look for neither friends nor helpers among them. . . .

Baydāwī (d, c. 1315–16), in his celebrated commentary on the Koran, interprets this passage to mean: "Whosover turns back from his belief (*irtada*), openly or secretly, take him and kill him wheresoever ye find him, like any other infidel. Separate yourself from him altogether. Do not accept intercession in his regard."[9] Ibn Kathīr, in his commentary on this passage, quoting Al-Suddi (d. 745), says that since the unbelievers have manifested their unbelief they should be killed.[10] Abūʾl Aʿlāʾ Mawdūdī (1903–1979), the founder of the Jamāʿat-i Islāmī, is perhaps the most influential Muslim thinker of the twentieth century, being responsible for the Islamic resurgence in modern times. He called for a return to the Koran and a purified sunna as a way to revive and revitalize Islam. In his book on apostasy in Islam, Mawdūdī argued that even the Koran prescribes the death penalty for all apostates. He points to sura IX:11,12 for evidence:

> But if they repent and establish worship and pay the poor-due, then are they your brethren in religion. We detail our revelations for a people who have knowledge. And if they break their pledges after their treaty (hath been made with you) and assail your religion, then fight the heads of disbelief—Lo! they have no binding oaths in order that they may desist.

Mawdūdī argues that

> the following is the occasion for the revelation of this verse: During the pilgrimage (*ḥajj*) in A.H. 9 God Most High ordered a proclamation of an immunity. By virtue of this proclamation all those who, up to that time, were fighting against God and His Apostle and were attempting to obstruct the way of God's religion through all kinds of excesses and false covenants, were granted from that time a maximum respite of four months. During this period they were to ponder their own situation. If they wanted to accept Islam, they could accept it and they would be forgiven. If they wanted to leave the country, they could leave. Within this fixed period nothing would hinder them from leaving. Thereafter those remaining, who would neither accept Islam nor leave the country, would be dealt with by the sword. In this connection it was said: "If they repent and uphold the practice of prayer and almsgiving, then they are your brothers in religion. If after this, however, they break their covenant, then war should be waged against the leaders of *kufr* (infidelity). Here "covenant breaking" in no way can be construed to mean "breaking of political covenants." Rather, the context clearly determines its meaning to be "confessing Islam and then renouncing it." Thereafter the meaning of "fight the heads of disbelief" (IX:11,12) can only mean that war should be waged against the leaders instigating apostasy.[11]

Ḥadīth

Here we find many traditions demanding the death penalty for apostasy. According to Ibn ʿAbbās, the Prophet said, "Kill him who changes his religion" or "behead him."[12] The only argument was as to the nature of the death penalty. Bukhārī recounts this gruesome tradition:

> Narrated Anas: Some people from the tribe of Ukl came to the Prophet and embraced Islam. The climate of Medina did not suit them, so the Prophet ordered them to go to the (herd of milch) camels of charity to drink their milk

and urine (as a medicine). They did so, and after they had recovered from their ailment they turned renegades (reverted from Islam, *irtada*) and killed the shepherd of the camels and took the camels away. The Prophet sent (some people) in their pursuit and so they were caught and brought, and the Prophet ordered that their hands and legs should be cut off and that their eyes should be branded with heated pieces of iron, and that their cut hands and legs should not be cauterised, till they die.[13]

Abū Dāwūd has collected the following saying of the Prophet:

Ikrimah said: Ali burned some people who retreated from Islam. When Ibn ʿAbbās was informed of it he said, If it had been I, I would not have them burned, for the apostle of Allah said: *Do not inflict Allah's punishment on anyone.* But would have killed them on account of the statement of the Apostle of Allah, *Kill those who change their religion.*[14]

In other words, kill the apostates (with the sword), but certainly not by burning them, as that is Allah's way of punishing transgressors in the next world. According to a tradition of ʿĀʾisha's, apostates are to be slain, crucified, or banished.[15] Should the apostate be given a chance to repent? Traditions differ enormously. In one tradition, Muʿādh Jabal refused to sit down until an apostate brought before him had been killed "in accordance with the decision of God and of His Apostle."[16] But in Abū Dāwūd's version of this tradition, it seems they tried in vain to convert the apostate for twenty nights: "Abū Burdah said: A man who turned back from Islam was brought to Abū Mūsā. He invited him to repent for twenty days or about so. Muʿādh then came and invited him (to embrace Islam) but he refused. So he was beheaded."[17] Abū Dāwūd also gives an example of the Prophet forgiving an apostate—once the latter had agreed to come back to the fold, of course.[18] However, Ibn Ḥanbal and others have traditions according to which God does not accept repentance of an apostate.

Under Muslim law, the male apostate must be put to death, as long as he is an adult and in full possession of his faculties. If an underage boy apostatizes, he is imprisoned until he comes of age; if he persists in rejecting Islam he must be put to death. Drunkards and the mentally disturbed are not held responsible for their apostasy. If a person has acted under compulsion he is not considered an apostate, his wife is not divorced, and his lands are not forfeited. According to Ḥanafīs and *Shīʿa*, a woman is imprisoned until she repents and adopts Islam once more, but according to the influential Ibn Ḥanbal and the Malikīs and Shāfiʿīs, she is also put to death. In general, execution must be by the sword, though there are examples of apostates tortured to death, or strangled, burned, drowned, impaled, or flayed. The caliph ʿUmar used to tie them to a post and had lances thrust into their hearts, and the Sultan Baybars II (1308–1309) made torture legal.

Should attempts be made at conversion? Some jurists accept the distinction between *Murtadd Fiṭri* and *Murtadd Milli*, and argue that the former be put to death immediately. Others, leaning on sura IV.137 ("Lo! those who believe, then disbelieve and then (again) believe, then disbelieve, and then increase in disbelief, Allah will never pardon them, nor will he guide them unto a way"), insist on three attempts at conversion, or have the apostate imprisoned for three days. Others argue that one should wait for the cycle of the five times of prayer and ask the apostate to perform the prayers at each. Only if he refuses at each prayer time is the death penalty to be applied. If he repents and embraces Islam once more, he is released.[19]

The *murtadd*, of course, is denied a Muslim burial, but he also suffers other civil disabilities. His property is taken over by the believers; if he returns penitent, he is given back what remains. Others argue that the apostate's rights of ownership are merely suspended; only if the dies outside the territory under Islam does he forfeit his property to the Muslim community. If either the husband or wife apostasizes, a divorce takes place ipso facto; the wife is entitled to her whole dower, but no pronouncement of divorce is necessary. According to some jurists, if husband and wife apostasize together, their marriage is still valid. However, if either the wife or husband singly returns to Islam, their marriage is dissolved.[20] According to Abū Ḥanīfa, legal activities such as manumission, endowment, testament and sale are suspended. But not all jurists agree. Some Shīʿī jurists would ask the Islamic law toward apostates to be applied even outside the Dār al-Islām, in non-Muslim countries.

Finally, according to the Shāfiʿīs it is not only apostasy from Islam that is to be punished with death, but also apostasy from other religions that is unaccompanied by conversion to Islam. For example, a Jew who becomes a Christian must be put to death, since the Prophet has ordered in general that everyone "who adopts any other religion" shall be put to death.[21]

Documents

There are four major schools of law in Sunni Islam; I shall quote representative documents concerning apostasy from three of them. I shall also quote one modern Sunni pronouncement on apostasy, and a modern *Shīʿa* declaration.

Malik ibn Anas

Mālik ibn Anas (d. 795 C.E.) developed his ideas in Medina, where he is said to have known one of the last survivors of the companions of the Prophet. His doctrine is recorded in the work *al-Muwaṭṭaʾ*, which has been adopted by most Muslims in Africa, with the exception of Lower Egypt, Zanzibar, and South Africa.

1410: Zayd b. Aslam reported that the Apostle of Allah (may peace be upon him) declared that the man who leaves the fold of Islam should be executed.

1411: Muḥammad b. ʿAbd Allāh b. ʿAbd al-Qāriʾ reported that a man came to ʿUmar b. al-Khaṭṭāb from Abū Mūsā Ashar (Yemen). ʿUmar b. al-Khaṭṭāb asked him about the condition of the people there. He gave the information. ʿUmar b. al-Khaṭṭāb then said: Have you anything extraordinary to report? The man said: Yes. A man had left the fold of Islam and became an infidel. He asked: What treatment had been meted out to him? He replied: We caught him and beheaded him. ʿUmar declared: It would have been better if you had cast him in prison for three days and given him one bread each day and asked him to repent. Perhaps he would have repented and obeyed the commands of the Lord. ʿUmar added: Oh, Allah, I was not present there, neither did I give any order, nor did I feel happy when I learnt it. (chap. 440)

Abū Ḥanīfa

Abū Ḥanūfa (d. 767 C.E.), the founder of the Ḥanīfī, was born in Iraq. His school is said to have given more scope to reason and logic than the other schools. The Muslims of India and Turkey follow this school.

We shall quote from the greatest compendium of Ḥanīfī law, called the *Hidāya*, which was compiled by Burhān al-Dīn Alī al-Marghīnānī (d. 1197):

When a Mussulman apostatizes from the faith, an exposition thereof is to be laid before him, in such a manner that if his apostasy should have arisen from any religious doubts or scruples, those may be removed. The reason for laying an exposition of the faith before him is that it is possible some doubts or errors may have arisen in his mind, which may be removed by such exposition; and as there are only two modes of repelling the sin of apostasy, namely, destruction or Islam, and Islam is preferable to destruction, the evil is rather to be removed by means of an exposition of the faith;—but yet this exposition of the faith is not incumbent, (according to what the learned have remarked upon this head), since a call to the faith has already reached the apostate.

An apostate is to be imprisoned for three days, within which time if he return to the faith, it is well: but if not, he must be slain.—It is recorded in the *Jama Sagheer* that "an exposition of the faith is to be laid before an apostate, and if he refuse the faith, he must be slain:"—and with respect to what is above stated, that "he is to be imprisoned for three days," it only implies that if he require a delay, three days may be granted him, as such is the term generally admitted and allowed for the purpose of consideration. It is recorded from Abū Ḥanīfa and Abū Yūsuf that the granting of a delay of three days is laudable, whether the apostate require it or not: and it is recorded from Shāfiʿī that it is incumbent on the Imam to delay for three days, and that it is not lawful for him to put the apostate to death before the lapse of that time; since it is most probable that a Mussulman will not apostatise but from some doubt or error arising in his mind; wherefore some time is necessary for consideration; and this is fixed at three days. The arguments of our doctors upon this point are twofold.—First, God says, in the Koran, "Slay the unbelievers," without any reserve of a delay of three days being granted to them; and the prophet has also said "Slay the man who changes his religion," without mentioning anything concerning a delay: secondly, an apostate is an infidel enemy, who has received a call to the faith, wherefore he may be slain upon the instant, without any delay. An apostate is termed on this occasion an infidel enemy, because he is undoubtedly such; and he is not protected, since he has not required a protection; neither is he a Zimmee [Dhimmi], because capitation-tax has not been accepted from him; hence it is proved that he is an infidel enemy. It is to be observed that, in these rules, there is no difference made between an apostate who is a freeman, and one who is a slave, as the arguments upon which they are established apply equally to both descriptions.

The repentance of an apostate is sufficiently manifested in his formally renouncing all religions except the religion of Islam, because apostates are not a sect: or if he formally renounce the religion which he embraced upon his apostasy, it suffices, since thus the end is obtained.

If any person kill an apostate, before an exposition of the faith has been laid open to him, it is abominable, (that is, it is laudable to let him continue unmolested). Nothing however, is incurred by the slayer; because the infidelity of an alien renders the killing of him admissible; and an exposition of the faith, after a call to the faith, is not necessary.

If a Mussulman woman become an apostate, she is not put to death, but is imprisoned, until she returns to the faith. Shāfiʿī maintains that she is to be put to death; because of the tradition before cited;—and also, because, as men are put to death for apostasy solely for this reason, that it is a crime of great magnitude, and therefore requires that its punishment be proportionally severe, (namely, death), so the apostasy of a woman being likewise (like that of a man) a crime of great magnitude, it follows that her punishment should be the same as that of a man. The arguments of our doctors upon this point are twofold.

First, the prophet has forbidden the slaying of women, without making any distinction between those who are apostates, and those who are original infidels. Secondly, the original principle in the retribution of offences is to delay it to a future state, (in other words, not to inflict punishment here, but to refer it to hereafter), since if retribution were executed in this world, it would render defective the state of trial, as men would avoid committing sin from apprehension of punishment, and therefore would be in the state of persons acting under compulsion, and not of free agents: but in the case of apostasy of men the punishment is not deferred to a future state, because it is indispensably requisite to repel their present wickedness, (namely, their becoming enemies to the faith), which wickedness cannot be conceived of women, who are, by natural weakness of frame, incapable thereof: contrary to men.

A female apostate, therefore, is the same as an original female infidel; and as the killing of the one is forbidden, so is the killing of the other also. She is however, to be imprisoned, until she returns to the faith; because, as she refuses the right of God after having acknowledged it, she must be compelled, by means of imprisonment, to render God his right, in the same manner as she would be imprisoned on account of the right of the individual. It is written in the *Jama Sagheer*,—"A female apostate is to be compelled to return to the faith, whether she be free, or a slave"—The slave is to be compelled by her master;—she is to be compelled, for the reasons already recited; and this compulsion is to be executed by her master, because in this a regard is had to the right both of God and of the master. It is elsewhere mentioned that a female apostate must be daily beaten with severity until she return to the faith.[23]

Al-Shāfi'ī

Al-Shāfi'ī (d. 820 C.E.), who was considered a moderate in most of his positions, taught in Iraq and then in Egypt. The adherents of his school are to be found in Indonesia, Lower Egypt, Malaysia, and Yemen. He placed great stress on the *sunna* of the Prophet, as embodied in the *ḥadīth*, as a source of the *Sharī'a*.

We shall quote from the celebrated *Minhāj al-ṭālibīn* a manual of *Shāfi'ī* law compiled by al-Nawawī (1233–1277 C.E.):

Apostasy consists in the abjuration of Islam, either mentally, or by words, or by acts incompatible with faith. As to oral abjuration, it matters little whether the words are said in joke, or through a spirit of contradiction, or in good faith. But before such words can be considered as a sign of apostasy they must contain a precise declaration:

(1) That one does not believe in the existence of the Creator, or of His apostles; or

(2) That Muhammad, or one of the other apostles, is an imposter; or

(3) That one considers lawful what is strictly forbidden by the *ijmā'*, e.g., the crime of fornication; or

(4) That one considers to be forbidden what is lawful according to the *ijmā'*.

(5) That one is not obliged to follow the precepts of the *ijmā'*, as well positive as negative; or

(6) That one intends shortly to change one's religion; Or that one has doubts upon the subject of the truth of Islam, etc.

As to acts, these are not considered to be incompatible with faith, unless they show a clear indication of a mockery or denial of religion, as, e.g., throwing the Koran upon a muck heap or prostrating oneself before an idol, or worshipping the sun. No account is taken of the apostasy of a minor or a lunatic, nor of acts committed under violent compulsion. Even where the guilty person, after pronouncing the words or committing the acts, becomes mad, he may not be put to death until he has recovered his sanity. This favour, however, does not, according to our school, extend to the case of drunken-ness. Apostasy, and a declaration of having returned from one's errors, pronounced by a drunken person, have the ordinary legal consequences.

Witnesses need not recount in all their details the facts that constitute apostasy; they may confine themselves to affirming that the guilty person is an apostate. Other authorities are of the contrary opinion; but the majority go so far as to make no account of the mere denial of the accused, even where the assertions of the witnesses are made in general terms. But where, on the other hand, the accused declares that he acted under compulsion, and the circumstances render this assertion plausible, e.g., if he has been kept a prisoner by infidels, he has a presumption in his favour, provided he takes an oath; but this presumption does not arise in the absence of such circumstances. Only where the two witnesses required by law do not declare that 'the accused is apostate,' but that 'the words pronounced by him are words implying apostasy,' and the accused then maintain that he only pronounced them under compulsion, the presumption is in his favour, and it is not necessary for him to give more detailed explanations. Where, after the death of an individual whose faith has never been suspected, one of his sons who are both Muslims declares that his father abjured Islam and died impenitent, and adds the cause of the apostasy, this son alone is excluded from the succession, and his portion escheats to the State as a tax; but his deposition has no effect upon the rights of his coinheritors. The same rule applies also where the cause of the crime is not mentioned and the son limits himself to saying that his father died apostate.

An attempt should be made to induce the apostate to return from his or her errors, though according to one authority this is only a commendable proceeding. The exhortation should take place immediately, or, according to one jurist, in the first three days; and if it is of no effect, the guilty man or woman should be put to death. Where, on the contrary, the guilty party returns from his or her errors, this conversion must be accepted as sincere, and the converted person left alone; unless, according to some authorities, he has embraced an occult religion such as the Zend, whose adherents, while professing Islam, are none the less infidels in their heart, or some doctrine admitting of a mystic or allegorical interpretation of the Koran.

The child of an apostate remains a Muslim, without regard to the time of its conception, or to one of its parents remaining a Muslim or not. One authority, however, considers the child whose father and mother have abjured the faith to be an apostate, while another considers such a child to be by origin an infidel. (The child should be considered as an apostate. This is what the jurists of Iraq have handed down to us as the universally accepted theory.)

As to the ownership of the property of an apostate dead in impenitence, it remains in suspense, i.e., the law considers it as lost from the moment of abjuration of the faith; but in case of repentance it is considered never to have been lost. However, there are several other theories upon the subject, though all authorities agree that debts contracted before apostasy, as well as the personal maintenance of the apostate during the period of exhortation, are Charges upon the estate. It is the same with any damages due in consequence of pecuniary prejudice caused to other persons, the maintenance of his wives, whose marriage remains in suspense, and the maintenance of his descendant or descendants. Where it is admitted that ownership remains in suspense, the same principle must be applied to dispositions subsequent to apostasy, in so far as they are capable of being suspended, such an enfranchisement by will, and legacies, which all remain intact where the exhortation is successful, though not otherwise. On the other hand, dispositions which, by their very nature, do not admit of such suspension, such as sale, pledging, gift, and enfranchisement by contract, are null and void *ab initio*, though *Shāfiʿī*, in his first period, wished to leave them in suspense. All authorities, however, are agreed that an apostate's property may in no case be left at his disposition, but must be deposited in charge of some person of irreproachable character. But a female slave may not be so entrusted to a man; she must be entrusted to some trustworthy woman. An apostate's property must be leased out, and it is to the court that his slave undergoing enfranchisement by contract should make his periodical payments.[24]

A Sunni Muslim Pronouncement on Apostasy from Lebanon[25]

Several years ago a Lebanese family in Germany requested official information from the Office of the Muftū[26] in Lebanon regarding the law of apostasy in Islam. The translation of the response is as follows:

In the Name of the Merciful and Compassionate Allah, Dār al-Fatwā in the Republic of Lebanon, Beirut. Praise be to Allah, the Lord of the Universe; blessings and peace be upon our Master Muhammad, the Apostle of Allah, and upon his Family, his Companions, his Followers and those who have found the way through him.

A question has come: "What is the stand of the Islamic Law regarding the Muslim who has renounced Islam and embraced another religion?" The answer is, with Allah's help: Etymologically, *raddah* (renouncing) means to go back on a thing to something else. As far as religious law is concerned, it means the severing of the continuity of Islam. The *murtadd* (apostate) is the one who has renounced Islam. The state of *raddah* (apostasy), should it continue and he die in it, will nullify the value of his work. Such a person will have died outside Islam. This is based on the saying of the Exalted One (i.e., Allah, in the Qurʾān): "Those who among you renounce their religion and die as unbelievers, their works would have failed them."

The loss of the merit of one's works is linked to two conditions: apostasy, and dying in the state of apostasy. These two conditions are necessary and are not the same. Should the apostate renounce his apostasy and return to Islam, his status would be valid as long as he gave these two testimonies:

"I testify that there is no god but Allah, and that Muhammad is the Apostle of Allah."

(The second testimony) should be a clear declaration that he is free from every religion which is contrary to Islam; that he no longer adheres to the faith which had caused him to apostatize; that he is not innocent from the transgression he fell into on account of his apostasy.

The person who renounces his apostasy is not obliged to repeat the performance of everything he had accomplished prior to his apostasy (i.e., while he was still a practicing Muslim), such as the *hajj* (pilgrimage) and the prayers. His works will no longer be counted as having failed him, now that he has returned to Islam. But he must perform all that he has missed during the *raddah* and the period leading up to it. For he is still under obligation, (even) while he was in the state of apostasy, to perform all that is required of a Muslim.

Now, should the apostate (male or female) persist in his apostasy, he should be given the opportunity to repent, prior to his being put to death, out of respect for his Islam. A misunderstanding on his part may have taken place, and there would thus be an opportunity to rectify it. Often apostasy takes place on account of an offer (of inducement). So Islam must be presented to the apostate, things should be clarified, and his sin made manifest. He should be imprisoned for three days, so that he may have the opportunity to reflect upon his situation. This three-day period has been deemed adequate. But if the man or the woman has not repented of his or her *raddah*, but has continued to persist in it, then he or she should be put to death. (This is in harmony with) Muhammad's saying, may Allah's blessings and peace be upon him: "Kill him who changes his religion," as related by the Ḥadīth authority al-Bukhārī (in his Ḥadīth collection). He who executes the apostate is the imam (ruler or leader in Islam) or, with his permission, his deputy. When a person deserves capital punishment, in accordance with the will of Allah, the carrying out of the penalty is left to the imam or the one he has authorized. But if some person, other than the imam or his deputy, has not abided by this rule and executed the apostate, that person should be punished because he has usurped the function of the imam. This punishment is not specifically described. It is left to the judge to decide the amount of the punishment in order that it will keep people from usurping the role of the imam.

An apostate may not be buried in the cemetery of the Muslims, since by his apostasy he has departed from them.

According to Imām Abū Ḥanīfa, may the mercy of Allah be upon him, the female apostate should not be put to death, but must be imprisoned until she islamizes. Reference is then made to Khaṭīb al-Sharbini, Ibn Ḥajar al-Haythamī, and other authorities. Allah knows best. May Allah bless our Master Muhammad, his Family and his Companions. Thanks be to God, the Lord of the universe.

Beirut, the 14th of Rabīʿ al-Thani in the year 1410 A.H. 13 November 1989.
Signed:
Signed:
Deputy to the Muftī of the Republic of Lebanon

A Shī'a Muslim Pronouncement on Apostasy[27]

The following *Shī'a* pronouncement on apostasy in Islam appeared in the ultra-conservative Tehran daily *Kayhan International*, March 1986.

Introduction

In Islam, apostasy is a flagrant sin and guilt for which certain punishments have been specified in *fiqh* (Islamic law). Apostasy means to renounce the religion or a religious principle after accepting it. In other words, one's departure from Islam to atheism is called apostasy.

A person who abandons Islam and adopts atheism is called an apostate. There are special laws concerning apostates in the Islamic *fiqh*. In this lesson, we will be familiarized with them. With regard to the above-mentioned points, we will continue to discuss the issue of apostasy and apostates in the following parts: (There follows an outline.)

1. Types of apostasy: As it was mentioned, apostasy means to return from Islam to atheism and polytheism. That is why it can also be called "reaction." Therefore, from the standpoint of Islam and the Islamic *fiqh*, reaction is to actually give up *Tawḥīd* (monotheism) and return to atheism and polytheism. Reaction is to abandon monotheism and take up paganism, idolatry, and materialism. Reaction is to return from faith and knowledge to ignorance. Therefore, the exact examples of reaction in the current world, especially Muslim-inhabited regions, are apostate materialists, Marxists, and polytheistic capitalists and Zionists who have abandoned *Tawḥīd* and resorted to Trinity and racism. Heretical groups in the Muslim world, such as Ba'athists and the likes of them are reactionary and apostate. Because by denying the genuineness of Islam, or many of its rules, they have practically become apostate and contracted the fatal disease of apostasy and reaction.

Apostasy has two types: one is "voluntary" apostasy and the other is "innate" apostasy. Therefore, there are also two types of apostates: voluntary apostates and innate apostates who are treated according to different rules. In the jurisprudential book of *Taḥrīr al-Wassilah* voluntary and innate apostates are defined as follows:

> An apostate, that is, one who abandons Islam and takes up atheism, may be of two types:
>
> a. Voluntary apostate: a person whose parents, or either of them, were Muslim at the time of his or her development in the mother's womb and who takes up atheism after growing up.
> b. Innate apostate: a person who is born of atheist parents and who accepts Islam after growing up, but returns to atheism later.[28]

2. The way to prove one's apostasy: After the meaning of apostasy and its two types have been clarified, this question may come to mind: How can a person's apostasy be proven?

In response, I should say that, since Islam is an easy religion, it has adopted an easy and untroubled manner in this connection, which does not involve any slander and accusation. Here, before anything else, the judge attaches importance to the confession of the accused person. Whatever the charged person says about himself or herself, the judge takes it as an evidence. If the charged person confesses to his apostasy, his word will be accepted; if he denies the charge of apostasy and claims Islam, again his word will be taken as valid.

Taḥrīr al-Wassilah reads so in this regard:

> Apostasy is proven in two ways: First, the person himself confesses to his apostasy twice. Second, two just and truthful men bear witness to the person's apostasy. But women's testimonies do not prove apostasy in any case; either they bear witness individually, in a group or beside a man.[29]

There should also be several conditions or prerequisites in a person charged with apostasy to be convicted of this guilt. These conditions are: adulthood, wisdom, free will, and intention. Therefore, apostasy does not apply to children, lunatics, and those who have been forced to pretend it. Also, apostasy does not apply for a Muslim who utters a blasphemous word or commits a blasphemous act neglectfully or jokingly and without intention, or in a coma, or in anger; that is to say, he is still a Muslim and considered a Muslim.

> If a person utters or does something indicative of apostasy, and he claims that he was compelled to do so, or did not have real intention and uttered it unconsciously, his or her claim is accepted, even though there is already ample proof of his having done a blasphemous act.[30]

3. The punishment of apostates: The punishment that Islam has considered for voluntary and innate apostates differ.

a. Voluntary apostate: If this apostate is a man, the following punishment will be imposed upon him:

> His wife is separated from him (that is, she becomes forbidden to him) and, as though her husband is dead, she should not marry another man for a certain period of time and after that period, she can marry someone else if she wants.
>
> In addition to this, the property of a male apostate is divided among his lawful heirs. In this division, they won't await his death and his property is distributed among them while he is still living; of course, his debts are first repaid (and the apostate himself is executed). The repentance of a voluntary apostate is

not accepted and has no effect in regaining his property and wife. His inward repentance will be accepted by God (that is to say, the other worldly chastisement will be lifted from him).

In some cases, a voluntary apostate's apparent repentance is also accepted and as a result his prayers and worship will be accepted, his body will be clean and touchable again; he will be allowed to gain new property through legitimate ways such as trade, work, and inheritance. He can also marry a Muslim woman or marry his former wife again.[31]

This is the punishment of a male voluntary apostate. As you observe, Islam considers him a dead person and issues the rule of the dead about his property and wife.

The words of the great Faqih Imam Khomeini indicate that, if a voluntary apostate repents, he will be relieved of death punishment. However, some of the earlier Faqihs such as Allamah Helli believed that a voluntary apostate should be executed immediately and that his repentance was not acceptable.[32]

Imam Khomeini's statement in this regard is based on common law and rationality. Some of the former Faqihs like Eskafi and Sahib al-Massalik were of the same opinion. Concerning the documents invoked by the opponents of this opinion, Sahib al-Massalik says, "Reliable jurisprudential documents generally indicate that an apostate's repentance is acceptable, and any different interpretation of these documents is doubtful."[33]

A similar statement has also been narrated from the Sunnis. For example, alha Ibn Khuwaylid Asadi, a well-known apostate in the early years of Islam who was defeated after apostasy and rebellion against Muslims, repented after some time (and thus was pardoned). In the Nahavand battle, he was one of the commanders of the Muslims' army and was killed in that battle.[34]

But the punishment of a female voluntary apostate is as follows:

Her property remains in her ownership and is not transferred to her lawful heirs, unless she dies. (A female apostate is not executed on charges of apostasy.) She is separated from her husband without any need to remain unmarried for a certain period, of course if no intercourse has taken place between her and her husband. But if they have had sexual intercourse, she should remain unmarried for a certain period as of the moment of her apostasy just as if she were divorced. If the woman repents in the middle of the period of remaining unmarried, she will become the wife of her former husband without any need to hold marriage ceremonies again.[35]

Therefore, a female apostate is never executed but is imprisoned.

b. Innate apostate: An innate apostate is treated in this way:

His or her property is not transferred to the heirs as a result of apostasy. An innate man or woman is separated from his or her spouse as a penalty for apostasy. In case of repenting before the expiration of the period that the woman has to remain unmarried, they will again belong to each other. But if repentance is uttered after the expiration of this special period, they will no longer be each other's wife and husband.[36]

An innate apostate is not executed if he repents. This is a matter agreed on by all *faqihs* (Islamic jurists).

4. Apostate's repentance: The case of an apostate's repentance has become clear and, therefore, there is no need to explain it again.

5. A view of the Koranic verses about apostasy: There are many verses in the Glorious Koran and numerous narrations in Islamic historical and narrative books that help us have a deep understanding of the phenomenon of apostasy. Let us take a look at some of them:

O you who believe! Whoever from among you turns back from his religion, then Allah will bring a people, He shall love them and they shall love Him, lowly before the believers, mighty against the unbelievers, they shall strive hard in Allah's way and shall not fear the censure of any censurer; this is Allah's grace, He gives it to whom He pleases, and Allah is Ample-giving, Knowing. (V.54)

And they will not cease fighting with you until they turn you back from your religion, if they can; and whoever of you turns back from his religion, then he dies while an unbeliever—these it is whose works shall go for nothing in this world and the hereafter; and they are the inmates of the fire; therein they shall abide. (II.217)

Surely (as for) those who return on their backs after that guidance has become manifest to them, the Shaitan has made it a light matter to them; and He gives them respite.

That is because they say to those who hate what Allah has revealed: We will obey you in some of the affairs; and Allah knows their secrets.

But how will it be when the angels cause them to die, smiting their backs.

That is because they follow what is displeasing to Allah and are averse to His pleasure, therefore He has made null their deeds. (XLVII.25–28)

O you who believe! If you obey a party from among those who have been given the Book, they will turn you back as unbelievers after you have believed. (III.100)

And Muhammad is no more than an apostle; the apostles have already passed away before him. If then he dies or is killed, will you turn back upon your heels? And whoever turns back upon his heels, he will by no means do harm to Allah in the least, and Allah will reward the grateful. (III.144)

As you observe, these verses have approached apostasy from different aspects and meditation upon them will shed light on many issues.

6. Answer to a controversial question: In connection with the subject of apostasy and the punishment that the holy religion of Islam has considered for it, the narrow minded or the enemies of justice and truth may attempt to create doubt in the people's minds by raising a question and taking advantage of it opportunistically in their anti-Islamic propaganda. This is the question: Do the Muslims not claim that Islam is the religion of the freedom of belief and creed and that there is no compulsion in choosing one's opinion? Then why has Islam considered such heavy penalties and punishment for apostasy?

The answer to this irrelevant question is this: Yes, Islam and the Glorious Koran have denied compulsion and coercion in belief, and the Exalted God says so in the Glorious Koran: "There is no compulsion in religion" (II.256). But the issue of apostasy differs from the free adoption of an opinion or belief.

In other words, I should say that from the viewpoint of the Islamic *fiqh*, there is a skeptic who is seeking the truth and there is also an obstinate apostate. These two are basically different from each other.

A skeptic is one who does not want to take up a creed and follow a religion in a hereditary way. He or she is doubtful and hesitant of what parents and family or society have inculcated upon his or her mind about God and Islam, and doubts whether they are true or not. That is why he doubts and thus embarks on studying and searching for the discovery of truth and reality.

Not only is this doubt not reproachable and bad from the viewpoint of Islam, but it is also praised. Because the Glorious Koran reproaches ancient nations for having imitated their ancestors in religion and creed. Even research facilities should be provided for the searching and studying of a skeptic out of the Muslims' public treasury. Because the root of this doubt lies in honesty, sincerity, and knowledge. Doubt is a very good passageway, but a very bad place to stop in.

However, apostasy is a matter of treason and ideological treachery, which originates from hostility and hypocrisy. The destiny of a person who has an inborn handicap is different from the destiny of one whose hand should be cut off due to the development of a dangerous and infectious disease.

The apostasy of a Muslim individual whose parents have also been Muslim is a very infectious, dangerous, and incurable disease that appears in the body of an *ummah* (people) and threatens people's lives, and that is why this rotten limb should be severed.

An apostate is an adversary who has penetrated the Islamic *ummah* as the faith column of the enemy of Islam and Muslims and who has taken advantage of his natural situation.

Apostasy is escape from the pattern of creation and nature and that is why the word "voluntary" has been adopted for such an apostate and that is the reason why the punishment of a voluntary apostate is heavier than that of an innate apostate. Can the penalty of escaping from the path and pattern of nature and creation be anything other than annihilation? This is the same thing that has been crystallized in the penal code of Islam.

The antiapostasy punishments of Islam are proper laws to rescue mankind from falling into the cesspool of treason, betrayal, and disloyalty and to remind the human being of his ideological commitments. A committed man should not violate his promise and vow, especially his promise to God. All the punitive laws of Islam have a similar goal. For example, they ask, why is a thief's hand cut for stealing five hundred or one thousand tomans? This is the denial of the value of the human being! But the fact is that a thief's hand is not cut off for the sake of a hundred or a thousand tomans, but his hand is severed for having deprived the human society of security. In other words, a thief's hand is cut for the revival of human values.

An objective and real proof of the fact that apostasy always has a treacherous and warlike nature and revolves around high political and social positions indeed, and not around the free adoption of a belief, as it is alleged, can be seen in the events of the early days of Islam.

After the demise of the Prophet of Islam (Praise Be Upon Him), most Arab tribes became apostate under the influence of their errant, arrogant, and idolatrous chiefs. These apostates were led by the false claimers of prophethood. Their first step after the Prophet's death was to attack Medina and other centers of Islam. In the wars that the bellicose apostates waged against Muslims, fifty or sixty thousand people were killed and the number of casualties is unprecedented in Arab history.

Their most heinous ringleaders were "Ablaha ibn Ka'b" known as "Asswad Ghassi"; in Yemen "Musaylima Kadhdhab" at *Ḥaḍramawt*, and "Ṭalḥa Ibn Khuwaylid Asadi" in the Bani Asad tribe. These wars, and similar wars, which occurred later, show the tyrannical nature of apostasy and justify the necessity of a decisive combat against it.[37]

Another example, which is expressive of the insincere nature of the sinister phenomenon of apostasy, is the ruthless inhuman murder of faithful Muslims by Marxian apostates in Iran under the Shah's regime under the pretext of "changing their ideology." They committed these crimes as "revolutionary assassinations." Yet instead of assassinating the ringleaders of Sawak (the Shah's secret police), they murdered anti-Shah and anti-U.S. Muslims who worshiped God. This is the shameful face of apostasy.

Case Studies

Nawal al-Saadawi [Nawāl al-Saʿdāwī][38]

The well-known Egyptian feminist writer Nawal al-Saadawi appeared before the Personal Status Court of North Cairo on July 30, 2001. A case was filed against her in May, branding her an apostate and calling for a divorce from her husband, Sherif Hitata, on the basis of some remarks she made in the Egyptian weekly newspaper *al-Midan*. If either the husband or the wife apostasizes from Islam, a divorce takes place ipso facto. Ms. al-Saadawi was quoted as saying that the pilgrimage to Mecca, the *hajj*, one of the five pillars of Islam, was a relic of a pagan custom. She also apparently criticized the Islamic law of inheritance, whereby a woman receives only half of what a man does.

The charges against Nawal al-Saadawi are based on the *hisba* law, which allows an individual to file a complaint "on behalf of society" against another individual. On May 23, 2001, the public prosecutor (the sole authority competent to decide whether or not a complaint under the *hisba* law, introduced in 1996, can lead to prosecution) stated that there was no justification for any such charge against Nawal al-Saadawi.

On June 18 the Personal Status Court of North Cairo briefly examined the complaint against Nawal al-Saadawi but postponed its decision. On July 9, with an Amnesty International delegate in attendance in court, the decision was again postponed. Earlier, in May 2001, Amnesty International had written to the public prosecutor expressing its concerns about the case raised against the Egyptian feminist. The letter stated that if Nawal al-Saadawi is tried in relation to comments published in *al-Midan* newspaper, Amnesty International would defend her right to freedom of expression.

The Personal Status Court eventually dismissed all charges against Ms. al-Saadawi, who said the decision was a victory for the freedom of expression and against the reactionary forces which use religion as a pretext to supress freedom of opinion and belief.

Dr. Nasr Abu Zayd[39]

In 1995 Dr. Nasr Abu Zayd (sometimes spelled Zeid), a university professor, faced similar charges to those leveled against Nawal al-Saadawi. On June 14, 1995, a Court of Appeal ruled that Dr. Nasr Abu Zayd had insulted the Islamic faith in his writings. It ordered a divorce from his wife, a professor of French literature, on the grounds that as a Muslim she should not remain married to an apostate. The Court of Cassation upheld the ruling in August 1996. Dr. Nasr Abu Zayd and his wife fled at first to Madrid and then to the Netherlands, where he is visiting professor of Islamic studies at Leiden University.

Amnesty International pointed out that

the right to freedom of opinion and expression is guaranteed by international and regional treaties, including the International Covenant on Civil and Political Rights (ICCPR) and the African Charter on Human and Peoples' Rights, to which Egypt is a state party. Article 19 of the ICCPR states,
"1. Everyone shall have the right to hold opinions without interference.
Everyone shall have the right to freedom of expression; this right shall include freedom to seek, receive and impart information and ideas of all kinds, regardless of frontiers, either orally, in writing or in print, in the form of art, or through any other media of his choice."[40]

Dr. Nasr Abu Zayd is a formidable scholar who has tried to bring to the study of the Koran modern literary and philosophical techniques that place texts in their historical context. One of Zayd's key arguments[41]

is the idea that, once the Quran was revealed to Muhammad, it entered history and became subject to historical and sociological laws or regularities [*qawanin*]. Irreversibly rent from its divine origins, the text became humanized [*muta'annas*], embodying the particular cultural, political, and ideological elements of seventh-century Arabian society:
The Quran—the pivotal point of our discussion so far—is a fixed religious text, from the standpoint of the literal wording, but once it has been subjected to human reason [al-`aql al-insani] it becomes a "concept" [mafhum], which loses its fixedness as it moves and its meanings proliferate. . . . It is imperative here that we affirm that the state of the original sacred text is a metaphysical one about which we can know nothing except that which the text itself mentions and which always comes to us via a historically changing humanity. . . .[42]
From the moment of its enunciation, the divine text was shaped, and continues to be reshaped, through the operation of human reason, such that the distance now separating it from the divine is so vast as to render the text all but human. . . .[43]
In other words, the abrupt break with the divine occurring at the moment of revelation results in the total secularization of the text, which henceforth becomes a book like any other: "Religious texts, in the final analysis, are nothing but linguistic texts, belonging to a specific cultural structure and produced in accord with the rules of that culture."[44]

Mahmud Muhammad Taha

Another attempt at reforming Islam from within ended in tragedy. A Sudanese theologian, Mahmud Muhammad Taha, tried to minimize the role of the Koran as a source of law. Taha felt it was time to devise new laws that would better meet the needs of the people in the twentieth century. To propagate his principles, Taha founded the Republican Brethren. The religious authorities in Khartoum did not take kindly to his ideas and in 1968 declared Taha guilty of apostasy, for which, under Islamic law, the normal punishment is death. His writings were burned, but Taha himself managed to escape execution for seventeen years. He was again tried, and at age of seventy-six was publically hanged in Khartoum in January 1985.[45]

NOTES

1. "Apostasy," in *Encyclopedia of Religion*, ed. Mircea Eliade (New York: Macmillan/Free Press, 1995), p. 355.

2. Ibid.

3. Bernard Lewis, *Islam and the West* (New York: Oxford University Press, 1993), p. 175.

4. For example, James Hastings, ed., *Encyclopaedia of Religion and Ethics* (Edinburgh: T & T Clark Ltd., 1910); Mircea Eliade, ed., *Encyclopedia of Religion* (New York: Macmillan, 1995).

5. The whole of this section on apostasy in Islam has leaned heavily on W. Heffening's excellent, terse article, "Murtadd," in *Encyclopedia of Islam*, 2d ed. (Leiden: E. J. Brill, 1999); S. Zwemer, *The Law of Apostasy in Islam* (New York: Marshall Brothers Ltd., 1924); and "Apostasy from Islam," in *Dictionary of Islam*, cd. T. Hughes (1885; reprint, Delhi: Rupa & Co., 1988).

6. Al-Rāghib al-Iṣṭahānī (d. 1108 C.E.), *al-Mufradāt fī Gharīb al-Qurʾān* (Cairo, 1324 A.H.).

7. For example, J. Schacht, *An Introduction to Islamic Law* (Oxford: Oxford University Press, 1991), p. 187: "The male apostate from Islam, however, is killed; it is recommended to offer him return to Islam and to give him a reprieve of three days"; Bernard Lewis, *The Middle East* (New York: Scribner, 1995), p. 229: "Apostasy was a crime as well as a sin, and the apostate was damned both in this world and the next. His crime was treason—desertion and betrayal of the community to which he belonged, and to which he owed loyalty; his life and property were forfeit. He was a dead limb to be excised."

8. Zwemer, *The Law of Apostasy in Islam*, pp. 34–35. See also al-Rāzī, *al-Tafsīr al-Kabīr* (Cairo, 1308 A.H.), vol. 2, lines 17–20.

9. Zwemer, *The Law of Apostasy in Islam*, pp. 33–34.

10. Ibn Kathīr, *L'interprétation du Coran*, trans. Fawzi Chaaban (Dār al-Fikr: Beyrouth, 1998), vol. 2, p. 128.

11. Abūʾl Aʿlāʾ Mawolūdī, *The Punishment of the Apostate according to Islamic Law*, trans. Syed Silas Husain and Ernest Hahn (1994), available online at www.answering-islam.org.

12. Ibn Māja, *Ḥudūd*, *bāb* 2; al-Nasāʾi, *Taḥrīm al-dam*, *bāb* 14; al-Ṭayālisī, no. 2689; Mālik, *Aqḍiya*, tr. 15; al-Bukhārī, *Istitābat al-murtaddīn*, *bāb* 2; al-Tirmidhī, *Ḥudūd*, *bāb* 25; Abū Dāwūd, *Ḥudūd*, *bāb* 1, Ibn Ḥanbal, i, 217, 282, 322.

13. al-Bukhārī, *Saḥiḥ*, trans. M. M. Khan (Delhi: Kitab Bhavan, 1987), vol. 8, pp. 519–20.

14. Abū Dāwūd, *Sunan*, trans. Ahmad Hasan, vol. 3, *Kitāb al-Ḥudūd*, chap. 1605, *Punishment of an Apostate*, hadith no. 4337 (New Delhi: Kitab Bhavan, 1990), p. 1212.

15. al-Nasāʾī, *Taḥrīm al-dam*, *bāb* 11; *Qasāma*, *bāb* 13; Abū Dāwūd, *Ḥudūd*, *bāb* 1.

16. al-Bukhārī, *Maghāzī*, *bāb* 60; *Istitabāt al-murtaddīn*, *bāb* 2; *Aḥkām*, *bāb* 12; Muslim, *Imāra*, tr. 15; Abū Dāwūd, *Ḥudūd*, *bāb* 1; Ibn Ḥanbal v, 231.

17. Dāwūd, *Sunan*, hadith no. 4342, pp. 1213–14.

18. Ibid., hadith no. 4346.

19. al-Shāfiʿi, *Umm*, I, 228; Abū Yūsuf, *Kharāj*, 109. Cited by Heffening in "Murtadd."

20. "Apostasy from Islam," p. 16.

21. T. W. Juynboll, "Apostasy," in *Encyclopaedia of Ethics and Religion*, ed. Hastings, p. 626.

22. Mālik ibn Anas, *Al-Muwaṭṭaʾ*, trans. M. Rahimuddin (New Delhi: Kitab Bhavan, 1981), pp. 317–18.

23. Burhān al-Dīn Alī al-Marghīnānī, *The Hedaya, or Guide: A Commentary on the Mussulman Laws*, trans. Charles Hamilton (London, 1791), vol. 2, pp. 225–28.

24. Nawawī, *Minhāj al-ṭālibīn: A Manual of Mohammedan Law according to the School of Shāfiʾi*, trans. E. C. Howard (London: Thacker, 1914).

25. Reproduced here with the kind permission of Dr. Ernest Hahn. It first appeared on the Web site www.answering-islam.org/Hahn/2statements.htm.

26. A *muftī*, a skilled legal expert in *Sharīʿa* (Muslim canonical law) who issues a legal opinion in the form of a *fatwā* (Islamic legal pronouncement) in response to a question. *Dār al-Fatwā*, lit., "the house of pronouncement."

27. Reproduced here with the kind permission of Dr. Ernest Hahn. It first appeared on the Web site www.answering-islam.org/Hahn/2statements.htm.

28. Ayatollah Imam Khomeini, *Taḥrīr al-Wassilah*, vol. 2, p. 367.

29. Ibid., p. 496.

30. Ibid., p. 495.

31. Ibid., p. 367.

32. *Tabsarat al-Motammenin*, new edition, p. 179.

33. *Jawahir al-Kalam*, new edition, vol. 41, p. 608.

34. Muhammad Ahmad Bashmil, *Horub al-Raddah* (Beirut), pp. 88, 106.

35. Khomeini, *Taḥrīr al-Wassilah*, vol. 2, p. 367.

36. Ibid.

37. Refer to Bashmil, *Horub al-Raddah*.

38. Amnesty International, "Egypt: Feminist Writer Threatened by Forced Divorce for Comments on Islam," AI Index (MDE 12/022/2001) [online], web.amnesty.org/80256 8F7005C/4453/0/4A84A51086D5C55480256A95003BAD5A?Open [July 27, 2001].

39. Ibid.

40. Ibid.

41. Charles Hirschkind, "Heresy or Hermeneutics: The Case of Nasr Hamid Abu Zayd," *Stanford Electronic Humanities Review* 5 [online], www.stanford. edu/group/SHR/5-1/text/hirschkind.html [February 26, 1996].

42. Nasr Abu Zayd, *Naqd al-Khitab al-Dini* [The critique of religious discourse] (Cairo: Dar al Thaqafa al Jadida, 1993), p. 93.

43. Ibid., p. 96.

44. Ibid., p. 193.

45. Daniel Pipes, *The Rushdie Affair: The Novel, the Ayatollah, and the West* (New York: Birch Lane Press, 1990), pp. 75–76.

2

EARLY HISTORY OF APOSTASY IN ISLAM
Zindīqs, *Atheists, Dualists, Mystics, and Freethinkers*

INTRODUCTION

Muslims are triumphalists, especially when they parrot the journalistic cliché that Islam is the fastest-growing religion in the world or when they present the testimony of someone who has "embraced Islam"; Islam, "that least huggable of faiths," as Rushdie calls it.[1] Many Muslims seem incapable of believing that any born Muslim could possibly wish to leave the most perfect of religions. This incomprehension is well illustrated by Dr. James L. Barton and analyzed by Frithjof Schuon. Dr. Barton gives us this conversation he had in Turkey at the end of the nineteenth century:

> A high official once told me that Turkey gives to all her subjects the widest religious liberty. He said, "There is the fullest liberty for the Armenian to become Catholic, for the Greek to become an Armenian, for the Catholic and the Armenian to become Greeks, for any one of them to become Protestants, or for all to become Muhammadans. There is the fullest and completest religious liberty for all the subjects of this empire."
>
> In response to the question, "How about liberty for the Muhammadan to become a Christian?" he replied, "That [is an] impossibility in the nature of the case. When one has once accepted Islam and become a follower of the Prophet,

he cannot change. There is no power on earth that can change him. Whatever he may say or claim cannot alter the fact that he is a Muslim still and must always be such. It is, therefore, an absurdity to say that a Muslim has the privilege of changing his religion, for to do so is beyond his power." For the last forty years the actions of the official and influential Turks have borne out this theory of religious liberty in the Ottoman empire. Every Muslim showing interest in Christian things takes his life in his hands. No protection can be afforded him against the false charges that begin at once to multiply. His only safety lies in flight.[2]

Schuon, a Western convert to a mystical variety of Islam, explains the Muslim mindset:

> The intellectual—and thereby the rational—foundation of Islam results in the average Muslim having a curious tendency to believe that non-Muslims either know that Islam is the truth and reject it out of pure obstinacy, or else are simply ignorant of it and can be converted by elementary explanations; that anyone should be able to oppose Islam with a good conscience quite exceeds the Muslims' power of imagination, precisely because Islam coincides in his mind with the irresistible logic of things.[3]

But of course, history furnishes us with countless examples of those who have struggled free from the all-encompassing, suffocating embrace of Islam to breathe the bracing air of intellectual freedom.

One of the first individual apostates was ʿUbaydallāh b. Jaḥsh, who embraced Islam and then left it during the Prophet's lifetime. Along with three friends, ʿUbaydallāh came to the conclusion that

> their people [the pagan Arabs] had corrupted the religion of their father Abraham, and that the stone they went round was of no account; it could neither hear, nor see, nor hurt, nor help. "Find for yourselves a religion" they said; "for by God you have none." So they went their several ways in the lands, seeking the *ḥanīfiya*, the religion of Abraham. . . . ʿUbaydallāh went on searching until Islam came; then he migrated with the Muslims to Abyssinia taking with him his wife who was a Muslim, Umm Ḥabība, daughter of Abū Sufyān. When he arrived there he adopted Christianity, parted from Islam, and died a Christian in Abyssinia.

After ʿUbaydallāh's death, the Prophet married his widow, Umm Ḥabība.[4]

We also have the evidence of the so-called wars of apostasy (the *riddah*) when many tribes that had adopted Islam reverted to their ancestral religion even before the death of the Prophet. Some scholars argued that these wars were political rather than religious.[5] But as Montgomery Watt has pointed out, the leaders of the *riddah*, often called the false prophets, represented themselves as possessing prophetic aspirations, hence it was not wholly devoid of religious character.[6]

Save a remnant here and there, faith was vanishing, and the Arabs throughout the Peninsula were relapsing into apostasy. Yet Islam was to be the Faith of all Arabia;—"Throughout the land there shall be no second creed," was the behest of Muhammad upon his deathbed. False prophets must be crushed; rebels vanquished; apostates reclaimed or else exterminated; and the supremacy vindicated of Islam. It was, in short, the mission of Abū Bakr to redeem the dying Prophet's words.[7]

The rebellions were crushed with much cruelty, which included the mutilation of writers who had mocked the Prophet in earlier days. The subsequent history of Islam provides us with many examples of individual apostates, but since history is written by the victors, we do not have many details. Nonetheless, the names of the apostates have become familiar through the works of those who tried to refute the arguments of these former Muslims turned agnostic or atheist: al-Rāwandī, al-Rāzī, al-Maʿarrī,[8] ʿUmar Khayyām, Ibn Dirham, and Ibn al-Muqaffaʿ, to whom we will now turn.

We know from the Koran itself that there were Arab skeptics in Mecca who did not accept the "fables" recounted by Muhammad—they scoffed at the notion of the resurrection of the body, they doubted the divine origins of his "revela tion," and even accused him of plagiarizing the pagan Arab poets; certain verses of the Koran are even now attributed to the pre-Islamic poet al-Qays. As J. M. Robertson suggests, it is thanks to these Meccan freethinkers that we have so few miracles attributed to Muhammad in the early days of Islam, for these opponents of Muhammad disbelieved in a future life and miracles, and they put to Muhammad challenges that "showed they rationally disbelieved his claim to inspiration. Hence, clearly, the scarcity of miracles in [Muhammad's] early legend, on the Arab side." But, as Robertson concludes, "On a people thus partly 'refined, sceptical, incredulous,' whose poetry showed no trace of religion, the triumph of Islam gradually imposed a tyrannous dogma, entailing abundance of primitive superstition under the aegis of monotheistic doctrine."[9]

Pagan Arabs lacked any deep religious sense, they were not wont to thank superior powers for their worldly sucesses. Thus, it is not surprising that these pagan attitudes prevailed in the early years of Islam. Arabs converted out of cupidity and hope of booty and success in this world. Many outwardly confessed their belief but in fact had no inclination toward Islam and its dogma and ritual. Aloys Sprenger estimates that at the death of Muhammad the number who really converted to Muhammad's doctrine did not exceed a thousand. If things went wrong, the bedouins were ready to drop Islam—apostasize—as quickly as they had adopted it. The fact that Islam restricted wine drinking and sexual intercourse, "the two delicious things," did not endear Muhammad to them, either.

The Arabs also resisted the institution of Muslim prayers and ridiculed the movements of the body connected with it. As Ignaz Goldziher says,

there are countless stories, unmistakably taken from true life, which describe the
indifference of the desert Arabs to prayer, their ignorance of the elements of
Muslim rites and even their indifference towards the sacred book of God itself
and their ignorance of its most important parts.[10] The Arabs always preferred to
hear the songs of the heroes of paganism rather than holy utterances of the
Koran. It is related that ʿUbayda b. Hilāl, one of the chiefs of the *Khawārij*, used
to ask his men, while they were resting from battle, to come to his tent. Once two
warriors came. "What would you prefer?" he asked them, "that I should read to
you from the Koran, or that I should recite poems to you?" They replied: "We
know the Koran as well as we know you; let us hear poems." "You godless
men," said ʿUbayda, "I knew that you would prefer poems to the Koran."[11]

We have the evidence of al-Jāḥiz that the Arabs mocked and derided the Koran.[12]
We might here quote a Muslim leader of the early days who is reputed to have said:
"If there were a God, I would swear by his name that I did not believe in him."

THE UMAYYADS (661–750 C.E.)

The Umayyads have always been considered "godless" by their opponents. The
ignorance of Islamic doctrine and ritual continued well into the first Islamic century; indeed, Islam can not be properly said to have existed in the sense of a fixed
dogma until later. We can get a glimpse of the kind of atmosphere that the caliph
al-Walīd II (ruled 743) grew up in by the verses he addressed to the Koran, referring to the threats made by the Koran against the stubborn opponents:

> You hurl threats against the stubborn opponent, well then, I am a stubborn oppo-
> nent myself.
>> When you appear before God at the day of resurrection just say:
>> My Lord, al-Walīd has torn me up.[13]

Walīd II is said to have stuck the Koran onto a lance and shot it to pieces with
arrows repeating the above verses. Walīd II certainly did not abide by the inter-
dictions of the Koran. An intensively cultivated man, he surrounded himself with
poets, dancing girls, and musicians, and lived the merry life of the libertine, with
no interest in religion.

ZINDĪQS, OR FROM DUALISM TO ATHEISM

In Islam, the term *zindīq* was, at first, applied to those who secretly held dualist
doctrines derived from Iranian religions, such as Manichaeism,[14] while publicly

professing Islam. Thus a *zindīq* was a heretic, guilty of *Zandaqa*, heresy. The term was later extended to mean anyone holding unorthodox or suspect beliefs likely to perturb the social order. Finally, *zindīq* came to be applied to all kinds of freethinkers, atheists, and materialists.[15]

Goldziher admirably sums up the different elements that make up what we call the *zindīqs*:

> Firstly, there are the old Persian families incorporated in Islam who, following the same path as the Shu'ūbīya, have a national interest in the revival of Persian religious ideas and traditions, and from this point of view react against the Arabian character of the Muhammadan system. Then, on the other hand, there are freethinkers, who oppose in particular the stubborn dogma of Islam, reject positive religion, and acknowledge only the moral law. Amongst the latter there is developed a monkish asceticism extraneous to Islam and ultimately traceable to Buddhistic influences.[16]

DJA'D IBN DIRHAM (EXECUTED C. 742 C.E.)

The first person to be executed on a charge of heresy, *zandaqa*, was Dja'd Ibn Dirham, on the orders of the Umayyad caliph Hishām, in 742 or 743 C.E. There is no indication that Dja'd was a dualist; rather, he was probably put to death for holding views, later associated with the Mu'tazilites, of the createdness of the Koran and of free will. He is also said to have denied the divine attributes, and as a consequence, held that "God did not speak to Moses, nor take Abraham as His friend." He is said to have been a materialist and his followers are said to have accused the Prophet Muhammad of lying and to have denied the resurrection.

Serious persecutions of the *zindīqs* began under the Abbasid caliph al-Manṣūr (reigned 754–775 C.E.). Many *zindīqs* were put to death under his reign, the most famous being Ibn al-Muqaffa' (executed 760 C.E.)

Ibn al-Muqaffa' was asked by the caliph al-Manṣūr to draw up an amnesty for Manṣūr's uncle, but the caliph was not at all pleased at the language used by Ibn al-Muqaffa' in the finished document. It is generally held that for this reason al-Manṣūr had Ibn al-Muqaffa' executed in a most horrific manner—his limbs were cut off one by one and fed into a blazing fire. But it is also very probable that Ibn al-Muqaffa''s unorthodox religious views played an important role in his condemnation.

Francesco Gabrieli,[17] Paul Kraus, and others have shown that an anti-Muslim work of a pronounced rationalist tendency was correctly attributed to Ibn al-Muqaffa'. The latter, according to Kraus, was the intellectual heir to the rationalist tradition that flourished at the time of the Sassanid king Chosroes Anusharwan, who is said to have fostered a "veritable hellenistic Aufklarung [Enlightenment]."

At any rate, from the perspective of the Manichaen faith, Ibn al-Muqaffaʿ attacked Islam, its Prophet, its theology and theodicy, and its concept of God. How do we reconcile Ibn al-Muqaffaʿ's rational skepticism and his adherence to Manichaean dualism? Gabrieli points out that intellectuals like Ibn al-Muqaffaʿ had already given an allegorical interpretation to the Manichaen mythology, and interpreted the universe and man's place in it in gnostic terms, rational and hellenistic.

Ibn al-Muqaffaʿ is also renowned for his translations from Pehlevi or Middle Persian literature into Arabic. His translation of *The Book of Kalīla and Dimna*, ultimately derived from the Sanskrit Fables of Bidpai, is considered a model of elegant style.

THE GRAND INQUISITOR

Under Manṣūr's successors, al-Mahdī (775–785 C.E.) and al-Hādī (785–786 C.E.) repression, persecution, and executions were applied with even greater ferocity. Special magistrates were appointed to pursue the heretics, and the whole inquisition was masterminded by the Grand Inquisitor, called the Sahih al-Zanādiqa. It was enough for a simple rumor to be aired for the Inquisitor to take immediate steps to incriminate the suspect. Often the *zindīqs* were arrested en masse, imprisoned, and finally brought before the inquisitor or the ruler, who then questioned them on their beliefs. If the suspects abjured their heretical religion they were released, if they refused; they were beheaded and their heads displayed on a gibbet. Some were crucified. Al-Hādī seems to have had some strangled also. Their heretical books were cut up with knives.

We have a glimpse of the whole procedure from this comic anecdote about Abū Nuwās (b. 762, d. between 806 and 814), the great lyric poet whose twin passions were beautiful boys and wine. One day he entered a mosque drunk as ever, and when the imam recited verse 1 from sura CIX:

"Say: O! You unbelievers . . . ," Abū Nuwās cried out, "Here I am!" Whereupon the faithful whisked him off to the chief of police, declaring that Abū Nuwās was an infidel, on his own admission. The chief of police then took Abū Nuwās to the Inquisitor. However, the latter refused to believe that the poet was a zindiq and refused to proceed any further. But the crowd insisted, and to calm a potentially dangerous situation, he brought a portrait of the prophet of the dualists, Mani, and asked Abū Nuwās to spit on it. Abū Nuwās did even better than that, he pushed a finger down his throat, and vomited on the picture, whereupon, the Inquisitor set him free. We know that on another occasion Abū Nuwās was in prison on charge of *zandaqa*. Heresy seems even to have penetrated the Hashimite family, the family to which the Prophet had belonged. Several members of the family were executed or died in prison.[18]

Ibn Abi ʾl-ʿAwjāʾ (executed 772) was one of the more interesting zindiqs. Apparently he believed that light had created good, while darkness had created evil; he also taught *metempsychosis** and the freedom of the will. Before his death, he confessed that he had fabricated more than four thousand traditions (ḥadīth), in which he forbade Muslims what was in fact permitted, and vice versa, and he made Muslims break the fast when they should have been fasting, and vice versa. He is supposed to have posed the problem of human suffering: "Why," he asked, "are there catastrophes, epidemics, if God is good?" According to al-Bīrūnī, Ibn Abi ʾl-ʿAwjāʾ was wont to shake the faith of simple people with captious questions about divine justice.

Ibn Abi ʾl-ʿAwjāʾ is said to have had a discussion with the imām Jaʿfar al-Ṣādiq that is recorded and reveals the full extent of his unorthodoxy: He believed in the eternity of the world; he denied the existence of a Creator. One day he asked Jaʿfar to justify the institution of pilgrimage, and refused to accept the answer that it was ordered by God, since this reply merely pushed the question further back to someone who was not present. He also cast doubt on the justice of some of the punishments described in the Koran. Ibn Abi ʾl-ʿAwjāʾ also accused some of the prophets mentioned in the Koran, especially Abraham and Joseph, of lying.

And like so many *zindīqs* of the period, he doubted the official dogma of the inimitability of the Koran. Even if we cannot specifically link the above dialogue with the historical figure of Ibn Abi ʾl-ʿAwjaʾ, it gives a true picture of the current *zindīq* beliefs. He was taken prisoner, and put to death in 772.[19]

Bashshār ibn Burd (c. 714/15—killed 784/85) was one of the poets who was eventually seized, charged with *zandaqa*, beaten, and finally thrown in a swamp. He was the descendant of a noble Persian family, though his father was a slave and, on being freed, a bricklayer. He had strong national sentiments, and did not miss an opportunity to glorify the memories of ancient Iran. He did not have a high opinion of the Arabs. He was born blind, and was considered physically very ugly, which may go toward explaining, in part, his celebrated misanthrophy. Bashshār b. Burd excelled as a writer of panegyric, elegy, and satire.

His religious views are difficult to esatablish with certainty, since he often concealed, the opportunist that he was, his true opinions. According to Vadja, he belonged to the *Shīʿa* sect of the *Kāmiliyya*, and anathematized the entire Muslim community. When charged with *zandaqa*, it was alleged that Bashshār did not pray in an orthodox manner. What is more, he is said to have mocked it by parodying, when drunk, the call to prayer.

He is also accused of being disrespectful toward the institution of pilgrimage. On one occasion, he left for the pilgrimage, solely to deflect any suspi-

---

*The migration of a soul from one body to another.

cion that he was a *zindīq*, but stopped at Zorara, where he spent his time drinking. As the pilgrims were returning he joined them, and pretended on arrival home to have completed the entire pilgrimage.

One of the charges often leveled at the *zindīqs*, and Bashshār b. Burd, was their continual undermining of the orthodox view of the miraculous nature of the Koran, which the orthodox considered inimitable. No one, in the orthodox view, was capable of reaching the perfection of the Koran. Goldziher gives this example of the *zindīqs'* irreverence:

> It is reported that at Basra a group of free thinkers, Muslim and non-Muslim heretics used to congregate and that Bashshār b. Burd did not forego character-ising the poems submitted to this assembly in these words: "Your poem is better than this or the other verse of the Koran, this line again is better than some other verse of the Koran, etc."[20]

Bashshār did in fact praise one of his own poetic products, when he heard it recited by a singing girl in Baghdad, as being better than the Surat al-Ḥashr. The way of expression of the Koran was criticized and the similes found wanting. Al-Mubarrad tells of a heretic who ridiculed the parable in sura XXXVII.63 where the fruits of the tree Zakkum in hell are likened to the heads of devils: "The critics say: 'He compares the visible with the unknown here.' We have never seen the heads of devils; what kind of a simile is this?"

Bashshār seems to have denied the resurrection and the last judgement in some of his verses. He may well have believed in metempsychosis, i.e., the trans-migration of souls. In some celebrated verses, Bashshār defends Iblīs (the devil), being made of fire, for refusing to prostrate himself before Adam, being made of ordinary clay. In another one of his verses, he prayed to the Prophet Muhammad to join with him in an attack upon the deity. He also seems to have held Manichaean beliefs laced with Zoroastrianism.

But, in the words of Régis Blachère, "Along with these beliefs there would seem always to have been a profound scepticism mingled with a fatalistic outlook leading *Bashshār* to pessimism and hedonism."[21] But out of prudence he was obliged to pay lip service to orthodoxy. This view of Bashshār being a skeptic is endorsed by Vadja, who argues that it seems totally out of character for someone as dissolute as he to adhere to a religion as ascetic as Manichaeism.

Ḥammād 'Ajrad (executed 777 C.E.) belonged to a circle of freethinkers based at Basra. Their reunions, already alluded to above, were attended by such unorthodox poets as Bashshār, Ṣāliḥ b. 'Abd al-Quddūs, Ibn Sinān of Harran, and Ibn Naẓīr, among others. Ḥammād was accused of not praying in an orthodox fashion and of preferring some of his verses to those of the Koran. He was accused of the dualist heresy and of composing verses the *zindīqs* recited in their prayers. Even if he was not high up in the religious hierarchy of the Manichaeans, Ḥammād was certainly a sympathizer to the extent that his religious poetry found its way into the liturgy of the Manichaeans. He was put to death by the governor of Basra.

OTHER FREETHINKERS OF BASRA

In our sources for this group, certain names keep cropping up, but often we do not have any other details about their views or works. Thus we are told that Qays b. Zubayr was a notorious atheist, that al-Baqili denied the resurrection, that Ibrahim b. Sayyaba was a *zindīq* and claimed that pederasty was the first law of *zandaqa*, and so on.

We do know a little more about Muṭīʿ b. Iyās, who gives every sign of being a *zindīq*. But the details we have of his life point rather to someone with a skeptical turn of mind with no real profound interest in any religion:

> He began his career under the Umayyads, and was devoted to the Caliph Walīd b. Yazīd, who found in him a fellow after his own heart, "accomplished, dissolute, an agreeable companion and excellent wit, reckless in his effrontery and suspected in his religion." When the Abbasids came to power Muṭīʿ attached himself to the Caliph Manṣūr. Many stories are told of the debauched life which he led in the company of *zindīqs*, or freethinkers. . . . His songs of love and wine are distinguished by their lightness and elegance.[22]

Abū ʿĪsā Muḥammad b. Hārūn al-Warrāq

Al-Warrāq was accused of *zandaqa*, and is important for, among other reasons, being the teacher of the Great Infidel himself, al-Rāwandī. Unfortunately none of his literary work survives, and we have only tantalizing glimpses of it in the quotations by other Arab scholars. Some of his works are also known from refutations. Al-Warrāq started as a Muʿtazilite theologian but seems to have been excommunicated for holding heterodox opinions. Al-Warrāq wrote a remarkable history of religions, where his objectivity, rationalism, and skepticism are given free rein. His critical examination of the three branches of Christianity of his time again reveal his dispassionate tone and rationalism, where there is no question of a dependence on revelation.

Al-Warrāq may well have had *Shīʿa* sympathies, but it is uncertain whether he was really a Manichaean. However, he does seem to have believed in the two principles, and very certainly in the eternity of the world. Louis Massignon correctly sums him up as an independent thinker and skeptic rather than someone who believed in any fixed system of thought.[23] A victim of the Abbasid persecution, al-Warrāq died in exile in 909 in Ahwaz.

Al-Mutanabbī

Al-Mutanabbī (915–965) is considered by many Arabs as the greatest poet in the Arabic language. Born in Kufa and educated in Damascus, al-Mutanabbī modelled himself on the poetry of Abū Tammām and set out consciously to make a name for himself. According to Blachère, al-Mutanabbī was influenced in his religious and philosophical development by a certain Abu ʾl-Faḍl of Kufa, who was a "complete agnostic," and an early patron of his works.[24] Under Abu ʾl-Faḍl's influence, al-Mutanabbī cast off Muslim religious dogmas, which he regarded as spiritual instruments of oppression. He then adopted a stoic and pessimistic philosophy. The world is made up of seductions that death destroys; stupidity and evil alone triumph there.

Not achieving the fame he dreamed of and felt he merited, al-Mutanabbī became determined to dominate by violent means. He began revolutionary propaganda, and then led a rebellion of a politico-religious character, where he claimed to be a prophet with a new Koran (hence his name *al-Mutanabbī*, in Arabic, "one who pretends to be a prophet"). He was defeated, captured, and imprisoned for two years in Hims. He was fortunate to be spared his life, since to claim to be a prophet is rank heresy, and equally to claim to have a new Koran is against all orthodox belief.

After his release, al-Mutanabbī was lucky enough to find patronage at the court of Sayf al-Dawla at Aleppo. For nine years, al-Mutanabbī sang the praises of this prince, and the odes he composed for him are considered the greatest masterpieces of Arabic literature. Al-Mutanabbī seems to have quarreled with Sayf al-Dawla, and was obliged to slip away from Aleppo to Egypt, where he found patronage with the Ikhshīdid ruler Kāfūr. He was to quarrel with the latter as well and obliged to flee. He was eventually killed by bandits while returning to Baghdad.

Al-Mutanabbī wrote a vast number of odes praising sometimes second rate patrons and at others the great Sayf al-Dawla. Some of the odes are full of bombast and some are sublime, but underneath them all we can discern a skepticism, a certain disillusionment with a world kept in chains by ignorance, stupidity, and superstition, from which only death can liberate us. But, as David Margoliouth points out, for many Muslims, al-Mutanabbī's odes are

> defaced by utterances which imply disrespect for the prophets and revealed religion. His most offensive line for Muslims is one in which he tells his patron, an Alid, "the greatest miracle of the man of Tihamah (i.e., Muhammad, the

Prophet) is that he is thy father"; in another he tells a patron that if his sword had hit the head of Lazarus on the battlefield, Jesus would not have been able to restore him to life; and that if the Red Sea had been like his hand, Moses could never have crossed it.[25]

Al-Sarakhsī (executed 899)

The spirit of philosophical inquiry, however, did eventually lead to a questioning of the fundamental tenets of Islamic belief, something that led people like al-Kindī's pupil Aḥmad b. al-Tayyib al-Sarakhsī into deep trouble. Al-Sarakhsī took an interest in Greek philosophy and was the tutor of the caliph al-Muʿtaḍid. He incurred the wrath of the caliph for discussing heretical ideas rather openly, such that the caliph was obliged to order his execution. According to al-Bīrūnī, al-Sarakhsī wrote numerous treatises in which he attacked the prophets as charlatans. Al-Sarakhsī was led into his religious skepticism by the rationalism of the Muʿtazilites, with whom he sympathized, and his philosophical enquiries.[26]

NOTES

1. S. Rushdie, *The Ground beneath Her Feet* (New York: Henry Holt, 1999), p. 74.

2. James L. Barton, *Daybreak in Turkey* (Boston: Pilgrim Press, 1910), pp. 256–57, quoted in S. Zwemer, *The Law of Apostasy in Islam* (New York: Marshall Brothers Ltd., 1924), pp. 44–45.

3. F. Schuon, *Stations of Wisdom* (London: John Murray, 1961), p. 64.

4. Ibn Isḥāq, *The Life of Muhammad*, trans. A Guillaume (Oxford: Oxford University Press, 1987), p. 99.

5. Julius Wellhausen, *Skizzen und Vorarbeiten* (Berlin: Verlag von Georg Reimer, 1884–99), vol. 6, pp. 7–37; Caetani, *Annali dell'Islam* (Milan: Ultico Hoepli, 1905–26), vol. 2, pp. 549–831.

6. Montgomery Watt, *Muhammad at Medina* (Oxford: Oxford University Press, 1956), pp. 147–48.

7. W. Muir, *The Caliphate, Its Rise, Decline, and Fall* (Edinburgh: John Grant, 1915), p. 16.

8. Full name: Abu ʾl-ʿAlāʾ Aḥmad b. ʿAbd Allāh b. Sulaymān al-Maʿarrī.

9. J. M. Robertson, *A Short History of Freethought Ancient and Modern* (London: Watts, 1906), vol. 1, p. 259.

10. Aghānī, IX, p. 89; XIV, p. 40. Some mixed up the poems of Dhuʾl-Rumma with the Koran: ibid., XVI, p. 112.

11. I. Goldziher, *Muslim Studies*, trans. C. R. Barber and S. M. Stern (London: Allen and Unwin, 1967–71), vol. 1, pp. 43–44.

12. al-Jāḥiẓ, *Bayān*, fol. 128a [II, p. 317].

13. Goldziher, *Muslim Studies*, vol. 2, p. 65, referring to *al-Masʿūdī*, VI, p. 10 (ed. F.

Gabrieli in *RSO* 27 [1934]: 41). There are interesting facts about the freedom in religious matters of these Umayyads in *Aghānī*, VI, p. 141; M. J. de Goeje and P. de Jong, eds., *Fragmenta Historicum Arabicorum* (Louvain, 1869), p. 114.

14. Mani or Manes (c. 216–76 C.E.), a teacher of Persian origin who, influenced by the Gnostic traditions of Persia, developed a theology of light and darkness, good and evil. He practiced severe asceticism, including vegetarianism.

15. B. Lewis, *Islam in History* (Chicago, 1993), pp. 285–93.

16. I. Goldziher, *Ṣāliḥ b. ʿAbd al-Quddūs und das Zindikthum wahrend der Regierung des Chalifen al-Mahdi*, in *Transactions of the Ninth Congress of Orientalists*, vol. 11, p. 105, quoted in R. A. Nicholson, *A Literary History of the Arabs* (Cambridge: Cambridge University Press, 1930), pp. 372–73.

17. F. Gabrieli, "La Zanadaqa au 1er siecle Abbaside," in *L'Elaboration de l'Islam*, ed. C. Cahen et al. (Paris: Centre d'études supérieures specialisé d'histoire des religions de Strasbourg, 1961).

18. G. Vadja, "Les Zindiqs en pays d'Islam au début de la période Abbaside," in *Revista degli Studi Orientali* 17 (1938): 184.

19. Ibid., pp. 173–229.

20. Goldziher, *Muslim Studies*, vol. 2, p. 363.

21. "Bashshār b. Burd," in *Encyclopedia of Islam*, 2d ed. (Leiden: E. J. Brill, 1999), vol 1, pp. 1080–82.

22. Nicholson, *A Literary History of the Arabs*, p. 291.

23. "Warrak," in *Encyclopedia of Islam* (Leiden: E. J. Brill, 1913–1934), vol. 4, p. 1218.

24. "al-Mutanabbī," in *Encyclopedia of Islam*, 2d ed., vol. 7, pp. 769–72.

25. D. S. Margoliouth, "Atheism (Muhammadan)," in *Encyclopaedia of Religion and Ethics*, ed. James Hastings (Edinburgh).

26. Majid Fakhry, *A History of Islamic Philosophy*, 2d ed. (New York: Columbia University Press, 1987).

3

AL-RĀWANDĪ
AND AL-RĀZĪ

AL-RĀWANDĪ (B. C.820–830 C.E.)

Al-Rāwandī started as a Muʿtazilite, but was expelled from their company for heresy. He then began a series of ferocious attacks on the Muʿtazilites and, thanks to a refutation of his work by al-Khayyāt, al-Rāwandī's book against his former colleagues is known in part the work is called the *Faḍīḥat al-Muʿtazila*, or the *Ignominy of the Muʿtazilites*. Al-Rāwandī never hesitated in broaching subjects long considered both taboo and dangerous, and it is not surprising that before long he was branded an infidel and a *zindīq*, both in the narrow sense of someone believing in dualism and in the wider sense of a freethinker. He was publicly accused by the Muʿtazilites, and eventually had to leave Baghdad because of government persecution. In his attacks on his former friends, al-Rāwandī showed their inconsistencies and deduced heretical conclusions from their principles.

As H. S. Nyberg[1] has shown, al-Rāwandī was condemned and expelled by the Muʿtazilites for his Aristotelian tendencies, which questioned the central orthodox dogma of the creation ex nihilo and of the creator. We know that al-Rāwandī wrote a book on the eternity of the world; however, this work has not survived. It is significant that it was often philosophers and doctors who took him seriously, and some even came to his defense—al-Haytham, for example, showed that the putative refutations of al-Rāwandī were plain wrong.

Al-Rāwandī undoubtedly taught dualism in one of his books and, for a time, turned toward Shīʿī doctrine of a moderate kind, finally cutting all intellectual links with the Muslim community and ending as an atheist.

The Muʿtazilites also accused al-Rāwandī of attacking the Prophet, the Koran, the *Hadīth*, revelation in general, in sum, whole of the *Sharīʿa*, in such works as the *Kitāb al-Dāmigh*, the *Kitāb al-Farīd*, and the *Kitāb al-Zumurrudh*. But as Nyberg and others have pointed out, al-Rāwandī was only drawing the logical conclusions of the principles held by the Muʿtazilites themselves.

The extracts we possess of al-Rāwandī's *Kitāb al-Zumurrudh* show exactly why he was seen as a radical and dangerous heretic: It contains a trenchant criticism of prophecy in general and the prophecy of Muhammad in particular, maintaining that reason is superior to revelation. Either what the so-called prophets say is in accordance with reason, in which case prophets are otiose and unnecessary since ordinary human beings are equally endowed with reason, or it does not conform to reason, in which case it must be rejected. For al-Rāwandī all religious dogma is contrary to reason and therefore must be rejected: "The miracles attributed to the prophets, persons who may reasonably be compared to sorcerers and magicians, are pure invention." As for the Koran, far from being a miracle and inimitable, is an inferior work from the literary point of view, since it is neither clear or comprehensible nor of any practical value, and is certainly not a revealed book. Besides, its putative literary miraculousness "is hardly relevant, as probative evidence, in regard to foreigners to whom Arabic is an alien tongue."[2]

Al-Rāwandī attacks all religious ritual as futile, and says any knowledge acquired by the so-called prophets can be explained in natural and human terms. According to at least one authority, al-Rāwandī rejected the very possibility of a satisfactory rational answer to the question of God's existence and the rationality of His ways.[3]

Al-Rāwandī's other views seem to include the eternity of the world, the superiority of dualism over monotheism and the vanity of divine wisdom. Al-Maʿarrī, in his *Risālat al-Ghufrān*, attributes the following lines to al-Rāwandī, addressed to God:

> Thou didst apportion the means of livelihood to Thy
> creatures like a drunkard who shows himself churlish.
> Had a man made such a division, we should have said to him,
> "You have swindled. Let this teach you a lesson."

No wonder Al-Maʿarrī exclaimed in horror, "If these two couplets stood erect, they would be taller in sin than the Egptian pyramids in size."[4]

Abū Bakr Muḥammad b. Zakarīyā Al-Rāzī (865–925 c.e.)

Perhaps the greatest freethinker in the whole of Islam was al-Rāzī,[5] the Rhazes of medieval Europe (or Razis of Chaucer), whose prestige and authority remained unchallenged until the seventeenth century. Max Meyerhof also calls him the greatest physician of the Islamic world and one of the great physicians of all time,[6] while for Gabrieli, he remains the greatest rationalist "agnostic" of the Middle Ages, European and Oriental.[7] Al-Rāzī was a native of Rayy (near Tehran), where he studied mathematics, philosophy, astronomy and literature, and, perhaps, alchemy.

It is possible that Al-Rāzī studied under that shadowy figure the freethinker Ērānsharī, who, according to al-Bīrūnī, "did not believe in any of the then existing religions, but was the sole believer in a religion invented by himself, which he tried to propagate."[8] Ērānsharī may thus have influenced Al-Rāzī's rather similar dismissal, as we shall see below, of all religions.

It was at Baghdad that Al-Rāzī learned medicine. At that time Baghdad was a great center of learning, and Al-Rāzī had access to libraries and well-equipped hospitals, one of which he later directed.

Al-Rāzī is credited with at least two hundred works on a wide variety of subjects, with the exception of mathematics. His greatest medical work was an enormous encyclopedia, *al-Ḥāwī*, on which he worked for fifteen years, and which was translated into Latin in 1279. Al-Rāzī was a thorough empiricist, and not at all dogmatic. This is evident from his extant clinical notebook, in which he carefully recorded the progress of his patients, their maladies, and the results of the treatment. He wrote what was perhaps the earliest treatise on infectious diseases—smallpox and measles. It is based on his own painstaking empirical observations, not neglecting any aspect of those diseases that might help in their treatment—heart, breathing, and so on. He wrote on a vast number of medical topics —skin diseases, diet, diseases of the joints, fevers, poison, and so on.

Al-Rāzī was equally empirical in his approach to chemistry. He shunned all the occultist mumbo jumbo attached to this subject, instead confining himself to "the classification of the substances and processes as well as to the exact description of his experiments." He was perhaps the first true chemist (as opposed to an alchemist).

Al-Rāzī's general philosophical attitude was that no authority was beyond criticism. He challenged tradition and authority in every field to which he turned his attention.

Though he had great respect and admiration for the great Greek figures of the past—Socrates, Plato and Aristotle, Hippocrates, and Galen—he was not at all overawed by them:

He does not hesitate either to modify their philosophical conclusions if he believes that he knows better, or to add to the store of accumulated medical knowledge what he has found out by his own research and observation. Whenever, for instance, he treats a particular disease he first summarises everything he can find in Greek and Indian sources, . . . and in the works of earlier Arabic doctors. He never fails to add his own opinion and his own judgment; he never adheres to authority as such.[9]

Like a true humanist, al-Rāzī has boundless faith in human reason. As al-Rāzī himself wrote in his book of ethics, *The Spiritual Physick*:

The Creator (Exalted be His Name) gave and bestowed upon us Reason to the end that we might thereby attain and achieve every advantage, that lies within the nature of such as us to attain and achieve, in this world and the next. It is God's greatest blessing to us, and there is nothing that surpasses it in procuring our advantage and profit. By Reason we are preferred above the irrational beasts, . . . By Reason we reach all that raises us up, and sweetens and beautifies our life, and through it we obtain our purpose and desire. For by Reason we have comprehended the manufacture and use of ships, so that we have reached unto distant lands divided from us by the seas; by it we have achieved medicine with its many uses to the body, and all the other arts that yield us profit . . . by it we have learned the shape of the earth and the sky, the dimension of the sun, moon and other stars, their distances and motions. . . .[10]

Al-Rāzī denied the Islamic dogma of creation ex nihilo. For him, the world was created at a finite moment in time, but not out of nothing. Al-Rāzī believed in the existence of the five eternal principles: creator, soul, matter, time, and space. "The ignorant Soul having desired Matter, God, in order to ease her misery, created the world conjoining her with matter, but also sent to her the Intellect to teach her that she would be finally delivered from her sufferings only by putting an end to her union with Matter. When the Soul grasps this, the world will be dissolved."[11] Al-Rāzī seems to be even impugning the Muslim Unity of God, "which could not bear to be associated with any eternal soul, matter, space or time."

In *The Spiritual Physick*, al-Rāzī is absolutely unique in not once referring to the Koran and the sayings of the Prophet—a practice common in such works—or to any specific Muslim doctrine. A. J. Arberry describes his attitude as "tolerant agnosticism" and "intellectual hedonism," and "though its origins in classical philosophy are obvious, it reflects very characteristically the outlook of the cultured Persian gentleman, constantly down the ages informing Iranian thought and life."[12] He advocated moderation, disapproved of asceticism, enjoined control of one's passions by reason, and, under the influence of Plato's *Philebus*, developed his theory of pleasure and pain—"pleasure is not something positive but the simple result of a return to normal conditions, the disturbance of which has caused pain."

On life after death he reserved judgment, and tried to allay the fear of death by reason, in a manner reminiscent of Epicurus. His attitude to death is summed up in a poem he wrote in old age:

> Truly I know not—and decay
> Hath laid his hand upon my heart,
> And whispered to me that the day
> Approaches, when I must depart—
> I know not whither I shall roam,
> Or where the sirit, having sped
> From this its wasted fleshly home,
> Will after dwell, when I am dead.[13]

This is like a breath of fresh air after the dogmatic certainties of al-Ghazālī and his beloved, pathological imagery of the torments of hell.

At last, we come to those views of al-Rāzī that earned him universal condemnation from Muslims for blasphemy. Ibn Ḥazm, Nāṣir-l-Khusraw, al-Kirmāni, and even al-Bīrūnī joined in the chorus of reproach. Unlike al-Kindī, al-Rāzī sees no possibility of a reconciliation between philosophy and religion. In two heretical works, one of which may well have influenced the European freethought classic *De Tribus Impostoribus*,[14] al-Rāzī gave vent to his hostility to the revealed religions. Al-Rāzī's heretical book *On Prophecy* has not survived, but we know that it maintained the thesis that reason is superior to revelation, and salvation is only possible through philosophy. The second of al-Rāzī's heretical works has partly survived in a refutation by an Ismaili author. Its audacity will be apparent as soon as we examine, with the help of Paul Kraus, Shlomo Pines,[15] and Gabrieli, its principal theses.

All men are by nature equal, and equally endowed with the faculty of reason, which must not be disparaged in favor of blind faith. Reason further enables men to perceive in an immediate way scientific truths. The prophets—these billy goats with long beards, as al-Rāzī disdainfully describes them—cannot claim any intellectual or spiritual superiority. These billy goats pretend to come with a message from God, all the while exhausting themselves spouting their lies and imposing on the masses blind obedience to the "words of the master." The miracles of the prophets are impostures, based on trickery, or the stories regarding them are lies. The falseness of what all the prophets say is evident in the fact that they contradict one another—one affirms what the other denies, and yet each claims to be the sole depository of the truth, thus the New Testament contradicts the Torah; the Koran, the New Testament. As for the Koran, it is but an assorted mixture of "absurd and inconsistent fables," which has ridiculously been judged inimitable when, in fact, its language, style, and its much-vaunted "eloquence" are far from being faultless. Custom, tradition, and intellectual laziness lead men to blindly follow their religious leaders. Religions have been the sole cause of the bloody wars that have ravaged mankind. Religions have also been resolutely hostile to philosophical speculation and to scientific research. The so-called holy scriptures are worthless and have done more harm than good, whereas the "writings of the ancients like Plato, Aristotle, Euclid and Hippocrates have rendered much greater service to humanity. . . . The people who gather round the religious leaders are either feeble-minded, or they are women and adolescents. Religion stifles truth and fosters enmity. If a book in itself can constitute a demonstration that it is true revelation, the treatises of geometry, astronomy, medicine and logic can justify such a claim much better than the Quran, the transcendent literary beauty of which, denied by al-Rāzī, was thought by orthodox Muslims to prove the truth of Muhammad's mission."[16]

In his political philosophy, al-Rāzī believed one could live in an orderly society without being terrorized by religious law or coerced by the prophets. Certainly the precepts of Muslim law, such as the prohibition of wine, did not trouble him in the least. It was, as noted earlier, through philosophy and human reason— not through religion—that human life could be improved. Finally, al-Rāzī believed in scientific and philosophical progress—the sciences progressed from generation to generation. One had to keep an open mind and not reject empirical observations simply because they did not fit into one's preconceived scheme of things. Despite his own contributions to the sciences, he believed that one day they would be superseded by minds even greater than his.

It is clear from the above account that al-Rāzī's criticisms of religion are the most violent to appear in the Middle Ages, whether European or Islamic. His heretical writings, significantly, have not survived, and were not widely read; nonetheless, they are a witness to a remarkably tolerant culture and society—a tolerance lacking in other periods and places.

NOTES

1. H. S. Nyberg, *Deux Réprouvés: 'Amr Ibn Ubaid et Ibn ar-Rawandi dans classicisme et déclin culturel (symposium de Bordeaux)* (Paris: Centre d'études supérieures specialisé d'histoire des religions de Strasbourg, 1957), pp. 131–35.

2. "Ibn al-Rāwandī," in *Encyclopedia of Islam*, 2d ed. (Leiden: E. J. Brill, 1999), p.

3. "Ibn al-Rāwandī," in *Encyclopedia of Islam*, supplement, p. 95.

4. Quoted by R. A. Nicholson in "The Risalatul Ghufran," in *Journal of the Royal Asiatic Society* 1900, 1902.

5. P. Kraus and S. Pines, "al-Rāzī," in *Encyclopedia of Islam*, pp. 1134–36.

6. M. Meyerhof, "Thirty-three Clinical Observations by Rhazes," *Isis* 23, no. 2 (1935): 322 f.

7. F. Gabrieli, "La Zandaqa an 1ᵉʳ Siècle Abbasiole," in *L'Elaboration de l'Islam* (Paris, 1961).

8. Alberuni [al-Bīrūnī], *India*, trans. Edward Sachau (London: Kegan Paul, 1914), p. 627.

9. R. Walzer, *Greek into Arabic* (Oxford: Oxford University Press, 1962), p. 15.

10. Al-Rāzī, *The Spiritual Physick*, trans. A. J. Arberry (London: John Murray, 1950), pp. 20–21.

11. S. Pines, "Philosophy," in *Cambridge History of Islam*, ed. P. M. Holt, Ann Lambton, and Bernard Lewis (Cambridge: Cambridge University Press, 1970), vol. 2B, p. 803.

12. Introduction to al-Rāzī, *The Spiritual Physick*, p. 11.

13. Ibid., p. 7.

14. See M. Hunter and D. Wootton, eds., *Atheism from the Reformation to the Enlightenment* (Oxford: Oxford University Press, 1992).

15. Kraus and Pines, "al-Rāzī," p. 1134–36.

16. Pines, "Philosophy," p. 801.

4

SUFISM,
OR ISLAMIC MYSTICISM
AND THE REJECTION
OF ISLAM

A s R. A. Nicholson, one of the greatest scholars of Sufism, said, the earliest Sufis were ascetics and quietists rather than true mystics. These
early Sufis were inspired by Christian ideals, seeking salvation by shunning the
meretricious delights of this world. Eventually, asceticism was seen as only the
first stage of a long journey whose ultimate aim was a deep and intimate knowledge of God. Light, knowledge, and love were the main ideas of this new Sufism.
"Ultimately they rest upon a pantheistic faith which deposed the One transcendent God of Islam and worshipped in His stead One Real Being who dwells and
works everywhere, and whose throne is not less, but more, in the human heart
than in the heaven of heavens."[1]

Sufis were undoubtedly influenced by certain passages in the Koran, but the
historical development of Sufism owes as much or more to the influence of Christianity, Neoplatonism, Gnosticism, and Buddhism (the Sufis learned the use of
the rosary from Buddhist monks, among other, more substantial matters).

In this chapter, what is interesting for us is the way in which later Sufis made
a complete break with the formal system of Islamic law, asserting that the shackles
of the law do not bind those who have attained knowledge.[2] This was true of individuals as much as whole orders of dervishes. Many Sufis were good Muslims, but
some were only nominally Muslim, while a third group were "Muslim after a

fashion." One of the most important figures in the history of Sufism, Abū Saʿīd (d. 1049) had nothing but contempt for Islam and all positive religion, forbidding his disciples to go on pilgrimage to Mecca, and so on. Bāyazīd (d. c.1581) also set little value on the observance of the precepts of the *Sharīʿa*.

The Bektāshī order seems to have come into existence around the beginning of the sixteenth century. Heavily influenced by Christian and Gnostic ideas, the Bektāshīs rejected as worthless all external ceremonies of Islam and all other religions. There was even a group of dervishes, collectively known as the *mala-matiya*, who deliberately committed the most outrageous acts possible to draw upon themselves the contempt of the populace. This in turn enabled them to show their own contempt for the contempt that others had of them.

The great achievement of the Sufis was their insistence that true religion had nothing to do with the doctrinal and legal system of orthodoxy, which only restricted man's religious horizon. In the mystic's vision there were no heavenly rewards and hellish punishments; the written word of God was abrogated by a direct and intimate revelation. Instead of being ruled by fear, the mystic is more concerned with the love and knowledge of God, detachment from the self, and "the divine service is regarded as a service of hearts," rather than the observance of external rules that have to be obeyed blindly.

The more Sufism moved toward pantheism, the more it produced

> a series of works, which, under pretence of orthodoxy and devoutness, in reality substituted for the personal God and the future life of Islam notions that were irreconcilable with either and were supported by an interpretation of the Quran so far-fetched as to be ludicrous and irreverent. The most famous of these are the poem of Ibn al-Farīd [1161–1235] . . . and the treatise of Ibn ʿArabī [1155–1240] . . . "Gems of Maxims." Both these works at different times brought their owners into danger, and were the cause of riots (see Ibn Iyās, History of Egypt, . . . where the latter book is described as the work of a worse unbeliever than Jew, Christian, or Idolater). Of the comments on the Quran which this work contains it is sufficient to cite that on the story of the Golden Calf; according to Ibn ʿArabī. . . . Moses found fault with his brother for not approving of the worship of the Calf, since Aaron should have known that nothing but God could ever be worshipped, and therefore the Calf was (like everything else) God.[3]

Sufi philosophy had the consequence of erasing the boundaries between the different creeds—Islam is no better than idolatry, or as one student of Ibn ʿArabī put it, "The Koran is polytheism pure and simple."[4] Ibn ʿArabī himself wrote that his heart was a temple for idols, a Kaʿba for pilgrims, the tables of the Torah and the Koran; love alone was his religion. "I am neither Christian, nor Jew, nor Muslim," sings another mystic.[5] The Sufis did not lay much store by the different creeds and their particulars. As Abū Saʿīd wrote, "Until mosque and madrasa are quite effaced, the work of the dervishes will not be accomplished; until belief and unbelief are quite alike, no man will be a true Muslim."[6] And, to quote R. A. Nicholson, "Hafiz sings more in the spirit of the freethinker, perhaps than of the mystic:

> "Love is where the glory falls
> of thy face—on convent walls
> Or on tavern floors, the same
> Unextinguishable flame
>
> Where the turbaned anchorite
> Chanteth Allah day and night
> Church bells ring the call to prayer
> And the Cross of Christ is there."[7]

Several famous Sufis were, in the words of Goldziher, "subjected to cruel inquisition."[8] The early Sufis aroused considerable suspicion from the authorities and the orthodox, as can be seen from the history of the Sufi Dhu'l-Nūn (d. 860 C.E.). This Sufi had many disciples, and such influence over the people that he was denounced as a *zindīq* by the envious. The caliph Mutawakkil had him put into prison, but later released him seeing his moral qualities.

Perhaps the most famous mystic put to death for what were considered blasphemous utterances was al-Hallāj (executed 922 C.E.).[9] He spent many years in prison before being flogged, mutilated, exposed on a gibbet, and finally decapitated and burned, all because he advocated personal piety rather than dry legalism and tried to bring "dogma into harmony with Greek philosophy on a basis of mystic experience." Twelve years later, al-Shalmaghānī was put to death, also on charges of blasphemy.

Al-Suhrawardī (executed 1191) was at first patronized by the viceroy at Aleppo, but his mysticism aroused much suspicion among the orthodox, who eventually demanded his execution. The viceroy dared not oppose the "true believers," and had al-Suhrawardī executed.

Badr al-Dīn, the eminent jurist, was "converted" to Sufism after his meeting with Shaikh Husayn Akhtali. He got involved with an underground communist movement, and was arrested, tried, and hanged as a traitor in 1416. He had openly developed his heretical ideas based on the views of the mystic Ibn ʿArabī.

Another heretical sect was the Khūbmesīḥīs, who taught that Jesus was superior to Muhammad, and seem to have been centered in Istanbul in the seventeenth century. Adherence to this sect was liable to lead to imprisonment and execution. The sect was said to be inspired by the heretic Qābiḍ, who held similar views and was executed in 1527.

NOTES

1. R. A. Nicholson, *The Mystics of Islam* (London: Cambridge University Press, 1963), p. 8.

2. Cf. ibid., pp. 86–87; I. Goldziher, introduction to *Islamic Theology and Law* (Princeton, N.J.: Princeton University Press, 1981), p. 147.

3. D. S. Margoliouth, "Atheism (Muhammadan)," in *Encyclopaedia of Religion and Ethics*, ed. James Hastings (Edinburgh: T & T Clark Ltd., 1910), pp. 188–90.

4. Nicholson, *The Mystics of Islam*, p. 93.

5. Ibid., p. 161.

6. Ibid., p. 90.

7. Ibid., p. 88.

8. Goldziher, introduction to *Islamic Theology and Law*, p. 156.

9. "al-Halladj," in *Encyclopedia of Islam* (Leiden: E. J. Brill, 1913–1934), pp. 239–40.

5

ABU ꞋL-ʿALĀꞋ AHMAD
B. ʿABD ALLĀH
B. SULAYMĀN AL-MAʿARRĪ

Al-Maʿarrī (973–1058 C.E.), sometimes known as the Eastern Lucretius, is the third of the great *zindīqs* of Islam, and no true Muslim feels comfortable in his poetic presence because of his skepticism toward positive religion in general, and Islam in particular.

Born in Syria not far from Aleppo, al-Maʿarrī, or Abu Ꞌl-ʿAlāꞋ, as he is sometimes called,[1] was struck with smallpox at an early age. This eventually led to his total blindness. He studied in Aleppo, Antioch, and other Syrian towns before returning to his native town of Maʿarrat al-Nuʿmān. When he was beginning to make a name for himself as a poet, al-Maʿarrī was attracted by the famous center of Baghdad. He set out for Baghdad in 1008, but stayed only eighteen months.

Returning home, he lived in semiretirement for fifty years, until his death. Such was his fame, however, that eager disciples flocked to Maʿarrat al-Nuʿmān to listen to his lectures on poetry and grammar. His poetry was deeply affected by a pervasive pessimism. He constantly spoke of death as something very desirable, and regarded procreation as a sin. At times, at least, he denied the resurrection:

[1]

We laugh, but inept is our laughter;
We should weep and weep sore,
Who are shattered like glass, and thereafter
Re-moulded no more.

He is said to have wanted this verse inscribed over his grave:

[2]

This wrong was by my father done
To me, but ne'er by me to one.

In other words, it would have been better not to have been born:

[3]

Better for Adam and all who issued forth from his loins
That he and they, yet unborn, created never had been!
For whilst his body was dust and rotten bones in the earth
Ah, did he feel what his children saw and suffered of woe.

As for religion, all men unquestioningly accept the creed of their fathers out of
habit, incapable of distinguishing the true from the false:

[4]

Sometimes you may find a man skilful in his trade, perfect in sagacity and
in the use of arguments, but when he comes to religion he is found obstinate, so does he follow the old groove. Piety is implanted in human nature;
it is deemed a sure refuge. To the growing child that which falls from his
elders' lips is a lesson that abides with him all his life. Monks in their clois-
ters and devotees in the mosques accept their creed just as a story is handed
down from him who tells it, without distinguishing between a true inter-
preter and a false. If one of these had found his kin among the Magians, or
among the Sabians, he would have declared himself a Magian, or among
the Sabians he would have become nearly or quite like them.

For al-Ma'arrī, religion is a "fable invented by the ancients," worthless
except for those who exploit the credulous masses:

[5]

So, too, the creeds of man: the one prevails
Until the other comes; and this one fails
When that one triumphs; ay, the lonesome world
Will always want the latest fairy-tales.

At other times he refers to religions as "noxious weeds":

[6]

Among the crumbling ruins of the creeds
The Scout upon his camel played his reeds
And called out to his people—"Let us hence!
The pasture here is full of noxious weeds."

He clearly puts Islam on the same level as all other creeds, and does not believe
a word of any of them:

[7]

Hanifs [Muslims] are stumbling, Christians all astray
Jews wildered, Magians far on error's way.
We mortals are composed of two great schools—
Enlightened knaves or else religious fools.

[8]

What is religion? A maid kept close that no eye may view her;
The price of her wedding-gifts and dowry baffles the wooer.
Of all the goodly doctrine that I from the pulpit heard
My heart has never accepted so much as a single word.

[9]

The holy fights by Muslim heroes fought,
The saintly works by Christian hermits wrought
And those of Jewry or of Sabian creed—
Their valour reaches not the Indian's deed
Whom zeal and awe religiously inspire
To cast his body on the flaming pyre.

Yet is man's death a long, long sleep of lead
And all his life a waking. O'er our dead
The prayers are chanted, hopeless farewells ta'en;
And there we lie, never to stir again.
Shall I so fear in mother earth to rest?
How soft a cradle is thy mother's breast!
When once the viewless spirit from me is gone,
By rains unfreshed let my bones rot on!

Here, al-Maʿarrī, while admiring the Indian, more than the Muslim, and the Indian custom of cremation, still insists that death is not such a terrible thing; it is only a falling asleep. In his collection of poems known as the *Luzūmīyāt*, al-Maʿarrī clearly prefers this practice of cremation to the Muslim one of burial. On Judgment Day, according to Muslim belief, the angels Munker and Nakir open the graves of the dead and crossexamine them in a cruel fashion on their faith. Those found wanting are pushed back into the grave, where they await hell. No wonder al-Maʿarrī prefers cremation. Of course, all Muslims find the very idea of cremation totally abhorrent:

[10]

And like the dead of Ind I do not fear
To go to thee in flames; the most austere
Angel of fire a softer tooth and tongue
Hath he than dreadful Munker and Nakir.

Margoliouth has compiled the following sentiments from al-Maʿarrī's poems:

[11]

Do not suppose the statements of the Prophets to be true;
they are all fabrications. Men lived comfortably till they
came and spoiled life. The "sacred books "are only such a
set of idle tales as any age could have and indeed did
actually produce. What inconsistency that God should forbid
the taking of life, and Himself send two angels to take each
man's! And as for the promise of a second life—the soul
could well have dispensed with both existences.

Further thoughts on prophets reveal that al-Maʿarrī, did not consider them any better than the lying clergy:

[12]

The Prophets, too, among us come to teach,
Are one with those who from the pulpit preach;
They pray, and slay, and pass away, and yet
Our ills are as the pebbles on the beach.

Islam does not have the monopoly of truth:

[13]

Mohammad or Messiah! Hear thou me,
The truth entire nor here nor there can be;
How should our God who made the sun and the moon
Give all his light to One, I cannot see.

As for the *ʿulamāʾ*, the Muslim "clergy" or divines, al-Maʿarrī, has nothing but contempt for them:

[14]

I take God to witness that the souls of men are without
intelligence, like the souls of moths.
They said, "A divine!" but the divine is an untruthful
disputatious person, and words are wounds.

[15]

For his own sordid ends
The pulpit he ascends
And though he disbelieves in resurrection,
Makes all his hearers quail
Whilst he unfolds a tale
Of Last Day scenes that stun the recollection.

[16]

They recite their sacred books, although the fact informs me
that these are fiction from first to last.
O Reason, thou (alone) speakest the truth. Then perish
the fools who forged the religious traditions or interpreted
them!

Al-Ma'arrī was a supreme rationalist who everywhere asserted "the rights of reason against the claims of custom, tradition and authority":

[17]

Oh, cleave ye to Reason's path that rightly ye may be led
Let none set his hopes except upon the Preserver!
And quench not the Almighty's beams, for lo, He hath given to all
A lamp of intelligence for use and enjoying.
I see humankind are lost in ignorance: even those
Of ripe age at random guess, like boys playing mora [a child's guessing game].

[18]

Traditions come from the past, of high import if they be
True; ay, but weak is the chain of those who warrant their truth.
Consult thy reason and let perdition take others all:
Of all the conference Reason best will counsel and guide.

A little doubt is better than total credulity:

[19]

By fearing whom I trust I find my way
To truth; by trusting wholly I betray
The trust of wisdom; better far is doubt
Which brings the false into the light of day.

The thoughts in the above quatrain can be compared to Tennyson's "There is more truth in honest doubt, Believe me, than in all the creeds."

Al-Ma'arrī attacks many of the dogmas of Islam, particularly the Pilgrimage, which he calls "a heathen's journey." As Nicholson remarked,

> Al-Ma'arrī . . . regards Islam, and positive religion generally, as a human institution. As such, it is false and rotten to the core. Its founders sought to procure wealth and power for themselves, its dignitaries pursue worldly ends, its defenders rely on spurious documents whivh they ascribe to divinely inspired apostles, and its adherents accept mechanically whatever they are told to believe.[2]

[20]

O fools, awake! The rites ye sacred hold
Are but a cheat contrived by men of old
Who lusted after wealth and gained their lust
And died in baseness—and their law is dust.

[21]

Praise God and pray
Walk seventy times, not seven, the Temple round
And impious remain!
Devout is he alone who, when he may
Feast his desires, is found
With courage to abstain.

[22]

Fortune is (so strangely) allotted, that rocks are visited
(by pilgrims) and touched with hands and lips,
Like the Holy Rock (at Jerusalem) or the two Angles of Quraysh,
howbeit all of them are stones that once were kicked.

Al-Maʿarrī is referring to the two corners of the *Kaʿba* in Mecca in which are set
the Black Stone and the stone which is supposed to mark the sepulchre of Ishmael.

[23]

Tis strange that Kurash and his people wash
Their faces in the staling of the kine;
And that the Christians say, Almighty God
Was tortured, mocked, and crucified in fine:
And that the Jews should picture Him as one
Who loves the odor of a roasting chine;
And stranger still that Muslims travel far
To kiss a black stone said to be divine:—
Almighty God! will all the human race
Stray blindly from the Truth's most sacred shrine?

[24]

They have not based their religion on any logical ground, whereby they
    might decide between Shi'ites and Sunnis.
In the opinion of some whom I do not mention (with praise), the Black
    Stone is only a remnant of idols and (sacrificial) altarstones.

Here al-Ma'arrī is attributing an opinion to a critic, thereby protecting himself
from charges of heresy, but we know from [22] and [23] that he deems most of
the rites of the Pilgrimage, including the kissing of the black stone, to be superstitious nonsense. Religions have only resulted in bigotry and bloodshed, with
sect fighting sect, and fanatics forcing their beliefs onto people at the point of a
sword. All religions are contrary to reason and sanity:

[25]

If a man of sound judgement appeals to his intelligence, he
will hold cheap the various creeds and despise them.
Do thou take thereof so much as Reason delivered (to thee),
and let not ignorance plunge thee in their stagnant pool!

[26]

Had they been left alone with Reason, they would not have
accepted a spoken lie; but the whips were raised (to strike
them).
Traditions were brought to them, and they were bidden say,
"We have been told the truth"; and if they refused, the
sword was drenched (in their blood).
They were terrified by scabbards full of calamities, and
tempted by great bowls brimming over with food for largesse.

[27]

Falsehood hath so corrupted all the world,
Ne'er deal as true friends they whom sects divide;
But were not hate Man's natural element,
Churches and mosques had risen side by side.

*   *   *

Space forbids me from giving further examples of his merciless attacks on every kind of superstition—astrology, augury, belief in omens, the custom of exclaiming "God bless you" when someone sneezes. The patriarchs did not live to be hundreds of years old, holy men did not walk on water or perform any miracles, and so on.

Al-Maʿarrī further offended Muslim sensibilities by composing "a somewhat frivolous parody of the sacred volume" i.e., the Koran, and "in the author's judgment its inferiority was simply due to the fact that it was not yet polished by the tongues of four centuries of readers." As if this were not enough, al-Maʿarrī compounded his errors in the eyes of the orthodox by his work the *Epistle of Forgiveness*. Nicholson, who was the first to translate it into English at the beginning of the century, sums up its contents admirably:

> Here the Paradise of the Faithful [Muslims] becomes a glorified salon tenanted by various heathen poets who have been forgiven—hence the title—and received among the Blest. This idea is carried out with much ingenuity and in a spirit of audacious burlesque that reminds us of Lucian. The poets are presented in a series of imaginary conversations with a certain Shaykh ʿAlī b. Manṣūr, to whom the work is addressed, reciting and explaining their verses, quarreling with one another, and generally behaving as literary Bohemians.[3]

Another remarkable feature of his thought was the belief that no living creature should be injured or harmed in any way. Al-Maʿarrī, adopted vegetarianism in his thirtieth year, and held all killing of animals, whether for food or sport, in abhorrence. Alfred von Kremer has suggested that al-Maʿarrī was influenced by the Jains of India in his attitude to the sanctity of all living things.[4] In his poetry, al-Maʿarrī firmly advocates abstinence from meat, fish, milk, eggs, and honey on the ground that it is an injustice to the animals concerned. Animals are capable of feeling pain, and it is immoral to inflict unnecessary harm on our fellow creatures. And even more remarkably, al-Maʿarrī protests against the use of animal skins for clothing, suggests wooden shoes, and reproaches court ladies for wearing furs.

Von Kremer has justly said that al-Maʿarrī was centuries ahead of his time.

Al-Maʿarrī was charged with heresy during his lifetime, but he was not prosecuted or punished for reasons that both von Kremer and Nicholson have carefully analyzed.[5] Al-Maʿarrī himself said that it is often wise to dissimulate, and thus we find many orthodox passages in his poetry that were meant to throw the sniffers of heresy off the scent. At heart, he seems to have been a thorough skeptic who managed to ridicule practically every dogma of Islam.

NOTES

1. This is rather confusing, because, accordingly, he sometimes appears in dictionaries and encyclopedias under "A" rather than "M."

2. R. A. Nicholson, *Studies in Islamic Poetry* (Cambridge: Cambridge University Press, 1921), p. 173. This entire chapter is based on Nicholson's classic study of Islamic poetry.

3. R. A. Nicholson, "The Risalatuʾl-Ghufrān," *Journal of the Royal Asiatic Society* (1900): 637–720.

4. Alfred von Kremer, "Ein Freidenker der Islam," in *Zeitschrift der Deutschen Morgenländischen Gesellschaft* 29 (1876): 304–12.

5. Nicholson, *Studies in Islamic Poetry*; von Kremer, "Ein Freidenker der Islam."

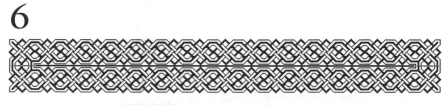

THE POET OF DOUBT
'Umar Khayyām: Medieval and Modern Iranian Freethought

'UMAR KHAYYĀM

In 1859, the year that saw the first edition of Charles Darwin's *On the Origin of Species*, there appeared *The Rubā'iyat of Omar Khayyam*,[1] the Astronomer Poet of Persia, an anonymous translation of the quatrains of an obscure medieval Persian poet who was better known as a mathematician. Unlike Darwin's classic, which was an immediate success,[2] the first edition of Edward Fitzgerald's inspired paraphrase went almost unnoticed and was remaindered. But it came to the attention of another skeptic, the poet Algernon Charles Swinburne, and later the pre-Raphaelite Dante Gabriel Rossetti, who between them launched *The Rubā'iyat [Rubā'iyāt]* on its career of extraordinary popularity that remains unabated and with felicitous consequences for the history of English poetry.[3]

The first that the West heard of 'Umar Khayyām's poetry, rather than his name, was probably in 1700, when Theodor Hyde in his *Veterum Persarum . . . religionis historia* gave a Latin translation of one of Khayyām's quatrains. In 1771 Sir William Jones, in *A Grammar of the Persian Language*, quoted without attribution a complete quatrain (in Persian *rubā'ī*, plural *rubā'iyāt*),[4] and part of another, generally ascribed to Khayyām:

[1]

Hear how the crowing cock at early dawn
Loudly laments the rising of the sun
Has he perceived that of your precious life
Another night has passed, and you care not?

[2]

As spring arrived and winter passed away,
The pages of our life were folded back.[5]

Several Persian quatrains were published in a Persian grammar compiled by
F. Dombay in Vienna in 1804.

Khayyām's quatrains are independent epigrammatic stanzas—in other words,
short, spontaneous, self-contained poems. Each *rubāʾī* stands on its own.
Fitzgerald, however, makes them a continuous sequence: The stanzas "here
selected are strung into something of an Eclogue."[6] Thus, far from being a close
translation, Fitzgerald's version is a paraphrase of "exceptional poetical merits."[7]
One English scholar, E. Heron Allen, compared Fitzgerald's version with the Persian text and established that forty-nine quatrains are faithful paraphrases of single
rubāʾī; forty-four are traceable to more than one *rubāʾī*; two are inspired by the
rubāʾī, found only in one particular edition of the Persian text; two reflect the
"whole spirit" of the original; two are traceable exclusively to Attar, the Persian
mystic poet (d. c. 1220); two are inspired by Khayyām but influenced by Hafiz, the
greatest Persian lyric poet (d. 1390); and three Heron Allen was unable to identify.[8]

One scholar admirably sums up the qualities that caught the late Victorian
imagination and that have endeared Fitzgerald's ʿUmar to so many:

> The Fitzgerald stanza, with its unrhymed, poised third line, is an admirable
> invention to carry the sceptical irony of the work and to accommodate the
> opposing impulses of enjoyment and regret. Fitzgerald's poem has a kind of dra-
> matic unity, starting with dawn and the desire to seize the enjoyment of the
> passing moment, moving through the day until, with the fall of evening, he
> laments the fading of youth and the approach of death. Several interests of the
> time, divine justice versus hedonism, science versus religion and the prevailing
> taste for eastern art and bric-a-brac, were united in the poem.[9]

Edward Fitzgerald himself sums up the delightful nature of ʿUmar and his
philosophy very accurately:

Omar's Epicurean Audacity of thought and Speech caused him to be regarded askance in his own time and country. He is said to have been especially hated and dreaded by the Sufis, whose practice he ridiculed, and whose faith amounts to little more than his own, when stript of the Mysticism and formal recognition of Islamism under which Omar would not hide. Their poets, including Hafiz, who are (with the exception of Firdausi) the most considerable in Persia, borrowed largely, indeed, of Omar's material, but turning it to a mystical use more convenient to themselves and the people they addressed; a people quite as quick of doubt as of belief; as keen of bodily sense as of intellectual; and delighting in a cloudy composition of both, in which they could float luxuriously between heaven and earth, and this world and the next, on the wings of a poetical expression, that might serve indifferently for either. Omar was too honest of heart as well of head for this. Having failed (however mistakenly) of finding any Providence but Destiny, and any World but this, he set about making the most of it; preferring rather to soothe the soul through the senses into acquiescence with things as he saw them, than to perplex it with vain disquietude after what they might be. It has been seen, however, that this worldly ambition was not exorbitant; and he very likely takes a humorous or perverse pleasure in exalting the gratification of sense above that of the intellect, in which he must have taken great delight, although it failed to answer the questions in which he, in common with all men, was most vitally interested.[10]

Fitzgerald will have no truck with those squeamish or puritanical scholars, like the Frenchman Jean-Baptiste Nicolas, who pretend to see something spiritual in 'Umar's verses, and who interpret every appearance of the word "wine" mystically:

And if more were needed to disprove Mons. Nicolas' Theory, there is the Biographical Notice which he himself has drawn up in direct contradiction to the Interpretation of the Poems given in his Notes. (See pp. 13–14 of his Preface.) Indeed I hardly knew poor Omar was so far gone till his Apologist informed me. For here we see that, whatever were the Wine that Hafiz drank and sang, the veritable Juice of the Grape it was which Omar used, not only when carousing with his friends, but (says Mons. Nicolas) in order to excite himself to that pitch of Devotion which others reached by cries and "hurlements." And yet, whenever Wine, Wine-bearer, &c. occur in the Text—which is often enough—Mons. Nicolas carefully annotates "Dieu," "La Divinité," &c.: so carefully indeed that one is tempted to think that he was indoctrinated by the Sufi with whom he read the Poems. (Note to Rub. ii. p. 8.) A Persian would naturally wish to vindicate a distinguished Countryman; and a Sufi to enroll him in his own sect, which already comprises all the chief Poets of Persia.

What historical Authority has Mons. Nicolas to show that Omar gave himself up "avec passion a l'étude de la philosophie des Soufis"? (Preface, p. xiii.) The Doctrines of Pantheism, Materialism, Necessity, &c., were not peculiar to the Sufi; nor to Lucretius before them; nor to Epicurus before him; probably the very original Irreligion of Thinking men from the first; and very likely to be the spontaneous growth of a Philosopher living in an Age of social and political barbarism, under shadow of one of the Two and Seventy Religions supposed to divide the world. Von Hammer (according to Sprenger's *Oriental Catalogue*) speaks of Omar as "a Free-thinker, and a great opponent of Sufism;" perhaps because, while holding much of their Doctrine, he would not pretend to any inconsistent severity of morals. Sir W. Ouseley has written a note to something of the same effect on the fly-leaf of the Bodleian MS. And in two Rubaiyat of Mons. Nicolas' own Edition Suf and Sufi are both disparagingly named.

No doubt many of these Quatrains seem unaccountable unless mystically interpreted; but many more as unaccountable unless literally. Were the Wine spiritual, for instance, how wash the Body with it when dead? Why make cups of the dead clay to be filled with—"La Divinité," by some succeeding Mystic? Mons. Nicolas himself is puzzled by some "bizarres" and "trop Orientales" allusions and images—"d'une sensualité quelquefois révoltante" indeed—which "les convenances" do not permit him to translate; but still which the reader cannot but refer to "La Divinité."[11]

For Fitzgerald the burden of Omar's Song, if not "let us eat," is assuredly "let us drink, for tomorrow we die!" Some may see Omar as a Sufi, but "on the other hand, as there is far more historical certainty of his being a philosopher, of scientific insight and ability far beyond that of the age and country he lived in, of such moderate worldly ambition as becomes a philosopher, and such moderate wants as rarely satisfy a debauchee; other readers may be content to believe with me that while the wine Omar celebrates is simply the juice of the grape, he bragg'd more than he drank of it, in very defiance perhaps of that spiritual wine which left its votaries sunk in hypocrisy or disgust."[12]

Here are some examples of Fitzgerald's paraphrase of Omar (from the first edition):

[3]

Dreaming when Dawn's Left Hand was in the Sky
I heard a Voice within the Tavern cry:
"Awake, my Little ones, and fill the Cup
Before Life's Liquor in its Cup be dry."

[4]

And, as the Cock crew, those who stood before
The Tavern shouted: "Open then the Door!
You know how little we have to stay,
And, once departed, may return no more."

[5]

The Worldly Hope men set their Hearts upon
Turns Ashes—or it prospers; and anon,
Like Snow upon the Desert's dusty Face
Lighting a little hour or two is gone.

[6]

Ah, Beloved, fill the Cup that clears
Today of past Regrets and future Fears—
Tomorrow? Why, Tomorrow I may be
Myself with Yesterday's Sev'n Thousand Years.

[7]

Lo! some we loved, the loveliest and best
That Time and Fate of all their Vintage prest,
Have drunk their Cup a Round or two before,
And one by one crept silently to Rest.

[8]

And we, that now make merry in the Room
They left, and Summer dresses in new Bloom,
Ourselves must we beneath the Couch of Earth
Descend, ourselves to make a Couch—for whom?

[9]

Ah, make the most of what we yet may spend,
Before we too into the Dust descend:
Dust into Dust, and under Dust, to lie,
Sans Wine, sans Song, sans Singer, and sans End!

[10]

Alike for those who for Today prepare,
And those that after a Tomorrow stare,
A Muezzin from the Tower of Darkness cries:
"Fools! your Reward is neither Here nor There!"

[11]

Why, all the Saints and Sages who discuss'd
Of the Two Worlds so learnedly, are thrust
Like foolish Prophets forth; their Words to Scorn
Are scatter'd, and their Mouths are stopt with Dust.

[12]

Oh, come with old Khayyam, and leave the Wise
To talk: one thing is certain, that Life flies;
One thing is certain, and the Rest is Lies:
The Flower that once has blown for ever dies.

[13]

And that inverted Bowl we call The Sky,
Whereunder crawling coop't we live and die,
Lift not thy hands to It for help—for It
Rolls impotently on as Thou or I.

From the fourth edition:

[14]

Some for the Glories of This World; and some
Sigh for the Prophet's Paradise to come;
Ah, take the Cash, and let the Credit go
Nor heed the rumble of a distant Drum!

But who was ʿUmar Khayyām? Very little is known for certain of his life and writings, particularly his poetry. He was born around 1048 in Nishapur, Persia, and died there in 1131. Khayyām was, according to George Sarton, "one of the greatest mathematicians of mediaeval times. His Algebra contains geometric and algebraic solutions of equations, including the cubic; a systematic attempt to solve them all and partial geometric solutions of most of them."[13] He also wrote on physics (specific weight of gold and silver), astronomy, geography, music, metaphysics, and history. While in Samarkand (Uzbekistan) Khayyām worked at the newly built astronomical observatory, and helped draw up a new calendar that was in many ways far superior to the Julian calendar, and certainly comparable in accuracy with the Gregorian one.

In one of our early sources of his life and poetry, *Mirṣād al-ʿIbād* (the Watch Tower of the Faithful), Khayyām is described as an atheist, philosopher, and naturalist: "Observation (of the world) leads to faith, the quest (for the Eternal) to gnosis. The philospher, atheist and naturalist are denied this spiritual level; they have been led astray and are lost. ʿUmar Khayyām is considered by the blind as a sage, an intelligent man. However he is so lost in doubt and shadows that he says in quatrains:

[15]

This circle within which we come and go
Has neither origin nor final end.
Will no one ever tell us truthfully
Whence we have come, and whither do we go?

[16]

Our elements were merged at His command
Why then did He disperse them once again?
For if the blend was good, why break it up?
If it was bad, whose was the fault but His?"

The constant themes of Khayyām's poetry are the certainty of death, the denial of an afterlife, the pointlessness of asking unanswerable questions, the mysteriousness of the universe, and the necessity of living for and enjoying the present:

[17]

No one has ever pierced this veil of secrets;
No one will ever understand the world.
Deep in the earth's our only resting place;
Cry out, "This is a story without end!"

[18]

The heavenly bodies that circle round the skies
Are full of mystery even to learned men;
Hold firm the thread of wisdom in your hand,
For those who plan their lives will be confused.

[19]

A drop of water fell into the sea,
A speck of dust came floating down to earth.
What signifies your passage through this world?
A tiny gnat appears—and disappears.

[20]

Long will the world last after we are gone,
When every sign and trace of us are lost.
We were not here before, and no one knew;
Though we are gone, the world will be the same.

[21]

Of all the travellers on this endless road
Not one returns to tell us where it leads.
There's little in this world but greed and need;
Leave nothing here, for you will not return.

[22]

I am not here for ever in this world;
How sinful then to forfeit wine and love!
The world may be eternal or created;
Once I am gone, it matters not a scrap.

[23]

When once you hear the roses are in bloom,
Then is the time, my love, to pour the wine;
Houris and palaces and Heaven and Hell—
These are but fairy-tales, forget them all.[14]

AL-MA'ARRĪ AND 'UMAR KHAYYĀM

The Koranic commentator al-Zamakhsharī (d. 1141), in a treatise composed just before 'Umar Khayyām's death, apparently mentions that 'Umar Khayyām visited his classes and seemed to be familiar with the Arabic stanzas of the Syrian al-Ma'arrī, who died in 1058, ten years after our Persian poet's birth. There is a remarkable similarity between the two poets in their imagery, sentiments, skepticism, and general philosophy of life. E. G. Browne pointed out the resemblance in his *Literary History of Persia*, first published in 1906.[15]

THE SIGNIFICANCE OF THE *RUBA'IYAT*

We do not know exactly when the *rubā'ī* as a verse form first entered Persian poetry but, as Avery points out, it "became a favourite verse form among the intellectuals, those philosphers and mystics in eleventh- and twelfth-century Persia who were in some degree non-conformists opposed to religious fanaticism, so that they have often been called Islam's free-thinkers."[16] Even if all the quatrains attributed to Khayyām are not really by him, for our purposes it is irrelevant. What is important is that there were many Persian intellectuals, poets, and philosophers who did not accept Islam and all its constraints on the human spirit, and who expressed their doubts, their skepticism, in the form of *ruba'iyat*, which they then attributed to Khayyām.

Some of the following Khayyām-like quatrains reveal a deep-seated skepticism about religion within Persian culture that Islam had not succeeded in stifling:

[24]

You who have chosen to take the Magian path,
You who have cast aside the Islamic faith,
You won't drink wine or kiss your love much longer;
Stay where you are, Omar, for death is near.

[25]

The Koran is held in deepest veneration,
And yet they read it only now and then.
The verse that is inscribed within the cup
Is read by all, no matter where or when.

[26]

Spend all your time with libertines and rogues;
Show your contempt for fasting and for prayer.
Hear the wise maxims of tent-maker Omar:
Drink wine, become a bandit, but do good.

[27]

How much more of the mosque, of prayer and fasting?
Better go drunk and begging round the taverns.
Khayyam, drink wine, for soon this clay of yours
Will make a cup, a bowl, one day a jar.

[28]

Take greetings from me to the Holy Prophet,
And ask him with respectful deference:
"Lord of the Prophet's house, why should sour milk
Be lawful under the Law, and not pure wine?"[17]

NINETEENTH AND TWENTIETH CENTURIES

'Umar Khayyām inspired many poets and freethinkers, and continues to influence modern writers. An early nineteenth-century traveler, Mountstuart Elphinstone, gives us a remarkable example in his *Account of the Kingdom of Caubul [Kabul]*. During his sojourn in the capital of Afghanistan, Elphinstone met a certain Mulla Zakki, who maintained that

> all prophets were impostors, and all revelation an invention. They seem very doubtful of the truth of future state, and even of the being of God. . . . Their tenets appear to be very ancient, and are precisely those of the old Persian poet Kheioom [*sic*, i.e., Khayyām], whose works exhibit such specimens of impiety, as probably were never equalled in any other language. Kheioom dwells particularly on the existence of evil, and taxes the Supreme Being with the introduction of it, in terms which can scarcely be believed.[18]

Sadegh Hedayat, the greatest Persian novelist and short-story writer of the twentieth century, first wrote about Khayyām in 1923, and then again in 1934. Hedayat was at pains to point out that Khayyām from "his youth to his death remained a materialist, pessimist, agnostic." Khayyām looked at all religious questions with a skeptical eye, continues Hedayat, and hated the fanaticism, narrow-mindedness, and the spirit of vengeance of the *mullas*, the so-called religious scholars. Khayyām was a freethinker who could not possibly accept the narrow, determinist, illogical dogmas of the religious class. Religion is but an ensemble of dogmas and duties that one has to follow without question, without discussion and without doubt. As Friedrich Neitzsche once said, it is certainty, and not doubt, which leads to religious fanaticism. Khayyām was a doubter par excellence. It is not difficult in our days, says Hedayat, to prove the absurdity of religious myths—disowned in their entirety by science—but imagine how it must have been for Khayyām, living in an intolerant epoch. Now we realize ʿUmar Khayyām's importance.[19]

Ali Dashti was born in 1896 of Persian ancestry at the holy city of Kerbala (in present-day Iraq), where he received a traditional religious education. He went to Persia in 1918 and lived in Shiraz, Isfahan, and finally in Tehran, where he became involved in the politics of the day. Dashti was arrested for the first time in 1920, and then again in 1921 after the coup d'état that brought the future Reza Shah to power. His prison memoirs, *Prison Days*,[20] made him a literary celebrity. He founded his own journal, *The Red Dawn*, in 1922.

Dashti's visit to Russia in 1927 was decisive for the development of his freethought. He gradually liberated himself from his religious upbringing, and by the time of his return to Persia, Dashti was a thorough skeptic. Dashti's skepticism found expression in his classic *Twenty-three Years*, where he leveled devastating criticisms at some of Muslims' most cherished beliefs.[20] The book was written in 1937 but was published anonymously, probably in 1974, in Beirut, since the shah's regime forbade the publication of any criticism of religion between 1971 and 1977. After the Iranian Revolution of 1979, Dashti authorized its publication by underground opposition groups. His book, whose title refers to the prophetic career of Muhammad, may well have sold over half a million copies in pirated editions between 1980 and 1986.

First, Dashti defends rational thought in general and criticizes blind faith, since "belief can blunt human reason and common sense," even in learned scholars. What is needed is more "impartial study." He vigorously denies any of the miracles ascribed to Muhammad by some of the later, overeager Muslim commentators. Dashti submits the orthodox view that the Koran is the word of God himself, that it is miraculous in virtue of its eloquence and subject matter, to a thorough and skeptical examination. He points out that even some early Muslim scholars "before bigotry and hyperbole prevailed, openly acknowledged that the arrangement and syntax of the Koran are not miraculous and that work of equal or greater value could be produced by other God-fearing persons."[22]

Furthermore, the Koran contains

> sentences which are incomplete and not fully intelligible without the aid of commentaries; foreign words, unfamiliar Arabic words and words used with other than the normal meaning; adjectives and verbs inflected without observance of the concords of gender and number; illogically and ungrammatically applied pronouns which sometimes have no referent; and predicates which in rhymed passages are often remote from the subjects. These and other such aberrations in

the language have given scope to critics who deny the Koran's eloquence. . . . To sum up, more than one hundred Koranic aberrations from the normal rules have been noted.[23]

What of the claim that the subject matter is miraculous? Dashti points out that the Koran

> contains nothing new in the sense of ideas not already expressed by others. All the moral precepts of the Koran are self-evident and generally acknowledged. The stories in it are taken in identical or slightly modified forms from the lore of the Jews and Christians, whose rabbis and monks Muhammad had met and consulted on his journeys to Syria, and from memories conserved by the descendants of the peoples of 'Ad and Thamud. . . . In the field of moral teachings, however, the Koran cannot be considered miraculous.
>
> Muhammad reiterated principles which mankind had already conceived in earlier centuries and many places. Confucius, Buddha, Zoroaster, Socrates, Moses, and Jesus had said similar things. . . . Many of the duties and rites of Islam are continuous of practices which the pagan Arabs had adopted from the Jews.[24]

Dashti ridicules the superstitious aspects of much ritual, especially during the pilgrimage to Mecca. Muhammad himself emerges as a shifty character who stoops to political assassinations, murder, and the elimination of all opponents. Among the Prophet's followers, killings were passed off as "services to Islam." He also examines the position of women under Islam and admits their inferior status. The Muslim doctrine of God is criticized as cruel, angry, and proud—qualities not to be admired. Finally, it is quite clear that the Koran is not the word of God, since it contains many instances of confusion between the two speakers, God and Muhammad.

Dashti died in 1984 after spending three years in Khomeini's prisons, where he was tortured even though he was eighty-three at the time. He told a friend before he died: "Had the Shah allowed books like this to be published and read by the people, we would never have had an Islamic revolution."[25]

Ali Dashti's study of 'Umar Khayyām first appeared in 1966. Dashti accepted 36 quatrains as being certainly by Khayyām, and, after much sifting, analysis, and comparison, he arrived at a total of 102 quatrains in all. Dashti constantly emphasizes Khayyām's philosophical doubt, particularly about the afterlife:

[29]

The withered tulip never blooms again.

[30]

. . . you will not return; once gone, you're gone.

[31]

For you're no gold, you foolish little man,
To bury till you're needed once again.

Dashti wrote:

The hope that buoys the theologians has no meaning for Khayyām. His mind is
obsessed with this tragic tragic destiny of man; he never leaves it alone, and it is
true to say that it is the starting-point of all his other speculations.

[32]

Drink wine, for long you'll sleep beneath the soil,
Without companion, lover, friend or mate.
But keep this sorry secret to yourself:
The withered tulip never blooms again.

Continues Dashti:

Khayyām waits within the prison of his thoughts like a man in the condemned
cell. All ways of escape are closed, and no ray of hope illuminates his spirit.

[33]

Why did we waste our lives so uselessly?
Why are we crushed so by the mills of Heaven?
Alas! Alas! Even as we blinked our eyes,
Though not by our own wish, we disappeared.

Let us cast aside everything that poisons our lives, one must not waste this
swiftly passing moment.

34

Rise up from sleep, and drink a draught of wine,
Before fate deals us yet another blow.
For this contentious sphere will suddenly
Take from us even the time to wet our lips.

[35]

Since no one can be certain of tomorrow,
It's better not to fill the heart with care.
Drink wine by moonlight, darling, for the moon
Will shine long after this, and find us not.[26]

NOTES

1. I have sometimes used the spelling Omar Khayyam, since Fitzgerald does so.

2. The first edition of *On the Origin of Species* appeared in November 1859, and the second appeared only two months later, in January 1860.

3. According to T. S. Eliot biographer Peter Ackroyd, when Eliot read Fitzgerald's Omar, "he wished to become a poet." Peter Ackroyd, *T. S. Eliot* (London: Abacus, 1984), p. 26. Here is how Eliot himself recounts his epiphanic moment, after a period of no interest in poetry at all: "I can recall clearly the moment when at the age of fourteen or so, I happened to pick up a copy of Fitzgerald's Omar which was lying about, and the almost overwhelming introduction to a new world of feeling which this poem was the occasion of giving me. It was like a sudden conversion; the world appeared anew, painted with bright, delicious and painful colours." T. S. Eliot, *The Use of Poetry & the Use of Criticism* (London: Faber, 1975), pp. 33, 91.

4. "The *rubāʿī*, plural *rubāʿiyāt*, is a two lined stanza, each line of with is divided into two hemistichs making up four altogether, hence the name *rubāʿī*, an Arabic word meaning 'foursome.' The first, second, and last of the four hemistychs must rhyme. The third need not rhyme with the other three, a point Fitzgerald noticed, so that he made the first, second and fourth lines of his quatrains rhyme:

> Dreaming when Dawn's Left Hand was in the *sky*
> I heard a Voice within the Tavern *cry*
> 'Awake my little ones and fill the Cup
> Before Life's Liquor in its Cup be *dry*.'"

Peter Avery, Introduction to *The Ruba'iyat of Omar Khayyam*, by Edward Fitzgerald (Harmondsworth, England: Penguin Books, 1981), p. 9.

5. Elwell Sutton, Introduction to *In Search of Omar Khayyam*, by Ali Dashti (New York: Columbia University Press, 1971), p. 13.

6. Edward Fitzgerald, Preface to *The Ruba'iyat of Omar Khayyam* (London: B. Quaritch, 1859), p.

7. V. Minorsky, "Omar Khaiyam," in *Encyclopedia of Islam* (Leiden: E. J. Brill, 1913–38), vol. 6, pp. 985–89.

8. Ibid., vol. 6, p. 988.

9. A. Ross, "Fitzgerald, Edward," in *The Penguin Companion to Literature* (Harmondsworth, England: Penguin Books, 1971), vol. 1, pp. 183–84.

10. Edward Fitzgerald, Introduction to *The Ruba'iyat of Omar Khayyam* (London: B. Quaritch, 1859).

11. Rather like those Catholic apologists who would have us believe that the Song of Songs of Solomon is a spiritual poem rather than a gently erotic one, which it obviously is. The King James Version has at the head of chapter 1 of the Song of Solomon (or the Song of Songs): "The church's love unto Christ."

12. Edward Fitzgerald, Introduction to *The Ruba'iyat of Omar Khayyam*, 3rd ed. (London: Macmillan, 1872).

13. G. Sarton, *Introduction to the History of Science* (Washington, D.C.: Williams & Wilkins, 1927), vol. 1, pp. 759–61.

14. These quatrains are not from Fitzgerald's translation but from those compiled by Ali Dashti in his *In Search of Omar Khayyam* (New York: Columbia University Press, 1971), pp. 187–99, and translated by Elwell Sutton into English. Dashti accepted 36 quatrains as being certainly by Khayyam and, after much sifting, analysis, and comparison, he arrived at a total of 102 quatrains in all.

15. E. G. Browne, *Literary History of Persia* (Cambridge: Cambridge University Press, 1956), vol. 2, p. 292; cited by Avery, Introduction to *The Ruba'iyat of Omar Khayyam*, pp. 24–25 and n. 7.

16. Avery, Introduction to *The Ruba'iyat of Omar Khayyam*, p. 13.

17. Quoted in Dashti, *In Search of Omar Khayyam*, p. 178.

18. Mountstuart Elphinstone, *Account of the Kingdom of Caubul* (London, 1815), pp. 209 ff.; cited by Avery, *The Ruba'iyat of Omar Khayyam*, app. 2, p. 113.

19. Sadegh Hedayat, *Les Chants d'Omar Khayyam*, trans. M. F. Farzaneh and J. Malaplate (Paris: José Corti, 1993), pp. 13 ff.

20. J. E. Knörzer, *Ali Dashti's Prison Days: Life under Reza Shah* (Costa Mesa, Calif.: Mazda Publishers, 1994).

21. Ali Dashti, *Twenty-three Years: A Study of the Prophetic Career of Mohammed* (London: Allen & Unwin, 1985).

22. Ibid., p. 48.

23. Ibid., p. 50.

24. Ibid., p. 56.

25. Amir Taheri, *Holy Terror* (London, 1987), p. 290.

26. Dashti, *In Search of Omar Khayyam*, p. 249.

7

APOSTATES
OF ISLAM I
Converts to Christianity

THE IMPOSSIBILITY OF CONVERTING MUSLIMS?

Herman Melville wrote in his diary of his visit to some American missionaries in Jerusalem in 1856, "In the afternoon called upon Mr. And Mrs. Saunders, outside the wall, the American Missionary.—Dismal story of their experiments. Might as well attempt to convert bricks into bride-cake as the Orientals into Christians. It is against the will of God that the East should be Christianized."[1]

Another American missionary, Dr. Samuel Zwemer, in his very useful book *The Law of Apostasy in Islam*, rather oddly quotes Canon W. H. T. Gairdner to the effect that "conversions from Islam in the East Indies and parts of Africa run into tens of thousands: and in other parts of the Moslem world, such as India, Persia and Egypt, they are regular and familiar phenomena," and then heads his first chapter, "Why So Few Moslem Converts?" and laments the "small visible result."[2] Zwemer is closer to Melville's opinion than to Canon Gairdner's. Could the meagerness of results, asks Zwemer, be due to the harshness of the law of apostasy in Islam? It certainly acted as a powerful deterrent. Even during the period of intense Christian missionary activity during the nineteenth century, it was applied mercilessly in public in the very city Zwemer himself was later to work in—Cairo—as this example from E. W. Lane shows:

89

> Apostacy from the faith of El-Islam is considered a most heinous sin, and must be punished with death, unless the apostate will recant on being thrice warned. I once saw a woman paraded through the streets of Cairo, and afterwards taken down to the Nile to be drowned, for having apostatized from the faith of Mohammad, and having married a Christian. Unfortunately, she had tattooed a blue cross on her arm, which led to her detection by one of her former friends in a bath. She was mounted upon a high-saddled ass, such as ladies in Egypt usually ride, and very respectably dressed, attended by soldiers, and surrounded by a rabble, who, instead of commiserating, uttered loud imprecations against her. The Kadee, who passed sentence upon her, exhorted her, in vain, to return to her former faith. He own father was her accuser! She was taken in a boat into the midst of the river, stripped nearly naked, strangled, and then thrown into the stream.[3]

Even in countries where executions of apostates have been abolished, the renegade's life is far from secure. An act of apostasy brings shame and social disgrace on the family of the apostate, who must be killed by family members to restore family honor and to expiate the collective humiliation. Even if the apostate survives attempts at poisoning, he will suffer from continuous social persecution and ostracism, and be treated as a traitor to his religion, his nation, and his culture.

Despite the paucity of converts, Zwemer does manage to give dozens of examples from history, and from his own experience as a missionary in Egypt. Zwemer quotes the following instances of persecution as found in the reports of the Egypt General Mission (1903–1922):

> A father saw his son reading the Bible, and taking it from him consigned it to the flames, and attempted to fatally injure the boy by throwing him over the balusters. Later the lad received a second copy of the Word of God; and a tract which for weeks he carried hidden in his pocket. When the father finally chanced to see it, he gave the boy a cruelly severe beating, and continued his ill-treatment until his son was forced to leave home.

We read that another convert was beaten daily with a native whip (only those who have seen them know what they are like). Since he remained obdurate, burning pieces of wood were brought and placed, red hot, on his body to force him to recant, but it was all of no avail. He said, "Kill me, and I will go straight to be with Jesus." Some of his companions suffered in a similar way. In one case a father decided to kill his son, so he poured paraffin oil all over him, and was just going to light it when an uncle came in and pleaded for the life of the boy. The father listened to the appeal, then banished his son from his home for ever.

> In 1912 a storm of persecution arose against A. T. His clothes were taken away, his Bible burnt. His father attempted to poison him. His uncle shot him, the bullet entering his leg. His father told him to make his choice between his for-

tune (some £2,000) and his faith, and with the chief men of the village actually entered his private apartments in the house (his harem, or wife's rooms), a terrible insult in Islam, to search for incriminating papers. Twice attempts were made to poison him; twice they attempted by bribes and threats to make his wife unfaithful to him. The whole story of this man is one of loneliness, poverty and contempt, cheerfully borne for Christ.

In 1923 a young man in one of the villages of the Delta accepted Christ and secured work as a cook. At home his Testament was burned, and his brothers made it very unpleasant for him; but that was as nothing compared to the storm which broke over him when, after due preparation, he decided to go forward and openly confess Christ in baptism. Relatives from far and near gathered at his home, threatening and cursing him: a cousin, who had been in jail, said that even if he hid in a fortress of brass he would get him out and kill him. Under the threats and hatred the young man's courage failed, and he promised not to be baptized then. Three times he has now come to the point of being baptized, and through fear has withdrawn each time. His brothers, who have often heard the Gospel, are dead against him-his own mother, who really loves him, would rather see him dead than baptized.[4]

The psychology of conversion is a complex subject in itself, and I doubt there is any one theory that would account for all the phenomena. A Muslim abandoning his faith for humanism or atheism is likely to give rational explanations why belief in any of the tenets of Islam is no longer intellectually tenable, and her reasons would differ substantially from a Muslim who converted to Christianity.

Ernest Renan was once asked whether it was true that he had, on abandoning Catholicism, embraced Protestantism. He replied testily, "It was my faith that I lost and not my reason."[5] James Joyce has a similar exchange:

—Do you fear then, Cranly asked, that the God of the Roman catholics would strike you dead and damn you if you made a sacrilegious communion?
—The God of the Roman catholics could do that now, Stephen said. I fear more than that the chemical action which would be set up in my soul by a false homage to a symbol behind which are massed twenty centuries of authority and veneration.
—Would you, Cranly asked, in extreme danger commit that particular sacrilege? For instance, if you lived in the penal days?
—I cannot answer for the past, Stephen replied. Possibly not.
—Then, said Cranly, you do not intend to become a protestant?
—I said that I had lost the faith, Stephen answered, but not that I had lost self-respect. What kind of liberation would that be to forsake an absurdity which is logical and coherent and to embrace one which is illogical and incoherent?[6]

Muslims who have converted to Christianity would be deemed, by Muslims who are now atheists and humanists, to have left one form of unreason only to adopt another. But what reasons do Muslim converts to Christianity give for their conversion? These converts evidently found something in Christianity that they felt was lacking in Islam. Many are attracted by the figure of Jesus, others find the Christian dogma of forgiveness of sins comforting, and still others are impressed by the charitable behavior of individual Christians around them. But if there is a common thread running through these conversion testimonies, it is that Christianity preaches the love of Christ and God, whereas Islam is forever threatening hellfire for disobeying, and obsessively holds up the wrath of God in front of the believer. In other words, the two religions have two totally different conceptions of God: In the former, God is near, loving, and protective, God the Father; in the latter, God is a remote, angry, tyrannical figure to be obeyed blindly. Or as one Muslim convert to Christianity was quoted as saying in a truly astonishing article that appeared in the Algerian Arabic daily *El Youm* in December 2000, "Christianity is life, Islam is death."[7] The article is worth quoting in full, since it lays to rest the myth of the impossibility of converting Muslims:

In Kabylie[, Algeria], people of all ages are converting to Christianity. . . . The (Protestant) church of Ouadhias has played an important role in the proliferation of the number of conversions in Kabylie, and it is considered the Mother Church, never having ceased its activities, even after Independence [1962] and the departure of the French and humanitarian missionaries.

. . . The media have played a great part in the conversions in Kabylie, the majority of radio stations have a strong following in this region, [many listening] to Radio Monte Carlo and particularly the popular broadcasts in Amazigh. As [one listener said,] *"80% of the reasons which impelled me towards Christianity came from Radio Monte Carlo."* There are also other radio stations such as "Miracle Channel" (7SAT) [a satellite channel received via dishes], and most of the faithful confirmed that they listen to these stations which broadcast the Christian message across the world.

. . . [T]he person responsible for the church at Ouadhias about the conversions [told a reporter] that there were more and more every day, his church alone celebrating 50 baptisms per year. The deterioration of the image of Islam during the crisis has played its part in this rise of conversions to Christianity and the adoption of its principles. What is happening and what has happened in Algeria, such as the massacres and killings [in the holy month of Ramadan, December 2000, alone, 340 people were killed, making a total of 2700 killed by the Islamists in the year 2000.[8]] in the name of Islam, has led many, when asked what the difference, in their view, was between Islam and Christianity, to declare: "Christianity is life, Islam is death." For Samia, a secondary school pupil, the proof of the difference between Islam and Christianity was the mixing and relationship between the sexes, the former forbidding it, and the latter allowing it.

...Bibles [are distributed] in three languages, Arabic, French, and Amazigh, and video- and audio-cassettes on the life of the Messiah, son of Mary, translated into Amazigh. . . . As to the financement of these places of worship, . . . the Churches of Ouadhias and Boghni [are] entirely supported by the gifts of the faithful. At the end of each month, workers pay in 10% of their salary, on top of the donations. . . .

. . . Protestantism is more developed in Algeria than Catholicism.[9]

This is indeed a very remarkable phenomenon; as the article notes, one church alone recorded fifty baptisms a year—in a country where a woman wearing lipstick could result in an entire family, elderly women and children included, having their throats cut.

Other recent accounts of conversions to Christianity in large numbers come from West Africa. A new reception center was inaugurated in Pambuegua, in Kaduna State in Nigeria, to accommodate the large number of former Muslims recently (in 2001) converted to Christianity. Many had been threatened with the death sentence under *Sharī'a* laws established by some Nigerian states, and all had their belongings and property looted by Muslims. Evidently, many hitherto Muslim Nigerians had been unaware of what it meant to have Islam applied to the letter, resented its intrusion into their way of life and their private lives, and decided to convert to Christianity. That is when their situation became truly dangerous.[10]

TESTIMONIES

Many conversion testimonies[11] from Islam to Christianity are moving, sometimes harrowing, and always witnesses to the converts' courage. They are all sincere personal records of deep religious experiences. Nonetheless, many are cloyingly sentimental, embarrassingly gushing about peace, harmony, and Christ's love.

Testimony 1. Why I Became a Christian, by Desert Son

I was born in Saudi Arabia as a member of a Muslim family. We were a very happy family, and I loved my relationship with them. I also felt very happy because I did all the things that God asked me to. I had learned one-sixth of the holy Koran by heart and a lot from the Hadith. When I was a teenager, I was an Imam for the mosque.

I was always very serious to do all that God ordered me to do—fasting during Ramadan, praying five times a day or more, *hajj*, and so on. I was, at that time, very much desiring to meet God at the last day, even when I had no guarantee. But I had always hoped for this. My hope grew when I started to think about fighting in the name of God (*jihad*) in Afghanistan. I was sixteen years old. My parents would not let me go because I was too young. So I decided to wait until I was old enough.

I always had love and respect for the Muslim people. There was no love or respect in my heart for the Christians, and the Jews were my first enemy, of course.

Far Away from God

After some time, the devil found his way into our home and our life, and my life became very hard. Slowly I drifted far away from God until the time that I believed in no God at all.

My life became busy. I had a very good job and earned a lot of money. Still, I was not happy because I was afraid for the day that I would die. Sometimes a question came to my mind—Will I be with God in heaven or not? And it was very frightening to think about this, even for seconds, that I would not be there. What about my future?

A Little Prayer

One day I had a big problem in my life. I was in my room looking through the window up to the sky. Then I remembered God, and I wanted to pray to him to ask him for help, but which God should I pray to? Allah? I was sure that he was very angry with me because I had not prayed for a very long time. Or Jesus? I knew he had done a lot of miracles in the lives of other people. Then I said, "Jesus help me!" I don't know why I spoke like this. I sat down on my bed and spoke to myself, "What is this stupid thing you just did?" Anyway, I did not expect anything to happen or the problem to go away. However, one and a half days later, my problem was solved! I decided to find out who this Jesus is. Is he God, as the Christian people say, or is he a prophet, as I know from Islam? At this time, I left my country and went to Europe.

The Dream

On the third day, my circumstances became very difficult for me, and I decided to go back to the Middle East. During that night I had a dream. I was standing in a cross shape with a low wall around it. In my right hand, I had a big stack of white, unwritten papers. I was standing at the cross beam, and I was looking to a small group of people who were standing at the top. They all wore long white clothing, but one of them was different. He was standing at the right side, and with his left hand he was leading the people through a door in the wall. Beyond the door was light, and I could not see what was in there. One moment I was standing in the dream, and the next moment I was seeing the cross from above. It was difficult for me to understand this. When I woke up the next morning, I felt a very beautiful happiness in my heart that I never had before. And I felt a love in my heart and from inside my body a very special feeling. I felt also I just wanted to walk and to walk and to ask every one I met, Do you know Jesus? It was more than a great feeling. It was happiness that I had never known before in my life.

After one year of reading the Bible in an honest way, I understand now what happened to me. I found my way to God, the real God, the Lord Jesus Christ.

I hope now for all the people I love, my family, my friends, and everyone else to change also and begin to read the Bible in an honest way. I am sure that God will help them to find their way.

My Life Now

I feel love in my heart, and I am very happy to know Jesus. When I was a Muslim, I could never imagine that the Christians were right. After that, I found out how much God loves me, and I became a Christian. Yes, he loves me, he loves you, and he loves the whole world. Jesus Christ loved us, and he still does. And don't forget in the last day nobody can save us, only Jesus Christ.

Dear Brother/Sister: Come to know Jesus before it is too late.
John 8: 12:

> When Jesus spoke again to the people, he said, "I am the light of the world. Whoever follows me will never walk in darkness, but will have the light of life."[12]

Testimony 2

I was born in a mixed parentage family. My father is a devout Muslim and my mother a Christian who was converted to Islam upon marriage to him. I was raised up in a normal Muslim locality and community, where all I saw through Islamic glasses and never a view beyond Islam. I took for granted what I was trained and taught, that is, Islam was the ultimate in everything, i.e., religion, scientific facts, etc. all existed in the Koran. During my teens I saw the other facet of Islamic life or rather now started viewing things more objectively. I started going to college and made new friends from other communities. My mom stumbled upon the fact that my dad was a womanizer and later on my mom realized the sad truth that he had secretly married his two mistresses. No doubt there was never enough money in the house to give us a decent lifestyle or education. The worst thing about this all was my dad was justifying all his illicit actions and relationships by quoting the Koranic verses at random. At first I thought he was bullshitting his way through, but upon reading the facts, i.e., the verses, I was stupe-fied to realize that these nonsensical verses did exist. He even threatened our very existence as a family by scaring my mom with the three most dreaded syllables for a woman married to a Muslim man: "talaq talaq talaq [I divorce thee, I divorce thee, I divorce thee]." But one fine day my mom, being a woman of strong character, decided to call if off before he could.

Later on I went on to work in another country and came across my mother's relatives (whom I was not much in touch with when I was in India). For the first time, though I was in a totally Islamic-dominated culture, I got more close to my mother's family. At first I couldn't make sense of why I saw so much peace, love, and family stability reign among non-Muslim families, i.e., you dont get to see two or more wives bickering with each other. I questioned my beliefs and values for the first time, and slowly started my way toward the truth. I worked in the hotel industry in the Middle East and all that I saw was the other side of Islam: the holier-than-thou locals womanizing, drinking, etc., but on the hide. I always pondered if my religion, Islam, was so divinely ordained by Allah and so perfect then why hadn't it made an impact on these Muslims. All I could say about my coreligionists was that they were only good in criticizing and being judgmental of other creeds by quoting the Koran! In fact now at this point I started delving deeper into this subject. I surfed the Web for these sites where I could come across unbiased material critically evaluating all religion, and started studying comparative religion. My interaction with my mother's family and their col-leagues helped me see the truth more clearly without the "horse's eyepads" one is forced to wear as a Muslim.

Two years ago, I did what I really wanted to do and be. I had gone on a vaca-tion to India and baptized myself a Christian. I would like my previous co-religionists to know that no missionary has converted me with false propoganda, etc., as they always claim when a Muslim converts and leaves his religion. I have seen a true dark side of Islam, which cannot be denied, as it is written in clear Arabic, and Yusaf Ali's English translation can vouch for it; and I have see the true love of God in the Bible and in the behavior and actions of Jesus's followers and the humanist, secular values of the Western world. Now I am a peace with myself . . . and would never like to tread that dangeraous path of Islam again.[13]

CASE STUDIES

Kuwait

Amnesty International reported the case of "Robert" Hussein Qambar ʾAli, a con-vert to Christianity who was declared by a Kuwaiti Islamic court an apostate on

May 29, 1996.[14] Robert Hussein, a forty-five-year-old Kuwaiti businessman, converted from Islam to Christianity in the early 1990s. In his interviews with news agencies, Hussein revealed that since his conversion became public he has received numerous death threats and lived in constant fear for his life. His conversion was denounced equally in mosques and parliament. He was forced to change his residence often as a security measure. His marriage broke up because of family opposition to his conversion.

A lawsuit to declare Hussein an apostate was brought against him by three independent Islamist lawyers. If successful it would have stripped Hussein of his civil rights. Hussein first appeared in an Islamic family court, which has jurisdiction over personal status and family matters, on March 6, 1996, where he confirmed that he had become Christian and proposed changing his name to "Robert Hussein," but insisted that the three-judge panel had no jurisdiction in the case. He asked for his case to be sent to the Constitutional Court on the grounds that Article 35 of the Kuwaiti Constitution allows for freedom of thought and belief. The said article reads, "Freedom of belief is absolute. The state protects the freedom of practising religion in accordance with established customs, provided that it does not conflict with public policy or morals."

At a further hearing before the Islamic court on April 24, the Islamist lawyers asked the court to strip Hussein of his nationality and civil rights for offending against Islamic law by abandoning his Islamic faith. Hussein again asked to be put before the Constitutional Court, adding that he felt he was being punished as if the court had already found him guilty of apostasy. He reported that "for six months I haven't seen my kids, my family, my home. I blame the Kuwaiti government. They do not come forward and say 'this man is protected by the Constitution.' " Those lawyers who showed a willingness to defend him asked for fees of $1 million (U.S.), which he could not afford to pay.

On May 29, Hussein was declared an apostate by the Islamic court. The presiding judge was later asked if the ruling would be taken as permission to kill Hussein and replied, "That is possible," but added that killing an apostate would be a violation of Kuwaiti criminal law, under which there was no penalty for apostasy as there was in Islamic law. Hussein lodged an appeal against the Islamic court decision to the Court of Appeal. The first hearing was set for September 15, 1996.

Amnesty International notes that "Article 18 of the International Covenant on Civil and Political Rights (ICCPR), which Kuwait ratified in May 1996, upholds freedom of religion, including the right to change one's religion. General commnet 22(48) on 'Freedom to have or to adopt a religion or belief,' made by the United Nations Human Rights Committee [UNHRC] on July 1993, expressly recognizes that Article 18 of the ICCPR entails the right to replace one's current religion or belief with another, or to adopt atheistic views."

While Hussein is not facing any penalty imposed by Kuwaiti authorities, the mere fact of being labeled "an apostate" makes him a target for human rights abuses by nongovernmental actors. Various religious figures have pronounced that apostates from Islam should be punished by death. Even a member of the National Assembly demanded that Hussein be stoned to death. To allay Hussein's fears and to appease international public opinion, the Kuwaiti department of of legal advice repeated that freedom of religion is protected under Kuwaiti law and that the putative death threats were baseless.

With the help of various religious and human rights organizations Hussein came to the United States. "It is his dream that one day the people of Kuwait will be free, not only from the tyrannical rule of the Amir of Kuwait, but free to think, to explore and to find the truth for themselves." He currently resides in the United States with his wife and daughter. Husein has since published his story in *Apostate Son*.[15]

Yemen

A Somali living in Yemen since 1994, Mohammed Omer Haji converted to Christianity two years ago and adopted the name "George." He was imprisoned in January 2000 and reportedly beaten and threatened for two months by Yemeni security police, who tried to persuade him to renounce his conversion to Christianity. After he was rearrested in May, he was formally put on trial in June for apostasy under Article 259 of Yemen's criminal law. Haji's release came seven weeks after he was given a court ultimatum to renounce Christianity and return to Islam or face execution as an apostate. Apostasy is a capital offense under the Muslim laws of "sharia" enforced in Yemen.

After news of the case broke in the international press, Yemeni authorities halted the trial proceedings against Haji. He was transferred on July 17 to Aden's Immigration Jail until resettlement could be finalized by the UNHCR, under which Haji had formal refugee status. One of the politicians who tabled a motion in July 2000 in the British House of Commons was David Atkinson: "Early Day Motion on Mohammed Omer Haji. That this House deplores the death penalty which has been issued from the Aden Tawahi Court in Yemen for the apostasy of the Somali national Mohammed Omer Haji unless he recants his Christian faith and states that he is a Muslim before the judge three times on Wednesday 12th July; deplores that Mr. Haji was held in custody for the sole reason that he held to the Christian faith and was severely beaten in custody to the point of not being able to walk; considers it a disgrace that UNHCR officials in Khormaksar stated they were only able to help him if he was a Muslim; and calls on the British Government and international colleagues to make representations immediately at the highest level in Yemen to ensure Mr. Haji's swift release and long-term safety and for the repeal of Yemen's barbaric apostate laws."

Amnesty International adopted Haji as a prisoner of conscience in an "urgent action" release on July 11, concluding that he was "detained solely on account of his religious beliefs." The government of New Zealand accepted Haji and his family for emergency resettlement in late July after negotiations with the Geneva headquarters of the UNHCR.[16]

THE NUMBER OF CONVERTS TO CHRISTIANITY IN THE WEST

Hass Hirji-Walji, the son of Indian Ugandans, tells how he was atttacked in a park in Minneapolis in 1975 by three men. They knocked him to the ground, held a knife to his throat, and asked him to profess Islam. He was saved by the chance arrival of some children from a nearby school. Hirji-Walji had recently converted to Christianity, and his story had been published in a magazine with a large circulation. This account had attracted the attention of some Muslim Arabs who decided to deal with the apostate themselves.[17]

Prof. James A. Beverly recounts a more recent tale of an apostate living in North America who received death threats and was granted police protection.[18] Even in the West, Muslim apostates fear for their lives and find it difficult to come out in public; hence, the difficulty in finding reliable statistics for conversions in the West. However, we do have some figures for adult baptisms in French Catholic parishes. The latter parishes also record the religion of origin of those baptized. In the year 2000, 2,503 adults were baptized, of which 9 percent were of Muslim origin; thus, 225 Muslims apostasized in France alone in 2000.[19] Unfortunately, I do not have figures for any other Western country.[20]

NOTES

1. Herman Melville, *Journal of a Visit to Europe and the Levant*, ed. Howard C. Horsford (Princeton, N.J.: Princeton University Press, 1955).

2. S. Zwemer, *The Law of Apostasy in Islam* (London/New York: Marshall Brothers Ltd., 1924), pp. 14–15.

3. E. W. Lane, *An Account of the Manners and Customs of the Modern Egyptians* (1836; reprint, New York: Dover, 1973), p. 108.

4. Zwemer, *The Law of Apostasy in Islam*, pp. 60–62.

5. I have never been able to remember where I heard this story. If anyone knows the source I would be grateful if they would contact me in care of the publisher.

6. James Joyce, *A Portrait of the Artist As a Young Man* (1914–15; reprint, Harmondsworth, England: Penguin Books, 1992), pp. 264–65.

7. From *El Youm* [al-Yawm], Algiers; reprinted in *Courrier International* 531 (January 4–10, 2001): 29. Translated from the French by Ibn Warraq.

8. Statistics from *Courrier International* 531 (January 4–10, 2001).

9. From *El Youm* [al-Yawm], Algiers; reprinted in *Courrier International* 531 (January 4–10, 2001): 29. Translated from the French by Ibn Warraq.

10. "L'Actualité interreligieuse," *Actualité des Religions* 31 (October 2001): 14.

11. Many testimonies can be read at www.answering-islam.org/Testimonies/index. html. For a full bibliography, see Jean-Marie Gaudeul, *Appelés Par le Christ: Ils Viennent de l'Islam* (Paris: Cerf, 1991); English edition, *Called from Islam to Christ* (Monarch Publications, 1999).

Other collections of testimonies include: W. M. Miller, *Ten Muslims Meet Christ* (Grand Rapids, Mich.: W. B. Eerdmans, 1980); A. T. Wallis Jr., *Indonesian Revival: Why Two Million Came to Christ* (Pasadena, Calif.: Gabriel Resources, 1977); and Jan Tamur, *Ex-Muslims for Christ* (Birmingham, England: Crossbearers, 1980).

12. Posted at www.answering-islam.org/Testimonies/desertson.html. Quoted with the permission of Desert Son, who can be contacted at desertson1@yahoo.com.

13. Posted at www.secularislam.org. Reprinted with permission from the Institute for the Secularisation of Islamic Society.

14. Amnesty International, "Kuwait: Hussein Qambar 'Ali: Death Threats," AI Index (MDE 17/05/96) [online], web.amnesty.org/802568F7005C4453/0/893E69A437755B52 80256900006933ED?Open&Highlight=2,Qambar [August 1, 1996].

15. Robert Hussein and Sharon Green, ed., *Apostate Son* (Colorado Springs: Najiba Publishing, 1998).

16. *Christianity Today*, August 28, 2000.

17. Hass Hirji-Walji and J. Strong, *Escape from Islam* (Eastbourne, England: Kingsway Publications, 1981), pp. 99–102.

18. J. A. Beverley, "Something Terrifying and Intolerable," *Faith Today* (January/ February 2000): 11.

19. "Les Pentes Croisées du baptême," *Le Figaro*, Paris, April 12, 2000, p. 9.

20. Please contact me in care of the publisher if you have statistics on this subject.

8

APOSTATES
OF ISLAM II
*Converts to Hinduism, Humanism,
Deism, Atheism, and Agnosticism*

CONVERTS TO HINDUISM

There is a certain amount of anecdotal evidence that many Muslims in India are reverting to the religion of their ancestors, Hinduism. More scientific evidence comes from the work of the Australian anthropologist Dr. Thomas Reuter, of the University of Melbourne, who conducted ethnographic fieldwork among the indigenous people of highland Bali, Indonesia.[1] Reuter's research into Hindu revivalism and religious conflict in Javanese society has shown that Hinduism has been reclaiming parts of the Indonesia archipelago it once dominated for a millennium: "Even Java, the island at the heart of what is now the world's largest Muslim nation, is witnessing mass conversions from Islam to Hinduism. Expectations of a new golden age among followers of this revival movement are an expression of utopian prophesies and political hopes more widely shared among contemporary Indonesians."[2]

Though the number of conversions in Java are hard to quantify, according to Reuter's own estimates there have been tens of thousands over the last twenty years, more in some years than others.[3] There is also a return to Hinduism in Kalimantan, Sulawesi, and Sumatra. Up to now there has been no systematic persecution of the Hindus, but unfortunately the signs are that the situation is changing for the worse.

MODERN CONVERTS TO ATHEISM AND HUMANISM

In *L'Islam en Questions*, published in France in 1986, twenty-four Arab writers replied to the following five questions:

(1) Does Islam retain its universal vocation?

(2) Could Islam be a system of government for a modern state?

(3) Is an Islamic system of government an obligatory step in the evolution of the Islamic and Arab peoples?

(4) Is the phenomenon of the "return to Islam" that is observable in the last ten years in the majority of Muslim countries something positive?

(5) What is today the principal enemy of Islam?

It is clear from their replies that a majority of these Arab intellectuals do not see Islam as the answer to the social, economic, and political problems besetting the Islamic world. The majority are the fervent advocates of a secular state. Nine writers give an emphatic and categoric "no" to the question 2, "Could Islam be a system of government for a modern state?" while another six are equally emphatically for a secular state. Even those writers who give "yes" as an answer to question 2 do so in a very tentative way, hedged with qualifications such as "provided rights are respected" or "as long as we have a modern interpretation of Islam." Almost all of them find the "return to Islam" a negative phenomenon and consider religious fanaticism as the greatest danger facing all Muslims.[4]

One of the writers in the book is Rachid Boudjedra, a novelist, playwright, essayist, communist, and self-confessed atheist. He is scathing about religion in Algeria—the hypocrisy of the majority (80 percent is his figure) of the "believers" who pray or pretend to pray only in the month of Ramadan, the holy month of fasting; who go on pilgrimage for the social prestige; who drink and fornicate and still claim to be good Muslims. As to the question, Could Islam be a system of government for a modern state? Boudjedra unequivocally replies:

> No, absolutely not, it's impossible; that is not just a personal opinion, it's something objective. We saw that when Nemeiri [head of the Sudan] wanted to apply the Sharia: it didn't work. The experiment ended abruptly after some hands and feet were chopped off. . . . There is a reaction even amongst the mass of Muslims against this sort of thing—stoning women, for example, is hardly carried out, except in Saudi Arabia, and extremely rarely. . . . Islam is absolutely incompatible with a modern state. . . . No, I don't see how Islam could be a system of government.[5]

It is generally not known that Boudjedra has had a *fatwa* pronounced against him since 1983 and that he remains in Algeria despite death threats, trying to carry on as normally as possible, moving from place to place heavily disguised. To compound his "errors," in 1992 Boudjedra wrote a ferocious attack on the Front Islamique du Salut (FIS), the Islamicist party that was all set to win the elections in 1992, exposing it for what it is: an extremist undemocratic party, even comparing it to the Nazi party of the 1930s. Boudjedra has nothing but contempt for those who remain silent and those who are not only uncritical of the Islamicists, but who pretend to see something "fertile" in this regression to medieval times.

The number of atheists in Algeria, I suspect, is high, but for obvious reasons we do not have reliable statistics. We do have them for young men of Algerian descent living in France. They make for very startling reading. In 1995 the French daily *Libération* conducted a thorough survey. Here are some of its findings:

Thirty percent of those men born in France and both of whose parents were born in Algeria declared themselves to be without any religion. This percentage is higher than the national average; 27 percent of all Frenchmen describe themselves as without any religion. Sixty percent of those men born in France with only one parent born in Algeria declared themselves to be without religion, more than double the national average! The figures for women remain almost unchanged: 30 percent women born in France and both of whose parents were born in Algeria said they were without religion. This percentage is even higher than the national average: 20 percent of all Frenchwomen say they are without religion. Fifty-eight percent of women with one parent born in Algeria said they were without any religion, almost three times the national average.[6]

CASE STUDIES

Pakistan

In 1933 a student of Cambridge University organized a dinner at London's Waldorf Hotel. The menu included oysters and good wine. Out of this convivial and certainly un-Islamic setting was born the idea of Pakistan, a separate homeland for the Muslims of India. There is further irony in that the man revered in present-day Pakistan as the Great Leader and founder of the nation, Muhammad Ali Jinnah, was an atheist. Religion never played an important role in Jinnah's private life[7] and, according to one historian, had Jinnah been alive today "he would have to be flogged publicly for his personal habits. Mr Jinnah not only chained-smoked Craven-A cigarettes but also liked his whisky and was not averse to pork."[8] At a press conference on July 4, 1947, a journalist asked Jinnah if Pakistan would be a religious state. Jinnah replied, "You are asking a question that is absurd. I do not know what a theocratic state means."[9] Then, on August 11, the day he was elected president of the Pakistan Constituent Assembly, Jinnah gave a moving speech that included the following sentiments: "We are starting the state with no discrimination . . . we should keep that in front of us as our ideal, and you will find that in course of time Hindus will cease to be Hindus and Muslims will cease to be Muslims, not in the religious sense, because that is the personal faith of each individual, but in the political sense as the citizens of the nation."[10]

Far from being a theocratic state, with over 135 million Muslim fundamentalists, Pakistan has a large, liberal, secular-minded middle class, in whose lives religion does not play an important part. Here is how one British journalist and novelist of Pakistani origin described the social milieu in Lahore (Pakistan), where he grew up:

> I never believed in God, not even between the ages of six and ten, when I was an agnostic. This unbelief was instinctive. I was sure there was nothing else out there but space. It could have been my lack of imagination. In the jasmine-scented summer nights, long before mosques were allowed to use loudspeakers, it was enough to savour the silence, look up at the exquisitely lit sky, count the shooting stars and fall asleep. The early morning call of the muezzin was a pleasant alarm-clock.
>
> There were many advantages in being an unbeliever. Threatened with divine sanctions by family retainers, cousins or elderly relatives—"If you do that Allah will be angry" or "If you don't do this Allah will punish you"—I was unmoved. Let him do his worst, I used to tell myself, but he never did, and that reinforced my belief in his non-existence.
>
> My parents, too, were non-believers. So were most of their close friends. Religion played a tiny part in our Lahore household. In the second half of the last century, a large proportion of educated Muslims had embraced modernity. Old habits persisted, nonetheless: the would-be virtuous made their ablutions and sloped off to Friday prayers. Some fasted for a few days each year, usually just before the new moon marking the end of Ramadan. I doubt whether more than a quarter of the population in the cities fasted for a whole month. Café life continued unabated. Many claimed that they had fasted so as to take advantage of the free food doled out at the end of each fasting day by the mosques or the kitchens of the wealthy. In the countryside fewer still fasted, since outdoor work was difficult without sustenance, and especially without water when Ramadan fell during the summer months. Eid, the festival marking the end of Ramadan, was celebrated by everyone.[11]

Iran

I suspect Iran is also a country where the majority of the population is totally disillusioned with Islam. In chapter 6 I adumbrated the freethinking tradition in Iranian culture. There is enough evidence to suggest that this tradition is alive and well in the twenty-first century. I have given talks to large groups of agnostic and anti-Islamic Iranians in Washington, D.C.; Paris; and Los Angeles in the last five years. Further anecdotal evidence comes from Dr. Ali Sina, the Iranian-born former Muslim who runs the Web site for Faith Freedom International.[12] An Iranian scholar once wrote to Sina saying that a census carried out in the 1980s among Iranian exiles in the Netherlands showed that 50 percent declared themselves agnostics or atheists. Indeed, one has only to visit a few Iranian Web sites to verify that a comfortable majority are anti-Islamic.[13] Many are communist,[14] as is the following writer found on the Web:

> A mainstay of cultural backwardness and sexist in Iranian society is Islam. If we want to fight sexist we have to lock up Islam. We have to launch a massive antireligious and secularist campaign; something that began somewhat with the Constitutional Revolution. The cultural and ideological barrier in Iranian society to women's liberation is Easternism and Islam. The struggle against both requires in the first step a powerful struggle against the Islamic Republic, which is the main protector of this culture and ideology.
>
> But things have changed—sadly, though, at the cost of the blood of hundreds of thousands of people, the destruction of the lives of millions, and the displacement of millions. Never before has the movement for secularism and atheism, for modern thought and culture, for free relationships, for women's liberation, been so massive. Things have changed. Hatred of religion and backward and Easternist culture is very widespread. The youth and women in Iran are the champions of this struggle; a growing struggle that has already shaken the ground under the feet of the Islamic system.
>
> As advocates of freedom and equality, as defenders of equal rights for women, we have to settle accounts with Easternism and religion. Only a secular system that ensures unconditional freedom of expression and organisation can also ensure triumph over sexist culture. In the 21st century it is high time that women were free and equal, decided their own fate, had their own independent identity, enjoyed sexual freedom and, in one word, had full and independent status. Today worker-communism is a force that is unequivocally fighting Islam and backwardness, for women's full equality and liberation.[15]

Salaheddin Mohsen

On June 18, 2000, an Egyptian writer on trial for atheism and blasphemy against Islam rooted his defense in the right to free speech. "I have an opinion and I expressed my opinion in these books," Salaheddin Mohsen, in detention since April 2000, told a state security court when his trial opened. Prosecutors put him on trial after he admitted under questioning in 2000 that he did not believe in Islam and sought to promote secular thought in four recent books. Mohsen "is sick in the heart and an example of atheism," prosecuting lawyer Ashraf al-Ashmawi told the court. "He mocked Islam and its rites and duties and was proud of his insolence against religion under the slogan of enlightenment and freedom of creativity." Mohsen "claimed that Islam is the reason for the nation's backwardness, that Muhammad is not a prophet but wrote the Koran and that the Koran is full of strife and contradictions," Ashmawi said. Mohsen is charged with "using religion to promote, by writing, extremist ideas to denigrate the Islamic religion, provoke and damage national unity." Mohsen, age fifty-two, promoted rationalism in four books and tried to establish an atheist organization in Egypt.

The court found him guilty in August 2000. Explaining that it did not want to turn him a hero, the court then gave him a suspended sentence of six months' imprisonment. The court's decision was appealed by the prosecution to the office for the ratification of court sentences, which is attached to the presidency. Following abrogation of the sentence and an order for retrial, Salaheddin faced a second trial and has now been given three years' hard labor for "deriding religion."[16]

Syria

In April 1967, just before the Six Day War, an issue of the Syrian army magazine *Jayash al-Sha'b* [*The People's Army*] contained an article attacking not just Islam but God and religion in general as "mummies which should be transferred to the museums of historical remains." It is worth quoting at length.

The author argued that the only way to build Arab society and civilization was to create

> a new Arab socialist man, who believes that God, religions, feudalism, capital, and all the values which prevailed in the pre-existing society were no more than mummies in the museums of history. . . . There is only one value: absolute faith in the new man of destiny . . . who relies only on himself and on his own contribution to humanity . . . because he knows that his inescapable end is death and nothing beyond death . . . no heaven and no hell. . . . We have no need of men who kneel and beg for grace and pity.[17]

Mobs took to the streets in many of the major cities of Syria leading to violence, strikes, and arrests. When the old ruse of blaming everything on a Zionist-American conspiracy failed to quell the violence, the article's author, Ibrahim Khalas, and two of his editors on the magazine were court-martialed, found guilty and sentenced to life imprisonment with hard labor. Happily, they were released after a short period in prison.

In 1969, after the disatrous defeat of the Arabs by Israel in 1967, a Syrian Marxist intellectual produced a brilliant critique of religious thought. Sadiq al-Azm was educated at the American University of Beirut, received his doctorate in philosophy from Yale University, and has published a study of the British philosopher Bishop Berkeley. His devastating criticisms of Islam and religion were not appreciated by the Sunni establishment in Beirut, and he was brought to trial on charges of provoking religious troubles. He was acquitted, perhaps because of his political connections since he came from a distinguished Syrian political family. Nonetheless, al-Azm thought it prudent to live abroad for a while.

Sadiq al-Azm takes to task the Arab leaders for not developing the critical faculties in their people, and for their own uncritical attitude toward Islam and its outmoded ways of thought. Arab reactionaries used religious thought as an ideological weapon, yet no one submitted their thought to

> a critical, scientific analysis to reveal the forgeries they employ to exploit the Arab man. . . . [The leaders] refrained from any criticism of the Arab intellectual and social heritage. . . . Under the cover of protecting the people's traditions, values, art, religion, and morals, the cultural effort of the Arab liberation movement was used to protect the backward institutions and the medieval culture and thought of obscurantist ideology.[18]

Every Muslim has to face the challenge of the scientific developments of the last 150 years. Scientific knowledge is in direct conflict with Muslim religious beliefs on a number of issues. But, more fundamentally, it is a question of methodology—Islam relies on blind faith and the uncritical acceptance of texts on which it is based; whereas science depends on critical thought, observation, deduction, and results that are internally coherent and correspond to reality. We can no longer leave religious thought uncriticized; all the sacred texts must be scrutinized in a scientific manner. Only then will we stop gazing back and only then will religion stop being an obscurantist justification for the intellectual and political status quo.

NOTES

1. Thomas Reuter, "Great Expectations: Hindu Revival Movements in Java," *Australian Journal of Anthropology* 12, no. 3 (2001): 327–338.

2. See Dr. Reuter's Web page on the University of Melbourne Web site: www.geography.unimelb.edu.au/staff/reuter.html.

3. Personal communication with Thomas Reuter, March 4, 2002.

4. Luc Barbulesco and Philippe Cardinale, *L'Islam en questions* (Paris: Grasset, 1986).

5. Ibid., pp. 213–14.

6. Immigration Supplement, *La Libération*, Paris, March 22, 1995, p. 5.

7. Stanley Wolpert, *Jinnah of Pakistan* (New York: Oxford University Press, 1984), p. 18.

8. M. J. Akbar, *India: The Siege Within* (Harmondsworth, England: Penguin, 1985), p. 32.

9. Ibid., p. 34.

10. Ibid.

11. Tariq Ali, "Mullahs and Heretics," *London Review of Books* 24, no. 3, February 7, 2002.

12. Online at www.faithfreedom.org.

13. A few examples are: www.geocities.com/hammihaniarani and www.geocities.com/frydon47/mazdak.html.

14. For example, the Worker-Communist Party of Iran, online at www.wpiran.org/english.htm.

15. Azar Majedi, "Future Is Ours" [online], www.medusa2000.com/azaspeech.htm.

16. Fatemah Farag, "Re-drawing the Line," *Al-Ahram* [online], August 3–9, 2000, weekly.ahram.org.eg/2000/493/eg9.htm.

17. Quoted in B. Lewis, *Islam in History* (Chicago: Open Court, 1993), p. 5.

18. Sadiq al-Azm's book is important and deserves to be better known, but as far as I know it remains untranslated from the original Arabic. More recently, Sadiq al-Azm has very courageously defended Salman Rushdie in an article in *Die Welt des Islams* 31 (1991): 1–49. See Sadiq al-Azm, *Critique of Religious Thought* (Damascus, 1969).

9

APOSTASY, HUMAN RIGHTS, AND ISLAM

The very notion of apostasy has vanished from the West, where one talks of being a "lapsed Catholic" or "nonpracticing Christian" rather than an "apostate." There are certainly no penal sanctions for converting from Christianity to any other superstitious flavor of the month, from New Ageism to Islam. In Islamic countries, on the other hand, the issue is far from dead, as the examples given earlier attest.

Article 18 of the Universal Declaration of Human Rights (UDHR) states: "Everyone has the right to freedom of thought, conscience and religion; this right includes freedom to change his religion or belief, and freedom, either alone or in community with others and in public or private, to manifest his religion or belief in teaching, practice, worship and observance."[1]

The clause guaranteeing the freedom to change one's religion was added at the request of the delegate from Lebanon, who was a Christian.[2] Lebanon had accepted many people fleeing persecution for their beliefs, in particular for having changed their religion. Lebanon specially objected to the Islamic law concerning apostasy. Many Muslim countries objected strongly to the clause regarding the right to change one's religion. The delegate from Egypt, for instance, said that "very often a man changes religion or his convictions under external influences with goals which are not recommendable such as divorce." He added that he feared in proclaiming the liberty to change one's religion or convictions the UDHR would unwittingly encourage "the machinations of certain missions well known in the East that relentlessly pursue their efforts with a view to converting to their faith the populations of the East."[3] Significantly, Lebanon was supported by a delegate from Pakistan who belonged to the Ahmadi community, which, ironically, was to be thrown out of the Islamic community in the 1970s for being "non-Muslim." In the end, all the Muslim countries except Saudi Arabia voted for the UDHR.

During discussions of Article 18 in 1966, Saudi Arabia and Egypt wanted to suppress the clause guaranteeing the freedom to change one's religion. Finally a compromise amendment proposed by Brazil and the Philippines was adopted to placate the Islamic countries. Thus "the freedom to change his religion or belief" was replaced by "the freedom to have or adopt a religion or belief of his choice."[4] Similarly, in 1981, during discussions on the Declaration on the Elimination of All Forms of Intolerance and Discrimination Based on Religion or Belief, Iran reminded everyone that Islam punished apostasy by death. The delegate from Iraq, backed up by Syria, speaking on behalf of the Organisation of the Islamic Conference, expressed his reserve for any clauses or terms that would contradict the Islamic *Sharī'a*, while the delegate from Egypt feared that such a clause might be exploited for political ends to interfere in the internal affairs of states.[5]

The various Islamic human rights schemes or declarations, such as the Universal Islamic Declaration of Human Rights (1981), are understandably vague or evasive on the issue of the freedom to change one's religion, since Islam itself clearly forbids apostasy and punishes it with death. As A. E. Mayer says:

> The lack of support for the principle of freedom of religion in the Islamic human rights schemes is one of the factors that most sharply distinguishes them from the International Bill of Human Rights, which treats freedom of religion as an unqualified right. The [Muslim] authors' unwillingness to repudiate the rule that a person should be executed over a question of religious belief reveals the enormous gap that exists between their mentalities and the modern philosophy of human rights.[6]

As for the constitutions of various Muslim countries, while many do guarantee freedom of belief (Egypt, 1971; Syria, 1973; Jordan, 1952), some talk of freedom of conscience (Algeria, 1989), some of freedom of thought and opinion (Mauritania, 1991). Islamic countries, with two exceptions, do not address the issue of apostasy in their penal codes; the two exceptions are the Sudan and Mauritania. Article 126.2 of the Sudanese Penal Code of 1991 reads, "Whoever is guilty of apostasy is invited to repent over a period to be determined by the tribunal. If he persists in his apostasy and was not recently converted to Islam, he will be put to death." The Penal Code of Mauritania of 1984, article 306, reads, "All Muslims guilty of apostasy, either spoken or by overt action will be asked to repent during a period of three days. If he doesnot repent during this period, he is condemend to death as an apostate, and his belongings confiscated by the State Treasury." This applies equally to women. The Moroccan Penal Code seems only to mention those guilty of trying to subvert the belief of a Muslim or try to convert a Muslim to another religion. The punishment ranges from a fine to imprisonment for up to three years.[7]

The absence of any mention of apostasy in some penal codes of Islamic countries, of course, in no way implies that a Muslim in the country concerned is free to leave his religion. In reality, the lacunae in the penal codes are filled by Islamic law. Mahmud Muhammad Taha was hanged for apostasy in Sudan in 1985, even though the Sudanese Penal Code of 1983 did not mention such a crime.[8]

In some countries, the term *apostate* is applied to some who were born non-Muslim, but whose ancestors had converted from Islam. The Baha'is in Iran in recent years have been persecuted for just such a reason. Similarly, in Pakistan the Ahmadiyya community were classed as non-Muslims, and subjected to all sorts of persecution.

There is some evidence that many Muslim women in Islamic countries would convert from Islam to escape their lowly position in Muslim societies, to avoid the application of an unfavorable law, especially *Sharī'a* laws governing divorce.[9] Muslim theologians are well aware of the temptation of Muslim women to evade the *Sharī'a* laws by converting from Islam, and take appropriate measures. For example, in Kuwait in an explanatory memorandum to the text of a law reform says: "Complaints have shown that the devil makes the route of apostasy attractive to the Muslim woman so that she can break a conjugal tie that does not please her. For this reason, it was decided that apostasy would not lead to the dissolution of the marriage in order to close this dangerous door."[10]

NOTES

1. Available online at the United Nations Web site: www.un.org/rights/50/decla.htm.

2. Sami A. Aldeeb Abu-Sahlieh, "Le Délit d'Apostasie Aujour'hui et ses Conséquences en Droit Arabe et Musulman," *Islamochristiana* 20 (1994): 93–116; A. E. Mayer, *Islam and Human Rights* (Boulder, Colo.: Westview Press, 1991), p. 164.

3. Abu-Sahlieh, "Le Délit d'Apostasie," p. 94.

4. Ibid.

5. Ibid.

6. Mayer, *Islam and Human Rights*, p. 187.

7. Abu-Sahlieh, "Le Délit d'Apostasie," p. 98.

8. Sami A. Aldeeb Abu-Sahlieh, *Les Musulmans face aux droits de l'homme* (Bachum: Verlag Dr. D. Winkler), p. 110.

9. Mayer, *Islam and Human Rights*, p. 167.

10. Sami A. Aldeeb Abu-Sahlieh, "Liberté religieuse et apostasie dans l'islam," *Praxis juridique et religion* 23 (1986): 53; quoted in Mayer, *Islam and Human Rights*, pp. 167–68.

PART 2

TESTIMONIES
SUBMITTED
TO THE
ISIS WEB SITE

10

INTRODUCTION

Ibn Warraq

T he testimony section on the ISIS Web site* has the following words of encouragement to former Muslims to contribute their stories:

Here we are not celebrating those who have left one form of unreason only to adopt another form of unreason, but those who confront unflinchingly a world devoid of fantasy, who look the world in the face without the crutches of irrational dogma.

We wish to encourage ex-Muslims to declare themselves, to liberate themselves, to make them take conscience of the fact that there are many who think like them, and who have taken the same lonely road to rationalism, and humanism, and some to Christianity.

Rest assured that we will jealously guard your secret. You may wish to submit your testimony anonymously, that is perfectly understandable and honourable even. For many ex-Muslims living in the West often travel back to the Islamic country of their birth, where they still have close relatives who themselves might be endangered by the apostates public declaration.

Here are some guidelines if you wish to write a testimony, but of course you have no obligation to follow any of them. If you know exactly what you want to say, just write directly on our Web site.

---

*The Institute for the Secularisation of Islamic Societies, www.secularislam.org.

1. Were your parents religious?
2. What was their mother tongue?
3. Did they know Arabic?
4. How often did they go to the Mosque?
5. Education: did you go to Koranic school?
6. Do you understand Arabic?
7. Did you read the Koran? Did you understand it?
8. When did you start questioning religion? Islam?
9. Was there someone who encouraged you in your freethought?
10. Were you influenced by any book?
11. Were freethought books available to you at home? In town? At friends'?
12. Do your parents know about your present feelings?
13. Does anyone else in your family or circle of friends know?
14. What is their reaction?
15. Do you feel threatened?
16. Have you been attacked physically for your beliefs?
17. How would you describe yourself now?
    a) atheist b) humanist c) rationalist d) agnostic e) deist f) secularist?
18. Perhaps a mixture of the above (e.g., some call themselves "atheist humanists," others "secular humanists")

Looking forward to reading your testimonies. Remember they can be powerful agents of change, and a source of inspiration and solace for others. Good Luck.

11

TESTIMONIES FROM THE
ISIS WEB SITE

The following testimonies were written between February 2001 and April 2002.

MY VIEW OF ISLAM AND WHY I LEFT IT

My reason for leaving Islam is very simple: I read the Koran. For me it was as easy as just reading the Koran and using a little reason, logic, and thinking. I thought the story of the Noah's Ark that is recorded in the Koran is one of the most bizarre stories I have ever heard. Apparently the world was overrun by water and the only survivors were the people who had followed Noah. Noah had, it seems, the ability to communicate with animals to ask them to come aboard the ship, so that their species would not become extinct.

Back then the early Arabs looked around themselves and they saw a few camels and a couple of dogs and they thought that these were all the animals in the world. They were unaware of the fact that there are over a billion species in the world and some that have not even been discovered yet. What about the animals that did not live in Arabia? Did Noah fly on a winged horse like Muhammad, to go and collect the animals from all around the world? What about the species that we are unable to see without a microscope? How did Noah collect them? Most important, in the research of earth biology we have discovered all the facts about the earth and its past. Can anyone find in any book of earth biology any evidence that proves that the earth was once completely covered by water?

This was enough for me to realize that the Koran is just a book of fables.

People will tell you that according to the Koran the sun sets in a pond, or that mountains are pegs that Allah installed on the earth to keep it from moving, and so on, but the only flaw of the Koran is not what is in it. The biggest flaw of the Koran is what is not in it. There are many many crimes a person can commit, yet the Koran mentions only the punishments for a mere three or four. I was astonished at the fact that the Koran mentions nothing about punishment for rape. The word *rape* is not even mentioned once in the Koran, as if it were not worth bringing up.

Apparently Allah thought it worthwhile to insist to his prophet on the necessity for praying and for paying alms over one thousand times, but rape is not worth mentioning. When you read the Hadiths about the obvious rape of Safiyah, the Jewish woman, by Muhammad, and the way he backs it up with a verse from the Koran, you also realize that rape is not considered a crime. It then all starts to come together and make sense.

There are an unlimited number of acts of kindness that we can do to help each other and make this world a better place for everyone, yet you do not see these in the Koran. How can the Koran be a perfect guidance from God when it lacks so many important issues?

What I have done for the last six months on the Internet is debate with Muslims and try to show them the light of truth. When you debate with a Muslim and he does not know what to say, he always says, "God is the author of the Koran because that's what it says in the Koran." It is absurd to prove something by itself. Sometimes when I hear these responses I feel like giving up on exposing the truth about Islam and religion, but then I realize that I would be abandoning my dear friends, like Dr. Ali Sina and the many people who have given their lives for the truth.

ANONYMOUS

I was was nine years old when my grade four teacher was teaching us about history. He asked us how we can know the truth about what really happened in the past. We did not know the answer to his question. What he offered us as the answer was this: "Only the Koran holds the truth." It did not make any sense to me at the time because I thought, What if the Koran itself is not true, either? However, I did not dare to voice my view. I did not pay the matter much attention. I grew up to be a Muslim but I always had my doubts about the whole thing. As I grew older, I started to look at religion as a social phenomenon. Now, there is no doubt in my mind that Judaism, Christianity, and Islam are all man-made. However, I found the Islamic message to be particularly disturbing mainly because it requires at its core suppression and persecution of all those that oppose it.

ANONYMOUS

I was born in a Pakistani family in the West. I was a major fundamentalist Muslim. I had absolute faith in Islam and I loved it very much. However after reading the Koran a few times I started to wonder about some of the verses. There were things in the Koran that were making me nervous, also the many stories about Muhammad were also cause for concern. The conquest and subjugation of the Jews was rather disturbing; so, too, was the rape of many women. I did not want to believe this and I started to say to myself that these stories are lies.

However the thought of my faith was eating my mind, slowly, slowly I was being torn apart by this dilemma. I finally wrote down some of the problems I had with the Koran and the story of Muhammad. I went to mosque and asked the *maulawi* [learned man, especially in religious matters] sahib about these issues I had with Islam. He tried his best to explain but I knew that he wasn't going to be able to justify some of the atrocities committed by Muhammad. However the part where he got stuck was the ʿĀʾisha question: How can a man of more than fifty years old have sexual feelings for a girl of only six? After he gave me an unsatisfactory answer I just went quiet and walked away. I was out the door and I looked back. He looked at me and he put his head down. I think he knew I was not going to come back.

Since then I have been rather heartbroken as I have lost my faith. Islam is a falsehood, a pure hoax. I felt that I might as well believe in Santa Claus or the bogeyman! I wish I could believe again, but as a normal and respectable human being I cannot believe in a man who is a pedophile! Simple as that. I can't comprehend the fact that a man of that age can fantasize about a six-year-old, and then have sex with her while she was still playing with her dolls! And why is it that a woman is lower than a man? Is my mother lower than me? Why is it that a Muslim man can have four wives? Can a woman not have four husbands, then? And why did Muhammad have more than four wives? Doesn't he believe in practice what you preach? Also, how can I believe a man with such low moral character? How can I believe in a man who does things I myself find abhorrent and disgusting? A man like him today, instead of being in a mosque, would actually be in prison with a seven-year jail sentence for rape and child molestation. For the cultural reasons given for this act (by the so-called scholars) of Muhammad's marriage with a six-year-old are irrelevant! No sane man in any time or place would have sexual feelings for a baby!

This is reason enough for denouncing Islam, for this man is not from God. And Islam is just the ramblings of some dillusioned Arab madman. All this religion has done is cause pain and misery for the world, especially India, where the mass murder of Hindus was unforgivable. No country suffered more than Hindu India. As for other religions, at least the so-called enemies of Islam, such as Sikhism, Hinduism, and Buddhism, etc., do not have their religious leaders doing such disgusting things or being complete hypocrites! I'm still a right-wing conservative but I am not a sucker and I am not going to let this nutcase ideology ruin my life anymore. Even Jesus was not anything like this fiend Muhammad! I'm just glad I got out while I could, and I just hope that all the other Muslims finally get their facts right and come to their senses. They should dump this evil satanic cult immediately, and do with the Koran as is done with all other piles of useless trash: Commit it to the flames!

ANONYMOUS

I find it difficult to accept the fact that Allah asked women to pray with the scarf on, with long sleeves, etc., when, surely, God is above all this unimportant issues and can see what is in our souls and hearts. Also, it is almost sacrilegious to assume that God is humanlike and would get offended or influenced in any way by the clothes people wear. We are naked many times and God is present around us at all times, so I don't understand the point of being alone in the house, feeling like praying, and having to look for particular garments to pray in. If it helps people to concentrate in their contemplation that is fine, but to claim that God would not accept a good human being just because this human being did not have appropriate garments (when alone) is completely ridiculous.

ANONYMOUS

In regard to women being required to pray with a scarf and long clothes on: This is something that has perplexed me, and, interestingly enough, I have not encountered another Muslim who also finds it strange. *Hijab* as an identifier or a protector is reasonable, but *hijab* as a uniform for prayer does not make sense. Prayer reflects a personal bond with God. What does *hijab* have to do with it?

Having to always have to put on prayer clothes before I can worship God always seemed to me a bother. It makes prayer much more formal, uncomfortable, and impersonal, for although God is supposed to be closer to you than your jugular vein, putting on *hijab* to pray implies that God is not as close to you as you would think (similar to putting on *hijab* in front of nonrelatives or strange men).

I never understood how covering added anything positive to prayer. I still do not (the "out of respect for God" explanation just doesn't cut it) and that is one of the many reasons, big and small, for my gradual disbelief in Islam.

ANONYMOUS

Born in to a Muslim household in the West, I learned to "read" Arabic somewhere around age five. I finished the Koran, so I'm told, at age six. In all my life, every time I pick up a book, it has always required a superhuman effort on my part to read it to the end. This, I am certain, is at least partly a consequence of my early forced reading of the Koran. It is obvious to me (from my experiences) that any forced adherence to rules, be they religious, political, or social, inflicts psychological damage on a mind. This damage is especially severe when the compelled individual is a child. What was the cause of my lame excuse to cover up Allah's ignorance?

ANONYMOUS

Although I am no longer a Muslim, I still enjoy listening to the Koran recitation by the voice of Al Shaikh Mustafa Ismail. I have a large collection of his tapes and I listen to them quite often. I found Surat Al-Namal (Ants) particularly amusing and perhaps down right funny. It talks about how Suliman was walking down the valley of the ants. One ant was warning the other ants and was saying, "Get down to your homes lest Suliman and his soliders destroy you while they are unaware." Suliman, who understands the language of the ants, laughed and smiled at what they were saying.

You will find these stories and much more in the Koran beautifully described, and the reading by Mustafa Ismail makes them even more beautiful. Great stories for kids, don't you think so?

There are also good adult stories. The story of Yosef is one that is particularly erotic. I know that most of these stories were borrowed from previous works by Jewish authors. But the Islamic edition is far superior from a literary point of view. I may be biased because Arabic is my mother tongue and so I have a taste for Arabic-language literature. One of my favorite Om Kalthoum songs is "Nahg El Burda," which is purely a religious song.

I like my Islamic cultural heritage and I enjoy it. Of course I am not taking any of it seriously. I understand why people still cling to their belief. They simply need it. I have nothing to offer these people because what they need is not the truth, they need to believe in something to ease their anxiety and their fear of death. If religion makes them feel good, let them. Where I draw the line is when they start to interfere in my own life. Fortunately, this is rather difficult because I no longer live in a Muslim country.

ANONYMOUS

This page has been an eye-opener for me. As a convert to Islam, I thought that I had stumbled upon a religion that promoted unity and, above all else, love. Now, two years later, I am struggling with this religion. When I pick up the Koran, all I see are threats against me, about what will happen should I turn my back. I see depicted before me a vengeful creator, a jealous God. Something isn't right. Where is the love in all of this? I have always believed that God would love me unconditionally; now I am being told that our infinite and divine creator has conditional love for us?! Something definitely is not right here.

ANONYMOUS

Repeated and completed Dear Enlightened Minds (peace be to you).

One of the unfortunate things that happened in my life was that my mother was a religious fanatic and I was raised in an atmosphere of religious superstition. Later, when the good vibrations became my fortune, I questioned my beliefs and found out that I followed Islam because of fear. I did not find the Koran inspiring but used to praise it because of fear and irrationality. Religious fear gripped me during my adolescence and late teens and I became an unbalanced personality. It was not easy to leave religion because I was living in an Islamic society, which is constantly sodomized by religious superstition. But gradually it dawned on me that if I wanted to live my life I would have to throw away the mask of being a Muslim. And so I believe in a power that is beyond my comprehension and that is orbiting the planets; thus, you could call me a deist. Yes, I agree that Islam has certain good points—but bad as well. In Islam the status of women is inferior, which I observed deeply, and I cannot understand the marriage between the Prophet of Islam and ʿĀʾisha. In my view *mullahs* or the ulemas twist this incident or avoid talking about it. From my boyhood I heard that the Prophet was fifty years old and she was nine years old, but later in an esteemed newspaper I saw an article that said a scholar had discovered that she was nineteen years old. I could not buy that. But I see a positive development: The world is getting smaller and through the blessing of the Internet the people of the world will get closer and will realize that one man's religion is another's superstition and they will act rationally rather then emotionally about religion and religious personalities.

ANONYMOUS

I embraced Islam many, many years ago, when I was young and impressionable. Drawn and influenced by religious propaganda, I honestly felt compelled to accept the reality that the Bible was a corrupted text and that the Koran was unquestionably infallible and correct in all aspects. Today I realize that the scholarship in Islam is, in reality, no better than that of Christendom in authenticating and contriving arguments. I have seen some of the most ridiculous irrational arguments used to justify beliefs, it is astounding. Some people have audacity, I will grant them that! Unfortunately, Christianity and Judaism have been used as a yardstick to gauge and prove the authenticity of Islam in most cases. And we all know how reliable those sources are! Oh well, as Rodney Dangerfield would have said: "Who knew?"

ANONYMOUS

Being from an ultraconservative society in an country where life revolves around the *Sharī‘a*, I was shocked but delighted to have come across this Web site. Having been exposed to liberal societies and thoughts while studying abroad from an early age, and having to endure an uneasy reintegration into my own society each time I returned, I knew from early on that my situation would be untenable. One of the most unconvincing aspects of Islam that, more than anything, turned me away from it is the portrayal of Allah in weak, deficient human terms. This all-powerful, all-knowing God is shown to have emotional problems, i.e., gets angry, vengeful when his "faulty creation," man, goes astray for the most ludicrous of sins. Is Allah so unsure of himself that he needs his own creation to pray to him five times a day and to praise him continually? Doesn't this God have better goals for his creation than this pursuit? Why not let man create or pursue better, more worthy objectives, such as figuring ways of overcoming hatred, war, intolerance, poverty, etc.? It seems the main focus is prayer, fasting, pilgrimage and mindless worship that serves no other worthy objective than to please him. Is this what gets him off? This omnipotent creator of the universe seems to have the character of a weak, emotionally unbalanced, deficient human being. Did he create us in his own image— or did we or Muhammad create him in our own image?

ANONYMOUS

I am delighted to have found your Web site. I wish I had known about it a year and a half ago, because it might have saved me a lot of grief. Here is my story:

I am female, born and raised in the West in a family that could be labeled "Christian" but does not belong to any such church or organization. In college I became a "freethinker," read parts of the Bible at one point, although not in depth, examined other religions, such as Judaism and Buddhism. But not Islam. Just the mention of the word "Islam" conjured images of religious zealots who strap dynamite to themselves and walk into a mall, of women punished for not veiling themselves properly, and so on. Islam just didn't seem like a "warm and fuzzy" religion.

Two years ago I met a man from the Middle East. I must admit that I was not happy with the fact that he was a Sunni Muslim. But he was charming and gentle, nothing like what I saw on television. Since it was not in my nature to be prejudiced anyway, I allowed our relationship to continue. We had so much in common (we often finished each other's sentences) that I put the issue of religion on the "back burner," so to speak.

We were married six months later, in a civil ceremony. I was very much aware that my new husband had an extensive library of Islamic materials and that he prayed five times a day. But that didn't bother me. After all, I did not consider myself much of a Christian. Sure, I believed in the crucifixion and resurrection of Jesus Christ. I remember how thinking about this every year at Easter would move me to tears. If that is enough for one to be a Christian, then I certainly was one. But I had never studied the Bible in depth (in fact, I had only read bits and and pieces of the Old Testament). I was far from those people who know each chapter and verse by heart.

Then one day, while my new husband and I were discussing nothing special, he got on the topic of religion. He was really good at this, since he had studied extensively, like I said, and had debated people far more knowledgable in Christianity than I. He knew what to say and what to omit.

I agreed to convert to Islam because it all sounded good. I was presented with a picture of the Prophet Muhammed: a kind, gentle man, very Christlike, in fact, who only fought when provoked. The other things, like terrorism and hate, are not a part of real Islam, my husband claimed. He even showed me a copy of the so-called Gospel of Barnabas. It was supposedly written by a "true" disciple of Jesus. This "gospel" appeared to verify the Muslim point of view.

I had a few remaining apprehensions, of course. But they were squashed by the following: One, my husband was the very example of good manners and values. I had never met a Christian (nor Jew nor Buddhist nor atheist) who even compared to him in this. He assured me that I would never be forced to wear *hijab* except in prayer. Two, I did not have anything to offer up as argument; that is, I was ignorant about how to argue for the Christian viewpoint. And finally, I wanted our relationship to remain intact. I feared that if I refused, we'd be well on our way to getting a divorce.

After converting, I started reading about Islam. First, I read translations of *hadith* on the Internet. I was often disturbed by them. In some cases, the Prophet is described as brutal, not exactly Christlike. When I tried questioning my husband on this, a heated argument would follow. It seems that he had neglected to tell me one thing: That he had been allowed to marry me as a Christian, and as long as I remained Christian I could ask questions because I was an unbeliever anyway. But now that I had become Muslim, any doubt about anything the Prophet did or said, any disrespect toward the Prophet, would make me an apostate. Apostasy, my husband said, would also automatically annul our marriage.

So I went back to reading, hoping I'd discover that I was wrong, that I'd find that Islam was the truth. But it seems that the more I looked, the more I realized how wrong it really was. I am not going to go into details here about what I discovered. Suffice it to say that much of it is already mentioned on this site.

But I will mention that the Prophet consummating a marriage to a nine-year-old troubled me especially. I find it funny that someone is debating this. I have already asked my husband and he has confirmed it. He even showed me the book with the English/Arabic side by side. ʿĀʾisha was nine when the Prophet took her to bed. The *hadith* could certainly be interpreted that she was as young as eight (depending if they used solar or lunar months) but she was certainly no older than nine. My husband said that this was acceptable, since this was "in the old days" and ʿĀʾisha had started menstruation. Beyond that, he did not want to discuss it. Again, I was warned that if I apostated, the consequences would be grave.

I have now managed to read all of the following: Most Web sites out there dealing with both Muslim and Christian viewpoints; the Koran in three English translations; both the Old and New Testaments. The Gospel of Barnabas, as it turns out, is a forgery, and there are even some Muslims out there who attest that it is. It's so ironic that in the last six months I have read more about religion than I ever had before or ever expected to.

My conclusion, much that I hoped for the contrary, is that Islam is a lie. Of course, all those born into it, including my husband, perpetuate the lie because they are so afraid of the threats in the Koran. The description of the hellfire and the torture in the graves is like a nightmare out of a horror novel. The torture in the grave[1] especially (my husband fears this so much that he turns pale when he talks about it) is nowhere to be found in any non-Muslim writing.

I can see that everything written in the Koran has a very human motivation. For example, Muslims drank until ʿUmar approached Muhammad and told him that something must be done about the situation, since some were praying while drunk. Conveniently, Muhammad then "got a revelation" that alcohol was now forbidden. There are many such examples.

Actually, it would be nice to live like that. To have a "convenient revelation" for everything. So that every time someones asks why, I could just say, "Because God says so." In the end, more was done for Muhammad through Islam than Muhammad ever did for his followers. Think about it: He got people to donate all their money to him, he got first pick of the most beautiful women, he got loyal followers who adored him as a prophet, he got young men to fight his battles, he got to rule a nation. In the end, he got conquered by the law that governs us all: We all die. And he did, in fact, die as a result of being poisoned. He died a quite ordinary death.

Compare Muhammad to Jesus: Jesus got no wife, no home, no guarantee of daily bread or lodging, and, in the end, he even gave up his life. He did not even get to grow old, as Muhammad did. And no one has been able to match the miracles Jesus performed. Above all, Jesus is the only one who broke the rule: He conquered death. And by showing us that through him this rule can be broken, he offers the same to us all if we just believe.

Now that I've reached this point, i.e., become a closet Christian, I am debating what I should do about my present situation. I will admit that I am weak and perhaps a little frightened of what might happen to me if I reveal my true beliefs to my husband. As a Christian, though, I would like to try to make this work by praying for a miracle that my husband should find the right path, perhaps try to find a time when I can approach him carefully with some ideas.

And you, out there, what do you think I should do? I am not interested in any Muslims who try to slander me (if I see such commentary here, rest assured that I will ignore it, especially if it contains vile language). I ask this of non-Muslims who might be able to offer suggestions. And, certainly, I also welcome that any Christian out there add me to their prayers that my husband finds the truth. I love and pray for you all.

ANONYMOUS

I could not remain a Muslim because Islam hates women. I think I always knew this, but as I got older that knowledge became more acute. Islam wants women to cover themselves, to stay indoors, to obey men, however stupid those men are. Islam says that women are inferior in every way. Islam distorted my father's feelings. He did not want us, his own daughters, to be happy or fulfilled. He only wanted us to be good Muslims and for daughters this means to be suffering Muslims. What sort of religion forces fathers to make their daughters suffer? What sort of father thinks that his daughter's hair is shameful? What sort of father tells her she cannot sing and dance when she is happy? A Muslim father.

This is why I am not a Muslim. My children, boys and girls, will be able to feel the wind in their hair. They will not be ashamed. They can sing and dance as much as they like. Nothing they do will shame me, as long as it is done with life and joy. Islam has no joy. Islam is a cult of tears and death.

Anonymous

Dear ISIS, I thank god for finding your site. Oops! How can I thank god when I do not believe in one? It is hard to break and old habit of language. Anyway, I want to thank your organization for providing a forum for those of us who, out of no choice of our own, were born into an Islamic family. I am so glad to find like-minded folks who not only share my nonreligious ethos but also share my Islamic heritage of birth. I never knew in my lifetime I would find a forum of ex-Muslims. When I get a chance to collect my thoughts I will share my testimonial. Until then accept my deep gratitude for providing this service.

Anonymous

I was just browsing the net after a local radio station aired a news item about Dr. Yunis Shaikh. Up until this point I wasn't even aware of an atheist movement in Pakistan! It didn't take long to find this excellent site, and to be quite honest I feel like this is the best thing that has ever happend to me!

Born to into a Muslim family, I was the typical religious fundamentalist, trapped in my own world of consipiracies; the Jews were behind everything I took on the cause of the Palestinian people as something personal. I became heavily involved with a group of Muslims going under the name "Young Muslims UK"—boy oh boy! This organization single-handedly managed to convert me from a Koran-quoting nutcase into a fully fledged atheist.

Having been brought up in an area where there weren't any other Muslims, I hadn't previously met anyone of the same background as me. When my father decided it was time for me to get involved with some other Pakistani Muslims, that is when I realized how stupid the whole thing was.

Prior to joining this organization I hadn't read the Koran in English, instead I read it in Arabic (believing that this would bring me *Swaab*—blessings). When I did read it for the first time I became very worried by the amount of violence in it. Subsequent late-night sessions with the Koran convinced me that I was reading a guide to war.

When I asked "Where did Allah come from?" in one of the weekly circles I was told that this question was inspired by the devil. As I had thought of this question, I took this personally! Well that was the start of my intense hatred for all organized religion. However, most of my family and Pakistani friends think I am a confused Muslim. I prefer it like this as it allows me to ask awkward questions and see them get mad.

Well I am glad I have found this site and I am going to be doing a bit of online and telephone campaigning on behalf of Dr. Yunis Shaikh. Let's use this as an opportunity to bring the world's focus on the babarism that is tolerated under the banner of "cultural differences." Human life is human life in all cultures. To the people behind this site . . . you have done an excellent job!

ANONYMOUS

I am a woman who was born in a supposedly "liberal" Muslim state. However, I learned at a young age that in any Muslim country, women do not count for much. I was told that men were smarter, better, and stronger than women. When I was married, my husband continued to try to reinforce male superiority over me. He continually told me that he was the boss and I was to do what he told me to do. He reminded me that if I wanted to leave the country, I had to have written permission from him. My own parents died shortly after my marriage, but I watched his own parents repeat the cycle of abuse that my husband was pulling me into. My mother-in-law was forced to be a slave of my father-in-law. He would stay out all night at cafés, laughing with his friends and soliciting prostitutes. My mother-in-law was suffering from ill health, but she was scared to leave the house to go see a doctor without permission from her husband. Her husband would always deny permission so that he wouldn't have to pay the doctor the money he wanted to use on entertainment. I learned to detest the religion that had made me and my mother-in-law into slaves. I started to refuse to wear *hijab*. My husband's beatings did not change my mind. Then I read the Koran for the first time critically. It was a disgusting book full of hatred and intolerance. When my husband and I immigrated to the United States, I bought a copy of Ibn Warraq's *Why I am Not a Muslim*. As I read the book, I felt like I was being liberated. Thank you, whoever you are, Ibn Warraq. Keep writing!

ANONYMOUS

Congratulations to you brave souls of this Web site! I came close to marrying a Muslim man. I was sent to study Islam and the Koran with a woman authorized by Mecca to teach, and to declare "ashado ina la ila ha ila allah; ashado Muhammad ul-rassul allah." After listening to the rules about exactness of praying, fasting times for the Ramadan month (i.e., if you live in Finland and Ramadan occurs in the summer then you can only eat between 3 A.M. and 4 A.M.), clothing while reading the Koran etc., I asked some more philosophical questions. She replied that I should not ask questions and simply submit to Allah and then I would have peace.

I tried reading the Koran and didn't find anything that gave me peace; on the contrary—once I was in a restaurant in Eygpt, and while waiting for my food to arrive I discovered the copy of a Koran on the bookshelf and took it to read. There was a family sitting close by and the woman suddenly started shouting "haram! haram!" and took her family, and slightly embarrassed husband, out of the restaurant yelling at the manager on her way out that an infidel was dirtying the Koran. I felt sick. There are many other stories about how I came to discover that Islam was in fact a dangerous cult, but have little time and space to tell all. Of course I ended up admitting to my fiancé at the time that I now believed that Islam was false and a dangerous delusion. He was very upset and shocked, but something in his eyes told me that there was doubt for him, too, yet he could never bring himself to admit it and would always live a life suppressing the truth. So I will end by asking a question: How can we Westerners from non-Muslim backgrounds, i.e., those of us who would be dismissed as simpy infidels, do something in support of your wonderful cause for the secularization of Islam?

ANONYMOUS

I was born in the East and moved to the West when I was four. My parents are moderately religious Muslims, though not fundamentalists. My paternal grandfather was a teacher of the Koran, though he only had the luxury to do this because he was wealthy and didn't really need to work. I have been told that my family (paternal) has been Muslim for some six hundred years.

My father is a chemist by trade, and throughout my formative years he spent most of his time in the laboratory. My mother didn't instruct me about religion much; my parents just told me the basics about Muhammad, Islam, and Allah. I knew about Hindus because my parents would make fun of them and say disparaging things, and my mother also told me about Christians when I was six. All in all, I didn't think much about religion until I was eight or so.

I was in the public library one day in third grade when I had an epiphany of sorts (excuse the term). I realized that God didn't really need to exist, from what little I knew of science there didn't seem any direct evidence. Though I was nominally Muslim, I'd always had a somewhat Aristotelian view of God as the Prime Mover. I had stumbled onto Occam's razor and onward toward atheism, without knowing what it really was. For about a year I was very depressed, not understanding that there were other people that didn't believe in God.

The first inkling I had of "others" was when my father's Ph.D. advisor mentioned offhand that he didn't believe in God, that he was an "atheist." It jolted me. The next few years were pretty difficult for me, because I had no familial support and had to keep quiet about it. In sixth grade I had a "conversion" experience, but it lasted maybe six months at the most. Over the next few years I went from being

Muslim to deist to Buddhist to agnostic to atheist. I simply didn't seem to be the type of person that had "faith."

During and after college I became involved in freethought organizations and discussions. I am interested in religion from a social perspective, and do a fair amount of reading apologetics and creationist tracts (they call it "intelligent design" now).

Islam is a dangerous religion. I believe that it is the only real competition to the West out there, and it knows it's backed up against a corner. I do not know what is going to happen with all the Islamic minorities in the West, because they are belligerent and quite frankly traitorous in the long term. I only hope to continue my life and enjoy living in a free country.

ANONYMOUS

My "apostasy" against Islam came about through a sustained critical analysis of the fundamental tenets of all religions, thus opening the way toward self-criticism.

Born into a Muslim family and raised in the West, I have experienced first-hand the atavistic savagery of Islamic culture, its antihuman doctrines, and the futility of being a Muslim living in the West. It slowly dawned on me that the Koran was not the infallible, immutable word of God, but a fascist slur on humanity, a human document with little relevance to the modern condition as well as the realization of the countless contradictions, historical inconsistencies, and errors, and some of the most intolerant verses ever written. Islam is perhaps the most intolerant religion on Earth, a proseletyzing ideology that ruthlessly crushes dissent.

My liberation from the fetters of Islamic tradition have allowed me to think more freely and independently, and I am able to pursue my hopes and dreams with an unflinching resolve.

ANONYMOUS

First off all greetings to all ex-Muslims on earth. I'm Mustafa, a secular feminist who is supporting women to face the threat of fundamentalism. The best example is what happened in Afghanistan and what is happening in other countries. Women are equal to men and we cannot accept any legislature that is against this, like the Islamic *Sharī'a*. Islam gives men the right to beat women, to prevent them from having an education and work. It gives men the right to marry four women and to veil them with *burqas* and *niqabs* and *hijabs*. So to all women in Islamic countries, fight for your rights, no democracy without secularism and the total blocking of *Sharīʿa* laws and banning of Islamic education and veil. At last, I would like to greet the great feminists in the Islamic world, like Tujan Faisal and Khalida Messaoudi and others: We really love you all.

ANONYMOUS

I'm a thirty-year-old male who was born in Pakistan but moved to the West with my family when I was five. I was forced to attend religious training with ignorant and cruel *mullahs* who whould twist my ear and scold me severely everytime I mispronounced a Koranic recitation. The garbage they would churn out as divine truth was appalling. Needless to say, I developed a deep-seated fear of God and of not obeying his law.

It was very difficult growing up in the West, where I made friends of all races and religions, and had to reconcile that with the fascist, absolutist doctrines of Islam. So I created a mental schizophrenia where I ignored the real barbaric and xenophobic nature of Islam with the reality I was experiencing. In my heart I always felt that the inequality of women was wrong, that non-Muslims were just as equal and human as Muslims, that science provided much more reasonable explanations of the world than the myths of Islam ever did. But I was too paralyzed by fear and by not wanting to upset my family, so I never said anything.

Then puberty hit! When I realized that I was attracted to boys and fell in love with them instead of girls, I had an extremely difficult crisis of the soul. I knew the extreme contempt that Islam had for homosexuality, and I felt that I would suffer the torments of hell for feeling the way I did. I tried committing suicide in college, but was saved by a friend. That was the turning point. I decided I was no longer going to be a slave to a barbaric, fascist, sexist, homophobic, totalitarian, obscurantist, cultlike, joyless, loveless, fear-mongering (should I add more adjectives?), horrible horrible horrible ideology!

Today, free of Islam and religion, I feel more liberated and powerful and in control of my life than I could have ever imagined. My relations with my family are very strained, having come out twice: first as a gay man and then as an atheist/secular humanist. When it rains it pours! But I have created a family for myself based on people who share my values and who accept and love me for who I am.

I wish all Muslims around the world would have the same opportunities to unchain themselves from the lies they're brainwashed into believing. I realize I'm very privileged in the West where I have the freedom to choose my life's path. I'm so grateful for this Web site, and truly want to bring the message to the 1.3 billion individuals who need to see the light of truth. Peace to all.

NOTE

1. Muslim, *Ṣaḥīḥ*, trans. Abdul Hamid Siddiqi (New Delhi: Kitab Bhavan, 1997), book 4, Hadith no. 1214, p. 290:

> ʿAisha reported: There came to me two old women from the old Jewesses of Medina and said: The people of the grave are tormented in their graves. I contradicted them and I did not deem it proper to testify them. They went away and the Messenger of Allah (may peace be upon him) came to me and I said to him: Messenger of Allah! there came to me two old women from the old Jewesses of Medina and asserted that the people of the graves would be tormented therein. He (the Prophet) said: They told the truth; they would be tormented (so much) that the animals would listen to it. She (ʿAisha) said: Never did I see him (the Holy Prophet) afterwards but seeking refuge from the torment of the grave in prayer.

PART 3

TESTIMONIES OF BORN MUSLIMS
Murtadd Fiṭri

12

INTRODUCTION
The Allah That Failed
Ibn Warraq

Given that I am rather skeptical of the very possibility of a scientific survey of apostates, it is difficult for me to make any psychological, socio-logical, or anthropological generalizations based on fewer than fifty personal testimonies that would be valid outside this particular group. No quick portrait of the typical apostate is likely to appear—some are young (students in their teens), some are middle-aged with children, some are scientists, while others are econo-mists, businesspeople, or journalists; some are from Bangladesh, others are from Pakistan, India, Morocco, Egypt, Malaysia, Saudi Arabia, or Iran. Our witnesses, nonetheless, do have certain moral and intellectual qualities in common: for instance, they are all comparatively well educated, computer literate with access to the Internet, and rational, with the ability to think for themselves. However, what is most striking is their fearlessness, their moral courage, and their moral commitment to telling the truth. They all face social ostracism, the loss of friends and family, a deep inner spiritual anguish and loneliness—and occasionally the death penalty if discovered. Their decisions are not frivolously taken, but the ineluctable result of rational thinking.

I had once thought of calling this whole anthology *The Allah That Failed*, as a homage to the famous testimonies of former communists collected together in *The God That Failed*.[1] There are very useful analogies to be drawn between communism and Islam, as Maxime Rodinson[2] and Bertrand Russell have pointed out, between the mindset of the communists of the 1930s and the Islamists of the 1990s and twenty-first century. As Russell said,

> Among religions, Bolshevism [Communism] is to be reckoned with Muhammadanism rather than with Christianity and Buddhism. Christianity and Buddhism are primarily personal religions, with mystical doctrines and a love of contemplation. Muhammadanism and Bolshevism are practical, social, unspiritual, concerned to win the empire of this world.[3]

Hence the interest in the present situation and its haunting parallels with the communism of the Western intellectuals in the 1930s. As Arthur Koestler said, "You hate our Cassandra cries and resent us as allies, but when all is said, we ex-Communists are the only people on your side who know what it's all about."[4] And as Richard Crossman wrote in his introduction to *The God That Failed*,

> Silone [an ex-Communist] was joking when he said to Togliatti that the final battle would be between the Communists and ex-Communists. But no one who has not wrestled with Communism as a philosophy and Communists as political opponents can really understand the values of Western Democracy. the Devil once lived in Heaven, and those who have not met him are unlikely to recognize an angel when they see one.[5]

Communism has been defeated, at least for the moment; Islamism has not, and unless a reformed, tolerant, liberal kind of Islam emerges soon, perhaps the final battle will be between Islam and Western democracy. And these former Muslims, to echo Koestler's words, on the side of Western democracy are the only ones who know what it's all about, and we would do well to listen to their Cassandra cries.

NOTES

1. A. Koestler, ed., *The God That Failed* (London: Hamish Hamilton, 1950). Other former Communists in the collection included Ignazio Silone, André Gide, Richard Wright, Louis Fischer, adn Stephen Spender.

2. Maxime Rodinson, "Islam et communisme, une resemblance frappante" [Islam and commonumism, a striking resemblance], *Le Figaro*, Paris, September 28, 2001.

3. Bertrand Russell, *Practice and Theory of Bolshevism* (London: Allen & Unwin, 1921), pp. 5, 29, 114.

4. Koestler, *The God That Failed*, p. 7.

5. R. Crossman, Introduction to *The God That Failed*, ed. A. Koestler (London: Hamish Hamilton, 1950), p. 16.

13

WHY I LEFT ISLAM

My Passage from Faith to Enlightenment

Ali Sina (Iran)

I was born to a religious family. From my mother's side I have a few relatives who are Ayatollahs. Although my grandfather was a skeptic, in the family where I grew up religion has been the pivot around which our lives revolved. My parents were not very fond of the *mullahs*. In fact, we did not have much to do with our more fundamentalist relatives. We liked to think of ourselves as believing in the "real Islam," not the one taught and practiced by the *mullahs*.

I recall discussing religion with the husband of one of my aunts when I was about fifteen years old. He was a fanatical Muslim who was much concerned about the *fiqh* [Islamic jurisprudence]. It determines the way a Muslim should pray, fast, run his public and private life, do business, clean himself, use the toilet, and even copulate. I argued that this has nothing to do with the real Islam, that it is a concoction of the *mullahs* and that too much attention to *fiqh* diminishes the relevance of the real Islam, which is a religion to unite man with his creator.

I believe that I was lucky to have open-minded parents who encouraged me to think critically. They tried to instill in me the love of God and his messenger, yet upheld humanistic values like equality of rights between men and women and love for all humankind irrespective of their faiths. In a sense, this is how most modern Iranian families were. In fact, the majority of Muslims who have some education believe that Islam is a humanistic religion that respects human rights that elevates women and protects their status. Most Muslims still believe that Islam means "peace."

I expended my early youth in this sweet dream: advocating the "real Islam" as I thought it should be and criticizing the *mullahs* and their deviations from the real teachings of Islam. I idealized an Islam conforming to my own humanistic values. Of course, my imaginary Islam was a beautiful religion. It was a religion of equality and of peace. It was a religion that encouraged its followers to go after knowledge and be inquisitive. It was a religion that was in harmony with science and reason. I thought science got its inspiration from this religion. The Islam that I believed in was a religion that sowed the seeds of the modern science, which eventually bore its fruits in the West and made modern discoveries and inventions possible. Islam, I used to believe, was the real cause of the modern civilization. The reason the Muslims were living in such miserable state of ignorance in comparison to the un-Islamic West was all the fault of the self-centered *mullahs* and the religious leaders who, for their own personal gain and dominance, had misinterpreted the real teachings of Islam.

Muslims honestly believe that the great Western civilization has its roots in Islam. They recall great Middle Eastern scientific minds whose contributions to science have been crucial in the birth of Modern science.

Omar Khayyam was a great mathematician who calculated the length of the year with a precision of 0.74% of a second. Zakaria Razi can very well be regarded as one of the first founders of empirical medicine who based his knowledge on research and experimentation. Ali Sina's monumental encyclopedia of medicine was taught in European universities for centuries. There are so many more great luminaries with "Islamic names" who have been the pioneers of modern science when Europe was languishing in the medieval era or the Dark Ages. Like all Muslims, I used to believe that all these great men were Muslims, that they had been inspired by the wealth of hidden knowledge that is in the Koran, and that if the Muslims today could regain the original purity of Islam, the long lost glorious days of Islam would return and the Muslims would lead the advancement of the world civilization once again.

Yet the reality was harsher than dreams. Iran was a Muslim country but it was also a corrupt country. The chance of getting to university was slim. Only one in ten applicants could get to university and often they were forced to choose subjects that they did not want to study because they could not get enough points for the subjects of their choice. The regime of the shah was a repressive regime and freedom of thought was suppressed. People feared each other as each person could turn out to be a secret agent of the dreaded Sazamane Etelaat Va Amniate Kechrar (SAVAK; Iranian secret police). I was always outspoken and hardly had any "tact" to keep my mouth shut when my life was in danger. The level of education in Iran was not ideal. Universities were underfunded, as the shah preferred building a powerful military force and becoming the gendarme of the Middle East to building the infrastructure of the country and investing in education. Because of all these factors, my father thought I would be better off if I left Iran and continued my education somewhere else.

We considered America and Europe but my father, acting upon the advice of a few of his friends, thought another Islamic country would be better for a sixteen-year-old boy. We were told that the West is too lax in morality, that its people are perverts, that the beaches are full of nudes, that they drink and have licentious lifestyles and all that could represent a danger to a young man. So I was sent to Pakistan instead. Pakistan, being an Islamic country, was safe. People were religious and therefore moral.

This, of course, proved to be untrue. I found people there to be as immoral and corrupt as Iranians. Yes, they were very religious. Yes, they did not eat pork and I saw no one consuming alcohol in public, but I noticed they had dirty minds, they lied, they were hypocrites, and they were cruel to the women and, above all, filled with hatred for the Indians. I did not find them better than Iranians in any way. They were religious, but not moral.

In college I did not take Urdu (the national language of Pakistan, much influenced by Persian); instead I took Pakistani culture to complete my A-level FSc (fellow of science). I learned about the reasons for the partition (of India) and for the first time about Muhammad Ali Jinnah. He was presented as a very intelligent man, the father of the nation, while Gandhi was spoken of in a derogatory way. Even then I could not but side with Gandhi and condemn Jinnah as an arrogant and ambitious man who was responsible for breaking up a mighty nation and causing millions of deaths. I did not see difference of religion enough reason to break up a country. The very word *Pakistan* seemed to be an insult to the Indians. They called themselves *pak*, or "clean" to distinguish themselves from the Indians, who were *najis* ("unclean"). The irony is that I never saw a people dirtier than the Pakistanis, both physically and mentally. It was disappointing to see another Islamic nation in such intellectual and moral bankruptcy. In my discussions with my friends I failed to convince anyone of the "real Islam." I condemned their bigotry and fanaticism, while they disapproved of me for my westernized and un-Islamic views. I recall when I spoke about the *hijab* ("the veil"), arguing that this has nothing to do with woman's chastity, I was accused of preferring to see women's underwear. When I spoke of women's rights and their freedom I was asked whether I enjoyed watching my wife making love to another man.

I decided to go to Italy for my university studies. I concluded that there was nothing I could learn in an atmosphere filled with bigotry and stupidity. In Italy people drank wine and ate pork. But I found they were more hospitable, more friendly, and less hypocritical. I noticed people were willing to help without expecting something in return. I met an elderly couple who were very hospitable to me. They called me on Sundays to have dinner with them and not stay home alone. They did not want anything from me, they just wanted to have someone to give their love. I was almost a son to them. Only those who have come to a new country, who do not know anyone and cannot speak even the language, can appreciate how much the help and the hospitality of a local is worth.

Their house was sparkling clean and the floor was marble and always shiny. This was quite in contrast with my idea of Westerners. Although my family was very open toward other people, my religion had taught me that the non-Muslims are *najis* (IX.28) and one should not take them as friends. I had a pocket copy of the Koran that I still have and used to read from it often. The verses were underlined with a Parsi translation. I came across this verse:

> O you who believe! Take not the Jews and the Christians as awliya' (friends, protectors, helpers, etc.), they are but awliya' to one another. . . . (V.51)

I had difficulty understanding the wisdom of such verses. I wondered why I should not befriend this wonderful elderly couple who apparently had no other motive in showing me their hospitality than just making me feel at home. I thought they were "real Muslims" and tried to raise the subject of religion, hoping they would see the truth of Islam and embrace it. But they were not interested and politely changed the subject. I don't think I was ever stupid enough to believe that all nonbelievers will go to hell. I suppose I read this in the Koran before, but never wanted to think about it. I simply shrugged it off or wanted to close my eyes, not wishing to see it. Of course, I knew that God would be pleased if someone recognized his messenger, but I never thought he would actually be that cruel to burn someone in hell for eternity, even if that person is the author of good deeds, just because he was not a Muslim. I read the following warning:

> If anyone desires a religion other than Islam (submission to Allah), never will it be accepted of him; and in the Hereafter He will be in the ranks of those who have lost (All spiritual good). (III.85)

Yet I paid little heed and tried to convince myself that the meaning has something else than what it appeared to be. At that moment it was not a subject that I was ready to handle, so I did not think about it.

I hung around with my Muslim friends and noticed that when it was convenient for them they lived a very immoral life. Most of them found girlfriends and slept with them. That was very un-Islamic, but what bothered me most was the fact that they did not value these girls as real human beings who deserved respect. These girls were not Muslim girls, and therefore were used by them just for sex. This attitude was not general. Those men who were less religious were more respectful and sincere toward their girlfriends, and some even loved them and wanted to marry them; but, paradoxically, those who were more religious were less faithful toward their girlfriends. But I had such high esteem for religion in my mind that it was hard for me to relate the immoral and callous behavior of the Muslims to what was being taught in Islam. I always thought that the true Islam was what was right. If something was immoral, unethical, dishonest, or cruel, it could not be Islam. Years later I realized that the truth is completely the reverse. I found many verses that were disturbing and made me rethink my whole opinion of Islam.

The funny thing was that the same very people who lived, according to me, unethically and immorally were the ones who called themselves Muslims, said their prayers, fasted, and were the first to defend Islam if anyone raised a question about it. They were the ones who would lose their tempers and enter into fights if someone dared say a word against Islam.

Once I met a young Iranian man at the university restaurant. I sat next to him and became his friend. Later I introduced him to two other Muslim friends of mine. We were all of the same age, but he was an erudite young man full of virtue and wisdom. All of us were captivated by his charm and his high moral values. We used to wait for him and sit next to him during the lunch hour, as we always learned something from him. We used to eat a lot of spaghetti and risotto and were craving for a good Persian ghorme sabzi and chelow. Our friend said that his mother had sent him some dried vegetables and invited us to go to his house the next Sunday for lunch. We found his apartment very clean, unlike the houses of other guys. He had made us the delicious *ghorme sabzi* that we ate with a lot of gusto and then we sat back chatting and sipping our tea. It was then that among his books we found some Baha'i books. When we inquired, he said that he was a Baha'i. Of course that did not bother me at all, but my two friends on the way back said that they do not wish to continue their friendship with him any more. I was surprised and asked, Why? They said that being a Baha'i makes him a *najis* person and had they known that he was a Baha'i, they would not have befriended him. I was puzzled and asked why they thought he was najis if we all were complementing him on his cleanliness and had never seen any impropriety from him. We all agreed that he was morally superior to the Muslims we knew, so why this sudden change of attitude? Their response was very disturbing. They said that the name itself had something in it that made them dislike this religion. Then they asked me whether I knew why everyone disliked the Baha'is. I told them I didn't know, because I didn't dislike anyone. But since they disliked the Baha'is perhaps they should explain their reasons. They did not know why. This man was the first Baha'i they had come to know this close, and in fact he was an exemplary man. So I wanted to know the reason for their dislike. There was no particular reason, they said. It's just they knew that they should not like the Baha'is.

I am happy that I did not continue my friendship with these two idiots, yet I learned how prejudice is formed and operates.

Later I realized that this prejudice and hatred that Muslims harbor in their hearts against almost all non-Muslims is not the result of any misinterpretation of the teachings of the Koran but because the Koran teaches hate and prejudice. There are many verses in the Koran that call believers to hate nonbelievers, to fight with them, to call them *najis*, to subdue and humiliate them, to chop off their heads and other limbs, to crucify them kill them wherever they find them.

I left religion on the back burner for several years. Not that my views about religion had changed or I didn't consider myself religious anymore, I just had so much to do that I had less and less time to expend on religion. I simply lived the way I thought I was supposed to live according to my understanding of how a good Muslim should live. Meanwhile I learned more about democracy, human rights, and other values, like equality of rights between men and women, and I liked them.

The Islamic revolution of Iran was a curse to my country. I was not there to see it firsthand, but what I heard about it was nauseating. The *mullahs* tried to impose a reign of terror that they called "Islamic." Lives became cheap. They executed the Iranians by hundreds. Anyone who disagreed with them was sent to jail, executed, or murdered. Young girls were killed, but before killing them they raped them because, according to the Muslims, this would impede God sending them to Paradise. Minorities became fair game. Many of them were executed for no other reason than belonging to another religion. Baha'is especially suffered the most, for they were regarded as apostates. I followed the news from abroad and I was shocked to see my people had stooped to such depths of barbarity.

Someone told me that he knew Khomeini prior to his rise to power. He said that once he saw Khomeini trying to kick a fly out of his room with a flyswatter. This person asked Khomeini why he didn't kill it, to which Khomeini responded that the fly is a creature of God and should not be killed. I wondered what made this man, who would not hurt a fly, murder so many people so heartlessly. He murdered thousands of Iranians. He massacred thousands of Iraqi prisoners of war. How could he do that? The Islamic regime in Iran started torturing people, beating them, stoning women accused of adultery, and made of Iran a giant prison and a huge torture chamber. Is that what Islam was all about? Then came along the Taliban in Afghanistan, who even surpassed the Iranian *mullahs* in cruelty. Yet all the time I tried to convince myself that this is not the "real Islam."

On one occasion Khomeini made a speech in which he called upon the Iranians to kill the enemies of Islam. He condemned those Muslims who would pay attention only to the few verses of the Koran that speak about tolerance. He called those who wanted to present Islam as a religion of peace hypocrites, and told everyone that Allah had ordered Muslims to be harsh with the enemies of Islam and that forgiveness was un-Islamic. He asked why we always talked about a few verses of the Koran that mention forgiveness and tolerance and neglected the entire Koran that tells you to be harsh with the infidels and the "hypocrites." This is a widely published speech and is available on the Internet.[1] Some Iranians accepted what he told them, and their bigotry and hate increased. The crimes perpetrated by the revolutionary guards and the *basijis* (a military force created to maintain Islamic rule in Iran) are so heinous that is unbelievable that a human being can commit such cruelties to another human being. At the same time, many Iranians continued to believe that what Khomeini said was not the real Islam.

One day I decided that it was time to deepen my knowledge of Islam and read the Koran from cover to cover to find out the real Islam on my own. I found an Arabic copy of the Koran with an English translation. Before that I had read the Koran, but only bits and pieces of it. This time I started to read all of it. I read a verse in Arabic, then I read the English translation moving back to Arabic, and did not go to the next verse unless I was satisfied that I had understood it in Arabic completely.

It didn't take me long before I came upon verses that I found hard to accept. One of the first verses that I found puzzling was this one:

> Allah forgiveth not that partners should be set up with Him; but He forgiveth anything else, to whom He pleaseth; to set up partners with Allah is to devise a sin most heinous indeed. (IV.48)

I found it hard to accept that Gandhi would be burned in hell forever with no hope of redemption because he was a polytheist, while a Muslim rapist and mass murderer could hope to receive Allah's forgiveness. This raised a disturbing question: Why is Allah so desperate to be known as the only God? Why should he even care whether anyone knows him and praises him or not? I learned about the size of this universe. Light, which travels at a speed of three hundred thousand kilometers per second, takes 20 billion years to reach us from the galaxies that are at the edges of the universe. How many galaxies are there? How many stars are there in these galaxies? How many planets are there in this universe? The thought of that was mind-boggling. If Allah is the creator of this vast universe, why would he be so concerned about being known as the only god by a bunch of apes living in a small planet down the Milky Way?

Now that I lived in the West, had many Western friends who were kind to me, who liked me, who had opened their hearts and their homes to me and accepted me as their friend; it was really hard to accept that Allah wanted me not to take them for friends.

> Let not the believers take for friends or helpers unbelievers rather than believers: if any do that, in nothing will there be help from Allah. (III.28)

Wasn't Allah the creator of the unbelievers? Wasn't he their god, too? Why should he be so unkind to them? Wasn't it better if the Muslims befriended the unbelievers and taught them Islam by setting a good example? By keeping ourselves aloof and distant from the unbelievers, the gap of misunderstanding would never be bridged. How in the world would they learn about Islam if we did not associate with them? The answer to this question came in a very disconcerting verse: Allah's order was to "slay them wherever ye catch them" (II:191).

I thought of my own friends, remembered their kindness and their love for me, and wondered how in the world a true god could ask anyone to kill another human being just because he did not believe in a religion? That seemed absurd, yet this concept was repeated so often in the Koran that obviously there was no doubt about it. In one verse Allah tells his prophet: "O Prophet! rouse the Believers to the fight. If there are twenty amongst you, patient and persevering, they will vanquish two hundred: if a hundred, they will vanquish a thousand of the Unbelievers" (VIII.65). Why should Allah send a messenger to make war? Shouldn't God teach us to love each other and be tolerant toward each other's beliefs? And if really Allah was so concerned about making people believe in him to the extent that he would kill them if they disbelieved, why would he ask us to do his dirty work and why would he not kill them himself? Are we supposed to be Allah's hitmen or mercenaries?

Although I knew of *jihad* and never questioned it before, I found it hard to accept that God would have recourse to such violent measures to impose himself on people. What was more shocking was the cruelty of Allah in dealing with the unbelievers:

> I will instill terror into the hearts of the unbelievers: smite ye above their necks and smite all their fingertips off them. (VIII.12)

It seemed that Allah was not satisfied with just killing the unbelievers. He enjoyed torturing them before killing them. Smiting people's heads from above their necks and chopping their fingertips were very cruel acts. Would God really give such orders? The following is what he promised to do with the unbelievers in the other world:

> These two antagonists dispute with each other about their Lord: But those who deny (their Lord),—for them will be cut out a garment of Fire: over their heads will be poured out boiling water. With it will be scalded what is within their bodies, as well as (their) skins. In addition there will be maces of iron (to punish) them. Every time they wish to get away therefrom, from anguish, they will be forced back therein, and (it will be said), "Taste ye the Penalty of Burning!" (XXII.19–22)

How could the creator of this universe be so petty as described in these verses? These verses of the Koran shocked me. I was shocked to learn how Allah ordered the killing of people, how he would torture them eternally in such a horrible way for no reason but disbelief.

I was shocked to learn that the Koran tells Muslims to kill the disbelievers wherever they find them (II.191), to murder them and treat them harshly (IX. 123), slay them (IX.5), fight with them (VIII.65), to humiliate them and impose on them a penalty tax even if they are Christians and Jews (IX.29). I was shocked when I learned that the Koran takes away the freedom of belief from all humanity, and says clearly that no other religion except Islam is accepted (III. 85). I was shocked to learn that Allah would relegate those who disbelieve in the Koran to hell (V.10) and calls them *najis* (filthy, untouchable, impure) (IX.28). I was shocked to learn that Allah orders the Muslims to fight the unbelievers until no other religion except Islam is left (II.193). I was shocked when I learned that the Koran says that the nonbelievers will go to hell and will drink boiling water (XIV.17), that it asks the Muslims to slay or crucify or cut the hands and the feet of the unbelievers, that they be expelled from the land with disgrace and that "they shall have a great punishment in the world hereafter" (V.33). I was shocked when I learned that the Koran says: "As for the disbelievers, for them garments of fire shall be cut and there shall be poured over their heads boiling water whereby whatever is in their bowls and skin shall be dissolved and they will be punished with hooked iron rods" (XXII.21). I was shocked when I learned that the Koran prohibits a Muslim to befriend an unbeliever even if that unbeliever is the father or the brother of that Muslim (IX.23, III.28). I was shocked to learn that the Koran asks the Muslim to "strive against the unbelievers with great endeavor" (XXV.52), and be stern with them because they belong to hell (LXVI.9). I was shocked to learn that the holy Prophet demanded his followers to "strike off the heads of the disbelievers," then, after making a "wide slaughter among them, carefully tie up the remaining captives" and enslave them (XLVII.4). I was shocked to learn that the book of Allah says that women are inferior to men and their husbands have the right to scourge them if they are found disobedient (IV.34), and that women will go to hell if they are disobedient to their husbands (LXVI.10). I was shocked to learn that the Koran maintains that men have an advantage over the women (II.228); that it not only denies women equal right to their inheritance (IV.11–12), but it also regards them as imbeciles and decrees that their testimony is not admissible in the court (II.282). This means that a woman who is raped cannot accuse her rapist unless she can produce a male witness. Muhammad allowed Muslim men to marry up to four wives and gave them license to sleep with their slave maids and as many "captive" women as they may have (IV.3). I was shocked to learn that the Prophet himself did just that and raped his female prisoners of war. That is why any time a Muslim army subdues another nation, they call them *kafir* and allow themselves to rape their women. Pakistani soldiers raped up to 250,000 Bengali women in 1971, after they had massacred 3 million unarmed civilians when their religious leader decreed that Bangladeshis were un-Islamic. This is why the prison guards in Islamic regime of Iran rape the women and then kill them after calling them apostates and the enemies of Allah.

After reading the Koran I was overtaken by a great depression. It was hard to accept all that. At first I started denying and seeking esoteric meanings to the apparent verses of the Koran. But it wasn't possible. The weight of the proof was too big. I found out that Khomeini was right, that the Taliban believe in the real Islam, that what I used to think of Islam was not the real Islam at all. I found out that Islam teaches nothing but hate, that the whole message of Islam is to believe in a deity without any proof, a deity who despises reason, who loves killing innocent people, who is expert in torture, who is ruthless, and who does not know elementary scientific facts about the universe that he allegedly created. This was hard to swallow, and I did not want to accept what I came to learn.

The passage from belief to freethinking and enlightenment has its stages. The first stage is shock, followed by denial. If one can overcome the denial one goes through confusion, guilt, dismay, anger, and finally enlightenment. The majority of Muslims are trapped in denial. They are unable or unwilling to admit that the Koran is a hoax. They desperately try to explain the unexplainable, to find miracles in it, and are not ashamed to bend all the rules of logic to prove that the Koran is right. Each time they are exposed to a shocking statement in the Koran or a shameful act performed by Muhammad, they retreat in denial. This is what I was doing. Denial is a safe place. It is the comfort zone. In denial you are not going to be hurt, everything is okay; everything is fine.

Truth is extremely painful, especially if one has been accustomed to lies all one's life. It is like telling someone that his father is a murderer, a rapist, or a criminal. This might be true, yet the child who adores his father will not be able to accept it. The shock is so great that the first thing he will do is deny it. He will call you a liar and he will hate you for hurting him. He will curse you, hold you as his enemy, and may even discharge his anger at you by physically attacking you.

This is the stage of denial. It is a defense mechanism. If pain is too big, denial will take that pain away. If a mother is informed that her child has died in an accident, the first thing she will do is to deny it. People who have lost a loved one often believe that this is all a bad dream and that when they wake up everything will be okay. But unfortunately, facts are stubborn and they will not go away. One can live in denial for a while, but he must accept the truth sooner or later.

Muslims are cocooned in lies. Because speaking against Islam is a crime punishable by death, no one dares tell the truth. Those who do tell the truth do not go far; they are silenced very quickly. So how would you know the truth if all you hear is lies? On the one hand, the Koran claims to be a miracle and challenges everyone to produce a Surah like it. On the other hand, it instructs its followers to kill anyone who dares criticize it. In such an atmosphere of insincerity and deceit, truth will never be known.

The fact of coming face-to-face with the truth and realizing that all we believed were lies is excruciatingly painful. The only mechanism and the natural way to deal with it is denial. Denial takes away the pain. Denial is soothing. Denial is bliss. But denial is hiding one's head in the sand. One cannot stay in denial forever. Sooner or later we have to face the truth and deal with it.

A great majority of Muslims live in denial. Those who don't are the fundamentalists who are so brainwashed that they actually think killing is good, bombing is holy, stoning is a divine mandate, beating wives is prescribed by God, hating the unbelievers is what God has told them to do, and so on. Apart from this group, which, unfortunately, constitutes the majority of the ignorant masses (see Afghanistan, Pakistan, Iran, Saudi Arabia, etc.), those Muslims who have come in contact with the humanistic values of the civilized world and like it either know nothing of the ugly truth of Islam or they deny it.

I do not think this group of Muslims will ever see the truth if they are kept cocooned in lies. All they have heard so far is the lie that Islam is good and that if only Muslims practiced the true Islam the world would become a paradise; that it is all the fault of the Muslims who do not practice the real Islam. This is a lie. Most Muslims are extremely good people. They are kind, generous, caring, hospitable, wonderful human beings. What is wrong is Islam. Those Muslims who do bad things *are* those who follow Islam. Islam rears the criminal instinct of the people. The more a person is Islamist, the more bloodthirsty, hate mongering, and zombielike she or he becomes. What made Khomeini, a man who would literally not hurt a fly, become one of the most despicable murderers of history was his belief in Islam. He believed that Islam is true and that to maintain that truth he was entitled to do what the Prophet of Islam did: kill the unbelievers and massacre the enemies of the true religion of Allah. Winwood Reade said, "A sincerely religious man is often an exceedingly bad man."[2] Khomeini proved this to be a truism.

Later, when I started to study the hadith, I learned many more horrible facts that I had never heard before. I learned, for example, that my beloved Prophet used to send assassins to terrorize his opponents in the middle of night, telling them to lie and act deceitfully if necessary. I learned that he ordered the murder of a 120-year-old man whose only crime was to recite a lyric ridiculing the Prophet. Another one of his victims was a poetess, mother of five small children, whose crime was also to compose poetry condemning Muhammad for murdering that old man. The assassin entered the house of this woman and pierced his sword in her chest while she was asleep with her baby nursing on her side. And the next day the messenger of Allah praised the assassin.

I wanted to deny what I was reading. I wanted to believe that the real meaning of what is in the Koran is something else. But I could not. I had read the whole thing and could no longer fool myself, saying that these inhumane verses were taken out of the context. What context? The Koran is a book without a context. Verses are jammed together haphazardly, often lacking any coherence. Yet the whole Koran is full of verses that teach the killing of the unbelievers and tell how Allah will torture them after they die. There are very few lessons on morality, on justice, on honesty, or on love. The only message the entire book conveys is to believe in Allah, and to achieve this, it coaxes people with celestial rewards of unlimited sex with fair *houris* in Paradise and coerces them with the threat of blazing fires of hell. This is the context of the Koran. That is it. When the Koran speaks of righteousness, it does not really mean righteousness as we intend it, but it means belief in Allah. Good actions are irrelevant; belief in Allah is the ultimate purpose of a person's life and of the entire creation.

After reading the Koran, my perspective of reality was jolted. I found myself standing face-to-face with the truth and I was scared to look at it. This was not what I was expecting to see. I had no one to blame, to curse and call a liar. I had found all those absurdities of the Koran and the inhumanities of its author by reading the Koran itself. And I was shocked. Eventually this shock made me come to my senses and face the truth. Unfortunately, this is a very painful process and I do not believe there is an easy way. The followers of Muhammad must see the naked truth and they must be shocked. We cannot keep sugarcoating the truth. The truth is bitter and it must be swallowed; only then the process of enlightenment starts.

But because every person's sensitivity is different, what shocks one person may not shock another. Even as a man, I was shocked when I read that Muhammad instructed his followers to beat their wives and called women "deficient in intelligence" (IV.34). Yet I have came to know many Muslim women who have no difficulty accepting these derogatory statements uttered by their prophet. Not that they like to be beaten, agree that they are deficient in intelligence, or believe that the majority of the inhabitants of the hell are women, as the Prophet used to say, but they simply block out that information. They read it, but it doesn't sink in. They are in denial. The denial acts as a shield that covers them, that protects them, that saves them from facing the pain of shock and disillusionment. Once that shield is up, nothing can bring it down. It is no use to repeat to them the same things over and over. At this point they must be attacked from other directions. They must be bombarded with other shocking teachings of the Koran. They may have a weak spot for one of them, and one of those stupid teachings may shock them. That is all they need: a good shock. Shocks are painful, but sometimes they can be lifesavers. Shocks are used by doctors to bring back to life, clinically dead patients.

For the first time, the Internet has changed the balance of power. Now the brutal force of guns, bombs, prisons, and death squads are helpless and the pen is almighty. For the first time Muslims cannot stop the truth by killing its messenger. Now a great number of them are coming in contact with the truth, and they feel helpless. They want to silence this voice but they cannot. They want to kill the messenger but they cannot. They try to ban the sites exposing their cherished beliefs; sometimes they succeed momentarily, but most of the time they don't. (Tripod was forced to shut down my site, now I have it hosted in two places.)[3] So the old way of killing the apostates, burning their books, and silencing them by terror does not work. Also, they cannot stop people from reading. So a great number of Muslims who never knew the truth about Islam are becoming shocked after they learn the truth for the first time.

Last year I met a lady on the Internet (Yahoo! clubs) who called herself Khadija an-Niqab. She had a Web site with her picture completely covered in a black veil and the story of how she had become a Muslim. She was very active and used to advise everyone not to read my writings. But when she read the story of Safiyah, an article I wrote about Muhammad's rape of a Jewish woman (after he had killed her father and husband, he tried to force himself on her on the same day) she was shocked. She asked for an explanation from other Muslims, who could not answer her. Then the door was open; she kept writing to me and asking questions. Finally she passed through the other stages that exist between the blind faith and enlightenment very quickly, and wrote a thank you letter for opening her eyes and withdrew from the Yahoo! Islamic clubs altogether.

I believe when people learn about the unholy lifestyle of the Prophet and the absurdities of the Koran, they will be shocked. At first they will deny, but when they recover from denial, they will be on their way to enlightenment. Our job is to expose Islam; to write the truth about Muhammad's unholy life, his shameful deeds, and his stupid assertions; and bombard the Muslims with facts. These people read what you write, they become angry with you, curse you, insult you, and tell you that after reading your articles their faith in Islam is strengthened. But that is when you know that you have sown the seed of doubt in their mind. They say all this to you because they are shocked. Now they have entered the stage of denial. The seed of doubt is planted and it will wait for the first chance to germinate. In some people it takes years, but given the chance it will eventually germinate.

Doubt is the greatest gift we can give to each other. It is the gift of enlightenment. Doubt will set us free, advance knowledge, and unravel the mysteries of this universe, but faith will keep us ignorant.

One of the hurdles we have to overcome is the hurdle of tradition and false values imposed on us by thousands of years of religious upbringing. The world still values faith and considers doubt something evil. People talk of men of faith with respect and disdain men of little faith. We are screwed up in our values. The word *faith* means belief without evidence; *gullibility* also means belief without evidence.

There is no glory in faithfulness. Faithfulness means gullibility, credulity, suscepti-bility, and being easy to fleece. How can one be proud of such qualities?

Doubt, on the other hand, means the reverse of the above. It means being capable of thinking independently, being capable of questioning and being skep-tical. We owe our science and our modern civilization to men and women who doubted, not to those who believed. Those who doubted were the pioneers, they were the leaders of thought, they were philosophers, inventors, and discoverers; but those who believed lived and died as followers and gave little or no contribu-tion to the advancement of science and human understanding.

Those who read my articles and are hurt by what I tell them about the Koran are lucky. They have me to blame. They can hate me, curse me, and direct all their anger toward me. But when I read the Koran and learned about its content, I could not blame anyone. So after going through the stages of shock and denial, I was confused and started to blame myself. I hated myself for thinking, for doubting, and for finding fault with what I regarded to be the words of God.

Just like all the other Muslims I was exposed to many lies, absurdities, and inhumanities inherent in Islam, but had accepted all that. I was brought up as a religious person. I believed in whatever I was told. These lies had been given to me in small doses, gradually, since my childhood. I was never given an alterna-tive to compare. It is like vaccination. I was immune to the truth. But when I started to read the Koran seriously from cover to cover and understood what this book had to say, I felt nauseated facing all those lies at once. I had heard all these lies before and had accepted them. It was as if my rational thinking was numbed. I had become insensitive to the absurdities of the Koran. When I found something that did not make sense I automatically overlooked it and said to myself that one has to look at the "big picture." The big picture, however was nowhere to be found except in my own mind. I had made a picture of Islam in my mind that was perfect. So all those absurdities did not bother me because I did not pay attention to them. But when I read the whole Koran I discovered a different picture very different from the picture I had made of it in my mind. The new picture of Islam emerging from the pages of the Koran was a violent, intolerant, irrational, arro-gant picture that was a far cry from my mental picture that depicted Islam as a religion of peace, equality, and tolerance.

My first reaction, of course, was denial. That was the easiest thing to do. I had to deny in order to keep my sanity. But for how long could I keep denying when the truth was out like the sun right in front of me? I was reading the Koran in Arabic so I could not say it is the question of the bad translation. I used dif-ferent translations to compare and make sure I did not misunderstand anything. I realized many translations in English are not entirely reliable. The poor transla-tors had tried very hard to hide the inhumanity and the violence of the Koran by twisting the words and adding their own words, sometimes in parentheses, to soften its harsh tone. When you read the Koran in Arabic and understand it, it is much more shocking than its English translations.

After reading the Koran and coming out of denial, I went through a period of depression. It was as if my whole world had fallen apart. I felt as if the floor on which I was standing was no longer there and I was falling into a bottomless pit. If I say that was like being in hell I am not exaggerating. I was confused and I did not know where to turn. My faith was shaken and my world had crumbled. I could no longer deny what I was reading. But I could not accept the possibility that this was all a huge lie. "How could it be?" I kept asking myself. "How could it be that so many people died for this religion for nothing? How could it be that so many people have not seen the truth and I see it? How could it be that great sears and saints like Maulana Jalaleddin Rumi did not see that Muhammad was an impostor and that Koran is a hoax and I see it?" It was then that I entered into another stage, and that was guilt.

The guilt lasted for many months. I hated myself for having these thoughts. I thought, God is testing my faith. I felt ashamed. I spoke with learned people I trusted, people who were not only knowledgable but also were wise and spiritual. I heard very little that could quench the burning fire that I had within me. One of these learned men told me not to read the Koran for a while. He told me to pray and read only books that strengthen my faith. I did that, but it did not help. The thoughts about the absurd, sometimes ruthless, sometimes ridiculous verses of the Koran kept throbbing in my head. Each time I looked at my bookshelf and saw that book, I felt pain. I took the Koran and hid it behind the other books. I thought if I did not think about it for a while, my thoughts would go away and I would regain my faith once again. But they didn't go away. I denied as much as I could, until I could no more. I was shocked and it was painful.

Then I went through the stage of confusion and bewilderment, pleading for help, and no one could help. Now I was in a deep state of guilt, ashamed of my thoughts and hating myself for having such thoughts. This sense of guilt was accompanied by a profound sense of loss and sadness. I am naturally a positive thinker. I see the good side of everything. I always think tomorrow is going to be better than today. I am not the kind of person who gets depressed easily. But this feeling of loss was overwhelming. I still recall that weight on my heart. I thought God had forsaken me and I did not know why. I did not remember hurting anyone ever. I had gone out of my way to help anyone who had crossed my way and asked me for help. I stopped eating meat because I did not want to destroy a life just to satisfy my taste buds, although the smell and the taste of a good steak drive me crazy. So why did God want to punish me in this way? Why did he not answer my prayers? Why had he abandoned me to myself and to these thoughts for which I find no answers?

This period of guilt lasted too long. One day I decided, enough is enough. I told myself that it was not my fault. I was not going to carry this guilt forever for thinking about things that make no sense to me. If God gave me a brain, it is because he wants me to use it. If what I perceive as right and wrong is completely twisted, then it is not my fault. He tells me killing is bad, and I know it is bad because I would not like to be killed, so why does his messenger kill so many innocent people and ask his followers to kill those who disbelieve? If rape is bad, and I know that it is bad because I do not want it to happen to people I love, why did Allah's prophet rape his captives of war? If imposition of religion is bad, and I know that it is bad because I do not like another person forcing religion on me that I don't want to accept, then why did the Prophet eulogize the *jihad* and exhort his followers to kill the unbelievers, take their booty, and sell their women and children as spoils of war? If God tells me something is good, and I know that it is good because it feels good to me, then why did his prophet do the reverse of that thing?

It was then that I felt liberated from guilt and entered the next stage, which is dismay, disillusionment, or cynicism. I felt sorry for all the religious people, and especially for all the Muslims who still believed in these foolish teachings. I felt sorry for all those who lost their lives in the name of these false doctrines. I felt sorry for all the women in virtually all the Islamic countries, who suffer all sorts of abuses and are so subdued that they do not even know they are being abused.

Then I became angry. I became angry for having believed in those lies for so many years; angry that I was for wasting so many years of my life chasing a wild goose. I was angry at my culture for it had betrayed me. I was angry at my parents for teaching me a lie. I was angry at my self for not thinking before, for believing in lies, for trusting an impostor. I was angry with God for letting me down, for not intervening and stopping the lies that were being disseminated in his name.

By then I knew that Muhammad was no messenger of God but a charlatan, a demagogue whose only intention was to beguile people and satisfy his own narcissistic ambitions. I knew that all those childish stories of a hell with scorching fire and a heaven with rivers of wine, honey, and milk, full of orgies, were the figments of the sick, wild, insecure, and bullying mind of a man in desperate need to dominate, destroy, and affirm his own authority.

But I could not be angry with my parents, for they did their best and taught me what they thought was the best. I could not be angry with my community, society, or culture because they, too, were just as misinformed as my parents and myself. When I looked carefully, I saw everyone as a victim. There are a billion victims who, in turn, have become victimizers. How I could blame the Muslims if they did not know what Islam stands for and honestly, though erroneously, believe that it is a religion of peace?

What about Muhammad? Should I be angry with him for lying, deceiving, and misleading people? How could I be angry with a corpse? Muhammad was a sick man who was not in control. He grew up as an orphan and had five foster parents before he reached the age of eight. As soon as he came to be attached to someone, he was snatched away and given to someone else. This must have been hard on him and was detrimental to his emotional health. As a child deprived of love and a sense of belonging, he grew up with deep feelings of fear and a lack of self-confidence. He tried to make up for it by becoming a narcissist. A narcissist is a person who has not received enough love in his childhood, who is incapable of loving, but instead craves attention, respect, and recognition. He sees his own worth in the way others view him. Without that recognition he is nobody. He is manipulative and a pathetic liar.

Narcissists have grandiose dreams. They want to conquer the world and dominate everybody. Only in these megalomaniac reveries do they find their narcissistic supply.

Famous narcissists include Adolf Hitler, Benito Mussolini, Josef Stalin, Saddam Hussein, Idi Amin, Pol Pot, and Mao Tse-tung. Narcissists can be very intelligent, but they are emotional wrecks. They are capable of thinking but incapable of feeling. They set themselves extremely high goals. Their goals always have to do with domination, power, and respect. They are the CEOs of big companies. They are cool, aloof, arbitrary, inflexible, and even ruthless. As Carl Jung put it, a narcissist "may be polite, amiable, and kind, but one is constantly aware of a certain uneasiness betraying an ulterior motive—the disarming of an opponent, who must at all costs be pacified and placated lest he prove himself a nuisance."[4]

A narcissist is nobody if he is neglected. Narcissists often seek alibis to impose their control over their unwary victims. For Hitler it was Nazism, for Mussolini it was fascism, and for Muhammad it was religion or monotheism. These are just tools in their quest for power. Instead of promoting themselves, they can promote these ideologies, causes, or religions, while presenting themselves as the only authority on and representative of these causes. Allah was Muhammad's own alter ego. He could wield control over everyone's life and death by telling them: This is what God has ordained.

Dr. Sam Vaknin, a psychologist specializing in narcissism, explains:

> Everyone is a narcissist, to varying degrees. Narcissism is a healthy phenomenon. It helps survival. The difference between healthy and pathological narcissism is, indeed, in measure. Pathological narcissism and its extreme form, NPD (Narcissistic Pathological Disorder), are characterized by extreme lack of empathy. The narcissist regards and treats other people as objects to be exploited. He uses them to obtain narcissistic supply. He believes that he is entitled to special treatment because he harbours these grandiose fantasies about himself. The narcissist is *not* self-aware. His cognition and emotions are distorted.[5]

The above perfectly describes Muhammad. Muhammad was a ruthless man with no human feelings. At first he molded his religion to appease the Jews and attract them, but when he realized that they are not going to accept him and would not become tools in his dreams of domination, he eliminated all of them. He massacred all the men of Banu Quraiza and Kheibar and banished every other Jew and Christian from Arabia. Surely if God wanted to destroy these people he did not need the help of his messenger.

So I found there was no reason to be angry at an emotionally sick man who was long dead. Muhammad was himself a victim of the stupid culture of his people, of the apathy and ignorance of his mother, who, instead of keeping him in the first years of his life when he needed her love most, entrusted him to a Bedouin woman to raise him.

Muhammad was a man with profound emotional scars. Vaknin says that a narcissist "lies to himself and to others, projecting "untouchability," emotional immunity and invincibility. . . . For a narcissist everything is bigger than life. If he is polite, then he is aggressively so. His promises outlandish, his criticism violent and ominous, his generosity inane."[6] Isn't this the image that the Prophet projected of himself?

I could not criticize or blame the ignorant Arabs of the seventh century for not being able to discern that Muhammad was sick and not a prophet, that his outlandish promises, his impressive reveries of conquering and subduing the great nations, when he was just a pauper, were caused by his pathological emotional complications and not due to a divine power. How could I blame those stupid Arabs for falling prey to a man like Muhammad when only in the last century, millions of Germans fell prey to the charisma of another narcissist who, also like Muhammad, gave them big promises of total domination, who was as ruthless as him, as manipulative as him, and as ambitious as him?

When I looked with care, I saw there is not a single person I could find to be angry with. I realized we are all victims and victimizers at the same time. The only culprit is ignorance. It is our ignorance that makes us believe in charlatans and their lies. It is because of ignorance that we let these impostors inseminate hate in us in the name of false deities, ideologies, or religions. It is our ignorance that does not allow us to see our oneness and hinders us from understanding that we are members of one body of humanity related to each other and interdependent with each other.

It was then that my anger gave way to a profound feeling of empathy, compassion, and love. I made a promise to myself to fight this ignorance that divides the human race. We paid dearly for our disunity. The disunity in the human race is caused by ignorance and the ignorance is the result of false beliefs and pernicious ideologies often concocted by emotionally unhealthy individuals for self-serving purposes.

Ideologies separate us. Religions cause disunity, hate, and antagonism. Humanity needs no ideology or any religion. As members of the human race, we need no ideology, cause, or religion to be united; but to be disunited, to fight and kill each other, we need to have an excuse, an ideology, a cause, or a religion— something for which we are willing to kill.

*   *   *

The process of going from faith to enlightenment is an arduous and painful one. Faith is the state of being confirmed in ignorance. We stay in that state of blissful oblivion until we are shocked and forced out of it. The natural and the first reaction to shock is denial. Denial acts like a shield. It buffers the pain and protects us from the agony of going out of our comfort zone. The comfort zone is where we feel at ease, where we find everything familiar, where we don't have to take new challenges or face the unknown. It is our cocoon. But growth doesn't take place in the comfort zone. In order to go forward and to evolve, we need to get out of our comfort zone. We won't get out of our comfort zone unless we are shocked. It is also natural to buffer the pain of the shock with denial. At that moment we need another shock, and we may decide to shield ourselves again with another denial. The more a person is exposed to facts and the more he is shocked, the more he tries to shield himself with denial. But denials do not eliminate the facts. They just shield us momentarily. When we are exposed to all the facts, we find ourselves unable to keep denying. That is when one of those facts will hit us and we are shocked. Suddenly, we find ourselves unable to keep our defenses up and all the denials come down. We can no longer keep hiding our heads in the sand, pretending that everything is okay. The first shock was a domino effect and we find ourselves being hit from all directions with facts that, up until now, we had kept at bay by denying them. Suddenly all those absurdities we had accepted and even defended do not seem logical anymore, and we are unable to accept them.

It is then that we are driven into the painful stage of confusion. The old beliefs seem unreasonable, foolish, and unacceptable, yet we have nothing to cling to. This stage, I believe, is the most dreadful stage in the passage from faith to enlightenment. In this stage we have lost our faith, but we have found no enlightenment. We are basically standing nowhere, experiencing a free fall. We ask for help, but all we get is the rehashing of some nonsense cliché. It seems that those who try to help us have no clue of what they are talking about, yet they are so convinced about it. They believe in what they don't know. The arguments they present are not logical at all. They expect us to believe without questioning. They bring the example of the faith of others, but the intensity of the faith of other people does not prove the truth of what they believe in.

This confusion eventually gives way to guilt. We feel guilty for thinking. We feel guilty for doubting, for questioning, for not understanding. We think it is our fault if the absurdities mentioned in our holy book make no sense to us. We think that God has abandoned us or that he is testing our faith. In this stage we are torn between our emotions and our intellect. Emotions are not rational, but they are extremely powerful. We want to go back, we desperately want to believe, but we simply can't. We have committed the sin of thinking. We have eaten the forbidden fruit from the tree of knowledge. We have angered our imaginary god. We are cast out of the paradise of ignorance. Now we find ourselves naked, ashamed, overtaken by guilt and with no way to return.

Then we enter the stage of anger. One day we decide that it is not our fault at all if all the mumbo jumbo taught to us in the name of the religion and truth make no sense. We decide to rebel. If the religions are stupid, it is not our fault. If they make no sense, why should we feel guilty? If they are from God certainly they should be logical and reasonable. If they are not reasonable, then perhaps they are not from God. Perhaps they are false doctrines. The fact that a billion people believe in something does not make that thing true. How many of those billion people actually sat down and questioned their beliefs? How many of them can answer our questions? How many of them are allowed to question without fearing persecution? Maybe all of them are in denial. There was a time when everyone thought that Earth was flat. Did this unanimous consensus make any difference to the shape of Earth? At this stage we become angry at ourselves and at everything else. We realize how much of your precious lives we lost believing in so many lies. That is when we enter the next stage, which is dismay.

In this stage we are overtaken by sadness. We ponder upon time lost. We think of so many people who believed in this nonsense and foolishly sacrificed everything for it, including their lives. How many millions of lives were sacrificed at the altar of these false religions? How many people voluntarily faced death and, in the case of Islam, how many people took the lives of other innocent people with a completely clear conscience? The pages of history are written with the blood of people who were killed in the name of Yahweh, Allah, and other gods. All for nothing! All for a lie!

But then we realize that we are the lucky ones for having made it this far, and that there are billions of others who are still trying to shield themselves with denial and not venture out of their comfort zone. There are billions of believers who are cocooned in lies and desperately try to stay there. At this stage, when we are completely free from faith, guilt, and anger, we are ready for understanding the ultimate truth and unravelling the mysteries of life. We are ready to be enlightened. The enlightenment comes when we realize that the truth is in love and in our relationship with our fellow human beings, not in a religion or a cult. Truth is a pathless land.

NOTES

1. www.islamistwatch.org
2. Winwood Reade, *The Martyrdom of Man* (London, 1948), p. 428.
3. main.faithfreedom.org
4. Carl Jung, *Collected Works* (Princeton, N.J.: Princeton University Press, 1976), vol. 6.
5. Sam Vaknin, *Malignant Self-Love—Narcissism Revisited* (Skopje, 1999).
6. Ibid.

14

A JOURNAL OF MY ESCAPE FROM THE HELL OF ISLAM

Sheraz Malik (Pakistan)

T his is the story of why I left Islam. I have kept my name secret for obvious reasons—in Islam, apostates (people who leave their religion) are given the death sentence. So if my identity is known, my life will be at risk. I can only tell that I am a male, originally from Pakistan. In this story, I explain what made me leave Islam, the defects in Islam, and why I think that Islam cannot be a religion from God. I explain the basic Islamic psyche and quote valid, recognized Koranic *ayahs* (verses) and *hadith* (traditions) to support my claims. These quotations have all been made in the correct context—it is an old habit of Muslim apologists to protest that the *ayahs* are taken out of context. The reader is welcome to verify the correct quotations by referring to the Koran and hadith themselves (online or in book form).[1] Many Muslims may think that my story is not true, or that I have falsified things. I say this because I understand the Muslim mindset—it hurts them to see anyone leave Islam. So to stop the hurt, they would rather label me a liar. But I have not lied. Every sentence of this story is truthful and real.

I was born to Muslim parents. I lived most of my life in Pakistan, which is an Islamic republic where more than 95 percent of the population is Muslim. My grandparents were religious Muslims, especially my grandfather, who was famous in the family because he was very pious and god fearing. Even though I had never met him, I liked to see his pictures, thinking of him as a sacred person—at that time, he was a role model for me. My family used to say that I bore a resemblance to him. In a secret way, only known to me, I used to think I was Allah's special child. I always felt closer to Allah (the Islamic God) than normal people did.[2]

Before my middle school exams, I started praying to Allah. I remember those nights. I would perform ablution with devotion, and wear simple clothes (called a *shalwar qameez* in local language Urdu). The *shalwar qameez* was faded and unironed, but soft and comfortable. I knew Allah liked simplicity, and this was my way of showing my respect and love for him. Then I would go to the farthest corner of the deserted living room of my house to start praying. I'd go to the living room as if I was going to a special altar to make contact with Allah. I'd leave the lights out, because I liked the darkness. I thought the darkness would prevent me from loosing my concentration in prayer, and keep my attention away from material things: the carpet, the walls, the curtains, and ornaments on the wall. I would want to give my full concentration to Allah. My favorite part of prayer was the *sadja* (kneeling down), I felt closest to Allah in those moments. I guess the *sadja* is the part of prayer when we show highest humility, bowing to Allah.

Perhaps I was just doing all that to get good results in my exams, which I did get. My parents were also happy with my results, and I got admission in the college I wanted. It was a well-reputed place, but the quality of education in our country was poor, especially the government education system, and this was the system which the college had. Anyway, I lost my religiousness after getting into college. It seems funny, but it was natural. We remember God when we're in trouble. Where would you remember God more? In Hawaii, lying on the beach, sipping lemonade, or when you're stuck in a concentration camp?

For many years, whenever I heard any strange noises in the night while going to sleep or whenever I had fear in my heart of burglars or thieves entering our house, I would recite the four *Quls* (four special *ayahs* of the Koran for warding off evil), blow air around to spread the "holiness," and then go back to sleep, praying to Allah to keep our house safe from burglars. I was definitely the extra-pious guy. While going to and from university, on the eight-hour bus journey, I would wait for darkness to fall and sometimes I would read Koranic *ayahs* or the *darood-sharif* (*darood* is the prayer for the prophet Muhammad), until I'd get tired and nod off to sleep. Even then, I'd keep reading the *darood*. On any long journey, in the nighttime or evening, I would see stars or far-off lights and imagine sometimes that they might be *jinns* (spirits). I would sense the power of Allah in all this creation and often this feeling would give me a chill in the spine. These would be moments in which I would read the *darood* with a lot of devotion and humility. My objective to read the *darood* was to be safe from evil and to gain the forgiveness of Allah so I may enter heaven when I die. I prayed to Allah to keep me in his "shadow" all the time.

After I got into university, I grew religious again. Why? Because it was a new place and I was lonely and didn't have any friends. I used to get some comfort by thinking that at least someone (God) loved me. Most "friends" I had were fake, and used to do leg-pulling all the time, which I hated. So at least I had some friend who was going to be with me all the time. I knew I couldn't have as much fun as the bad guys did, swearing, partying around, and not studying. I wasn't brought up like that. My parents were very strict and this had limited my ability to enjoy life tremendously.

I believed that I could depend on God at moments when people were making fun of me or having pity on me. I had a packet in which I kept special *ayahs* and recitals. These were my special, revered tools, which I used when I was in trouble, feeling mentally disturbed, or lost. I would lock my room, switch on the lamp, and read the *ayahs* with concentration, and praying to God to solve my problems. After praying, I felt God would help me. My university was in a scenic place, a clear sky, fresh air, and mountains around it. On and off, I would enjoy going to the roof of my dorm, which would be deserted at night. With the stars above me, away from the normal hustle and bustle of the other boys, I would feel that I was really close to God. I felt Allah around in the air. I would imagine there were Allah's angels around me. I developed a mark on my forehead, due to intensive praying. It was a special mark, and anyone who had it was a real faithful *namazi* (someone who prays).

So that's how I lived the first year of my university life. But slowly things started changing. Previously, I always believed that religious guys will go to heaven and will do better in life, because God is always with them. I thought that the guys who were not religious, who didn't pray, who swore, and who made fun of *maulvis* (religious people, often with a beard) were the guys who would go to hell.

Slowly I started seeing that there were some real losers in the group I met in the mosque. At the same time, I saw guys who never went to mosque, but were great people. My thinking that religion was the key to becoming a winner started to diminish slowly, and I started seeing that being a good person or not doesn't have to depend on religion.

Thus, I began to think that being a winner or not has little or no connection with religion. Surely the guy who never even went to Friday prayers but was a great person, who stayed happy, spoke his mind confidently, and had friends was better than the loser I met in mosque every day who was a hypocrite. Then, when I came back from university, I passed through a great depression, mostly due to my past life. I had suicidal thoughts. I started to wonder why I was thinking like this. Why was my life so sad? Why could I never be happy? Why were other people who were not religious happier than I was? I saw that they were happy, because they were free people and they were not unnecessarily afraid of anything. I started to find out why I was so suppressed. A large portion of my university years had also been spent in depression and even suicidal thoughts at times. I started to write a journal and put down all my thoughts in it. I read somewhere that keeping a journal can help us in our personal problems when they seem too difficult. Many people who leave Islam were victimized by it in various ways. The same is true for me as well.

I found that I was a suppressed human, mostly because of my abusive parents. Childhood scars are hard to heal, though possible. I found myself tied up in chains. Slowly, my depression turned into anger. I wanted to be free of these chains and my mind lashed out at anyone who tried to bind me into anything. I had started to write my thoughts in a journal, because I heard it helped to express ourselves. In my journal, I wrote:

> When I started thinking about my past life, I discovered that my low self-esteem was a result of my parents abusive behaviour towards me. No doubt about it. So it wasn't my fault that I had this low self-esteem. Having discovered that, I went on to tell God in my heart, that if he didn't pull me out of this shit, I would not forgive him. After all it was no fault of mine that I was in this shit. I was angry that my life had been spoilt due to no fault of mine.

I quote my journal to help the reader understand what was going on in my mind. Anger was the feeling that caused me to tell God that he *had* to pull me of this mess. These are my exact words I recorded in my journal at that time:

> God I will never forgive you if you don't pull me out this misery. I will definitely not be happy with you if you are not the primary being who helps me out of all of this, because it was not me who had the choice of my parents and thus my childhood. It was primarily you who put me here, so it will be you who will get me out of this. Yes.

In my mental pain, I reasoned with myself that God was definitely out there and he was the only one who could help me for sure. I wrote in my journal:

> God help me help myself.

At another point, I wrote down my feelings, in which I was talking to God:

> Was it my fault that I got the parents I did? Were things under my control when my mother didn't treat me with real love, affection and patience? No it's not. And I told God that if I didn't get better till the day I was married I would go ahead and kill myself. I don't want this life. It's my life, thank you for giving it to me but remember I didn't ask for it. And thanks a lot for giving me such a lovely childhood due to which I am in this present state of depression. I would rather give my life in charity than to live it. I am now because of what you put

me through. Now you have to pull me out of it. Of course I am trying and will keep trying. But if I don't get my objective met, I will kill myself. Punish me with whatever you can. But I would like to remind you that I did not ask you for my life and thus am not under any obligation to you. I would, if I were better and felt thankful towards you for giving me a better life and circumstances. Remember I haven't asked for any material things because they don't matter. This is my life and I have a right over it, the right to continue it or the right to end it. Of course you have infinite powers and you can do anything you want, end my life even right now etc, but I would like to tell you that this is my life and I have the right to do whatever I want to do with it. The one thing which I allow you to do (although you don't need anyone's approval) is to punish me for things, which I did and were harmful to other people. That is justice and that must be provided to everyone. But I have the right to end my life, and I don't think you should punish me for ending it. Well, for one thing, thanks for giving me such a lovely childhood due to which I am in this state. So, God, if I cant improve despite my varied efforts and I get the feeling that you are not helping me and will never help me, I will end this life. No point in going further. Do whatever you can to punish me but I will not allow this hell to continue. Thus, I again request you to help. Help me straighten out this mess which is not my fault, but *yours*. Definitely, there are people who had lovely affectionate, patient parents and their results are clear in their children. Tell me, does parenting have no effect on the personality of the child? Impatient, under-affectionate, easily irritable parents have a marked negative effect on their children. Why on earth do I have all these problems? Low self-esteem, depression? It's not my fault. Since it is not my fault, and one of the deepest desires of any human being is to feel satisfied and feel an overall sense of well-being. God, it is your duty to help me now. And if you're not gonna help me, thank you for this life but I would say goodbye to it. There's no point in living it. It's all unfair. All wrong. I am not begging you for help. I am telling you that it is your duty for you to help me, because you gave me this disadvantage. I've recognized it and want to correct it. You're the one who's going to help me correct it, if I cant do it myself. At least tell me what to do, or guide me. But primarily its your responsibility to correct it even if I fail to do it on my own, because remember, I didn't put myself on disadvantage on my own choice. Who would? I mean, mental injury just cant be compared to physical injury, I think you know this. And specially if having high SE is the most important thing to me. It's all so unfair. I look at other people and feel so much disabled and helpless and deficient. I mean, why on earth couldn't I have been satisfied with myself?

Then I thanked God:

By now, I've been helped by God (I acknowledge this) in recognizing my present state. I thank him for giving me the eyes to see it, where others are oblivious of it, like my sisters and mother. I know I was neglected in my childhood.

Now when I look back and see the process of my thoughts, they appear interesting. In Islam, suicide is not allowed. It is considered *haram* (unlawful), and the Prophet said that anyone committing suicide would be punished on the last day, by repeatedly killing himself forever. Here's the exact *hadith* I dug up from al-Bukhārī:

> Narrated Abu Huraira: The Prophet said, "Whoever purposely throws himself from a mountain and kills himself, will be in the (Hell) Fire falling down into it and abiding therein perpetually forever; and whoever drinks poison and kills himself with it, he will be carrying his poison in his hand and drinking it in the (Hell) Fire wherein he will abide eternally forever; and whoever kills himself with an iron weapon, will be carrying that weapon in his hand and stabbing his Abdomen with it in the (Hell) Fire wherein he will abide eternally forever."[3]

So you see, Islam does not permit suicide. But when I was in this phase of life of extreme depression; all I wanted was my depression to go away. If it was not going to go away, I decided I would kill myself. Suppose I had two choices: either to live my life pathetically and miserably, or to kill myself, end this pain, and finish this life. I could not see myself living this pathetic life, and on the other hand, there was Islam saying that I could not end it.

I reasoned that this is my life and I will end it if I want to. I did not ask God for this life. God was powerful and he had the power to solve my problems. If he didn't help me, I had the right to end my life. Recognizing the right to end my life was the beginning of my freedom. It is true that ending one's life is not the best solution, but one always has the right to end his life, just like he has the right to harm himself.

I moved ahead to decide that Allah (or God) did not need our prayers (called *namaz* in Urdu). God was an infinitely powerful being. He was not and could not be dependent on humans in any way. He did not need our praise or prayer. If it could be anyone who benefited from praying to God, it would have to be ourselves only. Then I reasoned that if it us who get the benefits of *namaz* (prayer) and not Allah, then we as individuals should have the choice whether to do that thing or not. After all, if I chose to cut my own finger, its absurd to punish me for cutting my own finger. Hell, it's *my* finger. I can cut it if I want to. The benefit or loss of cutting my finger is mine only. No other human will suffer due to my finger being cut. One could say that if all the humanity cut its fingers, maybe we would suffer as a whole, but again, our fingers are *ours*. This is the bottom line. I should be the one to decide whether to cut my finger or not. Thus, reading *namaz* is my choice. *I should not be punished for not reading* namaz. This was, of course, contrary to what Islam said. Islam said that *namaz* is compulsory.

In my journal, I wrote down the logic of not praying:

I feel this world is a great test. We have all been given a scene to deal with. We have to use our senses to see what to do. God doesn't need our religious acts, like saying something 100 times a day. It's very logical. Its really something stupid if they say that for every 100 times you say a certain word, there grows a tree in heaven for you, whose shade is so large that an Arabian horse would take 40 years to run and cover its diameter. It is downright absurd. I mean, that if prayer had the magical quality which people say it has (keeping you away from evil, etc. etc.), people who said regular prayers would really stand out in the crowd (I'm not saying they would be glamorous or something, but just that you know, it is like that anyone can distinguish between him and another person who doesn't pray). Anyone can say that these sorts of good deeds are rewarded when we die. First of all, what good deeds? Good deeds are something due to which someone benefits (you yourself or any other person). If it is Allah who benefits from our 'good' deeds, it is a wrong concept. The being, the entity, which has made black holes and the whole universe and complex things like humans and insects and what else not, surely can't benefit from my praying. God doesn't need our prayers. He doesn't get any pleasure form our praying. That would mean that his pleasure or satisfaction is dependent on what we do. And that means the balance of power has been shifted. God would then be dependent on us. Just like an infant is dependent on his parents, or plants are dependent on sunshine for their growth. Since God has infinite power, he is not dependent on anyone and is not inferior to anyone. Thus, we can rule the thing that God is happy when we pray to him or do something equally religious that has its connection only between God and us (like reciting something quietly to ourselves).

Still, we are given to reciting something when we are in pain or trouble. Why? Because we acknowledge God's power and the fact that he is our creator. We are asking him to help us. That is very logical. God has the power to help us. Although this just came to my mind that if god knows everything, he should also know when we are in trouble. So why doesn't he help us automatically? Because we have to ask for his help. It's again logical. The crying child gets the milk. Again, right now, I am asking god, please help me and keep helping me as much as possible, please? Just a prayer. When my prayer gets answered and to what degree is a complex question, to which I don't know the answer.

So one thing is clear. God's happiness is not dependent on our praying. Anyone can say, its actually you yourself who benefits from prayer. That is true. It's psychologically soothing as they say. It gives you support and hope when there is none from anywhere else. So following your religion strictly, is not the way of life. I believe we humans have the capability of thinking logically in any circumstance. Not everyone has it. But you can develop it inside you.

Anyway, this is my life and I'm gonna live it the way I want to. If I harm someone and he doesn't forgive me, that is god's work to provide that person with justice. I acknowledge that. And I fully deserve that punishment. But if that someone is me myself, I have already harmed myself. I have already punished myself. If you burn yourself, would your mother go ahead and beat you because you harmed yourself? I am only answerable for any harm, which I inflict on others. For my own harm, I am the only person who will suffer and not anyone else. God won't need to punish me if I harmed myself. And again, if I don't pray or do other religious things, I alone am responsible for any damage done to myself. I certainly don't have to be punished for that. Of course one of the major things is to decide whether a certain thing is harmful or not. Its all common sense.

About personal well-being and how it was the first important thing, as opposed to being close to God, I wrote:

For people like her, the concept is that if you are religious you automatically become satisfied. A great mis-concept. "Everything will be all right when you are closer to God." How about being closer to yourself first? That's more important. God comes afterwards. Isn't that true, God? If I am not close to myself, I possibly cannot be closer to anyone else, be it my wife, my children, my family, my friends, and God. It's this that is the first lesson to be learnt.

To trust yourself, to be kind to yourself, to be affectionate to yourself. Those who are too criticizing of themselves and always finding faults within themselves (consciously or unconsciously), never being able to praise themselves for anything good they did (if able, that too in a light manner), never being able to feel really proud over anything good they have done, these people are always unhappy with themselves. The first job is to be happy with yourself, honestly, sincerely. How can you be healthy with other people if you have conflicts within yourself?

At another point, I wrote about my personal struggle:

If this thing is not solved (I might discover this fact when I am old), I have told God many times in my heart that I will not forgive him for this. No matter how powerful he is (he can do anything since he created the world, even change hatred of him into love for him.), my dislike towards him will not change of my own will. I am sure he would not like that.

So my thinking had progressed to the point when I knew that the choice of reading *namaz* (prayer) had to be mine. And the idea of punishing me for not reading *namaz* was not logical. Anything that benefits me only should be my choice, and not my duty. I guess this was the point from which I started to develop some dislike for religion. I further probed my mind and decided that if the Prophet lived his life, I will live mine.

I also made another interesting observation. I reasoned with myself that if God is all-powerful, he is not affected by whatever I say or do. For example, my praise to God does not affect him. Likewise, God is not affected by anyone who abuses him, or anyone who says bad words to him in his heart. Imagine there are two men. One is a reasonable guy with a strong head on his shoulders. A passer-by comes and abuses the guy, hurling obscenities. This guy doesn't mind the abuse, and thinks the passer-by might be insane. He finds it funny and ignores the abuse. The passer-by abuses another person, but this guy is not like the first one. He becomes angry and his blood boils up, while he proceeds to give the passer-by a piece of his own mind, abusing him also.

Now decide, which is the stronger one? The one who was able to maintain an indifferent attitude or the one who got angered by the abuse? Shift this concept to Gods. There is one God who is affected by human abuses. Another who is not. Who is more powerful? Who is better? The God that is not affected by abuse, right? Great. So I decided that if God exists, he has to be the best god. He is not affected by abuse. I tested this thing by abusing God in my heart. It seemed to be working. I didn't see any lighting coming down, I didn't see the sky falling. God is there, and he isn't minding my abuse. Thank you, God, for not minding my abuse. I know you are powerful enough and sensible not to mind abuse from someone who is so much less in power than yourself.

This discovery was against Islam, too. Ask any Muslim, "Is swearing at God bad?" He will probably say, "*Astaghfirullah* |God forbid|, what kind of question is that?" And he will either be hurt or become angry at you. By now, I was fairly convinced that Islam had serious defects, but I didn't know that I would find more!

By this time I was ready to leave for abroad, to begin my studies. This was the second phase of the changing of my religious thinking. I was going to the United States and found that the people here were generally people of dignity and self-respect, while the country I was in was generally full of people who had no conscience.

Before coming to the United States, I made a tour of Medina, the holy city of Islam, with my near ones. There, when I saw people running around the *Ka'ba* (house of Allah), I thought these people are crazy. I saw the people doing *umrah* (a running ritual) and I ran (for the last time in my life), too, with them. Just to get the last hang of all this Islamic mentality and where it led us. What's all this running around and praying to God doing for the Muslims? Nothing! I looked at the global scene. Muslims are not doing well in the world. Their economy is in shambles, and their governments are corrupt. While I prayed I hurled abused to God and the Prophet and told them in my heart, *This is my life. I'll do whatever I want to do. You can go away.* I knew God would not mind my abuses to him, so I abused him, too. Why? To get rid myself of religious fear, to take these stupid fears out of my mind. At times I would laugh at what I was doing and sometimes a thought would come to mind, *Am I doing the right thing?* My mind would answer my own question with the same basic argument: *This is my life and I will definitely do what I want to do.*

This was what gave me back my peace of mind. So when I came to the

United States, I found the people over here were nice as well. Rather, much nicer. I saw the reason they are prospering. The reason was that they are not the losers the people of *my* country were. My country was Pakistan. Of course, there are all types of people everywhere, but there's a general personality level of every country and it is unique to that country. I knew that Pakistan's general level was way below the level of people in the United States.

Does religion even matter? No, it does not. Consider the following reasoning:

1. A person keeps the religion he is born to; that is, he has the same religion his parents have. In more than 90 percent of the cases, he keeps the religion. Very few people change their religion.
2. I did not have control over where I was born. Thus, I did not control which religion I was going to be born into.
3. So if the religion I have is only decided by where I was born, then is religion important?
4. Muslims say that it's important for everyone to be a Muslim, because according to Islam (XLVIII.13 and others), *kaafirs* (people who are not Muslims) will go to hell. Tell me, what credit is it of a Muslim to be a Muslim? What fault is it of a non-Muslim that he's not Muslim? None, right? You could say that non-Muslims can change their religions to Islam, after seeing the truth, but in fact the majority of people do not change their religion. Changing your faith brings you into difficulties, for example, opposition from your whole family and losing your links with your past. Bottom line: *In the vast majority of cases, you keep the faith you are born in, and it's difficult to change that faith.*

Thus I deduced that religion does not matter. To every Muslim I ask this question: "Why are you Muslim? Because your parents were Muslims, right?" To this, some answer that it was God who chose them to be Muslims. Well, why on Earth is it someone's fault if God did not "choose" him to be a Muslim? Is it that guy's fault? Why will he punished for not being a Muslim, when in fact it was God who chose that guy to be a non-Muslim?

There were several things that made me see that Islam was very much flawed. A very common belief in Islam is that Allah controls the destiny of all things. My question is, then, Why is man punished for his bad deeds? Since it is already decided by God that he'll do bad deeds, then why will the poor guy be punished for something that is not under his control?

Islam says do not eat *haram* things. *Haram* things are those forbidden in Islam. Again I thought, anything I eat affects me only. If I want to eat grass or garbage, is there any law in any country that says I should not do so? By eating garbage I am harming myself only. Thus, whatever I eat is my choice only. I will eat what I want to eat. And it's not logical to punish me for something I should not have eaten. To people who are thinking that I must follow God's orders because I am his slave: Well I am not! This I my life and I did not ask him for it. I owe God nothing. God, if he exists, can have only one thing for his creation, and that is love. God cannot hate or become angry with human beings for small, petty things such as missing prayer or eating something not allowed. The hell I care! Everyone around the world eats pork and *haram* chicken and beef as well. And they are healthier than Muslims.

I discovered that Islam does not give women equal rights to men. This was very absurd. Here is one of the several *ayahs* in the Koran (holy book) that clearly says that women are inferior to men and they have fewer rights as well:

> Men have authority over women because God has made the one superior to the other, and because they spend their wealth to maintain them. Good women are obedient. (IV.34)

It says, "Good women are obedient." Just like slaves are, right? This is unfair to women. After all, no one chooses before birth whether he or she is going to be born a man or a woman. In the same way, it does not matter if you're a man or a woman, and it does not matter what religion you have, because these things are not under your control. In most cases, we keep our sexes and we keep our religions, the same way we were born.

Islam says, "There shall be no compulsion in religion" (II.256). Then why will non-Muslims be punished? Also, if there is no compulsion in religion, why is it "mandatory" to say prayers? Forget my own reasoning, look at the following *ayah*, which completely contradicts the first one: "He that chooses a religion over Islam, it will not be accepted from him and in the world to come he will be one of the lost" (III.85).

When I came to the United States, I saw other nationalities and ethnic groups close up: nice Hindus, white people, Mexicans, Christians, Chinese, Buddhists, Indonesians, and so on. It is not possible that these nice people can burn in hell eternally. Take Mother Teresa or Princess Diana, for example. It's not possible for these nice women who had nice hearts to burn in fire forever. Muslims don't think about this. They take the burning in fire very lightly. Burn your little finger today, just the tip of it, and see how painful it is.

One other reasoning I had is that burning in hell forever is an infinite punishment. Now life is finite and a person can only commit a finite amount of sin. It is unfair to punish a finite amount of sin with an infinite amount of punishment. It doesn't make sense! You can always give more reward than he deserves to a person who does good, and no one will complain about this. But to give more punishment than what a sinner deserves is not justice. It is tyranny.

Islam is all about not paying attention to what really matters in life. That's why Muslim countries are generally pathetic losers. Look at their governments. What would happen to Saudi Arabia if the oil fields dried up? Pakistan, which doesn't have that much oil, is already dwindling. Poor economy, poor government, high corruption, inflation, and illiteracy. The thing is, after all this reasoning, it is virtually impossible to knock sense into Muslims. They will think I am the evil who is trying to lead them astray.

Islam is very clever in trapping its believers.

Muhammad said:

> Abu Huraira reported Allah's Messenger (may peace be upon him) as saying: No baby is born but upon Fitra. It is his parents who make him a Jew or a Christian or a Polytheist. A person said: Allah's Messenger, what is your opinion if they were to die before that (before reaching the age of adolescence when they can distinguish between right and wrong)? He said: It is Allah alone Who knows what they would be doing.[4]

Regarding the above *hadith*, common sense says that it's not possible for a baby to be a Muslim before it is born. This is just crazy and, again, it's a tool for Islam to show that God is so powerful that he makes infants Muslims before they are born and it is their parents who make them non-Muslim. Crazy indeed. We are born into whatever religions our parents have. If they are Christians, we are born into Christianity. If Muslims, we are Muslims, too.

My current beliefs are agnostic, that is, there is a possibility of God's existence. If God exists, he can have only love for humans. He cannot hate or be angry with humans. Also, any religion that forces anything on people and any religion that says that it is the right religion and all the others are wrong is nonsense. A person has a right to live life his own way. He will not be punished for exercising his freedom of thought and action, except where he has harmed other humans in ways he would not like others to harm him.

At least the certain truth I know, that I have the freedom to live my life any way I want to, and Islam, the religion that does not recognize my freedom, can certainly go to hell.

I know it's difficult for Muslims to think of leaving Islam, which prescribes the death sentence to people who leave it. Notice that they are the ones most dangerous to Islam, because they have seen the dark valleys, and they know it inside out.

At first when I read about Muhammad being a pedophile, I felt maybe the writer had overreacted a bit. After all, if Muhammad was really a pedophile, the evidence that supported this would have to be very light and hard to find. I thought, How could the leader of the fastest-growing religion be a pedophile? It sounded impossible! But I was wrong. I did my own research and will present here some *hadith* from al-Bukhārī. The collection of hadith made by al-Bukhārī is regarded as the most authentic hadith collection in Islam.

> Narrated ʿĀʾisha: The Prophet and I used to take a bath from a single pot while we were Junub. During the menses, he used to order me to put on an Izar (dress worn below the waist) and used to fondle me. While in Itikaf, he used to bring his head near me and I would wash it while I used to be in my periods (menses).[5]

Don't forget that the Prophet was more than fifty-four at that time, fondling a little girl who was only between nine and eighteen years old. Considering the worst case, nine years old is still considered very young. Muslims give all kinds of justifications when asked about this topic.

> Narrated ʿĀʾisha: that the Prophet married her when she was six years old and he consummated his marriage when she was nine years old, and then she remained with him for nine years (i.e., till his death).[6]

> Narrated ʿĀʾisha: I used to play with the dolls in the presence of the Prophet, and my girl friends also used to play with me. When Allah's Apostle used to enter (my dwelling place) they used to hide themselves, but the Prophet would call them to join and play with me. (The playing with the dolls and similar images is forbidden, but it was allowed for *ʿĀʾisha* at that time, as she was a little girl, not yet reached the age of puberty.)[7]

I bet ʿĀʾisha, the Prophet's wife, had a crash course in having sex. The girl hadn't even finished playing with her dolls and here comes a fifty-one-year-old man with a long beard, and he wants to marry her so that he can fondle her! Muslims would rather go deaf and dumb than be informed that the person they hold very dear and sacred in their hearts was actually a pedophile. Another *hadith* shows how obsessed our "dear" Prophet was:

> Narrated Anas bin Malik: The Prophet used to pass by (have sexual relation with) all his wives in one night, and at that time he had nine wives.

The Prophet had sex nine times every night. The Prophet paid much attention to his sexual desires, as the following *hadith* will reveal:

> Narrated ʿĀʾisha: Whenever Allah's Apostle finished his ʿAsr prayer, he would enter upon his wives and stay with one of them. One day he went to Hafsa and stayed with her longer than usual.[9]

Another *hadith* that shows how much Muhammad thought about sex is:

Narrated Maimuna: "Whenever Allah's Apostle wanted to fondle any of his wives during the periods (menses), he used to ask her to wear an Izar."[10]

I don't need to say more. For the Prophet, fondling of his wives was a normal and routine thing, and that, too, during menstruation, which is a painful thing for many women.

Here is another *hadith* about the Prophet.

Narrated Zainab bint Abi Salama: Um-Salama said, "I got my menses while I was lying with the Prophet under a woolen sheet. So I slipped away, took the clothes for menses and put them on.

"Allah's Apostle said, 'Have you got your menses?' I replied, 'Yes.' Then he called me and took me with him under the woolen sheet." Um Salama further said, "The Prophet used to kiss me while he was fasting. The Prophet and I used to take the bath of Janaba from a single pot."[11]

Here are more hadith, describing ʿĀʾisha, Muhammad's nine-year-old wife:

Narrated ʿĀʾisha: Allah's Apostle said (to me), "You have been shown to me twice in (my) dreams. A man was carrying you in a silken cloth and said to me, 'This is your wife.' I uncovered it; and behold, it was you. I said to myself, 'If this dream is from Allah, He will cause it to come true.' "[12]

Muhammad married her, because he dreamed of her. Imagine a fifty-one-year-old guy dreaming of some six-year-old girl (the *hadith* says she was six when they got married, and at nine years the marriage was consummated). The amazing thing is that all of this is supported by authentic hadith.

Even though Muhammad liked to fondle and kiss woman and have sex with them nine times every night, in reality, he had a disgust for them and thought were inferior, lesser mortals. The only thing he saw as likeable in women was that they could fulfill his sexual desires. The following *hadith* is self-explanatory:

Narrated Abu Said Al-Khudri: Once Allah's Apostle went out to the Musalla (to offer the prayer) o 'Id-al-Adha or Al-Fitr prayer. Then he passed by the women and said, "O women! Give alms, as I have seen that the majority of the dwellers of Hell-fire were you (women)." They asked, "Why is it so, O Allah's Apostle?" He replied, "You curse frequently and are ungrateful to your husbands. I have not seen anyone more deficient in intelligence and religion than you. A cautious sensible man could be led astray by some of you." The women asked, "O Allah's Apostle! What is deficient in our intelligence and religion?" He said, "Is not the evidence of two women equal to the witness of one man?" They replied in the affirmative. He said, "This is the deficiency in her intelligence. Isn't it true that a woman can neither pray nor fast during her menses?" The women replied in the affirmative. He said, "This is the deficiency in her religion."[13]

So women, all over the world, take notice of how poorly the Prophet of Islam, Muhammad, thinks of you. Tell me, O women, is the menses your fault? No, it is a part of your feminine character and in no way does it make you inferior or less religious. If it did, like Muhammad said, more women will go to hell because they menstruate and in that time they cannot pray to God, then tell me, is it your fault? No, it is not!

O Muslim women, take heed from this! Islam is an evil religion. Do not teach your children to be Muslims; rather, teach them to think on their own, instead of blindly following this religion whose leader had a big sexual appetite and thought poorly of women. Not only this, but Islam has many other faults. O women, you are half the world, which is a big number! You can help to eradicate Islam, this evil lie. You are closer to your children than your husbands are. Do not teach the Koran to your children! If possible, keep them away from this hateful, oppressive manual as much as you can.

In almost every Koranic *ayah*, the end is usually something like: "and Allah is Mighty, Wise." This is what brainwashes Muslims and stops them from doubting or having second thoughts about that particular *ayah*. The Koran wants its believers to believe all it says, without asking any questions or having doubts. If they doubt, they are threatened with "eternal hellfire." Here is a pseudo-*ayah* to illustrate:

And live life like losers and do not follow the transgressors. Verily, those who were not god-fearing, will have a painful end. And Allah is Mighty, Wise.

This is a bottom line of every Koranic *ayah*, for those who choose to see. Islam commands all to live life like losers. Those who don't follow Koran will suffer in the end. Anyone who feels a question coming to his mind: Live life like losers? Why? is hushed into silence by scaring him with God's might and wrath. Using your own head in Islam, to decide whether a certain *ayah* is valid or not, is not encouraged. The transgressor is he who thinks with his head. Here is a *hadith* that again, shows how much respect Muhammad had for woman, and how deep his thinking "really" was:

Narrated Sahl bin Sad As-Sa'idi: A woman came to Allah's Apostle and said, "O Allah's Apostle! I have come to give you myself in marriage (without Mahr)." Allah's Apostle looked at her. He looked at her carefully and fixed his glance on her and then lowered his head. When the lady saw that he did not say anything, she sat down. A man from his companions got up and said, "O Allah's Apostle! If you are not in need of her, then marry her to me." The Prophet said, "Have you got anything to offer?" The man said, "No, by Allah, O Allah's Apostle!" The Prophet said (to him), "Go to your family and see if you have something." The man went and returned, saying, "No, by Allah, I have not found anything." Allah's Apostle said, "(Go again) and look for something, even if it is an iron ring." He went again and returned, saying, "No, by Allah, O Allah's Apostle! I could not find even an iron ring, but this is my Izar (waist sheet) ." He had no rida. He added, "I give half of it to her." Allah's Apostle said, "What will she do with your Izar? If you wear it, she will be naked, and if she wears it, you will be naked." So that man sat down for a long while and then got up (to depart). When Allah's Apostle saw him going, he ordered that he be called back. When he came, the Prophet said, "How much of the Quran do you know?" He said, "I know such Sura and such Sura," counting them. The Prophet said, "Do you know them by heart?" He replied, "Yes." The Prophet said, "Go, I marry her to you for that much of the Quran which you have."[14]

In the *hadith* above, the woman was married to a certain man just because he knew a bit of the Koran. And she was never asked if she wanted to marry him or not. How degrading for a woman!

A *hadith* that shows Muhammad sees only four things in a woman: her wealth, her family status, her beauty and her religion. What about the goodness of heart, which matters the most?

Narrated Abu Huraira: The Prophet said, "A woman is married for four things, i.e., her wealth, her family status, her beauty and her religion. So you should marry the religious woman (otherwise) you will be a losers."[15]

Here are *hadith* where Muhammad says that women are evil omen:

Narrated Abdullah bin ʿUmar: Allah's Apostle said, "Evil omen is in the women, the house and the horse."[16]

Narrated Usama bin Zaid: The Prophet said, "After me I have not left any affliction more harmful to men than women."[17]

Even the Koran says that women are a degree lower than men, and men have authority over women. Also, the Koran wants women to be obedient to their spouses, just like slaves are to their masters (IV.34). Muhammad says that if a woman wants to be more religious, she cannot be so without the permission of her husband:

Narrated Abu Huraira: The Prophet said, "A woman should not fast (optional fasts) except with her husband's permission if he is at home (staying with her)."[18]

On top of this, as we already know, Muhammad says the majority of women will be in hell. To anyone who wants to be a Muslim woman I say, O Muslim women of the world: wake up! Do not let your life go to waste anymore! See the truth! Do not accept a religion that thinks so poorly of you! Islam is the religion of the devil! Allah is all-knowing and wise (emulating the same brainwashing tool used by the Koran). A woman also has to fulfill the sexual desires of her husband. Man's desires are above her own and if she does not agree to fulfilling her husbands desires, then angels will curse her:

> Narrated Abu Huraira: The Prophet said, "If a man Invites his wife to sleep with him and she refuses to come to him, then the angels send their curses on her till morning."[19]

Can these words be coming from a prophet of God? No. He was not a prophet. He was a great, clever liar. Now I will give some Koranic *ayahs* here, which show what Islam thinks of women. I have quoted the full *ayahs*, to show the true context. These *ayahs* show clearly that women are thought of something lesser than man and they have fewer rights as well.

> And the divorced women should keep themselves in waiting for three courses; and it is not lawful for them that they should conceal what Allah has created in their wombs, if they believe in Allah and the last day; and their husbands have a better right to take them back in the meanwhile if they wish for reconciliation; and they have rights similar to those against them in a just manner, *and the men are a degree above them*, and Allah is Mighty, Wise. (II.228)

Here is an *ayah* that says the testimony of two women is equal to the testimony of one man:

> O you who believe! When you deal with each other in contracting a debt for a fixed time, then write it down; and let a scribe write it down between you with fairness; and the scribe should not refuse to write as Allah has taught him, so he should write; and let him who owes the debt dictate, and he should be careful of (his duty to) Allah, his Lord, and not diminish anything from it; but if he who owes the debt is unsound in understanding, or weak, or (if) he is not able to dictate himself, let his guardian dictate with fairness; and call in to witness from among your men two witnesses; *but if there are not two men, then one man and two women* from among those whom you choose to be witnesses, so that if one of the two errs, the second of the two may remind the other; and the witnesses should not refuse when they are summoned; and be not averse to writing it (whether it is) small or large, with the time of its falling due; this is more equitable in the sight of Allah and assures greater accuracy in testimony, and the nearest (way) that you may not entertain doubts (afterwards), except when it is ready merchandise which

you give and take among yourselves from hand to hand, then there is no blame on you in not writing it down; and have witnesses when you barter with one another, and let no harm be done to the scribe or to the witness; and if you do (it) then surely it will be a transgression in you, and be careful of (your duty) to Allah, Allah teaches you, and Allah knows all things. (II.282)

Here is an *ayah* that allows this scene to happen: A man hates his wife so much that he wants to get rid of her. He can call four of his friends and everyone will testify that the woman was involved in sexual indecency. Then she can be confined in a place without food and water until she dies. Imagine the state of the woman's mind. Why is the same thing not provided for woman?

And as for those who are guilty of an indecency from among your women, *call to witnesses against them four (witnesses) from among you*; then if they bear witness confine them to the houses until death takes them away or Allah opens some way for them. (IV.15)

Wife battering is allowed in Islam:

Men are in charge of women, because Allah hath made the one of them to excel the other, and because they spend of their property (for the support of women). So good women are the obedient, guarding in secret that which Allah hath guarded. As for those from whom ye fear rebellion, admonish them and banish them to beds apart, and *scourge them*. Then if they obey you, seek not a way against them. Lo! Allah is ever High, Exalted, Great. (IV.34)

In Islam, inheritance for a woman is half the inheritance of a man:

Allah (thus) directs you as regards your Children's (Inheritance): *to the male, a portion equal to that of two females*: if only daughters, two or more, their share is two-thirds of the inheritance; if only one, her share is a half. For parents, a sixth share of the inheritance to each, if the deceased left children; if no children, and the parents are the (only) heirs, the mother has a third; if the deceased Left brothers (or sisters) the mother has a sixth. The distribution in all cases(s) after the payment of legacies and debts. Ye know not whether your parents or your children are nearest to you in benefit. These are settled portions ordained by Allah; and Allah is All-knowing, Al-wise. (IV.11)

In what your wives leave, your share is a half, if they leave no child; but if they leave a child, ye get a fourth; after payment of legacies and debts. In what ye leave, their share is a fourth, if ye leave no child; but if ye leave a child, they get an eighth; after payment of legacies and debts. If the man or woman whose inheritance is in question, has left neither ascendants nor descendants, but has left a brother or a sister, each one of the two gets a sixth; but if more than two, they share in a third; after payment of legacies and debts; so that no loss is caused (to any one). Thus is it ordained by Allah; and Allah is All-knowing, Most Forbearing. (IV.12)

THE UNIVERSAL DECLARATION OF HUMAN RIGHTS COMPARED TO ISLAM

The principles of Islam are against those promulgated by the United Nations (UN). The Universal Declaration of Human Rights (1948) says:

Article 1:

> All human beings are born free and equal in dignity and rights.

Article 18:

> Everyone has the right to freedom of thought, conscience and religion; this right includes freedom to change his religion or belief, and freedom, either alone or in community with others and in public or private, to manifest his religion or belief in teaching, practice, worship and observance.

But Allah and the Prophet say the opposite:

> Prophet, *make war on the unbelievers* and the hypocrites and deal rigorously with them. Hell shall be their home: an evil fire. They swear by God that they said nothing. *Yet they uttered the word of unbelief and renounced Islam after embracing it.* They sought to do what they could not attain. Yet they had no reason to be spiteful except perhaps because God and His apostle had enriched them through His bounty. If they repent, it will indeed be better for them, but if they give no heed, God will sternly punish them, both in this world and in the world to come. They shall have none on this earth to protect or help them. (IX.73,74)

> Narrated Abu Bruda: Abu Musa said. . . . Behold there was a fettered man beside Abu Musa. Muadh asked, "Who is this (man)?" Abu Musa said, *"He was a Jew and became a Muslim and then reverted back to Judaism."* Then Abu Musa requested Muadh to sit down but Muadh said, "I will not sit down till he has been killed. This is the judgment of Allah and his messenger," and repeated it thrice. Then Abu Musa ordered that the man be killed, and *he was killed.* Abu Musa added, "Then we discussed the night prayers."[20]

Narrated Ali: "Whenever I tell you a narration from Allah's messenger, by Allah, I would rather fall down from the sky, then ascribe a false statement to him, but if I tell you something between me and you, (not a Hadith), then it was indeed a trick (i.e., I may say things just to cheat my enemy). No doubt I heard Allah's messenger saying, "During the last days there will appear some young foolish people, who will say the best words, but their faith will not go beyond their throats (i.e., they will leave the faith) and will go out from their religion as an arrow goes out of the game. So, *wherever you find them, kill them, for whoever kills them shall have reward on the Day of Resurrection.*"[21]

Almost all Muslim countries mention in their constitutions that they believe in Allah and that the principles and laws set up in the country shall follow what is in the Koran and *sunnah*. For example, the preamble to Pakistan's constitution says:

Whereas sovereignty over the entire Universe belongs to Almighty Allah alone, and the authority to be exercised by the people of Pakistan within the limits prescribed by Him is a sacred trust; wherein the Muslims shall be enabled to order their lives in the individual and collective spheres in accordance with the teachings and requirements of Islam *as set out in the Holy Quran and Sunnah.*

Iran says in its constitution:

1. Continuous *ijtihād* of the *fuqahā'* possessing necessary qualifications, exercised *on the basis of the Qur'an and the Sunnah* of the Ma'sumun, upon all of whom be peace.

The Saudi Arabian constitution says:

Article 1: The Kingdom of Saudi Arabia is a sovereign Arab Islamic state with Islam as its religion; *God's Book and the Sunnah of His Prophet,* God's prayers and peace be upon him, are its constitution, Arabic is its language and Riyadh is its capital.

As you can see, the Muslim states profess their belief in the *sunnah* (*hadith*) and the Koran. The Koran and *hadith* also teach religious intolerance, as the above *hadith* and *ayahs* show. Thus, all these Muslim countries are abiding by constitutions that violate human rights and the principles of the UN. They have two options: (1) Change their constitutions and no longer involve the Koran or (2) change the Koran and declare that these verses are invalid from now on. Of course, that would not happen easily, but I'm just mentioning that it should. The changing of the Koran or the deletion of the Koran from the constitutions of the Muslim countries could begin the eventual, much-needed downfall of Islam.

Someone might think, If there is no Islam, then what is there? Christianity?

No. All religions that command humans are wrong, because freedom is the basic right of every human being. The UN also says this in article 1 of its Universal Declaration of Human Rights.

We are all human beings, born free to exercise our minds and bodies in ways that do not harm others. This is the only principle that humans are required to commit to, and it takes only common sense to deduce this. Do not do to another human what you would not want others to do to you. One does not need any religion to tell her this. We need to live simple lives. We need to love more and hate less. We need to be happy and satisfied and live in peace, like a loving family.

God or no God, there is certainly one truth: Islam is false. If there is God, then one possibility is that Islam was the tool of the devil, to lead men astray. The Koran says that Satan promised God that he would lead men astray. So, in the big picture, this is what is happening. Men are being turned into egotistic losers, while women are never given the chance to take advantage of opportunities, as the religion itself degrades woman and says that they are below man. Islam is the trap of the devil. It's the fastest-growing trap, too. If humankind needs to live in peace, all forceful religions, including Islam, must be eradicated from the earth. Islam is the religion whose believers hate the most, too, because believers of Islam in the extreme sense perform *jihad*, kill people in the name of religion and many other things. Of all the religions on Earth, Islam is the one that has the most hatred for nonbelievers. The results are observed by seeing the disastrous effects of Islamic terrorism in the world. It's true that most Muslims are peaceful human beings, but any person who truly follows Islam is required to

- hate non-Muslims vehemently; or, in the peaceful form, have a dislike and disgust for non-Muslims;
- fear an invisible God;
- be unhappy with her life, because she is, in reality, a slave to Allah, the imaginary God;
- live his life in vain.

Islam makes the whole of humanity—Muslims and non-Muslims—suffer. Peaceful Muslims become victims of the oppressive psyche of Islam, which sucks all the life out of them, while non-Muslims are made to suffer at the hands of Islamic terrorists. This world cannot rest until Islam and all other oppressive religions have been eradicated. Please think deeply about Islam. Do not take things for granted. Do not assume that the Koran is from God. I know that you all want to believe in God, because it's a survival instinct that we don't want to die. We want to keep living after we die. And to support this life-after-death philosophy, Islam and many other religions were created, sometimes due to creativity of man and sometimes due to man's desire to subjugate others. God might exist, but no one knows, since there is no proof to support his existence or absence. But certainly, Allah is not and cannot be a God. I wish you peace and inner happiness.

NOTES

1. Online Islamic resources can be found at many Web sites. One good, popular source is the Islamic Server of MSA/USC at www.usc.edu/dept/MSA.

2. I know now that Allah is a false, imaginary god, a creation of Muhammad's mind. *God* is a general term and, in reality, I know there is no religion from God and no one can scientifically prove or disprove the existence of a god.

3. al-Bukhārī, *Book of* Nikah *(Wedlock)*, vol. 7, book 62 of *Ṣaḥīḥ*, trans. M. Muhsin Khan (New Delhi: Kitab Bhavan, 1987), Hadith no. 670, pp. 450–51.

4. al-Bukhārī, *Book of Destiny*, vol. 4, book 31 of *Ṣaḥīḥ*, trans. Abdul Hamid Siddiqi (New Delhi: Kitab Bhavan, 1987), Hadith no. 6426, pp. 1398–99.

5. al-Bukhārī, *Book of Menses*, vol. 1, book 6 of *Ṣaḥīḥ*, trans. M. Muhsin Khan (New Delhi: Kitab Bhavan, 1987), Hadith no. 298, p. 180.

6. al-Bukhārī, *Book of* Nikah *(Wedlock)*, Hadith no. 64, p. 50.

7. al-Bukhārī, *Book of Good Manners* (al-Adab*)*, vol. 8, book 72 of *Ṣaḥīḥ*, trans. M. Muhsin Khan (New Delhi: Kitab Bhavan, 1987), Hadith no. 151, p. 95.

8. al-Bukhārī, *Book of* Nikah *(Wedlock)*, Hadith no. 142, p. 106.

9. Ibid., Hadith no. 143, pp. 106–107.

10. al-Bukhārī, *Book of Menses*, Hadith no. 300, p. 181.

11. Ibid., Hadith no. 319, pp. 191–92.

12. al-Bukhārī, *Book of* Nikah *(Wedlock)*, Hadith no. 15, p. 10.

13. al-Bukhārī, *Book of Menses*, Hadith no. 301, pp. 181–82.

14. al-Bukhārī, *Book of* Nikah *(Wedlock)*, Hadith no. 24, pp. 15–16.

15. Ibid., Hadith no. 27, pp. 18–19.

16. Ibid., Hadith no. 30, p. 21.

17. Ibid., Hadith no. 33, p. 22.

18. Ibid., Hadith no. 120, pp. 92–93.

19. Ibid., Hadith no. 121, p. 93.

20. al-Bukhārī, *Book of Apostates*, vol. 9, book 84 of *Ṣaḥīḥ*, trans. M. Muhsin Khan (New Delhi: Kitab Bhavan, 1987), Hadith no. 58, pp. 45–46.

21. Ibid., Hadith no. 64, p. 50.

15

ISLAMIC TERRORISM
AND THE GENOCIDE
IN BANGLADESH
Abul Kasem (Bangladesh)

As a young child I was brought up in a very strict Islamic way. My parents were devout Muslims, although not fanatics. I used to see them praying frequently, although at that very tender age I could understand very little of all the Islamic rituals they used to practice, like praying, fasting, paying *Zakat, fitrah*, and so on. My most memorable days were on the Eid day, when we used to wake up very early in the morning, wear our new dresses, eat special dishes prepared by my mum, then go to *Idgah* with my dad for the Eid prayer. I did not understand a single word of what the *imam* was saying or why the people were doing their body movements. When I asked my dad any question he used to tell me to keep quiet and that Allah will punish those kids who ask too many questions. Thus, I was introduced to the fear from the very beginning of my childhood. When I reached around seven or eight years, my father started to teach me Arabic in a very rudimentary way. He was not an expert in Arabic but had sufficient ability to read the Koran in Arabic.

After I finished learning the basic Arabic language, in about six to nine months' time, I was introduced to the Koran. I was forced to wake up every early morning and read the Koran with my older sister, who was quite good at it. My father and older sister used to guide me and correct my pronunciations. It was an unbearable tyranny to me. I dreaded waking up each morning and facing the

Koran. Once in a while I used to pretend to be sick just to avoid the daily morning chore. I was beaten by my father on many occasions for this trick. I was also admonished severely for not being able to pronounce Koranic verses in the correct way. This was really a torture to me. Many a time I used to ask my sister and father about the meanings of the verses. They had no idea. They only read the Koran without understanding a single verse. I was told to memorize the verses and never ask any questions on the Koran. Allah would surely punish me if I ask any questions on the Koran or any other matter about Islam.

Then I was introduced to *wudu* and prayer rituals. This was another torture to my young mind. I lost my childlike enthusiasm, exuberance, and curiosity. Islam became a great burden for me to carry, although I never complained or showed my displeasure for fear of being punished for transgression. I used to follow my dad every Friday to *Jumaa* prayer although I understood very little of why must I do that ritual.

That was how I was introduced to Islam. I was also brainwashed by the bombardment that Islam was the only religion for humankind and that Hindus and Christians are our enemies. I believed those words, spoken by my parents and relatives, and never questioned them.

After finishing my primary education I went to high school. The high school was in a small town in Bangladesh called Chandpur. There was a sizable number of Hindu students in my class. At first I avoided mixing with them, for I remembered of what I was taught during my childhood days. To my great surprise, I found that most of these Hindu students were quite friendly and would like to play and study with me. So I started to mix with them. Those were the young and innocent days of childhood, when most of us discarded the racial/religious prejudices and embraced any one who was friendly. At this stage I started to think about what I had been programmed on Islam.

RELIGIOUS RIOT AND THE SLAUGHTER OF A FRIEND

Now I am going to describe a few incidents that forced me to think about religion in general and Islam in particular.

I started to question the necessity of religion in our lives and the inhuman and illogical practices in many religions, including Islam. You might wonder what triggered my distaste for religion. It all started in my school days when I witnessed the slaughter of a dear Hindu friend of mine (along with his entire family) in Chandpur, Bangladesh. I can never erase that memory from my mind. That was a devastating experience. But more shocking was that many Muslims were actually happy about that slaughter and even went further, supporting the idea that we (Muslims) should kill more Hindus because the Muslims in India are being slaughtered, too. It was also declared by some Muslim clerics that killing of non-Muslims is an act of *jihad* and therefore anyone participating in *jihad* will be rewarded with heaven. At that tender age I knew very little of Islam and nothing about other religions. However, the little conscience inside me told me that what was being done and what was being practiced were not right. However, I had little power to change the course of events.

I personally visited the house of my slain friend and found that all the members of his family, including his parents, brothers, and sisters, were killed by axes and swords. I saw pools of blood in their kitchen and bathroom, where they hid to save their lives. The incident happened in the dead of night and no one came to help them. When I went back to my school, I was extremely ashamed in front of my Hindu friends. I was speechless and could say nothing. I feared that my Hindu friends might one day attack me. To my great surprise I found that my Hindu friends did not really bother very much and treated me as usual.

NIGHTS AND DAYS OF PAKISTANI BUTCHERS: REMEMBERING THIS BLOODY DAY AFTER THREE DECADES

This incident involves my life itself. I nearly died when Pakistani soldiers and their fanatic supporters attacked the university residential halls on the dark night of March 25, 1971. Here is my recollection of that horrifying experience.

In 1971 I was a final-year civil engineering student at East Pakistan University of Engineering and Technology (EPUET; now Bangladesh University of Engineering and Technology [BUET]). We were about to graduate when the political turmoil in East Pakistan got started. As we were preparing for our final examination, the university was closed due to the unrest all around us. The events I am about to tell brought into the fore one more time the inhuman butchery and atrocities committed by the Pakistani Islamic army as I witnessed with my own eyes. This was the most horrific experience of my life and, to put it mildly, had a profound impact on my views on religion and politics.

On the evening of March 25, 1971, I was staying at Shere-e-Bangla Hall of EPUET. Just a few days before that, political problems engulfed East Pakistan as General Yahya steadfastly refused to accept the mandate of the people of East Pakistan for full autonomy. The students were on strike. But it was exam time and I was preparing for my final-year examination, as I said it before. However, due to the political unrest the examination was canceled and many students had left the residential halls and went back home. I was, though, actively involved in student politics. Therefore, I decided to stay put in the hall so that should a need arise I would be available to join the movement. A few days before March 25 there were persistent rumors in the air that the talk between Mujib and General

Yahya was not progressing well and that there was the possibility of a military crackdown looming on the horizon. However, the government media cleverly played down this rumor by insisting that the talks were fruitful. Some newspapers even suggested that General Yahya was prepared to hand over the power to a civilian government, where both Bhutto and Mujib would have major roles. With this type of misleading information, many people thought that at last the Bengalis would have a chance to taste their freedom after a struggle of about thirteen years. But that did not happen. On the fateful night of March 25, 1971, the Pakistani Islamic army came out from the cantonment with fury to teach the Bengalis a lesson that they would never forget. And surely they never did.

This is my very personal recount of the nights and days on and immediately after March 25, 1971.

I went to bed a bit early, around 9:00 P.M. I had been quite tired all day and I quickly fell asleep. Suddenly, at around 11:00 P.M., my deep slumber was disturbed by the noise of constant barrage of gunfire. At first I thought that it must be firecrackers by Bengalis to celebrate their victory. But soon I realized my mistake. I opened the window. It was very dark. Not even the dim streetlights were burning. But I could barely see numerous military vehicles moving around, carrying soldiers with their automatic rifles. Occasionally, I could see very bright searchlights mounted on some of the military trucks and Jeeps. Many soldiers were running and shooting in the street. I saw that a large convoy of military vehicles had surrounded the whole of the EPUET area. As far as my eyes could go, I could see military men all around the campus. I could even hear the army people talking loudly in Urdu downstairs in our hall. I immediately knew what was going on. I thanked my lucky stars that I had switched off the room light before I went to bed. There was deafening noise from the machine guns and automatic rifles, which were not too far from where I stood. I could not believe what was going on. I was alone in the room; there was nobody to comfort me on that fateful night. Panic-stricken, I started trembling and fell down on my bed.

All of a sudden, a hail of bullets shattered the nearby window. The bullets hit the ceiling and walls and then hit the floor. A thought passed through my mind: I was going to die. Without thinking much I went under my bed to protect against stray bullets. I lay on my chest and grabbed the floor as if that was my life. The firing continued incessantly for almost the whole night. Then, suddenly, there was a lull. No machine gun or rifle sound. I thought it was over. I slowly came out from my hiding place and sat on my bed. I looked at my wristwatch. I could not see very well. It was 3:00 A.M. or so, I guessed. Suddenly, there was an extremely loud noise and the whole area was brightly lit. I could not resist looking. What I saw through the shattered window pane was utterly unbelievable. I saw a military tank throwing fire on the slums (*Bastee*). The slum was just next to our halls along the old railway track. I saw people running out of their hovels. As the slum dwellers came out to escape the fire, the Pakistani Islamic soldiers started shooting them with a machine gun that was mounted on a military truck. I could see only one truck with the machine gun near our hall, but I am sure there were many more on other sides as I could see the fires from these machine guns dropping like August showers in the darkness of the spring night. It was something I have seen only on TV and in movies about the Vietnam War. I could hear the desperate cries for help from those hapless victims. I closed the window, thinking that one of those bullets would be enough for me. I sat on the floor and suddenly realized that this was it. There was no escape for me.

Time passed and slowly the morning broke the silence of the eerie night. I could still see the military people from my window. I switched on my transistor radio at a very low volume to hear what was going on. The Dhaka radio station was dead. I switched to the Calcutta radio station. There was no mention of the affairs in East Pakistan, except that General Yahya Khan had left Dhaka after the final talks with Mujib. So I switched to Karachi. Now I got the news that I wanted so desperately to hear. There was a special announcement that General Yahya was going to speak to the nation. I heard him speaking. It was the voice of a heavily drunken person. I cannot recall all that he said, but there are a few words that I still remember. These words were: "Mujib's act is an act of treason. He will not go unpunished." Yahya Khan ended by saying that Mujib would be tried by a special military tribunal and punished. The news announced that Sheik Mujibur Rahman, along with Dr. Kamal Hussain, had been arrested and taken to West Pakistan for the trial. I also heard Bhutto saying, "Thank God. Pakistan was saved."

Meanwhile, the fire in the slum continued and I noticed a strange odor in the air. It took me some time to figure out that it was the smell of burning flesh. I did not hear any fire brigade siren, although there was a fire brigade office just next to our hall in the Palashi suburb. It was almost 8:00 A.M. and the fire slowly started to diminish after devouring the nearby shantytown. From my window I could see the tank moving away from our area. I again lay on my bed and started to search other radio stations for news. Suddenly, I heard soft knocking on my door. I froze. I felt that my blood circulation had suddenly stopped. In front of my eyes I saw nothing but white. I could not move from my bed. I just lay still. After a while there was another knock. Now it struck my mind that if it was the army they would not wait for my response. They would simply burst through my door and start shooting. There must be someone else, I guessed. So I went near the window close to the door and looked. I saw Monju, my next-door neighbor, crawling on his chest near my door. I gingerly opened a little of the door and asked him what was wrong. He whispered to me that something was wrong with his roommate, Ashraf. Monju asked me to follow him to his room. I opened the door silently and slowly crawled on my chest to Monju's room. I found Ashraf lying on the floor with his eyes wide open, but his mouth was shut and he was vigorously shivering. There was water all over. I asked Monju why was there so much water on the floor. Monju replied that it was not water. It was Ashraf's urine. He told me that Ashraf had urinated several times and now he could not talk. I called Ashraf very softly. He just stared at me but could not say anything. I knew what had happened. Ashraf had had a nervous breakdown. I told Monju that we should keep whispering to him that the military is gone and we are safe. Surprisingly, after we whispered to him for about fifteen to twenty minutes, Ashraf started to murmur a few words. After a while he simply whispered, "Please, please, do not leave me." I told Ashraf that whatever happened the three of us would remain together. If we died, we would die together. This assurance from us made Ashraf slowly come back to normal. All of us were very hungry and thirsty. So we ate stale bread and drank some water. Then we talked about how each of us passed the dreaded night.

It was around midday and we found that all the military personnel had left our area. There was no sound of gunfire, no sound of military trucks or vehicles. In fact, there was an eerie unbearable silence all around the campus. No buses, no rickshaws, no cars; hardly any people on the streets. We thought that it was our best opportunity to escape from the hall. We tuned our radio to AIR and heard about the indefinite curfew in Dhaka. But we decided to escape no matter what happened, even if that meant breaking the curfew and being shot at by the military. We decided that I would go to Monju's apartment at Azimpur government quarters. Both Monju and Ashraf used to live at Azimpur quarters. I crawled back to my room, put on my shoes, and grabbed my transistor radio. The three of us then slowly started to climb down the stairs, hiding ourselves as much as we could.

We went to the ground floor. To our disappointment we found the entry/exit gate was locked. The guards had locked the gate and fled. Later on, we realized that this action by the hall guards actually had saved our lives. In frustration, we came back to our rooms on the second floor. Then we decided to go to first floor and jump from the balcony. At first we thought of leaving the radios behind. Then we realized that the radio was the only means by which we would know what was going on in East Pakistan. The three of us then jumped into the garden. Luckily, the jump was a success. Then we quickly ran. While running across the hall compound, we saw the gruesome scenes of killing by the Pakistani Islamic army. In Liaquat Hall (I suppose it is Titumeer Hall now, but I'm not sure) we saw plenty of blood and a dead body, possibly the guard's. (Later, I learned that four students were killed at Liaquat Hall.) We quickly ran to the fire brigade center in Palashi. The center was very close to our residential hall. We thought of taking temporary refuge in fire brigade building before proceeding to the Azimpur colony. There was a small mosque inside the fire brigade compound. I saw four dead bodies there. All were riddled with numerous bullet holes. The floor of the mosque was flooded with blood. I thought that some fire brigade people tried to take shelter in the mosque, hoping that the Pakistanis would not commit murder in a place of worship. But how wrong they were! We saw many other dead bodies on the compound of the fire brigade. Some dead bodies were inside the fire brigade trucks and ambulance. They must have taken shelter inside these vehicles, hoping to escape the onslaught. Most likely none of the fire brigade people survived. Then we arrived at the road that separates the Azimpur colony from the Palashi. On the road we found many dead bodies scattered everywhere, mainly of rickshaw pullers.

There was a high wall at the entry of the Azimpur colony. We did not know what to do at that point. The curfew was on and if any army people saw us they surely would kill us. We had no choice but to jump over the wall. To our utter surprise, we jumped over the wall and fell on the other side of the wall. I still do not know how I did that. May be our adrenaline was running high after all that happened to us. I am sure that if I had to jump that wall again, I would fail.

After jumping inside the Azimpur colony we felt a little safer and we all heaved a great sigh of relief. Monju suggested that I go and stay with him. Ashraf was too nervous to say anything. So we escorted Ashraf to his quarters and then Monju and I headed toward Monju's apartment. When Monju's father and mother saw us they simply held us tight and started crying. We quickly went inside the bedroom and told our story. Monju's father said that they were certain that the Pakistani army had killed us as he had witnessed the army operation from the window. We realized how lucky we really were to be alive after that fateful night. Monju's mother prepared some food for us. We were extremely hungry. I finished all the food served to me. During this time we did not hear much gunfire in the area of Azimpur. But we could hear the nonstop machine gun firing in the distance. We carefully opened the window a little bit. All we saw was smoke and fire all around, a little away from Azimpur. We guessed that it was the Old Dhaka area, possibly near the Buriganga River and Sadarghat. After the liberation, it was found that the killing and destruction done by the Pakistani Islamic military was one of the worst in the Old Dhaka area. They killed virtually every person in the Hindu-dominated Shankari Patti in the Old Dhaka area. The fire and smoke were so terrible that at night the whole sky was red. In the evening we ate some food and we tried to sleep. But none of us could shut our eyelids. The whole night we searched the world on radio. At last we got news from the BBC of what was going on in East Pakistan. The Dhaka radio station was working again, playing mainly Urdu patriotic songs and Islamic verses. We were now sure that our dream of a free nation had suddenly vanished. The Pakistani army had captured us as slaves. The whole night we mostly talked about what would happen to the Bengalis since all our struggle was in vain. Finally, the morning came. At around 9:00 A.M. we heard on Dhaka radio that the curfew had been relaxed for six hours only. We found many people on the street. I suggested to Monju that I should go home and see if my family members were alive. As our house was in Nakhalpara (very close to cantonment and the airport), Monju and his parents were very reluctant that I should take the risk. However, after my constant insistence they let me go, but reminded me to return immediately to them if I had problems. I can never repay their debt. You can tell they were really concerned about me.

So I came open in the street. I found people all around me. No buses, no trucks. Hardly any rickshaws plying the street. There were occasional cars and military vehicles with fierce-looking soldiers and machine-gun-mounted trucks and Jeeps. I asked some people where were they headed to. Most of them replied that they did not know. They simply wanted to leave the city and go to villages where they felt they would be safe. Many of them headed toward Sadarghat, hoping that they could catch a steamer or a launch to go to the villages. I also did not know what to do. Since there was no transport I would have to walk all the way to Nakhalpara. I thought of going back to Monju's place. Then I changed my mind when I found that thousands of people are walking, many of them barefoot and with nothing but their clothes on. So I also started walking. Whatever happens to these people will also happen to me, I thought. The first place I came was Iqbal Hall (now Sergeant Zahurul Hall, I believe). The scene I saw in Iqbal Hall was beyond any description! The whole area was like a battlefield. I knew that Dhaka University Central Students' Union (DUCSU) vice president Tofail Ahmed used to live there. There were holes on the walls created by mortar shells. Those holes were visible from afar. When I arrived at the playground of the hall, I saw about thirty dead bodies all lined up for display to the public. Many of the dead bodies were beyond recognition due to innumerable bullet holes on their faces. That was a gruesome sight. Many people started crying. My friend Jafar used to live in Iqbal Hall. I did not see his body. Later I learned that his dead body was found in his bed. Needless to say, the displayed corpses were merely a small fraction of the students that Pakistani Islamic army had murdered in Iqbal Hall on that dreadful night. They simply displayed a few corpses to frighten and to break the morale of all Bengalis.

Anyway, I had to hurry along. I started to walk again and came to the central Shaheed Minar.* I saw that the entire Shaheed Minar was nothing but a heap of rubble. Many people could not believe what they saw. The army had totally destroyed the Shaheed Minar using powerful explosives, I guessed. Among all the cruelties inflicted on the Bengalis that night, I think the destruction of the central Shaheed Minar was the cruelest of all. I noticed some blood on the smooth, shiny floor of the Shaheed Minar, but I did not see any dead bodies. Maybe the Pakistani Islamic army decided to remove the corpses from the street area so that

---

*The Shaheed Minar was a tower constructed in Dhaka in memory of the dozens of protesters killed during the language movement in 1952. It became an important national symbol and annual celebrations took place around it.

their movement wouldn't be affected. I really cried when I saw the Shaheed Minar. Even the displayed corpses at Iqbal Hall could not bring tears to my eyes and make me cry. But I could not hold my tears when I saw the corpse of the Shaheed Minar. The shock was much too much for me.

I started to walk again and came to Jagannath Hall. The entire Jagannath Hall compound was like another battlefield. I saw the footprints of tractor vehicles. There were huge holes in the walls of the Jagannath Hall. I guessed that the army had used tanks in Jagannath Hall. In front of the Jagannath Hall lawn I saw a huge mass grave. The grave was so fresh and shallow that we could see some half-buried corpses. Some hands and feet were protruding from under the soil. It was a grotesque scene, to put it mildly. I do not know how many people were buried there. Judging from the size of the grave, my guess was at least a few hundred. After the liberation of Bangladesh many of us saw the video footage of this brutality of the Pakistani Islamic army. The video was taken secretly by a brave EPUET (now BUET) professor from the window of his apartment.

By the side of Jagannath Hall there was a small, narrow road. On the side of this road and on behind the back of Rokeya Hall there were a large number of washermen (*dhopa*) who used to live in small quarters with their families. Their number could be around fifty or more. I found that the Pak army had burned down the entire area. I could see the charred bodies of children and adults still in their burned beds. On the side of the *dhopa* quarter and by the side of the road, I saw another freshly dug shallow mass grave. I could see the feet and hands of children and adults sticking out from the grave, trying to tell the entire world what happened to them. All who passed by saw this terrible sight and shook their heads in utter disbelief.

After a long and tiring walk, I came to the Shahbag Hotel (now the Institute of Post-Graduate Medicine and Research). The building was intact. I looked at the Dhaka radio station. No sign of devastation, although there was heavy military guard, including tanks and armored vehicles, around the radio station. There was no damage to the Inter-Continental Hotel (now the Sheraton Dhaka). Then I came to the office of the daily newspaper the *People*. My friend Obaid was a subeditor with the *People*. Naturally I went to find his whereabouts. What I saw was unbelievable. The entire office of the *People*, along with a few shop houses, was burned to ashes. The place was still smoldering. When I went a little closer, I saw many dead bodies burned like charcoal. They were absolutely unrecognizable; only their shapes said that they were human. The area was filled with the smell of burned flesh. I do not know the fate of Obaid. I have still not heard anything about him, so I assume that he was burned alive in that inferno.

I came out from the ruins of the *People* office. As I was walking past the fashionable Sakura Restaurant (I am not sure if the restaurant is still in business or not), a car suddenly stopped near me. I was astonished to see my father, mother, and sisters all inside the car. My mother and sisters were weeping. My father asked me to get inside the car. My mother simply hugged me and started to cry loudly. I asked my father what had happened. My father said they were simply fortunate to be alive. Then he told me that we were all going to Dhanmondi to stay with our grandfather. My mother told me that she never expected to see me again, as they had heard that the army had killed each and every student in the residential halls.

Soon we arrived at my grandfather's house. My grandfather was happy to see us alive. We ate some food, then my mother narrated their fateful night of March 25.

So this was how it happened at our home on March 25, 1971. This was how Islam invaded our home and drove us out. The account was based on what I heard from my mother.

Around midnight everyone in our house woke up to noises of heavy vehicles, people marching in boots, loud shouting, bright lights, and gunfire. At first, they erroneously believed that it must be a victory celebration, because just before everyone went to sleep, there were rumors that Yahya Khan had agreed to transfer power to Mujib. However, when my folks opened the window they couldn't believe what they saw. It was shocking to see that the entire Nakhalpara area had been cordoned off by armored military trucks. Soldiers with rifles and machine guns were running all over the place. Also, there were very bright searchlights all around. My family also noticed Jeeps mounted with machine guns very close to our house. Naturally, everyone was frightened. Being nervous, my mother started praying without losing any time. A few minutes later they heard a loud banging at our front door. They were at a loss, not knowing what to do. My father summoned up the courage to open the entrance door. Four Islamic soldiers with pointed rifles immediately entered our lounge. They asked everyone to line up in the lounge. So my father, my younger brother, my brother in-law, my four sisters, my nephew and niece, and my mother all obliged by lining up in the crammed space. All of them were shivering in hot March night. Then one of the soldiers separated the males from the females. The males were ordered to remain in the lounge. All the females, including my mother, were ordered in the bedroom nearby. At that stage my mother started crying and fell down on the knees of the soldiers for their Islamic mercy. The soldiers simply dragged her to the bedroom. One soldier guarded the males while the other guarded the female quarter. The two other soldiers then started ransacking each and every item in every room, including the food in the kitchen. They even examined the newspapers and other documents, even though they did not understand a single word of Bangla.

One of the soldiers then found the shotgun that my father had always had with him. I have seen that shotgun since my birth. It was licensed and completely legal. I had seen my father go hunting with his favorite shotgun every once in a while when time permitted. The soldier who found the shotgun came immediately to the male captives. He demanded to know whose shotgun was that. My father calmly replied in broken Urdu that he was the lawful owner of the gun. The soldier then pointed his automatic rifle at my father and ordered him to follow him downstairs. My father knew that he had only a few minutes to live. At that stage my younger brother stood between the rifle and my father and told the soldier that he wanted to accompany my father. The soldier became furious at the insolence shown by my brother. The soldier threw my brother on the floor and started pushing my father with his rifle toward the exit door. My father then asked the soldier to look at the license of the shotgun. But alas, the soldier could neither read nor understand the English language. So the soldier said that he had to call his officer. Another army man was called to guard while he went outside looking for the officer.

After about fifteen minutes, the soldier returned with the officer. My father was not sure what was the rank of the officer. Thank God! The officer was not as brutish as the lower-ranking *jawan*. The officer showed little bit of courtesy for my elderly father. He asked my father to take a seat so that he could examine the document. After a thorough examination the officer asked my father why he had not surrendered his weapon to police station. My father replied that there was no directive to that effect. The officer then rebuked my father for being so stupid to keep the weapon in the house when there were so many miscreants in the area. My father agreed with him and asked for his forgiveness. The officer then said that my father's life would be spared but that they would have to confiscate the shotgun. Then he started interrogating everyone on various matters, including our religion and political affiliation. My father became the spokesman. He answered what the army men wanted to hear: that we are all Muslims and we had no connection with the Awami League or any pro-freedom party, and so on.

The officer then asked my father how many sons he had. My father replied two. He inquired about the whereabouts of his sons. My younger brother identified himself. He told the officer that he had finished his higher secondary certificate and waiting to go to EPUET (now BUET). The officer then asked my father about me. My father replied that I was about to graduate from EPUET. The army officer then demanded to know why I was not at home. At that point my father could guess the real reason these army people are barging into our home. He carefully said that I was very studious and I preferred to study with my friends, so I had not come home for a few days. The army officer then started to note down all the details about me and told my father that as soon as I returned home my father must contact him by telephone. I was simply lucky that my father did not disclose the university residential hall in which I was staying. The officer then warned my father not to leave our house, as they may come to investigate again. My father said no problem. Throughout this ordeal, my brother-in-law did not talk much because he was actively involved in National Awami Party (a leftist political party) politics!

When the interrogation of the male members was complete, the officer entered the bedroom to view his female captives. Needless to say, my mother feared what might happen to her daughters. My oldest sister was a schoolteacher. My next two sisters were in college and only my youngest sister was still in her childhood. My mother was so hysterical that she kneeled down to the two soldiers and begged them that whatever they wanted to do let them take her daughters out of her sight. The soldiers simply laughed and taunted my mother and sister with abusive language, accusing them of being pro–Awami League. They told my sisters that very soon they would take them to cantonment. At that stage my oldest sister gathered up some courage and told them in broken Urdu that they simply could not do that without a warrant of arrest.

The soldiers laughed heartily hearing the response from my sister and said that they were not police. They were army and they could do whatever they wanted. Luckily, at that point the army officer entered the bedroom. My sister asked the army officer why they were being harassed. The officer told my sister that he had information that there were many miscreants in our area. Their duty was to catch these miscreants and take them to cantonment for punishment. He then told my sister that he had found them very gentle, polite, and cooperative and so he would let all of them go free this time. But he wanted to let everyone know that they would come again. At last he showed some respect to my mother by apologising to her and saying good-bye to her in *chost* Urdu. But before the officer departed he whispered something to his recruits. The two soldiers then forced my older sister to open the steel *almirah* (safety box). They took all the money and jewelry that were there for safekeeping. Thus, we lost most of our valuables.

After almost thirty-six hours, the curfew was lifted for six hours. My family members heard the wailing sound of bereavement all around the area. The Pakistani army had taken many people from the Nakhalpara area to cantonment that night. Most of those taken were young students. It was a sheer miracle that my family members were spared. None were taken to the cantonment. It is not known how many of those unfortunate people lost their lives, because their whereabouts are not known. Be that as it may, most of them never returned home. All the residents of Nakhalpara realized that the area was absolutely unsafe. So most residents left Nakhalpara barefoot with only the clothes they were wearing. My family also left Nakhalpara immediately after the curfew was lifted. Through the grapevine we heard that Dhanmondi was a safe area, so we went to our grandpa's house over there in to seek refuge and secrecy. A few days later we heard the dreadful news from Chittagong. Two of my uncles were killed in Agrabad Railway colony in a military operation similar to the one in the Nakhalpara operation. The army calls those "mop-up operations." To us, the Bengalis, those operations were akin to serving the death notice or something similar to that.

A few weeks later, my younger brother secretly ventured to Nakhalpara to see with his own eyes the condition of our homestead. To his horror he found that everything, including a bag of rice, had been removed or stolen. So we became destitute right away. But that hardly dampened our spirits. We knew we were not alone in this struggle. Life became *Durbishoho* (extremely intolerable). It was a struggle every day for the rest of the nine-month period.

For the last thirty years I have wondered why the Islamic army targeted our house and our family. It has always been a mystery to me. Now I have some clue to the answer after such a long period of time. The Islamist Ashrafuzzaman Khan (then a member of the central committee of the Islami Chatra Sangha) used to live at Nakhalpara. This piece of information I got from the Internet.

As I wrote this recount, I learned that one hunded new killing fields have been discovered all around Bangladesh. Was I surprised? No, not at all! However, I wondered, Why did it take so long? Why did we have to wait almost thirty years to know that innocent folks were butchered just as cattle? Rest assured that many more killing fields will be found. The killing fields of Cambodia, Kosovo, Bosnia, Afghanistan, and the like, will be nothing when compared to the killing fields in Bangladesh. These are the Islamic killing fields. Let us not forget these Islamic killing fields. Let us not forget the sacrifice of 3 million people who shed enough blood to change the verdure of the monsoon-drenched land of Bengal. They certainly gave their lives so that we can enjoy the fruits of freedom from the tyranny of Punjabi masters and Pakistani Islamic oligarchy. I would ask every Bengalis not to forget the Islamic butchers of those nights and days when we remember the fallen angels of our land. The crime should never go unpunished.

What lessons have the Bengalis learned from this genocide? The answer is really pathetic: We pretend as if nothing happened in Bangladesh in 1971. We pretend that Islam had nothing to do with that genocide. Somehow or other we try to find other scapegoats, whoever that may be, except Islam. We pretend as if everything is fine and dandy with Islam. This is the biggest lie and the greatest cruelty: pretending that Islam had nothing to do with one of the most horrific genocides in human history. It pains people like me and many others who have seen and experienced the true color of Islam with their own eyes.

The Bangladesh genocide spawned the seed of deep religious distrust in my mind. At that time many of my friends also shared similar views with me. And naturally, I felt very happy that we had come to the end of religious tyranny.

But alas! As strange as it me seem now, many of those dear uni friends of mine have become fanatic followers of Islam now. Many of them I met in my overseas life. They have spent a good part of their lives in the Middle East. They openly support some of the actions by the Pakistani Islamic army and their fanatic followers. They strongly support the forced conversion of the entire world population to Islam. And only then, they say, there will be peace. Even in a country like Australia many of them dare to say "We came to Australia to rid the people of their sinful activities and convert them to Islam." One of their goals is to build a mosque in every suburb of Australia. Of course, these are laughing matters in place like Australia. Whenever I meet these old pals it really breaks my heart. When I ask them what had caused such a change in them, they readily admit that they were greatly influenced by the Arabs, even though many of them really hate the cruel treatment of them (in many cases slave treatment) by the Arabs. But nevertheless, they feel very grateful to the Arabs for giving them employment and good money. Many of these Bengalis are proud to dress like Arabs. They have literally wiped out the memory of genocide in Bangladesh, and some of them justify the genocide to purify Islam. This had led me to conclude that Islam is nothing but the preservation of Arab hegemony and the enslavement of the poor people of countries such as Bangladesh.

The strange thing is that none of these Islamists really want to migrate to any Islamic country. None of them chose to live in an Islamic society. Why? The simple truth is that none of those Arab countries want them. Those countries are for the Arabs only. Where is the Islamic brotherhood? The Arabs are very clever people. They have used Islam as a powerful bait to continue the age-old tradition of slavery in the twenty-first century. My guess is that this will continue escalating while oil prices keep soaring. These fanatics use the openness, the fairness, and the democratic institutions in countries like Australia to propagate their poisonous doctrines.

Two years after this horrifying experience I went to the Asian Institute of Technology (AIT) in Bangkok for postgraduate study. There I saw another true color of Islam. Let me narrate that story in detail.

THE MINDSET OF THE PAKISTANI ISLAMIC ARMY FAVORING THE 1971 GENOCIDE

This account starts when I was in Thailand in 1973 to do my postgraduate studies in engineering. The institution was AIT, and as it was an international institution for postgraduate study there were students from many parts of the world, though the majority were from the Asian countries. There was a sizable number of Bangladeshi as well as Pakistani and Indian students. Bangladesh had just been liberated and most of us still had the fresh memories of the holocaust and never expected the Pakistanis to be friendly with us. But to our surprise, we found that most Pakistanis were quite nice a bunch of friendly, helpful people. They were extremely curious about what had happened in Bangladesh during that turbulent nine-month period. Many times we would have lengthy chat sessions with them. These Pakistanis were extremely religious (Islamic minded). They used to preach to us on all aspects of the last revelations of God, that is, Islam. They thought that our knowledge of Islam was incomplete, erroneous, and filled with Hindu practices. They used to preach to us like a priest gives sermons to his followers. Their devotion to Islam was so strong that they forced the canteen manager to open a counter for Muslim students so that they (the Muslims) can eat the food sanctioned by Islam (*halal* foods). Naturally, many Bengalis who were religious minded were greatly impressed by their words and practices. But a sinner like me was very skeptical about their words and actions right from the very beginning.

Then came the topic of creation of Bangladesh. Naturally, they sided with the Pakistani Islamic army, although they expressed sorrow for the lives lost. When they heard that 3 million people were massacred and that the action of the Pakistani Islamic army could not be dismissed simply as an act of restoration of peace and order, they simply laughed. The reason was that they did not believe what had happened to our people in the occupied Bangladesh. When we asked them how many Bengalis were killed, they quoted a figure of three thousand. They also insisted that those killed were mostly Hindus, so we should not bother too much about the massacre. That was to say that the killing of Hindus was all right. We pointed out that the figure of 3 million was not invented by the government of Bangladesh but the figure was from reliable foreign sources such as the Agence France Presse, Reuters, and *Time* magazine. We also told them that a Pakistani journalist by the name of Anthony Mascarenhas has written a book titled *The Rape of Bangladesh*,[1] where he had quoted a similar figure. The Pakistanis simply dismissed those facts and said that the foreign journalists were bribed by India to write these figures. When we asked them how did they get the figure of three thousand, they said that that figure was released by the military authorities. And what about the two hundred thousand rape cases? They were adamant that not a single woman was raped. Such is the power of Pakistani Islamic oligarchy and Pakistani Islamic military to condition peoples' minds.

Now, the interesting point was that whenever the atrocities of the Pakistani Islamic army were mentioned to them, they were all adamant that we (the Bengalis) were to be blamed for that. Why? Simply, because we were not good Muslims. How? If we were good Muslims, we would not have voted for the Awami League. They told us that the right parties to vote were Islamic parties like the Pakistan Muslim League or Jamat-i-Islami. It was no secret to guess that most Pakistanis considered us (Bengalis) non-Muslims, as almost all of us voted for the Awami League. Therefore, they opined that the genocide was not really a genocide! It was getting rid of the non-Muslims. After all, the non-Muslims are not really human beings.

Everyone knows that Thailand—especially Bangkok—has plenty of seedy joints to have fun and frolic with young women. I shall admit that I went to one of those joints along with a couple of friends of mine. Being a sinner, I did not have serious problem with those things. However, one day we got the shock of our lives when we found these Pakistani Islamists sitting comfortably and blithely at the massage parlor and ogling the scantily dressed, amorous Thai sex kittens. Then they saw us. To our surprise, they expressed no shame and they even did not try to hide their faces. They openly welcomed us and shook hands with us as, per Islamic style. We were simply stunned and at a loss for words. The Pakistanis even told us which girls were good and sexually attractive, and so on. They were not ashamed or afraid to admit that they visited those joints quite frequently. Most of them had their favorite girls with whom they had plenty of erotic fun. Those things were absolutely unbelievable to me and I thought that I must have been in Mars or another planet or that God had changed his mind on sins and virtues.

A few weeks later, an opportunity came for me to ask one of these Islamists as to what would happen to them since they had committed the sin of *Zina* (illicit sex/adultery). He was very surprised at me for this impertinence. He told me that they had committed no sin. What? No sin! My brain must have failed to work! I simply could not hold my breath any longer to listen to what he had to say. He told me that Thais were not Muslims, so having fun with their girls was all right. In fact, he told me that that had been the practice in Islam for centuries. Whenever the Muslims defeated the non-Muslims, they could do whatever they wanted with non-Muslims. The Muslims could use the non-Muslim women as sex slaves and please themselves as they wished. A Muslim even had the right to kill the women if he wished. In simple language, the non-Muslims were not really human beings. They were inferior even to cattle and animals. Moreover, the Pakistani told me that the Prophet had allowed sex if a man was living overseas. I could not believe what I was hearing! He then quoted from memory many verses from the Koran and Hadith to support his views. I reminded my Pakistani Islamic friend that there was a small minority of Muslims in Thailand. So, if by accident he had sex with one of the Thai Muslim prostitutes, what will befall him? He answered glibly, "No problem. When I return to Pakistan I shall have a *Milad Mehfil* and ask for forgiveness." Finally, the *hajj* is there for him to receive forgiveness. But he said that that might not be necessary because he was very sure that none of the girls he had sex with were Muslims.

A Pakistani reading this account may be greatly offended, no doubt about that. Many Pakistanis will respond that the view of one person does not mean anything. No apology will be sought. Any Pakistani can form whatever opinion he thinks is suitable. It is up to him. Let us look at the wider implications of what my Pakistani Islamist said. Was it an individual's wrong interpretations of the holy books of Islam? Was it the mindset of a mentally sick person? Do not be fooled by these thoughts. For when we look back, we see that that was the mindset of Pakistani Islamic army recruits who unleashed a reign of terror leading into the massacre of millions of Bengalis. The Pakistani army did its Islamic duty in Bangladesh! Pakistanis may differ on many matters, but when the question of Islamic superiority comes, they are unanimous. This was the work of the Oligarchy, the army and the clerics of Pakistan. These groups have rigidly programmed the vast majority of Pakistanis with the thought that they have absolute superiority in Islamic matters. And this thinking got a further boost with the detonation of an Islamic bomb in 1998. We Bengalis have no problem with their superior thinking. The only trouble is that these dangerous Islamic thoughts have cost 3 million dear Bengali lives.

So, in simple language, the Pakistani Islamic army did not kill any human beings in Bangladesh. They only cleared the field of pests, just like a farmer spreads insecticide to free his crops from devastation. So in the case of the Pakistani Islamic army. They simply eliminated the non-Muslims and the not-so-good Muslims to protect the good Muslims, those who would follow them. The question of remorse or guilt does not arise at all. You see, the Pakistani Islamic army did not rape any women. They simply enjoyed the flesh of non-Muslims, as permitted by the Islamic religion. Even if there was some excessive force applied, there is no need to feel guilty about that. The ubiquitous *Milad* is there; the *Hajj* is there, too, to remove even the slightest trace of culpability.

A serial killer is a psychologically sick person. He gets pleasure in seeing the suffering of a dying person in his hands. But deep down, the serial killer knows that what he is doing is wrong. He is surely aware of the eventual punishment if he is caught. That is why most serial killers readily admit their crime and on many occasions regret of their actions when they recover from their sickness. What about the perpetrators of a Islamic genocide? They are perfectly normal. Most of them are really very nice, polite, and soft spoken (like the Islamic Circle of North America's leader, Ashrafuzzaman Khan). But there is one trait that separates them from the rest of us, and that is their uncompromising faith in the supremacy of what they believe and their inability to accept the existence of others who do not follow the same beliefs. Any means is justified to advance their beliefs, even if that means the annihilation of an entire race. That is why very few Pakistani Islamists have ever condemned the genocide of the Bengalis. That is why Islam will do that again if an opportunity lends itself. Since no crime has been committed, the question of trial of the perpetrators of genocide does not arise at all. Isn't it so?

This is the mindset of the planners and executioners of Bangladesh genocide by the Islamists. This is the mindset of Yahya Khan, Tikka Khan, Golam Azam, Ayatollah, and Ashrafuzzaman. This why we have Auschwitz, Kosovo, Bosnia, Palestine, East Timor, and so on.

Is Islam the only religion responsible for the genocide? Surely not. Every organized religion on Earth has sanctioned murder, rape, looting, and plundering, as long as that is directed toward the nonbelievers. Religion has a cousin to go with it. That is racism. Religion and racism go hand in hand. That is why we have Adolf Hitler, Radovan Karadzic, Slobodan Milosevic, Ratko Mladic, and so on.

Karl Marx said, "Religion is the opium of the masses." In today's world that is an understatement. If people take opium they become addicted and ruin their health.

There should not be any problem for humanity with that. Today, religion (especially Islam) has become a vermin for humanity. This cancerous virus has spread across the planet. I am not sure if we will find an antidote for this disease in our lifetime or not.

Why did I write this essay after all these years? It can be summed up by a quotation from Shakespeare. The famous bard wrote, "A little fire is quickly trodden out; Which, being suffered, rivers cannot quench."[2] The fire is still burning inside me, although the events of 1971 may be more like some specks of dust in the minds of Bengalis who to this day will not admit that Pakistani Islamists committed excesses in the name of religion.

It took me almost forty years to evaluate my belief in Islam and to come to a definite conclusion about its role in my life. Many times I had doubts about my feelings about Islam. Many of my Muslim friends told me that Islam is not what we see in the Pakistani army, Iran, Afghanistan, or Sudan. At some times I thought that maybe they are correct, maybe everything is fine with Islam. I thought that I could be mistaken. One billion followers can't be wrong! So I took Islam very seriously and started to read and comprehend the life force of Islam (that is, the Koran and *hadith*). I read the Koran several times. This time the study of the Koran was not to memorize or to use it for prayer purposes. I read each and every verse in the Koran with its translation and explanation from a few sources (Pickthall, Yusuf Ali Shakir, and Mawdudi). I studied the Koran like I studied mathematics, physics, and chemistry. I analyzed the Koran as if I was doing Ph.D. research on mathematical modeling of a scientific system. This time I found out the deepest secrets of the Koran. The secret is that the Koran can never be the words of Allah (or God). It is the monologue of a narcissistic person to catch all the attention of the world at any cost. The attention that Muhammad missed out when he was born was given posthumously to be raised by others. The more I read and try to understand the Koran the more disgusting it looks. Except a few passages, the *hadith* are more disgusting. It is absolutely impossible for a person with the slightest conscience to reconcile with the innumerable verses in the Koran that preaches, violence, cruelty, murder, rape, plunder, inhumanity, violation of basic human rights, and degradation of women. The Koran is absolutely against everything in humanity we consider civilized. We can probably forgive the inaccuracies, inconsistencies, and scientific blunders in the Koran, but can we forgive the Koran when we see what is being done to humanity in Islamic paradises (like Iran, Afghanistan, Sudan, etc.)? In these countries we see the Koran in action. This is the "real Islam" in practice. If this is the "real Islam" then imagine what will happen to the entire world if the Islamists find a way to force Islam on the world. Islamists often quote "there is no compulsion in religion" (II.256) to fool people. They give the impression that Islam is like other religions such as Chritianity, Judaism, and Hinduism. This verse is applicable only to Christians and Jews who have not converted to Islam. What the Islamists never tell you is that this verse is not applicable to Muslims or to people of other faiths. Muslims are not free to choose any religion other than Islam. A Muslim has to live and die with Islam whether he likes it or not. There is no escape for him from Islam. The punishment for apostasy in Islam is death. Most Muslims idealize Islam and try to think of Islam as a perfect religion. This is a complete illusion. In reality, Islam is the perfect tragedy for its adherents.

There are many verses in the Koran and *hadith* that are absolutely uncivilized and completely unsuited to humanity. Here are a few samples:

- The Koran tells Muslims to kill the disbelievers wherever they find them (II. 191), to fight them and treat them harshly (IX.123), slay them (IX.5), fight with them (VIII.65), even if they are Christians and Jews, humiliate them and impose on them a penalty tax (IX.29), strive hard against them (IX.73; XXV.52; LXVI.9).
- Sinners will be choked in liquid pus (XIV.16–17; LXXIII.12–13).
- The Koran denigrates humanity by saying that humankind has always been prone to be most foolish (XXXIII.72).
- The Koran takes away the freedom of belief from all humanity and says clearly that no other religion except Islam is accepted (III.85).
- It relegates those who disbelieve in the Koran to hell (V.10) and calls them *najis* (filthy, untouchable, impure; IX.28).
- It orders its followers to fight the unbelievers until no other religion except Islam is left (II.193).
- It says that the nonbelievers will go to hell and will drink boiling water (XIV.16).
- It asks the Muslims to slay or crucify or cut the hands and feet of the unbelievers, that they be expelled from the land with disgrace and that "they shall have a great punishment in world hereafter" (V.38).
- "As for the disbelievers," it says that "for them garments of fire shall be cut and there shall be poured over their heads boiling water whereby whatever is in their bowls and skin shall be dissolved and they will be punished with hooked iron rods" (XXII.19–22; LXXIV.26-27).
- If a unbeliever seeks mercy she will be given melted brass to drink and to scald her face (XVIII.30).
- The Koran prohibits a Muslim to befriend a nonbeliever, even if that nonbeliever is the father or the brother of that Muslim (IX.23; III.28).
- The Koran asks the Muslims to "strive against the unbelievers with great endeavor (XXV.52) and be stern with them because they belong to hell (LXVI.9).
- The holy Prophet demanded his followers to "strike off the heads of the dis-

believers"; then, after making a "wide slaughter among them, carefully tie up the remaining captives" (XLVII.4), acquire slaves after a slaughter (VIII.67).

- The Koran permits unlimited sex with female slaves and female captives of war (XXIII.6; XXXIII.50,52; LXX.30).
- The Koran prohibits the adoption of children by childless couples (XXXIII.4-5).
- As for women, the book of Allah says that they are inferior to men and their husbands have the right to scourge them if they are found disobedient (IV.34).
- The Koran insults women by saying that menstruation is an illness (II.222).
- It teaches that women will go to hell if they are disobedient to their husbands (LXVI.10).
- It maintains that men have an advantage over women (II.228).
- It not only denies women's equal right to their inheritance (IV.11–12), it also regards them as imbeciles and decrees that their individual witness is not admissible in court (II.282). This means that a woman who is raped cannot accuse her rapist unless she can produce a male witness.
- Muhammad allowed the Muslims to marry up to four wives and gave them license to sleep with their slave maids and as many "captive" women as they may have (IV.3). Muhammad himself did just that. This is why any time a Muslim army subdues another nation, they call them *kafir* and allow themselves to rape their women. That is why Pakistani soldiers raped up to two hundred thousand Bengali women in 1971 after they massacred 3 million unarmed civilians when their religious leader decreed that Bangladeshis were un-Islamic. This is why the prison guards in Islamic regime of Iran rape the women and then kill them after calling them apostates and the enemies of Allah.

I can go on quoting verse after verse from the Koran to show how dangerous and disgusting the Koran is. This is the "real Islam."

My decision to write this essay was not taken lightly. I gain nothing from this. In fact, I am putting my safety and security at risk. Any Muslim who reads my essay will surely find it very unpalatable. That is fine. I cannot convince all the billion or so Muslims in the world of my perception of Islam. All I ask them to do is to please read their holy scriptures thoroughly again. But this time please read and try to understand with an unbiased open mind. You will be surprised at what you will discover that you thought never existed in the Koran and *hadith*.

Islam was (and is) suffocating. The prohibitions in Islam are unbearable. The injunctions in Islam force Muslims all over the world to be alienated. Anything pleasurable, comfortable, and enjoyable is forbidden in Islam. I feel so relieved that after almost forty years of suffocation, finally I can breathe freely.

What alternative religion do I follow? The answer is that I follow no religion. All religions are oppressive and designed to subjugate people's freedom. I am now a freethinker and an agnostic.

Islam thrives because of oil prices. Once the world finds alternative sources of energy and the price of oil falls to $1.00 a barrel, Islam will surely die. Till then the world has to go through this Islamic madness.

The tragedy of Bangladesh can be put in a nutshell in the following way: Pakistan was created as a separate state for the Muslims of the subcontinent. It had two wings, West Pakistan (the Pakistan that is left now) and East Pakistan. The two wings were separated by a physical diatance of more than one thousand miles. India was in between the these two Pakistans. The founders of Pakistan wanted to implement an Islamic ruling system. Within a few years of the creation of Pakistan the truth became very clear. The truth was that West Pakistan became the center of power and East Pakistan became a colony of West Pakistan. The East Pakistanis revolted against this kind of apatheid treatment in the name of Islam. The East Pakistanis, with the leadership of Shekh Mujib and his party, Awami League, demanded full autonomy for themselves.

The ruling elite and the military of Pakistan were 90 percent West Pakistani. They saw a great danger in the demand for autonomy for East Pakistan. They tried to brainwash peoples' minds by saying that the plan for autonomy was an Indian plan and that granting autonomy to East Pakistan would destroy Islam in Pakistan. However, the vast majority of the people of East Pakistan did not believe in the propaganda of West Pakistan. In the general election of 1971, Sheikh Mujib and his Awami League won almost all the seats in East Pakistan. It was a clear mandate by the people of East Pakistan for autonomy. The military and the oligrchy of Pakistan refused to accept this mandate of the people of East Pakistan and declared that Islam was in danger. That was why they had the military crackdown with the connivance of the Islamists (a feeble minority) of East Pakistan. It was really a sort of *jihad* by the Pakistani Islamic army to protect and preserve Islam. The Pakistani rulers even declared that those who wanted freedom and the breakup of Pakistan were anti-Islam and required Islamic punishment.

All the atrocities commited by the Pakistani army clearly shows that it was nothing but a religious war. When I read the Koran and compare the actions of the Pakistani army I find an absolute link between the killings and the provisions in the Koran. To the Pakistani military, the Bengalis were not true followers of Islam, but hypocrites. So they wanted to get rid of these nonbelievers (the Bengalis) as per the provision in the Koran and *hadith*. The whole world knows the truth. The truth is that the genocide in Bangladesh was conducted by the Islmic army of Pakistan to save Islam and to completely annihilate the unbelievers.

Even if people do not accept my analysis of the role of Islam in the 1971 genocide in East Pakistan (Bangladesh), it remains true that the terrible events witnessed by my countrymen and me made me think very deeply about Islam. The people who perpetrated these crimes were Muslims who prided themselves in belonging to a superior religion, even a superior civilization, and yet they butchered fellow Muslims in a most savage way. Where was Allah's mercy? Why did Allah allow it to happen? These supposedly superior beings acted worse than even nonbelieving barbarians.

I looked at Islam, the Koran, and the historical behavior of Muhammad, the Prophet, and found that the source of violence was the Koran, which positively pushes Muslims to kill in the name of Islam, and in the acts of cruelty and murder carried out by the Prophet.

NOTES

1. Anthony Mascarenhas, *The Rape of Bangladesh* (Delhi: Vikas Publications, 1971).

2. *Henry VI, Part Three*, 4.8.7.

16

AN IRANIAN GIRLHOOD
AND ISLAMIC BARBARISM
Parvin Darabi (Iran)

I was six days old when my grandfather passed on his religion to me by reciting a series of Arabic words into my ear. I am quite positive those were the only Arabic words my grandfather could recite, and perhaps he did not know what he was reciting into my ear. We are Iranian and our language is Persian and a vast majority of Iranians, including my family, do not speak Arabic, the language of God. Religion is like the color of our eyes. It is hereditary.

For kindergarten I was sent to a neighborhood school where an old lady named Kobra was headmistress. I hated this school and the headmistress because she always looked so mean in those black shrouds she covered herself in. She wore black at all times. No laughter, no music, no play; just God and Islam. The school was dirty and all she did was read her Koran and prayer book. I knew she had no education and could not read, because when I would place her Koran upside down she would still read it just the same.

As a child I wanted to ride the tricycle like the boys did, but I was told that girls did not ride tricycles. When I went to school I wanted to learn how to play the violin; however, I was told, a good girl does not play musical instruments. When I wanted to ride a bicycle, I was told good girls do not ride bicycles. The same went for horses, swimming, and any other activities. From the time I was a little girl I learned the importance of virginity for a girl in Islamic culture. A girl must be a virgin when she gets married, and the marriage age for a girl is nine years. As a matter of fact, Khomeini, the founder of the Islamic Republic of Iran, stated that "the most suitable time for a girl to get married is the time when the girl can have her first menstrual period in her husband's house rather than her father's."

My family was not that religious; however, the culture of the family and the society we lived in was Islamic. The thought of being married and sent away to a total stranger at age nine used to send shivers down my spine. I had watched how the father of the girl who worked for our mother married her off to a man who had three sons older than she was. She was just eleven years old, an old maid by her father's standard.

I remember the time my father had a lamb sacrificed in front of our eyes in our yard. Watching how that poor animal struggled to get itself free and how it moaned and moved its legs and body after its throat was cut made me hate and curse the ritual for which this lamb had to die. The night following the lamb sacrifice my father's mother, the only religious person in our entire family, told me the story of Abraham and his son Ismael. She told me how God had asked Abraham to take his son to a place and sacrifice him in order to show his devotion to the Almighty. And that as he placed the knife over his son's throat he had heard a lamb and then had sacrificed the lamb instead. That was why we had to sacrifice the lamb that morning. The story was quite scary for me. I recall that for many nights I had nightmare about this story. I would dream about my father sacrificing me to show his devotion to God and then I would jump and find out I was still alive. I finally convinced myself that God would only ask men to sacrifice their sons, not their daughters. After all, why should anyone sacrifice a girl? In a way I felt happy being a girl.

My father's mother used to teach me about religion and Islam. She used to tell me that "God is great, knows everything, and has created man and the universe." But then she would ask me to pray in Arabic.

Grandma, doesn't God understand Persian?

Well no. You must speak to God in Arabic.

But you just said God made everything. Then if he made the Persian language how come he can't understand it?

Following these types of arguments, each time Grandma was cornered and did not have an answer to give, I completely discarded religion and Islam.

My dislike of religion was reinforced when I started studying *Sharīʿa* at high school. What I learned was so humiliating to women and so oppressive that I even hated to read the book.

I did not understand why divorce was a unilateral right of a man, why a woman had to surrender her children to their father's family when her husband divorced her or died. Why did women inherit only half as much as their male siblings and why could a boy do what he pleased while girls were denied all rights?

Why did we always have to wait for men and boys to finish eating before nourishing ourselves from their leftovers? Why was my body everyone else's property except mine? If I stood at our doorstep and talked to the neighbor boy, every male relative of ours made it his responsibility to force me inside the house.

The most disgusting thing to me was the process of *Khastegary* (matchmaking). In this process, women within a man's immediate or even extended family would search for a suitable girl for their male relative. Each time my family members visited a girl as potential wife for my uncle or my cousins, their evaluation of the poor young girl would make me sick. It was like they were buying a piece of furniture. The only important thing was her looks and physical features, and that she must be a virgin. In the case that the girl's virginity could not be proven her parents must pay the groom and his parents for all the wedding costs and the marriage would be annulled the next day.

When I was a teenager in Tehran, I went to a relative's wedding. This girl was only fourteen years old. Her parents were so concerned about her virginity that they were practically glued to the newly married couple's bedroom door. They stood there until the groom, a thirty-year-old man, came out of the room. They then entered and removed the bloody sheet from under their raped daughter and with jubilation offered the sheet to the groom's parents as the proof of their daughter's virginity. I never wanted to be treated in that manner on my wedding night.

There are so many laws in Islam that would turn off any educated person completely. One such law is the *Shī'a* custom of *Sigeh*, or temporary marriage. I call it religiously sanctioned prostitution. Marriage in Islam is a contract between a man and a woman's guardian for a specified length of time. In a permanent marriage, a man marries a woman for ninety-nine years, because no one is supposed to live that long. In reality most husbands die way before this period is over, since they marry in their late thirties or early forties. Then women who were given away by their guardians when they were quite young get a chance to live alone in peace the rest of their lives. In a temporary marriage, the man specifies the term of the contract. He asks a woman or her guardian if she would marry him for any amount of time from ten minutes to an hour, a week, or some months, for a specified amount of money. If her guardian agrees to the terms then they are married and the marriage is annulled when the time has elapsed.

Another barbaric Islamic law is that of the *Muḥallil*, when a man actually pays another man to marry his ex-wife for one night and have sex with her and divorce her the next day so that he can remarry her.

Years ago, one of our distant relatives divorced his wife under rage and then was sorry and wanted to get back with her. However, the *Mullā* would not remarry them unless she married another man, spent a night with this new husband (allowing him to have sex with her), and then was divorced the next day.

I recall what a circus this was. The ex-husband was desperate to find a man to pay to marry his ex-wife for one night and then divorce her the next day. Since his ex-wife was a very beautiful woman from a distinguished family, the man needed someone he could trust would divorce his ex-wife the next day. So finally they asked one of my father's workers to marry the woman. The ex-husband paid this man a substantial sum of money, he slept with the ex-wife for one night, and they were divorced the next day. Then the couple could get back together. What was appalling to me was the fact that none of the women thought much about the consequences of this one-night stand. Perhaps it was because they had all been raped on their wedding night by a strange man and getting raped again by another strange man was not such a big issue. Or maybe many of them wished that they would be divorced so they could marry another man who would treat them better than their ex-husbands.

Now that I think about this law, I find it appalling and humiliating to women. In these cases the women are not consulted and they are forced to accept the rape by a total stranger because their ex-husbands got mad and in a state of rage divorced them. Muslim apologists would tell you this law was put in place so men would not divorce their wives three times; basically, as a deterrent to divorce.

In Islam a man has the unilateral right to divorce (in itself a violation of women's rights) under following procedures. A man can divorce his wife once, by telling her "I divorce you," and if they are faced with each other the divorce is nullified and they can resume normal relations. A man can divorce his wife twice, "I divorce you, I divorce you," and then if they have sexual intercourse the divorce is nullified and they can resume their marital relation. However, once a man divorces his wife three times "I divorce you, I divorce you, I divorce you," in the presence of a witness, the man has to find a *Muḥallil* (a man who would marry his wife for one night and then divorce her) before he and his ex-wife can go back together. Many times these *Muḥallil* do not divorce the wife the next day, and there is nothing the ex-husband can do about it.

I found this law barbaric and inhumane for several reasons. First, the woman's feelings and rights are not considered and she is forced to be raped for one night by a total stranger. Second, the idea of a man paying another man to ravish his wife for an entire night is appalling. And finally, in the cases where the *Muḥallil* does not divorce the woman, she is forced to live a life in misery (unless the *Muḥallil* happens to be kinder than her ex-husband) away from her children by her first husband.

After this circus in the family, I decided that I did not want to be a Muslim; however, I did not have the courage to change. I left Iran with a small Koran in my pocket and passed under a large one coming out of our home on my way to the airport. Even though I had never prayed, fasted, been to a Mosque, or performed any religious ritual in my entire life, I still believed in God and his Prophet Muhammad when I left Iran in 1964 to come to the United States.

After I learned the English language well enough to be able to read books in

English, I read a part of the Koran in English. I had never read the Koran. When I left Iran it was not translated into Persian, or perhaps we did not know about it. I read some text of the Koran translated into English. I was appalled by such texts as the Sura of Lights, where God supposedly tells Muhammad "Prophet, tell your wives, daughters, and other women who believe in me to conceal their eyes and their treasures from the sight of strangers" (XXIV.31). My problem was to know how far a woman should be dressed to conceal her treasures, and besides, what are a woman's treasures? Was a woman's treasure under her belt or her brain? The way the Muslims in my family and neighborhood acted, it was clear that a woman's treasure was her virginity before marriage and her vagina after marriage. I resented that. After all, if the vagina is part of my body, why shouldn't I be in charge of it rather than my father or my husband, mother, and the rest of the clan? Then I read more in the Koran and in other books, and after reading all these sayings and proverbs I was convinced that religion was only to destroy a human's ability to think and act on his or her own behalf. I have listed some of these sayings below.

> Your wives are your tillage, go in unto your tillage in what manner so ever you will. (II.223)

> Good women are obedient, as for those from whom you fear rebellion, admonish them and banish them to beds apart, and scourge them. (IV. 34)

> Prophet Muhammad: "I was standing at the edge of fire (hell) and the majority of the people going there were women."[1]

> An Islamic leader in Indonesia: "It is better to wallow in mud with pigs than to shake the hand of a woman."

> An Islamic saying: "A woman's heaven is beneath her husband's feet."

> An Islamic saying: "Women should be exposed to the day light three times in their lives. When they are born, when they are married and when they die."

Later in my research on Islam I learned about the marriages of the Prophet to his first wife when he was twenty-four years old, sixteen years her junior. She was a rich, twice-divorced lady who proposed to Muhammad for his hand in marriage and he accepted it. Then, after she died at age seventy-two, when he was fifty-six years of age, he married a six-year-old girl. He supposedly had sex with her when she was nine years of age, and pronounced her mother of all Muslims at the time of his death, when she was only sixteen years old, so that she would never be able to marry another man.

In the last eight to ten years of his life, the Prophet Muhammad married some fifteen women. Muslim apologists say that these women were all widows and that they had no place to go and no one to take care of them, so God ordered his prophet to marry them. I find this excuse so preposterous. ʿĀʾisha, whom he married when she was only six years old, was a child. Zaynab was married to the Prophet's adopted son and was quite happily married till he asked his son, Zayd, to divorce his wife so he could marry her. In order to get the approval of the Quraysh tribe, he brought the excuse that "a Muslim man is not allowed to raise another man's child, therefore, Zayd is not his son, because he adopted Zayd prior to his ordination as a Muslim prophet." That is the main reason adoption is not legal in Islamic countries. And Reyhaneh was a beautiful married woman when her husband was decapitated by the Prophet's bandits and taken to the Prophet's bed the same night. These women were not widowed. They indeed had someone to take care of them.

When I read such stories my mind just exploded. How could so many people in this world follow a womanizer and a child molester? How could my grandfather make me a Muslim when I was six days old, to be a follower of such a criminal? Then I came to the conclusion that he did not know about it. Or if he did, it was because he had been raised in such a barbaric culture himself and did not know better.

When my son was born I did not give him any religion. I did not give him any religious education about God and his prophets, and I did not circumcise my son, either.

My faith in God was totally eroded on April 1, 1979, following the establishment of the Islamic Republic, or the government of God, in the country of my birth, Iran, when the country experienced a dramatic return to the Dark Ages by the establishment of the following Islamic laws.

Women were the first victims of the regression. More than 130 years of struggle was repudiated by the medieval religious rulers. Bereaved of their constitutional rights, they are socially reduced to inferior individuals and second-rank citizens.

In March 1979 Khomeini employed the *hijab* as a symbol of struggle against imperialism and corruption. He declared that "women should not enter the ministries of the Islamic Republic bare-headed. They may keep on working provided that they wear the *hijab*."

In 1980 Khomeini declared that "from now on women have no right to be present in government administration naked. They can carry on their tasks, provided they use Islamic dress." The ministry of education specified the color and style of the suited clothing for the girl students (black, straight, and covered from head to toe for children as young as six years of age).

To suppress the refractory women, the government set up special units. Patrols controlled whether women observed the Islamic habit on the streets. The

Islamic government went even further. During the last twenty-two years, women's conditions have continuously deteriorated. Nonetheless, in spite of the tortures (flagellation, stoning, imprisonment, and total segregation) Iranian women have not ceased their worthy struggle.

Hashemi Rafsanjani, president of the Islamic Republic of Iran recently discovered the difference between men and women. He says:

> Equality does not take precedence over justice. Justice does not mean that all laws must be the same for men and women. One of the mistakes the Westerners make is to forget this. The difference in the stature, vitality, voice, development, muscular quality and physical strength of men and women show that men are stronger and more capable in all fields. Men's brain are bigger so men are more inclined to fight and women are more excitable. Men are inclined to reasoning and rationalism, while women have a fundamental tendency to be emotional. The tendency to protect is stronger in men, where as most women like to be protected. Such differences affect the delegation of responsibilities, duties, and rights.

Under the Islamic rules, the family protection law has been abrogated. Polygamy has been reestablished. The Islamic Republic resolutely supports the practice of polygamy. Under the Islamic Republic, provisional marriage was sanctioned. Consequently, a man may marry four "permanent" and as many "provisional" wives as he desires.

Said Ayatollah Ghomi in 1979, "Most Europeans have mistresses. Why should we suppress human instincts? A rooster satisfies several hens, a stallion several mares. A woman is unavailable during certain periods whereas a man is always active."

According to Ayatollah Mutahari, one of the principal ideologues of the Islamic Republic of Iran, "The specific task of women in this society is to marry and bear children. They will be discouraged from entering legislative, judicial, or what ever careers which may require decision making, as women lack the intellectual ability and discerning judgment required for theses careers."

A man's testimony is equal to two women's. According to clauses 33 and 91 of the law in respect, *Qasas* (the Islamic Retribution Bill), and its boundaries, the value of woman witness is considered only half as much as of a man. According to the Islamic penal law that is being practiced by the present regime of Iran, "a woman is worth half of a man."

According to the clause 6 of the Law of Retribution and Punishment, "if a woman murders a man his family has the right to a sum paid to the next of kin as compensation for the slaughter of a relative. By contrast, if a man murders a woman, her murderer must, before retribution, pay half the amount of a man's blood money to her guardian."

According to the flea market situation prevailing in the Islamic Republic of

Iran the shameless assessment of life's worth is one hundred camels or two hundred cows. Clause number 6 regarding the *diya* (cash value of the fine) states that the cash fine for murdering a woman intentionally or unintentionally is half as much as for a man. The same clause adds that if a man intentionally murders a woman and the guardian of the woman himself is not able to pay half of the *diya* (the value of fifty camels or one hundred cows) to the murderer, the murderer will be exempted from retribution.

A married woman should always and unconditionally be ready to meet her husband's sexual needs, and if she refuses, she loses all rights to shelter, food, clothing, and so on:

> A woman should endure any violence or torture imposed on her by her husband for she is fully at his disposal. Without his permission she may not leave her house even for a good action (such as charitable work). Otherwise her prayers and devotions will not be accepted by God and curses of heaven and earth will fall upon her.

Khomeini stressed over and over that "all our societies' miseries come from universities." He also has said that "economy is a matter of donkeys" and "war is a blessing."

Women's "Freedom of Dress" of 1936 was declared as null and void:

> You may think by wearing the veil improperly, putting on transparent stockings or dressing indecently you are challenging the Islamic Republic. The day is not far when you regret your behavior. When the legislation regulates the problem, you will have no other choice. Stop hurting the decent feelings of our nation.

It has been reported that on August 15, 1991, the prosecutor general, Abolfazl Musavi-Tabrizi, said that "anyone who rejects the principle of Hijab is an apostate and the punishment for an apostate under Islamic law is death."

Girls condemned to death may not undergo the sentence as long as they are virgins. Thus, they are systematically raped before the sentence is executed:

> To rape women prisoners, especially virgin girls, who are accused of being against the regime, is a normal and daily practice in the Islamic Republic's prisons, and by doing so, the clergies declare that they adhere to the merits of the Islamic principles and laws, preventing a virgin girl to go to Heaven. Mullahs believe that these are ungodly creatures and they do not deserve it, therefore they are raped to be sure they will be sent to hell.

Article 115 of the Islamic constitution clearly states that the president of the country should be a man elected out of all God-fearing and dedicated men; this brings the conception that a woman can neither be president nor possess the rank of *Valiat-e-Faqih* (the religious spiritual leader) or the position of leader of a Muslim nation.

Iranian women are prevented from marrying foreigners unless they obtain written permission from the Ministry of Interior. The Ministry of Interior's director general for the affairs of foreign citizens and immigrants, Ahmad Hosseini, stated on March 30, 1991,

> marriages between Iranian women and foreign men will create many problems for these women and their children in future, because the marriages are not legally recognized. Religious registrations of such marriages will not be considered as sufficient documentation to provide legal services to these families.
>
> Married women are not allowed to travel abroad without presenting a written permission from their husbands.

In accordance with a draft resolution presented to the Majlis (the Islamic parliament) in May 1991, unmarried women and girls are not allowed to leave the country. According to Keyhan of May 23, 1991, although there was no law forbidding girls from leaving the country, authorities in practice create many obstacles for those who wish to leave. The authorities are allegedly particularly "severe with those unmarried women and girls who have won scholarships to study abroad."

The latest reports of the various international organizations such as Amnesty International and the United Nations' Human Rights Commission give a clear picture of the circumstances that Iranian women, as well as Iranian men and children, are suffering from a lack of all basic human rights.

According to the official reports, between 1988 and 1990, five thousand executions have taken place in the Islamic Republic of Iran. It was also declared that during the first months of 1991, the number of executions was three times that of the entire year 1990. From the other angle, by adopting the Islamic Criminal Code in 1982, a series of barbaric, savage, degrading, and antihuman laws were put in force. With such a turn around to the Dark and Middle Ages, any illiterate *mullah* has the jurisdiction over all civil and penal codes and can issue any verdict. The accused has no right to appoint defense lawyers and does not enjoy the principle of innocence until it is proven otherwise.

In such a system the way is paved for any kind of abuse of justice, which is contrary to the Universal Declaration of Human Rights. On his last visit to Iran, during the year 1991, Professor Reynaldo Galinde Pohl, special representative of the United Nations Human Rights Commission, interviewed the Islamic Republic's minister of justice, Mr. Hojatolislam Esmail Shoushtari:

> Referring to the penalties of amputation and stoning, he (The Minister) indicated that Iran's system of government was Islamic, thus Islamic laws were enforced

and some penalties could not be changed. Murder, for example, was punished by the death penalty, and that rule could not be changed; however, judges were empowered to negotiate with the victims' relatives to replace the death penalty by another, and that did happen in 95 per cent of cases. Theft was punished by amputation and adultery by stoning (to death). Those penalties could not be changed, because they were punishments especially established under Islam.

The Islamic Republic of Iran has a law for the size of the stone to be used in stoning. "It should not be so large as to kill at the first blow and small as pebbles."

The only thing the Islamic Republic has brought to the Iranian people is poverty and misery. I just wonder why God is discarding them? At the time of the revolution, Khomeini told people that God was on their side. If this is what we will get by having God on our side, I am pleased to not have him on mine.

That is when I realized that religion and God were only to control people. They are big businesses raising money for the clergy to live happily ever after by making others feel guilty for what humans must do. As my friend and colleague Dr. Ahmad said, there are three religions, or three big businesses: one collects money on Fridays, one on Saturdays, and one on Sundays.

NOTE

1. al-Bukhāri, *Book of* Nikah *(Wedlock)*, vol. 7, book 62 of *Ṣaḥīḥ*, trans. M. Muhsin Khan (New Delhi: Kitab Bhavan, 1987), Hadith no. 124, p. 94; Hadith no. 125, pp. 95–96.

17

LEAVING ISLAM
AND LIVING ISLAM

Azam Kamguian (Iran)

I left Islam long before I lived Islam. This is what I shall be discussing in my testimony. I do not intend to talk about Koranic verses in an abstract way. Rather, I shall be describing what these verses meant in real life, my life, along with the lives of millions of people.

My being a Muslim, as with all other children who are accidentally born into Muslim families, was hereditary. My parents were ordinary Muslims. They started prayer and fasting in their late thirties. My father was relatively open-minded, but my mother indoctrinated us and used religious rules for protecting her children. I was the youngest of six children. The home environment was more suitable for my education and growth than for that of my siblings. We had a big study with all kinds of books, including science and other nonfiction as well as fiction. That room was an important part of my world, a part that helped save me from the harm of religion, from the harm of Islam and superstition.

Now, in writing this testimony, I am trying to remember scenes from my childhood. My older brother and sister prayed and fasted for a short period of their lives, when I was four or five years old. Under my mother's indoctrination, I myself prayed and fasted between the ages of nine and eleven. I cannot remember praying and fasting at any other time. I also remember that my mother took me to some religious ceremonies of which I have some horrifying images and memories. I am talking about *Tasouaa* and *Ashoura*, when men hit themselves and their small children with clusters of heavy chains and swords, for the pleasure of Imam Housein. They shed their blood and the blood of their small children violently for Islam's sake.

My doubts about God began seriously when I was twelve years old. From that age, I began to read books on evolution, science, and the history of human social evolution, and asked questions constantly. That was a significant period in my life, the period of doubts and of search for the truth. When I was fifteen, an important incident marked my life and blocked off any possible fate of a person who could have believed in God and religion. My youngest brother, who was older than I, eighteen years old, was recruited by one of the darkest Islamic factions, the anti-Bahais, who were called *Hojatieh*. That was the oddest possible phenomenon. My brother had been interested in music, cinema, and reading books. We were very close and loved each other. We watched movies, went to theaters, and enjoyed our time together. He was learning to play a musical instrument and was extremely intelligent, one of the top students in math and physics in the country. All of a sudden, he started to read the Koran and Ali Shariati's books. Shariati was widely read and admired across the politico-religious spectrum in those years. My brother also began to take part in activities harassing and intimidating Bahais. Gradually, I became familiar with one of the ugly faces of Islam.

He invited me to participate in their discussion meetings, which I did, and the more I did, the more deeply I felt about our differences. In that period, I mainly read scientific and materialistic books. So when they gave me books written by Motahari and Makarem Shirizi, two famous *mullahs* of the time, I told them that these books are extremely ridiculous and I wouldn't read them. And that is why Shariati became popular. He was a non-*mullah* educated in Paris. He used philosophical, sociological, and even Marxist concepts and terminology in the framework of anticolonial, "anti–cultural imperialism," to attract the anti-shah youth of the time to Islam. They urged me to read Doctor's (that is what he was called) books, especially *Fatemeh Fatemeh Ast* ("Fatima is Fatima").[1] I read the book and refuted it with my rational understanding at that time. Years later, in 1996 when I was working on my own book, *Islam, Women, Challenges and Perspectives*,[2] I referred to Shariati and that book. Shariati introduced Fatima, the daughter of the prophet Muhammad and wife of Ali, the first *imam* of Shiism, as his ideal role model against the traditional woman and the Westernized woman, whom he saw as the modern "doll," the agent of the enemy.

The dominant theme in Shiite discourse in the 1970s was disdain for changing the status, dress, and conduct of women. The attitude cohered with the dominant anti-imperialist tendencies, which targeted Western economic and cultural influences as the root cause of all national problems. "Emancipated" women in religious and Easternist discourse were the most obvious sign of modernism and "imported" values. Women were considered the symbol of Western influence and the idea of women's rights and women's liberation were attacked. Gender equality was presented in Shiite discourse as a Western plot, and women who advocated secular reforms as agents of the West.

For Shariati, "Fatima answers how to be a woman, inside and out, in the home of her father, in the home of her husband, in her society, in her thoughts and behavior and in her life."[3] I saw clearly that Shariati's model woman aspired to nothing for herself. She used her voice only as a daughter, a wife, and a mother, never for herself and for her wants. She was an obedient, silent, and weak woman, who only sacrificed for her men. Shariati required women to be living martyrs, sexless creatures, free from all wants, the guardians of primitive traditions. He saw women's sexuality as the "exploiter's conspiracy" to divert the attention of the male masses. Fatima's sexlessness as a role model was praised because colonialism and imperialism could exploit women's sexuality. Shariati's conception of women did not differ from Islamic law and tradition.

Back in those years when I was fifteen, I confidently declared my atheism to the Islamists. Between fifteen and sixteen, I became an atheist definitely, in my feelings, understanding, and rational thoughts. From that time on, I broke from religion and God completely. There is no particle of God or religion in my soul or in my blood. As I stated before, in this testimony I do not intend to quote from the Koran, *hadith*, or other Islamic sources to refute Islam or religion in general. I shall instead write about living Islam, living under the rule of state Islam in Iran since 1979.

In my late teens, Iran was pregnant with revolution. The atmosphere of the time was for change, a profound demand for fundamental change in society. People were marching and fighting for freedom and justice. Unfortunately, the revolution was defeated by the Islamic tradition. The final decades of the twentieth century witnessed another holocaust, an Islamic one, because of which thousands have been executed, decapitated, stoned to death, and tortured by Islamic governments and Islamic movements. That was the beginning of a dark era that has not ended. That was the beginning of the rise of political Islam in the world, a period in history that most probably could be compared to the 1930s. There have not been and there are no limits to murder and repression: Young and old, women and men are all legitimate targets of Islam's blind and bloody terror. Any voice of dissent and freedom has been silenced on the spot. The robe, turban, and Koran continue to drive millions of people into Islamic dungeons. The conduct of Islamic movements is primarily in the form of opposition to the freedom of women, women's civil liberties, freedom of expression in the cultural and personal domains and the enforcement of brutal laws and traditions against people, and the killing, beheading, and genocide of people from young children to the elderly.

Yet this is a period in Iranian history of which humanity all around the world is largely unaware, a period during which crimes of such dimension and intensity were committed against people by the Islamic Republic of Iran and other political Islamic groups that, were they better known, would appall the wider world. In Iran, violence has another dimension: one that is based on Islam. The very statement that an Islamic Republic exists somewhere means that unparalleled and brutal violence exists in it. The very fact that people are forced to abide by laws based on something some god or prophet is reported to have said somewhere is a form of mental violence. If anyone protests against such laws, they are subject to suppression and punishment. And questioning Islam means suffering the worst and the most ferocious kinds of punishment. Iran is the most transparent picture of what Islam is capable of. I will try to pass you briefly through this period of bloodbath, of the atrocities committed and the brutal antiwomen laws and practice by Islam in power.

I have lived thousands of days in Iran when Islam has shed blood. In the name of Allah, a hundred thousand have been executed in Iran since 1979. I have lived days when I, along with thousands of men and women throughout the country, looked for the names of our lovers, husbands, wives, friends, daughters, sons, colleagues, and students in the papers that announced the names of the executed on a daily basis. Days when the soldiers of Allah attacked bookstores and publishing houses and burned books. Days of armed attacks on universities and the killing of innocent students all over the country. Weeks and months of bloody attacks on workers' strikes and demonstrations. Years of brutal murder and suppression of atheists, freethinkers, socialists, Marxists, Bahais, women who resisted the misery of *hijab* and the rule of sexual apartheid, and many others who were none of these, those who were arrested in the streets and then executed simply because of their innocent non-Islamic appearances. Years of mass killing of youth that kept the keys to heaven in their fists during the Iran-Iraq war. Years of brutal assassination of opponents inside and outside of Iran.

I, along with thousands of political prisoners, was tortured by order of the representative of Allah and *Shari'a*. Tortured, while the verses of the Koran were played in the torture chambers. The mechanical voice reading the Koran was mixed with our cries of pain from the lashes and other brutal forms of torture. Thousands were shot by execution squads who recited Koranic verses while conducting the killings, regarding as blasphemous those who were simply political opponents of the regime (they were called *mofsedin fe al-arz va moharbin ba khoda va rasool khoda*); the death of blasphemers is required by the Koran. They prayed before raping female political prisoners, for the sake of Allah and in order to enter heaven. Those who were in prisons and not yet executed were awakened every day at dawn only to hear more gunshots aimed at their friends and cellmates. From the numbers of shotguns you could find out how many were murdered on that day. The killing machine did not stop for a minute. Then, fathers and mothers and husbands and wives who received the bloody clothes of their loved ones had to pay for the bullets. Islamic Auschwitz was created. Many of the best, the most passionate and progressive people were massacred. The dimension was and is beyond imagination.

Then, love, happiness, smiling, and any free human interaction were all forbidden and Islam took over completely. This is what happened to my generation. But it was not limited only to that generation. It had bloody consequences for the parent generation and also the next generation. In other words, Islam ruined the lives, dreams, hopes, and aspirations of three consecutive generations. During those years, millions of children were brainwashed by Islamic education and manipulated by Islam and Allah. The crimes committed by the Islamic Republic of Iran and the political Islam in the region is comparable to the crimes committed by fascism in the period between 1933 and 1945 and the genocide in Rwanda and Indonesia.

With this regime's downfall, the world will finally be given an opportunity to know the truth—victims will speak out, prisons and torture chambers will be exposed, torturers will make heart-wrenching confessions, Islamic prosecutors and judges will reveal what they did to their victims behind prison walls. Then people all over the world will see what a despicable phenomenon political Islam is.

I haven't mentioned what happened and is still happening to women in Iran. Women were and still are firsthand victims of Islamic regimes and Islamic forces. In Iran reigns a regime of enslavement of women and of the rule of sexual apartheid, where being a woman is itself a crime. In Iran women are legally the inferior sex and, according to Islamic doctrine, this inferiority is rooted in the nature of women.

Women's inequality is God's commandment in Islam, enshrined in immutable law by Muhammad and eventually recorded in scripture. According to the Koran, a woman is equal to half a man; it allots daughters half the inheritance of sons. It decrees that a woman's testimony in court, at least in financial matters, is worth half that of a man's. Under *Shari'a*, compensation for the murder of a woman is half the going rate for men. In most Islamic countries these directives are incorporated into contemporary law. Family law in these countries generally follows the prescriptions of the Koran. The legal age of marriage for girls, polygamy, divorce laws, and the rights of women regarding custody of their children are all specified according to the Koran. Women's rights are compromised further by a section in the Koran that states that men have "preeminence" over women, that they are "overseers" of women, that the husband of an insubordinate wife should first admonish her, then leave her to sleep alone, and finally beat her (IV.34). That is why wife beating is so prevalent in Muslim inhabited countries. Life under Islamic law leaves women with battered bodies and shattered minds and souls. Still, beatings are not the worst of female suffering. Each year hundreds of women die in "honor killings": murders by husbands or male relatives of women suspected of disobedience. Female genital mutilation is also closely associated with Islam. Sexual anxiety lies at the heart of most Islamic strictures on women. The veil and *hijab* are justified by Islam on the basis that women arouse the lust of men other than their husbands. This is the general condition of the lives of women living under *Sharī'a* law, but the rights of women living under Islamic regimes such as the Islamic Republic of Iran are violated even more. In Iran:

- Women are stoned to death for engaging in voluntary sexual relations.
- Women do not have the right to choose their clothing; *hijab* is mandatory.
- Women are segregated from men in every aspect of public life. The penalty for breaking the rules of segregation and *hijab* is insult, cash fines, expulsion, deprivation of education, unwanted marriage, arrest, imprisonment, beating, and flogging. I call this *sexual apartheid*.
- Women are barred from taking employment in a large number of occupations simply because these jobs would compromise their chastity. A married woman can be employed only if she has the consent of her husband. The main duty of women is considered to be taking care of home and children and serving their husbands.
- Women are not free to choose their own academic or vocational field of study.
- The legal age of marriage for girls is nine years. Women have no right to choose a husband without the consent of their father or, in the absence of the father, the paternal grandfather.
- Women do not have equal rights to divorce. Only under extreme conditions such as insanity of their spouse can they file for divorce. In the event of divorce, the father has legal custody of boys after the age of two and girls after the age of seven. The mother loses this minimal right as soon as she remarries.
- Women do not have the right to acquire passports and travel without the written permission of their husbands/fathers.
- Women have no rights to the common property of the family.
- Women are officially declared temperamental. Their decisions are considered to be based not on reason but on sentiments. They are, on these grounds, barred from the profession of law, and deprived of the opportunity to become judges.
- In courts of law the testimony of two women counts as that of one man, and the testimony of any number of women is invalidated in the absence of a minimum of one male.

During the years that the Islamic government has been in power, thousands of women have spent time in prison and been tortured for having ignored Islamic regulations concerning *hijab*, segregation, and sexual relationships.

Since I have discussed Islam in a sociopolitical context and my testimony is based on living Islam, I need to discuss some important related issues and concepts such as political Islam, cultural relativism, the inverted colonialist mentality of Western intellectuals, and secularism. What do I mean by political Islam? How does cultural relativism justify Islam and backward Eastern culture in the region? What do I mean by the inverted colonialist mentality of Western intellectuals and how does it serve to promote Islamic fanaticism and racism? What is my interpretation of secularism? Let's start with political Islam.

Essentially, Islam is a set of beliefs and rules against human prosperity, happiness, welfare, freedom, equality, and knowledge. Islam and a full human life are contradictory concepts, opposed to each other. Islam with any kind of interpretation is and has always been a strong force against secularism, modernism, egalitarianism, and women's rights. Political Islam, however, is a political movement and current that has come to the fore against secular and progressive movements for liberation and egalitarianism, against cultural and intellectual advances, and against the oppressed who are fighting for justice, freedom, and equality in the region. This movement was supported and nurtured by the Western governments. Political Islam is a contemporary reactionary movement that has no relation to the Islamic movements of the end of the nineteenth century. It is the result of a defeated project of Western modernization in Muslim-inhabited Middle Eastern countries from the late 1960s and early 1970s and a decline in the secular-nationalist movement. The Westernization project failed and the political crisis heightened. Dominant nationalism has generally remained in a political coalition with Islam.

The rise of political Islam has domestic as well as international bases. In the Middle East and Asia, political Islam, like most other reactionary movements, was born in the context of poverty, economic misery, and political oppression, and in periods of political crises. Among the hungry and destitute, the Islamic movement gained support with the promise of salvation for the dispossessed and in the absence of a strong egalitarian, secular political force, they gained ground. Islamic rhetoric in the region, in countries under dictatorship where no opposition was tolerated—where progressive, socialist, women's rights groups, civil rights movements, and workers' organizations were brutally crushed—found a way to the hearts of deprived people. The anti-imperialist rhetoric added flavor to this appeal.

After the Islamic Republic of Iran took power, this movement got a chance and came out of the margins in the Middle Eastern countries. It was in Iran that this movement organized itself as a government and turned political Islam into a considerable force in the region. Thus, the Islamic Republic's downfall will facilitate the disintegration of Islamic sects worldwide.

When I came to the West in the early 1990s, I was faced with the fact that the majority of intellectuals, mainstream media, academics, and feminists, in the name of respecting "other cultures," were trying to justify Islam by dividing it into fundamentalist and moderate, progressive and reactionary, Medina's and Mecca's, Muhammad's and Kholafa's, folksy and nonfolksy. For people like me, the victims of Islam in power, it was suffocating to listen to and have to refute endless tales to justify the terror and bloodshed committed by Islamic movements and Islamic governments in Iran and in the region.

Western liberal and left-wing intellectuals have a strong sense of guilt about the West's past colonial history and are apologetic to the Third World as such. They consider the Third World a given entity, where people are keen to suffer under the rotten rules of Islam, are happy to be deprived of the human civilization in the twenty-first century. To them, women desire sexual apartheid, girls love to be segregated, people hate civil rights and individual freedom in the Third World. In their view, people are the allies of Islamic movements and Islamic governments in the Third World. This is a distorted image of reality. I call this *inverted colonialism*. In this picture, people who are fighting for civil rights and secularism, and against political Islam are nonexistent in the Third World. According to their view, human rights are relative to culture, and the culture of the Middle East is an unchangeable, uniform, barbaric culture. I call this *inverted racism and colonialism*. There is an ongoing battle, particularly over the last twenty or more years, between progressive movements in the Middle East and the West on one side, and political Islam on the other side. The records of the daily struggle of people and the non-Islamic opposition in Islam-ridden countries and the news of the daily resistance of the youth and women in Iran demonstrate the reality of peoples' needs and expectations in the Third World. The self-centered mentality in which everything should revolve around the guilt of Western pseudo-intellectuals is appalling. Freedom of expression, equality of men and women, and the right for a secular state applies to people in the Third World, too. Isn't it shameful that we have to argue about it?

According to cultural relativism, human rights are a Western concept and not applicable to people living in non-Western parts of the world. Cultural relativism is a racist idea because its essence is difference. The idea of difference always serves racism. According to cultural relativism we must respect people's culture and religion, however despicable. This is absurd and amounts to a call in many cases for the respect of brutality. Human beings are worthy of respect, but not all beliefs must be respected. If a culture allows women to be mutilated and killed to save the family's "honor," it cannot be excused.

Cultural relativists stamp us as Islamic and define Iran as an Islamic country. Contrary to this definition, Iran is a society keen for progress and sympathetic to Western achievement. More than twenty years ago, women walked in the street without veils. Although the Islamic Republic has been trying to impose the veil on women for twenty-three years with killing and acid throwing, flogging and daily propaganda, women have immediately pushed back their veils as soon as knife and acid have been withdrawn. Similarities to the West have always been seen as high values and virtues. That is why the Islamic Republic cannot control the people of Iran. The young generation that was born under the Islamic Republic is keener on Western culture and civilization, and has more enmity against the Islamic Republic and more hatred for Islam than my generation did.

Secularism must be defended actively and resolutely in Muslim-inhabited countries and in Islam-ridden communities in the West. The shameful idea of cultural relativism and the systematic and theorized failure to defend people's, particularly women's, civil and human rights in these countries and communities have given a free hand to political Islam to intimidate people and incite the youth. Universal human and civil rights must be the standard.

Why are secularism, separation of Islam from the state, separation of religion from education, and other secularist demands so urgent and pressing in Iran as well as in the region? Why do we have to push for secularism now in the twenty-first century, two hundred years after the West? What does secularism mean to me?

In the West, with the emergence of capitalism, a profound political, cultural, and philosophical movement emerged and criticized backward and antiquated ideas and beliefs. The Enlightenment, defense of individual freedom and civil liberties, the battle against the church and backward culture, caused a deep change in society's horizon and values and advanced the society. Western society shook off backward feudal and religious thoughts and beliefs.

In Iran, however, capitalism emerged under a repressive regime. Thus, the society did not experience the Enlightenment, and we did not have an array of giant thinkers and philosophers at the forefront of the movement for change. Rather, we had a repressed and closed society together with an army of intellectual dwarfs who were and are up to the neck against modernism, progress, and women's liberation. In the West, there was battle against religion and for secularism and freethought. In Iran, backward intellectual midgets took shelter under the robes and turbans of *mullahs* against modernism and advancement. These "intellectuals" theorized the "despicable" ideology of "westoxiction" or "Westernism." Together with this domestic situation, the dominant tendency internationally was anti-imperialism and anticolonialism. A complete system of anti-modernism and antisecularism emerged. That is why the 1979 revolution for freedom and justice was defeated by the Islamic movement. When the Islamic tendency took the upper hand, following deals struck by Western governments to fob off Khomeini and the Islamic movement on a people's revolution, society was disarmed completely.

Iranian society has changed dramatically and deeply since 1979. The movement for secularism and atheism, modern ideas and culture, individual freedom, and women's liberation and civil liberties has been widespread and deep. Disgust for religion and the backward ruling culture is immense. Women and the youth are the champions of this battle, a battle that threatens the basic pillars of the Islamic system. Any change in Iran will not only affect the lives of people living in Iran, but will have a significant impact on the region and worldwide. Secularism is not only realizable but is also, after the experiences of Iran, Afghanistan, the Sudan and Algeria, an urgent and pressing need and demand of the people of the region.

Based on my discussion of the socioeconomic situation in the Middle East, political Islam, the backward Eastern culture, and particularly after the Iranian experience, the 1979 revolution, I believe that the demand for secularism must be comprehensive and maximalist. It must push for absolute and complete separation of religion from the state and other vital demands as follows:

- Freedom of religion and atheism. Complete separation of religion from the state. Omission of all religious and religiously inspired notions from laws. Religion to be declared the private affair of individuals. Removal of any reference in laws and identity cards and official papers to the person's religion. Prohibition of ascribing people, individually or collectively, to any religion in official documents and in the media.
- Complete separation of religion from education. Prohibition of teaching religious subjects and dogmas or religious interpretation of subjects in schools.
- Raising of public scientific knowledge and education.
- Prohibition of any kind of financial, material or moral support by the state or state institutions to religion and religious activities and institutions.
- Prohibition of violent and inhumane religious ceremonies. Prohibition of any form of religious activity or ceremony that is incompatible with people's civil rights and liberties. Prohibition of any religious manifestation or conduct that disturbs people's peace and security, or is incompatible with regulations regarding health, safety, environment, and hygiene. Prevention of cruelty against animals.
- Protection of children under sixteen from all forms of material and spiritual manipulation by religions and religious institutions. Proselytizing activity by religious sects targeted at children under sixteen should be prohibited.
- All religious denominations and sects should be officially registered as private enterprises, subject to regulations and laws.

I finish my testimony with the hope that in the coming years of the twenty-first century, we will witness development and progress in Islam-ridden societies and in Muslim communities in the West. All freedom lovers and secularist forces around the world should take part in a joint effort to combat political Islam, to promote secularism, egalitarianism, and freedom in those societies. Humanity must achieve victory over Islam.

Notes

1. Ali Shariati, "Fatemeh Fatemeh Ast" (Fatima is Fatima) in *Collected Works* (Tehran: Chapakash, 1994), vol. 21.

2. Azam Kamguian, *Islam, Women, Challenges and Perspectives* (Stockholm: Nasim Publications, 1997).

3. Ibid., pp. 201–202.

18

THINKING FOR ONESELF
Faisal Muhammad (Pakistan)

I was born in 1947 in Lahore. Being a reflective child from the very beginning, I always wanted to find out for myself the truth about human existence. Although my father was a religious person, he was not devout. My parents were divorced and my mother made the wise decision to let me stay with my father. She believed that in Pakistani middle-class society a divorced woman with few economic resources could not provide the protection and support required for a child to get proper education. With a heavy heart she made the decision to let me live with my father and stepmother.

My father had developed a fancy for a woman barely eighteen years old when he himself was forty. He pronounced the *talak* (divorce) quickly to get rid of my mother and bring in his new wife. I was only three at that time. I grew up denied love and affection, but my father saw to it that I went to the best school in town. I could never accept the narrow interpretations of Islam that were offered to my various questions. For a while I became interested in Sufism but soon found out that my sufi master was a liar and a bigot, notwithstanding his pretensions of being a scholar and teacher of mysticism. Whenever he talked about the Hindus who had lived in Lahore before 1947, he forgot his message of human love and the fanatic in him would take over. During unguarded moments he would acknowledge that many Hindus and Sikhs were good people, but whenever I directly probed the subject he would give the standard version of all Hindus being *kafirs* and therefore killing them or turning them out of Lahore was all right.

Sometimes I would go around Lahore on my bike and, without any particular plan or objective, go through different parts of the city. This would include Krishan Nagar and Sant Nagar, which were not far from where I lived. These were middle- and lower-middle-class Hindu localities before partition. Here one could still read Hindu and Sikh names inscribed in stone at the entrance. Sometimes the house was named "Sunder Nivas" or "Bharat Nivas." I often wondered who were the people who lived there and why were they driven out at partition. By chance I got hold of novels and short stories written by Krishan Chander, Rajinder Singh Bedi, Saadat Hasan Manto, and other writers. Their great works on partition opened new vistas before me. I began to see the pernicious role played by religion and fanaticism in society. I think at about that time I became skeptical about religious beliefs. In 1968 I began studying at the Punjab University. It was the year when the student movement in Pakistan was radicalized. Many of my new friends were leftists and some of teachers were Marxists. Thus began a long association with Marxist politics and I read all the great works on Marxism.

By that time I had realized that Islam, like many other religions, was a primitive moral code that had outlived its usefulness in the present time. Muslim societies all around were corrupt, repressive, oppressive of non-Muslims, and eminently amenable to male chauvinism and domination. The ruling class could always invoke the most reactionary edict from the Koran to oppose progress and reform.

I read a great deal of original Islamic literature and studied the life of Muhammad and his various successors in depth. It was quite clear that he had established a totalitarian system in which there was no scope for innovation and freethought. Nothing impressed me, but I have never been able to grasp how so many millions of people continue to follow his teachings blindly and fanatically. Perhaps a lack of modern education and fear of death combine to render them victims to threats about punishment and hellfires. Although the Islamic god is presented as the most merciful, the Koran is replete with references to severe punishments.

The totalitarian system of Marxism and the undemocratic practices of the communist groups and parties in Pakistan also proved a disappointment. I have subsequently become a humanist and a rationalist. I think only a secular democracy can provide freedom of choice and belief. I think that Islam is currently the most backward-looking ideology in the world. It is indeed a threat to world peace but most crucially its venom is directed at freethinkers of Muslim origin.

19

A RATIONALIST LOOK
AT ISLAM
Husain Ahmed (Pakistan)

I have often wondered if, for a Muslim, I was brought up in a deeply religious family. I was born into a *Shī'a* family, and my earliest memories are of going to my native town from Delhi with my mother and siblings for the Muharram (observed by the *Shī'a* in commemoration of the martyrdom of al-Husayn, son of Ali and Fatima, the Prophet's daughter)—my father joined us later—but they were ten days spent in enjoyable and high excitement. The children certainly looked forward to it every year as a social occasion.

My father only started to pray regularly later in life, but he used to fast and in the month of Ramadan would also pray. *Shī'a* men often pray at home and so did he. My mother not only prayed and fasted but also, later in life, said the optional prayer of the *tahajjud* in the small hours of the morning.

My sister was taught to read the Koran but my three brothers were not. When I was four years old I was sent to a Koranic school. I was singled out for this treatment because of the very special nature of the school, which had only recently moved into our neighborhood. The *mullah* (religious scholar) who owned it was, I think, a brilliant educator. He jealously guarded his method of instruction by insisting that on admission the child must not be above the age of four—otherwise, he may well remember later in life how he was taught. I remember being quizzed about it by some relatives but not being able to explain. He taught us in class—I cannot remember how many children there were—and the doors were bolted from inside. We all sat on the floor and I vaguely remember him introducing the alphabet in a way that we found entertaining. He associated every letter with an assuming remark or rhyme, which were to recall every time he wrote a letter on the blackboard. I now know that this method is called *mnemonics* and is highly effective in enhancing memory.

He kept several canes by his side, but I do not think he ever used any of them. He did, however, distribute sweets at the end of each day. There were other stratagems he employed to encourage the children, which I can vaguely remember, but none of them went to heart of his system, which at the end of just three months resulted in the child being able to haltingly but correctly read any part of the Koran. He rightly asserted that since the child did not understand the meaning, why did it matter whether he was reading the last or the first verse?

At the end of three months we were taught by another *mullah* who simply made us fluent in reading. Six months later we were examined by some eminent *mullahs*, who then gave us our certificates as part of the graduation ceremony!

With most Muslim children, if they are going to receive any education at all, it will start with learning to read the Koran. The irony of supposedly the most difficult and profound book being taught to the most immature minds is completely lost on the majority of Muslims. To add to the irony, reading literally means *reading*. There is no attempt at teaching even the rudiments of the Arabic language. The child learns to read without understanding a single word. The contrast with secular education, where the reading material is made as inviting and interesting as possible, could not be more striking.

Most children are taught to be able to read on sight, but a few commit the whole book to memory. They are given the appellation *Hafiz* (preserver, protector, guardian), which they write before their names and which gives them an elevated status in society. In adulthood they usually earn a living by becoming teachers of the Koran. Some of them go on to specialize in the techniques chanting the Koran and are called *Qari* (reader). There are various schools of chanting and numerous treatises are devoted to the subject.[1]

Because blind boys are often encouraged to train as *Hafiz*, a blind man is often automatically addressed as *Hafizji* (Mr. *Hafiz*), even though in fact he may not have memorized the entire Koran.

Most public gatherings commence with a recitation from the Koran. In his autobiography the eminent British philosopher A. J. Ayer recounts attending a conference in Pakistan that opened with just such a recitation. If Ayer (who was well-known humanist) chose to read a paper on some aspect of moral philosophy it may well have been preceded by a *Hafiz* or a *Qari* reciting verses from the Koran containing the most blood curdling threats to nonbelievers or promising torture in hell to any transgressors of its moral codes, such as homosexuals! Of course, almost none of the believers would have had any clue as to the meaning of what had just been recited. Those very few suffciently familiar with Koranic Arabic, who may have understood, would not have possessed the mindset to appreciate the irony.

Since to this day most children are taught traditionally, which can mean at least two to three years of drudgery, I have great affection for my first Koranic teacher, whose innovative mind I admire. But what a sad and shameful waste of talent! If only he had had proper training as a secular educator and pursued a career in that field. Much later my mother used to remark that he charged a bigger fee than what my brother was paying at his college!

I am sure that there are some *ulama* (religious scholars) who are as clever as any other scholars, and one wishes that instead of devoting their lives to harming humankind they had pursued careers that promote its welfare. In most Islamic countries there is even a ministry of religious affairs employing a large and well-educated (often abroad) workforce.

I think my parents took great pride in my being able to read the Koran at such a tender age (and so did I!) but there was no coercion on their part to recite it regularly afterward. Similarly, although I was taught to pray I was never forced to pray regularly. I did pray for a brief period but it was only because the local Sunni community were opposing the building of a *Shī'a* mosque. My attendance at the prayers was more a political gesture than an act of piety!

All my siblings had a special day made of their first fast. Many friends and relatives were invited to mark the occasion. When I came of age for fasting to commence, the Partition [of India, in 1947] took place and everything was so dislocated and disorganized that I never had a ceremony arranged for me—the result being that I have never fasted! Although my parents were committed to religion in their own lives, they seemed unwilling to impose it on us and I remember appreciating that as a youngster.

Looking back, I think I also had exposure to the views of some relatives who were unusual for a Muslim community. I had an uncle who, although not irreligious, was of Sufi persuasion. He used to attack traditional religious practices, and one of his remarks sticks in my mind because of its clever wordplay. He was fond of saying that it was wrong to call Muhammad, the Prophet, *rahmatul 'ālamīn*, "blessing for the world"; it was nearer the mark to call him *zahmatul 'ālamīn*, "trouble of the world." (In Urdu, the only change needed to pass from one meaning to the other is a single dot, whereby an *r* becomes a *z*.) His argument ran as follows: Since the vast proportion of humanity from its inception has not received the message of his prophethood or has not believed in it, it will land in hell. How can he then be anything but a curse for the world at large?

I noticed that my father did not object to or resent this clearly blasphemous statement, which was later repeated in front of other people. I thought it such a clever remark that I often used to tell it, until one day I mentioned it to a Muslim sociologist who was studying at the London School of Economics. She was completely taken aback and muttered something to the effect that she did not find it amusing. She was clearly affronted. I now only tell it to known atheists or people I know to be broad-minded.

My relatives fall along a continuum from atheism to unquestioning commitment to religion. One obviously avoids discussing religious issues with those who are religious or are known to take umbrage, but most are happy to participate in discussions in spite of their views. Anything less than this I would find very uncongenial. Most family occasions turn into political or religious debates! Some distant relatives live in India as they were members or supporters of the Congress Party. Most of them are atheists, and some female relatives are married to Hindus.

Knowing from an early age that people can be atheists and perfectly respectable, or can make clever remarks even at the expense of Muhammad without meeting explosive wrath, gave me some encouragement in thinking critically. I think I had my earliest doubts at about the age of fifteen. They stemmed from what I saw as injustices imposed by, or at least allowed by, Allah. I regarded the imposition of *purdah* (veil) on women in the former category. Why were women enjoined to endure the humiliation and hardship of concealing themselves from head to toe when they were clearly the victims of men's lascivious behavior? Men were not to blame entirely, either, because that is the way they were created.

Why were men allowed four wives and not women four husbands? Why did Muhammad marry so many times? How could he marry a nine-year-old? At that time I was unaware of other discriminatory teachings against women, for example, that a woman is allowed only half the inheritnace and her evidence in court is only counted as half. I think the verse "Men have authority over women because God has made the one superior to the other, and because they spend their wealth to maintain them. Good women are obedient" (IV.34) leaves one in no doubt about women's status. Why, if he is just, does he prefer some of his creatures to others?

For some time the answer that those were the mores of Muhammad's time satisfied me. Later I realized the weakness of this argument. Since Islam is intended to provide guidance for all times, its injunctions cannot be time bound. What it teaches should be valid for all times. If polygamy can be allowed then why not female infanticide, which was also practiced by the seventh-century Arabs? Similarly, Muhammad is supposed to be the perfect man for all times. His conduct should meet the criterion of perfection for all times and in all cultures. It would be a different story if the Muslim claim was simply that Muhammad was perfect for his time and Islam an ideal ideology for seventh-century Arabia.

My other preoccupation with injustice was in the form of poverty, which I saw everywhere around me. How could Allah be at the same time just and

responsible for allowing poverty to exist? He is omnipotent and so could eliminate it if he so wished. I was told a parable concerning Moses, who apparently
had asked God just that question. God, presumably, made no reply. However, that
very night there was a violent storm and Moses' thatched roof was blown over
and damaged. Moses was unable to repair it and became depressed. Just then God
chose to speak to Moses to deliver a homily. He told Moses to go and find a
thatcher but to remember that thatchers existed only because some people were
poor enough to do menial jobs. Poverty was inevitable because otherwise everyone would be equal and why would anyone work for anyone else?

Of my three brothers, two had no great interest in religious matters. The one
just above me in sibship had always been religiously inclined. My mother's half
serious explanation for it was that she was fasting when he was conceived. At an
early age he abandoned the conventional *Shī'ī* doctrine under the influence of
Jamā'at-i-Islāmī. A few years later he converted to Ṭulū-i Islām (the dawn of
Islam) and has remained faithful to it.

I came across the Ṭulū-i Islām literature, which I avidly read, and for a short
period I accepted it. What appealed to me about it was that its founder, Ghulam
Ahmad Parvez, completely rejected the *hadith*, which he regarded as totally unreliable. He claimed to base his theology on the Koran alone, which he interpreted
in a very unique way. He claimed that the Koran advocated an economic system
that was socialistic and against private ownership of land. This meant the elimination of feudalism and the doing away of poverty. Into the bargain he also threw
in progressive policies about women and criticized the institution of slavery and
the death sentence for apostasy, which he alleged were un-Koranic. Like every
other group of Islamicists, he insisted that his was the only true and valid interpretation of the Koran. In claiming this he ferociously attacked *mullahs* and conventional Islam, which made his "message" the more attractive to the likes of me.

The spell of Ṭulū-i Islām, however, lasted for only a short time. I came to England at the age of nineteen and soon after, perhaps in 1958–59, came across copies
of Bertrand Russell's *Mysticism and Logic* and *Sceptical Essays* in a secondhand
bookshop, and went back to being an atheist. I had just become aware of his existence and his stature (it may have been partly because of the Campaign for Nuclear
Disarmament) and read these two books eagerly. They may have provided the spark
that rekindled what I think is my natural bent of mind. I cannot remember waking
up one morning and saying to myself that I had again rejected religion. The process
was gradual, but I did become aware of describing myself and thinking of myself
as an agnostic, which was a term I had picked up from Russell.

I think I crossed the Rubicon when my fellow students set me a litmus test.
They challenged me to eat pork if I really did not believe in the Koranic injunctions. I hesitated a few times and explained it in terms of the revulsion I felt,
which was instilled in me from an early childhood. I then thought about it and

began to eat it. The brainwashing done in the name of religion is truly on a mind-boggling scale that cannot be matched by any other institution.

Soon after a baby is born in a Muslim family the *azan* (the call to public prayers recited by the *muezzin*, the crier, five times a day from the minaret of a mosque) is said in his or her right ear. As soon as a child is old enough to say a few words, he or she is taught to memorize the *kalimah* (the creed of the Muslim, "There is no deity but God, Muhammad is the Apostle of God"). At an early age boys and girls begin to fast. Both are called to prayers five times a day. The Koran is recited by the congregation of friends and relatives when anyone dies. It is a sign of piety and not at all unusual for both Muslim men and women to recite the Koran for long periods every day. Most children learn to recite the Koran before secular education starts, which seems odd—the supposedly most difficult book is the first to be taught, and in a foreign language! In the month of Ramadan it is recited for hours in congregations every night.

I am astonished that even in secular societies like the United Kingdom, for instance, on BBC Radio 4, a religious program called "Thought for the Day" is broadcast every weekday. Would any political party dare to broadcast its propaganda this often? How would the "free world"—led by America—have reacted to the communists carrying out similar magnitude of propaganda?

I had started reading the *New Statesman* at this stage and in its back pages came across atheist and humanistic organisations. I came across an advertisement for the *Humanist* (not the *New Humanist* yet) and sent off for a sample copy, and probably briefly subscribed to it. I started my degree course in 1960 and remember asking a friend at Manchester to also write for a copy. I stopped subscribing while at Manchester, for lack of money. Knowing that very eminent thinkers shared one's views and that there were societies that promoted them was an extremely comforting and liberating experience.

When I came back to London in 1963 I got in touch with whatever body H. J. Blackham headed and probably subscribed to it. In 1967 (I remember the year because I had just passed the driving test and drove to South Kensington) Blackham's organization ran a course for volunteers to act as marriage guidance counselors for humanists. Blackham was very encouraging and asked me to be a trainer. I was at that stage working in the learning disability field and did not myself have the right experience. I did, however, agree to participate as a volunteer. There were about thirty volunteers who were divided into two groups for training puropses. The group I was in was taken by a social worker, and the other group by a clinical psychologist called Elkan. I only went to one training day, as they were held on Saturdays or Sundays and I was living in Surrey. I wrote to Blackham and excused myself and had a nice reply from him. After that I think my association with that organization ceased.

At the height of the Rushdie affair, a journalist from Pakistan wrote a very moving letter to the *Observer* about the plight of nonbelievers in that country, who cannot even share their views with their young children just in case, in their innocence, the children happen to betray their secret. Those who were not unfortunate enough (or fortunate, according to Muslims!) to be born Muslim can only imagine the terror apostates who publicly proclaim their apostasy must experience.

I began to think anew about my own reasons for not believing. The arguments I came up with, I am sure, are commonplace, but I have not come across them in writing, including Bertrand Russell's *Why I Am Not a Christian* (which, as one would expect, is basically a philosophical treatise) and will record them here for what they are worth. They are not in order of the importance I attach to them or in order in which I became aware of them—which, anyway, I cannot now remember.

Why would Allah choose to send all his messengers to the same very small area of the world? The Muslim tradition says that there were 124,000 prophets, some more major than others. some of them came in twos or threes (also stated by the Old Testament), for example, Moses and Aaron, Abraham with Isaac and Ishmael, Jacob and Joseph. If humankind was being favored by so many prophets at one time, why then stop?

It cannot be that humanity is no longer in need of guidance. In fact, a contrary case can be made. Never before have human beings possessed the means of destroying the whole planet. If guidance was needed at any time it is needed now.

The Muslim explanation for why God sent Muhammad to Arabia when he did is that conditions there were so bad at that time that guidnace was needed. Among the evil practices mentioned are interminable tribal wars and female infanticide. But surely other societies at other times have had both. What about tribal and nationalistic warfare in other parts of the world, some occurring even at present? What about infanticide practiced by other societies, such as, sacrifices made to their gods by the Incas and the Aztecs? What about the young women burned alive in suttee by Hindus? Why were none of them sent any prophets?

I cannot help feeling that that tiny proportion of humankind whose dwelling happens to be *Hijaz* is, for some unknown reason, unduly favored by Allah. They first had a monopoly on his guidance and now have a near monopoly on his other great blessing—the oil!

Why could the sending of the guidance not go on indefinitely? But even if at some stage it had to come to an end, surely the time to send the last guidance would have been now, not only, as mentioned before, because we have unprecedented means of destruction but also because we possess means of communication we have never had before? Even if the last messenger had come to a very remote, preliterate society in recent times, the whole world would have become aware of his or her existence and the ideal state he or she might have created.

In fairness, the same arguments apply to the other two revelatory religions. Why did God choose to send his only son when he did? He should either have chosen to be more prolific and sent his sons (and a few daughters!) at different times to different parts of the world or sent his only son at an optimal time, which, for reasons mentioned above, appears to be now. However, someone in a distant future may take a different view of what may have been the optimal time. Only God can look into the future!

One consolation for not having prophets in our midst is that we are also spared the prospect of meeting the fate that Lot's or Noah's contemporaries did! Why were they singled out for punishment?

My agnosticism took me back to the Koran. I knew the saying that the best informed about religion are the irreligious. I considered it my duty to read the Koran in its entirety and form my own judgment. My reaction can be summed up in one word: disappointment.

I had hoped that at least in a few of the verses I would find food for thought. Although no classicist or philosopher, I had enough exposure to these disciplines to know that one acquires a different perspective on the human condition when one comes across a truly profound view or thought one had not been aware of before. The same applies to great literature. There are numerous couplets in Ghalib's poetry (Urdu and Persian poet, 1797–1869) that leave me stunned by what they reveal about the human condition. I think when I say this to my Muslim friends they think I am saying it to produce an effect, but in reality I only state it for what I consider to be a matter of fact.

It is only with some difficulty that I manage to restrain myself from challenging them to produce a verse in the style of the Koran that could rival the couplet by the great Persian poet Saadi (c. 1215–?1292):

> Be aware of the status of Human Being
>   Humanity [i.e., the essence of civilization] consists in respecting other human beings.

Now I can see that in the translation the couplet has entirely lost the appeal it has in the word play on the words "human" and "humanity." It does not also sound as majestic as it does in the original. This is exactly the argument the apologists for the Koran give. They say that the Koran can be understood and appreciated only in the original.

I readily concede that the majesty of the language would be lost in the translation, but the sentiment or the philosophy should come through, as it does in Saadi's couplet. One can wholeheartedly respond to its message, whose significance one sees immediately and whose lofty ideal one can appreciate. What comes through in the translation is that the Koran's contents are terribly mundane and inextricably embedded in its milieu and are ephemeral.[2]

The Koran is particularly difficult to translate because of its alleged poetic

language. which it obviously employed to its advantage in impressing contemporary Arabs. Allah should have known that by making use of the poetic language
he was running a greater risk of ambiguity, which would result in his message
being misinterpreted. He should have used the most prosaic language in order to
avoid any risk of creating nuances and linguistic subtleties. If the language had
not been so imprecise (or poetic) there would not have been numerous sects and
so many radically divergent schools of thought. A very prosaic language would
have been easier to translate.

Another striking aspect of the language of the Koran is the abrasiveness of
the tone it employs. Instead of presenting a reasoned case for Islam with convincing arguments, the emphasis is on threats and coercion. I do not know how
many verses are devoted to it, but the threat of punishment awaiting humankind
in the form of hell is ever present. The other refrain is how Allah knows best and
how everything is known to him.

Natural phenomena are mentioned with great monotony as self-evident arguments in support of the existence of God without any attempt at proof (e.g., XVII.
90; XXV.33; LXXXVIII.17).

The Koran is also very repetitive. Some bitterness comes through when it is
claimed that Allah will guide whoever he wants to and will lead astray whoever
he does not want to, or that some people do not accept the guidance because he
has already sealed their hearts:

> Would you guide those whom God has confounded? He whom God confounds
> you cannot guide. (IV.88)
>
> The hypocrites seek to deceive God, but it is He who deceives them. . . . You
> cannot guide the man whom God has confounded. (IV.143)[3]

If that is the case, how can a just God punish people for their inability to convert to the true faith if he is responsible?

It also does not seem just that he will forgive who he will and punish who he
pleases (II.284; V.18; V.40; IV.48) or that he sends devils down to incite unbelievers to do evil (XIX.83).

He labels unbelievers as senseless men (XXIX.63). Who created them senseless? There is a touch of Emperor's Clothes in XXIX.43. Why did he not create
everyone wise?

Apologists, who in general have liberal views, tend to pretend that Islam has
a record of tolerance. They try to make their case in two ways. First, they cite the
examples of some Muslim rulers who were tolerant. They ignore the fact that
usually those rulers tended not to be very religious. Secondly, they point to verse
II.256: "There is no compulsion in religion," ignoring the numerous verses that

mention how unbelievers will be tortured in hell. How can there be choice if, by opting for unbelief, one guarantees eternal damnation for oneself? It is like a parent saying to a child that he has complete freedom to help himself to a cake, but to bear in mind that if he does eat the cake he will be severely punished.

An author of books on Islam who is popular in the West because of his liberal views made just such a claim for Islamic tolerance in one of his books. I wanted to write to him to challenge his claim, but had my doubts if he would reply. In order to make sure that the absence of reply could not have been because he had not received my letter, I confess to employing a ruse. I first wrote to him simply congratulating him on the excellence of the book he had written. He promptly wrote back thanking me and pointed out that another book was in the pipeline based on his forthcoming television series about Islam. Having established that he would receive my letter I wrote to him a second time, making the case against Islamic tolerance along the lines I have done above.

I also pointed out that Muhammad's own conduct did not show any tolerance. After the conquest of Mecca the first thing he did, accompanied by Ali, was to march to *Ka‘ba* and destroy all the idols in it. What provision did he make for those who had not converted to Islam so they could continue with their practices of worship? Even if he had claimed the *Ka‘ba* for the Muslims he could have told the unbelievers to move their idols to another place, where they could continue to worship them in safety. Is it any wonder that the Koran is replete with verses concerning the hypocrites—those who professed to embrace but in reality remained unbelievers?

I was not entirely surprised when he chose not to reply. I sent him a reminder, but with no more success.

The liberal press in the West is prone to publishing pro-Islam material. They cannot entirely ignore Islam, as it is increasingly in the news, and I think they are reluctant to publish anything against it for fear of promoting what the very active Islamist lobby has vociferously termed *Islamophobia*. At least that is how I explain it to myself when I get very frustrated at the newspapers for never publishing any letters I have sent putting across the alternative point of view in the most nonoffensive language possible. If I only could point out to these well-meaning editors, who have succeeded in suppressing even the mildest criticism of Islam, that to give offense on religious grounds is to truly adhere to the Prophet's *sunna* (exemplary code of conduct)! Surely those who had not converted to Islam and who had for centuries worshipped those idols in the *Ka‘ba*, which Muhammad considered his duty to destroy at the first opportunity, must have felt a little offended. It is repeatedly mentioned in the Traditions that Muhammad was offered all kinds of inducements: the leadership of his clan, all the wealth he desired, in return for giving up his criticism of the Meccan deities. That he chose to reject all these enticements in favor of proclaiming the truth (and giving offense to the Meccans, including friends and relatives) is proudly reported by Muslims. It seems that it is the duty of every Muslim to uphold and wage the holy war (II. 216) in spreading their brand of the truth, but this right is denied to the apostates, who pay for speaking out by forfeiting their right to live. No one must give offense to Muslims, but it is a great virtue for Muslims to practice iconoclasm.

I sometimes notice that I have given offense to Muslims by not using what I think should be called "religionist" language—luckily not meriting a death sentence! Just as race and gender are used in racist and sexist language, religious expressions are employed in the religionist language. From an early age Muslim children pick up the habit of including in their speech expressions like "God willing" (*Inshallah*), when expressing their intention to do something, or "By the grace of God" (*Mashallah*), when admiring something or someone. I went through a phase when I decided that the religionist language was no more acceptable to me than the racist or the sexist. I deliberately stopped using these expressions and sometimes found that the person I was talking to would interject them in my sentence at the appropriate time. On these occasions I was made to feel that I had committed more than a faux pas.

Even if I were not a humanist, I think I would find it totally unacceptable that homosexuals (IV.16; VII.81) or people who attempt suicide (IV.29) should in any way be punished. Should a merciful Allah punish a whole people because some of its members practiced homosexuality (VII.81; XXVI.160 ff)?

Muslims start their prayers (and the pious among them many other activities) with the following: "In the name of God, the compassionate and the merciful." You wonder what would God have done if he had not been merciful and compassionate! Tortures of hell aside (V.33), he is also responsible for any misfortune that befalls anyone (LXIV.10). This verse, incidentally, contradicts another, IV.79, which seems to allow some sort of free will.

It is just as well that my brothers and my son take no notice of IX.23. I wonder how I would feel if this threat were real for me. Would I have concealed my thoughts from them as I do from Muslims I cannot or do not know well enough to trust? Would I act like a *munafiq* (hypocrite)?

In writing this article I am also taking the risk of being disgraced in this life (XXII.9), but in view of the damage Islam has done and is doing to Muslims, I have come to the conclusion that it is worth taking!

NOTES

1. In fairness to Islam, Christians have the Gregorian chants and the Latin Mass.
2. Here are some examples of what I call the Koran's ephemeral contents, with my comments in square brackets.

When you (Prophet) are with the faithful, let one party of them rise up to pray with you, armed with their weapons. After making their prostrations, let them withdraw to the rear and then another party who have not prayed come forward and pray with you; and let these also be on their guard, armed with their weapons. It would much please the unbelievers if you neglected your arms and your baggage, so that they could swoop upon you with one assualt. But it is no offence for you to lay aside your arms when overtaken by heavy rain or stricken with an illness, although you must be always on your guard. God has prepared a shameful punishment for the unbelievers. [These are evidently instructions given to the Prophet about how to pray in time of war, and are of no use to anyone else at any other time. What has the last verse got to do with the pre-ceding verses?] (IV.102)

Believers, take neither Jews nor Christians for your friends. [I take it that most Muslims regard this verse as anachronistic! If not, why do they not act on it, but, if yes, are there other verses in the same position?] (V.51)

Believers, remember God's goodness to you . . . [This is very long, and to do with the Battle of Uhud and with no general message for mankind.] (XXXIII.9 f)

It was he who drove the unbelievers . . . (LIX.2)

Further examples of ephemeral verses to do with Muhammd's life with no general "eternal" message for mankind:

Those who invented that slander . . . (XXIV.11)

Prophet, say to your wives, "If you seek this life and all its finery, come, I will make provisions for you. . . ." (XXXIII.28)

Believers, make room in your assemblies when you are bidden so to do: God will make room. . . . (LVIII.11)

Yet no sooner do they see some commerce. . . . (LXII.11)

Prophet, why do you prohibit that which God has made lawful to you. . . . (LXVI.1)

(b) Embedded in its milieu.

Those of you who divorce their wives by declaring them to be their mothers . . . (LVIII.2)

The evil-doers mock the faithful. . . . (LXXXIII.29)

3. See also V.42; VI.39; VI.125; XXX.29; LXXIV.30; LXXIV.55; XVI.93; XX.16; XLII.8; XVIII.17; XVIII.57; XVI.109; XVII.45; XXV.51; XXXIX.36).

20

FLOODS, DROUGHTS, ISLAM, AND OTHER NATURAL CALAMITIES

Syed Kamran Mirza (Bangladesh)

Many times I have been asked by my friends and peers why I am not a true believer in Islam, although I belonged to a Muslim family. I never thought that I would ever disclose my own belief to the public for fear of social insult that may be inflicted upon me, as the apostate in Islam is punished by death. Things have changed a lot at the beginning of the twenty-first century and Islam has begun to be scrutinized, criticized, and evaluated by many freethinkers among Muslims throughout the world. Especially after the horrendous incident of September 11 by the Jihadi Muslims of Bin Laden's al-Qaeda on the soil of the United States, Islam has fallen into a hot pan of criticism by the entire world. I thought this was the time to be fair to my friends and admit that I am no longer a believer in Islam. The erosion of my belief system started over a long period, slowly and gradually. Dear readers, let me take you to my childhood in a remote village of Bangladesh to discover how I was changed.

I was born in a traditional Muslim family of Bangladesh. My parents were devout Muslims and their mother tongue was Bengali. They both used to pray regularly, observe fasting (Ramadan), and follow other conventional rituals of Islam. Nonetheless, neither of my parents were fanatic Muslims in any way. My father was quite a liberal person of honest personality, despite his regularities in prayers and daily Koran recitations. My father established a beautiful mosque in our house at his own expense in which he used to recite the Koran in Arabic with a sweet melodious voice. He also performed the pilgrimage (*hajj*) to Mecca. My father was a middle-class *zaminder* (landlord) who loved people of all religions equally. As a result, he had many friends from the local Hindu community.

In my early childhood days, I underwent religious education every morning from 6 to 8) in the *maktab* (Koranic school) before I went to primary school of general education at 10 A.M. In the *maktab* I learned all those suras/rules/methods required to observe five daily prayers, and also learned to read the Koran in Arabic. However, I never understood the meaning of any word of the Koran or the suras, which used to bother me very much. From my boyhood, I was very inquisitive, wanting to know about the religion of Islam. I wanted to know about the meaning of Allah, the Prophet, and angel. I often questioned *mullahs* about Allah, as to who he is and how he looks, where he lives, what he eats, angels, hell, heaven, and myriad other things related to the religion of Islam. Nevertheless, I was never satisfied with their answers. I was always trying to judge everything with human logic, which angered the *mullahs*. I used to ask my father who Allah was and where he lived. My father used to answer: "Allah is very big and powerful, and Allah lives over the sky (other side of the sky) with his many angels who help him in every business. Allah looks over all of us from the sky, decides the fates of everybody, decides every action taken on Earth." Then my father also talked about the dangers of hell and the good life of heaven, which I had already learned from those *mullahs* in the *maktab*. In those early childhood days I was praying regularly, but I did not attempt to read the Koran because I was not interested in something that I did not understand. One day, I asked my father if he understood the Koran which he read so routinely. My father replied: "I also do not understand what I am reading, but *Huzur* (*pir*) told me to read it everyday which will bring immense *sawaabs* (recompense, reward, profit) for me and for my family. Allah will reward me for reading the Koran daily. You don't need to understand the meanings of the Koran. Just by reading the Koran you will get lots of *sawaabs*."

I could not conceive what my father told me about reading the Koran without understanding the meaning, and I did not read the Koran again until recently, in translation. Fortunately, my father never forced me to read the Muslim holy book, but he asked me to pray regularly, which I was doing anyway. I was proud and happy to be a born Muslim, since I learned from *mullahs*, learned men, and my elders that Islam is the ultimate truth and best religion in the whole world. The Koran is the infallible words of Allah, who loves only the religion of Islam, and all other religions are simply bad, people of other religions are all *kafirs* and destined to go to hell. Muslims are impeccable human beings, and Allah loves only Muslims. Only we, the Muslims, are supposed to go to heaven and nobody else can enter the gate of heaven. I was also told that only Muslims would be prosperous in this world and hereafter. Among the peoples of the entire world, Muslims are the only perfect and good human beings, and so on. Also, I learned from the *pirs* (holy men) and *mullahs* that someday the entire world will be converted to Islam. Even though I was praying daily (*namaaz*), I did not observe fasting. I used to enjoy attending *Waaz Mahfils* (sermons) to listen to all those myths about Islam and prophets, but I had hard times digesting those incredible stories of Islamic miracles and the like, which were recounted by village *maulanas* with their extreme, loud voice of fanatical zeal. I used to make fun of those illiterate village *musullees* (devotees) who used to weep with their endless tears of fear induced by the dreadful scenarios of hell fires as described by a fanatic *maulana*. However, I could hardly believe such cruel tortures would be inflicted by a merciful Allah, nor could I imagine all those fanciful lifestyles of Islamic heavens described by *mullahs*.

Life went on, and when I was in the eighth grade, my father was preparing to transfer me to a good high school in a district town for a better education. At that time, something happened to me that gave a big shake-up to my belief system in religion. My father and most of other adult Muslims in our village were *mureed* (disciples) of one famous *pir* of Barisal (southern district of Bangladesh). This *pir* used to visit our area during the monsoon period in a decorative boat (popularly called *Pinnish*) with his several disciples, cooks, and servants. At the time my father was planning to send me to the district town, that *pir* arrived at our house with his gang of followers. There was a big festival of celebration for Pir Shaheb in our house, with lots of delicious foods being prepared to serve the wise man and his retinue. At that moment, when the *pir* heard from my father about the plan of sending me to a district town high school, the *pir* asked my father not to send me to a high school. Instead, the *pir* asked my father to send me to a *madrassah* (religious school) for religious education by which he (father) could please Allah. My father basically agreed with his *pir*. Later when he disclosed this matter to our family, everybody in my family (elder brothers, sisters, and mother) including me were furious and vehemently protested at this silly idea of the *pir*. My father dropped the suggestion of the *pir* upon pressure and agreed to send me to the high school. Later, when the same *pir* came to our house next year, we learned from his close disciples that the *pir* himself had three sons, all of whom he had sent to Dhaka to study in a good high school, and one of his sons would study medicine. The *pir* never sent any of his own children to *madrassah* to please Allah; on the contrary, he advocated his disciples to send their children to *madrassah*. We discussed this hypocritical attitude of the *pir* with our father. He was shocked to discover this hypocritical attitude of the *pir*. I, too, was very much disturbed by the selfishness of the *pir*. For the life of me, I could not understand why he was suggesting to my father that he send me to *madrassah* while his own children were studying in the English school. But such was life in rural Bangladesh in those days.

While in the school at district town, I was still praying regularly and following some of the Islamic rituals, and, of course, still believed in Allah, hell, and heaven. I was always inquisitive about Islam, religion, and Allah. Whenever I got the chance, I asked questions about religion. One thing that was very strange to me was the fact that religion and poverty go hand in hand. I mean, poor people are always very deeply religious, and the rich and affluent were mostly liberal or nonreligious. Although *mullahs* told me that Allah loves Muslims or religious persons, I could never see the proper reflection of that in real life. If Allah really loves Muslims, then how could he not see the distress and sufferings of the poor Muslims? While I was still in our village home, I was very fond of attending various religious gatherings like *Waz Mahfil, Urus* (festival of rituals to commemorate the birth or death of a famous *pir*), *milad mahfil* (meetings), and the like. There in the *Waz Mahfil* I had many opportunities to listen to religious sermons by *maulanas* who, on the one hand, used to proclaim ample rewards from Allah for devout Muslims in this world and hereafter, and little or no success for the infidels in this world and dreadful punishment of hell in the hereafter. On the other hand, the same *maulana* used to say that sometimes Allah let Muslims remain poor and to suffer the abject poverty to test their *īmān* (devoutness to Allah, faith). This flip-flop attitude of Allah used to bother me a lot, and I just could not conceive this idea of testing *īmān*. The entire thing looked to me incongruous and did not make any sense

SOME CHILDHOOD EXPERIENCES

Maulawi Kader Mullah was our village *mullah* who taught me the Koran and methods of prayer. This *mullah* was very poor but an honest, amiable type of person. I liked him because of his simplicity and honesty. This Kader Mullah used to recite the Koran twice a day without fail, in addition to his daily prayers and other rituals. As a child I wished him financial success, as he was so poor that he could hardly get two square meals a day. His son was my playmate and most of the time he was poorly fed or sometimes not fed at all because there was no rice at home. Many a time I fed him from my house with whatever I was able to save for him. This Kader Mullah never saw any happiness in his life, although in my judgment he was the most devout Muslim. Many years later when I inquired about Kader Mullah, I was told he had died of a serious sickness; his family suffered untold misery of poverty and one day they left the village for an unknown destination. Poor Kader Mullah died of malnourishment and disease. This cruel incident was a shocking surprise to me, and I never understood why a Muslim like Kader Mullah had to suffer to such an extent when almighty Allah is so merciful? Kader Mullah did his humble *Munājāt* (supplication for blessings extending his two hands) to get enough food five times each day for sixty years. Yet the merciful Allah never heard his prayers even once!

Cholera and Smallpox Eradication

In my school period (in the 1950s), I saw that village people always took the help of *pirs*, saints, and *mullahs* in order to get well from their diseases. There was no good doctor in the rural areas of the erstwhile East Pakistan, and sick people had to depend mostly on quack doctors, *pirs*, saints, and *mullahs*. They used to depend on *pani para* (hydrotherapy) received from the famous *pir* or saints of the locality. Every year during wintertime, cholera and smallpox were almost epidemic in rural East Pakistan. The *mullahs* used to give religious sermons in *Waz Mahfil* that Allah was sending cholera and smallpox to punish the sinners. Needless to say, the village people did not have the faintest idea at all as to what caused cholera or smallpox! They strongly believed that these diseases were purely sent by Allah as punishment. Our local *maulawi shaheb* (preacher) used to advise us to perform more regular prayers to avoid *ghazab* (curse from Allah, wrath of Allah) and he used to arrange cholera and smallpox elimination prayers every year in our village. These "cholera-driving" methods were really very interesting. The *pir* from Barisal used to arrive at our village and the entire village was informed about the ceremony of the cholera-driving prayer at night. It used to start after *Esha* prayer (last prayer of the day). The *pir*, along with his several assistant *mullahs*, used to stand at the center of the *Uthan* (open space of every house), and hundreds of village *musallees* (devout Muslims) and their children would gather around them, all extending both their hands toward the sky. Then the real drama of rituals would begin. First, the big *pir* used to recite some *dua* (supplication) in Arabic (which we never understood) for a few minutes, and after that the remaining small *mullahs* would recite in loud voices some incredible sermons and *Zikirs* (chanting) together for a few minutes. Then the big *pir* used say in Bengali that he has asked the devil of cholera and smallpox to leave this home immediately. After that, the joint rituals of *Zikir* in chorus used to begin, in which everybody would participate. For about twenty minutes, everybody performed *Zikirs* in loud voices, and then there was a final *Munājāt* (supplication) by the *pir* and that would conclude the cholera/smallpox driving ritual. The total time taken for this entire sermon was about an hour. Then we would go to another house and do the same, running from house to house until we had completed the entire village. To complete the entire village took the whole night, and we would return home the next morning. The pious *pir* used to return with a big chunk of cash and materials collected from each house for this job wonderfully done. The villagers would heave a sigh of relief, knowing that destructive cholera and smallpox could enter their houses no more. These ridiculous sermons of disease eradication used to happen every year until the mid-1960s, when village people somehow realized this nonsense ritual had no value in eradicating cholera and smallpox from their villages. The villagers were smart enough to know that cholera and smallpox were still afflicting the poor villagers with poor hygiene.

Natural Calamities

In my childhood, I heard from *mullahs* and *pirs* that Allah sends rains, storms, thunder, earthquake, and other natural calamities according to the needs and performances of humankind on Earth. In the monsoon, we had rain every day, causing floods, and the deluge used to bring all kinds of misery to our people. Then, in summertime, we saw continuous drought drying up ponds and canals and burning crops. To get rid of drought, people used to perform special prayers to Allah for rain. All these activities used to raise more and more questions in my mind about Allah and his whimsical purposes. I could not comprehend the acts of God in such a way. Why so much rain when we did not need it? Again, why so much drought when the land was already too dry? In 1954 there was a devastating flood submerging two-thirds of erstwhile East Pakistan (now Bangladesh). I was a young boy still living in our village. I still remember vividly how the entire village was under water; all crops were under water and the cultivating lands around our house looked like an open sea. Moreover, it was raining almost every day making peoples' lives ever more precariously miserable. I could not understand the purpose of rain when there already was water—water everywhere. There was a sea of water submerging entire villages, on top of that, the rain was falling from the sky—cats and dogs every day and night. I was thinking and questioning: Why is Allah pouring water from the top when we are already inundated below? What was the purpose of pouring water over the water? How could a merciful, benevolent, and wise Allah justify this kind of unjust act? All those questions used to bother me very much. In spite of all this, people in the village were devout Muslims despite their extreme poverty.

Communal Riots

In our neighboring villages Hindu families lived peacefully with Muslims side-by-side for centuries, until 1947 when Pakistan was created by Jinnah as a consequence of his two-nation theory. First, during the partition (1947), there was a Hindu-Muslim riot in our area and many Hindus were killed because they were a very tiny minority in that area of densely populated Muslims. During that riot, I was a mere child so I did not quite understand why there was riot between Hindus and Muslims! Only thing later I learned from the seniors that Hindus are *kafirs* and bad people, so they have to die.

There were several good affluent Hindu families near our village and I had some school friends from those Hindu families. Several of them were very good friends of mine, with whom I used to go to school and play and eat together in their houses. I noticed that many times local Muslims were hostile toward those Hindus whenever any riots occurred in neighboring India. These scenarios of riots used to bother me very much, as it was very hard for me to conceive why Hindus in East Pakistan (now Bangladesh) had to die for crimes committed by some Hindus in Delhi or Bombay. One day I asked one local *mullah* if he supported killing of local Hindus for his Muslim brother in Delhi or Bombay. I was simply stunned and horrified by his reply. The *mullah* told me: "*It is the sacred duty for the Muslims to kill* kafirs. *Hindus are* kafirs, *therefore it is our duty to kill them!*" I asked him if it is written in the Koran or *hadith* to kill Hindus. The *mullah* replied, "Yes!" At that time, it was not possible to verify the *mullah*'s assertion, since I did not understand a word of Arabic and there was no translated Koran available to me.

Later, in 1963, there was another riot in East Pakistan (as it was then called) during which I lost one of my Hindu university friends who left Pakistan for India as a refugee because his father was killed in that riot. After a few months, when I returned to my village home during summer vacation, I was told that most of those Hindu families that we had in our locality had left for India for fear of losing their lives in riots. I also learned that, along with some other Hindus, one of my boyhood friends, Nani Gopal, died in the riot of 1963. That news broke my heart. When I tried to remember the handsome childish face of Nani Gopal, I could not accept that terrible news. I was searching for answers for this tragedy, but nobody could answer my questions. I wanted to know how a religion could advocate killing humans of other beliefs. I wished I could ask Allah about this!

After my graduation from the university, I became a lecturer in the same institute. Immediately after that, I was sent to an Eastern European communist country for higher studies. I lived four long years in that communist country, where I got some experience that has changed my perspective about the world. I was told back home that a communist country is a godless country where people are generally nonbelievers. Before I arrived in that country, I thought the communist country must be poor because God does not love them, therefore these communists must be devoid of any glad tidings from Allah. In addition, I thought, communist people would be not good people and they would be devoid of any morality, or they may not be compassionate, either. At the beginning, I was somewhat suspicious about the general population in that country, and I was reluctant to socialize or talk with them. However, to my surprise, I found most people in that country were gentle, cordial, and very friendly. Ordinary people were very curious to know about me and my country, mt people, and so on, with much sympathy.

In those days, the number of foreigners was very small in that country;

nonetheless, there were quite a few foreign students from the Middle Eastern and African countries in various universities. One day, I was sitting alone in the corner of a *kavarna* (tea stall) and was drinking a cup of tea when a middle-aged gentleman suddenly came to my table and asked permission to join me. Out of politeness I said yes, and he sat down next to me and immediately ordered two beers. When I asked, "Why two beers?" He replied, "One is for you and the other one is for me, if you have no objection." Then we talked about various issues, and I found him a very courteous and kind person. He told me that he was observing me from the other corner and I seemed to him very sad and lonely. He said during the Second World War he was in France, a foreign country for him, and he knew very well how painful it was to be alone in a foreign land. After a pause, he offered me friendship with his family, so that I would not suffer the same ordeal as he. He had two sons and one of them was just my age and was studying medicine. He gave me his phone number and address before he said good-bye to me.

I found them to be a good, respectful family who really extended their friendship to me. I used to go to their house almost every weekend to enjoy dinner with them. As long as I was staying in that country, this family gave me everything I missed—love, care, good advice, and lots of compassion. We discussed many different issues, like politics and social matters, with ease, but I found disappointing their comments when I brought up religious issues. The man I called "Uncle" (by his wish) was a die-hard communist and never believed in any deity at all. Sometimes he used to make some jokes about Islam, especially the system of four wives (polygamy), women's inferiority to men, the Prophet's polygamous habit, and the like, which hurt my feelings. You see, I was still proud of being a Muslim, and I loved the prophet Muhammad, Allah, and other features of Islam. It was difficult for me to take sarcastic jokes about Islam from others, even though I was not a practicing Muslim. This kind of joke about the Prophet's polygamous habits and other fallacies of Islam were common weapons thrown to me by many other friends and by some of the university teachers who used to question me about Islam. Sometimes I got so hurt and annoyed with their questions that I tried to answer with all my knowledge, and I was always defensive. I tried to defend our Prophet by whatever logic was possible. Nonetheless, I could not sell my logic to them.

Most of all, it was a mystery to me how these people were so good in all other aspects in spite of the fact that they were godless people. If they did not believe in Allah, hell, and heaven, then how and why were they good human beings? What made them such moral and perfect human beings without a belief in God? Back home in Bangladesh, I thought only the Muslims were good people and rest of the world's populations were simply bad people or not as perfect as Muslims. I found the majority of the people in that communist country were basically good, more sincere and honest than the people of Bangladesh. Out of one hundred people I could find ninety good ones; on the contrary, I could not find even twenty good people out of one hundred Bangladeshis. How was that possible? Besides, I found these communists were light years ahead of Muslims in the fields of science and technology. Otherwise, why would I come there for my higher studies? Compared to Bangladesh, this communist country was much richer and more developed. I pondered why. I found all the Muslim countries were desperately poor. Yet we, the Muslims, were claiming that we were God's chosen people! These are some (I have mentioned a few out of many) valid questions that used to bother my mind. I wanted to find the reason why Muslims were so poor. Why is the person who is super-pious desperately poor? Why did Kader Maulawi have to die in dire poverty and in hunger? Does Islam, or overreligiosity, have anything to do with our poverty?

Another question brewing in my mind was the fact that the scientific field is totally under the control of the West. Out of one hundred famous scientists, I could not name even five Muslim scientists! Does religiosity have anything to do with it? My faith in religion was getting thinner and thinner day by day, and I decided to explore Islam more in detail. I decided to read the Koran and *hadith* when I got a chance in the future. Nevertheless, I still maintained my faith in Allah and his prophet, but with some skepticism. Finally, in 1969, my higher education was over and I achieved my Ph.D. from that communist country, and I left for home.

After returning home, I joined my alma mater as a teacher. Within a year, I got married. Life was really very romantic for a few months until the freedom struggle of the Bangalee nation began in March 1971. Being a staunch freedom-loving Bangalee, I supported *Muktijuddh* (freedom fighting) wholeheartedly. But I was shocked to discover that most Islamists (Islamic clerics—*mullahs, maulanas, qari, hafez, madrassah* students) were generally supporting the Pakistani military junta in their cruel suppression of Bangalee movement. These *mullahs* were supporting the Jamā'at-i Islāmī (religious party) of erstwhile East Pakistan. *Mullahs* and *madrassah* students were the nucleus of paramilitary forces (Razakar, Al-Badr, and Al-Shams) formed by the Pakistani military junta's chief intelligence officer, Maj. Gen. Rao Farman Ali Khan. The Pakistani military junta unleashed terror on the Bangalee nation with its fake slogan of saving Islam. They were killing Bangalee men, women, and children by the thousands daily throughout the country, burning thousands of homes, raping thousands of Bangalee women, and looting properties in the name of saving Islam. "Save Pakistan to Save Islam" was their slogan. And our Bangalee *mullahs* were brainwashed by this fake slogan of the Pakistani rulers, and they decided to dedicate their lives to protect Pakistan. These *mullahs* were supporting the oppressive Pakistani force with their minds and bodies. They were practically sold out to Pakistani army generals because the military tricked them into believing that by serving the military they were serving Islam.

I could not understand what Islam had to do with our freedom struggle for the Bengali nation. This betrayal of *mullahs* was the turning point in my faith, in my religious beliefs. In those days I was commuting between my university town and Dhaka, and I saw thousands of villages that were burned to ashes, many hundreds of innocent peoples who were killed in the rural areas of Bangladesh. In one such incident, local *razakars* (*mullahs* and *madrassah* students) took my childhood friend Anwar Ali, a twenty-six-year-old young man from a neighboring village as a *Muktijuddha* (freedom fighter) suspect. These heartless Islamists tortured him for three days and nights, and eventually killed him with a bayonet. He was the only child of a village doctor popularly called "Doctor Uncle." In my childhood, Doctor Uncle used to treat me with fatherly affection. When the war was over, I went to see our Doctor Uncle in his village. On seeing me, both Doctor Uncle and his wife began crying like babies, rolling on the bare ground. That terrible scene was heartbreaking. I was trying to figure out how those *mullahs* (*Razakars*) could be so cruel as to snatch the only child of these unfortunate parents. I could not understand how those persons, after reading the Koran and *hadith* (so-called Allah's books), turned into such devilish human beings? Therefore, I immediately decided to investigate what was in the Koran and *hadith* that could make people worse than a ferocious lion.

That day, I started to read the Koran bit by bit. I purchased two translated Holy Korans, one in English and one in Bengali. I also purchased some renowned *sahih hadiths* books.[1] I also gathered the Bible, Bhagavat Gita, and some chapters of the Upanishads. I was reading the Koran, first very slowly but systematically from the beginning, and my intention was to finish the Koran. Before that, I had read the Koran selectively, some verses here and there with no clear-cut idea of what it was. The more I read the holy book, the more I was dismayed. My intention was to search divinity, philosophy, science, ethics, morality, social, and political issues in the Koran. But alas, the Koran was a book with no chronology, no philosophy, no science at all (but had plenty of erroneous science), plenty of problems in ethics and morality, ample redundancies, unfit social and political teachings by today's standards, and, above all, it had ample superstitious scriptures. I also found out that the Koran was a book full of hatred, cruelty, unethical matters—no divinity at all. Some of the hateful verses that bothered me most are:

> O ye who believe! Take not the Jews and the Christians for your friends and protectors. They are but friends and protectors to each other. . . . (V.51)

> If anyone desires a religion other than Islam (submission to Allah), never will it be accepted of him; and in the Hereafter He will be in the ranks of those who have lost (All spiritual good). (III.85)

> And fight them on until there is no more tumult or oppression, and there prevail justice and faith in Allah altogether and everywhere. (VIII.39)

Fight those who believe not in Allah nor the Last Day, nor hold that forbidden which hath been forbidden by Allah and His Messenger, nor acknowledge the religion of Truth, (even if they are) of the People of the Book (Christians and Jews), until they pay the Jizya with willing submission, and feel themselves subdued. (IX.29)

If you meet those who are infidels or non-believers, you cut their heads off and tie things around their necks, start a war and God will give victory and those who will die in the war fighting God will not forget their acts. (XLVII.4)

My childhood religious teacher (Huzur Shaheb, a *mullah* who taught me about religion) always used to tell me that Islam is the best religion, Allah's chosen religion, and the most peaceful religion. It is beyond my comprehension how religious scriptures can dictate to kill other human beings! I will never understand how a so-called religion of peace can dictate to kill. At the same time, I could not believe in a deity who advocates the killing of other humans. This was when I lost my faith in Islam completely and became a secular humanist. To me, all people are the same, and I do not make any distinction between any religions. Finally, I came to terms with the notion that religious identity is not at all important to me.

My conclusion was that the Koran was man-made, as other holy books that predate Islam were, and I came to the realization that the Prophet himself primarily created it for his own self-serving, adventurous ambitions. Along with his own self-serving scriptures, he plagiarized verses from various books such as the Bible, Book of the Zoroastrians, other older religions, and local folklore. The Koran is full of folklore and mythological stories of ancient Arabia. Many verses were purely self-serving for Muhammad. Many verses are so unethical that no divine power would have ever uttered such silly things! Then I also read the *hadith*—*sahih Bukhari, sahih Muslim, sahih Tirmidhi*,[2] and others—and I found that the *hadith* are full of superstition and even worse than the Koran. Then I read the entire Bible and I found that the Bible is not holy, either; it is also full of junk talk and did not sound divine to me at all. One thing I should mention here that in the Bible there is a decent chronology and redundancy is very rare. In the New Testament, I found some good philosophical parables and also I found some good humane talks by Jesus. However, overall, there is no doubt that this book was also man-made. Other books, such as the Gita and the Upanishads, are all more or less the same—man-made books. But the Bible and other religious books do not have hateful dictums, as is the case with the Koran. And that is for sure!

My conclusion about religion in general is that all religions are man-made. Either all those prophets were pathological liars, or they were ambitious psychopaths who wanted to establish social order in the name of a supreme being. I do not believe for a moment that religion in general has any import toward one's morality, and I do believe that a person can be morally rich even without a religion. Most psychologists, philosophers, and scientists overwhelmingly reject religious models of human morality, and for good, valid reasons biologists reject the laughable biblical and Koranic creation theory.

Religion has some good things in it, but in general, bad things outweigh the good things, which has created a division among humans rendering racial and sectarian competition leading to immense miseries and intolerance among people. Moreover, in this material world we perhaps do not need any personal God or Allah or Bhagavan who will reward people for their kowtowing or sycophancy, some supreme, jealous God who severely punishes humans who do not kowtow to him and even punishes those who have not commited bad acts in the world. We perhaps need a very compassionate and a merciful God who would help people in their times of misery and sorrow. As modern science is progressing day by day and humans are getting knowledge about their surroundings, people all over the world are realizing that it is science, not religion, that gives humans knowledge and courage to fight natural calamities and tackle other social and medical problems. Besides, in my opinion, in this era of scientific revolution, one does not need to believe in any puritanical, superstitious deity, which only benefits people in an imaginary way and not in the real sense. Religion unquestionably makes divisions and creates prejudice among people. Therefore, we should believe in just one religion, and that is "Human Religion"—in other words, we should believe in humanity. This would invariably stop any future bloodbath and would spare future generations from the bondage of religious slavery. The time has finally come to slay the dragon of monotheism because these religions have done more harm to humanity than all other religions put together. Therefore, the sooner we get rid of all the religions, the better it will be for future generations. And this is my heartfelt wish.

NOTES

1. Especially the collections of traditions of al-Bukhārī (d. 870 A.D.) and Muslim (d. 875 A.D.). Their compilations are often called *Ṣaḥīḥ*, meaning "sound" or "authentic."
2. al-Bukhārī (d. 870 A.D.), Muslim (d. 875 A.D.), al-Tirmidhī (d. 892 A.D.).

21

LIBERATION FROM MUHAMMADAN IDEOLOGY

Shoaib Nasir (Pakistan)

I was born to Muhammadan parents in 1971. I first finished the Koran in Arabic when I was about five years old. After reading it for the first time, I told my mother that since I did not understand a word of it I would like to read it in Urdu. Consequently, my mother gave me another copy of the Koran with a Urdu translation. That translation opened my eyes, even at that age, to an ideology I did not think anybody could adopt in good conscience. I was particularly perturbed by Muhammad's narcissism. Every other line seemed to reiterate that he was Allah's beloved last prophet (read: sidekick). I found the book mostly disgusting. Further, one thing that really bothered me was the fact that under Islamic law one could not preach any other religion in the country. However, when Muhammadans went to other countries, they wanted (and still do with even more fervor) the freedom to practice, preach, and convert others. I can say with utmost confidence that I have never seen such a shameless display of hypocrisy in any other ideology. I also think that only Muhammadans can pull it off; I do not think there are too many people on this planet dishonest enough to have such blatant double standards.

At the age of five or six, my comparative study was based on the fact that in Muhammad's ideology people were not allowed to eat pork, but in Christianity they were. I found myself confused in terms of which of the two ideologies was revealed by Allah. I asked my mother. Fortunately, she did not give me the

Muhammadan pat answer that Allah revealed only Muhammad's ideology and the rest of the religions were its corrupted version.

My earliest memory is of being disrespectful to Muhammad's ideology. My mother always asked me to carry Muhammad's book above my head respectfully. I always carried it above my head when I was in sight. Once I neared the cabinet, I would put the book on the floor and step on it before I put it in the assigned place. Such was my contempt at that age toward a religion I believed was a madman's musing. Similarly, if I dropped the book, I was supposed to kiss the book and touch it with my forehead; in short, I had kissed the book many times long before I actually got to kiss a girl.

When religion was made mandatory in the school system I remember reading accounts of assassinations by Muhammad's sidekicks. I remember being horrified by accounts of beheadings, especially when the accounts said that such-and-such companion of Muhammad's beheaded the enemy with one big stroke. I also did not like Muhammad's wallowing in accounts of what happened in hell. The accounts made it seem as if Muhammad's only grievance at the time was that his enemies happened to be rich. It seemed that the only reason for Muhammad's sick mind conjuring up images of hell was his passive-aggressive anger. The accounts reeked of jealousy.

In short, such was the violence against my innocence against my will.

I also had a chance to see the film *Buddha* when I was about six or seven. I asked my father what he was about. What my father told me about him seemed more appealing than what I had seen in Muhammad's teachings. Buddhism seemed far more enlightened than anything else at the time. From that point onward, I used to tell everybody at school that I was a Buddhist. Once, when I was seven, I was questioned by a friend's mother. It so happened that this friend told his mother that I had told everybody that I was a Buddhist. During the break, she asked me how I was a Buddhist and if I was born to Buddhist parents, and so on. I told her that my parents were not Buddhist, only I was.

When I was about ten, I realized that people generally did not want me to play with girls because Muhammadanism asked people to separate boys from girls. I guess Muhammad understood how to make people submissive—by regimenting every single act. Following Freudian principles, one can argue that Muhammad gave women back to his followers only in heaven after taking them away for so long.

At the age of eleven, partly due to peer pressure and partly due to confusion accompanied by my attaining puberty, I practiced Muhammadanism blindly for about one and a half years. I offered prayers, observed fast, and so forth. Finally, at about thirteen, I came home one day and announced to my mother that there was no god, and religion was just a sham. A few days later, the *muezzin* at our mosque was caught raping a six-year-old boy. However, due to the community's senselessness, the *muezzin* was released without any charges being brought against him. This was the same *muezzin* who, while claiming to be upright and beyond reproach, for the past six years had preached anti-Semitism and hatred for the West.

Nineteen eighty-eight was a great year in my life. I was sixteen and fortunate enough to read Bertrand Russell's *Why I Am Not a Christian*. It was a whiff of fresh air in my life. Having grown up in Zia-ul-Haque's regime, I had lost all hope. After reading the book I decided to stand up for who I was and finally decided not to go to the mosque even for the perfunctory family ritual of Eid prayers twice a year. I'm glad to say that I haven't stepped inside a mosque in the last fourteen years. I had mixed feelings, though, because now my father had to go to Eid prayers by himself. However, my contempt for the religion was so strong that I could not convince myself to go with him.

Nineteen eighty-eight was also great because on August 17, in a great turn of events, Zia was blasted out of existence. A few days before his death he had decided to introduce Muhammad's *sharī'a*. Following Khomeini's principles, Zia wanted to introduce mandatory attendance at all five prayers. He had not finalized at this point what kind of punishment he would introduce; however, he did mention that people would get a lashing in public for not showing up at the mosque. When I finished watching his national address, I looked at my brother. He asked me what was going to happen to us and where we would go. Since no countries other than Thailand and Singapore gave the inhabitants of a terrorist/rogue state visas, I said to my brother firmly that I would leave for Singapore but I would not offer prayers. Luckily, Zia disappeared into thin air on August 17, 1988. I often wonder about the last few minutes of his life. I wonder how he behaved.

In 1988 I also thought out my project on Muhammad, of which I had some vague idea even before then and on which I have been working since. Zia's regime was full of persecution of atheists and secular people. He had heavily armed the student faction of Jamā'at-i Islāmī (fundamentalist organization) to Muhammadanize the country. He had also hired many *jammat* people to teach kids at primary and secondary school level, so by the time the students joined the university and the workforce they were thoroughly brainwashed. By the way, during his regime, "secularism" in Urdu was translated as "religionless," which goes against the grain of Muhammad's ideology, where religion is the basis of everything. People with an ideology different than Muhammad's were punished by the Jamā'at-i Islāmī and and its student wing, *jamiat*. In grade 11, I saw people's kneecaps being broken by *jamiat* members. I also saw students being tortured for having bought a female classmate a soft drink at the University of the Punjab cafeteria. A male student's naked body was found in Sheikh Zaid Hospital compound in Lahore early one morning. He was dead; the doctors who performed the autopsy said that every single hair on his body had been plucked and hot iron had been applied to his body. In short, in doctors' words, he looked like a boiled chicken.

At about eighteen, I had a chance to read Salman Rushdie's great book *The Satanic Verses*. It was banned and one could be put to death if found in possession of the book. I could not get the original; however, I found a photocopied version.

At about nineteen, I was doing a master's degree. I had finally managed to eat pork, courtesy of the American Center. I had become a social drinker as well. Eating pork had been on the top of my list for quite some time. Symbolically speaking, it was for me the last rite of passage required to part ways with Muhammadanism completely. My next step was to read more about the fact and fiction in what Muhammad had so carefully crafted in barbaric Arabia, thinking that he had arrived at some critical juncture in human history without accepting the fact that far superior cultures had already come into existence around the world. Anyway, Rushdie's book had gone in only so much depth. He had only scratched the surface; I was positive that the ideology had more filth hiding deep below.

One of my main goals at that time was to move to the Western part of the planet, so I could do more research on Muhammad and do a better project. I finally left for good in 1995, about a year after finishing my master's degree. My move to the West has completely disillusioned me. Academic clerisy, for the most part, has decided to jump on the political correctness bandwagon and not criticize Muhammad and his ideology at all. In most religious studies programs, professors criticize every religion on the face of the earth except the aforementioned. Some libraries have not even considered ordering Ibn Warraq's *Why I Am Not a Muslim* and *The Quest for the Historical Muhammad*. However, I can find every other book written by Western apologists of Muhammad's ideology. Incidentally, Muhmmad's ideology has the largest number of spin doctors, both Muhammadans and non-Muhammadans, who fail to question the fact that most world religions contradict Islam: they teach us not to kill, not to plunder at any cost. However, Muhammad's ideology in the name of Allah makes a virtue out of everything abhorrent in human nature. Also, some books have ridiculous arguments telling critics not to criticize the aforementioned ideology since it's the fastest growing religion in the world. In my mind, its growth makes it all the more necessary for us to criticize, and then let the ideology stand trial.

22

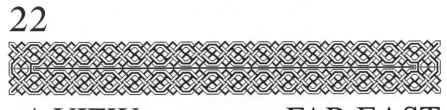

A VIEW FROM THE FAR EAST
Shah Ismail (Far East)

I was born in the Far East forty years ago. Born and bred a Muslim in a pre-dominantly Buddhist nation, I grew up feeling we were far superior in every aspect to nonbelievers, a concept upheld by Muslims around the world, even though their economic and social status are significantly behind the non-Muslims (Samuel Huntington wrote in *The Clash of Civilizations and the Remaking of World Order* that Muslims are convinced of the superiority of their religion; but obsessed with the inferiority of their economic standing).[1] I echoed the thoughts and teachings of Muslim elders, who told us that we were fortunate to be part of this purest and truest religion whose followers are given automatic entry to heaven just for being Muslims. Then I realized that everything we do as Muslims, from helping a starving orphan to playing matchmaker between a male and female, is all predicated on this concept of a choice between "heaven" and "hell," instead of doing things out of the goodness of our hearts. For a long while I, too, was fantasizing and salivating over my eternal resting place in heaven where I believed I held a ticket as a favor from Allah for being a slave to him. As my curiosity grew, I began to focus and search for the depth of heaven and what it had to offer. Lo and behold, I learned that Allah would provide us Muslim men (or boys, in my case) with seventy-two beautiful virgins, twelve pearl-like boys, honey, wine, fruits, water, milk, and a couch. Oh, boy! as a teenager with hormones raging, there were times when I fantacised about being married to those virgins, a common lure *mullahs* use in recruiting young Muslim men to fight the *jihad* (the same ploy that Muhammad used in attracting many Arab men to fight with him against his enemies fourteen hundred years ago).

The more I realized that I was the chosen one, the more I felt disconnected from *kafirs* (unbelievers), thus building a wall of prejudice toward them. The wake-up call for me was when I was sixteen years old and visited Singapore during a school break. I toured a popular attraction site called Tiger Balm Garden in Singapore. In it was a series of depictions in statues and art delineating what hell was like if you were a sinner. It was full of monsters, hydras, dragons, half-human-half-animal creatures—all busy torturing sinners in the worst forms imaginable, or perhaps unimaginable to civilized human minds (it makes me wonder if Almighty Merciful God could be that cruel to his children!). As I exited the garden, I noticed a big sign over my head that read, "Those who fail to pay their federal tax to the government of Singapore shall be doomed to face such eternal damanation as well," signed by Mr. Lee Kwan Yu, the president of Singapore.

On the way back to my hotel, I couldn't help but to think that hell was a scare tactic applied by the Caliphates, as used by the heads of governments today in both politics and religion alike.

As a kid growing up and as someone who attended Islamic congregations, mosques, and funerals, I noticed that the *mullahs*, *muftis*, and Muslim elders all preached how fearful Allah is, while being most merciful; how vengeful, while being most forgiving; how hateful, while being most loving; and so on. Of many funerals, I saw how women were prohibited from attending the burial of their loved ones. *Mullahs* reason that a woman's presence is a sign of disrespect for the dead at the burial ground. And women in general seem to have no significant role to play in Islamic society other than to be cooks and mothers. Men are clearly in charge of their women, dictating everything to them, from what their proper attire should be to how to conduct their behavior, especially in the presence of other men—all under the pretext of preserving dignity, which in actuality is control over their women. Islam is centered so much on women and sex that it has become an obsession in many Islamic countries today. My sisters were first sheltered by their father and brothers (myself included) and then later sheltered by their husbands—which is the norm in most Muslim families even in the twenty-first century. Consequently, the more Muslim women are brought up to be dependent on their men (father/husband), the more they become unproductive in society. I remember my American-born niece once commenting that she never saw a Muslim woman participating in the Winter Olympics or a team from any Muslim country playing in women's soccer tournaments in recent years. I am grateful that my niece lives in the United States, where she is free to be who she wants to be without a man controlling her mind and body, unlike the way her mother was brought up in her native country.

In the late 1970s I came to the United States as a young student eager to go to college in a land foreign to a Muslim mind like myself. Feeling lonely, I turned to Allah at least five times a day. At that time, revolution broke out in Iran, which later resulted in the taking of fifty American hostages. Most of my friends in college learned of this religion, Islam, for the first time and became curious, especially when seeing on television thousands of men and women in Iran chanting "Death to America" while holding the Koran in one hand and a gun in other hand. In my Monday morning sociology class, I was asked to stand before the class and to give a lecture on Islam (Islamic Course 101) by Professor Boon to her curious thirty or more students, who apparently had little or no knowledge of it. And I did give a talk as a confused but proud Muslim who felt it was my duty to spread the word of Allah to these nonbelievers, despite my limited knowledge of Islam and the Koran. As with all religions, I lectured on how peaceful, tolerant, forgiving, and merciful the religion founded by the Prophet Muhammad was. The truth was, like most Muslims today, I had read the Koran over and over, yet never comprehended the contents of it as it is written in Arabic, a language foreign to millions of Muslims. Consequently, we subconciously become the *taliban* (students) of *imam* who interpret the Koran as they see fit.

In my native country, we have a self-appointed *mufti* who periodically pronounces *fatwas*. Though the *mufti* has never attended a modern school, Muslims in my country look to the *mufti* for answers, everything from social and medical to judicial issues. My aunt, for instance, still embraces his teachings that the earth is flat and the moon landing by man was a Western hoax. Later I learned that it was the *mufti's fatwa* that women be barred from attending burial ceremonies. In our community, we were respected particularly not for what we had done but for our so-called title *Syed*—all Muslims with such a title claim direct descent from their beloved Muhammad. Since my grandfather was an *imam* who migrated from Yemen in his early years, his claim to be descended from Muhammad was an advantage that worked in our favor in our community. In actuality, Muhammad's two biological sons died in infancy, thus any claim of being a *Syed* by Muslims was baseless, though it remains unknown to most people today.

The more I observe Islam the more it becomes clear to me that it is a religion owned and manipulated by the Arabs for the Arabs in general. It is as though they have a monopoly on it and any challenge by non-Arabs will face fierce resistance. My feelings were confirmed during a visit to Saudi Arabia. Never have I seen a group of people wanting to safeguard this religion from the outside world as in Saudi Arabia. For example, while I was sitting in a shade watching worshipers circling the *Ka'ba* during *Umra* (lesser pilgrimage to Mecca), I saw a *mutawah* (religion police) who mercilessly dragged a ten-year-old boy by his arm while the kid cried, begging to be free. What was the crime? The boy was seen snapping a photo with his disposable Kodak camera. The *mutawah* was joined later by a uniformed policeman who took the boy into his custody without making any attempt to search for the boy's parents. I felt disgusted! Even a cult wouldn't treat children that way. What is it that they have that they want to hide so much from the outside world? That is precisely why Saudi Arabia is a nation most hostile to non-Muslims visiting their land. I know of no religion except Islam that bans others from visiting their places of worship, and it is certainly synonymous with a cult or mafia organization whose primary goal is to keep itself isolated from the outside world.

Now let us talk about logic in Islam (if there is any). During my trips to Saudi Arabia, I was annoyed by a customs official who ransacked my suitcase at the King Abdullah Aziz Airport in Jeddah. Attempting to crack a joke, I suggested to the officer that he get a dog to help him do his work. The officer was visibly insulted by my remark and reported to his boss who was a few feet away from him. The boss came over and warned me that if I ever made this remark again I would be jailed. So what was my crime? Dog, an animal most loyal and loving to man yet so abhorred by Muslims. Why? Because dogs are considered unclean and unsanitary. There are many *hadith* (traditions) that recommend the killing of dogs or describe how they are unacceptable to the Prophet, angels and God; e.g.: "The Prophet said: Angels do not enter a house in which there is a dog or there are pictures,"[2] and "Allah's Messenger ordered that dogs should be killed."[3] While the rest of the world adores this creature, it is unwelcome in the Islamic world. Then it dawned on me that Muslims are obsessed with cleanliness to the point of self-cleaning at least five times a day. I only wish that they cleaned themselves in their hearts more often than outer bodies.

Pigs! Muslims are more afraid of pigs than American cluster bombs. That is true! Today though you have a better chance of being struck by lightning twice in a row than to be infested by trichinosis—a disease that causes illness as result of meat, like pork, but is no longer a threat, thanks to modern medicine. Muslims are terrified of pork.

Intolerance! I knew that Islam was in deep water when I realized how intolerant it has become in my lifetime. Many Muslims, as if appointed by Allah, have taken the law into their own hands. In an Islamic country, the worst forms of crime are "apostasy," "blasphemy," and "heresy." One wonders who are they to speak for God? Recently, a medical professor named Dr. Yunus Shaikh from Pakistan was convicted by the Pakistani court of law. What was his crime? He dared to speak the truth that the Prophet Muhammad was not circumcised until he founded the religion Islam in his forties. He was found guilty of slandering Muhammad, even though the Prophet was not a Muslim until the revelation of the Koran was passed on to him by the Angel Gabriel when he was forty years old—by the messenger's own account.

It is no secret that scores of Muslims are killed every day for crimes against Islam as we enter the twenty-first century. Scientifically, we are behind. Socially, we are confused and messed up as ever. Technologically, we have yet to learn how to make a Q-tip. Politically, none of the fifty-seven Islamic nations has a democratic form of government.

In 1995 a house in Brooklyn was engulfed in a fire. In that house, a female cat had just given birth to seven kittens. Through the raging fire, the mother cat was seen risking her own life rescuing her baby cats, one by one, out of the house into a safe place. In the end, the mother cat was badly burned. The moral lesson here is that "honor killings" are still carried out today in some Muslim countries like Algeria, Jordan, Pakistan, and Saudi Arabia by parents, brothers, or uncles against Muslim girls in the name of preserving their image and dignity. Unthinkable, even in the animal kingdom! Again it is the case of Muslims being victimized by Muslims in Islam. Barbarism in its worst form! And more practices such as stoning, beheading, limb chopping, throat slashing, and genital mutilation are still condoned in many Islamic societies today.

In the aftermath of September 11 attacks by Muslim extremists in New York and Washington, I realized that Islam was doomed until Muslims dare to speak out and recognize their centuries-old shortcomings and collectively prepare for a major revision of the Koran, which they believe to be the unchangeable, untouchable word of God. The Christians and Jews did it a long time ago in order to adapt to this changing world. So long, Islam! Regrettably.

NOTES

1. Samuel Huntington, *The Clash of Civilizations and the Remaking of World Order* (New York: Simon and Schuster, 1996), pp. 102, 183, 185, 211.

2. al-Bukhāri, *Book of Dress*, vol. 7, book 72 of *Ṣaḥīḥ*, trans. M. Muhsin Khan (New Delhi: Kitab Bhavan, 1987), Hadith no. 833, p. 540.

3. al-Bukhāri, *Book of the Beginning of Creation*, vol. 4, book 54 of *Ṣaḥīḥ*, trans. M. Muhsin Khan (New Delhi: Kitab Bhavan, 1987), Hadith no. 540, p. 339.

23

AN ACCIDENTAL CRITIC
Taner Edis (Turkey)

I n my school days back in Turkey in the 1970s, I used to look forward to the religious instruction class each week. Not because I was at all devout—quite the opposite. Parents who so desired could opt their children out of the religion hour, and so I got to play outside for a while instead of enduring another lecture. Unfortunately, we usually couldn't get a ball game going, because only two or three of us out of a class of about fifty opted out.

Most kids who skipped religion class belonged to a minority faith such as the heterodox Alevi sect, or, like one of my close friends, Christianity. I was the rarest of the rare, going without even a nominal religion. In fact, I became somewhat notorious in school. Not only was I this half-American, equally fluent in English and Turkish, but I lacked religion. As kids will do, some of my friends pestered me about this. When a classmate preached to me about God, my sophisticated comeback was to ask, "Who's this 'Allah,' the neighborhood grocer?" To this day, I wonder how I survived school without being beaten up even once. I suspect that what I said was just too bizarre, so the other kids figured I was just weird this way and then we'd go back to playing ball or something.

*   *   *

The blame, naturally, lies with my parents. Religion was simply irrelevant to our lives when I was a child. My father is a hard-core Turkish secularist, with no patience for religion intruding on modern life. My mother, who grew up irreligious in California, seems at most slightly curious about religion, mainly as something other people do. They might have some vague beliefs in some sort of higher creative power, but even today, I'm not exactly sure. It was not anything that *mattered*.

Ours was also a household my friends compared to a library. I did not grow up, the way many others did, in a home where the Koran was one of but a few books, given pride of place. Our Koran was a tattered English translation, one among many hundreds of other books, one I would not even have noticed if I hadn't turned into a bibliomaniac and started looking through my parents' books. We had many children's science books, brought from the United States, and some childrens' encyclopedias both in Turkish and English. I was very impressed with them, fascinated by how much I could learn about the world just from books. I had plenty of fiction, fantasy, and fairy tales to read as well, even a number of Christian-lite Christmas books, which my mother brought out every December. When my Muslim friends spoke of God and his angels, of the wondrous Koran, it seemed obvious to me that these were also fairy tales. I was somewhat perplexed as to the whole business of believing them, but I didn't give it much thought.

My immediate environment beyond the family didn't encourage faith either. Few of our relatives and family friends were visibly religious, and when so, they seemed very liberal about it. We might visit a family who observed Ramadan and its monthlong fast during daylight hours, but they would immediately serve their guests tea and pastries, with no suggestion that there was anything wrong with our eating. They fasted, we did not, and that was all. Most others in our circle were nominal, unobservant Muslims. They believed in God and that the Koran was in some way a divine message giving a good moral foundation, but they didn't read the scriptures or care about doctrine. They only darkened the door of a mosque for funerals and such events. Where I grew up, faith was a personal business and some cultural color. It was not something people evangelized about, and almost no one turned Islam into a political statement.

So I never believed. I saw no great incentive for faith, except to please people who were not my immediate elders anyway. Adopting some vague, watered-down cultural Islam remained a live option for me, and my brother, I think, had some leanings in that direction as a kid. But in the end, religion was not important, and it was no great struggle to do without it.

*   *   *

Of course, this was not the result of any mature reflection. But the miracle stories of the devout sounded implausible and pointless, I was always pigheaded when it came to accepting popular opinion, and, just as important, I did not have any clear communal loyalties. I was a lot more impressed with my science books. Today I find, somewhat to my embarrassment, that my basic reasons for infidelity are much the same. I have to struggle to make sense of the very idea of a God, and when I get somewhere, it also becomes clearer that such a supernatural reality is improbable in the extreme. I still am not deeply rooted in any community and its beliefs. And I am even more convinced that modern science, though tentative and ever changing, is our best way of learning about the world. Religion just does not compare. I would like to say that I fell out of faith after a long intellectual and emotional struggle, that I knew Islam intimately as a devout believer and still came to see that it was false, harmful, or both. Then I might have had a more compelling story to tell. Unfortunately, Islam never had any attraction for me, and as I had occasion to learn more, my skepticism only deepened.

Today, my attitude toward Islam is complicated. I admit I respond to apologetics with irritation, and seeing many well-educated people I know still fawning over the Koran always leaves me puzzled. It seems the sanctity of the Koran is obvious to most people who grew up Muslim, though a preposterous notion to me. When presented as a serious description of the nature of our universe, Islam seems about as thoroughly mistaken as one could be. And I don't mean just popular Islam—polished intellectual defenses of religion that erect philosophical walls around the faith to protect it from criticism are, if anything, worse. On the other hand, I am more ambivalent about the social role of Islam. Most people seem to do better with a mythic perception of the world, and I hesitate to say that understanding the world as a godless, natural place is always a good thing. I mostly saw a low-key, tolerant Islam around me when growing up. So, though I sometimes get fed up and start thinking Islam is a curse in all its forms, I eventually simmer down and remember that rigid, orthodox Islam is not the whole story.

*   *   *

And yet I find myself a minor critic of Islam. I can't contribute to, say, arguments concerning the origins of Islam. I don't even speak Arabic, and at least in English and Turkish translations, the Koran seemed occasionally poetic but overall one of the most mind-numbingly boring books I have ever read. But in the occasional article or Internet rant, I can at least remind readers that not everyone from a Muslim country prays five times a day, and that some of us go so far as to reject much of Islam. When orthodox Muslim apologists exploit postcolonial guilt among Westerners, I can point out that however precarious in social support, there is also a tradition of opposition within the Islamic world. Plus I recently completed a book, *The Ghost in the Universe*,[1] in which I argue against theism, including its Islamic versions, in favor of a uncompromising scientific naturalism.

That I would join this argument is somewhat surprising, given my background. My parents were curious to find that I had developed an interest in religion, even as an opponent. This interest started in earnest when I came to the United States for graduate studies in physics and was intrigued by "weirdness"—paranormal and fringe-science beliefs that lack solid evidence but are still wildly popular. Gods and demons, of course, are the strongest supernatural beliefs of them all, and I certainly considered them weird.

My interest in weirdness first touched on Islam in a serious way when I began looking into the religious opposition to the theory of evolution, which has flared up in Turkey in recent years. For someone with my peculiar tastes, spending a lot of my time reading material I consider the most appalling intellectual garbage, this was a gold mine. The creationists spin the most outrageously bad arguments and plain intellectual dishonesty together to defend their faith, all the while claiming to be truly scientific and borrowing wholesale from the Protestant creationists who infest the United States. This has to appeal to anyone with a dark sense of humor. Today I continue to observe and write about Islamic creationism with a morbid fascination.

But I must confess my motivation to begin feverishly reading about religion was not limited to intellectual curiosity. The time I left Turkey was also when Islamist politics was gathering steam. The comfortable, self-contained social world of the secular Turkish elites and middle classes was being invaded by a populist, urban revival of Islam. Ever since the modern Turkish Republic was founded in the 1920s, secularists either controlled or constrained the state, always wary of an Islamic reaction to modernization efforts. Since the 1940s, however, religious conservatism has increased in influence. In the 1980s Turkey caught up with the rest of the Muslim world, when Islamists forsook the long tradition of political passivity among religious conservatives and made Islam into a radical political option.

The Islamist ideal society would make life very hard for secularists, so we naturally perceived the new Islamism and the revival of all things Islamic as a threat. But Islamists in Turkey also adopt heavy-handed identity politics. Some of our most bitter battles are over symbolic matters, such as university students being allowed to adopt Islamic dress or not. So secularists often respond with a defense of a modern identity, reasserting the ideals of the early Turkish Republic. For some, this includes elaborate, if implausible, statements about how orthodox Islam, rightly understood, is compatible with modern life. "We are all good Muslims here" is sometimes the rallying cry. I don't have that option, so I have to claim some living space for myself as an Enlightenment rationalist.

*   *   *

So I read about weirdness, about religion, and remained continually fascinated with supernatural beliefs both as intellectual claims and in their political aspect. Of course, I quickly encountered Western views of Islam. Much of it seemed disconnected from what I knew—not just the bomb-toting fanatics stereotype but also the notion of tolerant, misunderstood Islam. In either case, I was seeing rather condescending portraits put up for various Western purposes. I do appreciate how the Jews expelled from re-Christianized Spain found a home in the Ottoman Empire, and I'd like this to be better known. I am disappointed to find European notions of the marauding, barbarian Turk are still there below the surface, and I hope that people will come to understand that *jihad* and conquest was not *all* the Ottoman Empire was about. But still, I'm not entirely happy when I see Muslim history being used as little more than an object lesson in tolerance for the benefit of Christians.

So in the more popular works I read, I kept encountering ideal types, various "true" Islams that did not do justice to what I knew any more than the claims of Muslim apologists. And even in academic books I often encountered not so much an orientalist insensitivity as a reluctance to risk offending Muslims, overcompensating, I guess, for earlier scholarship on Islam that made it out to be an inferior version of Christianity. Digging deeper, though, I found plenty of interesting material.

Learning more about Islam was also a process of letting go of some of my own myths. I used to think that Islamic doctrine was more coherent than that of Christianity, that orthodox Islam was open to free inquiry before its long period of stagnation, that we had solid historical knowledge about the birth of Islam. After all, Turkish secularists propagate these myths as well, hoping to help rationalize an Islam that is stuck in the premodern world. Even those of us who reject Islam, like myself, too often treat orthodox Islam as a package deal, completed in all essentials at Muhammad's death. It was enlightening to discover the much more ambiguous situation the best of our modern knowledge indicates. Finding how the religion had a complex history, still in the making, changed my perspective, even as orthodox claims to divine revelations appeared ever less plausible.

I also came to appreciate the depth of Islam as a civilization, however much I dislike its oppressive and obscurantist sides. Atatürk, founder of the Turkish Republic and hero of every Turkish secularist, was certainly audacious in trying to move the country toward Western civilization. In the space of just about fifteen years, he led an effort to radically change almost everything in Turkish society. The young republic adopted European norms in all public matters, from weights and measures to Sunday as the official day off. Turkey discarded the old Arabic script in favor of the Latin alphabet, and Atatürk even outlawed traditional Muslim dress and had people wear European hats instead of turbans and other traditional headgear. Turkey was to become a new Western nation, with its own language and history, of course, and a private, liberal, emasculated Islam as a majority faith rather than a remnant of Christianity.

Yet knowing the depth of Muslim civilization and the commitment orthodox Islam inspires, I now also wonder if Atatürk's ambitions were completely realistic. Since his time, we have maintained some Western institutions and a secular elite, but all in all, Turkey is still uncomfortably caught between the modern and the premodern. We have McDonalds and trash TV, but most of our population is either peasants or removed from peasanthood only by a generation or two. Our urban elites, knowing what was a smart move for getting ahead in the world, adopted a private, liberal Islam. But elsewhere, for the large majority, religion is still a matter of communal allegiance, and dissent is still betrayal.

I now teach physics in a small Midwestern university, and comparing Turkey to the United States does not make me much more optimistic for the future of Turkish secularization. I think the idea of God is radically mistaken, but belief is amazingly robust. And the legacy of the European Enlightenment is culturally too thin. And so I see that here in America as well, God reigns supreme. Infidels have breathing space, though, because it is a pluralist country with many gods, and because we have become individual consumers instead of peasants. This is hardly an inspiring social scene, but I think I'll stay. At least here, it's much less likely that some Islamist loon will decide that I'm an enemy of Islam who deserves to be punished.

*   *   *

Though being shot is only a remote possibility, it isn't just an idle worry. In the last two decades, some of the most forceful Turkish critics of Islam have been either assassinated or forced into exile. Some in the Islamist press have targeted critics, printing names, addresses, photos. They do not explicitly ask that the traditional penalty against apostates—death—be carried out, but no doubt certain hotheads get the message.

I have some of the books written by the murdered critics. They seem uneven. Many of them wrote intemperately, even angrily. They sometimes lacked sophistication, and tended to emphasize the worst in Islam. It's easy, I guess, for popular criticism to end up as a mirror image of religious apologetics, especially when a writer falls out of faith through an intense personal struggle, and begins to think the religion that shaped much of his life was nothing but a lie. And if he comes to see Islam as an ideology that enslaves whole masses of people, that gives even more urgency to his writing. I don't have that level of personal anger when I approach Islam, but I'd like to see room for passionate attacks on Islam in Turkish culture, as well as a more quiet rejection. Though sometimes their arguments were obscured by their vehemence, I thought the murdered critics made some very good points as well. They could have been part of a public discussion Turkish culture would have greatly benefited from. They were silenced, though, by bombs and bullets.

Of course, the fringe element of Islamic terrorists does not represent the vast majority of Muslims. Yet terrorism and orthodox Islam are not entirely disconnected. It takes only a few rapists to make women fear going out at night, reinforcing a culture where women are thought to be in need of male protection and supervision. All too many in Turkey, I suspect, thought the murdered critics only asked for it with their provocative writings.

This became even clearer with the Salman Rushdie incident. Though Turkey is liberal compared to most of the Muslim world, The Satanic Verses was banned there, too. My mother wanted a copy, so I smuggled one in on my next visit. It was dismaying to see how even in Turkey, far from the ayatullahs, Rushdie was regularly condemned. Pundits would denounce Khomeini's infamous fatwa encouraging Rushdie's assassination, but they would make it clear how they did not condone Rushdie's actions either, sometimes going on to suggest less drastic ways of preventing his insult to Islam from circulating. I need not even mention what the Islamist press said.

At about that time, a group of secularist and Alevi intellectuals, including a well-known writer and notorious skeptic who spoke of having The Satanic Verses translated, held a meeting in a provincial hotel. Arsonists set fire to the hotel, and many were killed. Naturally, the culprits were never found, and those of the local populace who supported the violence suffered no consequences. In Turkey, this sort of thing happens every so often. It was just another episode of sectarian violence against Alevis, with some complete infidels massacred in the bargain.

*   *   *

Criticizing religion, I have found, does not go over well in Muslim culture. By this, I don't just mean that Islam discourages searching questions about its basic claims. That's true enough, but no different than just about any other faith. Sometimes I suspect, though, that Islam has an extra edge of defensiveness about it. After all, Islam was born with empire but shaped by political instability. And over the last few centuries Muslims have found their way of life repeatedly tested against an intrusive Western world, and have usually come out the losers. Perhaps, then, expressing doubt on basic matters, especially when outsiders can observe this dissent, seems to be an unacceptable display of weakness. When the community of believers faces crisis after crisis, another threat to its unity is the last thing it feels inclined to tolerate.

I'm not sure—that's all speculation on my part. Still, I've learned to be careful when arguing against the claims of orthodox Islam. Even Muslim academics working in Western universities can be very defensive about Islam, confusing criticism with insult. I don't know what to say. I might try and argue that one of the weaknesses of Muslim culture today is the limits it puts on criticism; but then, I am clearly not motivated to preserve the specifically *religious* aspect of Islamic culture.

Even at a more personal level, announcing not just passive lack of faith but active criticism is difficult. I worked on *The Ghost in the Universe* for a number of years, and naturally I would have liked to talk about what is something of a personal achievement. Strangely, though, I found myself having difficulty telling my Turkish friends what my book was about. Instead, I mumbled something about it involving science and philosophy, and told them they'd find out precisely what it was when it comes out. I'd like to see it translated into Turkish, if I could find the opportunity. I have an ego as big as anyone's—I like to see my work in print. But the Islamic revival in Turkey shows no signs of stalling, and sometimes I wonder if it would be such a good idea after all.

*   *   *

I get in black moods about Turkey. It's not news that the country's in bad shape, and that the secular nature of the state has eroded considerably in the last two decades. The Anatolian Enlightenment seems to have run out of steam halfway through; it now struggles against being swallowed up by Islamists on one side and the International Monetary Fund on the other. I shouldn't get carried away, though. Turkey's a volatile place where things can change quickly. If, for example, the European Union accepted Turkey as a member, this might change its prospects considerably. Acceptance would make economic sense for the Europeans, but the big snag is the cultural mismatch. Would the Europeans want to deal with a large population increasingly insistent on asserting an orthodox Muslim identity?

It might be significant that the example I just mentioned was a change in external circumstances. Internally, Turkish secularism seems shaky. It is true that secularized people have become more energized of late. In a land where even trivial acts can be political statements, attending a Western classical music concert can declare one's identification with Western culture, affirming the choices of the early Turkish Republic. Secularists are playing such symbolic politics with renewed vigor these days. But the political dynamism still seems to be on the Islamists' side. They set the agenda, they decide on the shape of the debate, and secularists react. And the least compromising secularists, the social democrats, have self-destructed as a political force. Then again, they were never popular favorites.

I'm not sure what Turkish secularists could have done differently. Perhaps, as conservatives keep accusing us, we kept insisting on imposing reform from above, losing contact with the real culture of the country. But then, secularists were never content to remain an elite, forgetting the impoverished peasantry. Some embraced socialism, most at least talked about the nationalist ideal of a confident Turkey joining the modern world in its democracy and prosperity. Rural Turks and recent urban immigrants, however, did not think much of those who presumed to speak for their interests, and thought even less of state-imposed modernity. They wanted prosperity, but by and large, they wanted to be prosperous as orthodox Muslims living in the land of Islam. With the exception of the heterodox Alevi minority, they rarely voted for the parties that claimed the legacy of the Turkish Revolution.

*　　*　　*

I'm starting to write like an academic—my prose is threatening to become bloodless, analytical, careful not to miss ambiguities in case a reviewer pounces on me. But I teach physics, not anything connected to Islam. So I have no incentive to spend much time thinking about Islam without some passion for the issues. So, I wonder now, what these days gets me fired up to oppose orthodox Islam?

There is, of course, my identification with education and the intellectual life. I'd like to keep religious influences away from the formal learning environment in universities. In particular, the pressures Turkish universities feel, and the amount of religion that has already seeped in, bother me to no end. Naturally, in a country caught between two civilizations, education is a highly political matter—the periodic American firestorms about canon and curriculum are trivial in comparison. Universities have become a battlefield for secularists and Islamists alike, and sometimes it amazes me that any learning gets done amid all the culture wars.

Secularists, no less than Islamists, play politics, trying to shape universities in their own image, but I don't want to suggest they are equivalent. An attempt to inject creationism into biology education is not the same as a political effort to keep evolution from being diluted. And, more important, a more secular vision must win out if a climate of open intellectual inquiry is to survive at all. Islamists always end up as fundamentalists. They would give us a scholarship in the traditional mold, based on transmitting received wisdom and protecting the faith from criticism. They would not promote an open engagement with the modern world.

So Islam, I think, is an intellectual nuisance. But again, this is a rather academic concern—it's almost like I don't want militant Islam to harm me and mine, and I do not care about the rest. Things may come to that. At this point, intellectual concerns *do* loom largest for me, at least at the surface. But whether I like it or not, no institution is isolated from the rest of society. Even in physics, someone has to pay for our computers and our instruments. So I can't just treat the questions Islam raises as invitations to an intellectual game, as items of weirdness for my collection. In the end, I find the full-blown orthodox Muslim community as imagined either by traditionalists or by Islamists to be a remarkably oppressive, closed society. I can try to escape the Muslim world or I can try to help those who want to change things. Usually, I have done some of both.

*   *   *

What really brings the issue home to me is the place orthodox Islam assigns women. It's no accident that the veil is always a flashpoint in the struggle between religious conservatives and secularists. In Turkey, the secular caricature of an ultraconservative is a man in medieval Islamic dress, with robe and beard, followed a few steps behind by multiple wives completely covered in their *carsafs*, all public identity erased. This, to secularists, symbolizes all the darkness, all the stagnation the Turkish Republic has been trying to leave behind.

Growing up in secular, middle-class neighborhoods, I did not see such scenes often. But when I did, it was disturbing. I would walk past a man exactly as in the stereotype, in Islamic dress, followed by black-clad nondescript figures with only eyes visible. I was bothered. I still am, especially when I see a short figure fully veiled, which means a daughter aged ten or eleven at most, who until a few months ago was free to play outside with her friends but now has to climb into a brown paper bag every time she sets foot in the street. I feel a gut-level revulsion in such cases, but curiously, also something like shame.

It continues. When I was in transit through a German airport and saw a Turkish immigrant worker family in Muslim dress, I was embarrassed to think that this was the image so many saw of Turkey. When I see Muslim women covering their hair in American universities, I am troubled again.

I am not entirely comfortable with my reactions. After all, a stock element in conservative Muslim literature is a heated denunciation of the modern lack of morals, evidenced by the half-naked women occupying the beaches. If I am dismayed to see women forced into, or, just as bad, consenting to a status that seems comparable to slavery, well, conservative Muslims are dismayed to see women volunteering to a status they see as comparable to whoredom. I used to give a hostile stare at ultraconservative families walking through our secular neighborhood. A university classmate's sister had to walk through a conservative neighborhood on her way to medical school. She ended up harassed to the point that she found it best to put on a head scarf when walking by.

To further complicate matters, many women among Islamists make a great show of covering themselves and recommending it to others. They don't seem forced into anything; they see a conservative role for women to be integral to a faith that gives them peace and meaning amid the chaos of modern life. Some of them are leaders among Islamists, even though their leadership is confined to "women's issues." Even in the industrialized West, most converts to Islam appear to be women.

I grew up among strong women, proud of the work my mother did, and my ideal is for men to live and work together with women as equals. But changing toward a society where the sexes are not segregated, where women have public identities, can be disturbing for both men *and* women. When growing up, a few of my friends took equality between the sexes as a given; my female classmates from college who entered professional life can't conceive of going around in a veil or being segregated from men in the name of religion. But then, many of my male friends never learned how to cook for themselves, sew, or clean a house. My mother made sure my brother and I could do such things, but we were exceptions. In my friends' parents' generation, the woman took care of the home, and no one thought to train the male children to do such things. My female friends work, but many still have to do all the housework.

Learning to live differently is hard, and no doubt many even among women find the certitudes of the old ways comforting. As elsewhere, Turkish women haven't begun to work out of feminist conviction but rather economic necessity; if they liked the accompanying measure of freedom, this was a side effect. Today, Turkish secularists nervously reassure each other that Turkey can never become like Iran, but I'm not so sure. Rigid gender roles keep men in their place as well as women; Muslim women can feel that with an Islamic separation of men from women, they would be protected from men violating the boundaries.

So I'm wary of denouncing too hastily how Islam treats women. Women's lives have a way of becoming battlegrounds for men, and I worry about pushing people around in the name of liberating women. In that case, perhaps the best I can do is to help, however modestly, to create an environment where women can decide for themselves, and help maintain a social space for those of us who do want to live modern lives.

But then, this does not quite work either. Personal freedom to choose and live according to one's identity seems wonderful, liberal, unobjectionable. Lately Turkish Islamists have been using such rhetoric often, claiming to defend personal freedom against an intrusive state that would impose secular lifestyles on all. But to many conservative Muslims, the very social climate supporting individual choice is unacceptable. It gives in to the modern, human-centered world, degrading the integrated community environment necessary for fully living out Islam. Without modern, autonomous persons who negotiate their differences within some semblance of a secular democracy, the whole notion of personal freedoms becomes too slippery. Even if I were to adopt the watered-down language of individual choice, shying away from asking how we might best live together, I would still be imposing my modern views on the debate.

I doubt there is a mutually acceptable solution to be reasoned out here. Moral condemnations fly fast and fierce on either side, but after all the talk, my interests differ from those of the Islamists. I'm not sure there's more to say.

*   *   *

Now, I don't want to reinforce the stereotype of the dour, inflexible Muslim who insists everyone should live according to Islamic law. Muslims can be more tolerant, at least those who are traditionalists rather than political Islamists. No uncovered Western tourist would be harassed when strolling through a conservative neighborhood; only a Turk, someone who *should* be a member of the community, faces demands for conformity. When I visited a Turkish village, they didn't expect me to conform to every community standard; they were very accepting of difference as long as it was clear that we belonged in different social worlds.

The secularized Muslims I grew up among were also very accepting. They lived modern lives; their part in the Muslim community was not so central to their identities. And so living together was no problem, especially since polite conversation stayed away from divisive matters like religion.

For that matter, many who start out conservatively learn that the different people they interact with are not all bad. I recently got in touch with a old school friend, by e-mail. He was one of the kids who didn't opt out of religion class; and in our conversation he remarked that he was surprised to find out, from my example, that not everybody was religious, and, contrary to what his grandparents said, going without faith did not automatically make a person a monster. So I seem to have contributed, in however small a fashion, to push him toward a more liberal Islam.

Yet I fear conservative, rigorous Islam will always lurk in the background, even if Turkey completes its halfhearted lurch towards social modernity. Even if the habit of understanding Islam an individual expression of faith spreads beyond the current minority, I wonder if this can work for long. After all, the Koran will still be there, held sacred by all. Some will decide to read it and take it seriously, and then they will find its premodern views are not so easy to interpret away. One of my friends once argued with me that the Koran was misinterpreted, that it did not allow women to be subordinated to men, and that there was no reason she should change her modern way of life. I didn't dispute her. I hope she keeps treating the Koran as a generic sacred object in the distance, revered but not consulted for God's commands for her life.

*   *   *

When I was a postdoctoral researcher in Louisiana, I became friendly with an Iranian computer specialist. He participated in a Koran study group, along with some other exiles from the Iran of the *ayatullahs* and some other Muslim families from various nations. The men typically worked in science- and technology-related fields. I expressed curiosity about their group, and visited their meetings a couple of times. The people there were all quite modern; some of the wives were Americans who had converted after marriage. None of the women covered their heads. The group's informal leader, a physics professor, was greatly impressed with Rashad Khalifa's 19-based Koranic numerology, and he would generally take charge of interpreting the passage chosen for each day after it was read. In keeping with Khalifa's views, this group generally rejected the prophetic traditions, insisting that the Koran and the Koran alone was the basis for Muslim faith and practice. The Iranians especially put a political coloring on this; they were prone to suspect the traditions harbored too many later fabrications designed to give clerics power—hence opening the way for criminals like Khomeini.

Interestingly, however, their attitude toward the Koran was as fundamentalist as any I've seen, and they almost always adopted the orthodox interpretations continuous with the traditions they ostensibly rejected. In many ways, they were like a Muslim version of an early Protestant sect—scripturally fundamentalist, but also sectarian and individualist, trying to assert independence of the wider community and tradition.

This sort of group is not unique; many in Turkey are also exploring ways to be Muslims without getting under the thumb of leaders of Sufi orders or that of the traditional religious scholars. Perhaps the current Islamic revival will produce something like the Protestant Reformation. In fact, after I started thinking this way, I found some Western scholars of Islam seriously discussing this possibility. I don't know—history does not repeat so easily, and I suspect in Islam it's much more difficult to break from the ideal of a unified overall community in favor of individualism. But in the long term, I hope something like the Reformation does happen. At first, the clash of rival fundamentalisms unleashed by individual interpretation would cause much misery. But *if* they would reach a stalemate, as happened in Europe emerging from the religious wars of their Reformation, the Muslim world might develop a similarly pluralist consensus about public life. We might get a modernized Islam with roots going deeper than the secularized elites in Turkey.

This would be wonderful. I don't expect most people will come to live without mythic perceptions of the world, without supernatural hopes. I would disagree with a Protestant Islam as strongly as before about its gods and demons, its claims of transcendent realities. But I could at least live in its social world.

*   *   *

I would be terrible as a political leader. Even as I wistfully hope for an individualist Islam to prevail, ambivalence about modern life creeps over me. Even someone like myself, a perpetual outsider to any organic community, has to feel some sympathy toward desires for a community that goes beyond a collection of individual consumers.

About a year ago as I write this, my brother and his wife had a son. They decided to name him "Bora." Talking to them, I found out that the current trend among secular Turkish professionals was to choose very short names for their children, names that could easily be pronounced in the Western world. The prospect for many of these kids is to become yuppies in a global economy, unlike the many graduates from nonelite universities who will face difficulty getting decent jobs, and who quite likely will find an outlet for their frustrations in Islamist politics. My nephew could end up living anywhere in the world—even now, many of my friends are scattered around the globe. I only visit Turkey once every couple of years.

Now I, and people like me, can easily survive, perhaps even thrive, in such an environment. But is it any surprise that many others might consider it a nightmare—our rootless wandering, our lives where claims of a transcendent purpose come as a distant echo we don't know what to make of? We contribute a small Turkish flavor to an indifferent modern culture, but how many of us can really feel at home?

*   *   *

Recently I visited Turkey in between semesters, after an absence of many years. It was Ramadan, and on a warm winter's day I got together with a high school friend I hadn't seen in nearly twenty years. We met at an outdoor café by the Bosphorus, ordered our glasses of Turkish tea, and caught up with each other's lives. It was lovely weather, with a great seaside view, on a weekend. Ordinarily, we would not have been able to find a seat without a lot of luck. But the rows of outdoor tables were deserted except for one other. These days, even middle-class citizens of Istanbul are a lot more observant of the Ramadan fast. This includes many socially modern people who want to demonstrate they are good Muslims as well.

My friend is a medical doctor, I a physicist. We move with ease in the secular realm, even the Western world. We not only use cell phones, we know how they work. When we discuss politics, the notion of conforming to a divine law is alien to us. As we sipped our tea, gazing at the scenery, I noticed an imposing old Ottoman fountain behind us. Unlike many left to crumble in back streets, it was clean and in good shape, and the inscriptions in the old Arab script were gilded. Probably to present something attractive to European tourists. Neither of us could, of course, read the script—Atatürk's reform adopting a Latin alphabet happened long ago. We, true children of the republic, stand at a remove from Islamic civilization.

The waiter who served us was fasting. I'm not sure I was much closer to his world than to that of the Ottomans. Just as the religion classes of my childhood, so with the culture of my land of birth. I have opted out.

NOTE

1. Taner Edis, *The Ghost in the Universe: God in Light of Modern Science* (Amherst, N.Y.: Prometheus Books, 2002).

24

ON BEING A WOMAN IN PAKISTAN

Qayyum (Pakistan)

Thank you for your concern about my rational thinking and the dangers surrounding me in this country. I am ready to face things, though I am very cautious about expressing my thoughts before others.

I was born into a conservative Muslim family. My mother was and still is very religious but my father was not that orthodox. He was not highly educated but he was very logical and rational in his thoughts and actions. When I was very small, I remember my father arguing with people on very sensitive religious issues and outwitting them through rational arguments. My father, a very simple, humble man of low profile, taught me to use reasoning and logic in my perception. In my childhood, I was never forced to go to mosque or recite the Koran, as is normally done in mediocre families in Pakistan. I studied in a Western type of convent school, where religion was not given much importance at that time (late 1950s). With this background I could have grown up an average materialistic, nonorthodox, Koranic Muslim. But I don't know how I had a knack for seeking the reality about the creator and creation. When I was in college, someone introduced me to Ṭulūꜥ-i Islām, an Islamic movement run by Ghulam Ahmad Parvez. I became a staunch supporter and fan of Parvez for his novel concepts derived from the Koran. As a student and disciple I lived with him in his house for about eight years. He was a man of very strong and dominant personality, although his personal life was not of a very high moral character. But as a true follower I always tried to justify his follies and lapses in character. There were numerous instances where he himself did not follow what he taught as Islamic teachings. I was so influenced by his charismatic personality that at one occasion I even went to jail for spreading his concept of Islam. Parvez was a bitter opponent of Mawdūdī; so was I. But to satisfy my thirst for Islam or to verify what all Parvez said about Mawdūdī, I once went to listen to the lecture of Mawdūdī. He was a very efficacious speaker, who could attract the audience. I made it my routine to go to the mosque, where Mawdūdī used to give lectures three times a week after *Fajar* prayers. When Parvez came to know this he threw me out of his house.

This was when I rationally analyzed the Islamic concepts given by Parvez. I was away from his magnetic influence and my mind was out of his overshadowing personality. I found out that what Parvez had preached throughout his life is contained in a very small portion of the Koran. A major part of the book teaches apartheid, damning of the non-Muslims, condemning of women.

This was the time when I approached some other Muslim scholars, like Dr. Israr, Maulana Amin Islahi, Dr. Wadood, Allama Tahir Qadri, and so on. But every time I came out to be a more steadfast atheist. It was like being "lost in the wilderness." My greatest companion and supporter in all my shortcomings, "Allah" was taken away from me. Then I came across the web site of Dr. Sina. It showed me a new path and new concept of god, the all-loving god, real creator of the universe, much more compassionate and caring than the religious god and above all the dirty, passionate Allah of the Muslims. This is in short my divine journey, which took almost thirty years. I will write more later. I love all living beings of this planet.

25

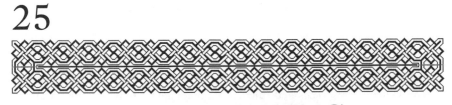

THE LIFTING OF THE VEIL OF BLIND FAITH
Sophia (Pakistan)

My reason for leaving Islam was the lifting of the veil of blind faith from my eyes. I am a Pakistani-born Muslim woman. I was raised in an liberal atmosphere and nobody pushed Islam over me, I adopted it myself. My mother died when I was a child, creating feelings of insecurity and being lost. I wanted a security blanket, which was Islam.

There is a search in the human heart to know the truth, and I thought the ultimate truth was Islam. Sure, there were unrealistic teachings in Islam but I attributed them to cultural reasons, to make Islam more acceptable during medieval times, but since then Islam has allowed *ijtihad* so these matters can be taken care of. Basically, my attitude was of those millions of Muslims who can see the unreasonable things in the Koran but justify them in every way possible. It is called *emotional inertia*: we don't want to change our emotional beliefs for the fear of losing identity. I wanted to preserve my faith in every way possible, so I lied to myself. The change started happening when I came to the United States to study and my psychology class introduced me to Freud. When I read his book *The Future of an Illusion*, everything made sense. God is an infantile fantasy. We, as humans, need it because the idea of facing this world on our own without any mystical help is traumatic. Ancient civilizations invented gods to look after them, parental figures. I saw religion as it was, a manipulative device engineered on socioeconomic basis to control. All major religions hate women because before Christianity and even Judaism, in the ancient world of Mesopotomia, the current Middle East, Mother Goddess was worshiped. Those were matriachal societies, where women were priests and rulers, so along came a religion with its divine patriarchal order that women were inferior and evil, thus ending the age of Mother Goddess. A simple question: If god* made women why is he so afraid of them that he wants them either in homes or in veils?

So when I understood the psychological compulsions for religion and god, I undertood Islam, a religion manufactured to impose ignorant Arab tribes on the world, a religion of men so horny they had women veiled from head to toe because they could not trust themselves not to pounce on them if they were unveiled. And when the blind faith was lifted from my eyes I also saw the man I sacredly used to call the prophet to be a narcisstic psychopath with illusions of ruling the world. He was charismatic, of course—so was Hitler—an expert in mass hypnotism, so grand were his illusions that every prayer not only sends blessing on him but also on his descendants, and he is above reproach, above question. Islam and the sayings of Muhammad are as divine as the rantings of a madman. It's more than a coincidence that the most confused and weak minds gravitate toward religion, the same way lost souls will gravitate toward some cult, in search of identity and a holy power above who tells them what to do, because these weaklings can not decide for themselves what life is. They need to be spoon-fed. If you have the misfortune of being born a Muslim, it becomes a part of who you are or who you perceive you are.

But now I am an atheist, or perhaps an agnostic. I believe religion, and Islam in particular, to be the biggest misfortune humankind had a chance of coming across. Islam is a sick and vile religion of which I was captive for twenty-one years, and finally—finally—I am free, and it feels good.

My Journey to Light

My name is Sophia. I am a twenty-two-year-old Pakistani woman of Muslim origin. I was born and raised as a Muslim. I am currently studying in the United States. I decided to walk away from my ancestoral faith and I believe it is perhaps the most important decision I have made in my life, and the most significant one, too. Islam was a very important part of my life, and being disillusioned by it and adjusting to the changes this disillusionment brought is an intellectual and emotional metamorphosis I am still going through. I was raised in a very liberal atmosphere and Islam was never imposed on me.

---

*The author chooses to use a lowercase "g" for "god."

I was brought up in what can be considered to be the most common mode of Islam these days, modernism combined with the very essential elements of Islam. Veil and prayer are not essential, but you must marry in a traditional way and live within certain parameters that Muslim society establishes. But I was not an indifferent Muslim; that is probably why I was disillusioned by it so bitterly. To disbelieve you must first also believe. I was raised on the Islamic mystic and sufi literature, Rumi and Omar Khayyam, and I believed that the true spirit of Islam was humanitarianism. And all the ugliness that I saw around me, the persecution of women, *mullahs* claiming that a woman belongs in the home and that one who crosses it deserves whatever she gets. The sudden rise in Islamic fundamantalism in Pakistan and, alarmingly for me, even in the so-called upper-middle class shocked me. I had one discussion with a newly converted fundamentalist who said that there is no such thing as moderate Islam, which is just a covenient idea made up by people who do not want to follow the book and their lives accordingly. So I read the Koran. You see, I had read only parts of it and that which I had read had been pretty mild, sublime stuff. When I read it all with Maulana Mawdūdī's translation, it was a mind-blower. Everything in it was so against the very modern and humane ideas I had grown up with and believed Islam was about. But I was pretty thoroughly conditioned. I talked with my professor who had a doctorate in Islamic studies and he told me that I should not take the Koran literally as a lot of it is symbolic and allegorical. That is why Islam has provision for *ijtihad* (the use of one's personal effort in order to make a decision on a point of law not explicitly covered by the Koran or the *sunna*). Needless to say, I was convinced and thus remained in the comfortable but self-deceptive state of neither believing nor disbelieving in which so many Muslims exist. They live their lives according to the idea, and the book they have never questioned or thought about. Sheep following sheep. That is how I look at them now.

My first rebellion was against a culture that teaches me to be subservient, to accept social sexual harrassment, and even to be killed. I worked with an organization in Pakistan where I witnessed acid being thrown over women because they married men they chose or they left men they chose to leave. Women were killed for disobeying, and thus dishonoring the family, beaten because they raised their voice against a man. Yes, all these things are directly related to religion. Islamic preachers will tell you all that is cultural and that Islam has played no role in this. Coincidentally, this culture seems to repeat itself in almost every Muslim country from Asia to Africa. The fact is that Islam particularly originated in the male-oriented lands of Arabia, to fulfill one man's dreams of glory and play to the fantasies and convenience of countless generations of men, pretty much explains why Muslim women are considered subhuman creatures. Four wives, countless mistresses (if you can afford them), and women who are just going to stay home as Allah thinks it is the best thing for them. If Allah so created women and supposing we are his creation, then why this division? Creators never choose and discriminate among their creations. It is not logical. I will not debate the fine points of Islamic *Sharī'a* because I am not educated enough for it, but I do have enough sense and self-respect to refuse a religion that gives me the status of property and defines my identity with relation to a man.

Human rights do not exist in Islamic societies. They cannot, as Islam specifically and religion generally do not believe in humans having the right to make choices. They tell you this is right and this is wrong. As for moderate Muslims, they just want convenience. Many of them do realize the idiosyncracies of Islam, but they lack the courage it requires to question their roots, the decisiveness to reject something that has formed the fabric of one's self. I, on the other hand, was very attracted to Islam's spirtual side. It provided an answer to great mysteries of life and made my decisions for me, giving me a strict guidelines to follow so I would not have to think and make my own choices, which would have been hairsplitting. Leaving your religion is a rebellion, and if you are in a Muslim county this rebellion can cost you your life.

I actually favor fundamentalism in one respect: Fundamentalists are honest, unlike so-called moderate Muslims. My reasons for leaving Islam were a combination of disillusionment coupled with the understanding I gained as to why we as humans need god and organized religion.

THE PRESENT

So now about my journey to freedom. I came to the United States for my studies as a psychology major, and that is where the unravelling of my faith started. The institute of religion is against the science of psychology, and with good reason. Understanding the dynamics of the human mind removes many cobwebs, the foremost being that of god. I refuse to use capital letters. Now I don't know whether I am an atheist or an agnostic, but I think all this is oversimplification of a very big mystery.

The truth of this universe is not so easily quantifiable that any aspect of it especially something as wonderous and amazing as the creation of it can be labeled as "god."

God exists for three reasons:

(1) To explain what cannot be explained easily, existential crisis, as Sartre called it. In our mortality and vulnerability we see the face of god.
(2) To fulfill a spiritual longing.
(3) To have someone to whine to and about when things go wrong.

In fact, god is quite similar to our mothers, isn't he? At least the father in all traditional religions, who created us and will now take care of us: all-knowing, all-seeing caretaker. An extremely comforting concept. Freudians call god an infantile fantasy, an adult replacement of another figure. So even if there is a supreme being who is the creator, from the way the world works he has pretty much left the world and us alone. This world runs according to its dynamics and so do we humans. There is no place for a god to be, unless you want to delude yourself.

Now after I resolved the conflict of god, everything else pretty much came apart. I understood religion to be what it was, why it is needed, and why it appeals to people. I have nothing aginst religion and god if it works for you, terrific. But I have a lot against Islam. When I was in college in Pakistan, my psychology professor discussed atheism and mentioned Freud's book *The Future of an Illusion*, which led to a discussion among us about whether god existed or not. We for a moment forgot we were not allowed to indulge in the luxury of rationalism. The next day men with beards and diapers over their heads threw stones at our class, shouting "*Murtads* (apostates) should be burned." You get the picture?

The more I read psychologists, historians, and philosophers, the more my belief strengthens that religion is a socioeconomic manipulation geared to take advantage of man's vulnerabilities.

Now more than ever it is important to speak out against Islam, especially if you are a Muslim. There are people living in subhuman conditions: millions of women living in the medieval age because thay believe that is the way of the world and that is their place, behind their husbands with heads bowed down. That is how the prophet intended it to be. Islam is a stifling chain around the neck of millions; it barely lets them breathe. Their lives and ideas are a hostage to this religion. If you are a gay man, you are condemned to a living a lie for the rest of your life. If you are a woman, your body, your soul, your thoughts are not yours—they are your father's, husband's, or other male relatives'. You will live the way they will want you to. I have nothing against believing in god or having a religion, most of us need it. Life would be very enigmatic, even traumatic, without it. Religion and god are the security blanket that a child clutches and goes to sleep with. But my security blanket also happened to be stifling in every way possible. I, as a woman, had no place in Islam. Women are supposed to be wives or sisters or mistresses; being human is not a right Islam grants them. I was raised in a culture that was hypocritical in its double standards, sadistic in its treatment of women, women were stoned and killed or harassed and the sublime religion provided it with a name and a justification. I believed at the time that Islam didn't have much to do with all that; there was a cultural Islam and there was a mystical Islam. How could that belief be so vile that had given birth to Sufism, Rumi, and all the mystic poetry? I had yet to make the distinction between spirituality and religion. Reading Saint Augustine's *Confessions* is a surreal experience, but should that be a basis for converting to Christianity? The answer would be no. I choose to listen to myself, to let all the doubts and my logic ask questions, rather than live a lie.

The end was my leaving Islam. I am quite vocal about my beliefs because religion might be a personal issue, but when your religion is Islam it is more than just a personal, spirtual choice. By being a Muslim in whatever form—liberal, moderate, or just as a namesake—we are in countless ways denying ourselves the right to be us. I often wonder what I would have been as a person in ideas and myself without Islam. If I had not been born a Muslim, I would have been a free woman in mind and spirit; now I am stifled. I have thrown away the choke around my neck, but I still have a long way to go toward being myself.

26

AUTOBIOGRAPHY
OF A DISSIDENT
Anwar Shaikh (Pakistan)

Anwar Shaikh has a personal story to tell, to confess, to expiate, that is fascinating, horrifying, tragic, and uplifting all at once. I shall let Anwar Shaikh unravel it slowly in his own words, recorded during an interview on May 14, 1997.—Ed.

EARLY LIFE

I was born on the first day of June 1928, in a village near the city of Gujrat (in present-day Pakistan). That day happened to be the day of *hajj* (or pilgrimage) as well. My family considered this a good omen since the *hajj* is one of the most sacred ceremonies of Islam, and so they called me Hajji Muhammad. That was the first name I was given, but as it happened I was also born circumcised, and this was seen as an even greater, more august omen, and accordingly they changed my name from Hajji Muhammad to Muhammad Anwar. "Anwar" means radiant. This is what prompted them to give me a sound Islamic education. They thought I was destined to be a stalwart of Islam.

I was born and brought up breathing Islam. My mother was not only deeply religious but also a scholar of Islam. She could recite at least half of the Koran from memory. She did all she could to teach me what she knew. My paternal grandfather was also very scholarly and religious, and on top of that the younger brother of my grandfather was a professional Muslim priest, a *mullah*. So I was under his care as well.

They, however, did not teach me Arabic grammar. I only started learning Arabic in sixth form, and my Arabic teacher happened to be, more or less, our next-door neighbor. I matriculated in 1946, loving Islam all the while. During that period I made myself familiar with the works of *hadith*, the Islamic Traditions, collected by such revered scholars as Bukhari, Muslim, Ibn Majja, and others. I was also lucky enough to come across many books on Arab culture and history, and the famous commentary on the Koran by Maulana Abul Kalam Azad.

LAHORE, 1947, INDEPENDENCE, AND THE PARTITION

I regret to say that 1947 was the darkest period of my life. We were told that murdering the non-Muslims, seducing their wives, and burning their properties, was an act of *jihad*, that is, holy war. And *jihad* is the most sacred duty of a Muslim because it guarantees him a safe passage to paradise where no fewer than seventy-two *houris*, that is the most beautiful virgins, and pearl-like boys wait for him. Such a reward is a great temptation!

It was during the first week of August 1947, when I was an accounts clerk in the railway office in Lahore, that I saw a train pull in from East Punjab. It was full of mutilated bodies of Muslims: men, women, and children. It had a terrific, horrendous effect on me. When I went home I prayed to the Lord asking him not to forget my share of *houris* and boys. Now this is true. I actually prayed and then I took up a club and a long knife, and I went out in search of non-Muslims. Those days were remembered for the curfew orders and everybody seemed terrified of everybody else. I found two men, Sikhs, a father and son. The father was perhaps not more than fifty, perhaps younger, and his young son. I killed both of them. Next day I did not go to work. I felt nauseated, but I wanted to kill some more non-Muslims. I encountered another Sikh at Darabi Road and I killed him too. Often memories of those terrible days haunt my mind; I feel ashamed and many times have I shed tears of remorse. If it had not been for my fanaticism, engendered by the Islamic traditions, those people might have been alive even today. And I might not have felt the guilt, which I still do.

Who told me that the act of *jihad*, the act of killing non-Muslims, was good? Well, if you read the Koran, you will find that in a certain sura God says that he has bought the lives of the Muslims in return for the rewards of paradise. They kill non-Muslims and get killed in this war effort, and the reward for these Muslims is paradise, and paradise is a huge garden inhabited by the most beautiful virgins, who live in palaces, and there are countless pretty pearl-like boys to serve them as well.

SKEPTICISM AND DOUBTS

When and how my skepticism about Islam began is a very strange episode. I was in Rawalpindi in the north of Pakistan, and I must have been twenty-five or twenty-six at the time. One day I was reading the Koran, which I had already read many times, of course, it was sura XLIX, called the Apartments. The first verse says,

> Believers, do not behave presumptuously in the presence of God and His Apostle. Have fear of God: God hears all and knows all. Believers, do not raise your voices above the voice of the Prophet, nor shout aloud when speaking to him as you do to one another. . . . Those who speak softly in the presence of God's apostle are the men whose hearts God has tested for piety.

It is supposed to be Allah telling the faithful to behave well in front of the Prophet. All of a sudden something struck me like lightening. I said, Why is it really for Allah to tell people to show reverence to Muhammad? Can't Muhammad tell the people these things himself? God was acting as a servant to Muhammad. This seems such a banal observation, but this is how my mind reacted to that: I came to the conclusion, all of a sudden, that it was Muhammad himself who was telling the people how to bow before him in the name of Allah, as though it were a command from Allah. By now, I felt that this veil of ignorance had been lifted from my mind.

I was no longer willing to study the Koran through faith. I started reading it critically and rationally, and as I went through it, I realized the Koran did not appeal to me anymore the way it used to do, the way it had for the last twenty-five years. It is at that time I started thinking about the nature of prophethood itself. As I read the Koran again, it appeared to me that prophethood is the ratchet with which someone raises himself above the status of God. It is not only that he wants to be worshiped and obeyed by ordinary people, but he even wants to be greater than God. If you read sura XXXIII.56, you will see it says, "Verily, God and His Angels pray for the prophet." In every other religion, it is man who worships God, but here God appears to be worshipping man.

The moment I started reading the Koran critically, it looked entirely another book to me. Now in the Koran there is a sura called "Women" (sura IV), and verse 82 says that if the Koran was not a book from God, it would contain many contradictions or inconsistencies. So I subjected the Koran to its own definition. And I found that all the important points had been contradicted by the Koran itself. I have written a book called *Faith and Deception*,[1] which demonstrates all these contradictions of the Koran. So you see when you read something rationally instead of blindly, as most of the faithful do, then the same verses, the same words, will have different meanings. That is how I went away from Islam gradually, simply by reading the Koran itself.

CARDIFF

I did not divulge my doubts to anyone, considering it a personal affair. Between 1947 and 1956 I started a small grocery business. When that failed I obtained a diploma and became a fully qualified teacher, and even served for a short time as a headmaster of a high school. In 1956 I decided to leave for Britain, and by chance ended up in Cardiff. My first three years in Cardiff were really tough, since I arrived with only £25 in my pocket. I was too proud to go on Social Security—I had to find a job before I ran out of money. I became a bus conductor, and kept the job for three years. I saved money, bought property, and became a mini-landlord, and I gradually increased the number of houses and I branched out into the construction industry. I became a property developer. I did this business for at least twenty-five years and I did it successfully. But just at the moment I had the chance to become very rich I decided to give it up because I wanted to do some writing.

I retired some twenty years before my time. I am glad that I have provided for my pension. I do not regret my decision. There comes a moment when you have to judge whether to do something really constructive, worthwhile, and creative or to make more money. I chose to do something constructive.

I used to subscribe to the *Freethinker*, and at the time I thought of myself not as a humanist but as a freethinker, that is someone who is not bound by any superstition; he says what he thinks and at the same time he respects the opinions of others. It is strange to say that I was impressed by the humanistic approach of the Rg Veda, which happens to be the sacred book of the Hindus. I was really struck by the fact that the Rg Veda says that their God, Indra, is the God of all mankind, he is the lover of all mankind. It was something unusual for me to learn that, having been brought up in the Islamic tradition, which teaches hatred of non-Muslims. I, from my own experience, came to realize that mankind is one large family, and the purpose of man's life is to look after his fellow beings, to improve the lot of the people, no matter where they are. So it is my own experience that eventually made me a humanist. My passion is humanity, the welfare and advancement of humanity.

ISLAM: THE ARAB NATIONAL MOVEMENT

The deeper study of the Koran, *hadith*, and Arab history led me to believe that Islam had been cleverly devised on the principle of divide and rule, and its purpose is to enable the Arabs to dominate the rest of the world. I have no doubt the Prophet wanted to raise himself to the same status as Allah. Muhammad loved Arabia and its culture, and his one desire was to create a strong, conquering Arab nation that believed in him and propagated his name. This could only be achieved by imperial dominance. For this purpose he took several steps. First, he divided humanity into two perpetually warring groups. He called his own followers the Hizbullah, the Party of God. Those who did not follow him were called Hizbushaitan, the Party of Satan. (You will find this truth in sura LVIII.) They are perpetually at war, and eventually the Party of God will emerge victorious. Muhammad, to make the Muslims dominant and, since at that time mainly Arabs were Muslims, to make the Arabs dominant, laid down that government belongs only to the Quraish, that is, the Prophet's own tribe. No non-Arab can ever head a truly Muslim government. This is the reason in the eight-hundred-year history of Spain, all the Muslim rulers belonged to the Quraish tribe, the tribe of Muhammad. The same is true of Arab government itself: For five to seven hundred years the rulers came from the Umayyad and Abbasid dynasty. They all belonged to the Quraish tribe, the tribe of Muhammad.

The device and philosophy of dividing mankind into two perpetually warring groups, reminiscent of Karl Marx's perpetual class conflict, is dangerous, it is based on blind faith, and far more destructive than fascism, since it advocates the annihilation of all non-Muslims. Indeed, it sees this extermination of non-Muslims as the greatest virtue, which guarantees paradise. Islam was created by the Prophet to impose Arab values on non-Arabs. To make sure that the non-Arab Muslims acknowledge the Arabs as their intellectual masters, the Prophet made Mecca the center of Islamic reverence, in such a way that it became an integral part of the Muslim faith. The Prophet made the *Ka'ba*, the cube-like shrine at Mecca, *the* central Arab shrine, as the House of Allah, and asserted that Allah himself had ordered Adam, the progenitor of humankind, to build this house for him. Now the beauty of it is that the *Ka'ba* is also the *qibla*—that is, the direction of worship. That means every Muslim, wherever he lives—India, Pakistan, Iran, Nigeria—should prostrate himself in the direction of Arabia, to bend in reverence toward it. Not only that, a Muslim grave must be dug in such a way that the body when buried faces the *Ka'ba*, that is, Mecca. So sacred is Mecca that nobody must defecate facing this city.

Again, every Muslim, no matter where he lives, must make a pilgrimage to Mecca provided he has the means to do so. This is a pre-Islamic custom of Arabia that the Prophet incorporated into Islam, to bring it all the economic benefits that a person can dream of. You must have in 1997 during the pilgrimage 3 million Muslims went to Mecca. Assuming every Muslim spends £2,000 to £3,000, which they are bound to, you can calculate the income from this ceremony alone. The people in Pakistan and India are known to sell their houses, their land—they auction the lot to raise money to go on pilgrimage.

Again, Allah speaks Arabic. The Koran is also in Arabic, which is a difficult language to learn. All Muslims must speak Arabic to earn Allah's blessings—see how Allah favors Arabia. In fact, this is the most effective device to impose Arabian culture on non-Arab Muslims.

This is what prompted me to write *Islam: The Arab National Movement*,[2] to waken all nations of the world to the dangers that lie ahead in the age of atom bombs.

FAITH AND DECEPTION

Faith and Deception is a book I wrote to take up the challenge thrown down by the Koran itself. The Koran claims that if it was not a book from God it would be full of inconsistencies. Now, I went through the Koran and all its major precepts and noted them down. I show that each principle is contradicted as you go through the Koran.

ISLAM, SEX, AND VIOLENCE

Islam, Sex, and Violence,[3] published in 1999, deals with the Muslim belief that a prophet is a completely innocent and infallible person. In sura XLVIII verses 1 and 2, Allah addresses Muhammad, saying, "May I forgive your sins of the past and any sins you may commit in the future." It surely nullifies this belief that a prophet is innocent and infallible, because if the Prophet had committed sins in the past and he was likely to commit them in the future, you cannot call him infallible.

In this book, I examine the lives of half a dozen prophets—and my account is based on the Bible and the Koran. I have illustrated the life of the Prophet with reference to sexuality, Koranic law and history. This book contains some hair-raising episodes that are fully documented from the books of Islamic Traditions, the *hadith*, the Koran, and Arab history. I was reluctant to publish this book for along time, it was for long preserved in the vaults of the bank. I honestly and sincerely believe that the contents of this book belong to the people throughout the world, because it will break the backbone of religion.

THE STATUS OF WOMEN UNDER ISLAM

The present low status of women in the Islamic world is all due to Islamic law, and the Koranic attitude. I discuss these matters in *Islam, Sex, and Violence*. The truth is that in Islam a woman is no more than a sexual toy. A man is free to play with her, and then divorce her at will. She is considered an unreliable witness in a court of law. Her brother is entitled to twice as much inheritance than she is. A man can have four wives at the same time; a man is legally entitled to beat her if she annoys him. She must be available for sexual intercourse whenever required. She must observe *purdah* (that is, cover her face) and must stay in the house; she must not join any social function. This is the reason why Islam has not produced one great woman in all the countries where the Muslims live. Benazir Bhutto and Tansu Ciller of Turkey are actually the marks of rebellion against Islam. Islam is not a rational religion because it has repressed women's rights for centuries.

The source of mischief is the *Sharīʿa*, and the lack of a separation of religion and state. Making religion a part of the state is the true source of trouble—economic and social conflict. It is since Europeans have separated religion and state, and have stopped making laws in the name of Christ, that they have learned to be free and claim their human rights. Until such time as this happens in the world of Islam, these countries are not going to have human rights at all. However, the truth is there is a very quiet revolution going on in these countries—they pay lip service to Islam but they are relying on the secular laws. They make their own laws in their own legislative assemblies but they give it a tinge of Islam, but I do not think they can do it for very long. By the end of the next century this Islamic magic will have vanished. All will try to be rational, instead of doing things in the name of God.

HUMANISM

I am a liberal humanist. I believe in the unity and dignity of people, who have the right to believe what they like. No one has the right to impose his beliefs on others. Faith must be a strictly personal affair. Believing in God or no god is immaterial, what matters is human dignity, human freedom, and human welfare. A human-loving atheist is a thousand times better human than a theist who hates his fellow beings on the grounds of religious bigotry. A true humanist is free from the restraints of race, color, and creed; he believes in human rights, civil liberties, and democratic principles.

*　　*　　*

In an interview with Tariq Ali in the Observer *in October 1995, Anwar said, "Whatever happens now, I will die confident in my humanist and rational beliefs and, if my writings have weaned even a few dozen people away from religious hatred and fanaticism, I feel I will have partially redeemed myself, even though nothing, nothing can bring my three victims back to life." Asked by another journalist if he expected to die violently, Anwar replied, "I want to die honorably."*

NOTES

1. Anwar Shaikh, *Faith and Deception* (Cardiff: Principality Publishers, 1996).

2. Anwar Shaikh, *Islam: The Arab National Movement* (Cardiff: Principality Publishers, 1995).

3. Anwar-Shaikh, *Islam, Sex, and Violence* (Cardiff: Principality Publishers, 1999).

27

NOW I AM GUIDED
Muhammad Bin Abdulla (Bangladesh)

I t was easy for me. Now I wonder how easy it was for me, something that is so difficult for others to achieve. Leaving one's religion seems suicidal. It seems to leave you psychologically an orphan and an outcast, since it brings hot waves of hatred from family, relatives, friends, society, workplace, and everywhere. However, before I left Islam it filled a need. Some moments are bound to come in life when we feel defeated, deserted, hopeless, and helpless. I admit that in those difficult moments one must have a place to go to, to beg without shame. Religion is the champion to fill the mental vacuum in those difficult moments. For me it was Islam.

And now it is no more. It was a slow, steady, and logical metamorphosis from a dark jail of humiliating, blind slavery to bright freedom, which can withstand any threat, temptation, greed or fear. I consider it *the* greatest achievement of my life. Thankfully it did not originate from any personal trauma, which could have fogged my vision. My disillusionment with Islam came from dependable sources like experience of life, decades of study of the Koran, Sahih Bukhari, biography of the Prophet, and history of Muslims written by Muslim Maulanas.

Want to have an unbelievably colorful journey through your own faith? Come with me. I will make you spellbound with utter surprise, pain, disbelief, and freedom at the end. You don't have to be a big scientist or academician; a little common sense will clearly show you a truth totally opposite what you have been shown and taught since childhood, if you are a Muslim.

I saw a well-equipped invading army indiscriminately killing millions of civilians and raping two hundred thousand women. Eight million uprooted people walked barefoot to take refuge in a neighboring country. The institution of Islamic leadership supported the invading army actively in capturing and killing freedom fighters and non-Muslims and raping women on a massive scale. Each of four thousand mosques became the ideological powerhouses of the mass-killers and mass-rapists. And these killers and rapists, these Islamists, were the same people of the same land as the freedom fighters and raped women. That was the civilians of Bangladesh and the killer army of Pakistan in 1971. All the Muslim countries and communities of the world either stood idle or actively sided with the killers and rapists in the name of Islam.

The message was clear. Something was very wrong, either with all the Islamic leaders or with Islam itself. How could each of the thousands of Islamic leaders have turned into killers and helpers of the killers?

Books invited me with open arms. I got hooked on the Koran, the 7,397 Ṣaḥīḥ (authentic or sound) *hadiths* of al-Bukhārī, Islamic jistory, biography of the Prophet, Sharī'a (Islamic law) of different sects, and hundreds of other issues of Islam. Books, the Internet, conventions, gatherings, Islamic lectures, cassettes, and videos crowded my study. The Earth kept revolving around the Sun silently. My life slowly went upside down, the real and final truth of my faith started moving in pain in the womb of time. All my other hobbies stepped back and started watching me curiously from a distance. When all this information was correlated, I started writing in the media and experienced interaction with people of all kind. Some praised me; some were inquisitive. Some wanted to cook me alive. I was on guard so that praise and hatred would not affect my vision. Decades passed; a mysterious door of truth started opening very slowly. Beautiful light came in. Things became clear, I was perplexed. Yes, yes, and yes. All those 1.2 billion Muslims are wrong. They are trapped in a wishful utopia, a fancy romantic dream-palace called Islam. All of them are wrong, just as all the people of the world were wrong when they used to believe that Earth was flat.

Muslim's beautiful palace of Islam floats in the air without any pillar of truth. They do not know. They do not want to know, they will never know it. While most Muslims pass peaceful lives, Islam is a perfect breeding ground for some killer *maulanas* to spring up time to time. They take their life force from the cruel instructions of the Koran and the Prophet's life. And the peaceful Muslims' obsession in the name of faith (*iman*) actively strengthens the killer Islamists. Muslims are taught to blindly believe every word of Koran and save the letters and words of the Koran and *hadith* even at the cost of human lives of other sects, women and non-Muslims.

My intense study continued. In Muhammad's biography, *Ṣaḥīḥ hadith* of al-Bukhārī, and Islamic history, I faced the unbelievable cruelty of the Prophet. I saw his enormous leadership, kindness, and forgiveness in cases of personal torture on him in the early, weak days of Islam. And only those incidents are always told to Muslims, not his cruelties of later years. During the early period of Islam his dedication was remarkable. When money and women were offered to him to stop preaching Islam, he declared, "Even if I am given the sun in one hand and the moon in the other, I won't stop preaching." And I also saw the same Prophet involved in slaughtering non-Muslim tribes, selling slaves of all ages, men and women, kids, young and old. I saw him driving his followers to kill others on the basis of faith, sleeping with his slave girls, marrying children, his lust (vividly described in our books) for his own daughter-in-law (the wife of his adopted son), grabbing the properties of non-Muslims and taking their most beautiful women, having sex within days of the slaughter of the women's husbands and fathers. Also I saw his extreme cruelty to establish Islam, cutting off hands and feet and passing red-hot iron in the eyes of his enemies before killing them, his cursing of non-Muslims, burning their orchards, destroying their idols. I saw him killing his enemy in sleep, permitting lying to his companion to kill opponents, his political game of deceiving during Khandak, hypnotizing his followers even to kill their non-Muslim fathers, brothers, and relatives. These are all recorded in our books, including *Ṣaḥīḥ hadith*, which I study. Of course I saw him establishing some unprecedented rights of women, then again setting cruel laws and insulting status for the same women. And yet he remains as "mercy to the whole world" to his mesmerized followers. No doubt from the desert of an incredible distance of fourteen hundred years, he still remains as mankind's "most influential man."

I faced the truth of the mess of the Koran and *hadith*. The Koran does not contain a single humane teaching that was not here before Islam. Mankind will not lose a single moral precept if Islam is not there tomorrow. Saying good words is easy; all those good words in the Koran can be said by any conscientious person, even an atheist. The Koran has a big portion dedicated to clear violence toward non-Muslims and Jews. There is no question of so-called misinterpretation. You cannot misinterpret "killing" as "kissing," or vice versa. Muslims did not misinterpret wife beating, marrying four wives, divorcing at will without showing any reason or excuse to anybody, sleeping with unlimited slave girls, getting involved in slave business, "cleaning" the Arab Peninsula of pagans, women's half inheritance, women's less credible witness in the court, or laws crushing non-Muslims. Umar did not misinterpret anything, but obeyed one of the Prophet's last three instructions when he "cleared" the Arabian Desert of non-Muslims. Don't we still see some of those torturous claws of Islamic "values" in some "laws" of Nigeria, Pakistan, and Afghanistan?

Unlike other religions, Islam controls Muslims in every second in every act, including using the left foot to step out and right foot to come into the house. It dangerously forces Muslims to establish an Islamic state even if it involves violence and killing non-Muslims. The Koran has no chronology. Some eighty-six thousand elements are sorted, divided, and blended there in a horrible, messy way. For any single topic, one has to jump around the whole Koran only to find one sentence here and another sentence there. Extremely important rules and laws are kept vague and dangerously left open to various interpretations and application by people of any depth and morals. There is no confirmation of the final instruction in case of different instruction on the same issue. The topic suddenly changes from North Pole to South Pole in the next line. Natural calamities are used as threats. The Koran's effort to trap people by scaring them is evident. An effort to hook people by lowly "bait," like sex with beautiful women in heaven, is also evident. These attitudes do not suit the grace and honor of a divine religion.

Islam is extrasensitive to and excessively obsessed with sex. Koranic handling of sex is crazy and overactive. Sleeping with slave girls is allowed without marrying them, but sex beyond wives and slave girls, even between consenting adults, is considered as one of the most, if not *the* most, destructive crimes in heaven and on Earth. Islam behaves as if all men of the world would jump on any woman at the first chance. To "protect" humankind from "sexual crime," Islam could not go beyond keeping women covered and segregated. Moral education with application of law and punishment was not given proper importance. That is an insult to men with morals and enlightenment. The whole attitude toward sex is seriously and clearly tilted in favor of men against women. The Koran did not foresee devastating crimes like genocide and mass-rape to put before so-called sex crimes. The Koran promises food for each person, but millions of people have died of starvation in the last thousand years. The Koran declares mercy to its followers but could not save hundreds of Hajis from burning to death in a fire during *hajj*.

In Islam human beings are used as coins to buy God's pleasure, as in the case of freeing slaves for "cleansing" from sin. Rich people are preferred as being able to free slaves and to perform *hajj*. Human beings are declared as enemies of God. Burning meteorites in the sky are described as arrows to Satan. *Jinns* are said to climb to the sky to listen to the gossip of the angels. The prophet Moses is described as running on the crowded road completely naked. Monkeys were stoned for adultery. After it "sets," the sun is described as prostrating itself to God to seek permission to rise the next day. Newborns are said to cry because Satan pinches them on their bodies. Yawning is said to be to God's disliking. Every aspect of Islamic attraction of heaven is attributable only to the desert. Not a thing in the Koran is beyond the precinct of Arabia. All its prophets and characters, problems and solutions, hopes and aspirations, incidents and accidents revolve around the only ancient Middle East. I have all these books with me, written by our *maulanas*. While not a single prophet of Islam is beyond the Middle East, all the gods of the Hindus are from India.

After consulting the Koran, the *hadith*, the Prophet's biography, and Islamic history for years with a guarded open mind, I related the past to the present. People tried reforming Islam. It never worked. Again and again Islam was mortgaged in the hands of killer leadership, while the rest of Muslim world only said, "This is not real Islam." It is indeed dangerous to humankind that nothing can stop Islam from breeding cruel killers time and time again. That is because many of the Prophet's deeds and Koranic instruction are always alive there to act as fertile ground for breeding killers. Things happened in Palestine, Chechnya, Bosnia, Kashmir, Indonesia, Egypt, Pakistan, and Bangladesh. The catastrophe of September 11 shook the whole world. I expected conflicting decisions of Islamic leadership in favor and against bin Laden based on geographic region. And how true my intuition was! Major Islamic leadership in North America and Europe "Islamically" denounced the cruelty of killing thousands by bin Laden. And the same leadership of the same Islam in Pakistan, England, and Muslim majority countries "Islamically" supported him as a hero. Once again the dual character of Islam became clear. Islam has two sets of teeth, like elephants. One is ivory, which makes it elegant and majestic. The other set of teeth is hidden inside its jaws and is used to chew and crush. All those sweet peace talks of Islam relate to the time and place of weak Islam in early years. But whenever and wherever Muslims were and are strong, they have another set of cruel laws and conduct. Tell me why the national flags of many Muslim countries have swords on the them. A sword is not for shaving beards, it is only for killing. With the hypocrisy and cunning game of sweet advice and cruel laws, the Koran has conclusively emerged as the most dangerous book for mankind as a whole.

The huge Muslim population of the Third World is frustrated because of various socioeconomic-political failures. The Islamic leadership there is completely ignorant of any solution to modern problems of international economics, national and international politics, sociology, and so on. It is only a century ago that the Islamic leaders started relating those failures to their faith. The Koran and hadith are the only things they knew. The Koran and hadith dangerously contain strong promises to Muslims to offer all the solutions of all the problems of the world for all time. So they were left with only one destiny: the violence embedded in the Koran and the biography of the Prophet. No other religion promises or demands so much at every step in life as Islam does. It urges Muslims to establish Islamic states and governments and to establish the *Sharīʿa*. A Muslim's life is never complete without that. This attitude served a strong purpose back fourteen hundred years ago, but now it has become a big liability for humankind, for Islam itself and Muslims themselves. This was a trap and they are still trapped in it. If Islam talks about any peace, it is the peace of the graveyard of non-Muslims, as proven from the biography of the Prophet to September 11, 2001, in New York.

Frustrated people, including Muslims and former Muslims, have been criticizing Islam increasingly. The world is so thirsty for social justice! If Islam could give a peaceful, just social system, as it promises, the whole world would embrace Islam. Instead, Islam today is a social liability to mankind as its leaders cause tremendous problem for human progress. It is true that if most of the Islamic leaders are wrong, there is something seriously wrong in Islam itself. The Prophet's cruelty to humankind and the continuous failure and violence of Islamic leaders are reasons enough to reject him and his religion. His attitude toward slaves, women, and non-Muslims clearly shows his limitation as only a talented human being with a clear vision of his goal without worrying about the cruel means of achieving that goal. There simply cannot be any divinity in cruelty to mankind.

The only reason behind Islam's establishment is the continuous support of the Muslim rulers for seven hundred to eight hundred years. Apart from that, Islam is nothing but another explosion of military power in human history, which died down with time. The only difference is, it was blended with divine faith in Islam's case. And as the faith spread, so did the Arabian language and dress, along with respect for Arabian fruits, water, and the like; that is imperialism with a coating of faith. The ritual of *Qurbān*, the "sacrifice," did not do any good to Muslims. It is nothing but slaughtering animals in the name of God to have a grand feast. It referred to the prophet Abraham, who left his wife and child in the open desert to die. Islam makes Muslims criticize social evils in other societies, but is blind to its own cruelties. It claims science in the Koran only after something is discovered, never before. And it ignores the fact that those scientists never embraced Islam. Islam hijacks the fruits of Muslim scientists as gifts of Islam.

Throughout my life I looked for any single moral code that was brought by Islam anew. There is simply none. All those Islamic social, familial, and other morals and sweet advice had always existed in the human mind long before Islam. Also, it is extremely unfair and dishonest to propagate the myth that before Islam the whole world was in "darkness." This is a shameless denial of so many thinkers' and philosophers' great contributions to human progress before Islam. We have ample proof that some societies before Islam had in fact more balanced, clear, and humane laws than the cruel imbalanced *Sharīʿa* laws of Islam. To be honest, I always felt ashamed whenever I read my books of *Sharīʿa* laws, both from Sunnis and *Shīʿa*. Islam definitely cleared up some primitive social systems of the ignorant desert people of that time. But its claim to bring "light" to the whole world is an insult to previous philosophers and scientists of all time in all places.

Society is driven less by constitutions, more by moral and applied institutions. That is why a country like England could be one of the most glorious nations of the world without a vividly written constitution. Islam as both an institution and a constitution failed measurably for all time. The bulk of world Muslims pass peaceful lives for two reasons. First, cruelty does not suit commoners continuously. Second, the cruel aspects of Islam are never disclosed to commoners. I say it again. If tomorrow morning there is no Islam on this planet, humankind has no sociofamilial value to lose except the occasional violence of a stubborn religious community that suffers from an artificial and dangerous superiority complex as the "best nation of mankind" with a "divine" license to look down upon others, both declared by their Koran.

I not only left Islam myself. I am leaving my vision in this article to talk for me when I am not here. I openly declare that anybody studying the Koran, *Ṣaḥīḥ hadith* of al-Bukhārī, the Prophet's biography, and the history of Muslims will have no way but to agree with what I said here. I am also teaching my kids to become decent and complete human beings with a concept of human brotherhood, which has been so much insulted and devastated by the dangerous concept and practice of Islamic brotherhood. I am teaching them to be guided by conscience, not by blind faith. Yes, now I am guided.

28

THE WIND BLOWING
THROUGH MY HAIR
Nadia (Morocco)

I left Islam not as a reaction against an Islamic fundamentalist or a restrictive upbringing. I left Islam for the simple fact that the religion is not logical, and I am by nature a very logical person. My parents were Moroccan immigrants to the United States. They loved America, but they also loved Islam. I was raised to be a Muslim, but in a very loving fashion. I wore a *hijab*, but I also wore typical American clothes—blue jeans and polo shirts. As a teenager, I was very proud to be a Muslim. It made me distinct from my classmates. I went so far as to believe that it made me superior. I reveled in the fact that I belonged to the "true" religion and that my religion held a monopoly on the word of God.

Around age twenty-five, I decided that I wanted to get married. Of course, I had to marry another Muslim. I did not have the freedom to marry outside of my faith, like Muslim men can do. I traveled back to my parents' homeland in search of a husband. It did not take me long to fall in love and marry a young man of my age. At first, he seemed to accept my "American" ways. However, before long he started to encourage me to change how I dressed, how I spoke, how I looked at people, how I ate, how I thought. The message was: You are not a good Muslim woman. He thought I was too forward and that I had no shame because I would say hello to his friends on the street. He almost died when I went so far as to shake hands with an American man I met one day. He was horrified that my shirts sometimes left a glimpse of my collarbone or that you could see the shape of my legs through my linen skirts.

It did not stop with my dress, though. He did not like me to watch singers or romantic shows on TV. He did not like me listening to love songs. And he almost fainted when I explained the theory of evolution to him. He began to preach to me about what Islam truly was. I listened. And then I read. I was sure I would prove to him that he didn't understand what Islam was at all. To my utter shock, I found out that it was I who didn't have a clue about Islam. Islam slowly transformed itself in front of my eyes from a benign, comforting faith to a demoralizing, vindictive cult. I kept trying to reassess my view. But the more I read the Koran, the more I realized that God could never have written those words.

I thought about divorcing my controlling husband, but despite his Hitler-like qualities, I am still terribly in love with him. I am sure that if he finds out that I am an apostate, he will kill me. Literally. So every day, I go through the ritual motions that the religion requires, disguising my true feelings of revulsion for the hate that Islam preaches. I did make one concession to my feelings when my husband and I moved to the United States: I took off my *hijab*. My husband almost went into seizures, but he hasn't been able to get that horrid piece of material back on my head again. To this day, I enjoy the feeling of the wind blowing through my hair, reminding me that although my life is repressed, my mind is not.

29

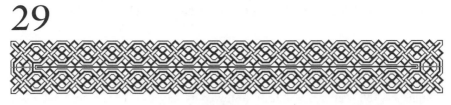

A PHILOSOPHER'S REJECTION OF ISLAM
Irfan Ahmad Khawaja (Pakistan)

I was born in Jersey City, New Jersey, in 1969 to Sunni Muslim parents who had come to the United States from Lahore, Pakistan, a few years earlier. My parents initially came to the United States intending merely to get their medical training here and go back, but circumstances conspired to keep them here, despite a few half-hearted attempts at return. They were (and are) certainly devout believers in Islam, but had had little religious education apart from the obligatory Islamiat required of students in Pakistan at the time. My mother is the more religious of the two, keeping most of the prayers and most of the fasts; she eventually performed *umra* (the lesser pilgrimage) in Mecca in 1996. My father is less overtly religious than my mother, and even toyed for a while with agnosticism, but is ultimately as devoted to Islam as she is. They were both great aficionados of the standard Islamic (or perhaps "Islamicate") prohibitions—against alcohol, pork, pre-marital sex, mingling of the sexes, intermarriage—and I'd go so far as to say that Islam's prohibitions constituted the core of its meaning for them.

I received my religious education from both my mother and my maternal grandmother. My grandmother played the role of "good cop" in this enterprise, filling my head at an early age with vivid stories of the lives of the prophets and the saints, along with apocalyptic tales of *qiyamat* (the day of judgment), *jahannum* (hell), and the grim fate of sinners (*Firawn* being her favorite example). My mother, in "bad cop" mode, managed to teach me Koranic Arabic as well as Urdu, also buying me some historical and religious books in English from the Islamic Center of New York. And so, every day the Arabic drill would commence, followed by Urdu drill, followed by recitation of *kalimas*,[1] and (as a reward for all that) an hour or so of Islamiat in English.

After some initial irritation at having to spend valuable playtime on all this, I actually came to enjoy the routine. In fact, I became something of a religious fanatic. I certainly believed all of what I had been taught literally and to the letter from early childhood until my teenage years. From ages nine to twelve, I voluntarily devoted at least half an hour every day to reading the Koran; I must have read it dozens of times in both English and Arabic by age eighteen. I finished my first Arabic reading of the Koran at age nine, and ended up memorizing at least half of its thirtieth section (*sipara*) by age twelve. (I still remember a good part of it.) At age ten, I made an abortive attempt to prepare my own translation of the Koran from Urdu into English from an Arabic-Urdu version that was floating around the house. That effort unfortunately failed after the first few sentences, when I discovered to my dismay that neither my Arabic nor my Urdu were nearly good enough to get me very far—a problem exacerbated by the fact that, according to my father, any error of translation on my part would spell instant damnation for falsifying the word of God.

I doubt I ever managed to say all *five* daily prayers on a regular basis, but I do remember regularly saying three or four, usually skipping *asr*, the most inconvenient of the bunch, because it interfered with track practice. I often took my prayer rug to high school with me, spreading it out in a secluded area to say *zuhr* prayers, sometimes reciting *maghrib* prayers[2] to myself on the late bus home after track practice. I fasted with great joy (I hesitate to say "relish") every Ramadan from ages nine until eighteen, and I'm sure that if I'd had any money after spending it on AC/DC records, I would have sent it away as *zakat* (alms) to the Afghan or Palestinian *mujahidin* (holy warriors). By age fourteen, I was pestering my parents to take us on *hajj*, and I was deeply puzzled and angered by their refusal to do so on the rather un-Islamic grounds that "it was inconvenient and unsafe" (which, of course, it is). "Someday we'll go on *umra*," my father assured me, which struck me a bit like his saying, "Don't worry, God will forgive us for aiming at second-best."

My steadfast belief in Islam began to unravel in high school, starting with a few sporadic crises of faith around age twelve, and eventuating in the irrevocable rejection of Islam at age sixteen or seventeen. (I practiced the rituals for a year or two after I left the faith.) I was fortunate to be sent to an expensive prep school and was also fortunate to have gotten an excellent education there, not only through my teachers, but through a group of bright and intellectually active friends, most of whom are now academics, physicians, or attorneys. A group of us—some Jews, a few Christians, and a Buddhist—would get together at lunchtime or during breaks in the day to discuss religious and philosophical issues. Those lunchtime conversations, along with prolonged bouts of agonized and solitary thought, gave rise to the questions that led me from faith to reason and eventually to apostasy.

The crucial turning point came in the summer of 1985, when I read Maxime Rodinson's *Muhammad* and Muhammad Haykal's *Life of Muhammad* in sequence, along with Thomas Carlyle's famous essay on the greatness of Muhammad.[3] I had previously only been acquainted with what I'd read about Muhammad from the Koran, and what I had read about him in the children's hagiographies my mother had bought for me from the Islamic Center. Rodinson's biography, then, came as a terrifying shock—hardly ameliorated by Haykal's inept apologetics or Carlyle's effusions.

The picture of Muhammad that Rodinson painted was not a flattering or admirable one, and it naturally provoked a series of uncomfortable questions about Muhammad and Islam. Could Rodinson conceivably be right about Muhammad? Could Muhammad have been as mercenary and hedonistic an individual as Rodinson had depicted? Could he really have sanctioned outright military conquest, summary execution, concubinage, and polygamy? Perhaps (I wondered) Rodinson was wrong, motivated by the desire to shame and humiliate Muslims and smear the Prophet. He was, after all, an orientalist and (worse) a Marxist—hardly trustworthy. More charitably, perhaps he was just honestly mistaken. He *was* a Judaized atheist—and so could hardly be expected to understand the deeper mysteries of our faith. But still, why was his biography so much better than Haykal's? Why did Haykal sound like such a fool? Why was he so defensive? Why was he utterly unable to answer any of the standard orientalist arguments despite spending pages and pages on the effort? For that matter, why was even Carlyle so unconvincing in his praise of Muhammad? These questions led me to wonder what was supposed to have been so admirable about Muhammad in the first place. Three problems seemed insuperable.

The first set concerned Muhammad's attitude toward violence—a live issue in the mid-1980s, when each day brought fresh news of another terrorist atrocity committed in the name of Islam. Muhammad was by common acclaim a "military genius." But how was that *admirable*? He was, we were told, a political genius as well—but it wasn't clear why that was admirable either; he was supposed to be a *prophet*, not a politician. Worse, nothing in his politics resonated with the tenets of my specifically American convictions: the Declaration of Independence, the Bill of Rights, the Gettysburg Address. It was unclear how one could admire Muhammad's accomplishments while *simultaneously* admiring those of the American republic.

The second problem was anti-Semitism. Anti-Semitism was a ubiquitous and shameful fact of life in the Pakistani-American community in which I'd grown up. (In fairness, the bigotry ran in both directions.) Because I had Jewish playmates, I found my elders' anti-Semitism deeply mortifying, but dismissed it as a deviation from Islam rather than an expression of it. Of course, there *were* those problematic passages in the Koran about the special wickedness of the Jews. Before I read Rodinson, those passages had been easy enough to ignore, but now the question haunted me like the return of the repressed: Why *was* there an undercurrent of anti-Jewish hostility in the Koran? The standard explanation was that the anti-Jewish verses, when "read in context," referred specifically to the "treachery" of the Jews of Medina. But what exactly had they done to merit that description? No adequate answer was forthcoming. More to the point, whatever the original "context" of the verses, why would an omniscient, omnipotent, and omnibenevolent God have made them part of his revelation? Couldn't he have foreseen what anti-Semitism would become in the future—and foreseen that his own words would come to abet it?

Islamic anti-Semitism would come back to haunt me later in life. I'll never forget a trip to Pakistan a few years ago during which a young cousin informed me of his great admiration for Adolf Hitler. Nor can I forget the conversation I had with another group of Pakistani cousins who quoted the Koran to me as indubitable "evidence" of the diabolical evil of Judaism and the Jews. One of them, my cousin Khawaja Saad Rafiq, went on to become special assistant to Prime Minister Nawaz Sharif in the late 1990s, and remains a prominent figure in the so-called Nawaz faction of the Pakistan Muslim League (PML-N). Apart from its penchant for corruption, the PML-N is notorious for its open support for the Taliban, for Kashmiri terrorism, and for its an on-again, off-again relationship with the fundamentalist Jamaat Islami. To add insult to injury, most of my immediate family has explicitly disavowed the legitimacy of my relationship with a Jewish woman—and disowned me as well. The legacy of the "treacherous Jews of Medina" dies hard.

Last but not least, there were the protofeminist problems. Why was the Koran obviously addressed to men rather than women? If God is genderless, why is he described in obviously androcentric terms? If God is just, why does he so obviously demote the status of women in his book? Actually, the question that had most perplexed me since the birth of my brother in 1975 was a rather specific one: Why did God make childbirth so painful and arduous? The question arose naturally from my mother's harping on the theme to make us feel guilty for our various transgressions against parental discipline. Little did she know where the harping would lead, and how unsatisfied I would be with the lame answer that women must suffer for Eve's sinful disobedience to God.

The questions kept piling up without end—and were not exactly mollified by the Koran's mind-negating announcement in Surah Al Baqara that "this is a book whereof there can be no doubt." As it turned out, there was more to doubt in the book than to believe. And before long, I was gripped by the thought that perhaps I had been duped into believing something that was not merely false, but so utterly irrational that the real question was not why I had come to have doubts about it, but why I had persisted so long in believing it. And yet I resolved to believe in it anyway, assuming that my mind had been polluted by Western culture and my own deficiencies of character, and that a just God would show me the route back to belief if only I used my mind properly and purged myself of sin. "God helps those who help themselves," I thought. And so I resolved to help myself.

The obvious way to do so was to go on a pilgrimage—and the obvious place to go was the public library. Searching the card catalog, and jotting down the names of prominent people who were writing about Islam in prominent publications (the *New York Times*, the *New Republic*, the *Nation*, *New York Review of Books*, etc.), I resolved to read Edward Said's *Orientalism*,[4] followed by the works of the arch-orientalist Bernard Lewis. Surely if the problem was that my mind had been polluted by Western culture, Said would help me see how that had happened, and Lewis's writings would acquaint me with the ways of the enemy.

I didn't understand all of Said's book at that age (seventeen), but I understood enough of it to see how useless it was for the enterprise I had in mind. It was true that Said scored a few polemical points against some of his opponents. But he said nothing at all in *Orientalism* or elsewhere (e.g., in his later book, *Covering Islam*[5]) to vindicate Islam from the obvious charges against it—charges that any thinking Muslim would have to acknowledge and take seriously. In fact, his work was an impediment to clear thought about Islam; it contained all the rationalizations one would need to retain one's prejudices about its benign role in the modern world. Said's modus operandi was as simple as it was predictable: He began by denying on nominalist and historicist grounds that there was any such thing as "Islam"; he then denied that "it" could possibly give comfort to terrorism, theocracy, anti-Semitism, or misogyny because after all, "it" didn't exist; he then let loose with a torrent of ad hominem abuse against anyone who had a dissenting view (especially Lewis, whom he consistently defames); and finally, he would switch grounds in the middle of the argument to insist that all of the bad things that ostensibly proceeded from Islam were really "distortions" of "it." (A classic example of every one of these moves is his recent essay "The Clash of Ignorance," in the *Nation*.[6]) This seemed to me to be an incoherent and disingenuous mode of argument, even when I was still a believing Muslim earnestly looking for a way to vindicate Islam in the face of Western criticism; my assessment of argument and author have not improved in the years since.

Contrary to my initial expectations, I found Bernard Lewis to be a much better guide to Islam than Said. Lewis was, above all, a clearer and more straightforward writer than Said, that it was always easier to filter out his prejudices and extract what was useful and informative in his prose. Amusingly, I matriculated at Princeton in 1987 with the intention of studying with Lewis, not realizing that as an "emeritus" professor—not an "eminent" one—he had long since retired! The dismaying truth was revealed to me on my first day at Princeton by a Turkish graduate student I met in the Near East Studies section of the library. After letting the cat out of the bag about Lewis's retirement, she told me not to fret too much at my mistake, since the fundamental mistake was to have wanted to study with Lewis in the first place.

By the end of the summer of 1985, my commitment to Islam had wavered, but not my commitment to theism. Surely it was possible, I thought, to reject Islam but believe in God? By year's end, that possibility had evaporated as well. I remember the circumstances exactly: It was on a plane ride back from Pakistan in January 1986, just a few days after visiting the Shah Faisal Masjid in Islamabad. The mosque, I believe, had just been built, and my proud Pakistani relatives were showing it off to me to inspire in me a deeper love of Islam and of Pakistan. For some reason, however, the tour had exactly the opposite effect: not only did the mosque *not* inspire me, but managed (in its similarity to the Kennedy Space Center *sans* rockets) to depress and alienate me. Saddened both by my reaction to the mosque and my alienation from those who took such pride in it, I settled down on the plane home to read the most depressing book I had at my disposal, namely William Barrett's *Irrational Man.*[7] In retrospect, the book strikes me as a fairly unconvincing piece of philosophy, but at the time, it had the genuine merit of keeping my mind focused directly on the issue of God's existence. With the book in hand, and the issue directly in mind, I decided for the first time in my life to confront the issue of God's existence in an honest, sustained, and objective way, suspending belief in him or against him, and simply resolving to go wherever my mind took me on the subject. By the end of a long and sleepless plane ride, I was more or less an atheist.

I can't quite reproduce the exact reasons by which I came to atheism all those years ago—I don't remember them, and I'm sure they were quite crude. But the basic reasons for rejecting theism remain the same for me now as then.

For one thing, it quickly became clear to me that God's attributes make no sense. Consider omnipotence. If God is omnipotent, he's capable of doing anything. But that proposition leads to obvious paradoxes—as clichéd as they are unanswerable. Can he make a rock that even he can't lift? Can he create something out of nothing? Can he make water water freeze at its boiling point? Can He make water molecules from a ratio of eighty-five hydrogen ions to thirteen hydroxide ions? Can he repeal the Law of Noncontradiction? To answer "yes" to any of these questions is to utter what is senseless. To answer "no" is to concede that the structure of the world puts limits on God's power. In neither case is omnipotence possible.

Nor does omniscience fare much better. If God is omniscient, he can foretell the future. But if he can foretell the future, the future must exist in a determinate way. If so, the future is already written, and we lack free will. But if we lack free will, we lack responsibility, and God contradicts himself when he holds us morally responsible for our actions by judging, rewarding, and punishing us. Since an omniscient being cannot be guilty of self-contradiction, this option seems impossible. On the other hand, if we have free will, God can't predict the future with certainty. Lacking a certain knowledge of the future, it follows that he lacks omniscience. Whether we have free will or not, then, omniscience fails.

Omnibenevolence fails even more miserably than the other two attributes. If God created the world, he is ultimately responsible for everything in it. Being omnibenevolent, he must be just, and being just, he must order the world so as to conforms to his own (Islamic) principle of justice—that every atom's weight of good is rewarded, and every atom's weight of evil is punished. And yet it is obvious that good goes unrewarded, and evil goes unpunished throughout history and throughout the world, thereby flagrantly contravening God's own principles in front of his face, indeed with his apparent sanction and, indirectly, by his own actions. Lacking any excuses of ignorance or incapacity, God merely watches mutely as justice is trampled and both injustice and misfortune take their toll. Since no agent of goodness can be indifferent to injustice and misfortune for which he is ultimately responsible, God cannot be omnibenevolent. In fact, He seems quite the reverse.

As a child, I had believed in God's existence on the strength of what has come to be called the *kalam* cosmological argument, which asserts that God's existence is necessary as the first cause of the universe. The argument says, in effect, that since time and causation cannot go backward infinitely, they must both have had a beginning—and that beginning is God. (I formulated a crude version of the argument for myself at age ten.) It's instructive to note that this impressive monument to Islamic philosophy has recently been developed in a sophisticated form by a non-Muslim philosopher (William Lane Craig); I have yet to encounter an ordinary Muslim who has heard of it, much less one who knows of its Islamic provenance.

Fascinating as it is, however, the *kalam* argument is unsound. For one thing, though there is a good justification for applying the concept of "cause" *within* the universe, there is no comparable justification for applying it to the universe as a whole. Second, the argument depends on the supposed impossibility of an infinite regress of times and causes, but I don't think its proponents have successfully established that such a regress *is* impossible. Finally, even if there was a beginning of time, there is no good reason to believe that that beginning is a deity worthy of worship, much less that it has the divine attributes of omnipotence, omniscience, or omnibenevolence. So the argument fails.

I had also believed in God because I was painfully aware of the fact that in this world, vice was too often rewarded, and virtue too often unrewarded. So I held out hope for another world in which the moral balances would finally be evened out. As the Koran says of the hereafter, "Whoever does an atom's weight of good shall see it, and whoever does an atom's weight of evil shall see it" (XCIX.7–8). It seemed inconceivable to me that the relationship between virtue and reward, and vice and punishment, could somehow rest on mere chance. And so, I reasoned, there must be a God to make everything work out in the end.

This was the most damaging and lasting falsehood I acquired from Islam. For one thing, the argument encourages passivity and resignation to misfortune and injustice on the grounds that "God will make everything work out." Worse still, the argument subordinates reason to hope in an insidious way, giving one a moral stake in the idea that fervent (and moralistic) wishes can override reality. Above all, it demotes the value of the world we actually live in, exaggerating the role of chance, depreciating the role of choice, and then maintaining the pretense that all chance contingencies can somehow be abolished in another, superior, chanceless realm. This was the hardest set of falsehoods to leave behind; its rejection brought the hardest set of truths to accept.

The falsehood of the view was most fully driven home to me while visiting Ground Zero a few months after the September 11 attacks. It was not until I saw the twisted remnants of the towers that I fully realized that *nothing* could compensate for the injustice and horror of what was lost that day—not even an identical and eternal replica of the World Trade Center in another realm and the resurrection of all the souls lost in it. Even if God were to create a replica of the place and bring all of its victims back to life, the brutal fact remains that the *real* World Trade Center was *not* a replica of anything, but a specific place in space and time, and loved precisely for its specificity. More to the point, the people who died there were specific individuals who were destroyed in a particularly awful and painful way. Nothing can ever undo the rupture in moral reality caused by their deaths; Nothing in the future can undo their suffering, or erase the evil that came into the world with the act. The only way to "replace" the buildings or "compensate" for the personal loss would be to undo what happened at 8:46 A.M. on September 11, 2001, so that the event never took place at all. And not even God in all of his supposed power claims *that* ability; possessing it would be an absurdity of its own.

In this light, I have been depressed not only by the Muslim reaction to September 11, but by the intellectually feeble reactions to it of Christians and Jews, who have managed to a fabricate a plethora of excuses for God despite his obvious absence that day at the crucial hour. Where, I feel like asking such people, *was* God on the morning of September 11? Did he not know what was on Muhammad Atta's mind? Were the airplanes too fast for him to intercept? Was his radar not on? Was he not nimble enough to catch the people jumping out of windows? Couldn't so "compassionate and merciful" a deity at least have given the firefighters some advance warning that the towers were going to collapse—or did even the good Lord have trouble that day with his Verizon Wireless service?

I don't think there are any other plausible arguments for God's existence, and since there aren't, and the plausible ones fail, I inferred (and infer) that God doesn't exist. What exists is just nature—and our place in it. I eventually found the guidance I was looking for from Islam in so-called Western philosophy, and especially in the works of Aristotle, John Locke, Benedict Spinoza, Friedrich Nietzsche, and Ayn Rand. It was Rand, in particular, who put things together for me into a coherent and integrated framework; Leonard Peikoff's *Objectivism: The Philosophy of Ayn Rand*,[8] is perhaps the best single-volume introduction to her thought.

Having rejected Islam, however, I don't bear any fundamental animosity toward it as such. My memories of life as a Muslim are mostly fond ones, and I learned many positive things from Islam. The Koran is neither inimitable, nor indubitable, nor consistent; nor is it the word of God. But it *is* a great work of literature, on par with Homer, Virgil, Milton, or Goethe, and I still read it from time to time in that spirit. Muhammad was not the Prophet of God, and is no moral hero. But he certainly *was* an important and in some ways admirable historical figure on par with Alexander or Napoleon, and should be ranked among them. The Muslim rituals are not exactly rational in their current form, much less commandments from God. But I have found some of them beneficial, at least in a secularized form. There is something to be said for the idea behind *salat*—of stopping in one's daily routine during the day to purify one's consciousness and reconnect with the world. So, in moderation, is there something to be said for the benefits of *sawm* (fasting) and *zakat* (charity); I try to practice both. Even *jihad* refers to certain spiritual, psychological, and political realities: Much of life *is* struggle against oneself and one's adversaries, and we need a word to capture this fact. Finally, while I don't think Islam deserves the credit for the achievements of the "Islamicate" world, I do cherish certain accomplishments of that world and wish they were more widely known. There is great value in the poetry of Rumi, Ghalib, and Iqbal, in the *qawwalis* of Nusrat Fateh Ali Khan, and the *ghazals* of Tahira Syed, in the novels of Neguib Mahfouz, and the architecture of the Alhambra, Cairo, Istanbul, Lahore, Delhi, and Agra. I've even come to make my peace with the Shah Faisal Masjid in Islamabad; on a clear day, its luminous white marble makes a striking contrast against the verdant green of the Himalayan foothills.

It is hard not to feel animosity, however, for what Islam has become in the last hundred years—and for what Muslims and their apologists have become in the process. The events and aftermath of September 11 are perhaps the most poignant reminder of this fact. Though I don't think that September 11 can be blamed on Islam as such, it certainly can be blamed on a certain form of Islam, and "a certain form of Islam" obviously bears some determinate relation to Islam itself. Even a *perversion* of Islam is, after all, a perversion *of Islam*, and given this, Muslims bear a special responsibility not only to repudiate the perversion, but to seek out its adherents within their midst and deal accordingly with them. At a minimum, that means refusing to make excuses for them; optimally, it calls for ruthless and unstinting criticism, and support for legal measures against them consistent with due process. (It should go without saying that I do *not* mean to be endorsing vigilante violence, or the spreading of false rumors, or anything of the sort.)

Suffice it to say that with a few rare and noble exceptions—I think of Fareed Zakariya (*Newsweek*), Fouad Ajami (*U.S. News & World Report*), Salman Rushdie, Neguib Mahfouz, Kanan Makiya, Irfan Husain (of the Pakistani newspaper *Dawn*), Wahiduddin Khan (the Indian Muslim thinker)—Muslims have been exceedingly slow to face reality and act accordingly. The Muslim communities of North America and the U.K. are perhaps the most remiss in this regard, consisting as they do of people who ought to know better but evidently don't. In my experience, the Muslim-American community is a hotbed of anti-Semitism, misogyny, chauvinism, and explicit apologetics for theocracy and terrorism. In Britain and Canada, I suspect, things are even worse than they are here. Despite this, you will rarely find prominent Muslim intellectuals—what to speak of such blatant fifth columnists as Shamim Siddiqi, Siraj Wahaj, or Hamza Yousaf—engaging in anything like the sustained, unremitting critique that Muslim-Americans or the broader Islamic *ummah* richly deserves.

The question I would want to pose to any thinking Muslim is this. Let's put aside my admittedly *kafir* objections to the existence of God, and focus on a specifically Islamic question, a question that any Muslim must face even from a strictly Islamic perspective. This is the question of Muhammad Iqbal's epic poem *Shikva and Javab-i-Shikva* (*Complaint and Answer to the Complaint*), written 1909–1913. Why is it, Iqbal asks, that

> *Rahmatan han teri aghyar kay kashano par;*
> *barq gir thi han to baycharay musulmanon par.*
> (Your blessings are showered on the homes of unbelievers, strangers all.
> Only on the poor Muslim, Your wrath like lightning falls.)

Islam was supposed to be a faith that guided and rewarded its followers in this world *and* the hereafter: *fi'dunia w'al akhira*. But it seems obvious that it has failed in this world: the Muslim world from Indonesia to the *Maghrib* is a veritable disaster area. It is easy, then, to agree with Iqbal's complaint but difficult to take seriously the answer to it that he puts in God's mouth: *kuch bi paygham-i-Muhammad*

kay thujhay pas nahin! ("Of Muhammad's message, nothing is left among you!")
I can't help wondering what wisdom the Prophet Muhammad could have imparted
to contemporary Muslims that would give them their rights and freedom, jump-
start their bankrupt economies, and give them the capacity to deal justly and reasonably with themselves and others. I don't pretend to know the answer, but then
again, as a non-Muslim, it's not my responsibility to know. What I *do* know is that
the answer is not to be found in the writings of Sayyid Qutb, Abul Ala Mawdudi,
Ruhollah Khomeini, Ali Shariati, or even Muhammad Iqbal. What I also know is
that by and large, Muslims have defaulted on the task of looking for it. Whether
the relevant answer *can* be found, I leave an open question.

For much of my adult life, I've endured the criticisms and pleas of Muslims
who, deprecating my atheism, have made the impertinent demand that I return to
the Islamic fold and redeem myself before their *ummah*. (It could be worse: There
are those who believe that apostasy like mine is grounds for assassination.) Be
that as it may, I now have a demand of my own that ought to become the demand
of every non-Muslim: Is it too much to ask of Muslims that they return to the
human fold? Humanity has endured enough at the hands of Muslims, and enough
in the name of Islam. Even as an atheist, I'm willing to concede that there are
better and worse forms of Islam, and that there is something inspiring and noble
about the better aspects of its better forms. Surely even Islam deserves better than
the indignities that contemporary Muslims have inflicted on it, and contemporary
Muslims deserve better than what Islam has now become. The question is: Do we
have to wait until *yawm al qiyamat* (the day of resurrection) before they manage
to get things right?

Notes

1. The Creed of the Muslim: "There is no Deity but God, Muhammad is the Apostle
of God."
2. *Zuhr* prayers: When the sun has begun to decline; *maghrib* prayers: a few mim-
nutes after sunset; *asr* prayers: midway between *zuhr* and *maghrib*.
3. Maxime Rodinson, *Muhammad* (New York: Pantheon, 1971); Muhammad
Haykal, *Life of Muhammad* (Delhi: Islamic Book Service, 1995); Thomas Carlyle, *Sartor
Resartus: On Heroes and Hero Worship* (London: Everyman's Library, 1971).
4. Edward Said, *Orientalism* (New York: Random House, 1979).
5. Edward Said, *Covering Islam* (New York: Vintage, 1997).
6. Bernard Lewis, "The Clash of Ignorance," *Nation*, October 22, 2001.
7. William Barrett, *Irrational Man* (New York: Anchor, 1962).
8. Leonard Peikoff, Objectivism: The Philosophy of Ayn Rand (New York: Dutton,
1991).

30

MY MALAISE

A Malaysian Ex-Muslim (Malaysia)

Before you read my story below, I would like you to know that a lot of details are omitted to prevent people finding out who I am. Some individuals and organizations may use my detailed info to hurt me in some way—just because I do not think Islam is right for me.

My parents made Malaysia their permanent home and that is where I was born and raised. By the laws in Malaysia, whoever is Malay or has a Malay ethnic background has to be Muslim. Since my dad is Malay, our whole family in Malaysia was registered as Muslim and had no other choice but to be Muslim

In regular school (from grade 1 to university), we had to learn Islam over and over. From ages eight to eleven, I was also sent to religious school (every day except weekends) in addition to regular school, which I hated! I hated to wear the veil because it is hot and humid all year long in Malaysia. I recall making fun of the teacher in religious school at the age of eleven because she kept on talking about nonsense (which she seemed to believe in). At least I just went to religious school from ages eight to eleven (other kids go from ages seven to twelve). I probably started late because my parents wanted to see if I could handle regular school alone. And I quit at age eleven because I wanted to do sports and the religious school's headmaster didn't want to let me take leave for sports practice. So, my parents said, "Hey! Quit then," which is good. My siblings had to go up to age twleve. But they were in a religious school that was only three times a week and only two hours a day instead of four to five hours.

In addition to all that, my parents insisted I learn the Koran. I hated that, too, because I hated reading Arabic and I had no idea what it was about. So what was the point of it? My parents just wanted me to be able to do well in religious studies at school and not feel left out among other children in Malaysia. Anyway, I used to make the Koran teachers want to quit coming to our house to teach. My mom has a lot of stories to tell when it comes to me making the Koran teachers want to quit. Later on, my dad would have a cane out (to beat me) to make sure I was learning the Koran and not making the teachers want to quit. This is another thing I used to do: when I changed teachers (because I made them quit by giving them a hard time) I used to flip the pages of the Koran a whole lot (hundreds of pages) and mark the page there as where the last teacher stopped. So the new teacher would start a page, which was hundreds of pages after the one I last read. That way I finished the Koran fast and didn't have to worry about wasting time on nonsense. Sometimes, I would do the same thing even if I didn't change teachers. I would try to trick the same teacher. Anyway, my parents still think I managed to go through the whole book.

Ever since I was young, I was doubtful about this whole Islam thing. With all the bizarre things going on according to the religious teachers and its difficult rituals, Islam was a nightmare to me. I recall one day (probably when I was about eleven years old) the Koran teacher was telling me we should believe in Allah, the prophets, the four books, and so on. I asked him did we only have to "believe" in them without knowing if they exist?! So he must believe in them without knowing if they exist.

In all schools, the teachers used to teach us that all non-Muslims (*kafirs*) are going to hell. When I told my parents this, they got mad. They said that isn't true. The teachers are not God, to judge who is going to hell or not. I think my parents just think the Koran teaches good things but they don't know themselves what is in there because they didn't study it. During my dad's time, no religious studies were taught in school.

For secondary school, I went to a school that was multiracial and multireligious. I began to make friends with people who were not Muslim. They were very nice people, nicer than the Muslims. They always respected me and never forced me to do anything religionwise. The Muslims were forcing me to practice Islam and giving me a hard time. I finally realized something was wrong with the idea that all Muslims will end up in heaven one day, but never the non-Muslims. So I decided that Islam is nonsense. Why is it that good people go to hell and bad ones go to heaven just because of what religion they follow? Not everyone is given the same chance to learn Islam. I realized my true friends in secondary school were never Muslim.

A factor that contributed toward my leaving Islam is the fact that women *have* to wear veils. They claim it is so that men don't look at sexy women. It is to protect the women from men staring at them. Well, there are Muslim men that turn me on and get me sexually aroused, and they don't have to wear a veil and cover up! I wish they would so that I could concentrate on other things rather than them. But this isn't in Islam for the men.

When I was in my last year in secondary school, we had to take the national exams. For Islamic education, I had to study about marriage in detail to do well. So I learned all the stuff and got the highest grade anyone can get for Islamic education. And guess what? Because I know it so well, I know that there is a lot of discrimination against women in Islam. Things like a father and grandfather can marry a girl/woman to whomever they want even if the girl/woman doesn't want to marry that person. That is disgusting! A man can beat his wife (after giving her advice and sleeping apart) if she doesn't do whatever he wants her to. That sounds horrible to me, too. I am strongly against corporal punishment on children, because of my own personal experience, and certainly against women! In addition, I learned that women couldn't be witnesses in Syariah courts and things like that.

Since there are parts that are horrible in Islam, I do not accept it as the true religion. Plus, the religion is extremely difficult for me to practice if I want to be comfortable with my lifestyle. So that is why I choose not to be Muslim. This has cost me a lot. I had to give up an education in a better university than the one I am attending now, a guaranteed respectable job, and everything I have in Malaysia to live in a foreign country. This is going to sound crazy, but I actually married another Muslim apostate from Malaysia so that he would help me move to this new home country of mine, as he had the money and in return he could stay here safely. This has disadvantages like it is hard to get other men to date me if they know I have a "husband." If Malaysian Muslims find out that we are not Muslim, many would torture us in some way. In Malaysia, there are *Pusat Pemulihan Akidah*s or faith rehabilitation centers, and perhaps even the death penalty (in one or two Malaysian states only) for Muslim apostates. I even gave up my Malaysian citizenship to be safer. The fact that Malaysian Muslims want to hurt us hurts me a lot, because why do they have to hurt us just because we view Islam differently? We wouldn't have treated them badly or anything. My "husband" said that they know their religion is nonsense. So anyone who tries to reveal this is somehow "changed" or killed to avoid more people knowing that it is nonsense. They are just so insecure about their religion that they have to get rid of people who know the truth about it!

After reading the Faith Freedom International and ISIS Web sites and confirming it by reading a translation of the Koran in English (translated by a Muslim!) and other translations online, I realized that there is more crap in the

Koran than I thought—all this killing the nonbelievers, keeping captives (slaves) and having sex with them, and so on. Even the *hadith* have a lot of inhumane stuff and I don't think they should be considered 100 percent true as they are based on what someone said hundreds of years ago.

Currently, I am a person of no religion. Many Muslim apostates who have been hurt and/or seen people get hurt in the name of Islam think that Islam should be totally destroyed. Of course, it would be great if it is possible. However, all I ask for from Muslims is freedom of religion, as I know that would help reduce the number of people suffering. Plus, if Islam were so great like Muslims claim, people would want to believe in it and practice it anyway without being forced.

31

A NIGHTMARE IN TUNISIA

Samia Labidi (Tunisia)

IN THE NAME OF MAN, THE BENEFICENT, THE MERCIFUL

When Ibn Warraq asked me to contribute to an anthology of testimonies by former Muslims, I decided to talk for the first time of the burden that religion imposes on minds and actions at the dawn of the third millennium.

Being a woman, I have experienced firsthand and to the full the grip of religion. As with all young girls of Arabo-Muslim origin, Islam was transfused into my blood as soon as I was born when the first words that were whispered into ears, and into my mind, were, "There is no God but God and Muhammad is his Prophet," the famous profession of faith that allows us to become Muslims. In the present case, it was a condemnation, without warning and without appeal, to being a Muslim. The child is the last one concerned in this forced baptism.

Gradually, it became clear that this profession of faith only had meaning from only one angle, that of men. I grew up in a traditional environment: the women inside and the men outside. I was lucky to be born in a rather tolerant milieu, which only paid lip service to Islam. Thus, prayers were confined to the days of religious festivals. Ramadan was the excuse for eating ten times more and better, alms to show that you were generous, pilgrimage to Mecca to purify oneself of the totality of one's sins forever.

In this atmosphere, governed inside the house by women and outside by men, I noticed the growing importance of the feminine universe developing in parallel to the masculine one, which was losing ground without being aware of it. In fact, Tunisia turned out to be the Arabo-Muslim country most favorable to the emancipation of women, thanks to secular-minded President Habib Bourguiba, who constantly fought against the archaisms of the institutions of the time. The Tunisian women have always been privileged, right up to the present, in contrast to their sisters in the rest of the Islamic world.

The double moral standard of men in Tunisian society is flagrant and shameful. The Tunisian male presents an open and modern personality on the out-side, in contact with the civilized world, and absolutely the opposite inside his family, where he has to preserve his image and almost bestial dominance. The passage from one to the other is effected mechanically, as though men were broken into this behavior right from birth.

From the ensemble of the dogma of the permitted and forbidden, which mixes up the trivial and important, man is able to pick and choose according to his needs and interests without worrying about divine sanction, such as the misuse of alcohol, which flows like water in the exclusively male evenings. On the other hand, a woman has to apply herself to this dogma in the smallest details; laxism is a one-way street and the dead end is reserved for the female of the species.

In a society where it is forbidden for women to occupy positions of power or importance, under the pretext that her emotions dominate her reason, her prin-cipal task consists in begetting and bringing up children. In a society where the woman inherits only half that of a man, where her testimony in a court is worth half that of a man, where a man is permitted to beat a woman when she deviates from customary behavior regarding her husband, it is very difficult for a woman to beat a path for herself and achieve her full potential.

My first contact with Islam was of the traditional kind without the least knowledge of the original texts. I went to Koranic school from the age of three without understanding the objective of this obligatory detour before rejoining the kindergarten. My memories are full of vivid impressions of strong and omni-present feminine personalities at the heart of my family, despite appearances to the contrary. My maternal grandmother, Omi Zohra, and my mother, Ouasilla, were real rebels against this injustice, which was difficult for them to give a name to.

In fact, the two women in my life did everything to ensure that their children were not subjected to the same punishments. My mother and, exceptionally, my father had done everything for their daughters to receive the same education as the boys without the smallest amount of discrimination. It is for this reason that I was able to continue my primary and secondary education without too much difficulty. Between tradition, Islam, and Tunisian culture of the old town of Tunis, we can see the ignorant but light presence of religion, which only tints in function of need the lives of Tunisians who know how to adapt it to satisfy their wants. In other words, it is rather tradition that has shaped Islam in the way it wants and not the other way around. It is obscurantism that has blackened the so-called light of religion and not the other way around; the last word is with the man molded and radio controlled by tradition.

I left the old quarter of Tunis with its bitter and sweet memories, dominated by its tradition and its hidden Islam, which was present only to comfirm and render credible habits deeply etched in the hearts and minds of men of the time. In the town of Ariana, in the suburbs of Tunis, we determined to start a new life, full of hope and promise. My parents set up in a modern villa that was meant to be the cradle of openness to the outside world and to tolerance. My mother was satisfied with the success of her children, her daughters particularly, in their studies. In fact, one of her daughters got into university to continue her, higher scientific research. A brilliant and independent future was smiling at her contrary to what her mother had lived through and suffered. Except the beginning of success constituted at the same time the beginning of failure; it was a double-edged sword that appeared on the horizon.

I had just begun my cycle of secondary school studies in the new environment, full of joy and unprecedented openness of spirit. An era of modernity swept through our family; we finally extirpated the clutches of archaic and suffocating tradition, and started to breathe new air. But this promising pause lasted only an instant before my family was infiltrated by the Islamic fundamentalists through the husband of one of my sisters. The sister who had succeeded in going up to university, the first to save the honor of women, flirted with the beginning of the movement of radical Islam in the mid-1970s in Tunis.

No one at the time gauged the impact that this encounter would have on the stability of our family. It was a mini Islamic revolution that was taking place in the heart of our home, from one day to the next a change of regime was in place; we went from one extreme to another. The intrusion of this son-in-law provoked a radical change with dramatic consequences for all of us: my father, my mother, my four sisters, my four brothers, and myself.

The Islamist seed was taking root gradually inside Tunisian families, among which was ours. The husband of my sister turned out to be one of the founding members of the Islamist organization Mouvement à Tendance Islamiste (MTI), known under the name of El Nahda (Renaissance). He represented the hard line of this movement, those who advocated military action. His strategy was to take control of his family-in-law to consolidate his power of oppression. He found husbands for the girls, one in the army, the other in business, and for me a fighter pilot who is now a political refugee in London. My eldest sister was already married before this infiltration, a narrow escape from the organizer's program.

As for the boys, he pulled strings to introduce one of them into military school, with the complicity of my father, who found himself once again suddenly at the head of the family, which he had always dreamed of. Islam made him into a powerful person with the help of Koranic texts. It was no longer the power conferred on him by tradition outside the house, his dominance now carried on into the interior, where it interfered with the trivial and the important. The three other boys were still young, they confined themselves to practicing religion to the letter and not in the traditional manner. From one day to the next, the entire family got down to work with passion to catch up for lost time and redeem the sins of the past.

As in the wake of all revolutions, there were various reactions. There were those who approved out of conviction, others out of obligation or out of weakness, and still others out of self-interest, and finally those who were totally opposed, like my mother and my eldest sister, who refused to let the new despotic regime take hold. Free will disappeared to leave the word to God and to Muhammad. Nothing could be decided or done without going back to the sacred texts to make sure that the act was in conformity with them.

At the time I was only eleven years old, but I was attracted by this sudden return to the "true Islam" as they called it, attributing greater rights to women than "traditional Islam." They dazzled us with the prospect of a situation far more honorable than that was reserved for us by Tunisian tradition or the Western world. At the beginning, the adherence of women to Islamism was in the spirit of a movement to liberate women from the chains of tradition and to save them from the devaluation that Western women experienced as sexual objects. To give back to woman her true place which was hers by rights pleased me.

I subscribed with heart and soul to this new Islam of the Islamists, which aimed to abolish the secular state. In my mind, it was only a return to our origins and our real Arabo-Muslim identity; I was totally unaware of the poltical aspects that were brewing at the time. The idea of God fascinated me, that of a perfect being one must resemble, as far as possible, to better understand him. I wanted to go back to this divine origin of the so-called creation. To win back paradise, for me, was nothing more than to be able to drink to the full at the source. I discovered finally that Islam was not what I had known during my traditional childhood.

I accepted putting on the Islamic scarf right from the age of eleven and become a follower of the "true Islam." I was an ardent practitioner, I knew the Koran by heart, I had mastered the *hadith* and exegesis as far as my young age would allow. I followed all the lessons about the legal element in Islam to improve my knowledge of and better penetrate the divine mystery. I wished to take an interest only in the basic fundamental elements of Islam independent of all the different interpretations of men who had monopolized this domain in tailoring the texts to their desires. I wanted to develop a personal point of view without having to refer to anyone else; I used the dogma to reach the essential, the quintessence of the so-called divine message.

The Islamic headscarf, which all women put on in the same way, had more a political rather than a religious connotation. I took it off only when I was with women or in front of men I could not marry. The rest of the body had to be entirely covered with a dress ample enough not to accentuate the form of the body, and simple enough not to attract the looks of men. The woman had to be a ghost who moved from place to place in silence, without rousing the smallest masculine desire. In brief, she was considered on the whole like a sexual organ, even her voice had to be not too feminine, lest, so they said, it entice the feeble hearts of men. I asked myself if the problem came rather from the bestial vision these men had of the feminine gender or of themselves.

On top of the five obligatory daily prayers, I was encouraged to add some more in order to redeem my past sins. On top of the fast of Ramadan, I was advised to fast every Monday and Thursday to have my unconscious errors pardoned. On the other hand, I was exempted from pilgrimage to Mecca and the Friday prayers at the mosque, because the woman is closer to the "real Islam" in her house, even more in her bedroom, not to mention her bed or even in her own body. I did not have the right to look men in the eyes or to shake their hands when greeting them. In short, mixing of the sexes was more than forbidden, as they said when a man finds himself alone with a woman, the devil is the third companion.

I had to say good-bye to outings for pleasure, to the beach in a swimming costume, to my friends who refused to follow me in my religious activities, to mini-skirts, to bursts of laughter, in short, to all the pleasures of life. I was buried alive inside the task that man wanted to condemn me for life. I resembled more a shadow than a living being worthy of the human condition. I saw my sisters around me sinking one after another into the madness of this interpretation, purely human and masculine, of the so-called divine texts. They were really far from the feminist revolution they had hoped to accomplish through their adherence. The spiral of circumstance was there and the trap was closing on them without them being able change anything. They had abandoned their studies and had renounced their careers in order to dedicate their lives and souls to the production of a new generation of Islamists who would save humanity.

I was lucky in refusing categorically the idea of marriage, which would have been the point of no return. There remained for me an opening to escape the depression that had taken hold of me. I wanted to flee this milieu by any means possible; it did not at all correspond to what I had imagined some years earlier. I saw the conflict growing larger daily between my parents, who were destroying themselves in front of everyone. All the quarrels were on the subject of the "real Islam" that my mother refused to admit as divine words.

As time went by, the disappointments succeeded one another in form and content. Having been through the main texts of the "real Islam," I did not find the answers to questions I posed on the subject of God, this perfect being, omniscient and inaccesible. I felt more and more chained up and crushed by the dogma that interfered in the smallest detail of one's daily life. My mind was sterilized gradually, unable to have access to freedom of thought, to myself. There formed an obstacle between me and myself, it prevented me from reaching my own innermost self to discover what was my real nature. Uniformity did not suit me. The ordinary did not resemble me. Everyone had to dress, talk, and behave in the same manner, like a herd of animals. Monotony invaded space and became burdensome, and my life was devoid of all originality. We fell back slowly and without being aware of it into a new legalized tradition, legalized by a so-called Allah who had forseen everything.

From the woman's point of view, the situation proved to be even worse. Tradition came back in force and with even more obscurantism in favor of men who were ready to progress in just about any domain except that of women. The shackling of women had to be pursued without any letup, otherwise men risked losing control of the situation. Women continued to be treated like incapable beings who need to be systematically under the guardianship of a close male relative in order to move, to exist, or even to breathe. I realized gradually that the promises of equal rights and duties they dazzled us with were but bait that lured us into a premeditated trap that closed over us immediately.

These revivers of Islam were only using women to reinforce their own power on a planetary scale. We were only puppets they used to go forward in their ignorance. I noticed that I had been an accomplice, without realizing it, to this deviance in the name of Allah. They made the latter say what they wanted without him intervening to contradict them. I began to see the real objective of this return to the "real Islam." I noted the political tinge of this fundamentalist faction in all the details of their actions. The aim envisaged is political power independent of all worries about respecting the so-called words of God, which enlightens their combat.

The philosophy of Bourguiba did not suit these fundamentalist revivers who wished to save the world from its slide and from the danger of the West, considered enemy number one of Islam and Muslims.

The masks fell gradually as they became more and more confident. I was terrified when I saw the true faces being uncovered, for me it was in the name of the devil and not God that they should have acted. They were convinced that they had the monopoly on God and the absolute truth, the totality of human salvation depended on their bloody actions, which they had put in motion with all impunity. Secret meetings proliferated in our home, in the villa of Ariana, the house of my adolescence. My parents were blind, seeing absolutely nothing coming.

The infiltration of Islamism into the heart of my family, as was the case in thousands of other families in North Africa and the Arabo-Muslim world, provoked the breakup of families, one after another. My family was the first victim of this deviation. My mother refused categorically to accept this situation and ended up asking for divorce. Her departure pushed me to think harder. I had started to question the ensemble of indoctrination to which I had been subjected. I suffered from the distancing of my mother who had seen all her hopes go up in smoke in the space of a few years.

I wanted to render her justice in the name of all women who had struggled for their independence in vain. It took a great deal of courage for her to renounce all that she had built up over years, to start from scratch in a country and cultural milieu she did not know at all. She left Tunisia for France, to the home of her brother, without having the slightest idea as to what awaited her on the other side of the Mediterranean.

I did not know how to liberate myself from these chains, which were getting heavier with time. I began by making a distinction between the different interpretations for the practice of Islam and the fundamental sources. I wanted to exonerate Islam from these crimes that they were committing in its name. Then I realized that the deficiencies were themselves ensconced at the heart of the so-called sacred text, that I could not exonerate Islam. The five pillars of Islam did not help me at all in my quest for the absolute; I found their repetitive application tedious and futile. I understood that I could achieve human dignity without them. The idea of God still interested me but I realized that I could experience God outside religion.

After seven years of religious observance and Islamic scarf, I decided to think for myself in suddenly stopping the dogmatic approach. The veil was lifted from my eyes, enabling me to see the world in color, in all its splendor. Finally, I was free to think, to eat, to dress in the way I wanted; in short, to behave as I felt in perfect harmony with my inner self. At the age of eighteen, I came out of the nightmare that had lasted seven years. It dawned on me that what I was looking for on the outside was to be found inside of me.

Scarcely free from this anguish, I decided to join my mother in Paris. By virtue of the negative images of the West that had been drummed into me, I was apprehensive about leaving but at the same time delighted at the possibility of discovering other cultures and new ways of thinking. After having known "traditional Islam" and the "true Islam," called Islamism or fundamentalism, I swung to the opposite end thirsty for the freedom to live by myself.

I arrived in Paris on July 14, 1983, having escaped the clutches of a religion that had deprived me of the best of myself. A new life opened up for me and took form in the university milieu, where I progressed through a double course in philosophy and sociology. At last, I was breathing to the full the freedom of thought through my passion for the great Greek or Western philosophers like Plato and Kant. This thirst to understand the meaning of my existence always followed me, but I no longer needed religion to put me in touch with the so-called divine. The paths that lead to God are as numerous as human beings, to each his or her path in accordance with her or his particular nature, where each being is unique.

My first reaction was to flee from every milieu that risked reminding me, to a greater or lesser degree, of the nightmare from which I had just escaped. Most of the people in my circle were French; my only Tunisian contacts were my mother and three of my brothers. I did not wish to hear anyone speaking of Islam and Muslims, all the while harboring a feeling of guilt and doubt about the degree of certainty of my choice. What if they were right about what they said of the West? I decided to throw myself into the unknown come what may, and to have confidence in my destiny, if ever one exists.

I thought I had finished with Islam and Islamism for good in turning a black page of my life. Suddenly I learned that my brother-in-law was settling in Paris, as a political refugee, after having failed in an attempted military coup d'état in Tunis against Bourguiba's regime, an attempt that had been thwarted just in time by President Ben Ali. In 1987 Bourguiba was removed from power because of the state of his health, whereby, in accordance with the Tunisian constitution, the prime minister took over the presidency.

Once again I was pursued by what I had wanted to flee with all my force four years earlier. Keeping a distance, I followed the evolution of this situation through my family. Now we were hunted on the one hand by Tunisian authorities for belonging to Islamic fundamentalist groups, and on the other by this brother-in-law who found us unequal to the task, not up to the level of his image as one of the founding members of the Islamist party MTI. In short, the less I heard talk of Islam the better I felt; the breakup of my family was only the beginning of the evil consequences of this self-seeking intrusion. Two other brothers-in-law were arrested and interrogated, even imprisoned after this abortive attempt provoking the destruction of other families close to mine.

At this time I had my first contact with my brother Karim, the first to settle in Paris to continue his studies; at the age of fourteen, he had come to my uncle's home while waiting for the arrival of my mother. In fact, the whole of my family did not know anything of his activities apart from my brother-in-law and my sister. At the time, he simply gave the impression of being a young man, fairly modern in his outlook, entirely integrated into French civilization. To us, he seemed to be traveling all the time, making him seem a bohemian in search of adventure. I dreamed of living like him but he constantly refused to let me accompany him on his voyages, avoiding answering but without raising suspicions.

It was in the summer of 1989 that I began to suspect the true nature of his activities. He was talking of the "true *Shīʿa* Islam" as opposed to the "true Sunni Islam." I discovered a new approach to this religion, which I could not seem to get rid of. I said to myself that I would find perhaps what I had been searching for in this doctrine claimed to be closer to the real version of Islam, given that it only relied on the line of the family of the Prophet through twelve infallible *imams*. I began to be interested in Twelver *Shīʿa*, which proved to be more philosophical and metaphysical than Sunni Islam.

Once again, I was intellectually intoxicated in my search for truth. I immersed myself in *Shīʿī* doctrine, reading assidulously the works of the famous Imam Ali, supposedly the esoteric repository of the prophetic secret. I confess that the *Shīʿī* approach is much more interesting and more seductive than that of the Sunnis, which is too down-to-earth in my view. What is interesting in the *Shīʿa* is that it does not put the accent on the dogmatic aspect of religion. Besides, one can discuss the nature of the divine without falling into blasphemy, which is far from the case in Sunnism, where it is forbidden to ask who God is.

In studying, I also discovered to my great surprise that the *Shīʿa* was the mastermind of the Islamic and fundamentalist terrorism in the world. It was through reading the poignant and unique testimony of my brother Karim, at the heart of the network based in Iran, that I ended up by understanding the true activities of my brother for several years. (He had been recruited by the Iranian Cultural Center in Paris.) For the first time someone was testifying from within a family and from within an international network whose tentacles reached out everywhere on the planet. It was when he handed over to me the account of his real-life experience written in Arabic that I began to realize the horror of this kind of enterprise, whose aim is to terrorize the world. I could no longer remain inactive faced with such barbarism being hatched in secret.

I was stupefied. I had the impression I was reading a science fiction novel that surpassed understanding. How could he have kept the true nature of his activities so hidden? I had the choice of believing his version of the facts and his desire to repent, and denouncing him; between giving and refusing help. I opted for the former solution, to give him the benefit of doubt, in agreeing to translate his testimony from Arabic to French, and above all to edit it so that it would act as a warning against this type of spiral.

After having been interested in Islam, in all its forms, as well as Christianity and Judaism, I became totally indifferent to religions. While my brother was training to kill innocents in the name of God, I led a completely modern life between the sea and mountains, between skiing and windsurfing, between my university studies and my small student jobs. But now, in thinking about his testimony, I decided to fight fundamentalism and Islamic terrorism with all the means at my disposal. I could no longer continue to turn a blind eye to what was being done in the name of God and Islam. One must have the courage and the conviction to denounce these deviations in order to preserve the rest of humanity from this religious dictatorship.

In 1993, while I was working on the French version of this testimony, limiting it to Karim's point of view, which insisted on distinguishing between Islam and Islamism, I learned of the interrogation in Paris of my brother-in-law, who was later put under house arrest because of his terrorist activities in France and Europe. This news confirmed my brother's written confession, and made me determined to go through with my denunciation of this evil that was corroding our societies in all impunity. I even decided to publish this documentary book under my own name in order not to give in to this fear that these terrorists wish to sow in the hearts of those who dare to criticize them.

It is under these circumstances that my book *Karim, Mon Frère. Ex-Intégriste et Terroriste* (Karim, my brother, ex-fundamentalist and terrorist)[1] came out in French in September 1997. Less than three months after its publication, my brother-in-law, SK, sued me for defamation from the place where he was under house arrest. I ended up winning this trial in the court of cassation, confirming in this way the facts related in the book, which retraced only a tiny part of his true activities. The law judged in my favor but the journalists preferred to support the thesis of this individual, according to whom it was the Tunisian secret service that was behind this testimony.

Since the media were only reflecting the state of mind of French society at the time, I cannot reproach them for supporting this type of individual, like my brother-in-law, who presented themselves as the victims of the regimes in place in their countries, whereas they themselves would have been capable of behaving much worse had they been in power for a while. In fact, in the book *Our Friend Ben Ali*[2] by Nicolas Beau of *Le Canard Enchainé* (a French satirical weekly) and Jean-Pierre Tuquoi of the *Le Monde* (a French daily), my book is presented as the work of the Tunisian secret service in a chapter given over to my brother-in-law,[3] who is described as a victim of the dictatorial regime of Ben Ali.

I invite these two eminent journalists to read my second book, *D. Le Zéro Neutre*,[4] and to tell me if it is still all a question of the Tunisian secret service. I also advise them to do their work as journalists in following my activities on behalf of associations, and as an editor and publisher for the last five years, and to tell me what they think of my combat against fundamentalism and Islamic terrorism. Alas, these fanatics of God have succeeded in convincing even the West, their supreme enemy, of their innocence and good intentions. They knew how to manipulate those who knew nothing of Islam, and to make these dupes agree with them.

We must reveal and admit that Islamism in the West is an imported product, not a local one. Many Islamists, fleeing their country of origin, were freely accorded political refugee status, and they were able to continue their activities in their host country as well as in their own from a distance. As a result, Islamism in its Western form established itself in the suburbs with a large Arabo-Muslim population. Now, the private domains of the Islamists and the home base of their activities are to be found in Europe and the United States. The attack is progressing on two parallel fronts; on the one hand they are sponsoring from a distance the establishment of Islamist states in Arabo-Muslim countries, and on the other they are undermining the West from the inside. Thus, it would be enough for the first half to invade the other half of the planet to establish international Islam. You would have to be a fanatic of God to imagine such a scenario.

At the time of the publication of my first book, I was struck by the ignorance and lack of interest of the public about the question of Islamism, as though it did not concern them. They kept repeating to me, "Well, yes, but how is it that we have never heard of this El Rissali terrorist network?" Today, I can reply that you have only to go on the Internet and type in "El Khat El Rissali" on an Arabic keyboard to get dozens of sites on this network in all languages. All the people cited in my book are to be found on these sites and are pursuing their fundamentalist and terrorist activities without being in the least worried. Their preparations for the coming of the famous *Mahdi* (the messiah who in *Shī'a* doctrine plays a stronger role than in Sunni Islam; while the Sunni wait passively for the messiah, the *Shī'a* actively prepare for his coming) are continuing, and the authorities are still doing nothing about them, claiming they have no proof. If the French authorities continue to do nothing, they will have more of September 11, 2001, to deal with.

Until this famous date, the West believed it was safe from any Islamist danger, despite the different attacks in France and other countries in recent years. When will the West realize that Islamist danger is planetary, that the Islamists are individuals who work and think on an international level in order to prepare for the coming of the *Mahdi*, who will govern according to their logic the entire earth in the name of Islam? When are we going to take seriously this danger that threatens all humans worthy of the name? Did we have to wait until the United States was attacked before reacting and protecting ourselves? What the Arabo-Muslim countries have been undergoing for decades to combat the rise of Islamist movements does not seem to have any importance for the Western countries. Shouldn't one ring the alarm bells instead of picking on the regimes in power?

In short, the book was ignored except in milieus concerned by the question, simply because the journalists were badly informed and because they considered the Islamist political opposition as any other ordinary opposition. My brother Karim's character was dubious, they said, and not very credible because he was a young man in search of divine truth and that he found himself, without realizing it, at the heart of an international terrorist network. Western journalists only listened to the bigger players, who were in fact capable manipulating them in no time at all. All the young penitents who wanted only to be heard and to be reintegrated into society were rejected because they were labeled Islamist for life.

The majority of young men who fall into this kind of trap are in search of identity, of an ideal. Generally they are cannon fodder to be sacrificed in order to advance on the battle field. It is the half-educated young men, on the edges of society, who are recruited to be turned into human bombs capable of producing great damage. Because they are uneducated does not mean that they are not credible. The so-called prophets were all illiterate, but that did not stop them from changing the face of the world. It is time to act and denounce Islamism without fear of reprisal.

How can you combat the Islamist menace if you do not give these penitents a new chance? They must be given a helping hand, just as I gave my brother one. Since then my brother and I have become a duo to combat fundamentalism and Islamic terrorism, whose worst acts are still to come. We began by creating an association in August 1997; then, in May 1999, we launched a cultural review that would allow young people to express themselves freely. Our objective was to encourage secularism in Arabo-Muslim countries, particularly the Maghreb (Northwest Africa). This sociocultural magazine is available in kiosks in Tunisia and Morocco, and for the moment has avoided censorship.

I did not want the new generation to undergo what I lived through during my adolescence. Seventy percent of the population is less than twenty-five years old; these young men and women are the ideal prey for the bloody Islamist criminals. Religion is but a subterfuge to attain political power. God is the first victim of this diabolical strategem.

Ultimately the solution lies in separating religion from politics, particularly in that part of the globe that is still suffering from this amalgam between the temporal power and the spiritual power. I know that our task smacks of the impossible since in Arabo-Muslim countries the word "secularism" is hardly pronounced. They do not even dare to think of it, and yet religion and nationalism remain the two greatest dangers that threaten humankind today.

It is only through this separation that young people can hope to advance effectively in their battle against fundamentalism and Islamic terrorism. The secular base is absolutely essential for the new foundation to be solid. One cannot construct on ruins that have had their day. We must learn to question ourselves and values and restart at zero, and we are not the first nor will be the last to do so.

It goes without saying that I am counting on Arabo-Muslim women who are more or less oppressed according to the interpretation that men wish to give to the so-called sacred texts. No religion is favorable to women for the simple reason that all religions are purely masculine products that try to protect the interests of men at all costs from women. Why are the monotheist religions so afraid of women? Perhaps because they know that the loosening of the grip of religion will come about through women.

After the first book, my brother and I were interested in writing a new one that would speak of the history of God and consist of seven volumes. The object of this project was to cure an evil by an evil; you can cut a diamond only with a diamond. We can undo the base of the monotheist religions only by turning their own arms against them. Well, the absolute arm of the foundation of religion is metaphysics, which is supposed to demonstrate the existence of God as creator of All. It is by using the same technique that my brother Karim started writing in Arabic his own subtle and elusive metaphysics to demonstrate the opposite, that is to say, the nonexistence of God.

In this way I published the first volume of this work, *D. Le Zéro Neutre*, in 2001. It treats of what I call atheist metaphysics, which, while seemingly talking of God, is in reality only referring to human beings. But you have to wait until you have read all seven volumes to be convinced of it. In fact, the characteristic of this book is to show that what one attributes systematically to God is nothing but human abilities whose ins and outs we still have not mastered. It is a book that believes in humankind, in all its divine splendor. Nothing exists outside him, the ensemble of human genius can only come from the interior of ourselves independently of all exterior intervention. God the protector does not exist, he is only the fruit of our imagination.

The idea of God is without doubt the most beautiful human invention, but it is nothing more than a human desire for perfection and omnipresence of which he has always dreamed. It is we who created God, and not the opposite. It is not a new discovery; it has been said so many times and in so many ways, but it is time to believe it. It is time to take our destiny in our hands and to have faith in our own people and ourselves, to believe in the huan, the merciful, and the compassionate.

The West has hitherto spoken only of Arabic Islam, but it is non-Arabic Islam that will make itself known more and more. The majority, and perhaps the most formidable part, of Muslims are non-Arab, including the *Shī'a*. We are not done with Islamism, which has only just started with the September 11 attacks, which proved clearly that terrorism is not blind but lucid, farsighted, and redoubtable. It is not the fruit of a handful of enlightened ones who dream of dominating the planet. On the contrary, Islamic terrorism is made up of individuals who have been trained for generations and who firmly believe in their bloody ideal.

Fatwas against innocent people whose only crime was to have tried to think for themselves are proliferating. Now it appears that Islam, which is full of contradictions, in trying to satisfy and seduce the greatest number of followers has run out of breath, it has nothing more to give. Humankind is growing up, slowly but surely; it no longer has need of legends that one recounts to children to help them become more mature, to keep them alive until they are capable of confronting reality themselves.

God the protector is no longer a factor of progress to whom one must keep going back in order to replenish ourselves. It is time to look at things in the face and to rely on ourselves to confront the imperfections of the so-called perfect creation. Today, it is true, these fundamentalists risk setting the earth ablaze with their heresy, but that does not stop the fact that they are living their last hours, because at the same time people are taking steps to avoid the worst. Fortunately, humanists, who believe in humankind, are far more present than one would think, and that among peoples of all races, colors, and religions.

Today in the West, we no longer have the right to criticize Islam, from near or far, at the risk of our lives. Even reformist practicing Muslims are fingered as criminals, simply because they dared to say that Islam should question itself and its values and adapt to the third millennium if it wants to remain on the scene, just as Christianity and Judaism has done.

Now, at the age of thirty-eight, I think I have thoroughly examined the religious question and I believe I have saved myself without too much damage because I acted in time. I can accept moderate religions that are followed in good faith, because I myself passed through the same beliefs and false hopes. On the other hand, they are incapable of understanding me since they have never dared to defy the grip of religion that flows in their blood. They have never thought it possible to live without the so-called divine radio control of our destiny. They are the slaves of their own beliefs because they are afraid of becoming adults. They prefer to continue in infantile tutelage, which religion offers in order to prevent us from growing up and taking our destiny in hand.

To end the influence of religion, and to help man to grow up, the secularists and atheists will have to work together on an international scale until secularism is accepted universally.

Today I prefer Vivaldi's *Four Seasons* to the four gospels; I prefer meditation and silent reflection to the five pillars of Islam. The really sacred temple can only be inside human beings. Religion does not have the monopoly of so-called divine truth; everyone must make his or her own way, respecting each other's individuality and difference.

The Islamists should know that we are as numerous as they and that we have as much conviction in the nonexistence of God as they have in his existence. I do not see that their faith will be superior to ours. We respect human life and preserve it with all our force, calling for a war of ideas instead of calling for a holy war and the shedding of innocent blood in the name of God.

As Euclid said, "What has been affirmed without proof can also be denied without proof." It is never too late to question oneself and to go ahead. Alas, God is too beautiful to be true.

NOTES

1. Samia Labidi, *Karim, Mon Frère. Ex-Intégriste et Terroriste* (Paris: Flammarion, 1997).

2. Nicolas Beau and Jean-Pierre Tuquoi, *Notre Ami Ben Ali* (Our friend Ben Ali) (Paris: La Découverte, 2002).

3. He has remained under house arrest for ten years now.

4. Samia Labidi, *D. Le Zéro Neutre* (Paris: Publibook, 2002).

32

AN ATHEIST FROM ANDHRA PRADESH
Azad (India)

I was fortunate to be born in a secular country like India. I was born in an economically backward Muslim family in a remote village in Andhra Pradesh in 1947. No one in my family had gone to school. My father was a farmer and I was the only male child who survived, with three sisters, out of eight issues.

My school going was an accident, my grandfather had sent me to school as a punishment because I refused to eat nontasty food in the house. After a month of this forcible practice of going to school it became a regular activity for me. My first standard teacher advised my grandfather not to discontinue my schooling, as I was showing much interest in studies. It happened to be a Telugu-language primary school.

By the time I reached third standard I was top of the class. One fine day the Urdu school administration realized that the standard in Urdu schools was dropping. It was a practice that only Muslim boys came to study in Urdu schools. The Urdu school administration decided that all Muslim children studying in Telugu schools should come back to the Urdu school. The Urdu school did not have a good reputation and none of its students had completed primary education and had gone on to high school. My Telugu schoolteachers advised my parents not to discontinue my Telugu school.

My father refused to obey the *fatwa* given by the Urdu school headmaster.

The matter was put to the village court. The village head summoned my father and me for a hearing. The village head tried to convince my father that the Urdu school was meant for the Muslim community. My father insisted that I was doing well in the Telugu school and there was no future for Urdu studies. The village head asked me a mathematical question to test my intelligence. The answer from me was instantaneous and it inspired the village head to support my father's decision. He gave a ruling that apart from this boy (me) all other Muslim children should go to the Urdu school. He offered to help my father by sending tutors to provide extra coaching for me, but this proved unnecessary.

After this incident the whole Muslim community boycotted our family, including our close relatives. My father was rigid in his decision; he did not yield to their pressure and continued my schooling in Telugu, where I was the top in every class till my high school education was completed. After that, knowing my father's financial position, I stopped my further studies and I was looking for job opportunities. Even in those days (1964) getting employment without a recommendation was difficult. After the schooling I was told to learn Arabic so that I could read the Koran and pray like other Muslim boys. I was able to read the Koran but without knowing or understanding the contents other than "Allah is the only God, Muhammad is His Prophet." After this I used to go to the mosque every Friday and listen to the *imam*'s preaching.

After one year of my schooling I got a first call from the district employment exchange to attend an interview for Indian Air Force selection for airmen category. Selection was purely on merit basis; hence, I got through the tests and was selected for technical trades. That was a turning point in my life. I was exposed to the greater world meeting people from different communities and cultures. Initially I was belittled by the Muslim boys, who had come from Uttar Pradesh and Kashmir, as I did not know how to read and write Urdu. Even my Hyderabadi Urdu accent was fun for them. Then I decided that I would have to overcome this inferiority. I started learning Urdu and was eventually able to read the magazines and write to some extent.

A Muslim colleague from Northern India felt that I should know more about Islam, like praying five times and fasting during Ramadan. I followed him in all these activities with utmost dedication. One day I found a flaw in him: he was following a girl to tease her. I knew he was a married man. I questioned him about this improper activity, and he covered it up saying it is permitted according to the holy text provided the girl gives her consent. In Indian terms it is adultery; how could it be permitted in Islam? I could not digest it and I could not argue with him, as he knew more about religion than I.

I used to visit my native place once a year and I got news from my friends about the local Muslim heads' atrocities against other women, such as the case where a lady teacher from the Urdu school was raped by a Muslim cleric, whom

I used to respect a lot for his knowledge of religion. Since the cleric was a close relative of the husband, the rape brought shame on the family, so the lady was forced to commit suicide for having such an affair! I used to also closely watch the activities of Muslim elders, but I had no answer for their evil deeds. They would say one thing in the mosque and do the opposite outside.

I was also astonished to hear about the communal riots in Meerut and Hyderabad. Why were these people fighting in the name of religion, saying that God is one? I used to also read a lot of Telugu literature, where modern Telugu writers expressed their radical views. I started doubting the existence of God. I started reading the Koran in Telugu, in a translation dating from the 1940s. The latest translators were skipping some of the objectionable sentences or giving them polished and softer meanings. To my surprise I found many objectionable and contradictory sentences in that so-called holy book. The only good sentence I found in that holy book was "When you go to some one's house knock the door and wait till it is opened." All the preaching in the Koran is against humanity, and there is no word in it like "humanity" or its equivalent. My belief against Islam became stronger. I started using the objectionable sentences of the Koran against those people who questioned my atheism. I have also read the Bible and the Hindu holy books; they are all the same. I understood these books were written by people who did not posses scientific knowledge.

Prophet Muhammad's preaching clearly indicates that he was selfish and a dictator, who kept his army (followers) intact by giving them booty of cash and women, which they collectively fought for and won. He also lured them by promising a place in heaven after death. Any dissident was mercilessly killed. Islam is not a religion of peace, but terror. For that matter, all religions and castes (in India) have a similar history of hate of others.

But I did not know what the alternative to religion and God was. As no one had expressed similar views to me, I unwillingly used to go to *Idgah* (the Muslim holy festivals, literally: place of *ʿīd*) twice a year, for *ʿīd al-fiṭrʿ* and *ʿīd al-aḍhā* (*Baqra ʿīd*) (the festival of the breaking of the fast of Ramadan, and the feast of sacrifice, respectively; the two principal Muslim festivals). My parents were also not so religious minded, hence they did not oppose my will.

In such circumstances I came across a periodical called the *Atheist*. I was surprised to learn that people like me existed. I rushed to the Atheist Centre to congratulate them and to know more about atheism. *We Become Atheists* by the late Mr. Gora[1] cleared all my doubts. Then I was about thirty years old. I openly denounced religion and told my Muslim friends I would only come to the mosque if God's existence could be proven by science. I was considered the wisest boy in my village, so they could not question my decision about religion. After that I never looked back. I started reading more and more intellectual articles, and listening to the lectures of learned humanists.

A critical situation arose in my life, that is, conducting the marriages of my children. I have one son and one daughter. When I was convinced about my beliefs and explained them to my wife, she, too, was convinced without much effort from me and we brought up our children in a nonreligious, scientific, and humanistic way. I took the opinions of my children as to which way they would like to live. They preferred the way I taught them. Then we (my wife and I) wanted to conduct their marriages in a nonreligious way, irrespective of the other family's religion (provided they had similar rationalistic views). There was some resistance from my close relatives who insisted that at least *Nikah* (the Muslim marriage ceremony) should be conducted. I was able to convince them that it was not necessary. Both my children's marriages have now taken place and they are living happily without "mental slavery."

Hence the need of the hour is "universal humanism," which can only be achieved by education for all and by getting rid of superstitions.

NOTE

1. Gora (1902–1975) was a well-known Indian atheist and social reformer. He founded the Atheist Centre in Vijayawada, India, in 1947. He was a prolific writer, in English and Telegu, of atheist tracts and books such as *An Atheist with Gandhi*; *Partyless Democracy*; *We Become Atheists*; and *Atheism, Questions and Answers.*

PART 4

TESTIMONIES
OF WESTERN
CONVERTS
Murtadd Milli

33

FROM SUBMITTER
TO *MULHID*
Denis Giron (United States)

Indeed I am an apostate from Islam, though from a decidedly heterodox form of the true *dūn* (religion). I was a *ḥadīth*-rejecting pseudo-Submitter,[1] and wholeheartedly considered myself a real Muslim. I suppose that being an apostate from a variant of the Submitter sect is to my benefit. The rabid foaming-at-the-beard neo-Salafi fascist types that would generally invoke Muhammad's words (*man baddala deenahu, faqtuluhu!* He who changes his religion, kill him!) would probably declare that I was never a "real Muslim," thus not a real *murtadd* (apostate), and thus not subject to execution for apostasy. In fact, much to the delight of the pious armchair *mujāhidin* (holy warriors) that would normally wince at the mere mention of a real apostate, I never recited the complete *shahāda*, the Islamic testament of faith that there is no God but Allah, and Muhammad is his Prophet!

You see, my pseudo-Submitter buddies informed me that the *shahaada* of Sunni lore is a statement of faith for "pagans," thus I never recited the second half of the testament of faith. *Wa Muhammadul Rasulullaah:* And Muhammad is the Messenger of Allah? Why is only Muhammad mentioned? Why the association of this particular messenger with *the* testament of faith in monotheism and not any other prophet? At the time, I thought this was a reasonable argument, and I, to this day, still feel there is a certain peculiar nature about only mentioning Muhammad. I could go on with humorous stories about Abu Hurayr, the *shahāda*'s first proponent, getting punched in the chest by his fellow frat brothers among the *sahaba*, companions of Muhammad, but I'm a *mulhid* (apostate, atheist) now, so I'll leave such discussions to the Muslims, both orthodox and heterodox.

More interesting than my tales from the land of Arabo-Judaic monotheist madness are the stories about how I got there, why I left, and what I think of those embarrassing times now that I look back in hindsight. You see, I was one of so many who were pulled from the ranks of disillusioned Christians, a deep resource of potential converts for missionaries of every ideology from Krisna consciousness to the Noachide faith.[2]

Being that I was a "revert"[3] from Christianity, I think I am in a position to ponder the mentality of such people as well as the psychology behind conversion from Christianity to Islam. No doubt Muslims who were once Christians will find my thoughts offensive, but I am convinced others who have traveled the Christian-Muslim-*murtadd* route will agree with much of what I have to say.

Indeed this is a route much traveled; so many disillusioned Christians have embraced Islam because they assumed it answered their questions that Christianity could not. Islam is very attractive to Christians who are troubled by the difficult, if not incomprehensible, concept of the Trinity. Many such people have been raised in what is portrayed as a monotheist religion (and Jewish monotheism still runs strong in the Old Testament), and are often unimpressed with their pastor or priest's attempts to explain the more mystical (if not polytheistic) concepts in trinitarian Christianity.

If they are not troubled by the Trinity, they are those who are aware of the Bible's many obvious contradictions. These are the Christians with a faith that is suffering from fatigue. They are at a point in their life where they can no longer believe the tenets of Christianity (or maybe they never really believed them at all).

Such Christians who begin to doubt the alleged truth of their creed, as was stated before, move on to become atheists, Buddhists, communists, New Age pagans, and so on. However, the ones that still desire to hold on to some remnant of the Bible, particularly belief in Jesus and the other messengers of God, are the ones who are most prone to converting to Islam.

It is now that we begin to form a picture of the early mentality of the Christian convert to Islam. Here is a man or a woman who still wants to believe in Jesus, minus the incomprehensible idea of a triune deity, and along comes their local Islamic missionary with his *dawaganda*[4] leaflet about "Jesus in Islam." The potential proselyte is told about how Jesus, whose real name was Eesa Ibn Maryam, was not a god; rather he was a devout messenger of Allah.

The new *mu'min* (believer) fallaciously assumes that Islam must be true in light of the "obvious accuracy" of the religion's version of the Jesus story. Many (dare I say most?) Christian converts to Islam feel that because the Islamic version is more "logical" the religion's validity and soundness have been established. In reality the Islamic account is just as absurd, but the more consistent monotheist feel to it makes for a more palatable myth.

Even more appetizing to the palate of the disenchanted Christian revert is the apparent internal consistency of the Islamic literature.[5] The Christian revert to Islam will have a few contradictions in the Bible memorized, and from there commits a subconscious bifurcation[6] fallacy: He assumes that because Christianity has been proven false, Islam automatically wins by default. Many an atheist who has discussed the validity of religion with a Muslim has been left puzzled by odd statements like "the Bible has been changed by man, but the Koran is still perfect and uncorrupted." In the mind of the Christian revert, attacking the Bible automatically validates Islam. This is the fallacious mode of thinking that subtly (and sometimes not so subtly) lines all their arguments.

Regardless of how poorly the Bible stands under criticism, this is not something that corroborates Islamic truth in any sense. Furthermore, the Koran is itself far from being free of error. Indeed, it has fewer contradictions than the Bible, but that is not surprising when one realizes that the Koran is roughly the size of the book of Psalms.[7] I could go into errors and contradictions within the Koranic text, but I suppose that issue should be touched on in *akhoona* (our brother) Warraq's other books.

Truthfully, I don't think it would really matter to anyone currently within the ranks of the *mu'mineen* (believers), as the vast majority of them believe in the Koran's perfection on blind faith. I am speaking from experience when I tell you that most Christians and Muslims will staunchly deny any error in their respective holy writs, and will maintain such a stance regardless of the evidence. While the Muslim seems to defend scripture better than his *Nasara* (Christian) tritheist counterpart, the reality is that their arguments are as weak and fallacy-ridden as those of any other Western monotheist. Muslims with strong *iman* (faith) will not hesitate to put forth any wild confabulation to salvage their most cherished beliefs.

Now the reader may be troubled by such claims if I don't back them up with a specific situation. The Muslim will claim it is a baseless claim, and the *kaafir* (disbeliever, infidel) will wish I cited an example. While I've already acknowledged that this is a discussion for another book, I will give one minor discrepancy. After that, we really must move on with my deconversion story.

To set the tone, let me give an analogy. Anyone who is familiar with the myriad contradictions in the Bible has heard the line about "what were Jesus' last words?" The reason this is a tough question is because the different gospel writers give slightly different final quotes for Jesus on the cross. Even a minor discrepancy makes one wonder about the claim of divine authorship.

The Koran often suffers from a similar problem with variant quotes. So many of the stories repeat ad nauseum, in the most unnecessary fashion. If one takes a closer look at the repeated stories, the minor differences in detail become apparent.

One story that is repeated many times is the discussion between Iblis and

Allah at the time of the creation of Adam. As the story goes, Iblis (a lone *jinn* oddly among angels), refused to prostrate before Adam when Allah told him to (maybe he thought it was a trick, and didn't want to get accused of committing *shirk*[8]). From there a conversation between Allah and Iblis takes place, and the exact wording of the discussion is never the same in the Koran.

So ask your Muslim friends, what did Allah say to Iblis? Did he ask, "O Iblis, why are you not with the prostrators?" (XV.32) Or did Allah ask, "O Iblis, what prevented you from prostrating before what I created with My hands? Are you too arrogant? Have you rebelled?" (XXXVIII.76)

While the questions are generally the same, the exact wording differs.

Furthermore, one wonders what Iblis's response was. Did Iblis turn to Allah and say, "I am not to prostrate before a human being, whom You created from aged mud, like the potter's clay" (XV.33)?

Or was it, "I am better than he; You created me from fire, and created him from clay" (XXXVIII.77)?

If you ask such questions, you'll see your monotheist counterpart squirm and clutch for straws as he desperately tries to concoct his hermeneutic miracle. I promise you, however, that he will eventually come up with an answer, and it will be the sort of deeply mystical, unfalsifiable, and wholly ambiguous flim-flam that could be used to reconcile any error in any religious text.

The nature of the Muslim mind is not that different from the nature of the fundamentalist Christian mind when it comes to defending the alleged word of God. They assume that the Koran is of a divine origin, and reject anything that would allow one to dispute this belief. This is why all discussions on the nature of Islamic scripture deteriorate into exhibitions of question begging and special pleading. After a while, one is tempted to yell: "*Ya Abdallaah* (O Servant of Allah), you cannot demonstrate the textual superiority by starting from the presupposition that this ancient manuscript is the word of God!"

While I can now sit from my quasi-intellectual perch and deride the Muslims (I find Islam ridiculous, hence I ridicule), I must concede that I can only speak of the Islamic psyche with such confidence because I was once drowning in such madness. Indeed, it is a fallacy to assume that one can determine the mental state of all Muslims by reflecting on one's own history, but I assure you that I have experienced a large enough number of interactions which lead me to feel justified in my generalizations. However, I acknowledge that this will be a gross stereotype if it is applied to the global *ummah* (Islamic community) in total.

That said, I still think my story can be a relevant tool for understanding the mind of the Muslim, particularly the Muslim revert from Christianity. However, I do not assume for a second that my conversion is original at all. It has been my goal to express how mechanical and robotic conversion to Islam is, and demonstrate that it is only apostasy that is mildly original.

My whole life I was raised as a nominal Christian. My father was a Catholic who seemed much closer to an atheist, and my mother was a Quaker of less-than-spectacular faith. While I believed in the myths of the Judeo-Christian story, it never played a major role in my life. I did not gain a passion for religion until the early 1990s, when, in my senior year in high school, I became a more pious (read: fundamentalist) Christian.

I joined the New York City Church of Christ and passionately immersed myself in diligent Bible study. Within a very short period of time I was having serious doubts about the trinity and other aspects of the Christian story. I was, without a doubt, a prime piece of revert meat for the Islamic predators who prey on disillusioned Christians.

In my freshman year in college at the City University of New York I came into contact with many Muslims who were eager to espouse the tenets of their faith. In high school I had only one Muslim friend, a nominal Sunni girl I still consider to be a close friend, despite the animosity I've developed toward mono-theist beliefs. In college my circle of friends was becoming increasingly Muslim.

The strange part of my rapid conversion is that my closet-Submitter friends were able to suck me in right from under the noses of the much larger Sunni cross-section within my social circle. The reason is obvious to anyone who has talked with a Western Submitter. As strange as this will sound, a lot of it can be pinned on the popular Islamic apologist Ahmed Deedat.

Western Muslims have, in the past, become drunk on Ahmed Deedat, though his popularity is starting to really disappear these days. His debates with Christians, along with his numerous booklets, have made up the heart of British-American *dawaganda* literature for the last two decades. Unfortunately, the Islamic literature cannot stand up to the standards that brother Deedat demanded the Bible be judged by.

Deedat's idea of the "Bible Combat Kit," where Muslims are encouraged to keep an inventory of contradictions, vulgar verses, and other embarrassing excerpts of the Bible, was one of the more popular aspects of Islam's missionary onslaught on the West. However, this caused some Muslims to ponder the idea of a "*Hadith* Combat Kit." As should have been expected, Muslims were beginning to doubt the use of the *ahadith* collections as a source of guidance considering the many contradictions, absurd stories, and vulgar tales found therein.

These problems became painfully apparent to me, and I leaned toward my pseudo-Submitter friends instead of the more Orthodox Muslims, whom I was already beginning to look down on as far as Islamic sectarian prejudice goes. Like my Submitter buddies, I was a closeted blasphemer. Such things are easier than one might assume, as any given local Muslim Students Association (MSA)[9] chapter is filled with *Ismailis, Qadianis, Alevis,* members of the *Ahmadiyya* movement, and various other blasphemers who keep their subtle *kufr* to them-selves. In fact, the first time I went to an MSA meeting, I was already an atheist!

I would try to discuss my anti-*hadith* views with my Sunni friends, but they would go on long rants about how *Shaytaan* (Satan) is always whispering in our ear, encouraging us to give up something more. I was told that first I'll give up the *ahadith*, then I'll give up the prayer, then the Koran, and finally I'll say, "I disbelieve in Allah." At that point *Shaytaan* is supposed to move away from me and say, "I will have nothing to do with you *Mulhid*, as I fear Allah." Let's be honest, this is an absurd story, and . . . well . . . *er* . . . maybe not, in light of my current state of theological bankruptcy. *W'ash-Shaytaanu 'Aleem!*[10]

Regardless, I rejected the "authentic traditions" of Orthodox Islam, but also felt that this left me outside the general Islamic community. I kept my beliefs mostly to myself, and only preached my beliefs within a closed circle. Muslim fears about the monolithic "Zionist Free Masons" who try to disrupt the truth of Allah's religion might not be so absurd in light of the fact that I was part of a small circle of heterodox Muslims that resembled some sort of ad hoc secret society.

We exchanged our thoughts on the sins of so-called Orthodox Muslims quite openly, save for when such sinners were around. Had a neo-Salafi savage witnessed some of our discussions at the pizza shop, he would probably flip through his Urdu translation of *The Protocols of the Elders of Zion*, looking for a precedent. In the end, this hypothetical discoverer of our blasphemous group would just yell, "*Astaghfirullaah!* Isn't this how Skull and Bones, the Illuminati, and the Bahais got started?!?"

At the time, I did not see a problem with this, as I felt I was a true Muslim; I was a Submitter. While today I sometimes answer the question, "How long were you a Muslim?" with "I was never Muslim; I was a pseudo-Submitter," I still see nothing incorrect about my previous beliefs in any Islamic sense. There is no set rule for proper interpretation of a theological text; hermeneutics is anarchy. I see no reason to assume my heterodox beliefs were any less "Islamic" than those practiced by members of the Orthodox fold. Besides, some of them probably had secret shrines dedicated to the Agha Khan in their homes.

Now there are the questions about what kind of a Muslim a Submitter is. Without the *Sunna*, how do you know how to pray properly? Well, to answer that now, I will admit that I've met Submitters who prayed five times a day and prostrated themselves, but this was not the case with all of us. There were times when I'd be at a friend's apartment and we'd rub our foreheads raw on the carpet, chanting *Allahu Akbar* and other meaningless phrases in a monotone voice that resembled that of an android. However, and this will horrify many Muslims, there were times when we would pray sitting up at a meal table before eating, with our hands clasped like Christians!

The argument that "with only the Koran you cannot know how to pray," which is a popular Sunni attack on the Submitters, was actually turned around by my Submitter buddies. Their logic[11] went along the lines of "The Koran does not say we have to pray like that, therefore we do not have to pray like that!" It's that simple. While I wonder about the more popular Submitters and their tendency to retain numerous Orthodox traditions, I think the version I experienced is still reasonable. What kind of an imbecile would assume that God, the being with infinite scope and knowledge, would actually be upset if you prayed a certain way? Furthermore, who takes seriously this madness that is the justification for five prayers a day? It stems from a *hadith* about Moses and Muhammad bargaining with Allah, getting the number of prescribed prayers down from fifty!

Reading through this, some might begin to realize that there is more than one kind of Submitter. While my group of friends considered themselves Submitters, I swear I never once saw Rashad Khalifa's translation of the Koran in hard copy. There was never any talk about the magic of the number nineteen (though there were silly discussions about the number of times words like "day," "night," and "month" appear in the Koran). We used the Ahmed Ali translation, which also offered a bit of subtle hostility toward the *ahadith* via the right interpretation.

The Ahmed Ali translation had one particular footnote that pointed readers toward Surah Luqman XXI.6, which spoke of those who spread *lahv-al-hadith* (frivolous stories), and essentially make the Koran *mahjura* (ineffectual). I'm not sure Ahmed Ali was a man who rejected the Orthodox traditions, but we sure believed he did back then. To this day I still see this as a relatively strong argument for the antihadith bunch, but I also acknowledge that there is no set logic in theism. *Ashkurullaah li'annani mulhid!* Thank God, I am an atheist.

Really, looking back on those days I still feel that the Submitters put forth a better argument than their Sunni brethren, despite the fact that I consider all theist arguments to be quite absurd. Under a relatively literal interpretation of the Koran, it does seem that the *ahadith* collections are being rejected. I am still fond of the verse that reads, *tilka aayaatullaahi nutloohaa ʿalayka bil haqqi fabi-ayyi hadeethi baʾdallaahi wa aayaatihi yooʾminoon.*[12]

The Sunni-Submitter debate probably fascinates me only because I once had a vested interest in that theological battle. The reality is that it is wholly absurd for the simple fact that both parties assume the Koran is of a divine origin. This is where I have to break with the Submitter minority that I have sympathy for. I have given Islam up altogether and, *inshati'l-laat*,[13] I will not have any lightning bolts hurled at me for this *kufurous*[14] decision. *Aʾoodhu bish-shaytaani min Allaahi ir-rajiim!*[15]

I finally broke from Islam in 1998, when I quite suddenly became an atheist. Prior to that, the bulk of my *dawa* (if you can call it that) was performed on the Internet. I was one of many anti-intellectual armchair cybermissionaries who went off to battle the evil Jochen Katz.[16] My name was briefly up there with the likes of Mohamed Ghounem[17] and other cyber-*mujahideen*.

My shift to atheism came at a time when I began to ponder the other religions. As a Muslim I was still caught in the fictional world where only Christianity and Islam were the possible religions; thus, if Christianity was false (which it is obviously was), then *la ilaaha illa'llaah*: There is no God but Allah. Of course, such an argument is totally unsound, as there is no reason to assume that Christianity's failures imply the truth of the first half of the *shahaada* or any other mindless Islamic chant.

Studying logic in college and learning about other religions made the space in my heart that was reserved for Allah shrink at a rapid rate. The real coup de grâce came in 1998 during a class on the religions of India at the City University of New York. There I was, the arrogant monotheist with half a brain, reading about the colorful beliefs in Hinduism. Castles made of beeswax, Siva replacing the head of his decapitated son with that of an elephant, Hannuman jumping over the ocean, and many other tales were, in my less than humble opinion, utterly ridiculous.

However, I stopped and wondered for a second, Why should I assume that these stories are ridiculous while at the same time believe that the myths of the Judeo-Christian-Islamic folklore are perfectly reasonable? The Hindu nationalist A. Ghosh[18] once wrote an article that is the embodiment of such questions. Do the Abrahamic[19] monotheists really believe stories about virgin births, sticks turning into snakes, talking babies, flying horses, men being swallowed by a big fish, and animals that speak human languages?

The Muslim will try to defend such fantastic myths by calling them "miracles." Unfortunately, is not this appeal to the belief that God can bend the rules of nature basically a justification for anything? The Muslims who laugh at the colorful stories that exist in the Hindu tradition are totally unjustified. Yes, Hannuman jumped over the ocean, as anything is possible for God.

The very concept of a "miracle" is difficult to believe. Ibn Warraq, in his first book,[20] gave the *Ikhwaan al-Kaafireen*[21] an interesting introduction to miracles in Islam, and a reason for his tendency not to believe them. I recommend others read that section if they have not already. Berkeley Professor John Searle expressed a similar feeling toward miracles:

> We no longer think of odd occurrences as cases of God performing speech acts in the language of miracles. Odd occurrences are just occurrences we do not understand. The result of this demystification is that we have gone beyond atheism to a point where the issue no longer matters in the way it did to earlier generations.[22]

So this appeal to the word "miracle" is mildly fallacious. A rational person can no longer accept such fantastic stories on blind faith. The Muslims' failure to provide evidence for the wild stories written in their religious literature will always be a point of friction between them and the Western freethinkers with whom I now align myself.

After I came to this conclusion, the floodgates of rational thought were open and could no longer be closed. Every rational argument I had ever heard began to make sense to me, and Islam began to seem more and more silly. My plunge into the world of *Ilhad* (atheism) was very rapid, and I even found myself using arguments traditionally used against Christianity to attack Islam. For example, Carl Sagan used to ridicule the ascension of Jesus into heaven on the grounds of our current understanding of the universe. Using that against Islam, we have to laugh off the whole story about Muhammad's night journey on his flying horse (which, by the way, is the beginning of the story that justifies the aforementioned rule about five prayers a day). If Muhammad left the nonexistent *Masjidul-Aqsa*[23] at the speed of light fourteen hundred years ago, he still would have not yet left our galaxy today!

Suddenly Islam, the most logical religion, looked as absurd as all the others. The more I pondered Islam, the more it seemed open to the same attacks the other religions were. The Koran, like the Bible, is an obvious compilation of variant traditions from a plurality of sources. Furthermore, the body of literature from which the vast majority of Islamic law is derived from is in as much a state of chaos as the Bible is; and finally, the historicity of the prophets is very much in question.

I suppose the historical lives of the heroes of the Abrahamic folklore is the subject I am most interested in. Some of this was touched on in Warraq's *Why I Am Not a Muslim*[24] when the discussion turned to the school of thought that holds that Jesus may not have been an historical character. To the Muslim, the question of Jesus' existence is absurd, but we must really call into the question the intellectual foundation of a religion that cannot present even the slightest bit of evidence to back up their fantastic stories.

The more I discuss prophet historicity, the more I begin to seriously doubt the existence of the heroes of Islamic folklore. While there is seemingly no evidence for the existence of the Jew named Jesus who is the center of discussion in the New Testament, there is even *less* evidence to support the existence of the Islamic Jesus, *Eesa Ibn Maryam*. Muslims have been so unable to come up with evidence that some have resorted to strange language games, asserting that the name Eesa is more historically accurate considering the fact that it *sounds* like the Aramaic Eesho.[25]

Jesus aside, I firmly believe that the further back you go in the prophetic line, the greater the chance that the hero in question never existed. Do you really believe that Moses was a real person? Why is it that despite the fact that the Egyptians wrote so much about their history and culture, they never recorded the existence of the amazing *yahoodi* who lived within their borders? Moses had a command over nature, freed a huge number of slaves, and even drowned a pharaoh and his army, yet the Egyptians seemed to have never heard of him!

Of course, the Muslims believe with all their hearts that these characters existed, taking a literal interpretation of nearly every tale found in their literature. There is even no question in their mind that Abraham or Adam (who was sixty cubits tall according to the *ahadith*) existed. The Muslims are so used to debating Christians that they are never prepared for an atheist who would question their myths in a way that no Christian ever would. One Muslim I have debated, who happened to have a Ph.D. from Cambridge,[26] was so exasperated by his inability to present evidence for the existence of Abraham that he threw logic out the window and shifted the burden of proof. He demanded that I justify my doubts by proving that his heroes *did not* exist![27]

Of course, prophet historicity becomes a moot point when one is an atheist. The very existence of God for me seems unreasonable. The existence of Allah, the provincial sky god of the Semites, is even harder to accept. Tribal war gods are something for primitive persons to believe in. No rhetorical question about the origin of the universe will ever prove that there is a mighty phantasm on the throne[28] recording our every move. To answer the questions about how the universe came to be, let me just say that even if there is a question we cannot answer, this does not mean that the sky god hypothesis automatically wins by default!

One could dedicate a whole book to atheist objections to Islam, but I shall not go into this subject much more at this time. The only thing I am trying to do here is add my name to the short but growing list of apostates from Islam. I believed that there was no God but Allah, and I believed that Muhammad was a messenger of Allah (so maybe I recited the full *shahāda* in my heart and deserve that death sentence after all). However, I woke up one day and abandoned this grotesquely ludicrous system of myths.

With a list of testimonies from the apostates we can encourage the others who have left Islam to come out of the closet. We are at the forefront of the first Western rationalist attack on Islam in history. While the Muslims assume their religion has withstood attacks from all comers, the reality is that it has never faced the kind of beating Christianity and its scriptures have.

This is why people like Ibn Warraq are so highly respected. He is a pioneer in this new genre of Islamic criticism. While centuries from now there will be scholars who will write criticisms superior to anything produced by Warraq or his contemporaries, it is brother Warraq who will go down in history as one of the key names in this battle.

The Muslims are already on the ropes when the fight has just begun. They have nothing left except a less-than-spectacular ability to fabricate stories to be later used as ad hominem attacks. I expect in the future there will be Muslims who will say Warraq is really a Jew, a Hindu posing as a Pakistani apostate, a Berber nationalist beer salesman, a Free Mason, Jochen Katz's brother, John Wansbrough's nephew, or some other obvious enemy of Islam. I promise you they will be reduced to name-calling.

We are the modern-day *jahiloonytoonies*[29] and we are reviving the war between *al-Ikwaan al-Muslimeen Wa'l-Ikhwaan al-Mushrikeen*[30] to have polytheism, idolatry, and blasphemy practiced within the borders of the Arabian Peninsula (well, not quite). This is, however, the call to join *al-jihaadul-kuffaa*—the infidel holy war.

However, I must reject and condemn all right-wing anti-Islamists who call for violence against Muslims. One of the greatest criticisms of Islam is that the tenets of the religion promote violence and intolerance towards polytheists, homosexuals, women who express their sexual freedom, and various other oppressed groups. Trying to meet violence with more violence only completes a viscous cycle, and removes one's right to criticize. For those of you who have a tendency to chant something awful like "Death to Muslims," please stop it now! I am in favor of death to Islam, and death to monotheism, but never death to Muslims. The practitioners of Islam are human beings, plain and simple. *Faqtulullaah!* Kill God!

Please jump on the *kufr* bandwagon and enjoy the ride. A market for criticism of Islam is rapidly opening up at a time when a critic of Christianity can go totally unnoticed, even among his infidel comrades. In the future these early Western criticisms of Islam will be seen as classics, much the way we now look back on Celsus' *On the True Doctrine*, or Julian the Apostate's *Against the Galileans*. I am a *Murtad*; I am *al-Kaafir al-Akabr*, the greatest infidel. My keyboard is my sword, and I'm off to battle. Won't you join us? *Takbir!*

NOTES

1. The Submitters are a sect that find their origin with Rashad Khalifa and his translation of the Koran that was obviously hostile to the use of *ahadith* collections as a source of guidance for Muslims. It should be noted that the murdered (martyred?) Khalifa and his followers were not the first Muslims to reject the extracanonical Islamic traditions, and other contemporary Submitters do not align themselves with Khalifa.

2. The Noachide faith is a sort of Christians for Moses, *Goyyim* for Torah theology where gentiles live by the Hebrew scriptures and the *Noachide Mitzvot* (commandments given to Noah), rejecting any notion of salvation through Jesus. Noachides are often quick to convert to Judaism, or sometimes become atheists or Muslims, thus their actual numbers are always small.

3. Muslims believe that every person is born a Muslim, but their environment causes them to renounce Allah at a time when they are just learning to walk and talk; thus, anyone who converts to Islam has actually "reverted" to the faith of his birth.

4. Muslims refer to proselytizing as "giving *dawa*," but such oft-repeated propaganda has been accurately termed *dawaganda*. This is a term that was originally coined by the great apostate from Islam Sadiqi az-Zindiki.

5. Actually, this is more along the lines of the internal consistency of the Koran. The Islamic literature overall is wholly inconsistent, with blatant contradictions between Koran and hadith, and even contradictions within the *ahadith* collections themselves.

6. The bifurcation fallacy occurs when a person assumes there are only two possibilities when really there are more. An example might be the Christian line about "either Jesus was God or he was lying. . . ."

7. Don't be fooled by the size of an English translation of the Koran you may have seen at a bookstore. The Arabic text of the Koran is roughly the same size as the Hebrew text of the book of Psalms. In fact, the book of Psalms has thirty-six more chapters than the Koran, and while no chapter of Psalms is as long as the longest *Surah* (*al-Baqarah*), no chapter of Psalms is as short as the shortest *Surahs* (*al-Ikhlaas, al-Falaq, an-Naas,* etc.).

8. Association of partners with God, anthropomorphism, polytheism, etc.

9. This is generally the official Muslim club at any college in the United States, including Jesuit schools like Fordham!

10. A play on *W'Allaahu 'Aleem!* My version could best be translated, "And Satan knows best" or "And Satan is knowledgeable."

11. I'm using the term "logic" here rather loosely, though I imagine, given the proper interpretation, the following is a valid syllogism:

(1) The Koran tells me what I have to do.

(2) The Koran does not say I have to pray like that.

Therefore, I do not have to pray like that.

12. "These are the *ayaat* of Allah, which We recite to you in truth. Then in which hadith [story, tradition, tale], after Allah and His *ayaat* will they believe?" (XLV.6) While it may seem obvious to some, other Muslims take a drastically different approach in coming up with an interpretation of this verse. One Shi a friend I knew tried to explain that this verse is talking about the reliability and authority of the Ayatollahs compared with any other religious source. I suppose the *Sunni Kuffaar* still dispute Ali Khamenei's alleged theological superiority despite this obvious sign from Our Lord.

13. Al-lat willing. This is a play on *Insh'allah* (God willing), only the future is attributed to the will of Al-lat (the daughter of Allah, according to stories about the beliefs of pre-Islamic Arabs).

14. *Kufr* = disbelief. *Kufrous* is another word coined by Sadiqi az-Zindiki, as in "my writings are *kufrous* in extremis."

15. I take refuge in Satan [to protect me] from the accursed Allah.

16. Jochen Katz was a Christian who put together a very popular Internet site called Answering Islam (answering-islam.org), which served as an early resource for *kuffaar* from all walks of life. The debates he had online created a web of names, both friend and foe to *akhoona* Katz, who would later build on a reputation from that time.

17. Mohamed Ghounem has written books based on his debates with Katz. He is also the president and founder of the Jews for Allah organization, a missionary group dedicated to converting the Yahoods to Islam. While his group is obviously quite similar to the Jews for Jesus movement, Mr. Ghounem attributes the idea to me!

18. A. Gnosh's "If Jesus Could Walk on Water, Why Could Not Hanuman Overfly

It?" was a response to Christian missionary ridicule. Though I have never seen a version of this article in a published journal, many copies of it exist on the Internet.

19. I use the word "Abrahamic" only because Judaism, Christianity, and Islam all find their origin with the mythical Abraham and his belief in one God.

20. Ibn Warraq, *Why I Am Not a Muslim* (Amherst, N.Y.: Prometheus Books, 1995), pp. 142–44.

21. "Brotherhood of disbelievers," although there's a slight abuse of Arabic here.

22. J. Searle, *Mind, Language, and Society* (New York: Basic Books, 1998), p. 35.

23. The "farthest Mosque," which is now in Jerusalem. The fact that the Koran makes reference to this place leads us to conclude one of two things: (1) The verse (XVII.1) is an interpolation that was inserted after the creation of this mosque, or (2) the story of the night journey is a sort of Islamic *Midrash* that was constructed to make sense of this wholly ambiguous verse.

24. Warraq, *Why I Am Not a Muslim*, pp. 147–53.

25. As far as I know, this theory finds its origin with a brilliant Islamic polemicist out of Houston names Shibli Zaman. While Zaman has a command of Semitic languages that many would envy, his claims about Eesa and Eesho seem to have very little etymological evidence upon deeper consideration of the roots of these names.

26. However, I must concede that his Ph.D. was in something like metallurgy, so my bragging about inflicting an intellectual defeat on the good doctor while I was still an undergrad is akin to boasting about being undefeated in Sumo wrestling matches against anorexics.

27. For those who don't know, the burden of proof is on the positive claimant. If I claimed there was a three-hundred-pound carnivorous mouse living in the Amazon, and you doubted my claim was true, who should be required to shoulder the burden of proof?

28. It should be mentioned that all of the Muslim criticisms against the Judeo-Christian scriptures on the grounds that anthropomorphic descriptions of God are a sin can be launched right back at the Koran and *Sunna*. The description of the throne of Allah leads one to believe that the anthropomorphic grandfather of Islam has a very physical backside to place in it. Muslims will try to claim the throne is metaphorical, but the Islamic literature depicts it as being very physical. It has a location (XI.7), it is held up and surrounded by angels (XXXIX.75; XXXX.7), and it was even mounted by Allah after the creation of the heavens and the earth (VII.54). While Muslims will try to claim that we cannot speculate on the divine meaning of *istawaa* (how exactly it is that a deity mounts something), the *ahadith* offer even greater examples of a physical throne. The traditions are filled with descriptions of Moses holding very specific parts of the throne, like the legs, the side, etc.

29. Yet again, this is a word coined by Sadiqi az-Zindiki. Like Voltaire's description of Dr. Pangloss as an expert in "cosmoloony-ology," *akhoona* Sadiqi has added "loony toony" to the name of the people of the *Jahiliyya* (pre-Islamic time of pagan Arab "ignorance").

30. The brotherhood of Muslims and the brotherhood of "pagans" (polytheists, associators, idolators).

34

A SPANISH TESTAMENT
My Experience As a Muslim
René (Spain)

I think any Westerner who comes across the authentic sources of Islam will be greatly surprised. There exists a great contrast between what we know about Islam and what it really is. Our sources are mostly biased and poor. Even if we talk with Muslim inmigrants, it is surprising how little they know about their own religion.

At the end, I joined Islam because I thought it was true; I thought Muhammad was a sincere man sent by Allah to become a guide for all of us. Maybe I was a bit immature back then, but after spending a lot of time on this and seeing so many good things on Muhammad and his teachings, I was convinced that everything was true.

While being a Muslim, I remember the generous hospitality of my Muslim friends I also remember one day that I was wearing some traditional Islamic clothing and, as I was walking down the street, a Spanish man shouted at me: "¡Moro!" [i.e., "Arab!"] That gave me a feeling of satisfaction. This is the kind of ignorance we must fight against, and we do not need any bombs, but dialogue and maturity.

Once within Islam, I tried to improve as a Muslim. One of my aims was to enrich my knowledge of Islam and spread it as much as I could. I used to translate Internet materials for my own Web page, *Textos sobre el Islam* (Texts about

This chapter originally appeared, in Spanish, on the Web site *Mi paso por Islam*, mallorcaweb.net/rene/islam.htm. Thanks to D. González García for his work on this translation.

Islam). It is not suprising, not even now, that I found everything to be true. What I regret now is not having done things properly. I should have searched for information against Islam and considered it before taking further steps. Maybe I devoted just 2 percent of my effort to search for information that would question Islam, and that is where I was wrong.

I suppose it is a human condition to search for evidence for that in which you believe and to leave aside those facts that could question your beliefs. Now I have learned to value the scientific method of examining issues objectively. Now more than ever!

I began thinking about the theory of evolution, and when enough evidence had accumulated I was forced to stop and reconsider. In a supermarket, I came across a book titled *El Catecismo de nuestros padres* (The catechism of our parents) by Enrique Miret Magdalena y Javier Sadaba. I was surprised and shocked at the same time. I thought that the book was serious, authoritative, and interesting. All of a sudden I read:

> First of all, let us consider and accept that Darwinism or neo-darwinist theories are as widely accepted in the scientific world as Einstein's physics or DNA structure. This hypothesis has been so thoroughly proven to be true that to doubt its aunthenticity is like having doubts about light. And not only in those aspects dealing with the evolution of the species and, more specifically, the human being, but in those aspects which could be considered as more controversial. Let us just think about natural selection and the survival of the fittest and which takes us to genetic principles. Although Darwin did not have access to the later discoveries on genetic developments, in his theory we can find them implicitly.[1]

That was shocking for me because I liked that book, but Islam does not accept evolution. Added to that, I found more proofs. I watched an excellent documentary by some Spanish scientists about thirty ancestors of *Homo sapiens* found in Atapuerca. I did not want to delay my search any more. It was clear to me that the method was correct and scientifically rigorous. I knew well the C-14 method and other techniques; I knew what they were talking about.

The more information I gathered, the more my eyes opened. The same happened to me when I once again asked my "Muslim brothers." This time I asked the wisest one I could find. His sectarian answer was, "The Jewish and demons confuse Muslims to take them away from Allah."

Let us make clear that Islam is not a sect, at least nowadays. And even though each major religion has its own sects, I was sure I was not in one of them. I knew well how dangerous sectarian behavior can be. One of the main characteristics of a sect is when its leaders reject anything that comes from outside the sect as something wrong or evil. I truly felt that his answer was a sectarian one, useful only when trying not to face the truth.

On the contrary, science has rational criticism as its leading principle, the principle that everything must be examined at any moment, taking into consideration all possibilities and not being attached to any of them.

From my point of view, Islam is much more rigorous than Christianity when dealing with legal, family, and administrative issues. Islam gives very specific and clear rules for almost everything in life; on the other hand, Christianity is much more ambiguous. And by same token, which was a great virtue at the beginning, it is now a flaw. Islam cannot change; it is the same as it was fourteen centuries ago. That is why it cannot adjust itself to new scientific discoveries.

There is within Islam no such a figure as the pope who could say that from now on Islam does recognize the theory of evolution as something true and well documented. I value this as a kind of sincerity. However, I must say that I do not support those who teach a "truth," later attack scientists who try to prove the opposite, and end up recognizing the discoveries made by those scientists already dead.

The Bible explains the myth of creation in a way similar to the Koran, but the situation differs greatly. Most Christians accept the myth of Adam as a way to explain their religion, not as a historical event. Islam was built on the idea that it is God the one who speaks, word by word and very clearly.

To deny the Koran in any of its parts or the words of Muhammad is simply to deny Islam. There is no room for other interpretations; the correct ones are those given by Muhammad, that is all. Since there is no doubt that evolution is a fact and that the natural-selection mechanism is what brought us to this planet, the Koran is not telling the truth; Muhammad is not telling the truth. Maybe he was a great person, but he did not tell the truth about our origins. Maybe his mysticism made him see something that he later interpreted or maybe he lied in order to reach a higher goal, such as creating a much better society. Probably a mixture of both; I do not know. What I do know is that:

(1) Not everything he said is true. Basically, he took the myth from the Bible and from it built his own doctrine. Maybe more than one of the *hadith* in which Islam is grounded was added freely after Muhammad's death. I find very surprising how many sentences are attributed to Muhammad or his followers. A lot of them are considered to be wrongly attributed, even by Muslim scholars.

(2) Allah is not the origin of Islamic teaching. OK, but that does not mean that there are no useful teachings for life in Islam.

In the *hadith* in Bukhari concerning the sex of the embryo we read:

Narrated Anas bin Malik: The Prophet said, "At every womb Allah appoints an angel who says, 'O Lord! A drop of semen, O Lord! A clot. O Lord! A little lump of flesh.' Then if Allah wishes (to complete) its creation, the angel asks, '(O Lord!) Will it be a male or female, a wretched or a blessed, and how much will his provision be? And what will his age be?' So all that is written while the child is still in the mother's womb."[2]

Narrated Anas bin Malik: The Prophet said, "Allah has appointed an angel in the womb, and the angel says, 'O Lord! A drop of discharge (i.e., of semen), O Lord! a clot, O Lord! a piece of flesh.' And then, if Allah wishes to complete the child's creation, the angel will say. 'O Lord! A male or a female? O Lord! wretched or blessed (in religion)? What will his livelihood be? What will his age be?' The angel writes all this while the child is in the womb of its mother."[3]

Narrated Anas bin Malik: The Prophet said, "Allah puts an angel in charge of the uterus and the angel says, 'O Lord, (it is) semen! O Lord, (it is now) a clot! O Lord, (it is now) a piece of flesh.' And then, if Allah wishes to complete its creation, the angel asks, 'O Lord, (will it be) a male or a female? A wretched (an evil doer) or a blessed (doer of good)? How much will his provisions be? What will his age be?' So all that is written while the creature is still in the mother's womb."[4]

From these *hadith*, considered to be the most authoritative, it can be clearly seen that it is Allah who decides the sex of the babies after fecundation. That is what it seems to those who were "lucky" enough to see a fetus back in those days.

But today, facts are clear, the sex of the fetus is defined exactly when the fecundation takes place, when the spermatozoon gives the chromosome Y or X to the fetus. It's not talking about when the part of DNA of sex becomes active. The mistake is to pretend that Allah makes the decision to complete his creation with the sex of the embryo weeks after the fecundation. The sex is detailed in all the somatic cells at that moment.

I would like to add that it is normal among Muslims to defend themselves from the mistakes found in the *hadith* by stating that, in fact, the Koran is the only book to be "protected" from mistakes. But the Koran is full of mistakes. There are even textual variants; Korans in North Africa are not the same as those of Saudi Arabia. For example sura 43 verses 18 and 19: In one version we find "angels from the Merciful" and in the other about "angels servers of the Merciful." What suprises me the most now is that, when they told me that the difference was not important, I just simply accepted it. Of course, the meaning remains the same, but that is not the question. The Koran was supposed to be protected from all mistakes and variants.

Lately, I have received several e-mails which reflect a deep anger toward my Web page and specially for what they consider a manipulation of the Koran. In their own words:

You say that the Koran is not protected, and to prove that you give the evidence of how a word changes its meaning in two different versions depending on the position of two points. I accept: if there were really two versions approved by all muslims then, there would something to think about.

There has never been any alteration in the Koran and there can never be any in the future. It is God's promise.

Words that could be taken as some kind of curse found in one e-mail:

God damn you. You will understand why some people like you deserve capital punishment. Although you will also have seen how this punishment is only materialized in very few and rare occasions. Because the greatness of the Islamic law is beyond the narrow minds of people like you, Westerners who are not able to understand and see it.

And from another e-mail:

You are an enemy of the Koran, enemy of the truth, enemy of God and enemy of the Islam, and I am your confessed enemy.

I told the latter writer that if he had patience with me and addressed me in a civilized manner, I could discuss the issues with him. In *The Demon-Haunted World: Science As a Candle in the Dark* by Carl Sagan, we find a similar example of medieval thinking: "In 1993, the highest and supreme religious authority from Saudi Arabia, the sheik Abdel-Aziz Ibn Baaz, issued a fatwa stating that the world was flat."[5]

And so, my answer is the following saying, attributed to Galileo: "And nevertheless, it moves." It seems like it is my turn to defend the right of free speech. I prefer the evidence from those words instead of writing some kind of argument for which I am not prepared. At the end, truth stays despite our lack of critical sense or our lack of tolerance.

I want to add that I have received other e-mails from Muslims pleased at reading my Web page: "I like to research too and I thank you for your article because it gave me more fair information and increased my love for the people." Fortunately, not all Muslims are intolerant. In fact, Muslims used to be more tolerant.

A very subjective confirmation, but especially relevant for me, was when I was told that I never really had faith. It seems that that is what Muhammad said. Those who leave Islam prove that they never had faith. I am very sure I had faith.

Some people have told me that it seems like I value positively my experience of being a Muslim. Well, it is true; it is something that will be part of my life and, overall, I value it in positive terms. It is a subjective opinion, it is something emotional rather than rational. I would rather keep good memories about it.

But in order for these pages to give a wider picture of Islam, there are some other details I would like to give you. They are facts that are not seen at the beginning and which are given to you gradually (so to be less shocking), as you become a Muslim; typical of sects, although Islam should not be considered as such.

- I devoted, as I once calculated, around three and a half hours a day to Islam. At the beginning, a lot less is always asked for; but, in my case, I was criticized for doing "too little." This was unfair since sometimes I was the only one in the mosque in the strictly mandatory dawn prayer. Islam understands life solely as a worship to God, in a variety of forms such as at work. But it also includes purely religious obligations such as praying five times a day, which becomes ten or more, gathered in five groups, to get closer to God.
- Due to the amount of time it requires and the fact that you value your Muslim friendships over the rest, you end up leaving your "old" friends aside. (This might be different from one group to another, although it is probably common to all of them.)
- I almost ended up thinking that the Jews had to disappear from the Earth. "Certainly you will find the most violent of people in enmity for those who believe (to be) the Jews and those who are polytheists." says the Koran (V.82) There are also prophesies from Muhammad saying that Muslims will kill all Jews. Now, I clearly see how hideous that is and I regret it. It is just another form of senseless racism. Which does not mean that I accept all the pain and racism that the Palestinians are suffering at the hands of the Jews. It is a very difficult and controversial situation in which both sides hate each other and find it hard to live next to each other. This has caused around 2 million Palestinians to become refugees in neighboring countries (such as Jordan).
- War against those non-Muslim countries is clearly defined. It is not the idea that the teaching must be brought to those who do not have it and then discuss it; that happened a long time ago. What needs to be done is to impose and bring every country under the "fair laws of Allah for their own good" by means of military occupation. The first countries that need to be occupied must be those which were Muslim before. Muhammad himself gave an example of this by forcing the people of Taif to become Muslim. At the same time I believe the attacks against the World Trade Center, which took place in September 2001, are against Muhammad's teachings although I am also sure that Muhammad would declare war on any neighboring country in order to convert it to Islam and give them the laws inspired by Allah. It does not matter if this country is one thousand times more powerful. Allah was with them; in fact, an army was sent against some parts of the Byzantine Empire.

- The true science is the knowledge of Islam, Allah's teaching, and the Muhammad's *hadith*; that is how Islam defines it. Doubt itself, as a method, is rejected and considered to be a sickness. In science, doubt and criticism are needed in order to keep it "healthy" and to ensure that facts or theories are objectively analyzed. In my opinion, that is the greatest problem for Islam: It tries to be scientific in nature but it rejects a very important fact in modern science, to thoroughly question and examine everything, giving as much information as possible of the points for and against it.
- Anybody who tries to leave Islam must be killed. It is a current law since it cannot be changed; it was like that in ancient times, and now nobody can abolish it. Overall, Islam offers little religious freedom.

During the last centuries and in the Western world, we have improved considerably regarding the definition and defense of freedom. The Islamic world must increase its cultural background, adding values such as objectivity, doubt as a scientific method, and individual freedoms. Those who do not want to contrast "their" truth against others in order to test it, are the most likely to be wrong.

My experience within Islam had many positive aspects, besides those derived from meeting and discovering new people and a new culture from within. I keep very good memories and many of them will be part of my life for a long time; even leaving Islam was a positive and enriching experience. I keep in mind the thought of that feeling of fear of God, a feeling that at the same time paralyzes and stimulates you. You continue with your own life, but always try to keep in mind that God is watching you. That is why you always try to do things to please him. That is part of the whole idea of *jihad* (which could be translated as "effort"), not in the sense of war but in the sense of the *jihad akbar* (the great *jihad*, according to Muhammad), the fight in trying to improve oneself. An effort the Muslim can handle no more than he can do, no more than he regrets afterward. Muslims must always try to increase it, never to decrease it. Nowadays, when somebody tells me that this or that thing can be done because "nobody is going to see you" I think to myself "yes, only if it is the truth" and that is important for me.

NOTES

1. Enrique Miret Magdalena y Javier Sadaba, *El Catechismo de nuestros padres* (Madrid: Plaza Janés Ediciones, 1998), p. 61.

2. al-Bukhārī, *Book of Menses*, vol. 1, book 6 of *Ṣaḥīḥ* (New Delhi: Kitab Bhavan, 1987), Hadith no. 315, p. 189.

3. al-Bukhārī, *Book of the Prophets*, vol. 4, book 55 of *Ṣaḥīḥ* (New Delhi: Kitab Bhavan, 1987), Hadith no. 550, p. 347.

4. al-Bukhārī, *Book of* al-Qadr, vol. 8, book 77 of *Ṣaḥīḥ* (New Delhi: Kitab Bhavan, 1987), Hadith no. 594, p. 388.

5. Carl Sagan, *The Demon-Haunted World: Science As a Candle in the Dark* (New York: Ballantine Books, 1996), p. 325.

35

"FORGET WHAT IS AND IS NOT ISLAM"

Michael Muhammad Knight (United States)

I was raised Roman Catholic. At fifteen, I developed an interest in Malcolm X, which eventually led to my conversion to Islam. Malcolm's autobiography inspired a search for knowledge as well as a curiosity about Islam. I devoured any book on history, philosophy, and comparative religion I could find. I did horribly in high school, as I would sit in chemistry class reading Nietzsche, Will Durant's history volumes, Plato, or the Koran.

At sixteen, I contacted the local Islamic Center. My mother drove me to the mosque and witnessed my official conversion. Before even stepping foot in the mosque I had memorized the prayers and some Koranic suras in Arabic. The *imams* sat me down and witnessed my *shahadah*. From that point on, Islam and my independent studies became the focus of my life. The *imams* were impressed with my thirst for knowledge. Through them I was introduced to a young Muslim girl for an arranged marriage (we never married due to my eventual apostasy). They also arranged for me to study Islam for two months of my senior year in Islamabad, Pakistan.

I returned home with dreams of becoming a respected Muslim scholar. I was working on applications for the Islamic universities in Malaysia, Pakistan, and Saudi Arabia. However, my continual reading caused me to become disillusioned with formal Islam. My world fell apart.

Having been given a key by one of the local brothers, I took to only visiting my mosque at night when no one else was around. I would sit and pray, sit and cry, run and play, or stand on my head in the *mihrab*. Sometimes I brought a portable word processor and wrote stories. These night visits led to the writing of *Where Mullahs Fear to Tread, or The Sleepless Night*. The stories are a journal of my painful and gradual apostasy, told through allegorical science fiction tales of Muslims in outer space.

My work is rooted in Islam, the religion I was not born into, rather, the faith I chose to immerse myself in. What my work offers, more than anything else, is that it is something you don't see that much. For Christian societies, works of disillusionment, estrangement, and the like are nothing new. In fact they are cliché. For what is commonplace in America or Europe with Christianity, would get your head chopped off in Saudi with Islam. I feel *The Sleepless Night* is inherently an Islamic work—a true, *fisabillah* work of Islam. But it is an Islam that could only be free to flourish in the West.

My ultimate goal, I think, is to break down some of the walls Islam puts around itself. Islam in modern practice can be very rigid, very strict. It wasn't always that way. Islam has a rich heritage of skeptical philosophers, mystics, and humanist scholars who pursued their own truths in relative freedom. The climate in today's Islamic world is much different, largely due to governments' manipulating Islam as an instrument of oppression, combined with resentment of the West and all that it represents. I retain an emotional attachment to Islam, its characters and rituals. But I cannot fall into the formal categorization of Islam anymore. If someone had to ask me of my religion, I would reply that I am a Sufi. A Sufi, though not necessarily a Muslim Sufi. Perhaps an agnostic Sufi, if there can be such a thing. My own personal religion came from Islam. It has Islam at its foundations. However, it escaped that cage long ago.

While in Pakistan, I often visited the Dawah Academy's library, despite continual suggestions from my teachers to "stick with the Koran." After reading some books on Buddhism, I was fascinated with the idea that Buddha was one of the many prophets mentioned in the Koran. I found that throughout my Islamic life, I was searching for knowledge from a wide variety of sources: philosophers, the texts of other religions, history, and so on, but I was always advised to first learn Arabic and master the Koran before engaging in those studies. Then I found Attar's *Conference of the Birds* and read a line that changed my life: "Forget what is and is not Islam."

This, appearing in a spiritual text, a Sufi text, relating to the search for God. To find Allah, forget Islam. The idea threw me to the floor. Allah without Islam! *Staghfirallah!*

As I continued studying, certain ideas in Islam lost their power over me. For example, my mother had a dog in her house. I no longer admonished her that the angels would not enter. My female cousin wore shorts in the summertime. I lost my harsh attitudes about such practice. It just did not matter to me anymore.

I still considered myself Muslim, but ignored *Sahih Bukhari* (the collection of *hadith*). It made no sense to me and its credibility was shot by my continual reading. Muslims argue that there was a very scientifically sound system for determing the validity of *hadith*. How sound can any system be for separating real from false gossip three hundred years after all the involved characters have died? Hell, look at the rumor mills in your offices, schools, or even mosques and tell me you have a scientifically sound "he said that he heard from so-and-so that she heard him say such-and-such" system for finding the truth.

The final nail in the coffin was when I started reading Islamic history from the *Shīʿa* perspective. I learned things that I never see mentioned in Sunni sources: How what Muhammad called "the greatest generation of Muslims" all killed each other over politics. How ʿĀʾisha ordered arrows to be shot at the coffin of Husain. How Fatima was trampled to death by Muslims seeking Ali's pledge of allegiance to Abu Bakr. The religion was junked the day Muhammad died.

My reading brought many other issues to light, which have all been touched upon here: Muhammad's marriage to a child, the killing of apostates, and so on.

I am still a spiritual person. I even retain my old admiration for Imam Husain, who was praised by *kufrs* such as Charles Dickens for his noble, selfless sacrifice. But I cannot call myself a Muslim. I am a free man.

36

I MARRIED A MUSLIM
Faiza (United States)

I wish to commend Dr. Ali Sina on his most excellent and informative Web site.

I am a freethinker also, although my current situation does not allow for me to reveal myself publicly because of my husband, who would probably declare our marriage void if he knew what I truly believe. Although he is a Muslim and determined to stay as such, he is not a fundamentalist. Born in Morocco, he is one of those people who is very much against terrorism, insisting that it is not "true Islam." He is Muslim due to the circumstances of having been born to Muslim parents and eventually meeting a *sheikh* through a circle of friends when he was in his teens. It was the meeting of this man, who preached about the horrors of the so-called torture in the grave and hellfire that eventually cemented in my husband a fear of this deity called Allah, a fear prevalent in people who follow this religion.

I must admit that I, too, was frightened of the threats in Islam until recently. I would like to share this with you because it is a fine example of how we, as humans, are prone to fear, which, in my opinion is the driving factor of religion. A few years ago, I started at the point I am now, believing in a higher power much as you describe but rejecting conventional Judeo-Christian and Muslim beliefs as myths. Then late one night, I was flipping through channels (insomnia) when I came upon a program about people who have had near-death experiences. There was one woman whose heart had stopped beating during surgery. She described a beautiful afterlife, available to all; a higher power, loving to all, which she described as the light-in-the-tunnel about which most of us who have seen such programs have heard. She was saying how she no longer feared death. I had a tremendously wonderful feeling after hearing this woman's story. I thought about this quite a bit in the next few days. I also thought about the traditional concepts of hell in various religions.

I must have been doing a lot of thinking because, inevitably, this concept worked its way into my dreams. A few weeks later I dreamed that I was climbing a staircase. On the edge of each step stood creatures I could not see clearly, although I know they were there. As I climbed the staircase I said to one of them, "There is no hell." And it replied, "No, don't say that, there is a hell." "Really?" I said, "What's it like then?" "It is like this," said the creature, and, as soon as these words reached my ears, I fell from the staircase and plunged into a void, and as I fell, I had the feeling of being smothered by ever-increasing darkness. Like falling into a pool of viscous ink.

I have a pretty nifty imagination, don't you think? (There might be a career for me as a novelist.) Anyway, that was my take on the dream, and I thought nothing about it after that.

A year later, after I was married, my husband, while trying to get me to become a "serious Muslim" told me about something the Muslims believe in called the *sirat*, the bridge to heaven. Sinners supposedly slip off this bridge and plunge for many years until they reach hell. Now, as you can see, I got a twinge of fear hearing this. No, make that massive fear. As a result, I spent a good six months under the "trance" of Islam, reciting the *Fatihah* ad nauseam so that I could get it perfect for when I performed the prayer. And I started to study the Koran.

But, thankfully, my search did not stop there. I made it my quest to research this "wonderful" religion called Islam. I used my husband's extensive personal library, and, of course, the Internet. I am thankful for this curiosity because, had I not ventured to learn more about Islam, I might have become one of those people who post chastising messages against the Faith Freedom Web site. I saw the Koran for what it really is: a bunch of rehashed Bible stories, legends, and half-baked theories peppered with threats and served under the guise of poetry that is actually quite mediocre, at best.

At this point I can almost hear all those Muslims out there, "May Allah curse you!" "You will go to hell just like you dreamed!" and many other far harsher descriptions of reprimand from both human and divine sources. What more can I say to them Ali has not told them through the Faith Freedom site already? Human fear may be the most powerful emotion of all. Fear is fed by all things unknown. It is the puzzlement of primitive man when he sees strange things he does not understand, like women who menstruate every month but do not seem to wither and die from the bleeding. It is the bogeyman in a child's closet. It is the knowledge that we all die, and that no one can stop it.

Fear is the tool that molesters employ with children so that they can continue to do so for years with a simple "If you tell I will kill your parents." That's not so different than "Do this or else I will cut off your hand, foot, or head." Or "Do this or Allah will plunge you into the hellfire."

It's all about interpretation of unknown situations. My husband loves Jesus the way Muslims do. As a result, he has had numerous dreams of Jesus. A person ready to accept Christianity would have interpreted that dream as a sign to leave Islam and accept Christianity, whereas my husband is a Muslim who also dreams of Muhammad. He therefore interprets this dream as a sign of the validity of Islam. I know of a woman who once dreamed of a man who glowed like gold and was riding a horse. Someone told her that this was Saint George. So she believed it, and now is a devout Christian.

Muslims need to realize that they are not the only people who have been given so-called miracles and blessings, as well as "signs" appearing to be from God. If Islam is so universal, why do some Christians receive healings when they go to shrines bedecked with crosses and things that God supposedly despises? These healings are well documented. I read of a woman whose severed spinal cord fused "miraculously" as she recited a verse in the New Testament. Is God in the business of tricking people by giving them miraculous signs so that they may fall astray? If so, then that implies that God hates every person except the ones born to Muslim parents or the ones who come into contact with Muslims. And if these so-called *kafir* people receive healings from satanic sources, then what makes the Muslims so sure that the Koran is not from satanic sources as well? After all, if Satan can heal people miraculously, then it is not a big task for him to compose a poem with a few stories and so-called valid scientific information.

Of course, debating the issue from either side is ludicrous. There are entire countries out there filled with people who never get a chance to know what Islam is about. I asked my husband this, in the guise of wanting to know the truth, and he was not able to answer me. He shrugged and said something about "Allah's will."

Again, I don't think his fear will allow him to explore this further because it is very devastating to most people when they venture out of their comfort zones. Likewise, there are people out there who live their whole lives under the shadow of the Koran, never encountering any other point of view. The truth is that people believe what they are told and very few try to venture beyond this.

It was very painful for me to shed Islam because when I let go of it, although I felt relief at the separation, I also felt a void, a wound that bled invisibly as I tried to go about my daily life, and I desperately searched for something, anything, to soothe it. For weeks I tried to hang on to another religion as a bandage, but each attempt left me with doubts: Is this the right way? What if I'm wrong?

But I eventually realized that the best way to go about it was to just let the wound heal by itself, no bandages, no crutches.

So I wish to thank Ali for his Web site because I found material there that helped me confront and conquer my fears. Just like a parent who leads a child to the very closet that houses an alleged bogeyman so that he can see that, indeed, there is no such bogeyman. I needed someone to do that for me, and, even though I have never met him, his willingness to put himself on the line and write the truth on his Web site is exactly what I needed.

As soon as I came to grips with the truth, I was completely at peace, more at peace than I have ever been in my entire life. I sleep very well: no visitations from any divine source to warn me about my decision. I take this as a sign of sanity. Since I have let go of the fear that Allah was going to get me, my nights have been remarkably peaceful and nightmare-free.

A few weeks ago, my husband told me a story about a man who lived to a very old age and died twenty years ago. All his life this man preached Islam and was even the one who called the *Adhan* (Muslim call to prayer) in his little town every day until his final illness. On his deathbed, he asked for his family—he had had several sons and daughers who in turn had families of their own. After his family came to him, he asked for a copy of the Koran. He had tears in his eyes, so his family thought that he was going to recite a part of it for one last time, as they had seen him do so many times in the past. But when they put it in his hands he said, "I hereby renounce everything written in this book. It is a lie." And then the man died.

I was speechless when I heard this. I could see myself in this man, hopelessly "trapped" in the role carved out for him, afraid to tell others that he had found out the truth. I also wondered when this happened, exactly. Did he find out at the end of his life? Or did he go through decades of torturous pretense?

I asked my husband why he thought the man did this. My husband gave me the explanation given by his *skeikh*: That the man probably had too much vanity when he preached. That because of this, Allah sought to punish him by willing for him to utter these words right before he died, so that he would be denied the rewards of the hereafter. At this point, I was appalled at my husband's *skeikh* for saying this of an supposedly all-powerful deity. It makes Allah sound not only angry, but downright malicious and petty. Again, it's all about interpretation.

I am in the process of assessing my relationship with my husband. I know that I cannot tell him without divorcing him, and I need to consider not only myself but my children as well. My husband is not a malicious person, but who knows what he might do if he is provoked by the realization that I have apostated and do not wish to go back to Islam? I might gather up enough courage to run and build a life where I should not hide my belief. Or it may well be that I, too, will be like that old man, brave enough to tell the truth only on my deathbed.

37

DARK COMEDY
Ben Hoja (United States)

Melancholy is the blackest of the four humors—and the most incisive. While I enjoy on occasion phlegm-inspired gross-out-comedies and Three Stooges choler, mockery of absurdity is the bile closest to my heart. But despite my delectation of the satirical arts, I've never had the talent to do stand-up. If I did, *Allahu 'alim*[1] where my material would come from. "Have you heard the one about the 'half-Jew, half-Catholic' nerd boy who 'reverted' to Sunni Islam at age sixteen?"

The one joke without a punchline still manages to deliver a Wrestle-monomania smackdown to any notion of self-respect. I grapple with the former Johnnie Taliban[2] within, and imagine the relief of detachment—if it had only been some other schmuck pinned to the mat. But no, honest *shahadah*,[3] it was I who in the first days of the World Wide Web, in the licentious domain of the Great *Shaytan.us*,[4] was "muslimed" 'Abdul-Something-or-Another.

No, there wasn't a fetching Muslimah damsel to chase. No, I wasn't imprisoned with two scary bunkmates in a high-security penitentiary. No, I wasn't such a rabid Yusuf Islam aka Cat Stevens fan that I felt the need to join him. "On the Road to Find Out" there is only one tune to hum. Rather, it was a matter of abnormal endocrinology—an overactive absurdity gland. I had all the presenting symptoms: guilt by the gallon, worm-worthiness, intolerance of all divergent opinions, anhedonistic, yet, by the desires of adolescence, a hypocrite.

As I examine the etiology of my hyperreligious malady now, I realize the operation of hindsight bias—the past molded by present beliefs. My motivations for conversion were vintage *Homo sapiens*, as they were for apostasy. Not all the reasons or personal qualities that led me to Islam were diabolical, though the stern and hateful side found easy expression.

The negative pallor comes from the recognition that the sellers of eternal sanguinity make promises incommensurate with observed results. In Sufi terms, Islam seeks to have us pull the wool over our own eyes, condemning us to servile sheep-hood.[5] The wool weaves the illusion that all rays of goodness emanate from the heavenly herder, and that if we don't find that promised goodness the actual problem is that we are black sheep, shorn of any worth (IV.79). That I assented to Islam as the all-encompassing cure-all leads me to recount the litany of vulnerabilities that left me all too ready to be fleeced, and if the letter of the *hadith* were to be implemented—slaughtered.[6]

As I ponder retrospectively how I could have fooled myself, I see there were no major precipitators until junior high. In elementary school, I associated Catholicism, the religion of my upbringing, with absolute boredom. On one occasion, I hid my shoes in my clothes hamper to avoid going to the doldrums of Sunday mass, my mom shouting to high heaven before finally acceding. By way of contrast, during that time I had a massive surge of enthusiasm for science: marine biology, model rocketry, computer programming, and robotics. I would spend my time in catechism classes sketching sharks and F-16 fighter jets, wishing I could dispense with the exercise book telling me how to behave and go back home, where I was taking apart an old Atari game system for the robot that I was going to tell how to behave. I didn't think about God and its accompaniments to any degree, except on the handful of occasions that I observed Judaism.

Although my dad hadn't practiced Judaism since he was a kid (he stopped going to the synagogue when a rabbi wouldn't answer him who Cain went to live with in exile if Adam and Eve indeed were the first people on Earth), he did arrange it so that I experienced some of its holidays and passages. The foreignness of the synagogue, the Torah scrolls, and the Hebrew language all contributed to me perceiving Judaism as more interesting (and by virtue of that alone superior to Catholicism). My neighborhood friend's family was Jewish, and I attended a Passover Seder at their house, disliking the matzah-ball-soup but not minding the prizes from the hide-the-matzah-game.[7] I also went to my friend's sister's bat mitzvah, but didn't gain much from the experience, as I realized midway that I had worn pants with a broken zipper and had to hope no one would notice my fly being open, and my futile attempts to zip the unzipable. Though I had only brief "exposure" to Judaism, I've come across a school paper from that time where I identified myself as, of all things, a "CathJew."

During junior high, this dual designation began to raise insoluble questions.

How could both religions be correct? How could a person combine them? Although it wasn't yet anything close to an obsessive quandary, I was also confronted with a greater awareness that there were even more religions than Catholicism and Judaism. A girl I flirted with was Buddhist. In a small extracurricular group for an interscholastic creative competition, a Protestant had disparaging things to say about Judaism, Catholicism, and Mormonism. Islam, however, did not register. My only memory of it was when a social studies teacher gave a bare, imprecise outline of Muhammad's life and influences, explaining that he came into contact with Jewish and Christian ideas through his caravan travels.

But it was in other classes that I would learn a less impersonal lesson—the price for intellectualism. My math teacher perhaps meant well by praising me in front of the whole class for solving the extra-credit problem no one else solved, but the result was more ridicule and bullying. In other classes I likewise had the know-it-all audacity to raise my hand and provide answers, with just as beneficial results. My devotion to science (in writings from that era I foresaw attending MIT) was sufficient cause to be labeled forevermore as a dork, the preferred target for random abuse. Whereas in elementary school, on the rare occasions I ever got into an argument or fight, I'd fight right back (I played tackle football then—my nickname was "the Animal"), the ferocity and number of my opponents in junior high resigned me to avoidance, self-doubt, and alienation.

When an opportunity to flee from my tormentors came, I took it. I skipped the last year of junior high and hoped to start anew at an all-boys Catholic high school (yes, that desperate). Although in some measure switching to a parochial school from a public school reduced the amount of conflict, it did not eliminate it. For my first semester I benched football ("played" is not the appropriate verb). The many hours I spent in the weight room the summer before didn't overcome not having yet had a growth spurt. After being set upon anew by two rich, preppy, jock a-holes during the season, and having to deal with the same characters again when I tried lacrosse in the spring, I quit all sports.

The ease with which trifling troubles could make me yell "uncle" didn't stop with the pigskin and my thin skin. My first semester of high school, I got D's on a few grammar tests, "scraping by" with a B+ in English. No greater catastrophe. I quit my attempt to get perfect grades, disregarding how negligibly close I was to completing that goal. My hypersensitivity to perceived failure and the degree to which all humiliations replayed in a mental Möbius loop began to reach neurotic proportions.

Two humiliations suffice to explain in part why I didn't see anything to lose in the rigors of Islam. The summer before my freshman year, I went with my older brother to an amusement-at-my-expense-park where some of his friends were starring in a '50s musical theatre show held on a stage in a '50s-style diner. Unbeknownst to me, one of my brother's friends told one of his costars to select me from the audience as a dance partner during part of the show. That this costar also happened to be a cheerleader for a professional football team and the epitome of gorgeousness didn't magically impart knowledge of how to dance. A peck on the cheek from the lips of Venus at the end intermixed with the kiss of death felt by a thirteen-year-old at having just performed a dance best described as the John Ashcroft boogie in front of ninety people.[8]

Despite the anxiety it caused, when the first school dance of freshman year came, I vowed not to remain chicken of the funky chicken. Summoning a *mujaheed's* courage (and ever-present lust for booty), I asked a girl to dance. The dance floor was ours, as we gyrated and whirled and in general, "got down." So flashy were our moves that the sea of dancers parted to watch our acrobatic interpretation of "Kung-Fu Fighting," clapping with uproarious enthusiasm. Oh, wait a minute. I must've been thinking of the movies. Back in reality, where there was no chance I'd ever be mistaken for John Travolta, I left the cafeteria/disco inferno hall with the notion that if a bookie was placing odds on me finding a girlfriend, ten to one on one of the elderly priests haunting my school beating me to it.

Luckless in love, destined forevermore to be more celibate than the celibates, I had the further misfortune to be luckless in friendship. In my sophomore year my dad asked me whether I thought I needed to see a psychiatrist because of an certain Arabic numeral: s*ifr*—zero. I had no friends. I was upset that he mentioned it, since I was well aware it was true. I had acquaintances I would talk to on occasion, but mostly kept to myself, never hanging out with anyone on the weekends. I didn't want to frame it in psychological terms, because I had started framing it in religious ones. I tried to pretend loneliness was solitude.

My religiomania sprung from unrelenting introspective reflection, free from the corrective of having friends who might challenge my assumptions and force me to reconsider my beliefs. Since my parents could not afford to pay full tuition, I had to take part in work-study. My first year, I was assigned to clean the school chapel. I enjoyed it because the stained glass and tranquility put me in a reflective cast of mind. On one of those occasions I prayed to find out who God was. Although I tried to take Catholicism seriously briefly during that time—taking Communion and reading all of the New Testament—the question of which religion might be true lingered. A less presumptive question I pushed aside: *Is* there a true religion? I took for granted that atheism was meaningless, and that if it were true, all that would follow would be to kill oneself.

It was terribly ironic that in seeking only religious alternatives, I sought to kill myself—at least metaphorically speaking. I was all too willing to believe that I needed to be destroyed and remolded in the forge of an attested, ancient truth. The panoply of interests that had previously sustained some self-confidence withered as I became obsessed with excising the reject within—the gods infallibly and invariably concurring with my peers in their rejection. The notion that there was something fundamentally wrong with me found easy company with the notion that something was fundamentally wrong with the world. I resented the effortless enjoyment of life I witnessed from afar: the hypocrisy of classmates who read from the Apostolic Letters during Wednesday mass and bragged about their weekend beer runs and "home runs" on Mondays. If it turned out that American society was corrupt and needed to be razed, all the better the rationalizations for that resentment.

Throwing around counterfactuals—what ifs—I thoroughly believe that any number of different cultic ideologies could've channeled my resentment and self-loathing. For a year or so I was a regular viewer of a radical, anti-abortion Protestant television talk show that favored replacing the government with a theocracy and Mosaic punishments. That the ideology of my discontent happened to be Islam, and not neo-Puritanism, was virtue of my participation in Model United Nations (MUN), a competition where teams represent nations at mock assemblies and councils. Having given up sports, I tried MUN my sophomore year, representing Syria at a couple of tournaments. In the midst of reading about Syria, I also began to read the Koran and visit Islamic sites on the Web.

Though, true to fashion, I eventually quit MUN because I was petrified of speaking in front of large groups of people, my reading didn't cease, but redoubled, as I checked out large portions of the Islam section at the city library. As I had grown skeptical of the Catholic Church by learning more about its less-than-holy history and, through doubts about dogma like transubstantiation, I became particularly interested in the Muslim polemics that contrasted Islam to its predecessor religions. Ditties on the irrationality of the trinity, and the lack of priest-hood were quite enough—in a short time, Islam became the victor. The strange aspect of this acceptance was that I rarely felt inspired by the Koran, the ad naseum repetition and the disconnectedness of verses were apparent even then. The immemorial cliché that a person must read the Koran in Arabic to capture the unearthly beauty was enough to quiet the literary critic for a time. The veil of language and distance concealed hopes that the world could be as simple as the monotheist formulae would have it. Like foreign Judaism, the even more foreign Islam could transcend detailed questioning so long as it kept a due romanticizing distance. Even after the rites of faith became old *kufi*,[9] the eventuality of questioning could be deferred by deference to the parallel universe where true religion was practiced, free from the blatant defects of earthly praxis and interpretation.

Soon after I clung to Islam, the distance began to ebb, and the parallel universe no sooner had to be invented. I had never met a Muslim until my sophomore year. The first words a Muslim ever spoke to me were while I was in the lunch line, "Hoja, why do you always have a stick up your ass?!" "Najmuddeen" was a junior then, who knew of me from Model United Nations. Granted, Najmuddeen told the truth, though I'm not certain what precisely prompted him to say it, as I'd never said a word to him before, but he did so in a manner I thought belying his acculturation to the West. Despite the put-down, I did eventually broach the topic of Islam and had a few forgettable conversations at lunchtime and study period about it.

There wasn't any charismatic figure to brain-*wudu*[10] me, nor any Muslim of deep piety to inspire me. I didn't meet any more Muslims until midway through my junior year, when I outright converted to Islam. In the interim, to a few fellow students I mentioned my intention to convert to Islam when I went to college. They had varying reactions if they didn't have polygamy jokes on tap, from the hypertolerant liberal atheist who was supportive and thought religion had the power to promote good works to the nominal Christian who never tired of mentioning the brutality begot in the name of Islam, such as the suicide teen mine clearers in the Iran-Iraq war. To the latter I had only my aforementioned multiverse theory, that on a parallel earth there is an Islamic utopia, and the rhetorical strategy of *tu quoque*.[11]

Nearing the end of my sophomore year, the Oklahoma City bombing bolstered my view that Americans were unjustly biased against Islam. The day of the bombing, when it was unknown who did it, I had the experience of being told repeatedly, in sarcastic tones, "Good job. Good job. Way to go Ben." A day or two later, I spoke to Najmuddeen, asking if the local mosque was okay and expressing the hope that whoever committed the bombing would get strung up. He said it was okay, that it had last been vandalized during the Gulf War. When the primary suspects turned out to be white Americans, I saw it as a rebuke to charging Muslims with collective guilt whenever a pack of nutcases decided to use American targets for demolition practice (and then charged America with collective guilt for their assignation of blame).

Influenced by Muslim and leftist critiques of the West, I increasingly viewed Americans as caring only for their own tragedies, rather than having a broader circle of concern for all humans. I wrote an unpublished editorial at that time asking whether Americans were in a better position to understand the situation of the Bosnians and the Rwandans after being interrupted for a moment from pax Americana. Taking the sweeping thesis that Americans view non-Westerners as subhuman one step further, I began to feel the American government was responsible for inflicting massive tragedies throughout its history, from the genocide of Native Americans to the Vietnam debacle. Although I didn't learn of Noam Chomsky until I went to college, I read a few like-minded leftist activists such as former attorney general Ramsey Clark, who wrote a book that particularly excited my indignation: *The Fire This Time: U.S. Crimes in the Gulf.*[12] Among the book's claims were that U.S. Ambassador to Iraq April Glaspie gave a free hand to Saddam Hussein to resolve Iraq's financial and territorial disputes with Kuwait a few days before the invasion, the Pentagon overstated use of "smart" weaponry, and the seldom-mentioned civilian casualties were astronomic.

The practical effect of my disgust at the American government was that I harbored revolutionary fantasies that for the most part remained misshapen and ill defined, but added to my already opinionated and disputative nature. My first published letter to the editorial page of the city paper my sophomore year was a pro-life tirade in response to a feminist's column. The first letter I drafted relating to Islam corresponded to the eve of my "reversion," galvanized by a national basketball controversy involving a Muslim Denver Nuggets player and a question of allegiance.

Mahmoud Abdul-Rauf, fka Chris Jackson, refused to stand for the national anthem, contravening NBA league rules. When it became known, I was among the very few supporters of his position, as the "Love It or Leave It" crowd skewered him in the newspapers and on talk radio. In a letter to the editor and a call to a talk radio station, I expressed the view that a Muslim would be committing *shirk*, the worst possible sin, by paying reverence to a symbolic idol.[13] I seconded Abdul-Rauf's comments that the flag represented oppression, and opined that nationalism had led to most bloody century in history. When Abdul-Rauf eventually capitulated to the threat of suspension and the potential loss of income, I had to acknowledge that there was humor in complaining of societal oppression while making millions. But to me, it was non sequitur humor, as I saw as the primary oppression that which the United States exerted on poor-to-moderate-income countries, where the Cold War had lead to Machiavellian dealings, such as using Iraq in the 1980s to bludgeon Iran. The main domestic tyranny I saw was *Roe* v. *Wade*, although the Muslim positions on the matter were less decisively "pro-life" than the Catholic position (Abdul-Rauf probably had different tyranny in mind).

Amid the fallout from the Abdul-Rauf affair, Najmuddeen's mosque decided to have an open house. My dad, perhaps having misread "How to Tell if Your Teenager Has Become a Muslim Radical," was the one who suggested going to it, to what end I'm not sure. I hadn't gotten my driver's license yet, and was über-inhibited in experiencing new situations and people, even if it was Allah's happening hangout. If I hadn't gone to that open house, my phobia of new surroundings might not have dissipated, and I might have remained an *ummah*-less Muslim until finding another obsession. But a shoeless tour of the facility by a behejabed high school girl, followed by Arab desserts and refreshments, *da'wa* brochures,[14] and a video playing in the background about the scientific miracle of the Koran quieted my unease.

As soon as I got my driver's license, I heeded the pressure tactics of the *da'wa* literature that warned that you could die at any time, so you had better propel yourself into the arms of the mother *ummah*.[15] I told Najmuddeen of my intention, and he arranged so that I might meet a scholar *sheik* he knew at a scheduled time. Next I told my dad. He objected. He repeated the truism that it was possible to be a good person no matter what the religion, but said he didn't think

I was in a state of mind to have discretion. I said that a person ought to practice what he believes, and not let societal pressure dissuade him from what he thinks is right (if he possessed the true religion, that is). He asked me to wait, not to rush into something I might regret: "There's no reason to hurry." I said that I had been studying Islam for more than a year, and that I had read more about religion than most people do in their entire lives. My dad also wanted me to speak with my mom about my conversion, as she was already upset that I had avoided confirmation as a Catholic. I refused. I wanted him to tell her, rather than tell her directly. Ultimately, my dad didn't try to stop me through coercion, though he told me I was making a mistake.

Sadly, I didn't have flashing green lights and a *takbir*[16]-droning-megaphone to put on my car as I drove on the way to take my emergency *shahadah*. As I drove up the mosque's driveway, I saw Najmuddeen up front, dressed in a *shawar qamees*. We went inside and he showed me to the footbath and taught me to perform *wudu'*. We then went in to the *musallah*[17] where a few Muslims had gathered around the *sheik* for a class. Once the class was finished the *sheik* gave an overview of the *aqeedah*[18] of Islam, and asked if I had questions. I had two. I asked about *halaal*[19] food—if it was permissible to eat meat at American restaurants—and posed a rather tougher question about Islam's position on predestination and free will. I only remember the gist of the *sheik*'s answers. His answer to the second question was confusing and perhaps a bit contradictory. More important, my stomach protested against his answer to the first. But if *kaafir*-burgers had to be sacrificed for the true religion, so be it. *Ashhaduanlailahaillallahwa-muhammad-rasulullah.*[20]

Soon after the preliminary *salaams* and the welcomes, I prayed for the first time in congregation, already having learned the basics of *salat* from a free book on practicing Islam, courtesy of good ol' King Fahd and his merry band of *Wahabbis*. My emotion, though guarded as usual by my ever-stoic face, mixed excitement at possibly annihilating Ben Hoja with discomfort at having to meet so many people. Since I'm probably listed in the *Guinness Book* as possessor of the world's biggest personal bubble, I was also put off by the manner some welcomed me, with a hug. From the first day there was a process of adjusting to a subculture with customs sometimes diametrically opposite to that of the American culture I was accustomed to.

A few of my new "brothers" offered brief words of advice, perhaps some in anticipation of adjustment to minutiae like eating with one's right hand *sans* fork. The bromide that affords me the biggest groan today, probably because I don't recall the exact wording: "Remember, Allah has made Islam easy." Certainly elements of Islam were easy, but in many respects, particularly when it bent human nature, it was anything but. With the initial burst of convert momentum, I could give away my devil music to my brother and my CD player to my parents. I could give 2.5 percent of my wealth to noble Muslim charities (only to find years later that one of the them had its assets frozen after September 11 for terrorist ties). I could give up baloney for its metaphysical equivalent. But give up movies? Television? Glances at beautiful *kaafira* women alternating with the Koran-mandated look-away? My austerities were lopsided and inconsistent from the start.

I couldn't consider human appreciation for beauty, art, music, and bodily function humor as an implacable foe in my quest to abolish enjoyment of life—uh, I mean to follow the path of the Prophet *sal Allahu alaihi was salaam*. The party line was that Islam merely frees that appreciation from the taint of disobedience. As the iconoclast who destroyed the pencil-and-ink sketches that brought pride when I created them in art class, I was following two directives: the prohibition in the *hadith* of creating images of living beings, and my personal directive of abolishing Ben Hoja. I sought to purify myself from the taint of my personal *jahiliyya*,[21] even if much of what I did seems now about as rational and beneficial as the Taliban ban on kite flying. Living among the *kufaar* hordes, I had a ready-made excuse when I inevitability couldn't imitate the Rasulullah to the nth degree: "I'm surrounded!"

I didn't discuss the travails of "Learning to be a Super-*Wali*[22] in 30 Days" with Najmuddeen, but rather with compatriots who had similarly tried to slough off past selves. After the *'Asr* afternoon prayer at the mosque one day, two brothers, one an American convert in his midtwenties, the other a slightly older North African "born-again" repenting from his libertine days of wine and women, introduced themselves. After learning I was a convert, they took upon themselves the role of mentorship during my remaining year and a half in high school: giving me rides to the mosque, inviting me to meals, and taking me to hear speakers on Islam.

Our conversations during those occasions would drift from the ever-important *sunnah* of growing a beard to discussing how to annex America to *Dar-ul-Islam*, the realm of Islam. "Mahdi," the American convert, related his experience of his family rejecting his conversion, while telling me that my family's willingness to accept my conversion meant that they were prime recruiting material for the *deen*. Mahdi thought I had the potential to study abroad and become a Muslim scholar, so he encouraged such a course.[23] "All Americans would become Muslims if only they had ten good Muslim scholars to teach the faith correctly." My mentors encouraged me to adopt visible signs of Islam, stating that it aided *da'wa* and was *sunnah* to distinguish oneself from the unbelievers in appearance. To this end, "'Abd-us-salaam," the North African, gave me a white *kufi*.

The day after the Dhahran bombing of a U.S. airbase, I remember wearing the *kufi* on the bus to downtown to visit 'Abd-us-salaam and Mahdi at the Oriental rug shop they managed, self-consciously wondering if anyone was staring. Then it hit me. Whenever I wore a *kufi* in public, most non-Muslims would think it was a yarmulke. Good thing the confusion was limited to them, because as I became more familiarized with the *masjid* and its inhabitants, there were occasions when I was confronted with anti-Semitism that made me uncomfortable: e.g., finding a radical publication in the *masjid*'s foyer containing cockamamie theories equivalent to or perhaps derived from a white supremacist's ranting on "Zionist-occupied government," and several times hearing less than flattering remarks about the *Yahood* during Friday *khutbah* sermons or during social occasions.[24] Yet at the same time I was bothered by what was barely concealed, I harbored indignation at Zionism, buying into the theory that defensive military action against Israel was justified because it was a colonial oppressor (while rejecting suicide bombers on the Islamic grounds that it was an attack against civilians and a suicidal act).

When I spoke with Mahdi and ʿAbdus-salaam that day, lounging around rugs more expensive than my car, I asked them what they thought about the killing of American military personnel in Saudi Arabia. Mahdi the *hajji* gave the *Allahu Akbar* cheer in so many words—he felt it was a justified military attack. ʿAbdus-salaam demurred in his thick accent, "No brother, you gotta-to try to show them Islam." On previous occasions, Mahdi expressed the desire to kill one of the *munafeeq* hypocrite autocrats ruling in the Muslim world, even if—or perhaps because—it would give him martyrdom. In spite of the crazed fanatic you may imagine, Mahdi was on the whole personable and above average in intelligence. I didn't see a remote chance for his rhetoric to be translated into action, because he was saddled with a wife and baby and never came across as a military or gun nut. But between the two choices offered by ʿAbdus-salaam and Mahdi, I thought that Mahdi had the more correct Islamic interpretation, if one accepted the scapegoat premise that the U.S. government was the force of oppression responsible for most of the miserable state of the Muslim world. At the same time, my conscience quibbled with the thought that foot soldiers should perish for the sins of the generals. I questioned my consistency on the morality and immorality of violence: How could I think the slaughter of retreating Iraqi troops (having perhaps more hatred for Saddam Hussein than any American patriot) was immoral and then turn around and say that a sneak attack in an undeclared war against presumably low-level American airmen was any more moral?

Thankfully, I was not so completely impressionable or wholly convinced that I lapped up every extremist belief that came my way. Not that my armchair extremism didn't have jagged edges. I vacillated on the question of how best to deal with *ash-Shaytan al-Akbar*, while having little compunction in siding with the Arabs on *ash-Shaytan al-Asghar*. I floated the idea of an American Islamic party, to promote Islamic principles of governance, rather than envisioning any military confrontation with the United States. While formulating the party platform I had the problem of selecting model examples for Islamic principles. The "Islamophobic" American news media cunningly managed to hide the success stories of the modern Islamist project. Instead, they would publish stories about barbarian buttheads clamoring for legalized female genital mutilation in Egypt, slashing throats in Algeria, eye gouging in Afghanistan, and engaging in modern-day slavery in Africa.

"Culture not religion . . . un-Islamic . . . Allah will punish the unjust. . . ." I could explain away some of the nauseating injustices done in Islam's name and just plain ignore how the sexual strictures of Islam contributed in part to the continuation of pre-Islamic customs like clitoridectomy. But then there were some cases where I would know the direct origin of the justifications: the Koran and Sunnah, the way of life of the supposed exemplar of humanity. In a *da'wag*anda brochure on the perfect criminal justice of Islam, a Dr. Islam Akbar or a Mrs. Muslimah Kamela could spin whatever rationalization they wanted for slicing off hands and feet, and then proclaim such mutilation to be a necessary step in achieving a crime-free Muslim utopia. Though I could understand that stealing would have a greater detrimental influence in a society where each of its members struggles to obtain his basic needs, limb chopping didn't seem all that sensible to import to the West. A person doesn't face starvation if a crook makes off with an expensive home entertainment system, he faces a missed Seinfeld rerun. And yet the penalty for theft was just the tip of the sand dune. There were plenty more tricky questions in store for my conscience to contend with, if I didn't bury them in the sands of denial. I could not accept without lingering repugnance many of the teachings of the *ahadith*, such as the de facto permissibility of raping enemy women captured by Muslim forces in a *jihad*.[25]

Left to my own devices to defend the indefensible, I think now that I would have left Islam within a few short months, if it weren't for the social reinforcement of my new "brothers and sisters" and the adversarial feedback that my less-than-conciliatory remarks generated at school. If I were going to be voted "most likely to blow up a large building" in the yearbook, I might as well oblige by demolishing the perversions of Christianity and the fascism of the American government. I needed an intellectual distraction, because one surety of an American convert to Islam is that both non-Muslims and Muslims will ask him to explain his reasons for conversion. To Muslims, my usual answer was, "It just made sense to me," with a tinge of discomfort at not being able to expound upon those reasons to the extent that the Dalai Lama would convert to Islam upon hearing them. To non-Muslims, I parroted the latest astounding proofs peddled by *da'wag*andists like Ahmed Deedat and Maurice Baucaille: "Muhammad is mentioned right there in the very Bible the Jews and Christians tampered with!" "The Koran coincides perfectly with science, whereas the Bible is flush full of errors. The Koran contains the blueprint for cold fusion, interstellar space travel, and the Pet Rock! The mother of the books, the mother of invention."

Justifying belief in Islam, whether to myself or others, made me aware of the doubt that the Koran denies just a few *ayaat* into its pages: "This is the Book; In it is guidance sure, without doubt, to those who fear Allah" (II.2). Just a month after my conversion, I was again in the Islam section of the library, when I spotted a new addition to the collection: *Why I Am Not a Muslim*.[26] Under the premise that Islam and reality could not contradict and that any opponent of Islam could be shown to be factually or interpretively incorrect, I checked out the book. I didn't finish half of it. I remember being upset for a good while, half-wondering if I had made a mistake in converting to what might be a palpable lie. Not to be deterred, I searched the Internet for an antidote to soothe the inner zealot, which came in the guise of a review by an academically credentialed American convert who dismissed the book in a largely ad hominem attack as the work of a bitter ex-Muslim relying upon bigoted orientalists. But in my searches of the Internet I found that *Shaytaan* the accursed had yet more fronts from which to lead astray, such as a list of Koranic contradictions on a Christian missionary Web site. I created a Web site to counter the missionaries via the "cut 'n' paste" *Sunnah*,[27] but in the end I just slipped into the lazy logic of an intellectually defeated zealot. The missionaries were just evil or full of anti-Muslim hatred—and saying so was enough of a refutation.

As I was nearing the end of high school, sifting through stacks of college brochures, I was also considering what career I wanted. My favorite subject in high school was biology, so I envisioned myself as a research biologist of some variety. The more I read about Muslim reactions to the theory of evolution, the more I envisioned myself making a career out of reconciling science with Islam. Though I never fully doubted evolution, the Sunni Muslim views on the subject that I came across usually repudiated it. On one Web site of a Muslim association at a British university, the webmaster had posted wholesale a series of antievolution articles written by a Christian creationist. When I researched it further, the only article I found suggesting the complementary nature of human evolution and Islam was written by a member of the Ahmadiyya, a "heretical" sect.

I was capable of my own heresies. Writing my college application essay, I expressed the naive *Mutazili* hope that my philosophy (science) and religion could be reconciled. Responding to a critic I referenced who said that Islam had not reconciled with the theory of evolution, I went into my trademark style of tirade:

> [I]t would be hilarious if this stupid 17 year old actually figured out that there are very interesting statements in the Qur'an which talk about Allah being able to create his creatures in whatever form Allah wishes (like dinosaurs, aliens, jinn, monerans, whatever). It would also be a very comical occasion if this same 17 year old figured out that Adam (*'alai his salaam*) and Eve might have just been the first two homo sapiens to have been given free will and human souls. Another fascinating event would be if this same 17 year old decided to be open to many different theories of evolution over the past few billion years rather than just blindly accepting natural selection as the only mechanism for it.

Needless to say, I sometimes wonder if the admissions committee admitted me for the sheer entertainment value of the kook theories they figured I might spout on campus. "We have to let him in, Dr. Usuli needs a lab assistant to help with the Genii (*Jinn*) Genome Project!" Alas, unfortunately I cannot say today that I am on the verge of perfecting a Genii cloning technique, nor have I discovered the fossilized remains of a rapacious *kafirsaurus* or *mushrikodactyl* through a dig funded by the Islamic Paleontology Association.[28] My cryptozoology/parapsychology career was cut short soon after I started my freshman year.

I had decided to go to a private out-of-state university based on my usual decision-making criterion—the relative level of anxiety it provoked. I had already hung out with some members of the Muslim Students Association during a preview weekend, and from that experience I was ecstatic about meeting Muslim thinkers my own age. When I came to the university, I largely forgot about Mahdi and 'Abdus-salaam and the handful of other, mostly older Muslims I had met. I simply did not feel any deep friendship, though I had spent a great deal of time with them. I was also annoyed at Mahdi for repeatedly pointing out before I left that it would be difficult for me to afford the university I had selected while avoiding usury: "It must be tough." I had difficulty thinking of any other options that I could find acceptable, and so contrary to the mandates of the Koran I went ahead and took out the loans I needed to be able to go to school. When I saw the Mercedes and Audis of some of my fellow Muslim students, I tried to beg an exemption from Allah on the grounds that I didn't think the best education should be limited to the children of doctors or millionaires.

Legitimate or not, I started with the intention of studying neurobiology *fi-sabil-lillah*, only to find out within a week I didn't have the stomach or the brains for the level of work demanded in my science and math classes. I changed my major to indecision, all the while redoubling my efforts in my first-year Arabic class, which I already had a leg up on because I had learned the alphabet and some rudimentary grammar on my own during high school. My pronunciation of Arabic could only get better; once when I tried to speak Arabic in full guttural glory back home, an Algerian "brother" laughed in my face and told me I sounded like Hitler. By the end of my freshman year, I could understand patches of the Friday *khutbah* in Arabic, and decipher the meaning of portions of the Koran. My fitful efforts to download the entire Koran into my brain, however, met with meager success, as I found it dull to read the same *ayaat* over and over again. Rather than focus on rote memorization, I believed it more important to understand what I was reading.

Except maybe for *al-'arabiyya*, schooling was secondary in importance to me in comparison to the friends I made. Although I realize it would be a relatively bland experience for those who aren't social retards, for the first time in my teenage life I had what would be considered a halfway normal social life of going out to restaurants and movies with a circle of friends on the weekends. Sure, if our *iftar* parties ever got wild 'n' crazy, it'd be because we'd chugged kegs of Mountain Dew. And if we got to the part in the R-rated movie where the actress flashed her breasts, we might avert our eyes and say "*Aghstafirullah*," or, if we were a second too late, "*Subhana Allah*."[29] But for an outwardly stolid hermit, the idea of having simple fun was sheer *wahy*. It was a long-overdue revelation and a relief that life could be lived without needing to assign a purpose or goal to every action beyond enjoyment.

Despite this discovery, my rigid fixation on academic success, coupled with an inability to adapt intelligently to college life, began to wear on my health and mental well-being. I did not adequately prepare to handle the stress of going to one of the toughest universities in the nation by taking practical measures such as exercising regularly or becoming organized. I just thought it would be another of Allah's tests that I'd endure. Each new week, my ego took a flogging at the whip of tests, homework, TAs, and the discussion groups where every time I spoke up, I embarrassed myself (the whipping perhaps a penalty from Allah—a result of his omniscient foreknowledge that I'd take to drink once I started to believe my qualifications and ambition were third-rate). My mood took a nosedive as my sleep schedule became chaotic and I consumed large amounts of sugar and caffeine. The rest of my diet consisted of what I like to call carbo-con-queso—all cheese and all carbohydrates, all the time. There was no *halaal* meat in the dorm cafeteria to give greater balance, so I pigged out whenever I went to a restaurant with *halaal* food in a manner kosher only for tipping the scales. Ramadan only made my situation worse, because I have a susceptibility to migraines and more often than not I would be in agony beyond a growling stomach right around the breaking of the fast.

In an attempt to relieve some of my stress, headaches, and fatigue, I downed plenty a bottle of ibuprofen. When things really seemed bad, I bowed down to take my tranquilizer. Though I had prayed all five prayers every day since I had become a Muslim, in times of greater distress, I would often pray the extra individual prayer after the congregational *salat*. Sometimes, I would pray to Mr. Al Lah for an hour or two in a solitary, quiet room, my forehead pressed against a prayer rug, tears welling in my eyes. Similar to the calming rituals of an individual with obsessive-compulsive disorder, my mind sought relief in prostrating before an unseen benefactor.

Though I prayed for world peace and the usual yada yada, I prayed with more fervor for a selfish object: "*Allahumma*, come on man, you owe me. Somehow make this non-Muslim woman that I spend every walking thought about turn out to be as great as I imagine, and then if you could bring her to Islam, and then I don't know, make her see past this exterior to fall madly in love with me, well, that'd be swell." Yes, I was then well on my way to becoming the expert on psychokinetic courtship that I am today. My expert analysis: believing in magic if you don't have the luxury of extroversion, money, or looks will make you go psycho—or worse, look like a psycho—even if it turns out that the object of your wanton infatuation may not have even been a remotely good fit to begin with.

Grasping with greater recognition that what I did or I did not do then might have reverberations for the rest of my years, whether it be love, friendship, family, or career, near the end of my freshman year I was reexamining my aspirations and meditating upon the possible effects of my choices to date. I envisioned life if I followed the path of marrying the pious Muslimah. I followed the trail of stinky diapers, familial and financial responsibilities, indoctrination/ moral upbringing, and I saw at the end of this life I created a theological dilemma: Was it in any way moral to have children if there was a possibility that by existing they could go astray and suffer eternal torment? I was roaming hypothetical land, wondering if perhaps the only reason I would try to get the hookup that many of my friends anticipated for themselves was because I was too gutless to pursue who and what I wanted, feigning deep spiritual reasons for my cowardice.

In the summer before what was supposed to be my second year of college, grimness enveloped my vision. I came home broke, and very much needed to work and raise money. However much my parents pestered me, I could not summon the strength to find work. I slept as much as possible, often waking up each afternoon at one or two o'clock. When I couldn't be distracted by escapism, my waking thoughts were dominated by the emotional dilemmas my conversion to Islam generated. I pretended I was writing a roman à clef novel whose protagonist successfully navigated those very same dilemmas—only I couldn't figure out how. My family and the other non-Muslims I cared about were not going to convert to Islam by my giving them the Koran or sets of brochures proclaiming Islam's blanket superiority. I wasn't going to turn into a superhero, becoming the model son who, so the theory went, they would completely attribute to the influence of Islam. They appeared perfectly content with their religious beliefs, and I felt guilty about the lack of "live and let live" reciprocity inherent in shunning traditional family holidays like Christmas and Easter because of their Trinitarian roots.

One day during the summer, I was staying with relatives who lived a fair distance away on a farm. My mom was coming with my siblings to pick me up, but she was late, and various unpleasant scenarios entered my head as hours passed and we hadn't got a phone call, and I couldn't reach her cell phone. I watched cable with unease, until my aunt got a call from another of my aunts: "They've been in an accident, but they're okay." Our piece of crap American car crapped out right on the busy highway, and my mom couldn't pull over to the side of the road because of the volume and speed of traffic. They were in terror for a few moments, because they realized the traffic wasn't slowing behind them. A pickup truck slammed into the back bumper, pulverizing the trunk of the car and partially crunching the back seats. "*Alhamdullilah,*" praise be to Allah, they all got by with minor scratches.

That night, staying in the farm's guest house, I began to face the issues I had tried to duck because they seemed to offer no satisfactory reconciliation with the Koran and Sunnah. I imagined the alternative scenario, if it had been not a pickup truck but a Mac truck. Was I to believe that for mouthing the Apostle's Creed, my own mother would burn in hellfire for eternity just because it says so in some revered fourteen-hundred-year-old book? That a humorless, woman-beating Taliban idiot pronounces the proper magic formula of "*la ilaha illallah*" and believes it, and Allah's ticket counter issues admittance to paradise? I could not accept belief in such a God. There's no crueler wager than Pascal's. None more stupid, either.

My practice of Islam began to degrade while I sought a gentler, more humane interpretation that would not condemn human beings to an eternity of torture. I associated an "out" for my predicament in becoming a Sufi, as I vaguely recalled some Sufis equating hell with a metaphorical place of purification that would eventually be free of inhabitants. The fatal flaw in this attempt at an interpretational shift was that not one second of the sanctified tortures described in the Koran would be remotely humane. The project was akin to the different bibles that have come out attempting to sanitize or make more palatable any sexism or retrograde ideas within their pages. The new, sanitized version of the Koran would simply have the parenthetical "metaphorically speaking, of course" suffixed to every iteration of threats of hellfire or inhumane temporal punishments like amputation and crucifixion.

My hermeneutic quest was preempted by a *khutbah* I heard that summer. When the *imam* made reference to the *hadith* that said the prophet Adam was sixty cubits tall, with no hint of suppressed amusement, a profane voice descended upon me: "This is all fucking absurd." It was absurd that I even had to tell myself after two and a half years that it was absurd. It was absurd that I would question my judgment of absurdity based on another tall tale that there was an invisible creature whose sole purpose of existing was to try whisper subliminal advertisements for evil.[30] It was absurd to waste untold hours seeking the profoundest wisdom in a brier patch of overrated scribbling that I would have to spend the rest of my life making excuses for thanks to its ethical and intellectual bankruptcy: "Oh you who believe! Beware. *Shaytaan* loves dominoes and houses of cards."

I never returned to that *masjid* or any *masjid* again. But indicative of why religion is so successful at persisting, despite my melancholy state, I still, incredibly, harbored hope that some heresy would save me from having to stare the universe straight in its nonface. Brand X Islam with superdeluxe stain-fighting action could still come to the rescue. Only problem: I couldn't think of a Brand X I could trust. The closest competition was the Submitters, a newfangled anti-*hadith* sect, but I had spotted back when I was a Sunni the trick behind the numerological shell games they liked to say proved the Koran's divine origin.

When I came back for my sophomore year, I couldn't concentrate very long on any academic task beyond the difficulty level of reading the funny pages. Instead of going to classes, some days I would sit on a park bench and imagine dying or killing myself. I knew from the first week that things could not continue as they were, but I was at a loss to do much of anything. It was no matter, as random events plotted my course. Little more than a month after I returned, I dropped out of college, dropped out of Islam, said my goodbyes, and skipped town.

My apostasy at first did not feel like in measure a liberation, but rather a betrayal of the community and a descent into nothingness. I felt extreme guilt at the hospitality I enjoyed and the friendships I had forged. I felt like my existence was a contagion and, in a reverse of the movie *It's a Wonderful Life*, that it would have been *better* for all involved that I never had lived. My delusion dissipated over time, as I realized I wasn't equally close to everyone in the community and that even if they were affected in the least, I hadn't met anyone as hypersensitive as me whose hurt would likely last for long, or who would be isolated in any way by my leaving. In a reflection of the absolutist thinking that helped propel me into zealotry in the first place, I felt if I had so much as inflicted an ounce of hurt on any human being, I merited a place in hell whether it existed or not.

Freedom from religion doesn't necessitate individual happiness or success anymore than a religion guarantees it. In the half decade since I cast Islam aside, my life as a whole hasn't metamorphosed drastically for the better. After a sequence of unsuccessful pill regimens and dealing with a series of three therapists and three psychiatrists, I've given up on mental-health experts. I keep melancholy at bay by lowering my ambition and stress levels. I pay homage to the reality of the physical mind by trying to get eight hours of sleep and exercising three times a week. I have a handful of friends, and those I see rarely. I am a recluse. The few dates I've gone on went nowhere, and I haven't even tried for a long while. I've never had a romantic relationship even though, or perhaps because, I idealize it to be one of the greatest goods. What could've been, if the "younguns" I observe at theaters and restaurants are any indication, the best of times is beyond half spent, and if I think about where I'm at, instead of watching cable, reading a book, or surfing the Internet, I sometimes think about making a final exeunt.

On the other hand, after half a decade of *kufr*, I have been able to analyze with greater candor what might be the causes of my despair. There is no prefabricated answer I have to accept, no "Don't pop a Prozac, just dream of the gardens of *jannah*. Your struggles are all a test. 'Testing. 1. 2. 3. This is just a test.'" Although, I've acknowledged it two or three times prior to this year, each time letting it drift from my attention, the primary contributor to my long-term melancholy is my avoidant personality. I say "could be," because there is a danger in treating fickle categories as immutable, rather than as a starting point to analyzing whether one's behavior patterns are self-detrimental. If my behavior didn't cause me or anyone else the degree of grief it has, then regardless of whether the psychiatrists had "thunk" a standardized label for it, that label would then be best ignored.

Although if you asked me in the days of *iman* why I was Muslim, I would give you the proximate causes for my conversion wrapped in layers of emotive homilies and specious argumentation, I have found the ultimate cause in my most pronounced deficit—I simply find it hard to relate to people. Eric Hoffer in the book *The True Believer* summed up the persistence of my religiomania well: "The burning conviction that we have a holy duty toward others is often a way of attaching our drowning selves to a passing raft . . . take away our holy duties and you leave our lives puny and meaningless."[31]

I see no greater confirmation of this aphorism than when I once declared my love of becoming an automaton, ruled exclusively by calcified dictates: "One aspect of Islam that I love is that it is not a compartmentalized religion. If you are a Muslim, you have to strive to be a Muslim twenty-four hours a day, seven days a week in what you say, do, and think. Islam is not something that is secondary in life, but primary and central to the believers, the only reason for living."

Given these dour and embarrassing confessions, I must confess to the one salvation I gained by leaving Islam and religion—unconstrained laughter. Fear may have created the gods, but laughter can banish them. Not that Allah lacks a sense of humor. It's just that, speaking as a reviewer, Allah's dark sense of humor in the Koran was too sadistic for my taste. Sometimes I imagine that if Allah could perhaps tone down that overused *Shar'iah* routine, maybe relax a bit more on stage when the jokes on him or he's being heckled, trash all of his mean jokes on the *kufaar* and women, there would be more comedy in the world and less tragedy.

Notes

    1. *Allahu 'Alim*—Allah knows (best). Corollary: people don't know jack squat.

    2. The Californian Talib—John Walker Lindh

    3. *shahadah*—witness/testimony, the first pillar of Islam, the act of saying "I bear witness there is no God but Allah, and Muhammad is his Messenger" in front of at least two Muslims. It's a remarkable feat; bearing witness to things you have no manner of witnessing.

    4. *Shaytan*—Allah's fall guy, Satan.

    5. "The answer of the Believers, when summoned to Allah and His Messenger, in order that He may judge between them, is no other than this: they say, 'We hear and we obey': it is such as these that will attain felicity" (XXIV.51).

    6. Some believermobile out there probably has "Islam is the solution" plastered on the bumper. If there were greater honesty, it would also append "Or else."

Some Zanadiqa (atheists) were brought to ʿAli and he burnt them. The news of this event, reached Ibn ʿAbbas who said, "If I had been in his place, I would not have burnt them, as Allah's Apostle forbade it, saying, 'Do not punish anybody with Allah's punishment (fire).' I would have killed them according to the statement of Allah's Apostle, 'Whoever changed his Islamic religion, then kill him.'"

al-Bukhārī, vol. 9, book 84, of *Ṣaḥīḥ* (New Delhi: Kitab Bharan, 1987), Hadith no. 57, p. 45.

7. *Afikomen*

8. John Ashcroft, the U.S. attorney general who considers dancing a sin.

9. *Kufi*—Muslim equivalent of a yarmulke. Old hat.

10. *Wuduʾ*—the ritual washing that purifies for prayer.

11. *Tu quoque*—you too. Nanny-nanny boo-boo.

12. Ramsey Clark, *The Fire This Time: U.S. War Crimes in the Gulf* (New York: Thunder's Mouth Press, 1992).

13. *shirk*—in Islam, the sin of worshipping anything other than Allah, who still has his cosmic self-esteem issues to work out.

14. *Daʾwa*—the call to Islam, Muslim proselytizing. I just picture a vendor at a sporting event, "Get your faith here, faith here, good in the here and hereafter! Just like Christianity, except better! Red hots! Avoid the red hots! Malcolm X, the slugger against injustice, endorses our fine, 100 percent pure product. Along with the countless millions rushing to revert to the fastest growing belief, you can too!" The vendor always waxes over the no-returns policy.

15. *ummah*—community. The Koran says that Muhammad's *ummah* is da' best *ummah*.

16. *takbir*—saying "Allahu Akbar!" Arabic for Allah is da' bomb.

17. *musalluh*—place of prayer.

18. *aqeedah*—set of beliefs. What must be swallowed to gain entrance to Club Islam. The books. The prophets. The angels. The day of judgment. Burraq the flying horse.

19. *halaal*—permitted.

20. Arabic for "Supercalifragilisticexpialidocious." Polytheism is simply quite atrocious.

21. *jahiliyya*—the pre-Islamic days of ignorance, e.g., the ignorant American disbelievers going to the moon, curing polio, synthesizing antibiotics.

22. *wali*—Allah's buddy. Symptomatic of needing an imaginary friend at age sixteen.

23. I got the application for *al-Azhar* in Cairo, but never filled it out because the mangled English made me suspicious of the scholarly level of the institution.

24. One Muslim told me one reason he knew Islam was the truth was because Muslims never had a Holocaust. Perhaps he never heard of the Mongols. Apparently, it's off to mass-murderville if you're not in God's select group of favorites.

25. The Prophet doesn't condemn raping captive women, but rather casts disfavor on a primitive form of birth control!

Narrated Ibn Muhairiz: "I entered the Mosque and saw Abu Said Al-Khudri and sat beside him and asked him about Al-Azl (i.e., coitus interruptus). Abu Said

said, 'We went out with Allah's Apostle for the Ghazwa of Banu Al-Mustaliq and we received captives from among the Arab captives and we desired women and celibacy became hard on us and we loved to do coitus interruptus. So when we intended to do coitus interrupt us, we said, "How can we do coitus interruptus before asking Allah's Apostle who is present among us?" We asked (him) about it and he said, "It is better for you not to do so, for if any soul (till the Day of Resurrection) is predestined to exist, it will exist." ' "

al-Bukhārī, vol. 5, book 59, of *Ṣaḥīḥ* (New Delhi: Kitab Bharan, 1987), Hadith no. 57, p. 317.

26. Ibn Warraq, *Why I Am Not a Muslim* (Amherst, N.Y.: Prometheus Books, 1995).

27. The number of small Muslim Web sites consisting largely of articles cut and pasted from other Muslim Web sites leads me to believe there is a *hadith* somewhere that goes like so: "Narrated Abu Huraira: 'The Prophet, SAWS said that every true believer with AOL access should post a crappy Web site and cut and paste articles reminding of how great Islam is. Each digital *jihad* is greater in Allah's sight than a thousand years of fasting near the North Pole.'"

28. Allah doesn't directly mention it in the Koran, but he threw the asteroid at the dino-sinners because they disobeyed their prophet Barney the Purple One *ʿalaihis-salaam.*

29. *Aghstafirullah*—forgive me Allah; *Subhana Allah*—glory be to Allah

30. On second thought, it's not totally implausible. Maybe Iblis is related to Joe Camel.

31. Eric Hoffer. *The True Believer: Thoughts on the Nature of Mass Movements* (New York: Harper Perennial Library, 2002), pp. 14–15.

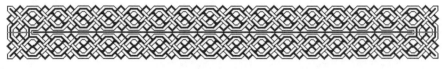

APPENDICES

A

ISLAM ON TRIAL
The Textual Evidence

MUHAMMAD AND HIS COMPANIONS

Muhammad's Cruelty

When some people from the tribe of Ukl who had reverted from Islam and killed a shepherd of camels were captured, Muhammad ordered that their hands and legs be cut off, and that their eyes be branded with heated pieces of iron, and that their cut hands and legs not be cauterized till they die.

Source: al-Bukhārī, *The Book of the Punishment of Those Who Wage War against Allah and His Messenger*, trans. M. Muhsin Khan, vol. 8, book 82 of *Sāḥīḥ* (New Delhi: Kitab Bhavan, 1987, Hadith no. 794, pp. 519–20).

A similar story is told about some men of Qays of Kubba of Bajila in Ibn Isḥāq's biography of the Prophet.

Source: Ibn Isḥāq, *The Life of Muhammad*, trans A. Guillaume (1955; reprint, Oxford: Oxford University Press, 1987), pp. 677–78.

Muhammad, the Prophet, orders the torture of a prisoner in order to discover the whereabouts of some hidden treasure. "Torture him until you extract it from him," Muhammad is quoted as saying.

Sources: Ibn Hisham, *al-Sīra al-Nabawiyya* (Cairo, 1955), vol. 2, pp. 328–38; Ibn Isḥāq, *The Life of Muhammad*, trans. A. Guillaume (1955; reprint, Oxford: Oxford University Press, 1987), p. 515; al-Ṭabarī, *The Victory of Islam*, trans. Michael Fishbein, vol. 8 of *The History of al-Ṭabarī* (Albany: State University of New York Press, 1997), pp. 122–23.

Muhammad revives the cruel practice of stoning to death for adultery.

Sources: Ibn Isḥāq, *The Life of Muhammad*, trans A. Guillaume (1955; reprint, Oxford: Oxford University Press, 1987) pp. 266–67; al-Bukhārī, *The Book of* Nikah *(Wedlock)*, trans. M. Muhsin Khan, vol. 7, book 62 of *Ṣaḥīḥ* (New Delhi: Kitab Bhavan, 1987), Hadith no. 195, p. 147.

> There came to him (Muhammad), a woman from Ghamid and said: Allah's Messenger, I have committed adultery, so purify me. He (the Holy Prophet) turned her away. On the following day she said: . . . By Allah, I have become pregnant. He said: Well if you insist upon it, then go away until you give birth to (the child). When she was delivered she came with the child (wrapped) in a rag and said: Here is the child whom I have given birth to. He said: Go away and suckle him until you wean him. When she had weaned him, she came to him (the Holy Prophet) with the child who was holding a piece of bread in his hand. She said: Allah's Apostle, here is he as I have weaned him and he eats food. He (the Holy Prophet) entrusted the child to one of the Muslims and then pronounced punishment. And she was put in a ditch up to her chest and he commanded people and they stoned her. Khalid b. Walid came forward with a stone which he flung at her head, and there spurted blood on the face of Khalid and so he abused her. . . . [Muhammad impressed by her repentance] prayed over her and she was buried.

Source: Muslim, *Kitab al-Hudud*, trans. Abdul Hamid Siddiqi, vol. 3, book 682 of *Ṣaḥīḥ* (New Delhi: Kitab Bhavan, 1997), Hadith no. 4206, pp. 916–17.

Crushing the head of a murderer between two stones.

Source: al-Bukhārī, *The Book of* Nikah *(Wedlock)*, trans. M. Muhsin Khan, vol. 7, book 62 of *Ṣaḥīḥ* (New Delhi: Kitab Bhavan, 1987) Hadith no. 216, pp. 165–66.

Islam, A Religion of Fear: Torture in the Grave:

> Aisha reported: There came to me two old women from the old Jewesses of Medina and said: The people of the grave are tormented in their graves. I contradicted them and I did not deem it proper to testify them. They went away and the Messenger of Allh (may peace be upon him) came to me and I said to him: Messenger of Allah! there came to me two old women from the old Jewesses of

Medina and asserted that the people of the graves would be tormented therein. He (the Prophet) said: They told the truth; they would be tormented (so much) that the animals would listen to it. She ('Aisha) said: Never did I see him (the Holy Prophet) afterwards but seeking refuge from the torment of the grave in prayer.

Source: Muslim, *Kitab al-Salat*, trans. Abdul Hamid Siddiqi, vol. 4, book 218 of *Ṣaḥīḥ* (New Delhi: Kitab Bhavan, 1997), Hadith no. 1214, p. 290.

Muhammad's Hatred of the Jews

"Kill any Jews that falls into your power," said the Prophet. (p. 369).

The killing of Ibn Sunayna,and its admiration leading someone to convert to Islam (ibid.).

The killing of Sallam ibn Abu'l-Huqayq (pp. 482-483)

The assassination of Ka'b b. al-Ashraf, who wrote verses against Muhammad (pp. 364-69).

The raid against the Jewish tribe of the Banu'l-Nadir and their banishment (437–45).

The extermination of the Banu Qurayza, between six hundred and eight hundred men (pp. 461–69).

The killing of al-Yusayr (pp. 665–66).

Source: [8] Ibn Isḥaq, *The Life of Muhammad*, trans. A Guillaume (1955; reprint, Oxford: Oxford University Press, 1987). Ibn Isḥāq, a Muslim historian, is our earliest source for the life of Muhammad in Arabic.

"Then occurred the *sariyyah* (raid) of Salim Ibn Umayr al-Amri against Abu Afak, the Jew, in (the month of) Shawwal in the beginning of the twentieth month from the *hijrah* (immigration from Mecca to Medina in 622 C.E.) of the Apostle of Allah. Abu Afak, was from Banu Amr Ibn Awf, and was an old man who had attained the age of 120. He was a Jew, and used to instigate the people against the Apostle of Allah, and composed (satirical) verses (about Muhammad).

Salim Ibn Umayr, who was one of the great weepers and who had participated in Badr, said, "I take a vow that I shall either kill Abu Afak or die before him." He waited for an opportunity until a hot night came, and Abu Afak slept in an open place. Salim Ibn Umayr knew it, so he placed the sword on his liver and pressed it till it reached his bed. The enemy of Allah screamed and the people who were his followers, rushed to him, took him to his house and interred him.

Source: Sa'd, *Kitab al-Ṭabaqāt al Kabīr*, trans. S. M. Haq (New Delhi: Kitab Bhavan, 1972), vol. 1, p. 32.

Bani An-Nadir and Bani Quraiza fought,[1] so the Prophet (Muhammad) exiled Bani An-Nadir and allowed Bani Quraiza to remain at their places. He then **killed** their men and distributed their women, children and property among the Muslims, but some of them came to the Prophet and he granted them safety, and they embraced Islam. He exiled all the Jews from Medina. They were the Jews of Bani Qainuqa', the tribe of 'Abdullah bin Salam and the Jews of Bani Haritha and all the other Jews of Medina.

> *Source:* al-Bukhārī, *The Book of* al-Maghazi *(Raids),* trans M. Muhsin Khan, vol. 5, book 59 of *Ṣaḥīḥ* (New Delhi: Kitab Bhavan, 1987), Hadith no. 362, p. 241.

Muhammad's Ordering of the Assassinations of His Opponents

The killing of poetess 'Asma' b. Marwan

> *Source:* [12] Ibn Isḥāq, *The Life of Muhammad,* trans. A. Guillaume (1955; reprint, Oxford: Oxford University Press, 1987), p. 675.

The gruesome details of Asma's killing, and the fact of her having her baby by her side are to be found in two other Muslim historians.

> Then (occurred) the *sariyyah* [raid] of Umayr ibn adi Ibn Kharashah al-Khatmi against Asma Bint Marwan, of Banu Umayyah Ibn Zayd, when five nights had remained from the month of Ramadan, in the beginning of the nineteenth month from the hijrah of the apostle of Allah. Asma was the wife of Yazid Ibn Zayd Ibn Hisn al-Khatmi. She used to revile Islam, offend the prophet and instigate the (people) against him. She composed verses. Umayr Ibn Adi came to her in the night and entered her house. Her children were sleeping around her. There was one whom she was suckling. He searched her with his hand because he was blind, and separated the child from her. He thrust his sword in her chest till it pierced up to her back. Then he offered the morning prayers with the prophet at al-Medina. The apostle of Allah said to him: "Have you slain the daughter of Marwan?" He said: "Yes. Is there something more for me to do?" He [Muhammad] said: "No. Two goats will butt together about her. This was the word that was first heard from the apostle of Allah. The apostle of Allah called him Umayr, "basir" (the seeing).

> *Sources:* Ibn Sa'd, *Kitab al-Ṭabaqāt al Kabīr,* trans. S. M. Haq (New Delhi: Kitab Bhavan, 1972), vol. 2, p. 31; see also al-Waqidi, *Muhammed in Medina,* trans. J. Wellhausen (Berlin, 1882), pp. 90 f.

Further cruelty of Muhammad, the Muslims, and the planning of murders of Muhammad's opponents is recounted in al-Ṭabarī's highly respected history, *The History of al-Ṭabarī*:

The death of Umm Qirfah (Fatimah bt. Rabiah b. Badr): "He [One of Muhammad's Commanders] tied her legs with rope and then tied her between two camels until they split her in two. She was a very old woman."

Source: al-Ṭabarī, *The Victory of Islam*, trans. Michael Fishbein, vol. 8 of *The History of al-Ṭabarī* (Albany: State University of New York Press, 1997), p. 96.

Muhammad orders the killing of those of whom he disapproves: "[Muhammad] gave charge concerning a group of men whom he named: he ordered that they should be killed even if they were found under the curtains of the Kaʿbah. Among them was ʿAbdallah b. Saʿd. The Messenger of God ordered that he should be killed only because he had become a Muslim and then had reverted to being a polytheist. . . . Also among them was ʿAbdallah b. Khatal [who] reverted to being a polytheist. He had two singing girls, Fartana and another with her. The two used to sing satire about the Messenger of God; so the latter commanded that the two of them should be killed along with him. Also among them was al-Huwayrith b. Nuqaydh, and Miqyas b. Subabah, ʿIkrimah b. Abi Jahl and Sarah. . . . According to al-Waqidi: the Messenger of God commanded that six men and four women should be killed."

Source: al-Ṭabarī, *The Victory of Islam*, trans. Michael Fishbein, vol. 8 of *The History of al-Ṭabarī* (Albany: State University of New York Press, 1997), pp. 178–81.

Captives killed after the Battle of Badr:

> Then the apostle began his return journey to Medina with the unbelieving prisoners, among whom were ʿUqba b. Abu Muʿayt and al-Nadr b. al-Harith. The apostle carried with him the booty that had been taken from the polytheists and put ʿAbdullah b. Kaʿb in charge of it. . . .
> When the apostle was in al-Safra, al-Nadr was killed by ʿAli. . . . When he was in ʿIrquʾl-Zabya ʿUqba was killed.
> When the apostle ordered him to be killed ʿUqba said, "But who will look after my children, O Muhammad?" "Hell," he said, and al-Ansari killed him.

Source: Ibn Isḥāq, *The Life of Muhammad*, trans. A. Guillaume (1955; reprint, Oxford: Oxford University Press, 1987), p. 308.

Muhammad's Life As a Brigand, Robber, and Plunderer of Caravans

Muhammad "took part personally in twenty-seven raids."

Source: Ibn Isḥāq, *The Life of Muhammad*, trans. A. Guillaume (1955; reprint, Oxford: Oxford University Press, 1987), p. 659.

Allah sanctions booty and terrorism: "When [the Battle] of Badr was over, Allah sent down the whole Sura *Anfal* (eighth sura) about it. With regard to their quarreling about the spoils there came down: VIII.1: 'They will ask you about the spoils, say, the spoils belong to Allah and the apostle, so fear Allah and be at peace with one another, and obey Allah and His apostle if you are believers' " (p. 321).

"The He taught them how to divide the spoil and His judgement about it when He made it lawful to them and said, VIII.41: 'And know that what you take as booty a fifth belongs to Allah and the apostle." (p. 324).

"Muhammad said, 'Booty was made lawful to me as to no prophet before me.' . . . Allah said, 'It is not for any prophet,' i.e., before thee, 'to take prisoners' from his enemies 'until he has made slaughter in the earth,' i.e., slaughtered his enemies until he drives them from the land" (VIII 67–69; pp. 326–27).

Source: Ibn Isḥāq, *The Life of Muhammad*, trans. A. Guillaume (1955; reprint, Oxford: Oxford University Press, 1987), pp. 326–27.

Muhammad's Intolerance of Other Religions

". . . I was told that the last injunction the apostle [Muhammad] gave [before his death] was in his words 'Let not two religions be left in the Arabian peninsula."

Source: Ibn Isḥāq, *The Life of Muhammad*, trans. A. Guillaume (1955; reprint, Oxford: Oxford University Press, 1987), p. 689.

The Apostle of Allah said, "I will certainly expel the Jews and the Christians from Arabia "

Source: Abū Dāwūd, *Sunan* (New Delhi: Kitab Bhavan, 1997), vol. 2, Hadith no. 3024, p. 861.

Muhammad's Attitude toward and Relations with Women

Muhammad's marriage to six-year-old ʿĀʾisha was consummated when she was nine years old, and he was over fifty years old.

Abu Bakr, later (632 C.E.) First Caliph, married his daughter to Muhammad "when she was [only] six years old. . . . ʿĀʾisha states: We came to Medina and Abu Bakr took up quarters in al-Sunh. . . . The Messenger of God came to our house and men and women of the Ansar gathered around him. My mother came to me while I was being swung on a swing between two branches and got me down. Jumaymah, my nurse, took over and wiped my face with some water and started leading me. When I was at the door, she stopped so I could catch my breath. I was then brought [in] while the Messenger of God was sitting on a bed in our house. [My mother] made me sit on his lap and said, 'These are your relatives. May God bless you with them and bless them with you!' Then men and women got up and left. The Messenger of God consumated his marriage to me in my house when I was nine years old."

Source: al-Ṭabarī, *The Last Years of the Prophet*, trans. Ismail Poonwala, vol. 9 of *The History of al-Ṭabarī* (Albany: State University of New York Press, 1990), pp. 130–31.

Narrated 'Aisha: that the Prophet married her when she was six years old and he consummated his marriage when she was nine years old, and then she remained with him for nine years (i.e., till his death).

Source: al-Bukhārī, *The Book of* Nikah *(Wedlock)*, trans. M. Muhsin Khan, vol. 7, book 62 of *Ṣaḥīḥ* (New Delhi: Kitab Bhavan, 1987), Hadith no. 64, p. 50.

Narrated 'Aisha: I used to play with the dolls in the presence of the Prophet, and my girl friends also used to play with me. When Allah's Apostle used to enter (my dwelling place) they used to hide themselves, but the Prophet would call them to join and play with me.

Source: al-Bukhārī, *The Book of Good Manners* (al-Adab), trans. M. Muhsin Khan, vol. 8, book 72 of *Ṣaḥīḥ* (New Delhi: Kitab Bhavan, 1987), Hadith no. 151, p. 95.

*   *   *

Muhammad married thirteen women, consummated his marriage with eleven women, two of whom died before him. Thus at his death, Muhammad left behind nine wives.

Source: Ibn Isḥāq, *The Life of Muhammad*, trans. A. Guillaume (1955; reprint, Oxford: Oxford University Press, 1987), pp. 792–94.

"My father reported to me that the Messenger of God married fifteen women [*sic*] and consummated his marriage with thirteen [*sic*]. He combined eleven at a time and left behind nine."

Source: al-Ṭabarī, *The Last Years of the Prophet*, trans. Ismail Poonwala, vol. 9 of *The History of al-Ṭabarī* (Albany: State University of New York Press, 1990), pp. 126–27; Ibn al-Athir, *Al-Kamil fi al-ta rikh*, ed. C. Tornberg (Beirut: Dar Sadir, 1965–67), vol. 2, p. 307.

Muhammad left behind two concubines at his death.

Source: al-Ṭabarī, *The Last Years of the Prophet*, trans. Ismail Poonwala, vol. 9 of *The History of al-Ṭabarī* (Albany: State University of New York Press, 1990), p. 141.

*   *   *

Muhammad compared women to domestic animals, and gave men permission to beat them.

Source: al-Ṭabarī, *The Last Years of the Prophet*, trans. Ismail Poonwala, vol. 9 of *The History of al-Ṭabarī* (Albany: State University of New York Press, 1990), p. 113.

Muhammad gives permission to husbands to beat their wives, and what is more, a man will not be asked as to why he beat his wife.

Source: Abū Dāwūd, *Sunan* (New Delhi: Kitab Bhavan, 1997), vol. 2, Hadith nos. 2141, 2142, p. 575.

Muhammad said, "the woman is like a rib, If you try to straighten her she will break. So if you want to get benefit from her, do so while she still has some crookedness."

Source: al-Bukhārī, *The Book of* Nikah *(Wedlock)*, trans. M. Muhsin Khan, vol. 7, book 62 of *Ṣaḥīḥ* (New Delhi: Kitab Bhavan, 1987), Hadith no. 113, p. 80.

Muhammad stood at the gates of hell and saw that the majority of those who entered it were women. Why? Because of the women's ungratefulness to men.

Source: al-Bukhārī, *The Book of* Nikah *(Wedlock)*, trans. M. Muhsin Khan, vol. 7, book 62 of *Ṣaḥīḥ* (New Delhi: Kitab Bhavan, 1987), Hadith nos. 124, 125, pp. 94–96.

The same *hadith* is found in: al-Bukhārī, *Sahih*: 29, 304, 1052, 1462, 3241, 5197, 5198, 6449, 6546 (Fath Al-Bari's numbering system); Muslim, *Sahih*: 80, 885, 907, 2737, 2738 (Abd Al-Baqi's numbering system); Al-Tirmidhī, *Sunan*: 635, 2602, 2603, 2613 (Ahmad Shakir's numbering system); Al-Nasā'ī, *Sunan*: 1493, 1575 (Abi Ghuda's numbering system); Ibn Mājah, *Sunan*: 4003 (Abd Al-Baqi's numbering system); Aḥmad, *Musnad*: 2087, 2706, 3364, 2559, 4009, 4027, 4111, 4140, 5321, 6574, 7891, 8645, 14386, 19336, 19351, 19415, 19425, 19480, 19484, 20743, 21729, 26508, 27562, 27567 (Ihya' Al-Turath's numbering system); Malik, *Muwaṭṭa'*: 445 (Muqata' Malik's numbering system); Al-Dārimī, *Sunan* 1007 (Alami and Zarmali's numbering system).

Muhammad said, a wife should never refuse a husband his conjugal rights even if it is on the saddle of a camel, or even on a scorching oven.

Source: '[31] Aynu, *ʿUmdad al-qārī sharhal-Bukhārī* (Cairo, 1308 A.H., Istanbul, 1309–1310 A.H.), vol. 9, p. 484.

Narrated Abu Said Al-Khudri: Once Allah's Apostle went out to the Musalla (to offer the prayer) o 'Id-al-Adha or Al-*Fitr* prayer. Then he passed by the women and said, "O women! Give alms, as I have seen that the majority of the dwellers of Hell-fire were you (women) ." They asked, "Why is it so, O Allah's Apostle?" He replied, "You curse frequently and are ungrateful to your husbands. I have not seen anyone more deficient in intelligence and religion than you. A cautious sensible man could be led astray by some of you." The women asked, "O Allah's Apostle! What is deficient in our intelligence and religion?" He said, "Is not the evidence of two women equal to the witness of one man?" They replied in the affirmative. He said, "This is the deficiency in her intelligence. Isn't it true that a woman can neither pray nor fast during her menses?" The women replied in the affirmative. He said, "This is the deficiency in her religion."

Source: al-Bukhārī, *The Book of Menses*, trans. M. Muhsin Khan, vol. 1, book 6 of *Ṣaḥīḥ* (New Delhi: Kitab Bhavan, 1987), Hadith no. 301, pp. 181–82.

Women, are the greatest calamity: The Prophet said, "After me I have not left any affliction more harmful to men than women."

Source: al-Bukhārī, *The Book of* Nikah *(Wedlock)*, trans. M. Muhsin Khan, vol. 7, book 62 of *Ṣaḥīḥ* (New Delhi: Kitab Bhavan, 1987), Hadith no. 33, p. 22.

Muhammad said, "People who make a woman their ruler will never prosper."

Source: Mishkāt al-Maṣabīḥ, trans. James Robson (Lahore, 1990), book 17, p. 785.

Muhammad's Racism

Abu Al-Darda reported Allah's Messenger (may peace be upon him) as saying: Allah created Adam when He had to create him and He struck his right shoulder and there emitted from it while offspring as if it were white ants. He struck his left shoulder and there emitted from it black offspring as if it were charcoals. He then said (to those who had been emitted) from right (shoulder): For Paradise and I do not mind and then He said to those (who had been emitted) from his left shoulder: They are for Hell and I do not mind."

Source: Mishkāt al-Maṣabīḥ, trans. Abdul Hameed Siddiqi, *Kitab-ul-Qadr* (Book of Destiny) (New Delhi: Kitab Bhavan, 1990), Hadith no. 119, p. 76–77.

"OUT OF CONTEXT"

It is quite common in this context to hear two arguments from Muslims and apologists of Islam: the language argument, and that old standby of crooked, lying politicians, "you have quoted out of context."

Let us look at the language argument first. You are asked aggressively, "Do you know Arabic?" Then you are told triumphantly, "You have to read it in the original Arabic to understand it fully." Western freethinkers and atheists are usually reduced to sullen silence with these Muslim tactics; they indeed become rather coy and self-defensive when it comes to criticism of Islam, feebly complaining, "Who am I to criticize Islam? I do not know any Arabic." And yet these same freethinkers are quite happy to criticize Christianity. How many Western freethinkers and atheists know Hebrew? How many even know what the language of Esra 4:6–8 is? Or in what language the New Testament was written?

Of course, Muslims are also free in their criticism of the Bible and Christianity without knowing a word of Hebrew, Aramaic, or Greek.

You do not need to know Arabic to criticize Islam or the Koran. Paul Kurtz does not know Arabic but he did a great job on Islam in his book *The Transcendental Temptation*.[2] You only need a critical sense, critical thought, and skepticism. Second, there are translations of the Koran, by Muslims themselves, so Muslims cannot claim that there has been deliberate tampering of the text by infidel translators. Third, the majority of Muslims are not Arabs, and are not Arabic speakers. So a majority of Muslims also have to rely on translations. Finally, the language of the Koran is a form of classical Arabic[3] that is totally different from the spoken Arabic of today, so *even Muslim Arabs* have to rely on translations to understand their holy text. Arabic is a Semitic language related to Hebrew and Aramaic, and is no easier and no more difficult to translate than any other language. Of course, there are all sorts of difficulties with the language of the Koran, but these difficulties have been recognized by Muslim scholars themselves. The Koran is indeed a rather opaque text, but it is opaque to everyone. Even Muslim scholars do not understand a fifth of it.

Let us now turn to "You have quoted out of context." This could mean two things: First, the historical context to which the various verses refer, or second, the textual context, the actual place in a particular chapter that the verse quoted comes from. The historical context argument is not available in fact to Muslims, since the Koran is the eternal word of God and is true and valid always. Thus for Muslims themselves there is no historical context. Of course, non-Muslims can legitimately and do avail themselves of the historical or cultural context to argue, for instance, that Islamic culture as a whole is antiwoman. Muslims did contradict themselves when they introduced the notion of *abrogation*, when a historically earlier verse was cancelled by a later one. This idea of abrogation was concocted to deal with the many contradictions in the Koran. What is more, it certainly backfires for those liberal Muslims who wish to give a moderate interpretation to the Koran, since all the verses advocating tolerance (there are some, but not many) have been abrogated by the verses of the sword.

The "Out of Context" Argument Used against Muslims Themselves

Now for textual context. First, of course, this argument could be turned against Muslims themselves. When they produce a verse preaching tolerance we can also say that they have quoted out of context, or, more pertinently (1) that such a verse has been cancelled by a more belligerent and intolerant one; (2) that in the overall context of the Koran and the whole theological construct that we call Islam (i.e., in the widest possible context), the tolerant verses are anomalous, or have no meaning, since Muslim theologians ignored them completely in developing Islamic law; or (3) that the verses do not say what they seem to say.

For instance, after September 11, 2001, many Muslims and apologists of Islam glibly came out with the following Koranic quote to show that Islam and the Koran disapproved of violence and killing: "Whoever killed a human being shall be looked upon as though he had killed all mankind" (V.32).

Unfortunately, these wonderful sounding words are being quoted out of context. Here is the entire quote:

> That was why We laid it down for the Isrealites that whoever killed a human being, except as a punishment for murder or other villainy in the land, shall be looked upon as though he had killed all mankind; and that whoever saved a human life shall be regarded as though he had saved all mankind.
>
> Our apostles brought them veritable proofs: yet it was not long before many of them committed great evils in the land.
>
> Those that make war against God and His apostle and spread disorder shall be put to death or crucified or have their hands and feet cut off on alternate sides, or be banished from the country. (V.32)

The supposedly noble sentiments are in fact a warning to Jews. "Behave, or else" is the message. Far from abjuring violence, these verses aggressively point out that anyone opposing the Prophet will be killed, crucified, mutilated, and banished!

Behind the textual context argument is thus the legitimate suspicion that by quoting only a short passage from the Koran I have somehow distorted its real meaning. I have, so the accusation goes, lifted the offending quote from the chapter in which it was embedded, and hence somehow altered its true sense. What does "context" mean here? Do I have to quote the sentence before and the sentence after the offending passage? Perhaps two sentences before and after? The whole chapter? Ultimately, of course, the entire Koran is the context.

The context, far from helping Muslims get out of difficulties only makes the barbaric principle apparent in the offending quote more obvious, as we have seen from sura V.32, just quoted. Let us take some other examples. Does the Koran say that men have the right to physically beat their wives or not? I say yes and quote the following verses to prove my point: "As for those [women] from whom you fear rebellion, admonish them and banish them to beds apart, and scourge [or beat] them" (IV.34).

This translation comes from a Muslim. Have I somehow distorted the meaning of these lines? Let us have a wider textual context:

> Men have authority over women because God has made the one superior to the other, and because they spend their wealth to maintain them. Good women are obedient. As for those from whom you fear disobedience, admonish them and send them to beds apart and beat them. Then if they obey you, take no further action against them. God is high, supreme. (IV.34)

If anything, the wider textual context makes things worse for those apologists of Islam who wish to minimize the mysogyny of the Koran. The oppression of women has divine sanction, women must obey God and their men, who have divine authorization to scourge them. One Muslim translator, Yusuf Ali, clearly disturbed by this verse adds the word "lightly" in brackets after "beat." even though there is no "lightly" in the original Arabic. An objective reading of the entire Koran (that is, the total context) makes grim reading as far as the position of women is concerned.

Finally, of course, many of the verses that we quote advocating killing of unbelievers were taken by Muslims themselves to develop the theory of *jihad*. Muslim scholars themselves referred to suras VIII.67, 39; and II.216 to justify holy war. Again, the context makes it clear that it is the battle field that is being referred to, and not some absurd moral struggle; these early Muslims were warriors after booty, land, and women—not some existential heroes from the pages of Albert Camus or Jean-Paul Sartre.

Let us take another example. Here I have tried to use where possible translations by Muslims or Arabophone scholars, to avoid the accusation of using infidel translations. However, many Muslim translators have a tendency to soften the harshness of the original Arabic, particularly in translating the Arabic word *jahada*, for example, sura IX.73. Maulana Muhammad Ali, of the Ahmadiyyah sect, translates this passage as: "O Prophet, strive hard against the disbelievers and the hypocrites and be firm against them. And their abode is hell, and evil is the destination." In a footnote of an apologetic nature, Muhammad Ali rules out the meaning "fighting" for *jahada*.

However, in his Penguin translation the Iraqi scholar Dawood renders this passge as: "Prophet, make war on the unbelievers and the hypocrites and deal rigorously with them. Hell shall be their home: an evil fate."

How do we settle the meaning of this verse? The whole context of sura IX indeed makes it clear that "make war" in the literal and not some metaphorical sense is meant.

Let us take another verse from this sura: "Then, when the sacred months have passed away, kill the idolaters wherever you find them. . . ." (IX.5) These words are usually cited to show what fate awaits indolaters.

Well, what of the context? The words immediately after these just quoted say, "and seize them, besiege them and lie in ambush everywhere for them." Ah, you might say, you have deliberately left out the words that come after those. Let us quote them then, "If they repent and take to prayer and render the alms levy, allow them to go their way. God is forgiving and merciful." Surely these are words of tolerance, you plead. Hardly. They are saying that if they become Muslims then they will be left in peace. In fact the whole sura, which has 129 verses (approximately fourteen pages in the Penguin translation by Dawood)—in other words, the whole context—is totally intolerant and is indeed the source of many totalitarian Islamic laws and principles, such as the concepts of *jihad* and *dhimmis*, the latter proclaiming the inferior status of Christians and Jews in an Islamic state. All our quotes from the Arabic sources in part 1 also, of course, provide the historical context of raids, massacres, booty, and assassinations, which make it crystal clear that real, bloody fighting is being advocated.

First the idolaters, how can you trust them? Most of them are evildoers (IX.8); fight them (IX.12, 14) ;they must not visit mosques (IX.18); they are unclean (IX.28); you may fight the idolaters even during the sacred months (IX.36). "It is not for the Prophet, and those who believe, to pray for the forgiveness of idolaters even though they may be near of kin after it has become clear they are people of hell-fire" (IX.113). So much for forgiveness! Even your parents are to be shunned if they do not embrace Islam: "O you who believe! Choose not your fathers nor your brethren for friends if they take pleasure in disbelief rather than faith. Whoso of you takes them for friends, such are wrong-doers" (IX.23). In other words if you are friendly with your parents who are not Muslims you are being immoral.

The theory of *jihad* is derived from verses 5 and 6 already quoted but also from the following verses:

> Believers, why is it that when it is said to you: "March in the cause of God," you linger slothfully in the land? Are you content with this life in preference to the life to come? Few indeed are the blessings of this life, compared to those of the life to come.
>
> If you do not fight, He will punish you sternly, and replace you by other men. (IX.38–39)

Whether unarmed or well-equipped, march on and fight for the cause of God, with your wealth and with your persons. (IX.41)

Prophet, make war on the unbelievers and the hypocrites and deal harshly with them. (IX.73)

The word that I have translated as "fight" is *jahid*. Some translate it as "go forth" or "strive." Dawood translates it as "fight," as does Penrice in his *Dictionary and Glossary of the Koran*, where it is defined as: "To strive, contend with, fight—especially against the enemies of Islam."[34] Hans Wehr, in his celebrated Arabic dictionary, translates it as "endeavour, strive; to fight; to wage holy war against the infidels."[5]

As for the intolerance against Jews and Christians, and their inferior status as *dhimmis*:

> Fight against such of those to whom the Scriptures were given as believe neither in God nor the Last Day, who do not forbid what God and His apostle have forbidden, and do not embrace the true faith, until they pay tribute out of hand and are utterly subdued.
>
> The Jews say Ezra is the son of God, while the Christians say the Messiah is the son of God. Such are their assertions, by which they imitate the infidels of old. God confound them! How perverse they are!
>
> They make of their clerics and their monks, and of the Messiah, the son of Mary, Lords besides God; though they were ordered to serve one God only. There is no god but Him. Exalted be He above those whom they deify besides Him! . . .
>
> It is He who has sent forth His apostle with guidance and the true Faith to make it triumphant over all religions, howver much the idolaters may dislike it.
>
> O you who believe! Lo! many of the Jewish rabbis and the Christian monks devour the wealth of mankind wantonly and debar men from the way of Allah; They who hoard up gold and silver and spend it not in the way of Allah, unto them give tidings of painful doom. . . . (IX.29–35)

The moral of all the above is clear: Islam is the only true religion, Jews and Christians are devious and money-grubbing, not to be trusted, and even have to pay a tax in the most humiliating way. I do not think I need quote any more from sura IX, although it goes on in this vein verse after verse.

The Koran

The Koranic references are given according to the verse numbering *used by Marmaduke Pickthall in* The Meaning of the Glorious Koran: An Explanatory Translation *(London: George Allen and Unwin, 1930). This translation is widely available in the English-speaking world, and is highly regarded by the Muslims themselves. Pickthall, a convert to Islam, used a lithograph copy of the Koran written by Al-Hajj Muhammad Shakerzadeh at the command of Sultan Mahmud of Turkey in 1246. Occasionally, Pickthall's numbering may vary, by two or three verses at the most, from the numbering in other translations currently available. However, I beg the reader not to panic if he or she does not find the verses referred to immediately but simply check a few verses before and a few after the ones given here.*

I have not always used Pickthall's translation *(only his verse numbering), since his style hardly makes for easy reading with his outdated "thees," "thous," and "hasts." I have used either other Muslim translations or the one by the Iraqi scholar N. J. Dawood.*

Translations used or consulted:

N. J. Dawood, The Koran *(Harmondsworth, England: Penguin, 1990).*

Muhammad Ali, The Holy Qur'an *(Woking, England, 1917).*

A. Yusuf Ali, The Holy Qur'an: Translation and Commentary, *2 vols. (Lahore, 1934).*

A. J. Arberry, The Koran Interpreted *(Oxford: Oxford University Press, 1964).*

R. Blachère, Le Coran *(Paris: G. P. Maisonneuve & Cie, 1949–51).*

Verses that Manifest Intolerance of and Incite Violence against Non-Muslims and Other Religions; Spread Mistrust of Different Communities

Fighting is obligatory for you, much as you dislike it. (II.216)

You shall not wed pagan women, unless they embrace the Faith. A believing slave-girl is better than an idolatress, although she may please you. Nor shall you wed idolaters, unless they embrace the Faith. A believing slave is better than an idolator, although he may please you. (II.221)

Let believers not make friends with infidels in preference to the faithful—he that does this has nothing to hope for from God. (III.28)

He that chooses a religion other than Islam, it will not be accepted from him and in the world to come he will be one of the lost. (III.85)

Believers, do not make friends with any but your own people. (III.118)

Did you suppose that you would enter Paradise before God has proved the men who fought for Him and endured with fortitude? (III.142)

Those of you who ran away on the day the two armies met must have been seduced by Satan on account of some evil they had done. . . . Believers, do not follow the example of the infidels, who say of their brothers when they meet death abroad or in battle: "had they stayed with us they would not have died, nor would they have been killed." God will cause them to regret their words. (III.155–58)

Never think that those who were slain in the cause of God are dead. They are alive, and well-provided for by their Lord. (III.169)

Therefore fight for the cause of God. (IV.84)

The believers who stay at home . . . are not equal to those who fight for the cause of God with their goods and their persons. (IV.95–96)

He that flies his homeland for the cause of God shall find numerous places of refuge in the land and great abundance. He that leaves his dwelling to fight for God and His apostle and is then overtaken by death, shall be rewarded by God. God is forgiving and merciful. (IV.100)

The unbelievers are your inveterate enemies. (IV.101)

Believers, do not choose the infidels rather than the faithful for your friends. (IV.144)

They [the Christians] denied the truth and uttered a monstrous falsehood against Mary.
  And because of their saying: We killed the Messiah Jesus son of Mary, Allah's messenger. They did not kill him nor did they crucify him, but they thought they did. (IV.156–57)

With those who said they were Christians We made a covenant also, but they too have forgotten much of what they were enjoined. Therefore We stirred among them enmity and hatred, which shall endure till the Day of Resurrection, when God will declare to them all that they have done (V.14)

As for the unbelievers, if they offered all that the earth contains and as much besides to redeem themselves from the torment of the Day of Resurrection, it shall not be accepted from them. Theirs shall be a woeful punishment. (V.36)

O you who believe! Take not the Jews and the Christians for friends. They are friends one to another. He among you who takes them for friends is one of them. (V.51)

Unbelievers are those that say: "God is the Messiah, the son of Mary." . . . Unbelievers are those that say: "God is one of three." (V.72–73)

Then God will say: "Jesus, son of Mary, did you ever say to mankind: 'Worship me and my mother as gods besides God'?"

"Glory to You," he will answer, "how could I ever say that to which I have no right? If I had ever said so, You would have surely known it. . . ." (V.116)

On the day when We gather them all together We shall say to the pagans: "Where are your idols now, those whom you supposed to be your gods?" They will not argue, but say: "By God, our Lord, we have never worshipped idols."

You shall see how they will lie against themselves and how the deities of their own invention will forsake them. (VI.22–24)

The idolaters will say: "Had God pleased, neither we nor our fathers would have served other gods besides Him; nor would we have made anything unlawful." In like manner did those who have gone before them deny the Truth until they felt Our scourge. (VI.149)

God revealed His will to the angels, saying: "I shall be with you. Give courage to the believers. I shall cast terror into the hearts of the infidels. Strike off their heads, strike off the very tips of their fingers!" (VIII.12)

That was because they defied God and His apostle. He that defies God and His apostle shall be sternly punished by God. We said to them: "Taste this. The scourge of the Fire await the unbelievers." (VIII.13–14)

Believers, when you encounter the infidels on the march, do not turn your backs to them in flight. If anyone on that day turns his back to them, except for tactical reasons, or to join another band, he shall incur the wrath of God and Hell shall be his home: an evil fate. (VIII.15–16)

Make war on them until idolatry shall cease and God's religion shall reign supreme. (VIII.39)

The basest creatures in the sight of God are the faithless who will not believe. (VIII.55)

Prophet, rouse the faithful to arms. If there are twenty steadfast men among you, they shall vanquish two hundred; if there are a hundred, they shall rout a thousand unbelievers, for they are devoid of understanding. (VIII.65)

It is not for any Prophet to have captives until he has made slaughter in the land. (VIII.67)

When the sacred months are over slay the idolaters wherever you find them. Arrest them, besiege them, and lie in ambush everywhere for them. If they repent and take to prayer and render the alms levy, allow them to go their way. God is forgiving and merciful. (IX.5)

Make war on them: God will chastise them at your hands and humble them. (IX.14)

It ill becomes the idolaters to visit the mosques of God, for they are self-confessed unbelievers. Vain shall be their works, and in the Fire they shall abide for ever. (IX.17)

Believers, do not befriend your fathers or your brothers if they choose unbelief in preference to faith. Wrongdoers are those that befriend them. (IX.23)

Believers, know that the idolaters are unclean. Let them not approach the Sacred Mosque after this year is ended. (IX.28)

Fight against such of those to whom the Scriptures were given as believe neither in God nor the Last Day, who do not forbid what God and His apostle have forbidden, and do not embrace the true faith, until they pay tribute out of hand and are utterly subdued. (IX.29)

But you fight against the idolaters in all these months since they themselves fight against you in all of them. (IX.36)

If you do not fight, He will punish you sternly, and replace you by other men. (IX.39)

Whether unarmed or well-equiped, march on and fight for the cause of God, with your wealth and with your persons. This will be best for you, if you but knew it. (IX.41)

Prophet, make war on the unbelievers and the hypocrites and deal rigorously with them. Hell shall be their home: an evil fate. (IX.73)

God has purchased from the faithful their lives and worldly goods and in return has promised them the Garden. They will fight for the cause of God, slay and be slain. (IX.111)

Believers, make war on the infidels who dwell around you. Deal firmly with them. Know that God is with the righteous. (IX.123)

Here are two antagonists who contend about their Lord. Garments of fire have been prepared for the unbelievers. Scalding water shall be poured upon their heads, melting their skins and that which is in their bellies. They shall be lashed with rods of iron.

Whenever, in their anguish, they try to escape from Hell, back they shall be dragged, and will be told: "Taste the torment of the Conflagration." (XXII.19–22)

Do not yield to the unbelievers, but fight them with this, most strenuously. (XXV.52)

When you meet the unbelievers in the battlefield strike off their heads and, when you have laid them low, bind your captives firmly. Then grant them their freedom or take ransom from them until War shall lay down her burdens. (XLVII.4)

It is He who has sent His apostle with guidance and the Faith of Truth, so that He may exalt it above all religions, much as the pagans may dislike it. (LXI.9)

The unbelievers among the People of the Book and the pagans shall burn for ever in the fire of Hell. They are the vilest of creatures. (XCVIII.6)

Anti-Jewish Sentiment in the Koran

Wretchedness and baseness were stamped upon them (that is, the Jews), and they were visited with wrath from Allah. That was because they disbelieved in Allah's revelations and slew the prophets wrongfully. That was for their disobedience and transgression. (II.61)

Have you not seen those who have received a portion of the Scripture? They purchase error, and they want you to go astray from the path.

But Allah knows best who your enemies are, and it is sufficient to have Allah as a friend. It is sufficient to have Allah as a helper.

Some of the Jews pervert words from their meanings, and say, "We hear and we disobey," and "Hear without hearing," and "Heed us!" twisting with their tongues and slandering religion. If they had said, "We have heard and obey," or "Hear and observe us" it would have been better for them and more upright. But Allah had cursed them for their disbelief, so they believe not, except for a few. (IV.44–46)

And for the evildoing of the Jews, We have forbidden them some good things that were previously permitted them, and because of their barring many from Allah's way.

And for their taking usury which was prohibited for them, and because of their consuming people's wealth under false pretense. We have prepared for the unbelievers among them a painful punishment. (IV.160–61)

Fight against such of those who have been given the Scripture [Jews and Christians] as believe not in Allah nor the Last Day, and forbid not that which Allah has forbidden by His Messenger, and follow not the religion of truth, until they pay the tribute [poll tax] readily, and are utterly subdued.

The Jews say, "Ezra is the son of Allah," and the Christians say, "The Messiah is the son of Allah." Those are the words of their mouths, conforming to the words of the unbelievers before them. Allah attack them! How perverse they are!

They have taken their rabbis and their monks as lords besides Allah, and so too the Messiah son of Mary, though they were commanded to serve but one God. There is no God but He. Allah is exalted above that which they deify beside Him. (IX.29–31)

O you who believe! Lo! many of the (Jewish) rabbis and the (Christian) monks devour the wealth of mankind wantonly and debar (men) from the way of Allah. They who hoard up gold and silver and spend it not in the way of Allah, unto them give tidings of a painful doom. (IX.34)

Why do not the rabbis and the priests forbid their evil-speaking and devouring of illicit gain? Verily evil is their handiwork.

The Jews say, "Allah's hands are fettered." Thei hands are fettered, and they are cursed for what they have said! On the contrary, His hands are spread open. He bestows as He wills. That which has been revealed to you from your Lord will surely increase the arrogance and unbelief of many among them. We have cast enmity and hatred among them until the Day of Resurrection. Every time they light the fire of war, Allah extinguishes it. Thay hasten to spread corruption throughout the earth, but Allah does not love corrupters! (V.63–64)

We made a covenant with the Israelites and sent forth apostles among them. But whenever an apostle came to them with a message that did not suit their fancies, some they accused of lying and others they put to death. They thought no harm would follow: they were blind and deaf. God is ever watching their actions. (V.70–71)

Indeed, you will surely find that the most vehement of men in enmity to those who believe are the Jews and the polytheists. (V.82)

O you who believe! Take not the Jews and the Christians for friends. They are friends one to another. He among you who takes them for friends is one of them. (V.51)

O you who believe! Choose not for friends such of those who received the Scripture [Jews and Christians] before you, and of the disbelievers, as make jest and sport of your religion. But keep your duty to Allah of you are true believers. (V.57)

Say: O, People of the Scripture [Jews and Christians]! Do you blame us for aught else than that we believe in Allah and that which is revealed unto us and that which was revealed aforetime, and because most of you are evil-doers? (V.59)

Among them [Jews and Christians] there are people who are moderate, but many of them are of evil conduct. (V.66)

He brought down from their strongholds those who had supported them from among the People of the Book [Jews of Bani Qurayza[6]] and cast terror into their hearts, so that some you killed and others you took captive. (XXXIII.26)

Say: "Shall I tell you who will receive a worse reward from God? Those whom[7] [i.e., Jews] God has cursed and with whom He has been angry, transforming them into apes and swine, and those who serve the devil. Worse is the plight of these, and they have strayed farther from the right path." (V.60)

Cruelty, Sadsim, and Unusual Punishments in the Koran

As for the thief, both male and female, cut off their hands. It is the reward of their own deeds, an exemplary punishment from Allah. Allah is Mighty, Wise. (V.38)

Those that make war against God and His apostle and spread disorder shall be put to death or crucified or have their hands and feet cut off on alternate sides, or be banished from the country. (V.33)

If any of your women commit fornication, call in four witnesses from among yourselves against them; if they testify to their guilt confine them to their houses till death overtakes them or till God finds another way for them. (IV.15)

The adulterer and adulteress shall each be given a hundred lashes. Let no pity for them cause you to disobey God, if you truly believe in God and the Last Day; and let their punishment be witnessed by a number of believers. (XXIV.2)

For the wrongdoers We have prepared a fire which will encompass them like the walls of a pavilion. When they cry out for help, they shall be showered with water as hot as molten brass, which will scald their faces. Evil shall be their drink, dismal their resting-place. (XVIII.30)

Here are two antagonists who contend about their Lord. Garments of fire have been prepared for the unbelievers. Scalding water shall be poured upon their heads, melting their skins and that which is in their bellies. They shall be lashed with rods of iron.

Whenever, in their anguish, they try to escape from Hell, back they shall be dragged, and will be told: "Taste the torment of the Conflagration."(XXII. 19–22)

Those who have denied the Book and the message We sent through Our apostles shall realize the truth hereafter: when, with chains and shackles round their necks, they shall be dragged through scalding water and burnt in the fire of Hell. (XL.70–72)

Antiwoman Sentiments in the Koran

O you who believe! Retaliation is prescribed for you in the matter of the murdered; the freeman for the freeman, and the slave for the slave, and the female for the female. (II.178)

Women shall with justice have rights similar to those exercised against them, although men have a status above women. God is mighty and wise. (II.228)

And call to witness, from among your men, two witnesses. And if two men be not (at hand) then a man and two women, of such as you approve as witnesses, so that if the one errs (through forgetfulness) the other will remember. (II.282)

If you fear that you cannot treat orphans [orphan girls] with fairness, marry of the women, who seem good to you, two or three or four; and if you fear that you cannot do justice (to so many) then one (only) or any slave girls you may own. This will make it easier for you to avoid injustice. (IV.3)

A male shall inherit twice as much as a female. (IV.11)

If a childless man have two sisters, they shall inherit two-thirds of his estate; but if he have both brothers and sisters, the share of each male shall be that of two females. (IV.177)

Men are in charge of women, because Allah has made the one of them to excel the other, and because they spend of their property (for the support of women). So good women are the obedient, guarding in secret that which Allah has guarded. As for those from whom you fear rebellion, admonish them and banish them to beds apart, scourge [beat] them. Then if they obey you, seek not a way against them. Lo! Allah is ever High Exalted, Great. (IV.34)

O you who believe! Draw not near unto prayer when you are drunken, till you know that which you utter, nor when you are polluted, save when journeying upon the road, till you have bathed. And if you are ill, or on a journey, or one of you comes from the closet, or you have touched women, and you find not water, then go to high clean soil and rub your faces and your hands (therewith). Lo! Allah is Benign, Forgiving. (IV.43; see also V.6)

If you ask his wives for anything, speak to them from behind a curtain. This more chaste for your hearts and their hearts. (XXXIII.53)

Prophet, enjoin your wives, your daughters and the wives of true believers to draw their veils close round them. That is more proper, so that they may be recognized and not molested. God is forgiving and merciful. (XXXIII.59)

Would God choose daughters for Himself and sons for you alone? Yet when a new-born girl is announced to one of them his countenance darkens and he is filled with gloom. Would they ascribe to God females who adorn themselves with trinkets and are powerless in disputation? (XLIII.16–18)

Prophet, We have made lawful to you the wives to whom you have granted dowries and the slave-girls whom God has given you as booty. (XXXIII.50)

[Forbidden to you are] married women, except those whom you own as slaves. (IV.24; see also XXIII.5–6; LXX.22–30)

Women are your fields: go, then, into your fields from whichever side you please. (II.223)

Why the Koran Is Not the Word of God

According to al-Suyūṭī (in *Al-Itqān fī ʿulūm al-Qurʾān* [Cairo, 1967], 10: I, pp. 99–101) there are at least five passages in the Koran that cannot be attributed to God. Suras VI.104 and VI.114 are the words of Muhammad:

No mortal eyes can see Him, though He sees all eyes. He is benignant and all-knowing. (VI.104)[8]

So that the hearts of those who have no faith in the life to come may be inclined to what they say and, being pleased, persist in their sinful ways. (VI.114)[9]

In sura XIX.64, it is the angel Gabriel who is speaking. Translators often slip in "angels" in brackets after "We," e.g., M. Pickthall.

We do not come down from heaven save at the bidding of your Lord. To Him belongs what is before us and behind us, and all that lies between. (XIX.64; see also XIX.9,21, LI.30)

Sura LI.50 is either spoken by the Prophet Muhammad, as Bell suggests, or a revealing angel as, Pickthall thinks: "Therefore seek Allah, lo! I come from Him to warn you plainly."

In the following verses, it is obviously angels who are speaking, as is indicated by Pickthall in a footnote:

> There is not one of Us but has his own position. Lo! We, even We are they who set the ranks. Lo! We, even We are they who hymn His praise. (XXXVII.164–66)

Finally, Sura 1, the *Fatihah*, is obviously a prayer offered *to* God by the faithful.

JIHAD

The totalitarian nature of Islam is nowhere more apparent than in the concept of *jihad*, the holy war, whose ultimate aim is to conquer the entire world and submit it to the one true faith, to the law of Allah. Islam alone has been granted the truth—there is no possibility of salvation outside it. It is the sacred duty—an incumbent religious duty established in the Koran and the Traditions—of all Muslims to bring it to all humanity. *Jihad* is a divine institution, enjoined specifically for the purpose of advancing Islam. Muslims must strive, fight, and kill in the name of God:

> Kill those who join other gods with God wherever you may find them. (IX.5–6)

> Those who believe fight in the cause of God. . . . (IV.76)

> I will instill terror into the hearts of the Infidels, strike off their heads then, and strike off from them every fingertip. (VIII.12)

> Say to the Infidels: If they desist from their unbelief, what is now past shall be forgiven them; but if they return to it, they have already before them the doom of the ancients! Fight then against them till strife be at an end, and the religion be all of it God's. (VIII.39–42)

> The believers who stay at home . . . are not equal to those who fight for the cause of God. . . . God has promised all a good reward, but far richer is the recompense of those who fight for Him. . . . (IV.95)

It is a grave sin for a Muslim to shirk the battle against the unbelievers, those who do will roast in hell:

Believers, when you meet the unbelievers preparing for battle do not turn your backs to them. [Anyone who does] shall incur the wrath of God and hell shall be his home: an evil dwelling indeed. (VIII.15,16)

If you do not fight, He will punish you severely, and put others in your place. (IX.39)

Those who die fighting for the only true religion, Islam, will be amply rewarded in the life to come:

Let those fight in the cause of God who barter the life of this world for that which is to come; for whoever fights on God's path, whether he is killed or triumphs, We will give him a handsome reward. (IV.74)

It is abundantly clear from many of the above verses that the Koran is not talking of metaphorical battles or of moral crusades; it is talking of the battlefield. To read such blood thirsty injunctions in a holy book is shocking.

Mankind is divided into two groups—Muslims and non-Muslims. The Muslims are members of the Islamic community, the *umma*, who possess territories in the *Dār al-Islām*, the Land of Islam, where the edicts of Islam are fully promulgated. The non-Muslims are the *Harbi,* people of the *Dār al-Harb*, the Land of Warfare, any country belonging to the infidels that has not been subdued by Islam but which, nonetheless, is destined to pass into Islamic jurisdiction either by conversion or by war (*Harb*). All acts of war are permitted in the *Dār al-Harb*. Once the *Dar al-Harb* has been subjugated, the *Harbi* become prisoners of war. The *imam* can do what he likes to them according to the circumstances. Woe betide the city that resists and is then taken by the Islamic army by storm. In this case, the inhabitants have no rights whatsoever, and as Sir Steven Runciman says in *The Fall of Constantinople, 1453*:

The conquering army is allowed three days of unrestricted pillage; and the former places of worship, with every other building, become the property of the conquering leader; he may dispose of them as he pleases. Sultan Mehmet [after the fall of Constantinople in 1453 allowed] his soldiers the three days of pillage to which they were entitled. They poured into the city. . . . They slew everyone that they met in the streets, men, women and children without discrimination.. The blood ran in rivers down the steep streets. . . . But soon the lust for slaughter was assuaged. The soldiers realized that captives and precious objects would bring them greater profits.[10]

In other cases, they are sold into slavery, exiled, or treated as *dhimmis*, who are tolerated as second-class subjects, as long as they pay a regular tribute.

It is common nowadays for the apologists of Islam, whether Muslims or their Western admirers, to interpret *jihad* in the nonmilitary sense of "moral struggle" or "moral striving." But it is quite illegitimate to pretend that the Koran and the books on Islamic law were talking about "moral crusades." Rather, as Rudolf Peters says in his definitive study of *jihad* says, "In the books on Islamic Law, the word means armed struggle against the unbelievers, which is also a common meaning in the Koran."[11] Apologists of Islam, even when they do admit that real battles are being referred to, still pretend that the doctrine of *jihad* only talks of "defensive measures," that is, the apologists pretend that fighting is only allowed to defend Muslims, and that offensive wars are illegitimate. But again, this is not the classical doctrine in Islam; as Peters makes clear, the Sword Verses in the Koran were interpreted as unconditional commands to fight the unbelievers, and furthermore these Sword Verses abrogated all previous verses concerning intercourse with non-Muslims. Peters sums up the classical doctrine as:

> The doctrine of Jihad as laid down in the works on Islamic Law, developed out of the Koranic prescriptions and the example of the Prophet and the first caliphs, which is recorded in the hadith; The crux of the doctrine is the existence of one single Islamic state, ruling the entire umma [Muslim community]. It is the duty of the umma to expand the territory of this state in order to bring as many people under its rule as possible. The ultimate aim is to bring the whole earth under the sway of Islam and to extirpate unbelief: "Fight them until there is no persecution and the religion is God's entirely." (sura ii. 193; viii. 39). Expansionist jihad is a collective duty (fard ala al-kifaya), which is fulfilled if a sufficient number of people take part in it. If this is not the case, the whole umma [Muslim community] is sinning.[12]

Here are more bellicose verses from the Koran, the words of Allah telling Muslims to kill, to murder on his behalf:

> Fight against them until sedition is no more and Allah's religion reigns supreme. (II.193)

> Fighting is obligatory for you, much as you dislike it. But you may hate a thing although it is good for you, and love a thing although it is bad for you. Allah knows, but you do not. (II.216)

> Whether unarmed or well-equipped, march on and fight for the cause of Allah, with your wealth and your persons. This is best for you, if you but knew it. (IX.41)

> Believers! Make war on the infidels who dwell around you let them find harshness in you. (IX.123)

O Prophet! Make war on the unbelievers and the hypocrites and deal sternly with them hell shall be their home, evil their fate. (LXVI.9)

O Prophet! Make war on the unbelievers and the hypocrites. Be harsh with them. Their ultimate abode is hell, a hapless journey's end. (IX.73)

O Prophet! Exhort the believers to fight. If there are twenty steadfast men among you, they shall vanquish two hundred; and if there are a hundred, they shall rout a thousand unbelievers, for they are devoid of understanding. (VIII.65)

When you meet the unbelievers in the battlefield strike off their heads and when you have laid them low, bind your captives firmly. . . . (XLVII.4–15)

Do not yield to the unbelievers, but fight them strenuously with this Koran. (XXV.52)

It is not for any Prophet to have captives until he has made slaughter in the land. . . . (VIII.67)

The cult of heroism and the cult of death is beautifully exemplified in the Muslim cult of martyrdom. The Koran promises paradise with its seductive *houris* to all those who die in the cause of Islam:

Allah has purchased of their faithful lives and worldly goods and in return has promised them the Garden. They will fight for His cause, kill and be killed. (IX.111)

You must not think that those who were slain in the cause of Allah are dead. They are alive, and well-provided for by their Lord. . . . (III.169–71)

If you should die or be killed in the cause of Allah, His mercy and forgiveness would surely be better than all the riches that amass. If you should die or be killed, before Him you shall all be gathered. (III.157–58)

Hadith

Hadith on *jihad* from al-Bukhārī, *Ṣaḥūḥ*, trans. Muhsin M. Khan (New Delhi: Kitab Bhavan, 1987), 9 vols.

From Volume 1

Muhammad said, "The person who participates in (holy battles) in Allah's cause and nothing compels him to do so except belief in Allah and His Apostles, will be recompensed by Allah either with a reward, or booty (if he survives) or will be admitted to Paradise (if he is killed in the battle as a martyr). Had I not found it difficult for my followers, then I would not remain behind any sariya [army unit] going for Jihad and I would have loved to be martyred in Allah's cause and then made alive, and then martyred and then made alive and then again martyred in His cause. (1:35)

From Volume 4

Abdullah bin Masud said, "I asked Allah's Apostle, 'O Allah's Apostle! What is the best deed?' He replied, 'To offer the prayers at their early stated fixed times.' I asked, 'What is next in goodness?' He replied, 'To be good and dutiful to your parents.' I further asked, 'What is next in goodness?' He replied, 'To participate in Jihad in Allah's cause.' " (4:41)

Muhammad said, "There is no Hijra (i.e., migration from Mecca to Medina) after the conquest (of Mecca), but Jihad and good intention [to fight in Jihad] remain; and if you are called (by the Muslim ruler) for fighting, go forth immediately." (4:42, 4:311)

A man came to Muhammad and said, "Instruct me as to such a deed as equals Jihad (in reward)." He replied, "I do not find such a deed." Then he added, "Can you, while the Muslim fighter is in the battle-field, enter your mosque to perform prayers without cease and fast and never break your fast?" The man said, "But who can do that?" (4:44)

Someone asked, "O Allah's Apostle! Who is the best among the people?" Allah's Apostle replied, "A believer who strives his utmost in Allah's cause with his life and property." They asked, "Who is next?" He replied, "A believer who stays in one of the mountain paths worshiping Allah and leaving the people secure from his mischief." (4:45)

Muhammad said, ". . . Allah guarantees the He will admit the Mujahid [one who fights in Jihad] in His cause into Paradise if he is killed, otherwise He will return him to his home safely with rewards and war booty." (4:46)

Muhammad said, "Last night two men came to me (in a dream) and made me ascend a tree and then admitted me into a better and superior house, better of which I have never seen. One of them said, 'This house is the house of martyrs.' " (4:49)

Muhammad said, "A single endeavour (of fighting) in Allah's cause in the forenoon or in the afternoon is better than the world and whatever is in it." (4:50)

Muhammad said, "Nobody who dies and finds good from Allah (in the hereafter) would wish to come back to this world even if he were given the whole world and whatever is in it, except the martyr who, on seeing the superiority of martyrdom, would like to come back to the world and get killed again (in Allah's cause)." (4:53)

Muhammad said, "Nobody who enters Paradise likes to go back to the world even if he got everything on the earth, except a Mujahid [one who fights in Jihad] who wishes to return to the world so that he may be martyred ten times because of the dignity he receives (from Allah)." (4:72)

Muhammad said, "Were it not for the fear that it would be difficult for my followers, I would not have remained behind any Sariya (army unit) but I don't have riding camels and have no other means of conveyance to carry them on, and it is hard for me that my companions should remain behind me. No doubt I wish I could fight in Allah's cause and be martyred and come to life again to be martyred and come to life once more." (4:216)

A man came to the Prophet and asked, "A man fights for war booty; another fights for fame and a third fights for showing off. Which of them fights in Allah's cause?" The prophet said, "He who fights that Allah's Word (i.e., Islam) should be superior, fights in Allah's cause." (4:65)

Muhammad said, "Anyone whose both feet get covered with dust in Allah's cause will not be touched by the (hell) fire." (4:66)

Al-Mughira bin Shu'ba said, "Our Prophet told us about the message of our Lord that ". . . whoever amongst us is killed will go to Paradise." Umar asked the Prophet, "Is it not true that our men who are killed will go to Paradise and their's (i.e., those of the pagans) will go to the (hell)fire?" The Prophet said, "Yes." (4:72b)

Muhammad said, "Know that Paradise is under the shades of swords." (4:73)

Once Allah's Apostle (during a holy battle), waited till the sun had declined and then he got up among the people and said, "O people! Do not wish to face the enemy (in a battle) and ask Allah to save you (from calamities) but if you should face the enemy, then be patient and let it be known to you that Paradise is under the shades of swords." He then said, "O Allah! The Revealer of the (holy) Book, the Mover of the clouds, and Defeater of Al-Ahzab (i.e., the clans of infidels), defeat the infidels and bestow victory upon us." (4:210)

Muhammad said, "Allah welcomes two men with a smile. One of whom kills the other and both of them enter Paradise. One fights in Allah's cause and gets killed. Later on Allah forgives the killer (i.e., he embraces Islam) who also get martyred (in Allah's cause)." (4:80)

Muhammad said, "He who prepares a ghazi going in Allah's cause is (given a reward equal to that of) a ghazi; and he who looks after properly the dependents of a ghazi going in Allah's cause is (given a reward equal to that of) a ghazi." (4:96)

Aisha (one of Muhammad's wives) said, "I requested the Prophet to permit me to participate in Jihad, but he said, 'Your Jihad is the performance of Hajj [the annual pilgrimage to Mecca].' " (4:127)

Anas said, "On the day (of the battle) of Uhud when (some) people retreated and left the Prophet I saw Aisha bint Abi Bakr and um Sulaim [two women], with their robes tucked up so that the bangles around their ankles were visible hurrying with their water skins. Then they would pour the water in the mouths of the people, and return to fill the water skins again and came back again to pour water in the mouths of the people." (4:131)

Muhammad said, ". . . Paradise is for him who holds the reins of his horse to strive in Allah's cause, with his hair unkempt and feet covered with dust. If he is appointed in the vanguard, he is perfectly satisfied with his post of guarding, and if he is appointed in the rearguard, he accepts his post with satisfaction." (4:137)

Muhammad said, "A time will come when groups of people will go for Jihad and it will be asked, 'Is there anyone amongst you who has enjoyed the company of the Prophet?' The answer will be 'Yes.' Then they will be given victory (by Allah). Then a time will come when it will be asked, 'Is there anyone amongst you who has enjoyed the company of the companions of the Prophet?' It will be said, 'Yes,' and they will be given the victory (by Allah). Then a time will come when it will be said, 'Is there anyone amongst you who has enjoyed the company of the companions of the companions of the Prophet?' It will be said, 'Yes,' and they will be given victory (by Allah)." (4:146)

Sahl bin Sa'd As-Sa'idi said, "Allah's Apostle and the pagans faced each other and started fighting. When Allah's Apostle returned to his camp and when the pagans returned to their camp, somebody talked about a man amongst the companions of Allah's Apostle who would follow and kill with his sword any pagan going alone. He said, 'Nobody did his job (i.e., fighting) so properly today as that man.' Allah's Apostle said, 'Indeed, he is amongst the people of the (hell) fire.' A man amongst the people said, 'I shall accompany him (to watch what he does).' Thus he accompanied him, and wherever he stood, he would stand with him, and wherever he ran, he would run with him. Then the (brave) man got wounded seriously and he decided to bring about his death quickly. He planted the blade of the sword in the ground directing its sharp end towards his chest between his two breasts. Then he leaned on the sword and killed himself. The other man came to Allah's Apostle and said, 'I testify that you are Allah's Apostle.' The Prophet asked, 'What has happened?' He replied, '(It is about) the man whom you had described as one of the people of the (hell) fire. The people were greatly surprised at what you said, and I said, "I will find out his reality for you." So, I came out seeking him. He got severely wounded, and hastened to die by planting the blade of his sword in the ground directing its sharp end towards his chest between his two breasts. Then he leaned on his sword and killed himself.' Then Allah's Apostle said, 'A man may seem to the people as if he were practicing the deeds of the people of Paradise while in fact he is from the people of the (hell) fire, another may seem to the people as if he were practicing the deeds of the people of hell (fire), while in fact he is from the people of Paradise.' " (4:147)

Muhammad said, "My livelihood is under the shade of my spear, and he who disobeys my orders will be humiliated by paying Jizya." (4:162b)

Umair said, "Um Haram informed us that she heard the Prophet saying, 'Paradise is granted to the first batch of my followers who will undertake a naval expedition.' Um Haram added, 'I said, O Allah's Apostle! Will I be amongst them?' He replied, 'You are amongst them.' The Prophet then said, 'The first army amongst my followers who will invade Caesar's city will be forgiven their sins.' I asked, 'Will I be one of them, O Allah's Apostle?' He replied in the negative." (4:175)

Muhammad said, "The hour will not be established until you fight with the Turks; people with small eyes, red faces, and flat noses. Their faces will look like shields coated with leather. The hour will not be established till you fight with people whose shoes are made of hair." (4.179)

Ali said, "When it was the day of the battle of Al-Ahzab (i.e., the clans), Allah's Apostle said, 'O Allah! Fill their (i.e., the infidels') houses and graves with fire as they busied us so much that we did not perform the prayer (i.e., 'Asr) till the sun had set.' " (4:182)

Aisha said, "Once the Jews came to the Prophet and said, 'Death be upon you.' So I cursed them. The Prophet said, 'What is the matter?' I said, 'Have you not heard what they said?' The Prophet said, 'Have you not heard what I replied (to them)? (I said), ("The same is upon you.").' " (4:186)

On the day of the battle of Khaibar, Sahl bin Sa'd heard Muhammad say, "I will give the flag to a person at whose hands Allah will grant victory." So, the companions of the Prophet got up, wishing eagerly to see to whom the flag will be given, and everyone of them wished to be given the flag. But the Prophet asked for Ali. Someone informed him that he was suffering from eye-trouble. So, he ordered them to bring Ali in front of him. Then the Prophet spat in his eyes and his eyes were cured immediately as if he had never any eye-trouble. Ali said, "We will fight with them (i.e., infidels) till they become like us (i.e., Muslims)." The Prophet said, "Be patient, till you face them and invite them to Islam and inform them of what Allah has enjoined upon them. By Allah! If a single person embraces Islam at your hands (i.e., through you), that will be better for you than the red camels." (4:192)

Anas said, "Whenever Allah's Apostle attacked some people, he would never attack them till it was dawn. If he heard the adhan (i.e., call for prayer) he would delay the fight, and if he did not hear the adhan, he would attack them immediately after dawn." (4:193)

Anas said, "The Prophet set out for Khaibar and reached it at night. He used not to attack if he reached the people at night, till the day broke. So, when the day dawned, the Jews came out with their bags and spades. When they saw the Prophet they said, 'Muhammad and his army!' The Prophet said, 'Allahu-Akbar! (Allah is Greater) and Khaibar is ruined, for whenever we approach a nation (i.e., enemy to fight) then it will be a miserable morning for those who have been warned.' " (4:195)

Muhammad said, "I have been ordered to fight with the people till they say, 'None has the right to be worshiped but Allah,' and whoever says, 'None has the right to be worshiped by Allah,' his life and property will be saved by me except for Islamic law, and his accounts will be with Allah (either to punish him or to forgive him.)" (4:196)

Ka'b bin Malik said, "Whenever Allah's Apostle intended to carry out a Ghazwa, he would use an equivocation to conceal his real destination till it was the Ghazwa of Tabuk which Allah's Apostle carried out in very hot weather. As he was going to face a very long journey through a wasteland and was to meet and attack a large number of enemies. So, he made the situation clear to the Muslims so that they might prepare themselves accordingly and get ready to conquer their enemy." (4:198)

Muhammad said, ". . . I have been made victorious with terror (cast in the hearts of the enemy). . . ." (4:220)

Abdullah bin Amr said, "A man came to the Prophet asking his permission to take part in Jihad. The Prophet asked him, 'Are your parents alive?' He replied in the affirmative. The Prophet said to him, 'Then exert yourself in their service.' " (4:248)

As-Sa'b bin Jaththama said, "The Prophet . . . was asked whether it was permissible to attack the pagan warriors at night with the probability of exposing their women and children to danger. The Prophet replied, 'They (i.e., women and children) are from them (i.e., pagans). ' " (4:256)

Abu Huraira said, "Allah's Apostle sent us in a mission (i.e., an army-unit) and said, 'If you find so-and-so and so-and-so, burn both of them with fire.' When we intended to depart, Allah's Apostle said, 'I have ordered you to burn so-and-so and so-and-so, and it is none but Allah Who punishes with fire, so, if you find them, kill them.' " (4:259)

Ikrima said, "Ali burnt some people and this news reached Ibn Abbas, who said, 'Had I been in his place I would not have burnt them, as the Prophet said, "Don't punish (anybody) with Allah's punishment." No doubt, I would have killed them, for the Prophet said, "If somebody (a Muslim) discards his religion, kill him." ' " (4:260)

Anas bin Malik said, "A group of eight men from the tribe of Ukil came to the Prophet and then they found the climate of Medina unsuitable for them. So, they said, 'O Allah's Apostle! Provide us with some milk.' Allah's apostle said, 'I recommend that you should join the herd of camels.' So they went and drank the urine and the milk of the camels (as a medicine) till they became healthy and fat. Then they killed the shepherd and drove away the camels, and they became unbelievers after they were Muslims. When the Prophet was informed by a shouter for help, he sent some men in their pursuit, and before the sun rose high, they were brought and he had their hands and feet cut off. Then he ordered for nails which were heated and passed over their eyes, and they were left in the Harra (i.e., rocky land in Medina). They asked for water, and nobody provided them with water till they died." (4:261)

Al-Bara bin Azib said, "Allah's Apostle sent a group of Ansari men to kill Abu-Rafi'. One of them set out and entered their (i.e., the enemies') fort. That man said, 'I hid myself . . . and came upon Abu Rafi' and said, "O Abu Rafi'." When he replied me, I proceeded towards the voice and hit him. He shouted and I came out to come back, pretending to be a helper. I said, "O Abu Rafi'," changing the tone of my voice . . . I asked him, "What happened to you?" He said, "I don't know who came to me and hit me." Then I drove my sword into his belly and pushed it forcibly till it touched the bone. Then I came out, filled with puzzlement and went towards a ladder of theirs in order to get down but I fell down and sprained my foot. I came to my companions and said, "I will not leave till I hear the wailing of the women." So, I did not leave till I heard the women bewailing Abu Rafi', the mercant of Hijaz. Then I got up, feeling no ailment, (and we proceeded) till we came upon the Prophet and informed him.' " (4:264; 4:267, 269 Muhammad said, "War is deceit.")

Jabir bin Abdullah said, "The Prophet said, 'Who is ready to kill Ka'b bin Al-Ashraf who has really hurt Allah and His Apostle?' Muhammad bin Maslama said, 'O Allah's Apostle! Do you like me to kill him?' He replied in the affirmative. So, Muhammad bin Maslama went to him (i.e., Ka'b) and said, 'This person (i.e., the Prophet) has put us to task and asked us for charity.' Ka'b replied, 'By Allah, you will get tired of him.' Muhammad said to him, 'We have followed him, so we dislike to leave him till we see the end of his affair.' Muhammad bin Maslama went on talking to him in this way till he got the chance to kill him." (4:270)

Anas bin Malik said, "Allah's Apostle entered (Mecca) in the year of the conquest (of Mecca) wearing a helmet over his head. After he took it off, a man came and said, 'Ibn Khatal is clinging to the curtains of the Ka'ba.' The Prophet said, 'Kill him. '" (4:280b)

Salarma bin Al-Akwa said, "An infidel spy came to the Prophet while he was on a journey. The spy sat with the companions of the Prophet and started talking and then went away. The Prophet said, (to his companions), 'Chase and kill him.' So, I killed him." (4:286)

Ibn Abbas said, ". . . The Prophet on his death-bed, gave three orders saying, 'Expel the pagans from the Arabian Peninsula. . . .' " (4:288)

Abdullah said, "When the Prophet returned (from Jihad), he would say Takbir thrice and add, 'We are returning, if Allah wishes, with repentance and worshiping and praising (our Lord) and prostrating ourselves before our Lord. Allah fulfilled His promise and helped His slave, and He alone defeated the (infidel) clans.' " (4:317)

From Volume 9

Ali said, ". . . no Muslim should be killed . . . for killing a kafir (disbeliever)." (9:50; 4:283)

Some Zanadiqa (atheists) were brought to Ali and he burnt them. The news of this event, reached Ibn Abbas who said, "If I had been in his place, I would not have burnt them, as Allah's Apostle forbade it, saying, 'Do not punish anybody with Allah's punishment (fire).' I would have killed them according to the statement of Allah's Apostle, 'Whoever changed his Islamic religion, then kill him.' " (9:57)

Classical Muslim Thinkers on Jihad

Finally, on the obligation of *jihad*, I shall quote from two Muslim thinkers greatly admired in the West. First, Ibn Khaldūn in his *Muqaddimah* writes: "In the Muslim community, the holy war is religious duty, because of the universalism of the Muslim mission and (the obligation to) convert everybody to Islam either by persuasion or by force."[13]

And now Averroes (Ibn Rushd), a much-romanticized figure in the West:

> According to the majority of scholars, the compulsory nature of the jihad is founded on sura II.216: 'Prescribed for you is fighting, though it is hateful to you.' . . . The obligation to participate in the jihad applies to adult free men who have the means at their disposal to go to war and who are healthy, . . . Scholars agree that all polytheists should be fought; This founded on sura VIII.39: Fight them until there is no persecution and the religion is God's entirely." . . . Most scholars are agreed that, in his dealing with captives, various policies are open to the Imam. He may pardon them, enslave them, kill them, or release them either on ransom or as dhimmi [non-Muslim, second class subject of the Islamic state], in which latter case the released captive is obliged to pay poll-tax (jizya). . . . Sura VIII. 67 "It is not for any Prophet to have prisoners until he make wide slaughter in the land." as well as the occasion when this verse was revealed [viz. the captives of Badr] would prove that it is better to kill captives than to enslave them. The Prophet himself would in some cases kill captives outside the field of battle, while he would pardon them in others. Women he used to enslave. . . . The Muslims are agreed that the aim of warfare against the People of the Book is two-fold: either conversion to Islam or payment of poll-tax (jizya). This is based on Sura IX. 29."

Source: Averroes [Ibn Rushd], *Bidayat al-Mujiahid wa-Nihayat al-Muqtasid* (Cairo, 1960), translated by R. Peters in *Jihad in Classical and Modern Islam*, pp. 27–40.

ANWAR SHAIKH AND THE INCONSISTENCIES OF THE KORAN

On Saturday, October 21, 1995, there appeared the following news items in the *Daily Sadaqat*, a newspaper in Lahore, Pakistan:

"All Pakistani clergy demand extradition of the accursed renegade Anwar Shaikh from Britain to hang him publicly."

"A renegade must be murdered—this is a fundamental rule of the Islamic Law—Anwar Shaikh must be called back, some lover of the Prophet is bound to kill him. America [*sic*] protects every insulter of the Prophet."

"If he (Anwar Shaikh) is not eliminated, more Rushdies will appear. He is an apostate for denying heaven, hell, revelation, Koran, Prophet and angels. The Muslims of the world are ready to behead the accursed renegade to defend the magnificence of their Prophet."

Those of us who feared that the shadow of the Rushdie affair would fall on all subsequent attempts to criticize this most criticizable of all religions were pleasantly surprised, not to say astonished, to find that someone had openly dared take a stand against religious fascism in the form of Islam. Anwar Shaikh, in five books published at his own expense since February 1989, the date of the infamous *fatwa* on Rushdie, denounces Islam in uncompromising terms: *Eternity*; *Faith & Deception*; *Islam, The Arab National Movement*; *Islam, Sex and Violence*; and *Islam, The Arab Imperialism*.[14]

I first came across Shaikh's name on the Net, where I also obtained his address. I wrote to him immediately, thinking that, at last, I had found a kindred spirit—an former Muslim willing to criticize his former religion. I was not disappointed. I met him a month later in his spacious and very comfortable house in the suburbs of Cardiff. Anwar is a large, affable man of great warmth, humor, and obvious defiance and courage. Now over seventy, he has health worries: He has had seven bypass operations and rarely leaves his home. He not only showed me his homemade wine—"Do you like wine? Ah, good, good, then you are a true humanist"—but insisted that I take away a whole flagon of several liters with me back to London on the train. He spends much of his time writing, not only diatribes against Islam but beautiful poetry in Urdu, which he publishes in his own journal, *Liberty*.

Anwar Shaikh worries about the secular future of Britain. As he said in an interview in 1995, "Britain is my home and unless you do something about Muslim fundamentalism there is going to be a huge fifth column in our midst. England must wake up. You [the British] spent hundreds of years getting Christian fundamentalism out of this country. Don't let fundamentalism come back."[15]

In more recent months (June, July, and August 2002), Anwar Shaikh has talked to me about his work in progress, *The Two Faces of Islam*. He begins with a quote from Sura IV.82: "What, do they not ponder the Koran? If it had been from other than God surely, they would have found in it much inconsistency," and takes up the challenge. He points out and discusses over a hundred inconsistencies in the Koran. Anwar Shaikh kindly let me have a look at his manuscript. Here are some excerpts from *The Two Faces of Islam*.

*   *   *

God declares in the Koran, Sura CXII, *Al-Ikhlas*, that He is totally independent. Again at Sura XXXI (Luqman): 12, the Koran emphasises that "Allah is free of all wants." And yet, God contradicts Himself, for the Koran tells us that "I (Allah) have created Jinns and Humans only to serve (worship) me." Sura LI.56.

On the one hand Allah is completely selfless, but on the other hand, He is motivated by desire, i.e., He has created humankind only for self-interest (worship).

The Koran also tells us that God leads astray whom He wills (Sura XVII. 97), but then God Himself will muster those He has led astray on the Day of Resurrection and shall punish them by throwing them into hell. What kind of justice is this? He Himself leads people astray, and then punishes them. How can Allah Himself be righteous if He deliberately misguides people?

XVIII.58: Surely we (Allah) have laid veils on their hearts lest they understand it, and in their ears heaviness and though thou (Muhammad) callest them to the guidance, yet they will not be guided ever.

III.178: And let not the unbelievers suppose that the indulgence We (Allah) grant them (unbeliever) is better for them. We grant them indulgence only that they may increase in sin, and there awaits them a humbling chastisement.

VI.126: Whomsover God desires to guide, He expands his breast to Islam, Whomsoever He desires to lead astray He makes his breast narrow, tight as if he were climbing to heaven. So God lays abomination upon those who believe not.

XIII.31: . . . If God had willed, He would have guided men altogether.

From the above quotes it is clear that the Koran's claim to be the code of guidance (Sura XXVII.1–6) does not hold good because God does not want to guide all people; He guides as well as misguides. In fact, according to the Koran, Allah is more inclined to misguide than guide. Because for misleading people, He has a special contingent of Satans:

XIX.83: Hast thou (Muhammad) not seen how We (Allah) sent the Satans against the unbelievers, to incite them to evil? So hasten thou not against them.

In view of these verses, how can the Koran claim to be the Book of Guidance? Obviously, Satans act under Allah's command to spread evil.

Whatever Allah does, He does it for His own glory without paying any heed to the consequences of His actions to humankind. The second chapter of the Koran, known as "the Cow," tells us that in the beginning when Allah declared to the company of angels that he was about to create man (Adam), there was a big uproar, with angels contesting the desirability of this project; the angels asserted that man "will do corruption there (on earth) and shed blood, while we proclaim Thy praise and call thee Holy "(II.30). Answering the angel's criticism, He said, "Assuredly I know that you know not."

Allah manipulates the situation by secretly teaching names of things to Adam, and then commands angels to reveal names of things if they claim to know so much. They cannot do so, and feel extremely embarrassed. To exploit the situation, Allah commands angels to prostrate before Adam (the first man). They all surrender except Iblis, the chief of angels. He is condemned by Allah and is banished from His Court. From his moment, Iblis is declared as satan, who is believed to be the Father of Evil. (Sura II.30–34) This interpretation cannot be true because:

According to the Divine Law as expressed by the Koran, the most serious and only unpardonable sin is prostrating before someone other than God. This is the biggest evil that there can be. Fancy, Allah commanding the Chief of Angels to commit the cardinal sin! Obviously, Allah is not All-Good. Then how can He guide people? Is it possible to call the Koran the Word of Allah, as the True Guide?

It shows that Allah is a manipulator, teaching Adam names of things quietly to humiliate angles, especially when they knew the truth about man, is not ingenuous. It certainly comes within the category of vice. How can then Allah guide?

Sura VII continues the story of Satan's disobedience. Allah asks Satan, "What prevented you to bow yourself, when I commanded you? "Satan replied, "I am better than he (Adam); You created me of fire, and him of clay." VII.12.

Having been infuriated by Satan's arrogance, Allah banishes him from His court. As he is about leave, he says to Allah, "Respite me till the day they (the dead humans) shall be raised (from their graves) ." And Allah, agreeing to Satan's request declares: "Thou art among the ones who are respited "VII. 15. Satan says, "Now for Thy perverting me, I shall surely sit in ambush for them (humans) on Thy straight path. . . ." Expelling him from the Divine Court, Allah says, "Go forth from it, despised and banished. Those of them that follow thee—I shall assuredly fill Hell with all of you."

From the above, it is clear:

Satan blames God for perverting him.

He asks God to respite him until the end of time to mislead people, without any interference from Him, and He agrees.

Having appointed Satan to mislead people, Allah threatens the misled with his intention to throw them in the blazing hell.

One wonders if Allah knows what He is doing. Being a manipulator, is He really capable of guiding others? Do these facts not contradict the Koran's claim of being the Divine Book of Guidance? To be continued.

NOTES

1. M. Muhsin Khan has added in brackets here "with the Prophet, violating their peace treaty," which is not in the original Arabic.

2. Paul Kurtz, *The Transcendental Temptation* (Amherst, N.Y.: Prometheus Books, 1986).

3. There seems to be some controversy as to what the language of the Koran really is. See my introduction to *What the Koran Really Says* (Amherst, N.Y.: Prometheus Books, 2002).

4. John Penrice, *Dictionary and Glossary of the Koran* (1873; reprint, New Delhi: Low Price Publications, 1990).

5. Hans Wehr, *A Dictionary of Modern Written Arabic* (Lebanon: Librairie du Liban, 1980), p. 142.

6. Translators and commentators refer this sura to the massacre of the Jews in the tribe of Qurayza by Muhammad. See Ibn Isḥāq, *The Life of Muhammad*, trans. A. Guillaume (1995; reprint, Oxford: Oxford University Press, 1987), pp. 461–69.

7. Muslim commentators point out that Jews are meant: e.g., Maulana Muhammad Ali, translator of *The Holy Quran* (1917; reprint, Lahore, 1995), p. 260, n. 714.

8. R. Bell agrees with al-Suyuti and also says in his commentary, "The end of the verse shows that the Prophet is speaking in his own words." R. Bell, *A Commentary on the Qurʾan* (Manchester, England: Victoria University of Manchester, 1991), vol. 1, p. 201.

9. R. Bell: "... verse 114 contains a perplexing mixture of pronouns. ..." Ibid., p. 203.

10. Steven Runciman, *The Fall of Constantinople, 1453* (Cambridge: Canto, 1990), p. 145.

11. R. Peters, *Jihad in Classical and Modern Islam: A Reader* (Princeton, N.J.: Princeton University Press, 1996), p. 1.

12. Ibid., p. 3.

13. Ibn Khaldūn, *The Muqaddimah*, trans. F. Rosenthal, ed. N. J. Dawood (Princeton, N.J.: Princeton University Press, 1967), p. 183.

14. A. Shaikh, *Faith and Deception* (Cardiff: Principality Publishers, 1996); *Islam, The Arab National Movement* (Cardiff: Principality Publishers, 1995); *Islam, Sex and Violence* (Cardiff: Principality Publishers, 1999); *Islam, The Arab Imperialism* (Cardiff: Principality Publishers, 1998); and *Eternity* (Cardiff: Principality Publishers, 1990).

15. *Express and Star* (Britain), July 17, 1995.

B

EX-MUSLIMS OF THE WORLD UNITE!

ISIS: Institute for the Secularisation of Islamic Society

Executive Directors: Ibn Warraq and Fatemolla
URL: www.secularislam.org
E-mail: info@SecularIslam.org

Mission Statement

We believe that Islamic society has been held back by an unwillingness to subject its beliefs, laws, and practices to critical examination, by a lack of respect for the rights of the individual, and by an unwillingness to tolerate alternative viewpoints or to engage in constructive dialogue.

The Institute for the Secularisation of Islamic Society (ISIS) has been formed to promote the ideas of rationalism, secularism, democracy and human rights within Islamic society.

ISIS promotes freedom of expression, freedom of thought and belief, freedom of intellectual and scientific inquiry, freedom of conscience and religion—including the freedom to change one's religion or belief—and freedom from religion: the freedom not to believe in any deity.

Statement of Principles

We share the ideals of a democratic society, and a secular state that does not endorse any religion, religious institution, or any religious dogma. The basis for its authority is in man-made law, not in religious doctrine or in divine revelation. In a theocracy of the type that Islamic fundamentalists wish to establish, sovereignty belongs to god, but in a democracy sovereignty belongs to the people. We therefore favor the firm separation of religion and state: without such a separation there can be no freedom from tyranny, and such a separation is the sine qua non for a secular state.

We believe in the primacy of the rule of law: a common civil code under which all men and women have equal protection of their rights and freedoms.

We endorse the Universal Declaration of Human Rights and the International Covenants on Human Rights without qualification. We are particularly concerned to promote and protect the rights of women and those with minority beliefs: all should be equal before the law.

We are dedicated to combating fanaticism, intolerance, violent fundamentalism, and terrorism by showing the intellectual inadequacy of the fanatics' programmes, the historical inaccuracy of their claims, the philosophical poverty of their arguments, and the totalitarian nature of their thought.

We defend the right of free inquiry, and the free expression of ideas. We therefore reserve the right to examine the historical foundations of Islam, and to explain the rise and fall of Islam by the normal mechanisms of human history.

Practical Goals

To create a network of secularists and freethinkers in Islamic countries.

To establish a women's network to provide mutual support and to highlight the plight and the achievements of women in Islamic societies.

To report on recent research findings on the origins of Islam and the Koran.

To provide an alternative source of information and comment for the media on Islamic issues.

To publicise acts of terror and oppression.

To honor the memory and promote the work and thought of those martyred in the cause of freedom of expression.

To attract writers, academics, politicians and activists as members of the institute and as contributors to the debate.

To establish a database of books, articles, and news reports; an annotated bibliography of texts of interest; and a suggested reading list.

To seek funding for institute activities, including the translation of important texts.

To publish a Web-based newsletter: "Secular Islam."

FAITH FREEDOM INTERNATIONAL

Executive Director: Dr. Ali Sina
URL: main.faithfreedom.org/
Email: faithfreedomintl@yahoo.com

Mission Statement

The world was shocked to watch in disbelief the events of September 11, and the brutal slaying of the young journalist Daniel Pearl made it clear that we are facing a ruthless and an evil force. Yet what happened is nothing compared to what is still to come. This evil knows no bounds. This hatred has no limits. It is inspired by an ideology that claims to be from God. It is backed by a billion or more people. No one is safe. Anyone could become the target of this hate. We may be at the threshold of another war of a world scale.

Yes indeed, this could be the beginning of the World War III. But unlike the previous wars, the enemy in this war is invisible and our guns, tanks, and fighter jets are worthless. This is not a war between the East and the West. It is not a war between haves and have-nots. It is not even a war between Muslims and non-Muslims. It is a war between the civilized world and barbarity.

Making war against terrorism is like fighting against viruses. Terrorists are our enemies, but they can be anywhere. They are among us, they live in our lands, they work our factories and offices, and they are our neighbors. Yet they will kill us when the order comes and the *fatwa* is issued. No one is safe at home or abroad. You could be used as a pawn and/or a bargaining chip and easily killed, as there are others who could replace you. Our cities, our water reservoirs, our planes, and our offices are no more safe. Why do they hate us and why do they want to kill us?

People just don't decide to become terrorists. Terrorists are motivated by a doctrine that instigates in them the hate and the will to kill. In order to combat the terrorism you have to combat their doctrine. The Quran is a book full of hate of the nonbelievers. To overlook this fact is a gross error that could cost millions of lives. Faith Freedom International was formed to combat this invisible enemy and stop Islamic terrorism by eliminating its cause.

Yes there are Hindu, Buddhist, and Christian terrorists, too. But these terrorists have chosen paths of violence despite the teachings of their religions. In Islam, terrorism is prescribed in the Quran; it is encouraged and recommended. The prophet of Islam laid the example of terror for all his followers to follow. He raided civilians, massacred his prisoners of war, raped their women, enslaved women and children, looted their belongings, assassinated his opponents, burned trees, and showed no mercy to anyone who dared to stand in his way. Muslim terrorists are doing just that. You cannot fight Islamic terrorism without fighting Islam.

Islam marches on two feet. One foot is represented by the Islamic apologists: those who call themselves doctors and write in good English painting a lovey-dovey picture of Islam and claiming it to be a "religion of peace." The tools of these so-called intellectuals of Islam are lies and deceit. The terrorists represent the other foot of Islam. This group executes the second phase of Islamic expansionism. Though an unwary person may think that these two groups are antagonists to each other, in reality they are executing the same plan and indeed are two faces of the same coin and very much interdependent.

The Faith Freedom International is a nonprofit organization formed by mostly ex-Muslims who know too well that Islam is the root cause behind Islamic terrorism. We know that good Muslims become terrorists when they decide to practice what the Quran teaches. This organization was formed by a group of writers and common citizens to expose the lies of the Islamic propagandists and reveal the true face of Islam. We care about the world and about peace. We believe that the majority of Muslims are not aware of the truth of Islam. They are fed with lies and they have believed in those lies. They are victims themselves. But ignorance is not an excuse. The truth is out and it is up to them to learn it, just as we did, and denounce this doctrine of hate, weaken it and eradicate it before it destroys more lives.

As the first step after Faith Freedom International was formed, we issued a statement and called Muslims to rethink their beliefs. If you are a journalist, we urge you to publish it in your media, and if you are not we ask you to circulate it around (no spamming please).

Our goal is to educate the born Muslims to abandon Islam and warn the fool-hardy to avoid it. There are many John Walkers and potential John Walkers that are victims of Islam and its lies. We have to stop this insanity.

Faith Freedom International is a humanist organization. We are secularists and believe in a secular society. However, we respect freedom of belief and religion. We are not against any faith. We are against hate.

Islamic terror machinery is fueled by billons of dollars. All those good Muslims who innocently support their mosques and pay their *khoms* and *zakat*, with every liter of oil that you pump into your SUV, Islamic terrorism is invigorated. Thousands of books and Web sites are spewing the lies to promote Islam, and this means more terrorism. With every new convert that falls into the trap of Islam a new potential terrorist is born. Some unscrupulous Western writers who have sold out their integrity have turned Islamic apologists, too. And our politicians have no choice but to play the political correctness game and echo the lie that "Islam is a religion of peace."

Who Is Going to Tell the Truth?

Faith Freedom International is the voice of the truth. We are dedicated to one goal and that is to expose the lies of Islam and call off its expansionist plans.

Islam is absolute darkness and therefore vulnerable to the light of the truth. However, Islam is vulnerable to truth but not to hate. Islam feeds on hate and no one can overpower Islam by hating the Muslims. Therefore efforts such as ours, who love our people and truly want to help them integrate with the rest of the world and emancipate from their backwardness, will bear fruit while hate that fundamentalists of other religions foment against Muslims will be counterproductive.

We declare Islam to be a false religion and challenge the Islamic apologists to prove us wrong. We believe Islam is evil. We believe Islam is endangering the peace of the world and the lives of every one of us including Muslims themselves. We urge the peace-loving people of the world, ex-Muslims and others, to help us fight this overgrown cult. This is indeed the fight of David against Goliath. We are a small group of people, with our own lives to run and works to do, but we are poised to face the second most spread "religion" of the world, some of whose followers are very violent who would not hesitate to kill us if they could lay their hand on us.

But we shall win. We shall win because light is more powerful than darkness and truth is more potent than lies. Islam is very powerful today. Its followers are fanatic and violent. But Islam is also vulnerable. Islam is absolute darkness and as such is very susceptible to light. Islam is founded on lies and therefore will crumble with a little blow of the truth. To fight Islamic terrorism we have to fight Islam Islam is terrorism. This is clear by just reading few pages from the Quran. You cannot fight Islamic terrorism through military force. Billions of dollars expended for armaments will not wipe it out. The United States is giving Egypt $3 billion annually, yet every child in a Madrassa of Egypt will rise his hand when his religious teacher asks, who is willing to become a martyr by blowing himself in order to kill the American *kafirs*. The United States expended billions of dollars to save the Kuwait from a brutal dictator such as Saddam Hussein. Today Kuwait is adamant against the United States invading Iraq and removing that madman by force. Unbelievable as it may seem, the Kosovars are anti-American and anti-Westerner even though the West waged a war to liberate them.

It would be a huge mistake if we neglect to see that the root cause of all this hate is Islam. The rise of Islamic fundamentalism that started with Islamic revolution in Iran soon inspired the rest of the Islamic world and is now rolling our planet into a total disaster.

Islamic terrorism can be eliminated only when Islam is eliminated. Just as communism fell apart from within, Islam will also collapse from within. Today it is ex-Muslims who have risen to slaughter this beast, but we need the help of the world to achieve our sacred goal.

Billions of dollars and millions of *Jihadis* willing to kill and die fuel Islamic expansionism. We are only a handful of writers and commoners, with nothing but the will to overcome hate and make the earth a peaceful planet.

We fight ignorance with knowledge. We are motivated by love of humanity. We endeavor to bring peace. We strive for equality of genders, for elimination of prejudices, for freedom of beliefs and expression, for democracy and for unity of humanity. Please help our cause and spread our message of love and unity.

ADVOCATES OF ARTICLE 18

Executive Directors: Armen Saginian and Syed Kamran Mirza
Address: P.O. Box 896, Glendale, CA 91209, USA
Tel.: (323) 666-4278
Fax: (323) 666-4271
Email: armen@cfiwest.org

Mission Statement

We uphold the principles enshrined in Article 18 of the Universal Declaration Of Human Rights (1948):

> Everyone has the right to Freedom of thought, conscience and religion; this right includes freedom to change his religion or belief, and freedom, either alone or in community with others and in public or private, to manifest his religion or belief in teaching, practice, worship and observance.

APOSTATES OF ISLAM

URL: www.apostatesofislam.com
E-mail: contact via Web site, www.apostatesofislam.com/forms/contactus.htm

Philosophy, Aims, and Hopes of this Web Site

The founder of Islam, Muhammad, ordered to kill anyone who left Islam, and he did so because he knew that if an ex-Muslim was allowed to live, he would shake the beliefs of all other Muslims.

Thus, it is extremely important for ex-Muslims to come out and form a group. This Web site serves this important purpose.

All religions are man-made and defective, but Islam is currently the most destructive religion and we protest against the hatred meted out to us and non-Muslims by Islam. We will work to expose the truth about Islam and help to relieve mankind of this destructive, harmful cult, which threatens peace on Earth.

We do not hate Muslims, but we do hate Islam. Muslims do not know the evil nature of Islam and do not want to know because they are afraid of Islam's imaginary hellfire. Nowadays, it is not safe to come out in the open and claim to have left Islam, but we must start revealing ourselves and the start of this revelation is this Web site, the growing online community of ex-Muslims.

As a reminder to Muslims who have difficulty in believing our claim of being former Muslims, it is important for them to note that Muhammad himself knew of people who had left Islam and he ordered them to be killed. So, ironically, for Muslims to refuse to believe that we left Islam is to disbelieve an important part of Islamic tradition, Hadith, which renders these Muslims apostates!

So, all Muslims must believe that we have left Islam, or else they could be committing the sin of "unbelief," i.e., *kufr*, and thus will be most likely punished in (imaginary) hellfire.

C

THE COUNCIL FOR SECULAR HUMANISM

The Council for Secular Humanism Web site (www.secularhumanism.org) provides timely information concerning the activities of the Council for Secular Humanism and also acts as a general educational resource on secular humanism.

The Council for Secular Humanism is North America's leading organization for nonreligious people. A not-for-profit educational association, the council supports a wide range of activities to meet the needs of people who find meaning and value in life without looking to a god. Its activities range from magazine publishing to campaigning on ethical issues, from conferences to support networks, from educational courses to conducting secular ceremonies, from local groups to international development. Officers of the Council for Secular Humanism include Paul Kurtz (Chairman) and Ed Buckner (Executive Director).

Secular humanism is a way of thinking and living that aims to bring out the best in people so that all people can have the best in life. Secular humanists reject supernatural and authoritarian beliefs. They affirm that we must take responsibility for our own lives and the communities and world in which we live. Secular humanism emphasizes reason and scientific inquiry, individual freedom and responsibility, human values and compassion, and the need for tolerance and cooperation.

Council activities include:

- Championing the Rights and Beliefs of Secular Humanists

  The Council for Secular Humanism campaigns for a more secular and ethical society. It presents the case for understanding the world without reference to a god, and works to separate church and state and defend the rights of people who do not accept religious beliefs.

- Serving the Needs of Nonreligious People

  The council gives practical support and services to nonreligious people. It runs courses and summer camps that educate children in critical thinking and ethical values. For rites of passage, such as marriage and death, it provides dignified nonreligious celebrations and memorials. And it runs a national support network for secular families and parents.

- Developing Secular Communities

  The Council for Secular Humanism supports local groups (both off-campus and on-campus) that provide a forum for ideas and a base for activities. Regular regional and national conferences bring secular humanists together to exchange ideas and explore topical issues. And the new Centers for Inquiry across America are providing the buildings and staff to develop a dynamic humanist presence at the grassroots level.

- Giving a Moral and Intellectual Lead

  The Council for Secular Humanism promotes rational, human-based viewpoints on important social and ethical issues. In particular, it tackles issues where traditional religion obstructs the right to self-determination, for example, freedom of choice in sexual relationships. reproduction, and voluntary euthanasia. The council also promotes critical thinking about supernatural and paranormal claims. The council conducts research, issues statements, and brings together leading thinkers for conferences and seminars.

If you support what we are working to achieve, please help us make a difference—join the Council for Secular Humanism! Associate Members receive the *Secular Humanist Bulletin*, a quarterly newsletter, in addition to other benefits including discounts on conference registrations, conference tapes, and selected titles from Prometheus Books.

The Council for Secular Humanism is committed to free inquiry, reason, and science; the separation of church and state; civil liberties; nontheism and humanist ethics. It does not endorse candidates or parties, nor does it take political positions as a corporate body. We open our pages to a wide range of opinions, including dissenting viewpoints; opinions expressed in columns and articles do not necessarily represent the views of the council.

D

A LIST OF WEB SITES
CRITICAL OF ISLAM

"Kafir" of AntiJihad created the following list of sites, including the descriptions and reviews, offering an alternative view on Islam. Since then, new sites have been added by "Raven" and "Kovac," who are also members of the same organization. I should like to thank them for their immense work. They were also kind enough to give me permission to reproduce it here, and even provided me the list in a form that my computer could handle for publication. The most current version of this list can be found at www.geocities.com/listislam.

Most, though not all, of the Web sites devoted to criticizing Islam are hosted and written by Christians, Hindus, or Jews. If you bear this in mind, and thus make allowances for the particular viewpoint from which they are written, then you will find most of the links here of immense value.

I do not necessarily endorse or agree with the tone or the entire contents of all the Web sites listed below. How could I, since I am an atheist, humanist, and rationalist? I have simply tried to give a comprehensive list of sites critical of Islam. But, of course, to the extent that they do criticize Islam in a rational way, bringing textual, historical, philological, and philosophical arguments to bear on Islamic doctrine and practice, I do approve of them.

ABOUT ISA

Perspective: Christian
Description: Tells Muslims about Jesus
Review: User-friendly and available in Indonesian and Turkish language. Please look out for an excellent comparison between the Bible and the Koran. Interesting essays on known forgeries such as the "Gospel" of Barnabas.
URL: www.aboutisa.com/
Contact: mail@aboutisa.com

ACTUALITÉ INTERNATIONALE

Perspective: French
Description: Good site in French about Islamic invasions
Review: Nice site with international news about "Islamic conquest" all around the world.
URL: aipj.net/
E-mail: aipj@aipj.net

AIME: D'AILLEURS OU D'ICI MAIS ENSEMBLE

Perspective: Secular
Description: AIME was created in 1997 aimed at the North African World, to promote secularism and equality between women and men, to reject fundamentalism and to take a critical look at religion.
Review: In French. Founded by a courageous Tunisian woman, Samia Labidi, whose brother was an Islamic terrorist at one point in his life. The site cannot as yet take on Islam directly, though it does advocate atheism quite openly. Launched a magazine in 1999 to spread its ideas. Needs to be encouraged.
URL: www.assoaime.net/
Contact: taimeatic@assoaime.net

AL NOUR

Perspective: Christian
Description: Tells Muslims about Jesus
Review: Easy-to-understand discussions on the fallacies of Islam and common Islamic allegations about the Bible.
URL: members.aol.com/alnour/index2.html
E-mail: FUZL@aol.com

AMERICA AT WAR
Perspective: Christian
Description: Salem the Soldier's homepage
Review: This site tells us about America and its war against Islamic terrorism.
URL: www.salemthesoldier.us/America_At_War.html
E-mail: info@salemthesoldier.us, salem83@aol.com

AN OPEN CHALLENGE TO MY MUSLIM FRIENDS
Perspective: Atheist
Description: Questions the Koran.
Review: Funny facts about Islam and astronomy. Includes a great drawing.
URL: humanists.net/avijit/
E-mail: avijitroy@hotmail.com

ANSWERING ISLAM
Perspective: Christian
Description: A Muslim-Christian dialogue
Review: This is not only the best Christian Web site, but probably the best Web
   site of all the Internet devoted to refuting and criticizing Islamic claims, doctrines, history, and the Koran. It is well-documented, and is one of the few
   anti Islamic Web sites that is very careful to give the proper references, and
   thus one has all the more confidence in its pronouncements. It is also very
   fair in that it gives ample space to Muslims to reply, and scrupulously
   removes any material that is shown to be erroneous
URL: www.answering-islam.org; German mirror: www.answering-islam.de/
E-mail: dialog@answering-islam.org; webmaster@answering-islam.de

ANSWERING THE CLAIMS OF ISLAM
Perspective: Christian
Description: Small site, many links
Review: The links are good. Several of the Islamic claims are addressed in a non-
   biased manner. The link about the Koran and Yemeni scrolls is interesting.
URL: usr.ijntb.net/thickman/islam.html
E-mail: Not available

ANTIJIHAD

Perspective: Kafir Unity

Description: An international network promoting unity among those who face the threat of Islamic terror

Review: Cool site for a crash course in resisting terrorism. Great links and forums. Only site with active campaigns.

URL: www.geocities.com/AntiJihad/home.html

E-mail: seeds@ca.tc

ANTIJIHAD: NORTH AMERICA

Perspective: North American

Description: North American branch of AntiJihad

Review: Call to North Americans to unite

URL: www.geocities.com/jihadisucks

E-mail: USKAFIR@yahoo.com

ANTIJIHAD: WEST AND SOUTH ASIA

Perspective: West and South Asian

Description: West and South Asian branch of AntiJihad

Review: Call to Israelis, Hindus, and other *kafirs* to unite

URL: www.antijihad.cjb.net/

E-mail: Israeli_guy@hotmail.co.il

APOSTATES OF ISLAM

Perspective: Ex-Muslim

Description: Online community of ex-Muslims who share their thoughts and experiences with Islam and why they left it

Review: Good site design; easy navigation; extensive content and categorized, searchable databases of the Koran and *hadith*

URL: www.apostatesofislam.com

E-mail: See Web site

ARGUMENTS AGAINST ISLAM BY AN EX-MUSLIM

Perspective: Apostate

Description: Contains quotes from the Koran and *hadith*. Made by a young Turk who has left Islam.

Review: Many interesting *hadith*

URL: www.geocities.com/heywantor/
E-mail: heywantor@yahoo.com

AWFUL TRUTH ABOUT ISLAM
Perspective: Secular
Description: Systematically dissects Islamist duplicity
Review: Small site, great facts
URL: www.geocities.com/the_awful_truth_about_islam/index.htm
E-mail: Not available

BAT YE'OR
Perspective: Academic
Description: Thoughts on Islam by an Egyptian woman
Review: Good site, great facts
URL: mypage.bluewin.ch/ameland/index.html
E-mail: Not available

BEHIND THE VEIL
Perspective: Christian
Description: An online book
Review: Truth seekers (both *kafirs* and Muslims) will find this book interesting. This is a thorough documentation on Islamic doublespeak and fallacies. Also see Answering Islam.
URL: answering-islam.org/BehindVeil/content.htm
E-mail: dialog@answering-islam.org

BHARATVANI INSTITUTE
Perspective: Hindu
Description: Hindu Web site, with online books by K. Elst, R. Swarup, and Sita Ram Goel critical of Islam
Review: An informative and a must-visit site for every Hindu who wishes to rediscover his roots and dharma.
URL: www.voi.org/
E-mail: bharatvani@usa.net

Blacks Who Oppose Islam

Perspective: Afro-American
Description: Still under construction. Facts on various issues such as modern slavery in the Islamic world.
Review: Really interesting site
URL: www.geocities.com/bwoi2002/
E-mail: Not available

Chechen Truth

Perspective: Pro-Russian
Description: Tells the truth about the Muslim-Russian war
Review: Informative site with many photos
URL: www.geocities.com/chechentruth/
E-mail: stalkercal@yahoo.com

CHICK Publications

Perspective: Christian
Description: Publishing house offering a lot of information about Islam
Review: Useful resource
URL: www.chick.com/information/religions/islam/
E-mail: Not available

Christliche (1) Christliche (2) Christliche (3)

Perspective: German
Description: Exposes Islam and the strategies this cult uses to conquer European/ Western societies
Review: Great Web site in German
URL: www.christliche-mitte.de/themen/islam/buchliste.htm
E-mail: islam@christliche-mitte.de

Committee to Defend Women's Rights in the Middle East—CDWRME

Perspective: Secular, Feminist, Women's Rights
Description: "The Committee to Defend Women's Rights in the Middle East— CDWRME—has been formed to promote women's rights and equality in the Middle East. We believe that secularism and the separation of religion from the state are the basic preconditions for women's liberation in the Middle

East. We believe in the universality of women's rights and combat the idea of cultural relativism that justifies women's oppression under the rule of Islamic law and Islamic governments. We try to create a network of women's rights activists in the Middle Eastern countries, we campaign around women's civil rights and individual freedom, and support the just struggle of women in the Middle East."

Review: The treatment of Women in Islamic countries remains inhuman, but there are courageous activists who battle for women's rights despite all sorts of dangers, obstacles, and prejudices.

URL: www.eclipse.co.uk/women/

E-mail: azam_kamguian@yahoo.com

COPTS

Perspective: Christian

Description: The official site of the persecuted (Christian) Copts in (Muslim) Egypt

Review: Daily documentation of Islamic atrocities on Christians of Africa, with links

URL: www.copts.net/index.asp

E-mail: us_copts@copts.com

CRITICAL ANALYSIS OF ISLAM

Perspective: Christian

Description: Christian-Islamic thoughts

Review: Good links. The testimony of ex-Muslims make good reading. Also available in Arabic.

URL: debate.org.uk/topics/coolcalm/

E-mail: Not available

CRUSADER AND JEW PRESS

Perspective: Israeli nationalist

Description: About Israel and the United States

Review: Many interesting articles

URL: cjpress.topcities.com/

E-mail: Not available

CRUSADERS CLUB

Perspective: Christian

Description: "We, the Undersigned . . . do commit ourselves, our wealth, and our families to join in a Holy Crusade to fight against Islam and its false god, false prophet, and false book."

Review: A great Christian site that knows what the real root of Muslim terrorism is

URL: www.faithdefenders.com/crusaders.shtml

E-mail: Not available; see site for 'Contact us' link.

DEMOCRATIC ALLIANCE

Perspective: American

Description: *Hadith* and links

Review: The site brings back memories of 9/11 and why it happened.

URL: www.salvation.at/democracy

E-mail: Not available

DHIMMI

Perspective: International

Description: "(We) still endure the ravaging effects of an ideological movement that is intolerant, discriminatory, racist and even genocidal: a Radical Islamist-Jihad culture."

Review: Interesting

URL: www.dhimmi.com/

E-mail: info@dhimmi.com

DIE KONSERVATIVE INFORMATIONSBASIS IM INTERNET: ISLAM

Perspective: Conservative

Description: This site offers a number of essays on the subject of the Islamization of Europe. In German.

Review: Informative, great!

URL: www.konservativ.de/islam/home.htm

E-mail: rolf.josef@eibicht.de

DRHOMA DARABI FOUNDATION

Perspective: Women's rights

Description: Pictures, campaigns, articles, and link

Review: A great Web site for women wanting to learn the hidden face of Islam
URL: www.homa.org/
E-mail: homa@homa.org

ENOUGH NET

Perspective: Israeli
Description: Pictures, campaigns, articles, and links
Review: Great Israeli Web site
URL: www.geocities.com/enough_nct/right-islam.html
E-mail: game_net2001@hotmail.com

FAITH FREEDOM FOUNDATION

Perspective: Apostate/humanist
Description: Huge site by a former Muslim. Has everything one might need.
Review: Excellent site! Also available in Indonesian.
URL: www.faithfreedom.org/; mirrors: www.golshan.com/; www.humanists.net/
  alisina/
E-mail: faithfreedomintl@yahoo.com

FOMI

Perspective: Norwegian
Description: Site of Forum against Islamization
Review: This Scandinavian site is mainly in Norwegian, with some information
  in English.
URL: rto73.0catch.com/index.htm
E-mail: Not available

FOMI—2

Perspective: Norwegian
Description: Well-indexed documentation of holocausts and genocide in the
  name of Islam
Review: Even though this site is in Norwegian, the pictures do not need a lan-
  guage
URL: rto73.0catch.com/Verdenrundt/Verdenrundt.htm
E-mail: Not available

FREEDOM SOCIETY
Perspective: Democratic
Description: Links
Review: Good links for global war against terrorism
URL: www.freedomsociety.4t.com/
E-mail: freedom_society007@hotmail.com

FREEMAN CENTER
Perspective: Pro-Israel
Description: Very much a pro-Israel site with learned articles defending a tough
    approach to the problems in the Middle East
Review: Very good articles on the theory and practice of Islamic terrorism, par-
    ticularly from Y. Bodansky
URL: www.freeman.org
E-mail: BSaphir@aol.com

FREETHOUGHT MECCA
Perspective: Humor
Description: Cold facts and logical reasoning unravelling hot rumors and claims
Review: A very funny and totally irreverent look at Islam and Christianity
URL: www.geocities.com/freethoughtmecca/home.htm
E-mail: freethoughtmecca@yahoo.com

GEO ISLAM
Perspective: French/secular
Description: Exposes Islamic teachings and goals in French
Review: Exposes Islamic worldwide expansion via immigration
URL: www.geo-islam.org/
E-mail: infos@geo-islam.org

HAMMIHAN IRANI
Perspective: Secular democratic
Description: Articles, *hadith*, and links on Islam and theocratic Iran
Review: Excellent content
URL: www.geocities.com/hammihanirani/; mirror: hammihan.20fr.com/
E-mail: Not available

HINDU AWARENESS!
Perspective: Hindu nationalist
Description: Essays and pictures
Review: Well written essays. The essay on Hindu-Muslim marriages is a must read for everyone.
URL: www.angelfire.com/country/army/index.html
E-mail: Not available

HINDU SITAH
Perspective: Hindu
Description: Hindus from India tell us about their struggle with Islamic and Koranic terrorism.
Review: Real eye-opener about Muslim *jihadi* activities in South Asia. A call for Hindus to unite and protect their motherland.
URL: hsita.cjb.net/
E-mail: hsitah9@yahoo.com

HINDU HOLOCAUST MUSEUM
Perspective: Hindu
Description: "The massacres perpetrated by Muslims in India are unparalleled in history . . ."
Review: Sheds light upon a virtually unknown part of history
URL: www.mantra.com/holocaust/
E-mail: hhm@mantra.com

HINDU STRUGGLE
Perspective: Hindu
Description: A huge collection of hateful quotes from Koran
Review: Islam exposed, good collection of quotes
URL: www.geocities.com/hinduunity
E-mail: hinduunity@yahoo.com

HINDUUNITY
Perspective: Hindu nationalist
Description: One-stop shop for details on Islamic atrocities
Review: A huge archive, frequently updated, and an excellent forum

URL: www.hinduunity.org/
E-mail: hinduunity@hotmail.com

HUAREN
Perspective: Indonesian Christian and Buddhist
Description: Pictures, eyewitness accounts, and details on recent atrocities
against *kafirs* in Indonesia
Review: Warning: Has graphic details and pictures of atrocities against Christians
in Indonesia
URL: www.huaren.org/atro/
E-mail: inquiry@huaren.org

HUMAN RIGHTS ABUSES IN ISLAMIC COUNTRIES
Perspective: Secular
Description: Multiethnic, multireligious organization committed to combating
abuses in Muslim countries; focuses on Islamic law
Review: Good reading. The inflammatory hadith and abuse of human rights are
clearly documented.
URL: www.hraic.org/
E-mail: hraic@hraic.org

INJIL.ORG
Perspective: Christian
Description: Tells Muslims about Jesus
Review: Easy read for Muslims who wish to renounce violence
URL: injil.org/
E-mail: Not available

INTO THE LIGHT
Perspective: Christian
Description: Tells Muslims about Jesus
Review: Thought-provoking Muslim-Christian discussions
URL: www.itl.org.uk/
E-mail: info@itl.org.uk

IRAN FREEDOM
Perspective: Nationalist, Zoroastrian
Description: Anti-Islamic Iranian nationalist site
Review: Cool effects, nice summary on the founder of Islam, and excellent links
URL: www.hope.at/iranfreedom
E-mail: Not available

INSTITUTE FOR THE SECULARISATION OF ISLAMIC SOCIETY (ISIS)
Perspective: Secular
Description: Promote the ideas of rationalism, secularism, democracy, and human rights within Islamic society
Review: A good source of quotations, event documentations, and skepticism. This site addresses issues ailing the current Islamic world.
URL: secularislam.org/
E-mail: info@secularislam.org

ISLAMANIACS!
Perspective: Hindu nationalist
Description: A brief history of Islam
Review: Annoying structure, but includes a lovely song
URL: members.aye.net/~abrupt/house/islam.html
E-mail: Not available

ISLAM CHALLENGES CHRISTIANITY
Perspective: Secular
Description: Questions and contradictions on the Koran
Review: Good layout, easy read; answers Islamic and Koranic "miracles"
URL: members.aol.com/AlHaqq4u/; mirror: debate.domini.org./newton/
E-mail: Not available

ISLAM EXPOSED
Perspective: Atheist
Description: Does what it says: exposes concealed truths
Review: Beautiful layout
URL: www.islamexposed.com/
E-mail: webmaster@islamexposed.com

ISLAM EXPOSED (ARCHIVES ONLY)
Perspective: Hindu nationalist
Description: Big archive, something for everyone
Review: Great resource
URL: www.geocities.com/heywantor/
E-mail: heywantor@yahoo.com

ISLAM FAITH EXAMINED!
Perspective: Christian
Description: A resource for the study of Islam
Review: Great material and good reading on claims of Islam and prophethood
URL: www.bible.ca/eo/islam.htm
E-mail: markcopeland@aol.com

ISLAMIC SOCIETY
Perspective: Secular
Description: Open directory and links to Islamic literature
Review: Great links, arguments
URL: dmoz.org/Society/Religion_and_Spirituality/Opposing_Views/ Islam
E-mail: Not available

ISLAMIC STUDIES IN CHRISTIAN PERSPECTIVE
Perspective: Christian
Description: Studies Islam from a Christian perspective, and tries to convert
    Muslims
Review: Great Web site, nice design, cool material on Islam and the Koran
URL: www.rim.org/muslim/islam.htm
E-mail: comments@rim.org

ISLAMIC TERROR SITES ON THE WEB
Perspective: Secular
Description: Gives a list of Islamic Web sites that promote *jihad*
Review: Great Web page, links updated regularly. Feel free to send them *jihadi*
    Web sites you come across.
URL: www.geocities.com/johnathanrgalt
E-mail: johnathanrgalt@yahoo.co.uk

ISLAMINFO

Perspective: Danish
Description: A Danish site with an alternative view on Islam, and Danish Islam-related news. In Danish.
Review: Excellent site for Scandinavians
URL: www.islaminfo.dk/
E-mail: Not available

ISLAM-ON-LINE

Perspective: Christian
Description: Persecution of Christians by Islam
Review: Great resource for persecuted Christians and Muslim converts to Christianity. Well-documented atrocities with insights into the *jihad* theory.
URL: www.islam-on-line.org/
E-mail: Not available

ISLAM REVIEW

Perspective: Christian
Description: About Islam, not Muslims
Review: Good Web design, good material, and good reading. An eye-opener to the mistreatment of blacks in Islam.
URL: www.islamreview.com/
E-mail: Feedback@IslamReview.com

ISLAM: THE GREATEST THREAT

Perspective: Secular
Description: Discusses "the greatest and most immediate threat to human civilization"
Review: Good page design, easy reading, a "gumbo" of quotations from the Bible, Hindu-Islamist dialogues, and the Koran
URL: www.geocities.com/Athens/Ithaca/3440/islam.html
E-mail: singhvj@rogers.com

ISLAM VIA HADIS

Perspective: Hindu
Description: A book by Ram Swaroop
Review: Rudimentary Web design, but great material on Islam and Islamists

URL: voi.org/books/uith/
E-mail: Not available

JESUS IS LORD

Perspective: Christian
Description: Facts notebook
Review: Basic design, but great material on Islamists. Interesting facts on black Islamic movement.
URL: jesus-is-lord.com/islam.htm
E-mail: webmaster@jesus-is-lord.com

JEWISH TASK FORCE

Perspective: Jewish
Description: Pro-America, Israel, and India
Review: Right-wing, patriotic Jewish Web site. Selected verses from the Koran. Facts backed by pictures on Islamic barbarism.
URL: www.jtf.org/
E-mail: Not available

KAFFIR RESISTANCE

Perspective: Antiterrorist
Description: "Our silence has only encouraged the Jehadis. If you wish to know what might happen to the US in future, take a good look at the problems faced by Israel and India. Focuses on South Asia."
Review: New site
URL: www.geocities.com/kaffir_resistance/
E-mail: J_A_S_O_N67@hotmail.com

KOMMT DER ISLAM?

Perspective: Kafir
Description: This site describes Islam as fascism wearing the mask of religion. It also shows the difference between Christianity and Islam, and calls for *kafirs* to unite. In German.
Review: Really interesting site; suggests what can be done about the problem
URL: members.aol.com/PetrusLotichius/Dokumente/stolz_islam_ text.htm
E-mail: Not available

KORAN AND KAFIR

Perspective: Hindu/Sikh

Description: Online book by A. Ghosh; "All that a *kafir* needs to know about Islam but is scared to ask"

Review: The page design could be better, but the material is fantastic.

URL: www.hindutva.org/KoranKafir/

E-mail: webmaster@RealIslam.org

LET US REASON

Perspective: Christian

Description: Answers to Islamic questions and claims

Review: Good material

URL: www.letusreason.org/Islamdir.htm

E-mail: administrator@letusreason.org

LIGHT OF LIFE

Perspective: Christian

Description: Investigates Islam from a Christian point of view

Review: Great Web design; good material comparing Allah with God from a Christian perspective

URL: www.light-of-life.com/

E-mail: webmaster@light-of-life.com

L'ISLAM, RELIGION OU SYSTEME POLITIQUE?

Perspective: Secular

Description: Defines Islamic ideology and roots. In French.

Review: Basic Web design; good discussions on Islam as imperialism rather than a peaceful religion; excellent references

URL: pages.intnet.mu/ramsurat/GauraKrishna/Islam.html

E-mail: Not available

LONE WOLF

Perspective: Secular

Description: Investigates "scientific" claims of Islam

Review: Basic design, advanced material

URL: www.geocities.com/lone_wolf_gc/

E-mail: lone_wolf@europe.com

LOVING A MUSLIM
Perspective: Christian
Description: Support group, memoirs
Review: Good page design, riveting stories
URL: www.domini.org/lam/home.html
E-mail: Not available

MARRYING A MIDDLE EASTERNER
Perspective: Western woman's
Description: Real-life experience
Review: One page of actual experiences
URL: www.domini.org/lam/warnings.html
E-mail: Not available

MASADA 2000
Perspective: Israeli nationalist
Description: Synopsis of the trouble spots
Review: Good design, good material on the truth
URL: www.masada2000.org/islam.html
E-mail: masada2ooo@hotmail.com

MENSCHENRECHTE AUF ISLAMISTISCH?
Perspective: Human rights
Description: An insight into the *Shariah*—Islamic laws—and how Muslims seek
    to have these laws recognized. Text in English and in German.
Review: Interesting
URL: people.freenet.de/frauenfokus/html/menschenrechte.htm
E-mail: Not available

MI PASO POR EL ISLAM
Perspective: Humanist-rationalist
Description: The story of a Spanish man who has been a Muslim. In Spanish and
    English.
Review: A moderate, intelligent analysis of Islam
URL: www.mallorcaweb.net/users/rene/islam.htm
E-mail: Not available

MUHAMMADANISM

Perspective: Christian
Description: Review of Islam
Review: Sophisticated site with excellent information on issues pertaining to
 Islam and Christianity
URL: www.muhammadanism.com/
E-mail: muhammadanism@yahoo.com

MUSLIM FREETHINKERS

Perspective: Apostate
Description: Its goal is to combat against dogmatism and blind faith.
Review: Good review of Ibn Warraq's *Why I Am Not a Muslim*, and some articles
 very critical of Islam
URL: www.geocities.com/muslimfreethinkers/index.htm
E-mail: humanism@canada.com

NATIONAL UNITY COALITION FOR ISRAEL

Perspective: Judeo-Christian
Description: A site promoting solidarity with the only democracy of the Middle
 East. Has some info about Islam.
Review: Lots of advice and arguments that will help one win any debate about
 the Jewish-Islamic conflict in the Middle East
URL: www.israelunitycoalition.com/
E-mail: voicesunited@israelunitycoalition.com

NEW HORIZONS

Perspective: Iranian
Description: Promotes the ideals of secularism, democracy, and rational inquiry
 to Iranians
Review: Good design, some material, good links for Iranians, small discussion board
URL: cfiwest.org/newhorizons/
E-mail: NewHorizons@CFIWest.org

ORTHODOX INFO (1) ORTHODOX INFO (2)

Perspective: Christian Orthodox
Description: Demonstrates the moral/ethical superiority of Christianity over
 Islam

Review: Good information about Eastern Europeans and Middle East Christians
who suffered under Islam
URL: www.orthodoxinfo.com/general/islam_definitivereply.htm
E-mail: jtalajaji@drmc.org

PERSIAN WORLD OUTREACH
Perspective: Christian/Iranian
Description: Promotes the love of Jesus
Review: Good design, news, good links for Iranians
URL: www.farsinet.com/
E-mail: feedback@farsinet.com

PRIMECHOICE
Perspective: Secular
Description: Q&A on Islam
Review: Basic design, good material and links
URL: www.primechoice.com/philosophy
E-mail: philosopherplus@hotmail.com

PROJECT: OPEN BOOK
Perspective: Christian
Description: A watchdog, keeping an eye on the persecution of Christians in the
Islamic world. Devotes some pages to the history of and theory behind the
persecutions.
Review: Good documentation of atrocities on Christians by Muslims
URL: www.domini.org/openbook/
E-mail: ireneaus@aol.com

PSYCHOHISTORY
Perspective: Secular
Description: Psychoanalysis
Review: On hatred of women and Islamic terrorism
URL: www.geocities.com/psychohistory2001/index.html
E-mail: liviolev@zahav.net.il

REAL ISLAM
Perspective: Kashmiri Sufism
Description: Writings of Anwar Shaikh
Review: Good design; great articles unraveling the myth of peaceful Islam
URL: www.realislam.org/
E-mail: webmaster@RealIslam.org

RIPOUBLIQUE BANANIÈRE DE FRANCARABIA
Perspective: French
Description: French Webring
Review: Good design, novel ideas, and excellent links in French
URL: francarabia.liberty-web.net/
E-mail: francarabia@liberty-web.net

RUSSIAN SOCIETY
Perspective: Russian
Description: A group of Russian students who want to protest against the evil religion of Islam
Review: Basic design; some pictures and notes on terrorism in Chechnya
URL: www.russian.5u.com/
E-mail: russian_society@hotmail.com

SAFFRON TIGERS
Perspective: Hindu nationalist
Description: Wake-up call for Hindus
Review: Well-designed Web site with a Shiv Sena perspective
URL: www.hinduunity.org/saffrontigers/
E-mail: saffronpower@rediffmail.com

SITA KA SANSAR
Perspective: Hindu-nationalist
Description: The personal Web site of a Hindu patriot; includes an "Islam exposed" section
Review: Well designed site, information on Hinduism and the truth on Islam
URL: www.hinduweb.org/home/general_sites/sita/
E-mail: sita@epatra.com

SOURCES OF ISLAM
Perspective: Academic/research
Description: Online book by W. St. Clair-Tisdall
Review: Good design, intricate details on the "origin" of the Koran
URL: www.truthnet.org/islam/source.htm
E-mail: truthnet@yahoo.com

STOPISLAM.COM
Perspective: Kafir
Description: A site with info about Islam and Islamic terrorism
Review: Professional layout and very informative; splendid!
URL: www.stopislam.com/
E-mail: webmaster@stopislam.com

SWORD OF TRUTH
Perspective: Hindu nationalist
Description: Hindu Web site; material on the writings of Anwar Shaikh and Islam
    in India
Review: Very informative discussions on topics related to Hinduism. Excellent
    source for Islamic doublespeak and atrocities. Anwar Shaikh's (ex-Muslim)
    articles are eye-openers.
URL: www.swordoftruth.com/
E-mail: feedback@swordoftruth.com

THE GOOD WAY
Perspective: Christian
Description: Tells Muslims about Jesus
Review: Cool Web site; great for Muslims attempting to understand Christianity
URL: the-good-way.com/
E-mail: info@the-good-way.com

THE ISLAMIC MONITOR
Perspective: Secular
Description: "The rising influence of Islam in the West will be the greatest threat
    to our rights to freedom of speech and religion."
Review: Basic design but great material for everyone. Essay on Jemmima Gold-
    smith is revealing.

URL: www.geocities.com/islamic_monitor/index.html
E-mail: islam_monitor@hotmail.com

THE ISLAMIZATION OF BETLEHEM BY ARAFAT
Perspective: Israeli
Description: Info about persecution of Christians in the areas ruled by Muslim
    terrorist Arafat. In the same site you will also, among other things, find a list
    of books about Islamization.
Review: Great site, especially for Christians
URL: www.acpr.org.il/cloakrm/clk117.html
E-mail: yoramtex@netvision.net.il

THE ISLAM THREAT AND THE ENEMY WITHIN
Perspective: British
Description: About the Islamic threat in the U.K.
Review: Beautiful site with video clips
URL: www.thekafir.co.uk/
E-mail: rami@thekafir.co.uk

THE KORAN: TESTIMONY OF ANTI-CHRIST
Perspective: Christian
Description: Essays; comparisons between Christianity and Islam
Review: The color combination of this Web site is tedious, but has good material
    for Christians.
URL: members.aol.com/AllahIslam/index.html; also see www.isnet.org/~djoko/
    Offsites/Religions/Islam/Oppose/Anti-Christ/ 00main.html
E-mail: Not available

THE PREVAILING MYTH
Perspective: Atheist
Description: Unravels the inherent logical inconsistency of Islam
Review: Basic design, but has good material and links on logical inconsistencies
    of Islam
URL: www.geocities.com/prevailingmyth/
E-mail: prevailingmyth@yahoo.com

THE QURAN
Perspective: Christian
Description: Examines Islam from a Biblical perspective
Review: Has useful information
URL: www.theKoran.com/
E-mail: Not available

THE TRUE FURQAN
Perspective: Islamic
Description: Preaching peace and brotherhood
Review: A testament for Muslims to shed the way of atrocity and adopt the way
   of peace
URL: www.islamexpose.com/
E-mail: Not available

THE TRUTH ONLY
Perspective: Israeli nationalist
Description: Tells the truth about the Arab-Israeli conflict
Review: Great, huge resource
URL: thetruthonly.tripod.com/TheTRUTHOnly/
E-mail: Not available

TIDENS TECKEN
Perspective: Christian
Description: This link leads to one of the great articles about Islam at the site
   Tidens tecken. In Swedish.
Review: Informative site with useful information on persecution against Christians in Islamic countries
URL: home.swipnet.se/~w-93281/islamfrf.htm
E-mail: ebrev@iname.com

TRUE FACTOR OF ISLAM
Perspective: Secular
Description: "Can you still say that Islam is the religion of peace?"
Review: Good read, good materials and links, and nice humor
URL: www.geocities.com/truefactor/
E-mail: stalkercal@yahoo.com

TRUE ISLAM

Perspective: Islamic
Description: Collection of *jehadi* thoughts, pictures, and *hadith*
Review: Strange reading, but has good collections of *hadith*. One can obtain insight into *jehadis'* thought process.
URL: www.hope.at/trueislam
E-mail: Not available

TRUTH ALONE TRIUMPHS

Perspective: Hindu nationalist
Description: Essays and links related to Islamic atrocities
Review: The twenty articles help understand Islam without the usual masquerade or frills. Eight links, including one to the Armenian genocide page.
URL: www.flex.com/~jai/satyamevajayate/
E-mail: zulfikark@usa.net; jai@mantra.com

VICTOR MORDECAI

Perspective: Judeo-Christian
Description: Home page on Islamism and threats to peace
Review: Great Web design and thought collection
URL: www.vicmord.com/
E-mail: Vicmord2001@yahoo.com

WELCOME HOME LOST SHEEP OF ISRAEL

Perspective: Judeo-Christian
Description: Has an article with information on the difference between the Judeo-Christian culture and Islam, and then suggests how we can solve the problem.
Review: Good article
URL: www.geocities.com/welcomehomelostsheepofisrael/Islam. htm
E-mail: yovela_@hotmail.com

WELCOME TO THE WORLD OF HINDU HOLOCAUST

Perspective: Hindu
Description: Documentation of the history of Islamic massacres against Hindus
Review: This is very useful information. Great!
URL: www.geocities.com/hindoo_humanist/
E-mail: Not available

WELTHERRSCHAFT
Perspective: German
Description: Religion and politics in Islam
Review: In German
URL: www.efg-hohenstaufenstr.de/downloads/texte/islam_weltherrschaft. html
E-mail: webmaster@efg-hohenstaufenstr.de

WENN DER PAPST DEN KORAN KÜSST
Perspective: Democratic
Description: Explores the al-Taqiyya strategy, and criticizes the politics of multi-
    culturalism, among other things. In German.
Review: A very good site
URL: www.moschee-schluechtern.de/texte/stolz/rezension_raddatz.htm
E-mail: info@moschee-schluechtern.de

WHAT ARAB CIVILIZATION?
Perspective: Assyrian
Description: A letter about Islamic "achievements" and "tolerance," written by an
    Assyrian
Review: Exposes many myths; excellent
URL: www.ninevehsoft.com/fiorina.htm
E-mail: Not available

"WHAT THE HELL IS GOING ON?"
Perspective: Israeli nationalist
Description: Under construction
Review: Has pictures and commentaries on Arafat's terrorism
URL: www.geocities.com/jihadisucks/index.html
E-mail: USKAFIR@yahoo.com

E

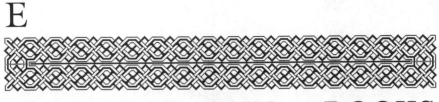

BIBLIOGRAPHY OF BOOKS CRITICAL OF ISLAM

REFERENCE

Encyclopaedia of Islam. 4 vols. and supplement. Leiden: E. J. Brill, 1913–1938. Reprint, 1993.
Encyclopaedia of Islam. 2d ed. Leiden: E. J. Brill, 1954—in progress.
Hughes, T. P. *Dictionary of Islam.* Delhi: Rupa & Co., 1988.

THREE EX-MUSLIMS WHO CONFRONT ISLAM HEAD-ON

Dashti, Ali. *Twenty-three Years: A Study of the Prophetic Career of Mohammed.* Translated by E. Bagley. London, 1985.
Shaikh, Anwar. *Faith and Deception.* Cardiff: Principality Publishers, 1996
———. *Islam, The Arab Imperialism.* Cardiff: Principality Publishers, 1998
———. *Islam, Sex and Violence.* Cardiff: Principality Publishers, 1999
———. *The Two Faces of Islam.* Cardiff: Principality Publishers, Forthcoming.
Warraq, Ibn. *Why I Am Not a Muslim.* Amherst, N.Y.: Prometheus Books, 1995.

CRITICAL BIOGRAPHIES OF MUHAMMAD

Cook, Michael. *Muhammad*. Oxford: Oxford University Press, 1983.
Margoliouth, D. S. *Mohammed and the Rise of Islam*. London, 1905. Reprint, Delhi: Voice of India, 1992.
Muir, William. *The Life of Mahomet*. London, 1894. Reprint, Delhi: Voice of India, 1992.
Rodinson, Maxime. *Muhammad*. New York: Pantheon Books, 1980.
Warraq, Ibn. *The Quest for the Historical Muhammad*. Amherst, N.Y.: Prometheus Books, 2000

THE KORAN

'Abd al-Fadl, 'Abdallah. *Is the Qur'an Infallible?* Villach, Austria, n.d. Available from Light of Life, P.O. Box 13, A-9503, Villach, Austria.
Cook, Michael. *The Koran: A Very Short Introduction*. Oxford: Oxford University Press, 2000.
Luxenberg, C. *Die Syro-Aramaische Lesart des Koran*. Berlin: Das Arabische Buch, 2000.
Sfar, Mondher. *Le Coran est-il authentique?* Paris, 2000.
Wansbrough, John. *Quranic Studies*. Oxford: Oxford University Press, 1977.
Warraq, Ibn. *The Origins of the Koran*, Amherst, N.Y.: Prometheus Books, 1998.
———. *What the Koran Really Says*, Amherst, N.Y.: Prometheus Books, 2002.

CRITICAL LOOK AT *HADITH* AND ISLAMIC HISTORY

Cook, M. *Early Muslim Dogma: A Source Critical Study*. Cambridge: Cambridge University Press, 1981.
Cook, M., and P. Crone. *Hagarism, the Making of the Islamic World*. Cambridge: Cambridge University Press, 1977.
Crone, P. *Meccan Trade and the Rise of Islam*. Princeton, N.J.: Princeton University Press, 1987.
Goldziher, I. *Muslim Studies*. 2 vols. Translated by S. M. Stern and C. R. Barber. London: Allen and Unwin, 1967–71.
Schacht, J. *The Origins of Muhammadan Jurisprudence*. Oxford: Clarendon Press, 1950.

THE MYTH OF ISLAMIC TOLERANCE

Vryonis, S., Jr. *The Decline of Medieval Hellenism in Asia Minor and the Process of Islamization from the Eleventh through the Fifteenth Century*. Berkeley, 1971.
Wistrich, R. *Antisemitism. The Longest Hatred*. London: Pantheon, 1991.
Ye'or, Bat *The Decline of Eastern Christianity under Islam. From Jihad to Dhimmitude*.

Seventh–Twentieth Century. Cranbury, NJ., 1996.
———. *The Dhimmi: Jews and Christians under Islam*. Rutherford, N.J, 1985
———. *Islam and Dhimmitude, Where Civilizations Collide*. Cranbury, N.J.: Fairleigh
Dickinson University Press, 2002

ARMENIAN GENOCIDE

Dadrian, V. N. *The History of the Armenian Genocide. Ethnic Conflict from the Balkans to
Anatolia to the Caucasus*. Oxford: Berghahn Books, 1995.
Sarafian, Ara, ed. *United States Official Documents on the Armenian Genocide*, 4 vols.
Watertown, Mass., 1995.

ISLAMIC MAYHEM IN INDIA

Elst, K. *Negationism in India. Concealing the Record of Islam*. New Delhi: Voice of India,
1993
Goel, Sita Ram. *Hindu Temples. What Happened to Them*. 2 vols. New Delhi: Voice of
India, 1998.
Lal, K. S. *The Legacy of Muslim Rule in India*, New Delhi: Voice of India, 1992.
———. *Muslim Slave System in Medieval India*, New Delhi: Voice of India, 1994.

ISLAMIC SLAVERY

Cotton, Samuel. *Silent Terror: A Journey into Contemporary African Slavery*. New York:
Harlem River Press 1999.
Fisher, Humphrey J., et al. *Slavery in the History of Black Muslim Africa*. New York: New
York University Press, 2001.
Gordon, Murray. *Slavery in the Arab World*. New York: New Amsterdam Books, 1990
Levtzion, N., and R. L. Pouwels, eds. *The History of Islam in Africa*. Athens: Ohio Uni-
versity Center for International Studies, 2000.
Lewis, B. *Race and Slavery in the Middle East*. New York: Oxford University Press, 1990.
Marmon, Shaun Elizabeth, ed. *Slavery in the Islamic Middle East*. Princeton, N.J.: Markus
Wiener Publishers, 1999.
Willis, John Ralph, ed. *Slaves and Slavery in Muslim Africa: Islam and the Ideology of
Enslavement*. London: Frank Cass & Co.,1986.
———. *Slaves and Slavery in Muslim Africa: The Servile Estate*. London: Frank Cass &
Co.,1986.

WOMEN UNDER ISLAM

Ascha, Ghassan. *Du Statut Inférieur de la Femme en Islam*. Paris: L'Harmattan, 1989.
Darabi, Parvin, and Romin P. Thomson. *Rage Against the Veil*. Amherst, N.Y.: Prometheus Books, 1999.
Goodwin, J. *Price of Honor*. Boston: Little, Brown, 1994.
Shaarawi, Huda. *Harem Years. The Memoirs of an Egyptian Feminist*. London: Virago 1986.

SEX IN ISLAM

Bouhdiba, A. *La Sexualité en Islam*. Paris: Quadrige/Presses Universitaires de France, 1974.
Bousquet, G. H. *L'Ethique sexuelle de l'Islam*. Paris: Desclée de Brouwer, 1966.
Murray, Stephen O., ed. *Islamic Homosexualities: Culture, History, and Literature*. New York: New York University Press, 1997.
Schmitt, Arno, and J. Sofer, *Sexuality and Eroticism Among Males in Moslem Societies*. New York: Harrington Park Press, 1991.

JIHAD: CLASSICAL AND MODERN

Benjamin, Daniel, et al. *The Age of Sacred Terror: Radical Islam's War Against America*. New York: Random House, 2002.
Dennis, Anthony J. *The Rise of the Islamic Empire and the Threat to the West*. Bristol, Ind.: Wyndham Hall Press, 2001.
Emerson, Steven. *American Jihad. The Terrorists Living Among Us*. New York: Simon & Schuster, 2002
Firestone, Reuven. *Jihad: The Origin of Holy War in Islam*. Oxford: Oxford University Press, 1999.
Peters, R. *Jihad in Classical and Modern Islam: A Reader*. Princeton, N.J.: Princeton University Press, 1996.
Pipes, Daniel. *Militant Islam Reaches America*. New York: W. W. Norton, & Co., 2002

CONVERSIONS

Gaudeul, Jean-Marie. *Appelés Par le Christ. Ils Viennent de l'Islam*. Paris: Cerf, 1991. Translated as *Called from Islam to Christ* (N.p.: Monarch Publications, 1999).
Miller, W. M. *Ten Muslims Meet Christ*. Grand Rapids, Mich.: W. B. Eerdmans, 1969, 1980.
Reuter, Thomas. "Great Expectations: Hindu Revival Movements in Java." *Australian Journal of Anthropology* 12, no. 3 (2001): 327–38.

Tamur, Jan. *Ex-Muslims for Christ*. Birmingham, England: The Crossbearers, 1980.
Wallis, A. T., Jr., *Indonesian Revival, Why Two Million Came to Christ*. Pasadena: William Carey Library, 1977.

ATHEISM, SKEPTICISM, AND FREETHOUGHT IN ISLAM

Badawi, Abd al-Rahman. *Tar'rikh al-Ilhad fi al-Islam* (History of atheism in Islam). Cairo, 1945.
Stroumsa, Sarah. *Freethinkers of Medieval Islam: Ibn al-Rawandi, Abu Bakr al-Razi and Their Impact on Islamic Thought*. Leiden: E. J. Brill, 1999.
Urvoy, Dominique. *Les Penseurs Libres dans l'Islam Classique*. Paris: Albin Michel, 1996.

NON-MUSLIM CRITIQUES OF ISLAM

Spencer, R. Islam *Unveiled: Disturbing Questions about the World's Fastest-Growing Faith*. San Francisco: Encounter Books, 2002.
Trifkovic, Serge. *The Sword of the Prophet: History, Theology, Impact on the World*. Boston: Regina Orthodox Press, 2002.